# AQUATIC
# PHOTOSYNTHESIS

**Paul G. Falkowski, PhD**
Institute of Marine and Coastal Sciences
Rutgers University
New Brunswick, New Jersey

**John A. Raven, PhD, FRSE, FRS**
John Boyd Baxter Professor of Biology
Department of Biological Sciences
University of Dundee
Dundee, Scotland

*b*
Blackwell
Science

# BLACKWELL SCIENCE

## Editorial Offices

Commerce Place, 350 Main Street, Malden, Massachusetts 02148, USA
Osney Mead, Oxford OX2 0EL, England
25 John Street, London WC1N 2BL, England
23 Ainslie Place, Edinburgh EH3 6AJ, Scotland
54 University Street, Carlton, Victoria 3053, Australia
Other Editorial offices:
Blackwell Wissenschafts-Verlag GmbH Kurfürstendamm 57, 10707 Berlin, Germany
Blackwell Science KK, MG Kodenmacho Building, 7-10 Kodenmacho Nihombashi,
    Chuo-ku, Tokyo 104, Japan

## Distributors

*USA*    Blackwell Science, Inc.
    Commerce Place
    350 Main Street
    Malden, Massachusetts 02148
    (Telephone orders: 800-215-1000 or 781-388-8250; fax orders: 781-388-8270)

*Canada*    Login Brothers Book Company
    324 Saulteaux Crescent
    Winnipeg, Manitoba, R3J 3T2
    (Telephone orders: 204-224-4068)

*Australia*    Blackwell Science Pty, Ltd.
    54 University Street
    Carlton, Victoria 3053
    (Telephone orders: 03-9347-0300; fax orders: 03-9349-3016)

*Outside North America and Australia*
    Blackwell Science, Ltd.
    c/o Marston Book Services, Ltd.
    P.O. Box 269, Abingdon, Oxon OX14 4YN, England
    (Telephone orders: 44-01235-465500; fax orders: 44-01235-465555)

The Blackwell Science logo is a trade mark of Blackwell Science Ltd., registered at the United Kingdom

Trade Marks Registry

Acquisitions: Jane Humphreys
Production: Irene Herlihy
Manufacturing: Lisa Flanagan
Typeset by Best-set Typesetter Ltd., Hong Kong
Printed and bound by Capital City Press
© 1997 by Paul G. Falkowski and John A. Raven
Printed in the United States of America
98 99 00 5 4 3 2

Library of Congress Cataloging-in-Publication Data

Falkowski, Paul G.
    Aquatic photosynthesis / Paul Falkowski, John Raven.
      p.  cm.
    Includes bibliographical references (p.    ) and index.
    ISBN 0-86542-387-3 (alk. paper)
    1. Photosynthesis. 2. Aquatic plants—Physiology. I. Raven,
John A. II. Title.
QK882.F36  1997
581.1'3342—dc20

                                                 96-36431
                                               CIP

*To Linda, Sári, Sasha, and Mirit*

# Contents

# Preface

Photosynthesis is one of the oldest and most fascinating processes in biology. The subject has attracted physicists, physical chemists, organic chemists, biochemists, geneticists, molecular biologists, physiologists, ecologists, geochemists, and evolutionary biologists. Indeed, research on photosynthesis can lend itself to so many lines of investigation that not only students but professional researchers and teachers as well are hard pressed to assimilate it all.

There are many textbooks on photosynthesis, and a few even discuss photosynthesis in aquatic ecosystems as part of a curriculum in aquatic science. For the most part, these texts consider flowering plants and green algae as the "norm." While many aspects of photosynthesis are common to all oxygen-evolving photosynthetic organisms, there is a great deal of taxonomic diversity in aquatic photosynthetic organisms that is manifested in photosynthetic processes. We have not found an introductory textbook that integrates biophysical, biochemical, and physiological concepts of photosynthesis in the context of the ecology and evolution of aquatic organisms. We felt, therefore, that it was time to write an accessible text that takes as the norm the diversity of taxa that contribute to primary productivity in aquatic systems.

Terrestrial plants are so much a part of the human experience that aquatic photosynthetic organisms are often overlooked. All terrestrial plants are derived from a single class of a single division of algae. There are a dozen divisions of eukaryotic algae that we know of, and at least one prokaryotic division. A division is the taxonomic equivalent of phylum. (To illustrate the depth of evolutionary diversity in the algae, it is humbling to consider that humans, birds, dinosaurs, and fish are all in the same phylum, Chordata.) The diversity in algae is manifested in many aspects of the photosynthetic apparatus. Perhaps the most obvious is the wide range of colors observed in algae. In fact, differences in color are often a clue to the taxonomic classification of the organism. In addition, however, aquatic photosynthetic organisms often differ from higher plants in choices of metals used in photosynthetic electron transport, the enzymes used to fix carbon dioxide, the location of genes encoding proteins in the photosynthetic system, and the architecture of the organisms themselves. A discussion of photosynthesis in aquatic organisms puts diversity at the center of the consideration of mechanisms, the ecology of natural populations, and the geochemical and paleoecological consequences of aquatic photosynthesis on the evolution of life on Earth.

This text is not meant to be a reference book that reviews all the latest discoveries in photosynthesis. Rather, it is our attempt to explain fundamental concepts, especially biochemical and biophysical mechanisms, not only in terms of molecular processes, but also in terms of underlying physical and chemical processes. We hope that this physico-chemical approach will help readers less familiar with physics and chemistry to understand and appreciate the biochemical and biophysical discussion. Similarly, our discussion of the phylogeny and structure of the aquatic photosynthetic organisms should help readers with less background in biology.

The book was written for advanced undergraduate or postgraduate students with a general scientific background. We presume no previous knowledge of photosynthesis. Each of the ten chapters, written in what we believe is a logical sequence, can be read on its own, used in a course, or assigned as supplemental reading for a course. Each successive chapter builds upon information in the preceding chapter, but each can also be read as a self-contained essay. We have provided references not only to review papers, but also to original research papers that we think will help an interested reader explore a specific subject in depth. We would consider the book a success if it helped the reader understand virtually any paper written on any topic related to photosynthesis.

The book was a collaboration between us, extending, in fits and starts, over a period of three years. During that time, we learned a great deal from each other and from discussions with numerous colleagues, students, and collaborators. We especially thank Richard Barber, John Beardall, Mike Behrenfeld, John Berges, William Cramer, Bruce Diner, Zvy Dubinsky, Dion Durnford, Diane Edwards, Jack Fajer, Graham Farquhar, Anthony Fielding, Elizabeth Gantt, Richard Geider, Sheila Glidewell, Govindjee, Howard Griffiths, Linda Handley, Garmen Harbottle, Geoffrey Hind, Andy Johnston, Todd Kana, Jon Keeley, John Kirk, Andrew Knoll, Robert Knox, Zbignew Kolber, Janet Kubler, Claire Lamberti, Julie LaRoche, Jeff MacFarlane, Enid MacRobbie, David Mauzerall, Michael McKay, Linda Medlin, Andre Morel, François Morel, Jack Myers, Bruce Osborne, Barry Osmond, Ondrej Prasil, Katherine Richardson, Slim Samulesson, Andrew Smith, Bob Spicer, Janet Sprent, Norman Sutin, Alan Walker, David Walker, Doug Wallace, John Whitmarsh, and Kevin Wyman for sharing their thoughts. We take full responsibility for any errors in fact or interpretation. We are indebted to our families for their patience and support, without which this project could not have been completed. We both thank our parents for their nurturing and guidance. JAR thanks his primary school teacher, the late Mrs. F. Ridgewell. PGF thanks the late Bill Siegelman for his encouragement and counsel through the years.

PGF  
JAR

# 1

# An Introduction to Photosynthesis in Aquatic Systems

Photosynthesis is the biological conversion of light energy to chemical bond energy that is stored in the form of organic carbon compounds. Approximately 40% of the photosynthesis on Earth each year occurs in aquatic environments (Falkowski 1994). Because we live on land, however, and the aggregate biomass of aquatic plants amounts to less than 1% of the total plant biomass on Earth, terrestrial plants are much more a part of the human experience (Table 1.1). Consequently, the role and importance of aquatic photosynthetic organisms are not appreciated by most students of photosynthesis.

Most of the detailed biochemical, biophysical, and molecular biological information about photosynthetic processes comes from studies of higher plants and a few model algae such as *Chlamydomonas* and *Chlorella* (Harris 1989; Rochaix 1995). Traditionally, model organisms have been chosen because they are easily grown or can be genetically manipulated rather than because they are ecologically important. There are significant differences between terrestrial and aquatic environments that affect and are reflected in photosynthetic processes. These differences have led to a variety of evolutionary adaptations and physiological acclimations of the photosynthetic apparatus in aquatic organisms that are without parallel in terrestrial plants. Moreover, there is sufficient knowledge of the basic mechanisms and principles of photosynthetic processes in aquatic organisms to provide a basic understanding of how they respond to changes in their environment. Such interpretations form the foundation of aquatic ecophysiology and are requisite to understanding both community structure and global biogeochemical cycles.

We strive here to describe some of the basic concepts and mechanisms of photosynthetic processes, with the overall goal of developing an appreciation of the adaptations and acclimations that have led to the abundance, diversity, and productivity of photosynthetic organisms in aquatic ecosystems. In this introductory chapter we briefly examine the overall photosynthetic process, the geochemical and biological evidence for the evolution of oxygenic photosynthetic organisms, and the concepts of life-forms and nutritional modes. Many of these themes are explored in detail in subsequent chapters.

## A DESCRIPTION OF THE OVERALL PHOTOSYNTHETIC PROCESS

The biological economy of Earth is based on the chemistry of carbon. The vast

**Table 1.1** Comparison of global net productivity/living biomass in marine and terrestrial ecosystems

| Ecosystem | Net Primary Productivity ($10^{15}$ grams/year) | Total Plant Biomass ($10^{15}$ grams) | Turnover Time (years) |
|---|---|---|---|
| Marine | 35–50 | 1–2 | 0.02–0.06 |
| Terrestrial | 50–70 | 600–1000 | 9–20 |

majority of carbon on Earth is in an oxidized, inorganic form;[1] that is, it is combined with molecular oxygen and is in the form of the gas carbon dioxide ($CO_2$) or its hydrated or ionic equivalents, namely bicarbonate ($HCO_3^-$) and carbonate ($CO_3^{2-}$). These inorganic forms of carbon are interconvertible but thermodynamically stable. They contain no biologically usable energy, nor can they be used directly to form organic molecules without undergoing a chemical or biochemical reaction. In order to extract energy from inorganic carbon or to use the element to build organic molecules, the carbon must be chemically reduced, which requires an investment of free energy. There are only a handful of biological mechanisms extant for the reduction of inorganic carbon; on a global basis photosynthesis is the most familiar, most important, and most extensively studied.

Photosynthesis can be written as an oxidation-reduction reaction of the general form:

$$2H_2A + CO_2 + Light \xrightarrow{\ Pigment\ } (CH_2O) + H_2O + 2A \tag{1.1}$$

Note that in this representation of photosynthesis light is specified as a substrate; some of the energy of the absorbed light is stored in the products. All photosynthetic bacteria, with the important exceptions of the cyanobacteria and prochlorophytes, are obligate anaerobes and are incapable of evolving oxygen. In these organisms compound A is, for example, an atom of sulfur and the pigments are bacteriochlorophylls (Blankenship et al. 1995; Van Niel 1941). All other photosynthetic organisms, including the cyanobacteria, prochlorophytes, eukaryotic algae, and higher plants, are oxygenic; that is, Equation 1.1 can be modified to:

$$2H_2O + CO_2 + Light \xrightarrow{\ Chl\,a\ } (CH_2O) + H_2O + O_2 \tag{1.2}$$

where Chl *a* is the ubiquitous plant pigment chlorophyll *a*. Equation 1.2 implies that somehow chlorophyll *a* catalyzes a reaction or a series of reactions whereby light energy is used to oxidize water:

$$2H_2O + Light \xrightarrow{\ Chl\,a\ } 4H^+ + 4e + O_2 \tag{1.3}$$

yielding gaseous, molecular oxygen. Equation 1.3 represents the so-called "light reactions" of oxygenic photosynthesis. The processes that constitute the light reactions will be discussed in Chapters 2 and 3.

Equation 1.3 describes an oxidation process. Specifically, it is a *partial reaction*, where electrons are extracted from water to form molecular oxygen. This process is the heart of one of two groups of reactions in oxygenic photosynthesis.

---

1. The terms *inorganic* and *organic* are archaic, originating from the time when inorganic carbon compounds were obtained from minerals and organic compounds were obtained from plant or animal sources. For our purposes, we assume that an organic molecule contains a carbon atom that is directly, covalently linked to a hydrogen atom.

The other reaction, the reduction of $CO_2$, also can be described by:

$$CO_2 + 4H^+ + 4e^- \rightarrow CH_2O + H_2O \tag{1.4}$$

As free electrons are normally not found in biological systems, the reaction described by Equations 1.3 and 1.4 requires the formation of an intermediate reducing agent that is not shown explicitly. The form of, and mechanism for, the generation of reductants will be discussed in Chapter 4.

Although the biological reduction of $CO_2$ may be thermodynamically permitted on theoretical grounds, by, for example, mixing a biological reducing agent such as NADPH with $CO_2$, the reaction will not spontaneously proceed. Enzymes are required to facilitate the reduction process. Given the substrates and appropriate enzymes, the reactions that lead to carbon reduction can proceed in the dark as well as the light. These so-called "dark reactions" are coupled to the light reactions by common intermediates and by enzyme regulation. Although there are variations on the metabolic pathways for carbon reduction, the initial dark reaction, whereby $CO_2$ is temporarily "fixed" to an organic molecule, is highly conserved throughout all photosynthetic organisms.[2] We will examine the dark reactions in Chapter 5.

## AN INTRODUCTION TO OXIDATION–REDUCTION REACTIONS

The term *oxidation* was originally proposed by chemists in the latter part of the 18th century to describe reactions involving the addition of oxygen to metals, forming metallic oxides. For example:

$$3Fe + 2O_2 \rightarrow Fe_3O_4 \tag{1.5}$$

The term *reduction* was used to describe the reverse reaction, namely the removal of oxygen from a metallic oxide, for example, by heating with carbon:

$$Fe_3O_4 + 2C \rightarrow 3Fe + 2CO_2 \tag{1.6}$$

Subsequent analysis of these reactions established that the addition of oxygen is accompanied by the removal of electrons from an atom or molecule. Conversely, reduction is accompanied by the addition of electrons. In the specific case of organic reactions that involve the reduction of carbon, the addition of electrons is usually balanced by the addition of protons. For example, the reduction of carbon dioxide to formaldehyde requires the addition of four electrons *and* four $H^+$, that is, the equivalent of four hydrogen atoms.

$$O{=}C{=}O + 4e^- + 4H^+ \rightarrow \overset{\displaystyle H}{\underset{\displaystyle H}{\overset{|}{\underset{|}{C}}}}{=}O + H_2O \tag{1.7}$$

---

2. Historically, the term *fixation* means to make nonvolatile. It is a term applied to the biochemical or chemical, but not physical, sequestration of a gas. Thus, adsorption of a gas by activated charcoal is not fixation, while the chemical reaction of $CO_2$ with an amine to form a carbamate is a form of fixation. Strictly speaking, the term fixation is not synonymous with chemical reduction, although the two terms often are used interchangeably in the vernacular.

Thus, from the perspective of organic chemistry, oxidation may be defined as the addition of oxygen, the loss of electrons, or the loss of hydrogen atoms (but not hydrogen ions, $H^+$); conversely, reduction can be defined as the removal of oxygen, the addition of electrons, or the addition of hydrogen atoms.

Oxidation-reduction reactions only occur when there are pairs of substrates, forming pairs of products:

$$A_{ox} + B_{red} \rightleftharpoons A_{red} + B_{ox} \tag{1.8}$$

In oxygenic photosynthesis, $CO_2$ is the recipient of the electrons and protons, and thus becomes reduced (it is the A in Eq 1.8). Water is the electron and proton donor, and thus becomes oxidized (it is the B in Eq 1.8). The oxidation of two moles of water (Eq 1.3) requires the addition of 495 kJ. The reduction of $CO_2$ to the simplest organic carbon molecule, formaldehyde, adds 176 kJ of energy. The energetic efficiency of photosynthesis can be calculated by dividing the energy stored in organic matter by that required to split water into molecular hydrogen and oxygen. Thus, the maximum overall energy efficiency of photosynthesis, assuming no losses at any intermediate step, is 176/495 or about 36%. We will discuss the thermodynamics of oxidation–reduction reactions more fully in Chapter 4.

## THE PHOTOSYNTHETIC APPARATUS

The light reactions and the subsequent movement of protons and electrons through the photosynthetic machinery to form chemical bond energy and reductants are reactions associated with, or occurring in, membranes (Anderson, Andersson 1988; Staehelin 1986). The fixation and subsequent biochemical reduction of carbon dioxide to organic carbon compounds are processes occurring in the aqueous phase, that is, not in membranes. The ensemble of the biochemical elements that facilitate these processes constitute the *photosynthetic apparatus*. In most anaerobic photosynthetic bacteria and cyanobacteria, the photosynthetic light reactions are organized on membranes that are arranged in sheets or lamellae adjacent to the periplasmic membrane (Blankenship et al. 1995; Bryant 1994; Fig 1.1a). The dark reactions are generally localized in the center of the cell. In eukaryotic cells, the photosynthetic apparatus is organized in special organelles, the chloroplasts, which contain alternating layers of lipoprotein membranes and aqueous phases (Staehelin 1986; Fig 1.1b).

The lipoprotein membranes of eukaryotic cell chloroplasts are called thylakoids,[3] and contain two major lipid components, mono- and digalactosyl diacylglycerol (MGDG and DGDG, respectively), arranged in a bilayer approximately 4 nm thick ($1 nm = 10^{-9} m = 10 Å$) in which proteins and other functional molecules are embedded (Singer, Nicolson 1972; Fig 1.2). Unlike most of the rest of the membranes in the cell, thylakoid membranes are not phospholipids (Murphy 1986). Like most biological membranes, thylakoids are not symmetrical; that is, some of the components span the membrane completely, whereas others are only embed-

---

3. Derived from the Greek *thylakos*, meaning "a sack."

ded partially (Cramer, Knaff 1990). The thylakoid membranes form closed vesicles around an aqueous, intrathylakoid space. This structure is analogous to the pocket in pita bread, the pocket being called the *lumen*. The proteins and pigments that constitute the two light reactions, as well as most of the electron transfer components that link them, and the catalysts involved in oxygen evolution and ATP synthesis are organized laterally along the membrane (Fig 1.3). In addition, although there are some important exceptions, thylakoid membranes contain the major light-harvesting pigment-protein complexes; hence, when isolated from cells, thylakoids are characteristically colored (Larkum, Barrett 1983).

Surrounding the thylakoids is an aqueous phase, the *stroma*. Soluble proteins in the stroma use chemical reductants and energy generated by the biochemical reactions in the thylakoid membranes to reduce $CO_2$, $NO_3^-$, and $SO_4^{2-}$, thereby forming organic carbon compounds, ammonium and amino acids, and organic sulfide compounds, respectively. The stroma also contains functional DNA (nucleoids), ribosomal (r), messenger (m), and transfer (t) RNAs, as well as all the associated enzymes for transcription and translation of the chloroplast genome (Kirk, Tilney-Bassett 1978; Reith, Munholland 1993).

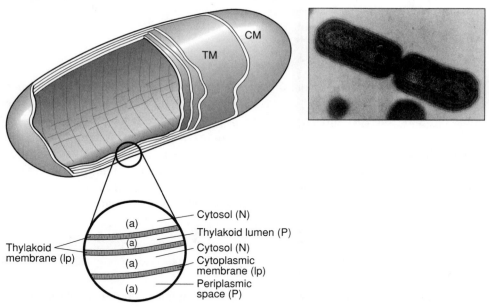

(a)

**Figure 1.1** Schematic representations and transmission electron micrographs showing the membrane structures of a cyanobacterial cell and an algal chloroplast. (a) The three-dimensional architecture of the photosynthetic membrane structure in a cyanobacterium. The thylakoids are depicted as sheets of membranes, each representing a pair of apposed membranes as shown in the enlargement. Not shown are the cell wall, ribosomes, or other internal structures. The N side of the membrane becomes electrically negative, while the P side becomes positive as a result of the active transport of protons during photosynthesis. In cyanobacteria the cell is surrounded by a wall and outer membrane, separated from the plasma membrane by a periplasmic space. TM—thylakoid membrane; CM—cytoplasmic membrane. Cytosol refers to the aqueous phase contained by plasmalemma excluding organelles. The wall is clearly visible in the transmission electron micrograph showing a longitudinal section of a cyanobacterium. (Courtesy of Michael McKay)

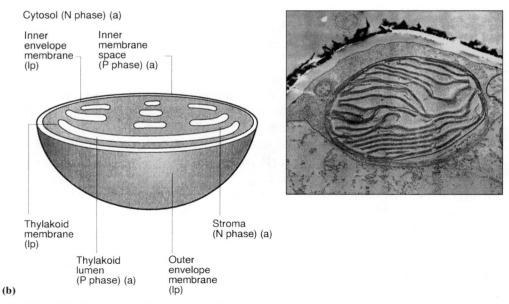

Cytosol (N phase) (a)

Inner envelope membrane (lp)

Inner membrane space (P phase) (a)

Thylakoid membrane (lp)

Stroma (N phase) (a)

Thylakoid lumen (P phase) (a)

Outer envelope membrane (lp)

**(b)**

**Figure 1.1** (b) The three-dimensional architecture of a chloroplast showing one or more (depending on algal class, see Table 1.4) envelope membranes that separate the organelle from the cytosol. Inset is a transmission electron micrograph showing the membrane structure in a diatom chloroplast.

The stroma, in turn, is surrounded by two to four plastid envelope membranes (depending on the organism) that, in some organisms, are connected to the nucleus and separated from each other by an aqueous intermembrane compartment (Berner 1993). The inner envelope membrane has a number of integral membrane proteins, which selectively transport photosynthetic substrates into the stroma and photosynthetic products out of it. The outer envelope membrane also has integral membrane proteins, called *porins*, which permit nonselective transport of solutes less than about 800 Da,[4] such as $CO_2$, $O_2$, inorganic phosphate, ATP, and so on (Raven, Beardall 1981b).

**The Role of Membranes in Photosynthesis**

The structure of the chloroplast illustrates some important features of photosynthetic processes. All photosynthetic organisms, whether they be prokaryotes, eukaryotic algae, or higher plants, use membranes to organize photosynthetic electron transport processes and separate these processes from carbon fixation (Bryant 1994; Drews 1985; Redlinger, Gantt 1983). Biological membranes serve many purposes, not the least of which is to control the fluxes of solutes between compartments within cells and between cells. Membranes are electrical insulators; that is, electrical charges can be separated between one side of a membrane and the other.

---

4. A Dalton (Da) is a unit of mass equal to $^{1}/_{12}$ the mass of the carbon atom.

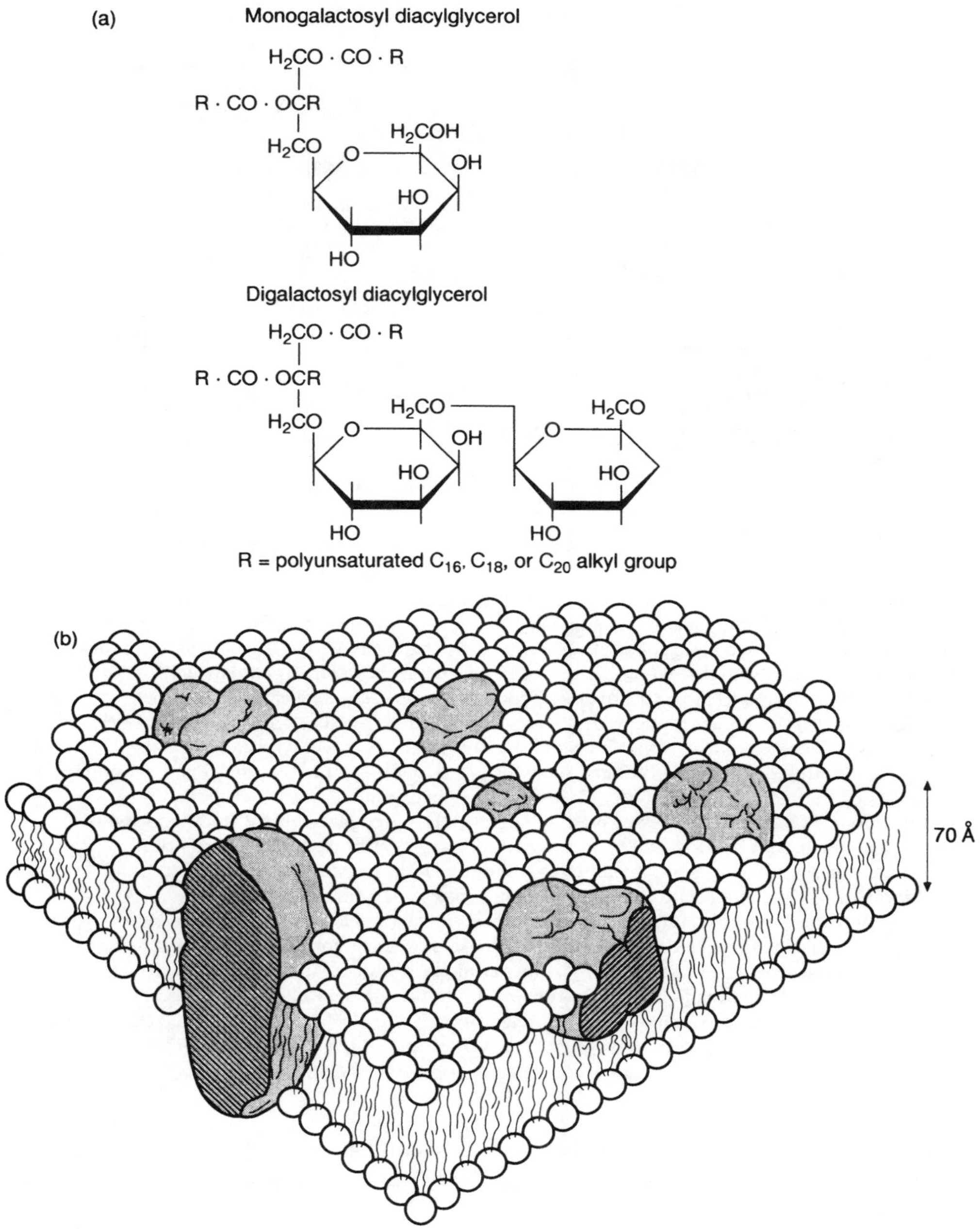

**(a)**  Monogalactosyl diacylglycerol

$$H_2CO \cdot CO \cdot R$$
$$R \cdot CO \cdot OCR$$
$$H_2CO$$

H$_2$COH, OH, HO, HO, O

Digalactosyl diacylglycerol

$$H_2CO \cdot CO \cdot R$$
$$R \cdot CO \cdot OCR$$
$$H_2CO$$

H$_2$CO, OH, HO, HO, O, H$_2$CO, HO, HO, O

R = polyunsaturated $C_{16}$, $C_{18}$, or $C_{20}$ alkyl group

**(b)**

70 Å

**Figure 1.2** (a) Structure of two of the most important lipids that make up thylakoid membranes: monogalactosyl diacylglycerol (MGDG) and digalactosyl diacylglycerol (DGDG). In the formation of membranes, the polar sugar groups face the aqueous phases, while opposing nonpolar alkyl groups are oriented toward each other to form a lipid bilayer. The width of the bilayer is approximately 4 nm. (b) A schematic diagram of a thylakoid membrane (modified from Singer, Nicolson 1972). Thylakoid membranes are largely composed of MGDG and DGDG with other polyunsaturated fatty acids. Proteins are oriented within the membrane in a nonrandom fashion. Some proteins span the membrane, whereas others may only partially protrude. The proteins will have specific "sidedness," with some functional groups facing the lumen and others facing the stroma.

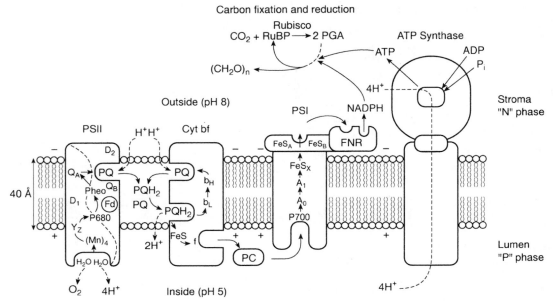

**Figure 1.3** Schematic cross-section through a photosynthetic (i.e., thylakoid) membrane showing the orientation and some of the major components of the photosynthetic apparatus. The complete membrane forms a closed vesicle. The electron transport chain is indicated by solid arrows; proton transport is indicated with dashed lines. Electrons extracted from water in photosystem II (PSII) are sequentially transferred to the cytochrome $b_6/f$ complex (cyt bf), and thence through either plastocyanin (PC) or another cytochrome (cytochrome $c_{553}$, also called $c_6$) to photosystem I (PSI), where they are used to reduce NADP to NADPH. Abbreviations: $Y_z$—a tyrosine that is the immediate electron donor to the PSII chlorophyll $P_{680}$. $P_{680}$ and $P_{700}$—the reaction center chlorophyll *a* molecules of PSII and PSI, respectively. Pheo—a phaeophytin *a* molecule. $Q_A$—a bound plastoquinone. PQ—free (i.e., mobile) plastoquinone. $PQH_2$—free plastoquinol (reduced form of plastoquinone). $b_L$ and $b_H$—low and high potential forms of cytochrome $b_6$. FeS—iron-sulfur components in the cytochrome $b_6/f$ complexes and on the reducing side of PSI. f—cytochrome *f*. PC—plastocyanin. $A_o$—the immediate electron acceptor from $P_{700}$ (a chlorophyll *a* molecule). $A_1$—phylloquinone. Fd—ferredoxin. FNR—ferredoxin/NADP oxidoreductase. NADPH—reduced nicotinamide adenine dinucleotide phosphate. ADP—adenosine diphosphate. ATP—adenosine triphosphate. Pi—inorganic phosphate. +/−—polarity of electrical potential difference across the membrane established in the light. RuBP—ribulose-1,5-bisphosphate. Rubisco—ribulose-1,5-bisphosphate carboxylase/oxygenase. PGA—3 phosphoglycerate. $(CH_2O)n$—generalized carbohydrate. The stoichiometry of protons, electrons, $O_2$, ATP, NADPH, and $CO_2$ is not indicated. (Courtesy of John Whitmarsh and Govindjee; adapted from Encyc Appl Phys 1995, 13:513–532)

From a bioenergetic viewpoint, however, a second important role is facilitating spatial organization of chemical reactions. These two roles of membranes are related to each other.

In themselves, chemical reactions are scalar processes—they have no intrinsic relationship to their spatial environment. The orientation of proteins and prosthetic groups within membranes allows the coupling of scalar photochemical reactions to vectorial fluxes of electrons, ions, and neutral solutes (Cramer, Knaff 1990). In the context of the photosynthetic apparatus, "vectorial" refers to a process whereby specific products of biochemical reactions accumulate only on one side of a thylakoid membrane, thereby forming concentration gradients across the membrane. The vectorial translocation of ions and electrons helps establish an electrical field across the membrane. Because membranes allow for spatial organization of enzymes and other proteins, mechanical (vectorially oriented) actions, on a molecular scale, can be coupled to the dissipation of the electrochemical (scalar) energy. For example, protons can be transported from one side of a membrane to the other at the expense of ATP hydrolysis, and vice versa. These processes, which would be energetically futile in solution, are highly profitable when employed by a membrane.

### Evolution of Oxygenic Photosynthesis: Geochemical Evidence

The evolution of biological membranes is obscure, but the origins of photosynthetic oxygen production can be traced from both geochemical and molecular biological evidence. Inferences based on these two apparently disparate areas reveal the integrated evolution of photosynthesis and the chemistry of the Earth's oceans and atmosphere.

Evidence of the timing and extent of photosynthetic metabolism comes from a variety of geochemical and geological sources. Based on the rate of abundance of natural radioisotopes in the Earth's crust, geochemists and astrophysicists date the formation of the Earth to about 4.6 billion years before present (ybp). The primordial atmosphere is thought to have contained mainly $CO_2$, $N_2$, $H_2O$, and CO with traces of $H_2$, HCN,[5] $H_2S$, and $NH_3$ but to have been devoid of $O_2$, and thus was neutral to mildly reducing (Holland 1984; Kasting et al. 1988; Kasting 1993a). Today the Earth's atmosphere contains 78% $N_2$, 21% $O_2$, and 0.035% $CO_2$ by volume, and is strongly oxidizing. All of the molecular oxygen present in the Earth's atmosphere has been produced as the result of oxygenic photosynthesis; the source of the original $O_2$ was photosynthetic activity in the primordial oceans (Kasting 1993a). Presently the photosynthetic supply to reservoir of atmospheric $O_2$ is approximately in balance with the consumption of the gas by respiration.

The development of aquatic photosynthesis coincided with a long and reasonably steady drawdown of atmospheric $CO_2$, from concentrations approximately 100-fold higher than in the present-day atmosphere to approximately half of the present levels (Fig 1.4). This drawdown was accompanied by a simultaneous evolution of oxygen from nil to approximately 21 kPa, that is, comparable to that of the present day. Over geological time scales, the drawdown of $CO_2$ was not stoichiometrically proportional to the accumulation of $O_2$ because photosynthesis and respiration are but two of the many biological and chemical processes that affect the atmospheric concentrations of these two gases.

One geochemical clue to the origin of oxygen can be gleaned from the distribution of uranium in sediments. Uraninite, $UO_2$, is a detrital mineral that was presumed to have been produced when the Earth was formed and naturally occurs in igneous rocks. Under anaerobic (i.e., reducing) conditions, the valence state of U is +4, and detrital $UO_2$, produced by the weathering of the igneous source rocks, is transported in sediments in aquatic environments without further chemical reac-

---

5. Note that HCN is, by our earlier definition, an organic molecule that existed in the Earth's atmosphere prior to the origin of life.

tion. However, when $O_2$ concentrations in seawater become greater than about 1% of the concentration that would be at equilibrium with the $O_2$ in the present-day atmosphere, U becomes oxidized to the +6 valence state. In the presence of anions such as $HCO_3^-$, a dicarbonate precipitate, $UO_2(CO_3)_2^{2-}$, can be formed by the reaction:

$$UO_2 + \tfrac{1}{2}O_2 + 2HCO_3^- \rightleftharpoons UO_2\left(CO_3\right)_2^{2-} + H_2O \tag{1.9}$$

The radioactive half-life for $U^{238}$ is 4.51 billion years. From knowledge of the oxidation state of uranium in relict sedimentary (i.e., metamorphic) rocks and the relative abundance of the parent isotope and its daughter products, it is possible to estimate the date of oxygen evolution. Assuming that the only source of oxygen was photosynthesis, this approach constrains the build-up of oxygen from oxygenic photosynthesis to between about 2.5 to 2.7 billion ybp (Holland 1984).

The paleochemical signatures of oxygenic photosynthesis can also be inferred from the precipitation of oxidized transition metals such as iron ($Fe^{3+}$) or manganese ($Mn^{4+}$) compounds found in sedimentary and metamorphic rocks. Iron is the most abundant transition metal in the Earth's crust. In its reduced, ionic form, $Fe^{2+}$, it is relatively soluble in seawater; in its oxidized, ionic form, $Fe^{3+}$, it is highly insoluble. The oxidized forms of iron are complexed with oxygen and hydroxides and vast quantities of $Fe^{3+}$-containing minerals precipitated in the Precambrian ocean,

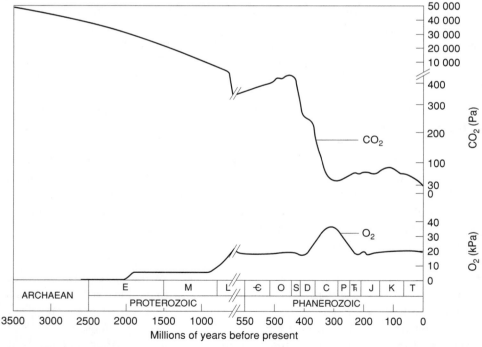

**(a)**

**Figure 1.4** (a) A reconstruction of variations in the partial pressures of $CO_2$ and $O_2$ in the atmosphere through geological time using data from Berner (1990, 1993) and Berner and Canfield (1989) for the post-Cambrian epochs (i.e., the Phanerozoic ). The absolute values and timing for the evolution of oxygen are not constrained in the Proterozoic epoch. (b) Major geological and biological epochs and their characteristics regarding the evolution of photoautotrophs in aquatic environments.

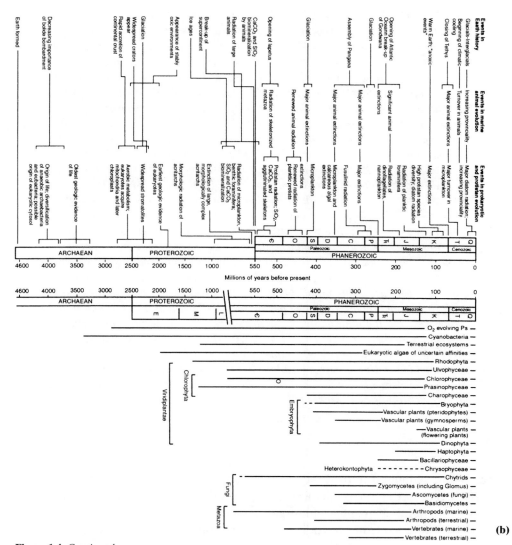

**Figure 1.4** *Continued*

forming the basis of metamorphic rocks in the Earth's crust. Based on the stratigraphy and elemental composition of these rock formations, the precipitation appears to have occurred over several hundred million years. It is inferred that the precipitation was brought about due to the endogenous production of oxygen by photosynthetic organisms in the Precambrian seas.

Best-guess reconstructions from geochemical and geological evidence suggest that photosynthetic oxygen production probably occurred primarily in relatively small, shallow regions of coastal seas, such as those inhabited by microbial mat communities as are found in many tropical continental margins in the modern ocean. The oxygen produced in such mats was largely consumed in situ by the oxidation of inorganic elements, leading to the precipitation of iron- and manganese-

## ❏ TERMINOLOGY OF GEOLOGICAL EPOCHS

*The terminology of geological epochs is a historical idiom that developed from the early investigations of rock formations. At the dawn of the 19th century, two British geologists, Rev. Prof. Adam Sedgwick and Prof. Roderick Impey Murchison, examined the structure of the exposed rock formations in Wales. The lowest—and therefore oldest—identifiable formation was called the Cambrian, a term derived from the latinization of "Wales." This epoch, subsequently dated by isotopic measurements, began approximately 550 million ybp. Consequently, all epochs prior to the Cambrian are called Precambrian. The Precambrian is subdivided into three major epochs: the Hadean (4800 to 4000 million ybp), the Archean (4000 to 2500 million ybp), and Proterozoic (2500 to 550 million ybp).*

*All epochs following the Cambrian are collectively called the Phanerozoic (meaning "obvious" or "visible" life). The Cambrian epoch was succeeded by a distinctly different formation, based on the fossils and mineralogy, and came to be known as the Ordovician, a term derived from the Latin word for a tribe that had inhabited the region. Similarly, the next epoch, Silurian, was named after another Welsh tribe, and Devonian was named after the county of southwest England where the original geological formation that defined the epoch was discovered. There are many parallel names in the geological literature for common geological epochs, based on the specific location in which the formations were discovered and the nationality of the discoverers. For example, the Carboniferous epoch, occurring between 375 and 310 million ybp, is subdivided into the earlier Mississippian and later Pennsylvanian epochs in many geological texts published in the United States (Table 1.2). Prior to the use of naturally occurring radioactive elements to date the various epochs, it was not possible to discern their absolute chronology (Turekian 1996).*

---

containing sediments to the Precambrian sea floor (Knoll, Bauld 1989). During this early period in the biogeochemical evolution of the Earth, there was a net oxidation of mineral elements, and organic compounds formed by photosynthetic processes were likely not reoxidized by heterotrophic metabolism, which left a net accumulation of photosynthetically fixed organic carbon in the environment. A small fraction of this organic carbon was deposited in shallow seas (Berner 1980). Geochemical aging (digenesis) and burial of these ancient deposits led to the formation of the petroleum and natural gas that literally fuel the industrial world in the present geological epoch.

Some aquatic photosynthetic organisms also precipitate inorganic carbon to form calcareous shells (Holligan, Robertson 1996). This reaction can be described as:

$$Ca^{2+} + 2HCO_3^- \rightarrow CaCO_3 + CO_2 + H_2O \tag{1.10}$$

Calcium carbonate is highly insoluble in seawater, and over hundreds of millions of years vast deposits of the fossilized remains of relict calcareous shells produced by a variety of marine organisms formed the bedrock of what subsequently became major mountain ranges, from the Alps and Andes to the Himalayas.

**Table 1.2** Scale of geological time: The major geological epochs

| Era | Period or Epoch | Beginning and End, in $10^6$ years before present | Approximate Duration, in $10^6$ years |
|---|---|---|---|
| | Quaternary | | |
| | Holocene | 0.010–0.001 | } 0.01 |
| | Pleistocene | 0.010–1.6 ± 0.050 | 1.6 |
| Cenozoic | Tertiary | | |
| | Pliocene | 1.6–5.1 | 9 |
| | Miocene | 5.1–24 | 15 |
| | Oligocene | 24–38 | 15 } 69 |
| | Eocene | 38–55 | 20 |
| | Paleocene | 55–68 | 10 |
| Mesozoic | Cretaceous | 68–144 | 76 |
| | Jurassic | 144–200 | 56 } 182 |
| | Triassic | 200–250 | 50 |
| Paleozoic | Permian | 250–285 | 35 |
| | Carboniferous | 285–360 | 75 |
| | Pennsylvanian | 285–320 | |
| | Mississippian | 320–360 | } 290 |
| | Devonian | 360–410 | 50 |
| | Silurian | 410–440 | 30 |
| | Ordovician | 440–505 | 65 |
| | Cambrian | 505–550 | 45 |
| Precambrian | Late Proterozoic | 550–700 | 150 |
| | Middle Proterozoic | 750–1500 | 750 |
| | Early Proterozoic | 1500–2500 | 1000 } 4200 |
| | Archean | 2500–4000 | 1500 |
| | Hadean | 4000–4800 | 800 |

## The Evolution of Photosynthetic Organisms: Biological Evidence

The evolution of oxygenic photosynthesis can also be reconstructed or inferred by comparing the features of extant photosynthetic organisms. The earliest photosynthetic organisms evolved approximately 3800 million ybp as anaerobic bacteria (Schopf 1983; Fig 1.5). These organisms used light energy to extract protons and electrons from a variety of donor molecules, such as $H_2S$, to reduce $CO_2$ to form organic molecules. Anaerobic photosynthetic processes were probably among the first energy-transforming processes to appear on Earth, and proceeded without the evolution of molecular oxygen (Blankenship 1992). Two basic types of anaerobic photosynthetic reactions appear to have evolved and have persisted to the present time. One, typified by the heliobacteria and green sulphur bacteria such as *Chlorobium*, uses iron-sulfur clusters as an electron acceptor; whereas the second, typified by the purple photosynthetic bacteria and *Chloroflexus*, uses phaeophytin and a quinone as an electron acceptor (Fig 1.6). The two types of bacterial reaction centers appear to have evolved independently; no known anaerobic photosynthetic bacteria contains both types of light reactions (Blankenship 1992).

Best-guess reconstructions of the scant fossil evidence suggest that some 100 to 200 million years following the appearance of anaerobic photosynthetic bacteria,

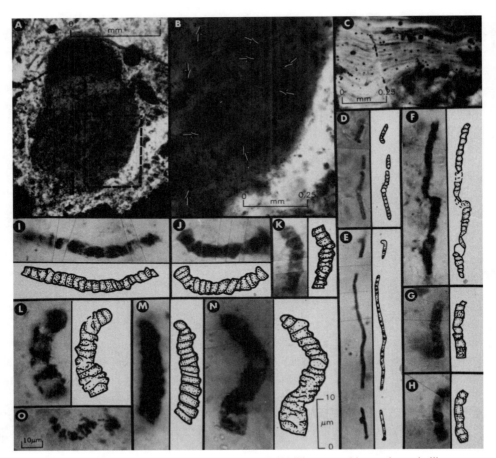

**Figure 1.5** Transmission electron photomicrographs of 3.45 billion-year-old cyanobacteria-like organisms. Microfossiliferous (A and B) and laminated stromatolite-like groups (C), and carbonaceous and iron-stained (L) prokaryotic fossil microorganisms (with interpretive drawings) shown in petrographic thin sections of the Early Archean Apex chert from northwestern Australia. Except as otherwise indicated, magnification of all parts is denoted by the scale in (N). (D) to (K) and (N) and (O) show photomontages of the sinous three-dimensional microfossils. (A) Microfossiliferous group; area denoted by dashed lines is shown in (B). (B) Arrows point to minute filamentous microfossils, randomly oriented in the group. (C) Portion of a group showing stromatolite-like laminae. (D and E) *Archaeotrichion septatum* (D, holotype). (F) *Eoleptonema apex* (holotype). (G and H) *Primaevifilum minutum* (G, holotype). (I, J, and K) *Primaevifilum delicatulum* (I, holotype). (L, M, N, and O) *Archaeoscillatoriopsis disciformis* (M, holotype). (Courtesy of J. William Schopf, with permission)

oxygen-producing photosynthetic organisms emerged in the oceans (Holland 1984). The fossilized outlines of these cells can be found in the oldest rocks on the Earth's crust and they are strikingly similar to extant cyanobacteria. Aquatic photosynthetic organisms filled the late Archean or early Proterozoic atmosphere with oxygen, permanently transforming the Earth and simultaneously poisoning most habitats for the anaerobic bacteria. Subsequently, the ecological and biogeochemical role of anaerobic photosynthetic bacteria has been one more of evolutionary curiosity than biogeochemical linchpin. In fact, there is clear fossil evidence of multicellular pho-

**(A)** **(B)**

**Figure 1.6** Approx. 1700 million-year-old (early Proterozoic epoch) fossil eukaryotic alga of unknown affinities from the Tuanshanzi Formation of the Changsheng Group of the Jixian region of north China. (A) Micrograph showing the ribbonlike blade and the holdfast by which it was attached to the substratum. Scale bar = 5 mm. (B) Scanning electron micrograph of the internal structure showing multicellular organization. Scale bar = 2 μm. (Courtesy of Prof. Zhu Shixing)

tosynthetic aquatic organisms, the forerunners of the modern-day seaweeds, 1.7 billion ybp, in the middle of the Proterozoic (see Fig 1.6). There is striking homology, however, between the proteins found in the two basic anaerobic photosynthetic bacteria and the photosynthetic apparatus of oxygenic cyanobacteria, unicellular eukaryotic algae, seaweeds, and higher plants (Barber 1992; Blankenship 1992; Bryant 1994; Michel, Deisenhofer 1988; Reith 1995). Based on this homology, it is assumed that the photoreaction responsible for the oxidation of water (photosystem II) is derived from an organism resembling the relict purple photosynthetic bacteria, while the second photoreaction (photosystem I), also found in all photosynthetic oxygenic photoautotrophs, arose from the green sulfur bacterial line. (We will discuss these two photosystems in Chapters 2, 4, and 6.)

Since the first appearance of aquatic oxygenic photosynthetic organisms, approximately 12 divisions (or phyla) of unicellular and multicellular algae have evolved, and there is no place on Earth where photosynthetic organisms cannot be found if liquid water and light are available for at least part of the year (Cavalier-Smith 1993a; Table 1.3). Although the earliest oxygenic photosynthetic organisms were prokaryotes, all but one of the 12 recognized algal divisions are eukaryotic. Eukaryotic cells appear to have arisen at least 2 billion years ago (Wray, Levinton 1996). Based on the structure of fossils that are at least 700 million years old, the first eukaryotic algae referable to a modern algal class resemble members of the extant red algal family, Bangiaceae.

**Table 1.3** The higher taxa of oxygenic photoautotrophs, with estimates of the approximate number of total known species, and their distributions between marine and freshwater habitats*

| Taxonomic Group | Known Species | Marine | Freshwater |
|---|---|---|---|
| Empire: Bacteria (= Prokaryota) | | | |
| Kingdom: Eubacteria | | | |
| Subdivision: Cyanobacteria (sensu strictu) | 1,500 | 150 | 1,350 |
| (= Cyanophytes, blue-green algae) | | | |
| Subdivision: Chloroxybacteria (= Prochlorophyceae) | 3 | 2 | 1 |
| | | | |
| Empire: Eukaryota | | | |
| Kingdom: Protozoa | | | |
| Division: Euglenophyta | 1,050 | 30 | 1,020 |
| Class: Euglenophyceae | | | |
| Division: Dinophyta (Dinoflagellates) | | | |
| Class: Dinophyceae | 2,000 | 1,800 | 200 |
| Kingdom: Plantae | | | |
| Subkingdom: Biliphyta | | | |
| Division: Glaucocystophyta | | | |
| Class: Glaucocystophyceae | 13 | — | — |
| Division: Rhodophyta | | | |
| Class: Rhodophyceae | 6,000 | 5,880 | 120 |
| Subkingdom: Viridiplantae | | | |
| Division: Chlorophyta | | | |
| Class: Chlorophyceae | 2,500 | 100 | 2,400 |
| Prasinophyceae | 120 | 100 | 20 |
| Ulvophyceae | 1,100 | 1,000 | 100 |
| Charophyceae | 12,500 | 100 | 12,400 |
| Division: Bryophyta (mosses, liverworts) | 22,000 | — | 1,000 |
| Division: Lycopsida | 1,228 | — | 70 |
| Division: Filicopsida (ferns) | 8,400 | — | 94 |
| Division: Magnoliophyta (flowering plants) | (240,000) | | |
| Subdivision: Monocotyledoneae | 52,000 | 55 | 455 |
| Subdivision: Dicotyledoneae | 188,000 | — | 391 |
| | | | |
| Kingdom: Chromista | | | |
| Subkingdom: Chlorechnia | | | |
| Division: Chlorarachniophyta | | | |
| Class: Chlorarachniophyceae | 3–4 | 3–4 | 0 |
| Subkingdom: Euchromista | | | |
| Division: Crytophyta | | | |
| Class: Cryptophyceae | 200 | 100 | 100 |
| Division: Haptophyta | | | |
| Class: Prymnesiophyceae | 500 | 100 | 400 |
| Division: Heterokonta | | | |
| Class: Bacillariophyceae (diatoms) | 10,000 | 5,000 | 5,000 |
| Chrysophyceae | 1,000 | 800 | 200 |
| Eustigmatophyceae | 12 | 6 | 6 |
| Fucophyceae (brown algae) | 1,500 | 1,497 | 3 |
| Raphidophyceae | 27 | 10 | 17 |
| Synurophyceae | 250 | — | 250 |
| Tribophyceae (Xanthophyceae) | 600 | 50 | 500 |
| | | | |
| Kingdom: Fungi | | | |
| Division: Ascomycotina (lichens) | 13,000 | 15 | 20 |

*The difference between the number of marine and freshwater species, and that of known species, is accounted for by terrestrial organisms. Dashes indicate that no species are known (by us) for their particular group in this environment. (Adapted from John 1996; Mabberly 1987)

## THE ORIGIN AND PHYLOGENY OF PHOTOAUTOTROPHS

The determination of evolutionary relationships has been greatly aided by molecular biological methods. Molecular techniques permit quantitative measurement of the genetic diversity of organisms. One of the most common approaches to deducing diversity compares nucleic acid sequences, especially those obtained from ribosomal RNA (Neefs et al. 1993). The two rRNA molecules that are commonly used in constructing phylogenetic trees are the 16S[6] and 18S rRNAs. Analysis of these data is particularly useful because of the large databases for these molecules from a wide variety of organisms. The 16S rRNA molecule, together with about 21 proteins, constitutes the small subunit of the 70S ribosome that is responsible for translating organellar and prokaryote messenger RNA (Hill 1990). The 18S rRNA molecule, together with about 30 proteins, constitutes the small subunit of the 80S ribosome that translates nuclear-encoded mRNA in eukaryotic cells. Both the 16S and 18S rRNA molecules contain both conserved and variable sequence regions (Fig 1.7). The distinction between conserved and variable regions is related to the frequency with which base substitutions are made at specific positions relative to the entire molecule. Thus, in regions of the molecule with sequence variations, the nucleotide base substitutions can be analyzed between 16S or 18S rRNA sequences from a wide variety of organisms. These sequences are compared using a variety of mathematical criteria to obtain a measure of the evolutionary "distance" or divergence between organisms. Assuming an ancestral origin of a sequence as the root (preferably using a sequence from an organism that is not represented by a taxon under investigation), each sequence can be related to the root to develop a branching tree or *cladogram* (Medlin et al. 1994).

A cladogram showing the phylogeny of prokaryotes, based on the analyses of 16S rRNA nucleotide sequences (Giovannoni et al. 1993), is shown in Figure 1.8. This analysis provided a basis for distinguishing between two major groupings of bacteria, the eubacteria and the archebacteria (Woese 1987). The latter are believed to have been among the first life-forms to evolve on the Earth and contain all the extreme thermophilic heterotrophic bacteria, methanogens, and extreme halophiles. The eubacteria contain all the gram-positive bacteria, green nonsulfur bacteria, cyanobacteria, and flavobacteria, and a group of gram-negative bacteria that, for want of a better name, are called "purple bacteria." The purple bacteria are further

---

6. S is an abbreviation for a Svedberg unit, which is a unit of relative mass named after a Swedish physicist who invented the ultracentrifuge. The unit is based on the rate of sedimentation of molecules or particles in a centrifugal field. The rate of sedimentation is related to a sedimentation coefficient, $s$, by: $s = dx/dt\,(\omega^2 x)^{-1}$, where $x$ is distance of the molecule or particle from the center of rotation after time $t$ (in seconds) in the rotating field and $\omega$ is the angular velocity in radians per second. A sedimentation coefficient of $1 \times 10^{-13}$ s is equal to 1S. Thus, a 16S rRNA molecule would sediment with a coefficient of $16 \times 10^{-13}$ s. The larger the coefficient, the larger the molecular mass of the molecule (i.e., the faster it sediments). The molecular mass can be related to the sedimentation rate by the Svedberg equation: $mw = RTs/D(1 - v\rho)$, where $R$ is the gas constant, $T$ is absolute temperature, $v$ is the partial specific volume of the sedimenting particle or molecule, $D$ is the diffusion coefficient, and $\rho$ is the density of the solvent. This equation only gives an approximate molecular mass because it assumes that the sedimenting particles or molecules behave like an ideal gas, meaning that the particles are perfect spheres and do not have any interactions between each other.

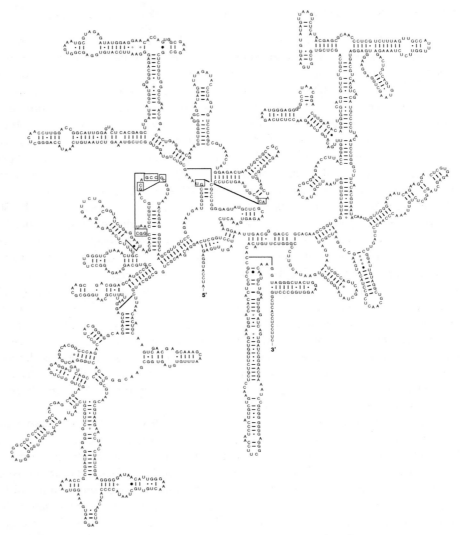

**Figure 1.7** The secondary structure of the small subunit (16S) rRNA from *Chlamydomonas reinhardtii*. The structure is inferred from homology with known structures in yeast and prokaryotes. Hollow circles and unpaired regions represent areas of generally higher variability between organisms.

subdivided into α, β, γ, and δ subdivisions. The α subdivision includes the rhizobacteria which are capable of nitrogen fixation and form symbiotic associations with legumes, and the rickettsias, which are intracellular pathogens of animals.

In addition to the nucleus, eukaryotic photoautotrophs contain two membrane-bound organelles, namely chloroplasts (often called *plastids*) and mitochondria. In eukaryotes, molecular phylogenies can be constructed from either 16S or 18S rRNA molecules (Falkowksi and LaRoche 1991). The former are found in the plastids whereas the latter trace the phylogeny of the nucleus. A cladogram for eukaryotes, based on 18S rRNA sequences, is shown in Figure 1.9. Other molecular cladograms

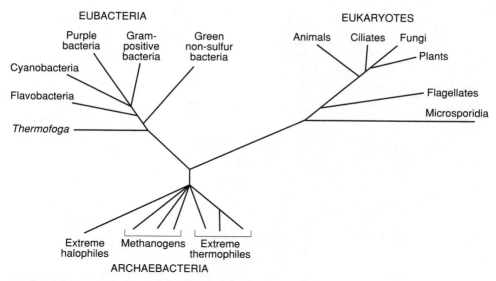

**Figure 1.8** Universal phylogenetic tree, indicating relationships among major taxa derived from RNA sequence comparisons. Modified from Woese (1989), with more detail on taxa of special interest to the subject matter of this book.

have also been published and alternative schemes to that shown in Figure 1.9 can be plausibly constructed. The alternative schemes often differ in some important details, and true phylogenetic relationships are not yet established for all algal divisions because the 18S rRNA data have not yet resolved the earliest relationships among major taxa of photoautotrophs.

The prevailing theory for the origin of these organelles is the so-called *endosymbiotic hypothesis* (Margulis 1974). This hypothesis suggests that progenitor eukaryotes originated as prokaryotic cells, which phagotrophically engulfed and incorporated other prokaryotes to form intracellular symbionts. The engulfed, ancestral prokaryote formed organelles. Thus, according to the hypothesis, chloroplasts arose from oxygenic cyanobacteria that presumably had themselves arisen from the genetic fusion of ancestral purple photosynthetic bacteria (with a photosystem II–like reaction center) with green sulfur bacteria (with a photosystem I–like reaction center). The template for mitochondria appears to have been a branch of eubacteria, the α-proteobacteria (Margulis 1974). The origin of plastid- and mitochondria-containing eukaryotes is, according to the endosymbiotic hypothesis, a result of arrested digestion of cyanobacteria and α-proteobacteria, respectively, that had been ingested by phagotrophic ancestral eukaryotes with endomembranes and a cytoskeleton. Such a proposal seems plausible because symbiotic associations of protists with eukaryotic and prokaryotic algae have been well documented, especially for the dinoflagellates (Schnepf, Elbrächter 1992; Taylor 1987).

One infers that the plastids of many eukaryotic algae arose from the ingestion of prokaryotes (i.e., a "primary" endosymbiosis), or of other eukaryotic, plastid-containing photosynthetic organisms (i.e., a "secondary" endosymbiosis) by eukaryotic phagotrophs. A major clue to the wholesale incorporation of a prefabricated

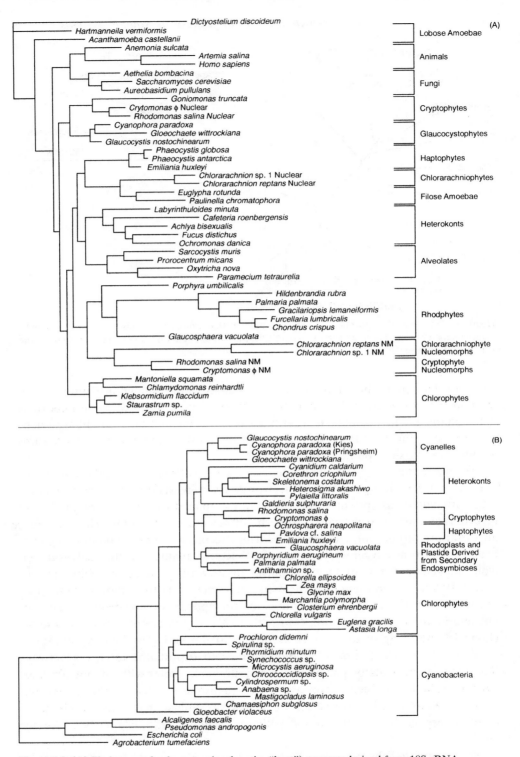

**Figure 1.9** (A) Phylogeny of eukaryotes (nuclear, i.e. "host") genome derived from 18S rRNA sequences using a "maximum likelihood" method (see Bhattacharya, Medlin 1995). Phylogenetic distance is proportional to the connecting lines. Note that the apparent close relationship between nucleomorphs of cryptophytes and chlorarachniophytes is an artifact (Palmer, Delwiche 1996). (B) A phylogenetic tree derived from analysis of plastid (i.e., "symbiont") genomes using plastid-encoded 16S rRNA sequences (Bhattacharya, Medlin 1995). (Courtesy of Linda Medlin)

## ❏ THE MOLECULAR CLOCK

*The analysis of sequence variation in establishing phylogenetic relationships is based on the observation that the number of nucleotide or amino acid substitutions separating a pair of species is proportional to the time back to a common ancestor. In the simplest models, the rate at which substitutions occur is assumed to be constant (although there is significant debate on this issue) for a specific molecule (Gillespie 1991). If it is further assumed that the substitutions, I, are random point processes, then the statistical probability, P, of change can be derived from a Poisson distribution:*

$$P[N(t) = I] = e^{-rt}(rt)^I / I!  \tag{1.11}$$

*where N(t) is the total number of substitutions at a particular point over time t, and r is the rate of substitution. This analysis forms the basis of the "molecular clock," from which it is possible to estimate rates of speciation within an algal class, or rates of divergence from a common origin. Each mutation represents a "tick." For example, geological evidence indicates that diatoms probably arose during the Jurassic period, some 200 million years ago (when dinosaurs roamed a conglomerated continent we call "Gondwana" and the Atlantic Ocean was just being formed). Based on the rate of substitution of bases in 18S rRNAs, it is estimated that 1% of the ancestral diatom genome has changed every 18 million years (Medlin et al. 1995; Fig 1.10).*

---

photosynthetic apparatus is the presence of extra membranes surrounding the plastids (Reith 1995; Fig 1.11; Table 1.4). In green algae, red algae, and higher plants the chloroplast envelope always contains two membranes (Berner 1993). In Euglenophyta and Dinophyta there are three plastid envelope membranes, whereas Chlorarachniophyta, Cryptophyta, Heterokonta, and Haptophyta have four (see Fig 1.11). In many cases, the outermost membranes form an endoreticular conduit from the cell's nucleus to the chloroplast.

Perhaps the most convincing evidence for the evolution of a plastid from a photosynthetic eukaryote is the presence of a nucleomorph[7] (the remnant nucleus of the endosymbiont) in the plastid compartment of cryptophytes and chlorarachniophytes (Gibbs 1992). In cryptophytes, the 18S rRNA from the nucleomorph more closely resembles red algal 18S rRNA rather than cryptophyte nuclear 18S rRNA, suggesting the plastids of the latter evolved from an endosymbiotic red algal-like organism (Cavalier-Smith 1993b; Douglas et al. 1991).

A key aspect of the endosymbiont hypothesis is that the incorporated organelle has become an obligate symbiont—chloroplasts cannot reproduce without their "host" cell. The obligate nature of the organelle is assured by the transfer of many of the genes necessary for its independent function to the nucleus of the host cell, as well as the loss of genes that would permit the endosymbiont to revert to a free-living existence. For example, all eukaryotic algae lack a complete suite of tRNAs in both the mitochondria and chloroplast. The missing genes are found in the

---

7. A *nucleomorph* is a nucleic-acid–containing, membrane-bound organelle located in the cytoplasmic region between the two sets of double membranes (i.e., a total of four in all) that surround the plastid.

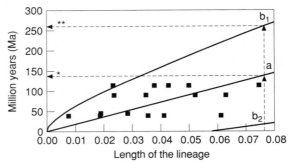

**Figure 1.10** Results of molecular clock calibrations in which dates of first appearances of diatom lineages in the fossil record are regressed against their measured branch lengths from a maximum likelihood tree. The straight line (a) is the regression line, forced through zero; the upper and lower curves (b1 and b2) are the 95% confidence limits for a new predicted value of time according to Hillis and Moritz (1990). Lower confidence limits, lower than zero, are reset at zero. The average age of the diatoms (* = 138 Ma) is the length of their median lineage in the maximum likelihood tree multiplied by the regression coefficient. The earliest possible age of the diatoms (** = 258 Ma) is the date corresponding to the point on the upper 95% confidence limit given the length of the median lineage of the group. Because of poor preservation in the fossil record from 110 Ma to 70 Ma, it is hypothesized that taxa with a first appearance date of 770 Ma emerge at 90 Ma or at 115 Ma if selected taxa can be linked to similar fossil taxa in 115 Ma deposits. Using these calibrations, the diatoms are evolving at 1% per 18.0 Ma +/− 5.3 Ma. (Courtesy of Linda Medlin)

nucleus, and the gene products must be imported into the respective organelles. Thus, the transcription and translation of organelle genes, which are essential for organelle function, are dependent on the supply of tRNAs encoded by the nucleus, thereby allowing nuclear control of organelle protein synthesis.

There is considerable variability among algae in the number of genes retained in the plastid genome, but a core of genes encoding essential plastid and mito-chondrial functions are present in all of the respective organelles (Valentin et al. 1993). In chloroplasts, this core comprises genes for the electron transport compo-nents required for the light reactions, as well as enzymes that catalyze key dark reac-tions. The organellar genes are not inherited by Mendelian genetics. As we will see in Chapter 6, this conservation greatly improves the ability to extrapolate specific biophysical, structural, and biochemical processes that are encoded in the chloro-plast genome from model organisms to large groups of otherwise disparate organisms.

The evolution of photosynthetic organisms was not simply linear, but rather branched. Understanding the mechanisms that led to the selection of individual species and the progenitor branches of the various algal classes in relationship to photosynthetic characteristics is an important aspect of phylogeny and physiologi-cal ecology. Historically, the systematics and classification of aquatic photosynthetic organisms have been based largely on the characteristics of organelles, especially chloroplasts and their pigments (Cavalier-Smith 1993b; Lee 1989). Because of the ease with which they can be assayed, photosynthetic pigments have been used to distinguish among algal classes. Two major groups of eukaryotic algae have been delineated in an informal taxonomy based on whether they contain (1) chlorophyll *b* (with or without chlorophyll *c*), the chlorophytes, or (2) chlorophyll *c*, the chro-mophytes (a few members of which have only chlorophyll *a* but most also have

**Table 1.4** Structure and pigmentation of the photosynthetic apparatus in the higher taxa of oxygenic photoautotrophs with aquatic members

| Cell Structure | PROKARYOTIC | EUKARYOTIC | | |
|---|---|---|---|---|
| Compartments | Thylakoids in cytoplasm; No membranes between thylakoids and plasmalemma | Thylakoids in Plastids | | |
| | | Plastids in the cytoplasm; Envelope of two membranes | Plastids in subcompartment of the cytoplasm | |
| | | | Envelope of four membranes | Envelope of three membranes |
| Taxa; *Thylakoid Arrangement* | Cyanobacteria Cyanobacteria *sensu strictu* (Cyanophyceae) (1) *Thylakoids single* | Biliphyta (1) Rhodophyceae Glaucocystophyceae *Thylakoids single* | Heterokonta (5) Bacillariophyceae Chrysophyceae Eustigmatophyceae Fucophyceae (= Phaeophyceae) Pelagophyceae Synurophyceae Tribophyceae (= Xanthophyceae) *Thylakoids in stacks of three* | Euglenophyta (4) *Thylakoids in stacks of one or more* |
| | Chloroxybacteria (3) (Prochlorophyceae) *Thylakoids in pairs* | Viridiplantae (4) Chlorophyta Bryophyta Lycopsida Filicopsida Magnoliophyta *Thylakoids in stacks of three or more* | Haptophyta (5) *Thylakoids in stacks of three* | Dinophyta (6) *Thylakoids in stacks of three or more* |
| | | | Cryptophyta (2) *Thylakoids in pairs* | |
| | | | Chlorarachniophyta (4) *Thylakoids in stacks of three* | |

Pigments and their location as indicated by suffix number:

(1) Chlorophyll *a*, β-carotene and other carotenoids in the thylakoid membrane; phycobilins on the N side of the membrane.

(2) Chlorophyll *a*, Chlorophyllide $c_2$ (± Mg-2,4 divinyl phaeoporphyrin $a_5$ monomethyl ester), β-carotene and other carotenoids in the thylakoid membrane; phycobilins on the P side of the membrane.

(3) Chlorophyll *a* (± divinyl-Chlorophyll *a*), Chlorophyll *b* (± divinyl-Chlorophyll *b*), β-carotene and other carotenoids on the thylakoid membrane.

(4) Chlorophyll *a*, Chlorophyll *b* (Mg-2,4 divinyl phaeoporphyrin $a_5$ monomethyl ester in some members of the Chlorophyceae, Prasinophyceae in the Chlorophyta), β-carotene and other carotenoids in the thylakoid membrane.

(5) Chlorophyll *a*, Chlorophyllide $c_1$ and/or $c_2$ and/or $c_3$ (or no Chlorophyllide *c* in Eustigmatophyceae); β-carotene and other carotenoids (usually including fucoxanthin and/or fatty acid derivatives) in the thylakoid membrane.

(6) Chlorophyll *a*, Chlorophyll *c*, β-carotene and other carotenoids including peridinin, some Chlorophyll *a*, all peridinin, in complexes on the surface thylakoid membrane, remaining pigments in the thylakoid membrane.

chlorophyll *c*). The red algae are sometimes included with the chlorophytes but also often simply are called rhodophytes (Reith 1995). By incorporating the myriad accessory pigments found in specific algal classes, this type of "chemotaxonomic" classification can be highly refined and has practical application in the rapid characterization of natural assemblages of aquatic organisms by employing chromatographic pigment analyses.

A further clue to the relationship among photosynthetic organisms can be gleaned from the ultrastructural organization of the thylakoid membranes. Being lipid bilayers, thylakoid membranes can aggregate via hydrophobic interactions.[8] In higher plant chloroplasts, highly appressed areas of thylakoids called grana lamellae are interconnected with lower density regions (often single thylakoids) called stromal lamellae (Staehelin 1986).

Whereas in higher plants this organizational differentiation within the thylakoids appears to be important in the lateral distribution of electron transport components along the membrane surface, this "typical" chloroplast structure is rarely found in algae. In cyanobacteria and red algae, thylakoids occur singly. The lack of any association between thylakoids in these organisms is likely a result of their major light-harvesting complexes, the phycobilisomes. These hydrophilic macro-

---

8. Hydrophobic interactions are brought about as a result of the thermodynamic relationship of molecules to water. Liquid water forms extensive hydrogen bonding networks. Hydrophobic molecules, such as lipids, tend to aggregate in aqueous phases, thereby minimizing the disruption of the hydrogen bonds. This is a low free-energy condition. Hence, the water "squeezes" the lipids together, forming bilayers. Subsequent, larger interactions can be brought about by the addition of hydrophobic proteins, or secondary lipids, to form heterogeneous, macromolecular complexes. Hydrophobic interactions are generally weak and can be readily disrupted by cold temperatures, organic solvents, detergents, and some small ions such as $Na^+$.

---

**Figure 1.11** Transmission electron micrographs showing the basic structure of chloroplast membranes in a variety of unicellular algae. (a) A section through the whole cell of the chrysophyte, *Ochromonas danica*, and (b) a detailed view of the thylakoid membranes. Note that the membranes form stacks of three. The chloroplast itself is surrounded by four membranes, the two inner membranes are designated chloroplast envelope membranes while the two outer membranes are the chloroplast endoplasmic reticulum. In (a) it can be seen that the chloroplast endoplasmic reticulum is continuous with the nucleus, and ribosomes on the membrane translate nuclear-encoded genes destined for the chloroplast. (c) A section through the chloroplast of the chlorophyte *Dunaliella tertiolecta* (inset a whole cell section). Note the large electron transparent region within the chloroplast, which corresponds to a site of starch accumulation. At the center of this structure is a pyrenoid. The thylakoid membranes can be aggregated to less aggregated, depending on growth conditions. Inspection of the whole cell reveals that the chloroplast in this organism follows the cell perimeter but with an opening. This structure is often called a "cup-shaped" chloroplast. (d) A whole cell section through a diatom, *Cylindrotheca guillardii*. As found in chrysophytes (a), the thylakoids form stacks of three membranes, and the chloroplast is surrounded by four. The outer membrane of the chloroplast can be seen to envelop a nucleomorph at the bottom of the cup-shaped chloroplast. The nucleomorph is the vestigial nucleus of the symbiont that gave rise to the chloroplast in this organism. (e) Section through a diatom, *Phaeodactylum tricornutum*. Thylakoids are found in stacks of three, except in the pyrenoid, where they are often paired. The chloroplast is also surrounded by four membranes, but unlike in chrysophytes or cryptophytes, the outer membrane seldom is connected to either the nucleus or a nucleomorph. (Panels a, b, d, and e courtesy of Sally Gibbs and Michael McKay)

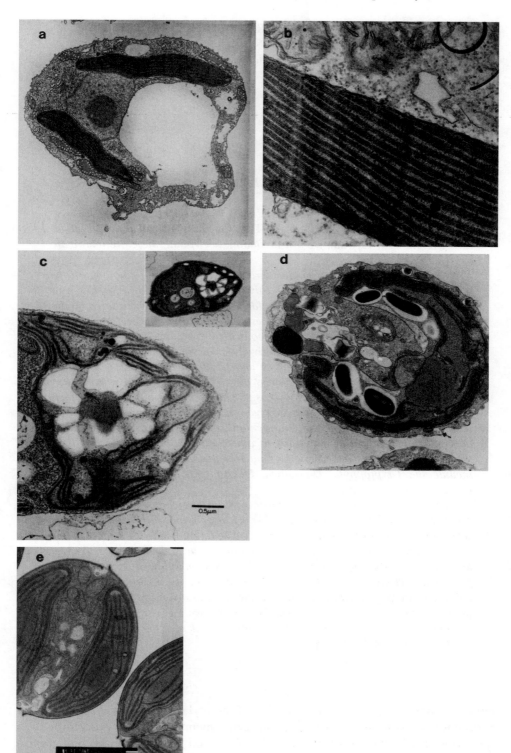

## ❏ NOMENCLATURE OF MAJOR GROUPS OF AQUATIC PHOTOSYNTHETIC ORGANISMS

*The hierarchy of taxonomic classification is basically as follows:*

*Empire*

*Kingdom*

*Subkingdom*

*Division = Phylum*

*Subdivision*

*Class*

*Order*

*Family*

*Genus*

*Species*

*Botanical texts frequently use the term* Division *while microbial and zoological texts use the term* Phylum; *from a taxonomic viewpoint, these are hierarchical equivalents.*

*Ironically, molecular biological criteria for classifying photoautotrophs, based on their "real" (i.e., evolutionarily meaningful) relationships, has sometimes caused more confusion than the older classification schemes based on morphology and/or pigmentation. This is especially true at the level of Divisions. Viridiplantae, for example, is a term coined by Cavalier-Smith to include the Chlorophyta and their higher plant derivatives. Excluded from Viridiplantae are two groups of algae, the Euglenophyta and Chlorarachniophyta, that obtained their plastids from unicellular members of the Chlorophyta but whose nuclear genome is only distantly related to those of higher plants and of Chlorophyta. Similarly, the Biliphyta covers the red algae and the Glaucocystophyta, which are related to each other by their nuclear genomes, but not the groups that acquired their chloroplasts by endosymbiosis of unicellular red algae and are only distantly related to them as far as their nuclear genome is concerned. The latter include the Cryptophyta, Dinophyta, Haptophyta, and Heterokonta (sensu Cavalier-Smith 1993a,b).*

*An informal taxonomic usage has evolved in the photosynthesis researcher population (no doubt encoded in their nuclear genomes through mutation and selection by their professors). Thus,* green algae *or* chlorophytes *refer to eukaryotic chlorophyll-b–containing organisms other than higher plants. Eukaryotes lacking either chlorophyll* b *and phycobilins, but containing chorophyll* c *and/or fucoxanthin (Heterokonta, Haptophyta) or peridinin (most Dinophyta) are often called* chromophytes. *Although most of the chromophytes are brown, yellow, or olive-green rather than bright green, the term* brown algae *is generally reserved for members of the Fucophyceae (Phaeophyceae), all members of which are multicellular and contain chlorophyll* c.

---

molecules are located on the stromal side of the thylakoid membrane and prevent hydrophobic associations between adjacent membranes. In prochlorophytes (prokaryotic cells that contain chlorophyll *b* but no phycobilisomes) and cryptophytes (algae with phycobilins located within the thylakoid lumen and not organized into a phycobilisome), thylakoids are paired. Chromophytes typically have thylakoids in stacks of three, whereas the chlorophytes sometimes have pseudo-grana, regions of appressed stacks of three or more membranes interspersed with less-stacked regions (Berner 1993). In no algal class is there compelling evidence of lateral heterogeneity of photosynthetic systems within the thylakoid membranes (e.g., Song, Gibbs 1995).

Although both pigment composition and ultrastructural organization of the photosynthetic apparatus have served to help establish phylogenetic relationships, because of parallel evolution and ill-defined evolutionary partnerships between pigments such an approach is limited (Bhattacharya et al. 1992). Plastid characteristics, whether they are encoded in the plastid per se or nuclear genomes, reflect the evolution of the endosymbiont that produced plastids as well as those inherited from the host (Douglas 1994; Lewin 1993). For example, the photosynthetic pigment, chlorophyll *b*, appears to have evolved several times in the prokaryotes (in the polyphyletic prochlorophytes) and once in the eukaryotic algal classes (producing the Chlorophyta, Euglenophyta, and Chlorarachniophyta from phycobilin-containing ancestors), hence phylogenetic trees based on pigment composition using chlorophyll *b* would be misleading (Palenik, Haselkorn 1992).

There are approximately 1500 species of prokaryotic photoautotrophs and 28,500 species of eukaryotic aquatic photoautotrophs extant. The ensemble of these organisms is, in the vernacular, called *algae* (from the Latin for "seaweed," although it also includes some higher plants, the seagrasses).[9] A summary of the formal names of the higher plant taxa of aquatic photosynthetic organisms is given in Table 1.3, together with estimates of their diversity and comments on their habitats (marine, freshwater, terrestrial). This arrangement is based on analyses of nuclear (i.e., 18S rRNA) characteristics; however, many of the prefixes for the classes (e.g., Chloro-, Rhodo-, Phaeo-, Xantho-, Chryso-, Cyano-, etc.) refer to plastid pigmentation, which is a more commonly found nomenclature in most texts.

One of the algal classes, the Charophyceae, was the progenitor of higher land plants and garnered a foothold in the terrestrial world about 500 million ybp. From the time of their invasion of land, higher plants have managed to diversify so extensively that an estimated 270,000 species of higher plants are extant (Table 1.3) and many more are extinct. Although there are many more species of terrestrial higher plants than there are of aquatic photoautotrophs, the genetic differences between the higher plants are relatively small compared with algae. Thus, although there are fewer recognized species of algae than there are of higher plants, there is a much larger evolutionary distance between and within algal divisions. For example, Ragan and colleagues (1994) point out that the genetic diversity within a single algal division, the Rhodophyta, is greater than that within the higher plants. Despite the great diversity of aquatic photosynthetic organisms, most of the molecular structures and functions that are essential for photosynthesis are highly conserved. This conservation suggests a common (i.e., single ancestral) origin of oxygenic photoautotrophs (Lewin 1993).

---

9. The study of algae is called *phycology*, a word derived from the Greek word for a marine plant or seaweed.

## SIMILARITIES AND DIFFERENCES IN THE PHOTOSYNTHETIC PROCESSES IN THE ALGAL CLASSES

People who study aquatic photosynthesis generally operate at two taxonomic levels. One is related to the general kind of organism they are dealing with—meaning, is it a diatom, a cyanobacterium, or a seagrass? This level of classification is at the level of divisions or of classes. A *division* or *class* is defined by the extent of similarities of the organisms within divisions (or classes) and of differences between organisms among divisions (or classes). Knowledge of the division or class confers considerable predictive value—for example, in the evolutionary origin of the photosynthetic pigments or enzymes involved in the photosynthetic process (Raven et al. 1989).

The other taxonomic level at which photosynthesis workers operate is that of the *species*. The concept of a species, which emerged from the studies of higher organisms in the 18th century, is not generally applicable for microbes in general, and for unicellular photoautrophs in particular. There is no simple, universally accepted definition of a species (Wood, Wood 1992). A species is usually defined as like organisms that exchange genetic information in nature and produce sexually viable progeny. Such a definition is restricted to sexually reproducing organisms and generally involves genetic variability within a species. For organisms that do not have easily demonstrable sexual reproduction, such as the majority of the phytoplankton, there can be many genotypes within a morphologically defined species. In the case of the marine prokaryote *Prochlorococcus marinus*, for example, only one species is recognized; however, many genotypic differences in photosynthetic responses are apparent. Even within a known sexually reproducing species, such as the diatom *Skeletonema costatum*, genetically (and biogeographically and ecophysiologically) distinguishable races can be distinguished (Gallagher et al. 1984). These races appear to be phenotypically different in their photosynthetic characteristics. Genetic variability within a species appears to be common in unicellular algae (Medlin et al. 1995).

In 1830, the British geologist and naturalist Charles Lyell wrote,

> The name of a species, observes Lamark, has been usually applied to "every collection of similar individuals, produced by other individuals like themselves." But this is not all which is usually implied by the term species, for the majority of naturalists agree with Linnaeus in supposing that all the individuals propagated from one stock have certain distinguishing characters in common which will never vary, and which have remained the same since the creation of each species. The more we advance in our knowledge of the different organized bodies which cover the surface of the globe, the more our embarrassment increases, to determine what ought to be regarded as a species, and still more how to limit and distinguish genera.

Operationally, a species may be defined as a morphologically identifiable entity of known environmental plasticity that has the same degree of similarity among members of a genus. This definition is somewhat arbitrary but often practical, although Lyell noted, "When the species are arranged in a series, and placed near to each other, with due regard for their natural affinities, they each differ in so minute a degree from those adjoining, that they almost melt into each other, and are in a manner confounded together." Because there is such propensity for confusion of what constitutes a species based on morphological characteristics, the phycological literature abounds in correction and renaming of organisms.[10]

## Life-Forms and Niches in Aquatic Photosynthetic Organisms

Species exist because of natural selection and are sustained because of genetic fitness. In the identification of species, morphological characteristics are frequent determinates; however, ecologists often adopt the concept of *life-form*, meaning the genetically determined gross morphology of an organism rather than its phenotypically determined growth form. Life-forms are presumed to confer a measure of evolutionary fitness, and therefore have been selected through the success offered to the species in a given environment. In aquatic systems, the life-form plays a key role in determining the ecological niche that an organism can occupy. With respect to photosynthesis, life-forms are critical to determining the rate of supply of substrates, especially $CO_2$ and other dissolved nutrients, and light. For example, small cells, with high surface-area-to-volume ratios, have an advantage over large cells with respect to the diffusion and acquisition of essential elements and molecules between the bulk fluid and the cell (Chisholm 1992b; Raven 1986). Thus, simply by virtue of size, small cells have a competitive advantage over large cells in environments where the diffusion of nutrients may be limiting growth. Large cells usually have a large storage capacity for nutrients (Raven 1984a). Hence, in environments where nutrients are delivered in pulses, such as continental margins or coastal upwelling areas, large cells often can acquire nutrients more rapidly and sustain growth for longer periods than their smaller counterparts (Malone 1980).

In the simplest sense, it is useful to distinguish between two basic life-forms in aquatic photoautotrophs, namely those organisms that are attached to a substrate, and those that are unattached and are free to float in the water (Lee 1989). The latter are commonly called *phytoplankton*, from the Greek *planktos*, meaning "to wander." Some phytoplankton are usually able to control their vertical position in the water column to some extent, either by changing their buoyancy and thereby facilitating sinking or floating, or by flagellar motility. In the context of photosynthesis, these vertical displacements may attenuate or enhance natural variations in irradiance resulting from turbulence; however, they do not significantly influence boundary layer thickness, and hence do not materially affect the diffusive exchange of nutrients between the bulk fluid and the organism. The boundary layer in relationship to carbon acquisition will be discussed in Chapter 5.

The attached organisms are both single-celled microalgae and multicellular macrophytes. The attached microalgae are usually associated with specific substrates

---

10. Because of the difficulty in applying the species concept to organisms that do not necessarily reproduce sexually, there have been proposals to define a species based on molecular biological criteria. For example, Annette Coleman (personal communication) has found in groups of green algae that a specific 116 nucleotide subset of the sequence between the 5.8S and the 18S rRNA gene (the second internal transcribed spacer region, or ITS2) determines the secondary structure of the primary RNA transcript. Interbreeders (members of a biological species) can differ at single nucleotide positions, but never by a compensating base pair change—a presumably more rare event. Since this region is present in essentially all eukaryotes, it could contribute to a molecular criterion for species.

in shallow waters. These organisms are often capable of movement that permits migration from the surface into the substrate. In some lakes and coastal ecosystems the single-celled, benthic organisms provide a significant source of organic carbon to the benthic community. The benthic macrophytes, or seaweeds, can reach exceedingly large sizes and can form layered canopies. From a photosynthetic perspective, the size of these organisms often has two consequences. First, the boundary layer becomes extremely large, necessitating continuous agitation to provide diffusive fluxes of nutrients to the blade or leaf of the plant. Hence, all macrophytes have relatively thin cross-sections and large benthic macrophytes are often found in surf zones or regions with large physical energy inputs that facilitate the physical movement of water and nutrients to the plant. This situation is analogous to that of cell size for microalgae, but is significantly different from that of terrestrial environments, where the diffusive fluxes of gases (e.g., $CO_2$) are four orders of magnitude higher in air than in water. Secondly, the canopy of the macrophytes can shade lower blades from light. This situation is highly analogous to terrestrial plant canopies; however, the degree of physiological acclimation that results in aquatic macrophytes is without parallel. The acclimation of the photosynthetic apparatus to irradiance will be discussed in Chapters 7 and 9.

### Nutritional Modes in Aquatic Phototrophs

While the life-form and shape of an organism begin to define the environment in which the organism may survive and grow, the nutritional mode can also be extremely important. By far the majority of the organisms in all of the higher taxa listed in Table 1.3 are capable of photosynthetic oxygen evolution and of growth with inorganic carbon as the sole carbon source and light as the sole energy source. If, as is also usually the case, other nutrient elements can also be used in the inorganic form, then this mode of nutrition is termed *photoautotrophy*, meaning light-dependent self-feeders (sometimes called *photolithotrophy*; Table 1.5). Obligate photoautotrophs are generally able to take up and metabolize at least some organic carbon compounds, but they can grow only if light and $CO_2$ are provided, and the presence of an exogenous organic carbon source also does not always enhance the light- and $CO_2$-saturated growth rate. Some of the obligate photoautotrophs have a requirement for one or more vitamins, supplied in nature by secretion or excretion from other organisms or by death and decay of other organisms. Obligate photoautotrophy is, by far, the major pathway for the biochemical reduction of inorganic carbon in aquatic environments and is the overarching subject of this book.

Earlier we had briefly mentioned that a second organelle, the *mitochondrion*, was also incorporated via the phagotrophic ingestion of a symbiotic prokaryote. This organelle oxidizes organic carbon at the expense of molecular oxygen to provide not only energy but also substrates for cell growth. This aspect of cell metabolism will be examined in Chapter 8. Mitochondria are found in almost all eukaryotic cells, whether photosynthetic or not.[11] Although all obligate photoautotrophs are photo-

---

11. Some eukaryotes, such as the flagellates *Giardia* and *Microsporidium*, have been considered as never having had mitochondria, but apparently these organisms lost them in evolution.

**Table 1.5** Definitions of carbon and energy acquisition mechanisms used by aquatic plants

| Term | Definition for an Organism Using It as an Obligate or Facultative Nutritional Mode | |
| --- | --- | --- |
| | Obligate | Facultative |
| Photoautotrophy (Photolithotrophy) | Light as sole energy source, $CO_2$ as sole C source; unable to grow in dark. | Able to grow photoautotrophically, or in light with organic C as supplemental energy and C source, or (in most cases) in dark on organic C. |
| Heterotrophy (Chemoorganotrophy) | Organic C as sole energy and C source (anaplerotic $CO_2$ needs satisfied from respired $CO_2$); cannot produce chlorophyll. | |

synthetic, not all photosynthetic organisms are obligate photoautotrophs. Some of the organisms in Table 1.3 are capable of using organic carbon as a supplement to, or a replacement for, light and $CO_2$ as the energy and carbon sources for growth (see Table 1.5). These organisms metabolize the externally supplied organic carbon by oxygen-consuming, heterotrophic metabolic processes, where mitochondrial respiration supplements, or in some cases replaces, chloroplast metabolism. Such organisms are called *facultative photoautotrophs*. An example of a commonly grown facultative photoautotroph is the freshwater chlorophyte, *Chlamydomonas* sp, which is often used to study the molecular genetics of photosynthesis. *Chlamydomonas* can use simple organic compounds such as acetate to supplement its photosynthetic nutrition. Facultative photoautotrophy (sometimes called *mixotrophy*) may be common in estuarine phytoplankton, where the concentrations of dissolved organic compounds are relatively high.

If cells can also grow in the dark with an exogenous organic carbon source, they are *heterotrophs* (sometimes called *chemoorganotrophs*). Some species of diatoms and many species of dinoflagellates and euglenoids, for example, lack photosynthetic pigments entirely and are completely dependent on heterotrophic metabolism. *Phagotrophy* (the ingestion of particles) is a form of acquisition of exogenous organic matter that is found in both facultative photoautotrophic and heterotrophic organisms. Phagotrophy by facultative photoautotrophs occurs in a number of diverse microalgal taxa, notably the Chrysophyceae, Cryptophyta, Dinophyta, and Haptophyta. As definitive tests for these alternative nutritional modes have been largely restricted to microalgae, the nutritional status of most larger aquatic photosynthetic organisms is sometimes unclear (Ramus 1992).

## THE STUDY OF PHOTOSYNTHESIS: A COALESCENCE OF DISCIPLINES

Since the middle of the 20th century, the main trends in photosynthesis research have been, broadly speaking, moving from biophysical to biochemical to molecular biological and structural processes on one hand, and toward large-scale—even global—investigations on the other, with each subdiscipline enhancing and modifying the previous research in the others.

From the late 1920s to the late 1960s, studies of the photosynthetic light reactions were primarily biophysical; photosynthesis was studied from the mechanistic perspective of physical chemistry, where the process was treated as a chemical reaction (Clayton 1980; Rabinowitch, Govindjee 1969). Using principles described by empirical mathematical equations, the early biological physicists treated photosynthesis as a "black box." In the early stages of research that approach was especially useful because it allowed for systematic analyses of complex processes without requiring a mechanistic understanding of the processes.

From the late 1950s through the 1970s, research expanded and became more diversified as biochemists and geneticists explored the nature of the molecules involved in the photosynthetic apparatus. During this period, there was special interest and subsequent progress in understanding the mechanism of carbon fixation, patterns of the flow of electrons and protons, and the generation of ATP in chloroplasts (Lawlor 1993). Interestingly, the reactions responsible for carbon fixation were first elucidated in *Chlorella* and directly extended to higher plants.

The 1980s hailed the beginning of the molecular biological era, which led to characterization of key genes and proteins responsible for the photosynthetic light reactions and the development of detailed working models of the "photosynthetic apparatus." By 1985 the light energy conversion system of a purple photosynthetic bacterium, *Rhodopseudomonas viridis*, had been crystallized and analyzed, and its structure could be related to its function at the molecular level (Michel, Deisenhofer 1986). This structure has been central to the development of conceptual models for the reaction centers in oxygenic photosynthetic organisms (Barber J 1992; Michel et al. 1988).

In the late 1980s, geochemists and biologists began to more fully appreciate the role that aquatic photoautotrophs have played in mediating major biogeochemical cycles of the Earth (Berger et al. 1987; Falkowski, Woodhead 1992; Sarmiento, Bender 1994). These organisms are not only essential to maintaining the steady-state gas composition of the atmosphere, but also appear to be responsive to climate feedbacks (Lovelock 1994). We will discuss the biogeochemical processes in the context of the Earth's climate and the evolution and ecology of aquatic photoautotrophs in Chapter 10.

With the powerful combination of biophysics, biochemistry, and molecular and structural biology, as well as geochemistry and remote sensing technologies, considerable progress has been made toward understanding not only the molecular mechanisms basic to water splitting and electron transfer and carbon reduction, but also the extrapolation of that information to the understanding of photosynthetic processes in natural aquatic ecosystems. Integrating that information requires an appreciation of both mechanistic, reductionist approaches to photosynthetic processes as well as the more observational and synthetic approaches used to understand the evolution and ecology of photosynthetic organisms. Let us begin with the reductionist approach by examining the physical nature of light and its absorption by the photosynthetic apparatus.

# 2

# Light Absorption and Energy Transfer in the Photosynthetic Apparatus

Photosynthesis begins with the absorption of light and the transfer of its energy to special structures, called reaction centers, where the energy is used in electrical charge separation. These three processes—absorption, energy transfer, and primary charge separation—constitute the so-called light reactions of photosynthesis, and are fundamentally similar in all photosynthetic organisms. An understanding of the light reactions requires some understanding of the nature of light itself, the process of light absorption by atoms and molecules, the relationship between light absorption and molecular structure, and the concept of energy transfer between homogeneous and heterogeneous molecules. In this chapter we discuss the nature of light and its absorption by pigments in the photosynthetic apparatus.

## THE NATURE OF LIGHT

Light is electromagnetic radiation that can be produced by a variety of energy-conversion processes. For example, when a moving charged particle, such as an electron, changes its direction (thereby giving up energy), electromagnetic radiation is emitted. Light is also emitted when matter is heated. In the sun, light is produced as a by-product of nuclear fusion reactions deep in the sun's core. The fusion reactions produce γ radiation. As the radiation is absorbed by the nuclei of neighboring atoms, intense thermal energy is produced. The thermal radiation diffuses toward the sun's surface, where a portion of the energy is given off as electromagnetic radiation. It takes on the order of $10^4$ years for the energy produced by nuclear reactions in the sun's interior to migrate to the surface. Thus, light from the sun that is intercepted by the Earth today was created before the pharaohs built the pyramids.

The two components of electromagnetic radiation, namely the electronic and magnetic oscillations, are at right angles to each other and propagate along and around an axis with a velocity $c$. The frequency of the wave, $\nu$, corresponds to the frequency of the oscillation of the charged particle from whence it emanates. The spectrum of emitted energy is not continuous, but is delivered in discrete frequencies or energetic packages, called *quanta*. The phenomenological behavior of light allows the postulation of massless particles that convey the properties of the electromagnetic radiation. These massless particles have an apparent momentum and are called *photons*, a term coined in 1926 by a chemist, GN Lewis.[1]

---

1. Lewis was trying to explain the apparent pressure of light when it impinges on a body—as, for example, when a radiometer in a vacuum turns when exposed to light. He wrote, "I therefore take the liberty of proposing for this hypothetical new atom [i.e., atoms of light], which is not light but plays an essential part in every process of radiation, the name photon."

The energy ($\varepsilon$) of a photon is directly proportional to the frequency ($\nu$) of the radiating wave. The proportionality factor is called Planck's constant, $h$:

$$\varepsilon = h\nu \tag{2.1}$$

where $h$ is $6.625 \times 10^{-34}$ J s.

In a vacuum, the velocity (distance/time) of the photons is a constant ($c = 3 \times 10^{10}$ cm s$^{-1}$) and independent of frequency. To meet this constraint, the product of frequency (time$^{-1}$) and wavelength (the distance covered in one frequency period), $\lambda$, must be constant, hence:

$$c = \nu\lambda \tag{2.2}$$

From Equations 2.1 and 2.2, it can be deduced that the energy of a photon is inversely related to its wavelength:

$$\varepsilon = hc/\lambda \tag{2.3}$$

Thus, the shorter the wavelength of the radiation, the greater the photon energy. It should be noted that because the energy of a photon is inversely proportional to its wavelength but directly proportional to its frequency, representation of light in the frequency domain is more readily interpreted in relation to energy. Hence, physicists, physical chemists, and spectroscopists often represent spectra in the frequency domain, where frequency is converted to units of reciprocal length (cm$^{-1}$; i.e., the number of waves of monochromatic radiation in a centimeter—called a *wave number* and denoted by the symbol $\kappa$). Biologists, by convention, usually represent spectra as a function of wavelength, opting for units of nanometers (i.e., $10^{-9}$ m or $10^{-7}$ cm). This convention is relatively inconvenient for biophysical calculations, and often requires conversion to wave number. A simple method for converting wavelength to energy is as follows: The energy contained in a photon at 1240 nm (i.e., in the infrared) is equal to 1 eV; hence the energy at any wavelength, $\varepsilon_\lambda$, can be calculated as $\varepsilon_\lambda = 1240/\lambda$. For example, the energy of a photon at 685 nm = 1240/685 = 1.81 eV.

The interaction of electromagnetic radiation with matter depends on the energy of the radiation (Table 2.1), and the study of the interactions forms the basis of molecular spectroscopy (Banwell, McCash 1994). The sun emits electromagnetic radiation over a large range of wavelengths—from high-energy gamma emissions, through ultraviolet, visible, and infrared, to low-energy radiowaves (Fig 2.1). Solar energy peaks in the visible region of the electromagnetic spectrum, between 400 and 700 nm. These correspond to frequencies between $7.5 \times 10^{14}$ and $4.3 \times 10^{14}$ s$^{-1}$. The lower wavelength light is perceived as a violet color by the human eye, while the longer wavelength appears red.[2] From Equation 2.3, it can be calculated that the energy in this region ranges between $5 \times 10^{-19}$ and $2.8 \times 10^{-19}$ joules per photon, which is equivalent to 3.1 to 1.7 electron volts (1 ev = $1.6 \times 10^{-19}$ joules; see Table 2.1). The oxidation of water requires a change in free energy of 1.23 V per electron.

On the scale of centuries, the spectrally integrated flux of light energy from the

---

2. Spectroscopists and astrophysicists often use the shorthand notations "blue shifted" or "red shifted" to indicate light absorbed or emitted at shorter or longer wavelengths, respectively.

**Table 2.1** The major regions of the electromagnetic spectrum and their interactions with matter

| Interaction with matter | Region | Wavenumber ($cm^{-1}$) | Wavelength (nm) | Frequency ($s^{-1}$) | Energy (joules/mole) | Energy (electron/volts) |
|---|---|---|---|---|---|---|
| Change of spin | Nuclear magnetic resonance | $10^{-4}$ | $10^{11}$ | $3 \times 10^{6}$ | $10^{-3}$ | $10^{-4}$ |
| Change of spin | Electron spin resonance | $10^{-2}$ | $10^{9}$ | $3 \times 10^{8}$ | $10^{-1}$ | $10^{-3}$ |
| Change of atomic orientation | Microwave | $1$ | $10^{7}$ | $3 \times 10^{10}$ | $10$ | $10^{-2}$ |
| Change of atomic configuration | Infra-red | $100$ | $10^{5}$ | $3 \times 10^{12}$ | $10^{3}$ | $0.1$ |
| Change of electron distribution | Visible and ultra-violet | $10^{4}$ | $10^{3}$ | $3 \times 10^{14}$ | $10^{5}$ | $1$ |
| Change of electron distribution | X-ray | $10^{6}$ | $10$ | $3 \times 10^{16}$ | $10^{7}$ | $10$ |
| Change of nuclear configuration | γ-ray | $10^{8}$ | $0.1$ | $3 \times 10^{18}$ | $10^{9}$ | $100$ |

(Modified from Branwell, McCash, 1994)

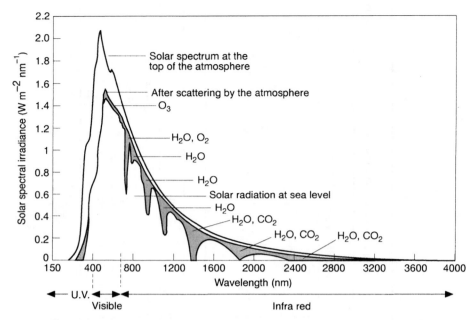

**Figure 2.1** The spectral irradiance distribution impinging at the top of the Earth's atmosphere and at sea level. Although there are very high energy photons emitted by the sun (i.e., cosmic and X-rays), the number of such photons relative to the visible and infrared is extremely small and is not shown. The difference between the solar spectrum at the top of the atmosphere and at sea level is due to both scattering of photons back to space and the selective absorption of photons by gases in the atmosphere. Visible radiation is commonly considered to range from about 400 to 700 nm.

sun is assumed to be relatively constant. The radiation incident at the top of the Earth's atmosphere corresponds to about $1373\,\mathrm{W\,m^{-2}}$ (Angstrom 1965). This is called the *solar constant*.[3] It should be noted that in the steady state, all of this energy is ultimately reradiated back to space; if it were not, the Earth would continuously heat up (Budyko 1982).

The initial fate of photons incident on the Earth's atmosphere is to be scattered or absorbed. Both phenomena are related to the electronic structure of atoms or molecules in the atmosphere and the interaction of these structures with light. *Scattering* is a process resulting in the change of direction of propagation of photons. *Absorption* is a process by which an electron in the absorbing matter is brought to a higher excited state. As the description of absorption requires some explanation of quantum mechanics, let us first examine scattering.

## SCATTERING OF LIGHT

All substances contain negatively charged electrons that oscillate around the positively charged nuclei of the contributing atoms or molecules. Let us consider the effect of light incident on some material substance. The electrical component of the incident light can interact with the electronic structure of the atoms or molecules

---

3. $1\,\mathrm{W} = 1$ joule per second.

and induce a transient displacement of the electrons with respect to the nuclei. The *dipole* moments that are induced by the incident light oscillate with the same frequency as the incident light, thereby becoming secondary sources of radiation. Because the phasing of the secondary waveform, but not the frequency, is changed, the "color" of the secondary light remains that of the incident light. All of the secondary radiators oscillate relative to each other with a fixed phase difference. If the atoms in the substance are held rigidly in place (as, for example, in a crystal) the secondary electromagnetic waves, generated by each of the individual light sources, will interfere with each and cancel themselves out in all directions except that of the direction of the incident light. The resulting waveform propagates in the direction of the incident light with a reduced velocity $u$. The reduction in velocity in light relative to that in a vacuum is called the *refractive index*, which is a function of the dipole density (the number of atoms or molecules per unit volume) and the strength of the dipole (the charge displacement of the electrons with respect to the nuclei). Under such conditions, the angle of the incident light is changed (i.e., the light is bent) but scattering of the light is not observed. This phenomenon is called *refraction*.

If the frequency of light exactly matches the frequency of the oscillation of the dipole of the atoms on the surface of the substance, the electromagnetic radiation cannot penetrate into the substance and is reflected. Hence, reflection is a special case of refraction.

In a gaseous phase at low pressure, the number of molecules or atoms (and hence, dipoles) per unit volume is relatively low. Under such conditions, the average path between dipoles is much longer than the wavelength of light, and the secondary waveforms have little chance of canceling each other out. Additionally, molecular vibrations due to thermal energy allow the molecules to change the phase of the secondary light according to the exact vibrational state of the molecule at the time of incidence, thereby further destroying the coherence between the secondary radiators. The result of this phenomenon is that light is scattered in all directions (i.e., it is isotropically distributed) relative to the source.

The angular distribution of scattered light is, to a first approximation, symmetrical about 90°; however, the scattering coefficient is inversely proportional to the fourth power of the wavelength (i.e., $1/\lambda^4$). Thus, the shorter the wavelength light, the higher the probability it has of being scattered. This type of scattering of light was formulated from theoretical analyses by Lord Rayleigh (1871) assuming spherical particles and is called *molecular* or *Rayleigh scattering*.[4]

Rayleigh scattering is only applicable for conditions where the molecules, atoms, or particles that interfere with the incident light are widely dispersed. Such conditions exist in low pressure gases or aerosols where intermolecular interactions are negligible, the size of the molecules is small relative to the wavelengths of the incident radiation, and the molecules are distributed randomly. Rayleigh scattering explains, for example, the color of the sky. To an observer looking at a clear sky at

---

4. Specifically, Lord Rayleigh, while convalescing from a vague illness contracted onboard a ship traveling down the Nile River (during his honeymoon), deduced that the scattering of light by small, widely dispersed particles could be described by the equation: $\sigma_m = [32\pi^3(n-1)^2]/(3\lambda^4 N^2)$.

any angle away from the solar zenith, the only light reaching the observer's eye will be that scattered by the (widely dispersed) molecules in the atmosphere. Because scattering is proportional to $1/\lambda^4$, light with shorter wavelengths is far more likely to be scattered—so the sky appears blue.

In water or other liquids, the density of the molecules is so great that the molecules interact and gradients in thermal energy within the fluid cannot be dissipated rapidly enough to permit a purely isotropic distribution. Consequently, at any moment in time, two adjacent but equal volumes of the fluid will, on purely statistical grounds, contain slightly different numbers of molecules. The minute differences in molecular density lead (by definition) to temporal and spatial variations in the refractive index. The fluctuations in the refractive index produce incoherences in the phases of the secondary (refracted) light, which allows the waveform to propagate in different directions from the primary light source. Hence, a collimated beam of light will become increasingly incoherent (diffuse) as it passes through a liquid. The optical manifestation of this process is light scattering, and even in the purest water (or any liquid), light is scattered as a consequence of fluctuations in the refractive index. This so-called "statistical fluctuation theory" of scattering (Einstein 1910; Raman 1922; Smoluchowski 1908) leads to a slightly different approximation of the wavelength distribution of the scattered radiation than molecular scattering and is more applicable to aquatic systems (Jerlov 1976; Morel 1974). The scattering of light given by density fluctuations in water is derived from empirical measurement and is inversely proportional to the wavelength to the power of 4.3 (Morel 1974). Thus, to an observer looking down at an infinitely long column of pure water, illuminated from above by white light, the light scattered back to the observer's eye will be color shifted toward shorter wavelengths, primarily in the blue and blue-green region of the spectrum (Fig 2.2).

Neither the atmosphere nor natural water bodies are pure gases or liquids; both contain particles. The scattering of light by particles in the atmosphere can be appreciated when we observe sunsets or look down at the clouds from an airplane window. The basic scattering, first described by the English physicist John Tyndall (1861), can be easily demonstrated by looking up at the projected light in a movie theater or at smoke from a cigarette. The particles scatter light nonrandomly with respect to direction.

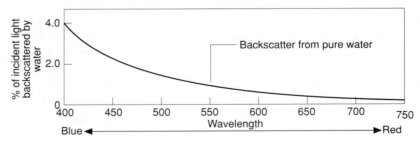

**Figure 2.2** The backscattering spectrum of pure water. To an observer looking down at a body of water, more blue photons will be reflected back than red photons; hence water will appear blue. The slope of the decay of the photons backscattered is inversely proportional to $\lambda^{4.3}$ (see text for an explanation of what causes the scattering).

The scattering of light by particles is not simply a function of their concentration (i.e., numbers per unit volume), but also of their size. This can be visualized by, for example, considering a large crystal of sugar 2 cm across (such as rock candy). Most of the light incident on the sugar is refracted and passes through the crystal; large crystals are relatively transparent to the naked eye. If the crystal is ground into a powder, the resulting material will scatter light and the powder will appear white. Thus, the same amount of sugar can transmit or scatter light, depending on the size and number of the particles. Smaller particles scatter light at larger angles (i.e., in backward directions), and high concentrations of small particles are extremely effective at scattering light.

Similarly, in aquatic systems, sediments, bacteria, and phytoplankton all contribute to the scattering of light; the smaller the particle, the greater will be its scattering ability. Particles are almost never distributed homogeneously, and their size is usually far greater than the wavelength of the incident radiation. Thus, the vertical distribution of scattered light is highly variable in natural water bodies. Both bacteria and phytoplankton tend to scatter visible light uniformly across the spectrum; the angular distribution of the scattered light is a complex function of the shape and size of the particle (Kirk 1991; Kirk, Tyler 1986; Morel, Ahn 1990).

There is a rich literature in aquatic sciences related to light scattering in oceans and lakes (Jerlov 1976; Kirk 1994b; Mobely 1994; Seliger, McElroy 1965), and it is not our intention or purpose to discuss the details of light scattering here. It is important, however, to understand that when light is scattered, a fraction of it may be detected outside of the system unless the photons are absorbed; hence the emergence of light from the ocean can be detected by satellites and this phenomenon forms the basis for the quantitation of photosynthetic pigments from space (Morel 1991b). We will discuss the nature of satellite-based measurements of photosynthetic organisms in Chapter 10. From a photobiological perspective, scattering means, by definition, that incident photons have not been absorbed but rather have changed their direction of travel. Thus, scattered light is available for photosynthesis. To be used in photosynthetic processes, however, the available light must first be absorbed. We shall discuss the absorption of photosynthetic radiation by photosynthetic pigments shortly, but first we must consider some of the basic concepts in the absorption of light by atoms and molecules.

## LIGHT ABSORPTION

Light absorption leads to a change in the energy state of atoms or molecules. The frequencies of visible light are such that the interaction is constrained to the oscillation frequencies of electrons (which is often the source of the light in the first place). The early spectroscopists in the mid-19th century, such as Bunsun and Kirchoff, heated elements or mixtures of elements in a flame and observed the colors emitted. For pure elements, the emission occurred at discrete wavelengths that are characteristic of the element. The spectral lines of the emitted radiation were characterized by eye, using a hand-held spectroscope, as being either *sharp* (s) or *diffuse* (d); later the terms *principal* (p) or *fundamental* (f) were added to describe other emission bands. As each element had a unique set of emission bands, spectroscopists could observe the specific emission and composition of unknown compounds. In fact, it was from the color of the emission that a number of elements were discovered. One contemporary manifestation of this technique is called *atomic absorption spectroscopy*, which is extremely sensitive and useful for characterizing specific elements, especially transition metals.

The absorption of photons by elements follows the same basic principle. For example, the emission of photons by the sun contains discrete gaps corresponding to the absorption of specific frequencies of radiation by a wide variety of elements in the solar corona. These gaps, called Fraunhoffer lines (after the German spectroscopist), are used to infer the elemental composition of the corona of the sun and other celestial bodies. Moreover, by looking at the absorption spectrum of infrared radiation from the scattered light in the sky, the gas composition of the Earth's atmosphere can be inferred with remarkable accuracy. This basic spectroscopic method formed the theoretical basis for deducing the effect of altered gas compositions of the atmosphere on the radiation budget of the Earth (Arrhenius 1896; Tyndall 1861).

By the end of the 19th century, it was realized that the frequencies of spectral emission at absorption lines of simple atoms such as hydrogen were separated in a predictable fashion and could be described mathematically by simple series functions. These series, named after their discoverers (e.g., the Balmer series, the Lyman series, etc.), provoked a search for the physical meaning of the emission and absorption lines and a reason for the mathematical order. Early in the 20th century it was hypothesized, based on rudimentary concepts of the structure of atoms, that the spectral lines correspond to different energy states of electrons. The Danish physicist Niels Bohr[5] tried to explain the spectral lines observed for hydrogen with a model for atomic structure; subsequently the Bohr model of an atom led to the theoretical development of quantum mechanics.

In quantum mechanics, the electronic structure of an atom is described by a probability function that is empirically related to electron density distributions through a set of equations developed by Schrödinger. The Schrödinger equations form, in turn, the basis for molecular spectroscopy (Branwell, McCash 1994). The Schrödinger equations describe the probability of finding an electron at a certain position in an atom. This probability is graphically represented as a cloud or shell with a designated, specific shape. The shape of the cloud corresponds to the spectral line designations s, p, d, and f. Each cloud or shell can be filled with only a prescribed number of electrons. Thus, the first shell, designated 1s, is occupied by up to two electrons. The s orbitals are spherical, and electrons within the first s orbital are designated as $1s^n$. The second shell, designated 2s, can also accommodate two electrons; the third, 2p, accommodates up to six electrons in three pairs of lobed clouds at 90° orientations; each lobe of the p orbitals, in the x, y, and z coordinates, accommodates a pair of electrons. For example, carbon contains six electrons; these can

---

5. Bohr had a reputation for being a klutz in the laboratory, and hence worked most of the time with pencil and paper.

### ❑ SCHRÖDINGER'S EQUATION

*The solution of the Schrödinger equation for a hydrogen atom is:*

$$\psi = f(r/a_o)e^{(-r/na_o)} \tag{2.4}$$

*where* $a_o = h^2/4\pi^2\,me^2$ *(*$= \hbar^2\,me^2$*), h is Planck's constant, and m and e are the mass and charge of the electron, respectively, r is the radial distance from the nucleus, $f(r/a_o)$ is a power series of degree (n − 1) in $r/a_o$, and n is the principal quantum number, which can only have integral values of 1,2,3 . . . ∞. The constant* $a_o$ *has dimensions of length, and thus* $(r/a_o)$ *is dimensionless. For a given set of values for r and n, ψ (or more strictly $\psi^2$) is a function that describes the probability of finding an electron at distance r from the nucleus for a given value of n.*

---

be written $1s^2$, $2s^2$, $2p^2$. It has 2p orbitals that are unfilled. The two p orbitals can accommodate four electrons.

The Schrödinger[6] equations predict the probability of finding an electron within a given orbital by a wave function, $\psi$, which is determined by three properties: (a) the mass and charge of the electron (which are constants), (b) a relative coordinate system for describing the position of the electron in relation to the nucleus (the mathematically convenient system adopted by theoretical physicists for this description was developed by an Irish mathematician, Hamilton, a century before the conceptual development of quantum mechanics), and (3) a set of unique numbers that describe the quantum state.

The mathematical series which describes the spectral lines could be thus related to properties of the electron. Four properties were introduced, and came to be called the quantum numbers. These (Table 2.2) describe the number in the shell designation, $n$, orbital angular momentum, $l$, the apparent magnetic spin field, $m$, and the intrinsic angular momentum, $s$. Using these properties, each electron could be uniquely described in relative spatial coordinates, and assigned a unique, discrete (i.e., quantized) status related to its energy status. No two electrons can simultaneously have identical quantum numbers in the same atom. By definition, absorption of electromagnetic radiation must lead to an increase in the energy status of one electron in the atom, and conversely, a decrease in the energy status of atoms results in the emission of electromagnetic radiation, i.e., a change in quantum number.

Let us now consider the physical principles of light absorption within the context of electronic states. Consider an electron within an orbital shell. In principle, the electron can be moved to another orbital shell as long as no other electron is there already (i.e., the shell is unoccupied). The energy gap between any two shells (i.e., any two quantum states) is fixed. Let us arbitrarily designate one state, with a lower

---

6. Later in his career, Erwin Schrödinger, who was Austrian by birth, became a serious student of Buddhism and was increasingly intrigued by biology. He wrote a book entitled *What Is Life?: The Physical Aspects of the Living Cell*, published in 1944. This book stimulated many interactions between biologists and physicists in the middle of the 20th century, and led many physicists to begin to experiment with biological systems.

**Table 2.2** A description of the quantum numbers

| Quantum Number | Allowed Values | Function |
|---|---|---|
| principal, $n$ | $1, 2, 3 \ldots \infty$ | Determines the energy and size of the orbital |
| orbital, $l$ | $(n-1), (n-2), \ldots, 0$ | Determines orbital shape and the electronic angular momentum |
| magnetic, $m$ | $\pm l, \pm(l-1), \ldots 0$ | Determines the direction of an orbital and the behavior of an electron in an external magnetic field |
| spin, $s$ | $\pm^1/_2$ | Determines the angular momentum of an electron spinning on its axis of rotation |

energy level (i.e., a more stable energy state), $E_0$, and an excited state, $E_1$. Consider an incident stream of white light, which can be thought of as a mixture of photons with a uniform energy distribution, $\overline{hc}/\lambda$.[7] Photons with energies exactly matching the difference, $E_1 - E_0$, will be selectively absorbed, thereby depleting the incident light field of the wavelengths corresponding to the absorbed energy. In the absorption spectra of pure elements, the energy gaps are discrete and the energy difference corresponds to the transitions of electrons to different orbitals. Conversely, the relaxation of an electron from a higher to lower energy level is accompanied by the radiative emission of energy. These transitions may or may not be (and usually are not) accompanied by a change in spin direction of the electron. The wavelength of the emitted radiation is related to the energy gap ($E_1 - E_0$) by

$$\lambda = hc \big/ \left( E_1 - E_0 \right) \tag{2.5}$$

If this transition proceeds from an excited state to a lower energy state, where no change in the spin direction of the electron has been induced, light may be reemitted (i.e., a "backreaction"). This phenomenon is called *fluorescence* (Fig 2.3). Thus, optical absorption and fluorescence spectra are quantitative measures of the excited states of electrons and the energy gaps between these states (Clayton 1980).

In atoms, the absorption of light occurs in clearly defined, narrow wavelengths that correspond to specific shell designations. In the formation of molecules, electrons are shared between atoms, forming bonds, and a great multiplicity of quantum configurations becomes possible, leading to absorption bands that are symmetrical around a maximum. In the simplest molecule, $H_2$, two electrons are shared between the two hydrogen nuclei. In the lowest energy, or ground state, the 1s orbital of both atoms is filled. Electrons in an s orbital have zero orbital angular momentum, and the single bond formed is symmetrical between the two nuclei. This type of bond is called a $\sigma$ bond. When $H_2$ is exposed to ultraviolet radiation, the absorbed energy leads to electronic transitions, populating higher, unoccupied orbitals. The alternative orbital configuration can be predicted by expansion of the Schödinger equation, and brings the nuclei closer to each other while separating the electron clouds (Fig 2.4). This configuration is less stable (i.e., it is a higher energy configuration) than the $\sigma$ bond configuration and is called an antibonding orbital, $\sigma^*$. Thus, absorption of radiation by a molecule promotes a destabilization of a bond by populating an antibonding orbital configuration.

---

7. In practice, there is no such thing as truly "white" light; all light sources have some spectral bias.

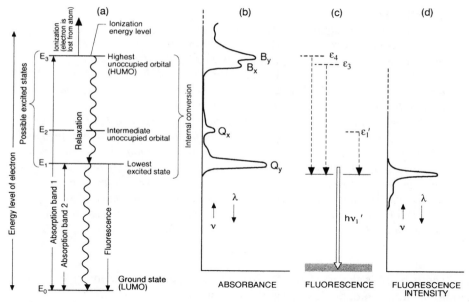

**Figure 2.3** Energy-level diagram showing excited states of an electron. Upon absorption of a photon, an electron populates an unoccupied orbital to form an excited state. There are numerous possible excited states ($\varepsilon_1$, $\varepsilon_2$, $\varepsilon_3$, etc.); the specific one induced is dictated by the energy of the absorbed photon ($h\nu_1$, $h\nu_2$, $h\nu_3$, etc.). Absorption of a photon with energy in excess of nuclear attraction leads to a loss of the electron, in a process called *ionization*. Electrons brought to higher excited states but retained within the atom or molecule return to lower excited states via nonradiative relaxation processes, where the energy is lost as heat. Electrons may return from the lowest excited state to the ground state via the emission of a photon. If the spin direction of the electron is maintained from the ground state to the excited state, the photon emission is called *fluorescence*. If the spin direction is reversed, the electron must "flip" its spin state before it can return to the ground state. The spin reversal takes more time than that for a direct return, but, as with fluorescence, may be accompanied by the emission of a photon; this process is called *luminescence* or *phosphorescence*.

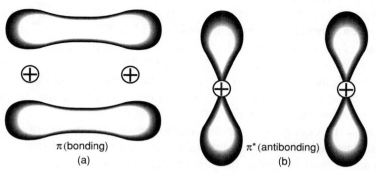

**Figure 2.4** A schematic diagram showing bonding and antibonding $\pi$ orbitals. The nuclei of the two atoms are represented by a + symbol, and the probability density distribution of the electrons is represented by the shaded cloud. A bonding configuration is represented in panel (a). Absorption of electromagnetic radiation by the molecule promotes antibonding configurations, represented by panel (b).

## ❑ ORBITALS

*The concept of electrons "populating" higher or lower orbitals based on their absorption of light can be thought of as comparable to an elevator in an apartment house without a basement. Electrons on the ground floor cannot go lower—they are in a "ground state." When light is absorbed, it "pushes a button" and the elevator goes up. The electron can only get out on floors that are unoccupied by another electron spinning in the same direction (an unoccupied orbital). Each atom or molecule has higher unoccupied molecular orbitals or "frontier orbitals"; the absorption of energy beyond the highest permitted unoccupied molecular orbital leads to the loss of the electron from the atom (i.e., when the atom becomes ionized). Once the electrons occupy a frontier orbital the orbital becomes an occupied molecular orbital. If there is a vacant lower unoccupied orbital, this condition is unstable, and the electron must ultimately descend from a HOMO to a lower unoccupied orbital (LUMO). As in the elevator analogy, energy in the form of heat or light is given up in the descent (see Fig 2.3).*

---

The $\sigma$ bond is the most stable (strongest) bond in a covalent linkage between nonionic atoms and, by definition, the lowest energy state of the molecule is when the $\sigma^*$ orbital is vacant. Because of the stability of the bond, the transition from $\sigma$ to $\sigma^*$ usually requires the absorption of light with significantly more energy than that available in visible radiation, hence molecules containing only $\sigma$ bonds are usually not visibly colored.

Unshared electrons in p orbitals may further form bonds where the orbital overlap of the shared electrons is physically above and below that of the $\sigma$ bond. p orbital bonds are called $\pi$ bonds. For each $\pi$ bond, there is an antibonding orbital configuration, $\pi^*$. Energy gaps between the ground state and the excited states of $\pi$ electrons are smaller than those for $\sigma$ bonds, and hence molecules possessing $\pi$ bonds often absorb long-wave UV and visible radiation. All $C=C$, $C\equiv C$, $C=N$, $C\equiv N$, and $C=O$ groups (i.e., all double and triple bonds) contain $\pi$ bonds.

In addition to the bonding electrons, all atoms possess highly stable, "nonbonding" electrons (called *n* electrons). Such electrons sit at low energy states in stable, fully occupied shells. Such electrons can, however, absorb radiation and be brought to higher energy states. Although the energy of radiation required for such a transition is often considerable, normally stable, nonbonding electrons can be coaxed into forming either $\sigma$ or $\pi$ bonds. Hence, the absorption of radiation can induce the following transitions: $n$-$\sigma^*$, $n$-$\pi^*$, $\pi$-$\pi^*$, and $\pi$-$\sigma^*$. The $\pi$ bonds are at lower energy levels than $\sigma$ bonds (it takes less energy to break a $\pi$ bond), and hence the transition to antibonding orbital configurations requires less energy (i.e., the absorption of longer wavelengths of light; Fig 2.4).

Although the energy of a photon must exactly match the energy gap between the ground state and the excited state before it can be absorbed, even if such a criterion is met it does not mean that the excited state will be occupied. The probability for photon absorption is greatly enhanced if the wavefunctions between the two states overlap. There is often a large overlap between the wavefunctions in the ground and excited states of $\pi$-$\pi^*$ transition, and consequently, this transition is often accompanied by the absorption of visible radiation. When plotted as a function of the frequency of light, the width of the absorption band is directly proportional to the energy required for the transition.

It must be stressed that the π electrons are *delocalized*; that is, they are shared between nuclei, and consequently the energy of the absorbed photon is not possessed by a single atom, but is communal property of the molecule. The larger the number of double bonds in a molecule, the greater is the delocalization. The electronic transitions induced by absorption are extremely rapid, on the order of $10^{-15}$ s, and do not initially induce changes in the nuclear orientations. However, as the number of unoccupied higher electronic orbital configurations increases with increased interatomic interactions (e.g., when a molecule possesses conjugated π bonds; ... C=C—C=C ...), the number of permitted quantum states becomes large; hence, absorbing molecules, rather than displaying sharp absorption lines like atoms, have absorption bands that sometimes can be quite broad (Fig 2.5). The breadth of the bands is further increased by rotational and vibrational (i.e., thermal) energy associated with the bond. The breadth of the absorption bands can be significantly decreased by cooling the molecules to low temperatures (e.g., liquid $N_2$ at 77 K, or liquid He at 4 K, is often used for this purpose), which reduces internuclear motions.

The frequency and intensity of absorption bands in complex molecules can be

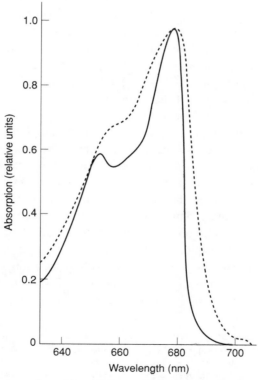

**Figure 2.5** Absorption spectra for a chlorophyll-protein complex at room temperature (dashed line) and at temperature of liquid nitrogen (77 K; solid line). Note how the absorption bands become sharper at low temperatures as a result of constraining molecular motions that contribute to small changes in electron density distributions.

predicted with reasonable accuracy by linear expansion of Schrödinger equations, considering individually and iteratively each atom in the molecule and every orbital configuration. Such an approach is computationally intensive, especially as the molecules of interest increase in number and variety of composite atoms, but such molecular orbital (MO) calculations can be extremely useful in predicting the absorption bands of unknown molecular structures and vice versa.

## Electron Spin Resonance

Electrons also spin on their axis. The spin can be related to the emitted electromagnetic radiation vectors of photons by showing that light is circularly polarized.[8] In fact, if circularly polarized light is absorbed, it transfers the angular momentum of the photon to the electronic transition. More importantly however, electrons, as spinning, charged particles, possess a magnetic moment (the spin was first inferred from the induction of magnetic field variations). To an observer looking along an axis of an electron orbit, the spin direction is either clockwise or counterclockwise. The magnetic spin vector, $s$, designated either $+1/2$ or $-1/2$, possesses an angular momentum of $\sqrt{[1/2(1/2 + 1)]}(h/2\pi) = \sqrt{3}/2(h/2\pi)$. There are $2(\Sigma s) + 1$ spin states. If an atom's shell is filled with two electrons, they must have opposite spins, and the sum of the magnetic vectors is zero. Thus, in an externally imposed magnetic field, for each electron that aligns parallel to the field another will align antiparallel, resulting in a zero magnetic moment for the atom or molecule (Fig 2.6). If, however, excitation energy is absorbed, and one of the two electrons moves to a higher energy state but maintains its original spin direction, the electronic spin status of the excited atom or molecule is given as $2(+1/2 + -1/2) + 1 = 1$. This excited electronic state is called a *singlet*. The relaxation of the electron from the singlet excited state to the ground state is the origin of fluorescence.

Sometimes when energy is absorbed by an electron and it is brought to another orbital level, it may reverse its spin state. The magnetic moment is then given by $2(+1/2 + 1/2) + 1 = 3$, and is called a *triplet*.[9] Before the electron can return to its former, lower energy orbital level, it must reverse its spin state. This de-excitation pathway takes a much longer time than that of fluorescence. For example, the relaxation for a chlorophyll triplet to the ground state occurs on the order of $10^{-3}$s whereas the relaxation of the singlet excited state occurs on the order of $10^{-9}$s. Photon emission from the deactivation of a triplet is called *luminescence* or *phosphorescence* (see Fig 2.6). The formation of triplets is much more likely from a singlet excited state than from the ground state. A molecule in a triplet state is far more likely to exchange an electron with its surroundings, thereby leading to oxidation and reduction reac-

---

8. Recall that light is composed of electrical and magnetic waves that travel along and *around* an axis. If the waves that travel along (normal to) the axis are isolated, the light is said to be *plane polarized*. If the waves traveling around the axis are isolated, they are *circularly polarized*. Circularly polarized light can be visualized by shining light through a circular polarizing filter onto a black disk, suspended at its center by a thread. As the light is absorbed, the disk will rotate in the direction of circular momentum imparted by the impinging photons.

9. The word "triplet" was introduced by GN Lewis, who first described the EPR signal for this species. Recall that Lewis also coined the word "photon."

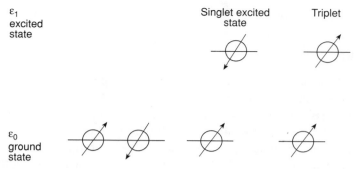

**Figure 2.6** A schematic diagram showing electron spin states for a pair of electrons in the ground state, an excited singlet state, and a triplet state. The arrow shows the direction of rotation of each electron. Symmetry in quantum mechanics requires that each pair of electrons that shares an orbital must spin in opposite directions. Absorption of the electromagnetic radiation may promote either a singlet or triplet excited state. Electrons return to the ground state from the singlet state directly; however, before an electron can return to the ground state from the triplet state it must flip (i.e., reverse its rotation). Some molecules, such as $O_2$, have a propensity to form triplets.

tions. Despite this propensity, however, the photochemical reactions in photosynthesis do not proceed from the triplet state, but rather from a singlet excited state.

The magnetic field strength of an atom or molecule can be quantified by exposing the material to an external magnetic field and exciting the molecule with microwave radiation. Because of their intrinsic magnetic moments, electrons in the atoms partially align with the external magnetic field, and the orbital undergoes a precession, comparable to the tracing of the cone along the axis of rotation by a spinning top. The rotation of the electrons can be perturbed by electromagnetic radiation in the microwave frequency domain ($10^{11}$ to $10^{12}$ cycles per second, which corresponds to wavelengths of about 1 cm). As microwave radiation is absorbed by the electron, the spin state can be altered (the electron can be "flipped") and hence adds to (enhances) or absorbs (reduces) the external magnetic field strength. The measurement of the resonance between electron spin state and magnetic field is called *electron paramagnetic* (EPR) or *electron spin resonance* (ESR) spectroscopy.

It is technically easier to vary the magnetic field strength than the microwave radiation frequency, and hence EPR spectra are plots of radiation frequency versus field strength. In a triplet configuration, three possible orientations of the electrons are detectable, namely those parallel, antiparallel, and perpendicular to the external field. A plot of the absorbed microwave radiation against field strength reveals three isomers for a triplet.

Some atoms and molecules, such as $O_2$, NO, $NO_2$, the metals Mn and Fe, and all the alkali metals in the first series of the periodic table, have unpaired electrons in the ground state and are naturally paramagnetic (i.e., they have natural EPR signals). Others may be made paramagnetic by oxidation or reduction, thereby producing an ion radical. The detection of transition metals and organic radicals has been particularly important in photosynthesis research; consequently, EPR techniques have been well exploited.

In practice, EPR spectra are often characterized by the so-called Landé splitting factor, *g*. The spin energy levels of an electron in an applied magnetic field are related to *g* by

$$g = \Delta E / \beta B_0 \tag{2.6}$$

where $B_0$ is the magnetic field strength (in Gauss) and $\beta$ is the Bohr magneton constant that relates magnetic field strength to energy ($9.273 \times 10^{-27}$ J/Gauss). The *g* factor for a free spinning electron is approximately 2.0023. Thus, EPR signals with *g* values close to 2 are interpreted to indicate the presence of a free radical. (Note that the *g* factor is independent of the absolute field strength.) The formation of free radicals is central to photosynthesis, and hence EPR spectroscopy has played an important role in helping to elucidate the kinetics and identity of the electron transfer reactions, especially in primary charge separations (Boussac, Rutherford 1992; Klimov et al. 1979; Rutherford, Inoue 1984).

In practice, EPR spectra can also be used to infer interactions between electrons and neighboring nuclei, and thus inferences can be made about the "environment" of functional groups. Two major disadvantages of EPR spectroscopy are that the instrumentation is usually large and nontransportable, and the detection limits for molecules of interest are such that relatively large concentrations of material are required. Thus, EPR methods are limited to laboratory applications and have not been much used in studies of photosynthesis in aquatic organisms.

## OPTICAL ABSORPTION

The first (and perhaps obvious) rule of photochemistry is that for light to promote a chemical reaction it must be absorbed. A second, and perhaps less obvious rule, is that each absorbed photon can only influence one molecule.[10] The portion of a molecule that absorbs light is called a *chromophore*, and four basic types of chromophores have emerged in photosynthesis, namely, open tetrapyrroles (found in the phycobilipigments), closed tetrapyrroles and their derivatives consisting of porphyrins (e.g., chlorophyll *c*) and chlorins (e.g., chlorophylls *a* and *b*), and the carotenoids (e.g., zeaxanthin, fucoxanthin, β-carotene). All four types of molecules are characterized by extensive π bond systems and all are visibly colored. We first consider the structures of these molecules in relation to their absorption characteristics and then the generation of singlet excited states.

Light absorption is most commonly measured with a spectrophotometer, in which a beam of monochromatic light is projected onto a sample (Fig 2.7). For simplicity, we will assume that the sample is a homogeneous solution of molecules in a cuvette and that the concentration of the molecules is small enough that they do not shade each other (i.e., the sample is "optically thin"). As the monochromatic beam of light, with intensity $I_0$, passes through the sample, some of the light may be absorbed by the molecules, reducing $I_0$ to I. The finite difference between $I_0$ and I is directly proportional to the concentration of absorbing molecules in the sample

---

10. This is called the *Stark–Einstein law*.

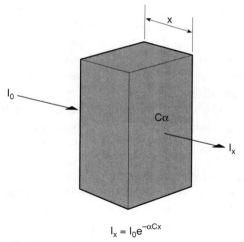

$$I_x = I_0e^{-\alpha Cx}$$

**Figure 2.7** A schematic representation of the integrated form of the Beer–Lambert law (Eq 2.8). A fraction of the photons in an incident beam of monochromatic light ($I_0$) can be absorbed by molecules (C) with a probability $\alpha$, in pathlength $x$, such that the emerging beam ($I_x$) contains fewer photons. The rate of photon absorption is described by an exponential function and is linearly proportional to the pathlength and concentration of the absorber. Thus, if $\alpha$ and the pathlength are known, the concentration of the absorber can be calculated. It should be stressed that the Beer–Lambert law assumes that scattering of light is nil. Such an assumption cannot be made for particles larger than the wavelength of the measuring beam, so it is difficult to measure the true absorption of light by membrane fragments, chloroplasts, or cells.

(C), the optical path length $x$, and the probability that the light will be absorbed $\alpha$, thus:

$$\frac{-dI}{I} = \alpha Cdx \tag{2.7}$$

where the negative sign indicates that the change in I is negative (i.e., the sample did not add light to the beam). As $x$ is finite, it is useful to integrate the equation with respect to $x$, to obtain

$$I(x) = I_0e^{-Cx\alpha} \tag{2.8}$$

which can be expressed in log form:

$$A = \log_{10}\left(I_0/I(x)\right) = Cx\epsilon \tag{2.9}$$

where $A$ is called the "absorbance," $\epsilon$ is the *extinction coefficient* and equals $\alpha/2.3$ (i.e., the natural log of 10). $A$ is dimensionless, and if the units of C are in moles/liter and $x$ is in cm, then $\epsilon$ has units liter mole$^{-1}$ cm$^{-1}$. The larger the value of $\epsilon$, the higher the probability that light will be absorbed. It should be clear that $\epsilon$ is a wavelength-dependent function. Equation 2.9 is known as the *Beer-Lambert law* and is used to derive the concentration of molecules in solution or in the gas phase from knowledge of the absorption, pathlength, and extinction coefficient.

A volume (e.g., a milliliter) can be expressed as a cubic function of length, such as cm$^3$, and hence it is possible to rewrite C in units of moles/m$^3$. If this notation is used, and the pathlength is a length (e.g., meters), the extinction coefficient must be expressed on a unit area basis. When so done, the ability of a molecule to absorb light at a given wavelength is called the *optical absorption cross-section*, σ (not to be confused with the same symbol used for a type of chemical bond). The optical absorption cross-section can be defined as (2.3 A/C x) with units of $m^2$/mole (or $cm^2$/mole, or $nm^2$/mole, etc.). Note that optical absorption cross-section and the extinction coefficient are alternative ways of expressing the same property, namely the ability of a molecule to absorb light at a specific wavelength. The optical absorption cross-section is convenient in that it can be used to calculate the rate at which molecules absorb light. For example, if the intensity of the incident beam light is expressed as quanta $cm^{-2}$ $s^{-1}$, the rate of light absorption is given by σI in quanta per mole (or molecule or gram) per second.

It should be noted that the optical and physical cross-sections are not related to each other. For example, the physical structure is related to internuclear distances, determined by bond type. The optical cross-section describes the probability of interaction between photons of a specific wavelength and the electronic field in the molecules. The optical cross-section for a chlorophyll molecule dissolved in an organic solvent is typically about $0.01\,nm^2$ ($0.01\,nm^2 = 10^{-20}\,m^2$) at 440 nm. This compares with a physical cross-section (based on the interatomic distances deduced from X-ray diffraction patterns of chlorophyll crystals) of about 0.14 nm across the plane of the molecule.

In living cells or in most biological material, absorption at a given wavelength is almost always a consequence of more than a single species of molecule. The total absorbance is related to the weighted concentration and extinction coefficient at any wavelength by

$$A = \left(\epsilon_1 C_1 + \epsilon_2 C_2 + \epsilon_3 C_3 \ldots\right) \tag{2.10}$$

Where $\epsilon_1$, $\epsilon_2$, and so on, are the extinction coefficients for components 1, 2, and so on, and $C_1$, $C_2$, and so on, are the concentrations of the components in the sample. If the number of components contributing to the total absorption is known and relatively small, the concentration of each component can often be accurately determined from knowledge of the extinction coefficients and by measurement of absorbance at more than one wavelength. However, complications often arise. The absorption properties of a chromophore are dependent on the environment of the molecule. These properties can vary from solvent to solvent or if an applied electrical field is introduced.[11] In vivo, the optical cross-section of pigment molecules is always smaller than in vitro. This modification is a consequence of spatial organization of the molecules within membranes, the organization of the membranes within the chloroplasts, and the organization of the chloroplasts within the cell. Thus, while it is possible to assume that optical absorption cross-sections are constant for a pigment dissolved in a specific solvent in vitro, the optical cross-sections in vivo are always smaller, highly variable, and must be empirically determined.

---

11. This is called the *Stark effect*, which occurs when an applied electrical field alters the electronic (i.e., quantum) configurations of the absorbing molecule.

## Optical Absorption Properties of Chlorins and Tetrapyrroles

The structure of all chlorophylls and porphyrins is based on chemical condensation of a repeating element, namely the nonessential[12] amino acid, δ-aminolevulinic acid (ALA). Two molecules of ALA condense to form porphobilinogen, which is a pyrrole containing two atoms of nitrogen (Beale 1990). The formation of pyrroles is an ancient metabolic pathway, and the products of pyrroles are used to synthesize hemes and enzyme cofactors, as well as bacteriochlorophylls and chlorophylls. The condensation of four pyrroles can lead to the formation of an open molecule with extensive conjugated double-bond systems. Such linear tetrapyrroles are the chromophores found in phycobilisomes of cyanobacteria and rhodophytes. However, tetrapyrroles can also condense to form a closed-ring system. Two basic types of closed rings are found: chlorins and porphyrins. Chlorins are distinguished from porphyrins by the saturation of a single C—C bond in ring 4 (Fig 2.8), which breaks the symmetry of the molecule and leads to important spectral consequences. In addition, all chlorins contain a fifth ring attached to ring 3 (sometimes called ring C). The fifth ring in a chlorin does not contain nitrogen. In chlorophylls (which are mostly chlorins), the nitrogen atoms in the rings are coordinated to a Mg atom. The removal of the Mg to form the corresponding phaeopigment (which can easily be achieved in vitro by the addition of weak acid) results in relatively minor spectral modifications.

All chlorophylls have two major absorption bands: blue or blue-green absorption bands, often called the B bands or (more commonly) Soret bands, and red absorption bands, called the Q bands.

By convention, spectroscopists draw axes obliquely though the four rings of pyrroles, designating the axis intersecting rings 1 and 3 as the y-axis, and that intersecting rings 2 and 4 as the x-axis (Fig 2.9). The Soret (blue) absorption bands reflect the population of three higher energy singlet states, which rapidly (on the order of 0.2 ps) decay to the lowest singlet excited state represented by the red absorption band.

The major red absorption band in both chlorophylls *a* and *b* is a consequence of a redistribution of the electrons associated with the π-π* transition on ring 4, oblique to the y-axis of the molecule. Hence the name for the resulting spectral bands, $Q_y$. (There is also the weaker $Q_x$ transition.) All photochemical reactions in photosynthesis proceed from the de-excitation of the $Q_y$ transition to the ground state. Thus, regardless of the energy of the absorbed photon, absorbed energy must be converted to the lowest singlet excited state (Butler, Katajima 1975a). This is achieved by dissipating the extra energy in the form of heat. In chlorophyll *b*, the methyl group on ring 2 (found in chlorophyll *a*) is replaced with a formyl group (CHO). This structural modification leads to the absorption of longer wavelengths (i.e., "red shifted") in the Soret region relative to chlorophyll *a* but a shorter wavelength absorption (i.e., "blue shifted") in the red region. Thus, the lowest singlet

---

12. The term "nonessential" means that all organisms can synthesize the substance. δ-aminolevulinic acid is not used for protein synthesis.

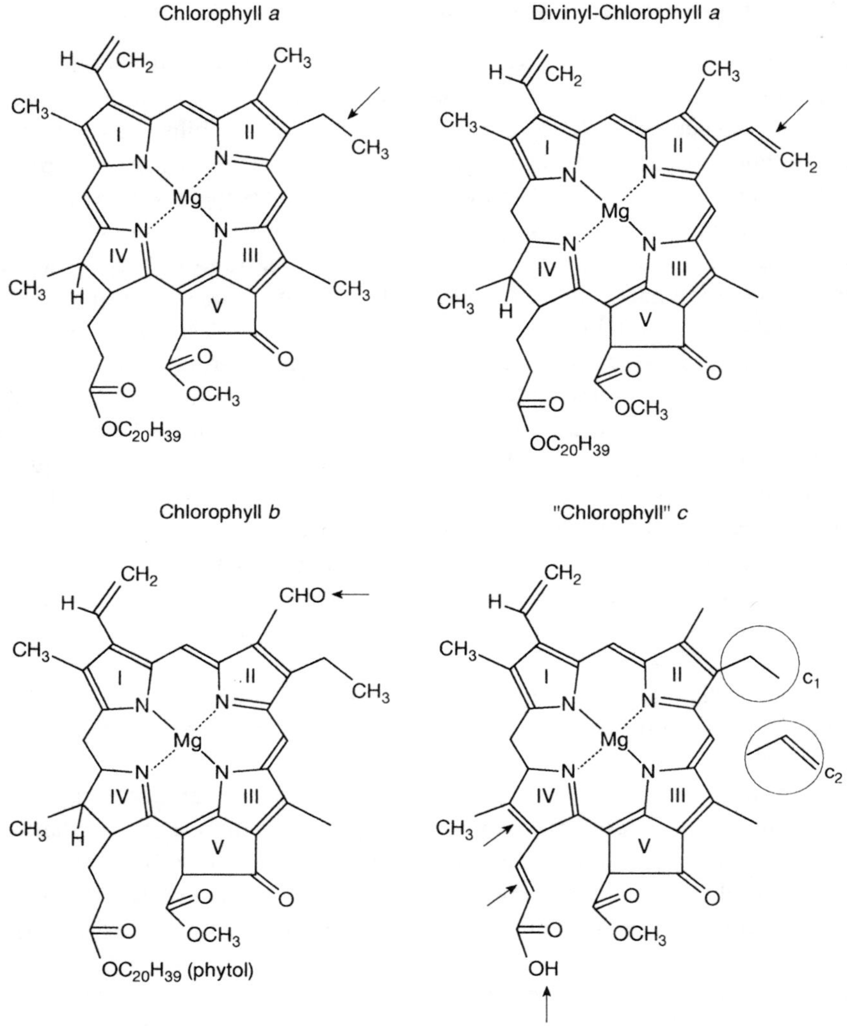

**Figure 2.8** (A) Structures of some "chlorophylls." All chlorophylls are made of four pyrroles, which are nitrogen-containing five-member rings. The four nitrogen atoms have electrons coordinated to a Mg atom. In true chlorophylls, a single bond in ring 4 is saturated, whereas in "chlorophyll" *c* a double bond is present in that position. The latter structure is derived from porphyrins, while the former is derived from chlorins. The consequences of the changes in the single bond in ring 4 are significant. When the bond is saturated (i.e., in true chlorophylls), symmetry is broken and delocalization of electrons in the rings leads to large absorption bands at lower energy states (i.e., in the red region of the spectrum). In porphyrin-derived pigments, however, a comparable absorption band is either missing or greatly attenuated. In chlorophylls *a*, *b*, and divinyl chlorophyll *a*, a 20-carbon alcohol group (phytol) is attached at ring 4; a comparable group is usually missing in the chlorophyll *c* structures. The phytol group helps to anchor the pigment within a hydrophobic domain of the protein and thylakoid membrane. In contrast, chlorophyll *c*'s are water-soluble pigments. Note that the difference between divinyl chlorophyll *a* and chlorophyll *a* is a single bond on a side chain attached to ring 2. The spectral consequences of this structural modification are relatively minor. (B) A stick diagram showing the internuclear bond distances in the ring system of a chlorophyll *a*. These distances are in angstroms. The x- and y-coordinate axes are also shown. The axes are reference axes from which spectroscopists ascribe changes in electron density to specific absorption bands.

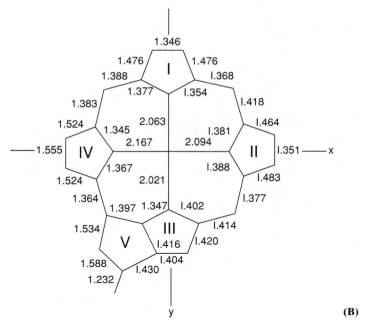

**Figure 2.8** *Continued*

excited state for chlorophyll *b* (i.e., the red band) is at a higher energy level than the corresponding state for chlorophyll *a*.

Unlike in chlorins, the double bond on ring 4 in porphyrins remains intact, and often the tetrapyrrole is symmetrical between the x- and y-axis. As a result of the symmetry, the $Q_y$ transition is either missing or very weak. One important exception are the chlorophyll *c*'s, which although called chlorophylls are really porphyrins[13] (Fig 2.10). Chlorophyll(ide) *c*'s are found in diatoms, dinoflagellates, chrysophytes, and other brown-colored algae. Like chlorophylls *a* and *b*, chlorophyllide *c*'s have a fifth ring attached to ring 3. This modification breaks the symmetry and consequently chlorophyllide *c*'s have a weak $Q_y$ band, which, as in the case for chlorophyll *b*, is found at a slightly shorter wavelength (i.e., higher energy) than that of chlorophyll *a*. Not only are the $Q_y$ bands of chlorophyll *b* and chlorophyllide *c* at higher energy levels than that of chlorophyll *a*, but they also overlap the $Q_y$ absorption band of chlorophyll *a*. As we shall shortly explain, these two phenomena allow excitation energy to be transferred efficiently from the former molecules to the latter.

In cyanobacteria and red algae, the major chromophores, called phycobilins (Fig 2.11), are linear tetrapyrroles that do not have an associated metal (Gantt 1981). Depending on the exact structure of the chromophore, these molecules absorb either blue-green, green, yellow, or orange light.

---

13. Actually the term "chlorophyll *c*" is a misnomer in two ways. Not only are the molecules really porphyrins, but they also generally lack a phytol chain that is found on "true" chlorophylls. If they were chlorins the correct term for the molecule would be chlorophyllide *c*; however, they are neither chlorins nor chlorophyllides.

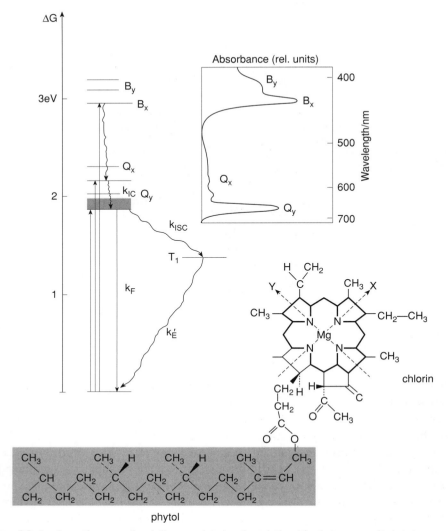

**Figure 2.9** A schematic energy-level diagram showing the relationships between excited states, absorption bands, and fluorescence in chlorophyll *a*. There is a series of higher excited states that are promoted by the absorption of blue light. These higher excited states, $B_y$ and $B_x$, correspond to the so-called Soret bands. Electrons in such molecular orbitals rapidly decay to lower excited states, $Q_y$ and $Q_x$, via radiationless processes (i.e., heat). The $Q_y$ band, which in vivo is centered at approximately 678 nm, represents the lowest singlet excited state. Electrons in that molecular orbital decay to the ground state with a relatively high probability of emission of a photon. The emission of the photon from the decay of the lowest singlet excited state is fluorescence. The peak wavelength of that emission occurs at a slightly longer wavelength (e.g., lower energy level) than the absorption maxima. In vivo fluorescence emission is centered around 685 nm in algae.

Carotenoids represent an extremely large group of biological chromophores that, depending on subtle structural changes, can demonstrate a remarkable range of spectral characteristics (Rau 1988; Rowan 1989; Siefermann-Harms 1985). The basic structural element consists of two unsaturated, 6-carbon rings joined by an 18-carbon, conjugated double-bond bridge. The flanking rings can be either in a *cis* or *trans* configuration, and natural isomers are often found. The isomers can often have

## ❏ THE SORET BAND

*JL Soret was a French physical chemist and spectroscopist who discovered holmium and iridium. In 1883 Soret described an intense blue absorption band at about 400nm in hemoglobin. Fourteen years later, this absorption band was observed in other porphyrins by an Indian spectroscopist, Gamgee, who dubbed it the "Soret" band. The appellation was adopted for porphyrins and chlorophylls and refers to the blue absorption bands in these and related molecules. The Soret band is found in all fully conjugated tetrapyrroles. The extinction coefficients in the Soret region are often extremely high, allowing for relative ease of detection at low concentrations of tetrapyrroles by optical absorption spectroscopy.*

---

markedly different spectral properties. The conjugated bridge-ring system permits extensive π bonding and thus potential interactions with photons in the visible wavelengths. In xanthophylls, oxygen is bound to the ring forming an alcohol or epoxide (Fig 2.12). Major photosynthetically important carotenoids include fucoxanthin, peridinin, lutein, violaxanthin, zeaxanthin, diadinoxanthin, and diatoxanthin. Spectrally, all of these carotenoids display blue and/or blue-green absorption bands that partially overlap the Soret bands of chlorophyll and, depending on the nature of

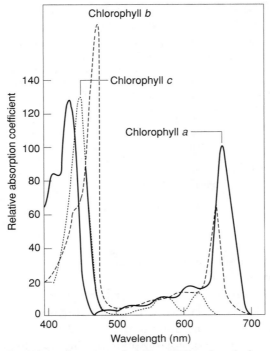

**Figure 2.10** The normalized absorption spectra for chlorophylls *a*, *b*, and *c* in acetone. Both chlorophylls *a* and *b* have relatively large absorption bands in the red region, while chlorophyll *c* has small absorption bands in the corresponding region. Note as well how both chlorophylls *b* and *c* have longer wavelength absorption bands in the blue-green region compared with chlorophyll *a*.

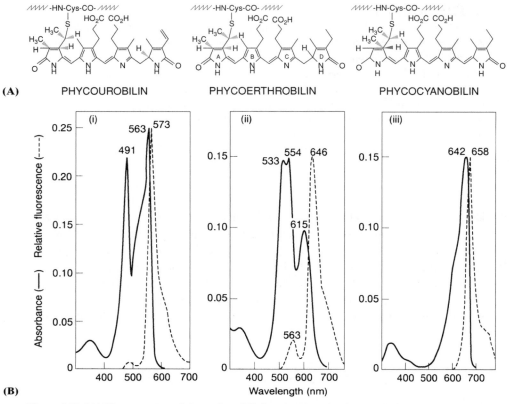

**Figure 2.11** (A) The structures of three phycobilipigments, namely phycourobilin, phycoerythrobilin, and phycocyanobilin. Each of these water-soluble pigments is an open tetrapyrrole that strongly absorbs visible light. The pigments are covalently linked to a protein via a sulfide bridge. (B) The absorption and fluorescence emission spectra of phycobiliproteins from the marine cyanobacterium *Synechococcus* WH8103. In this antenna system, (i) phycourobilin absorbs light at 491 while phycoerythrin absorbs at 563 nm, and the pigments transfer excitation energy at 573 nm. (ii) Phycoerythrobilin absorbs at 553 and 615 nm, and transfers excitation energy at 646 nm. (iii) Phycocyanobilin, at the center of the phycobilisome core, receives excitation energy at 642 nm and emits energy at 658 nm. The latter emission band overlaps the $Q_y$ absorption band of chlorophyll *a*, and hence energy is transferred from allophycocyanin to the reaction center. In vivo, fluorescence emission from phycoerythrin or phycourobilin is sometimes seen; however, in general, the transfer of excitation energy from shorter to longer wavelengths is very efficient.

the overlap, either facilitate the transfer of excitation energy to, or remove excitation energy from, chlorophyll.

In addition to promoting energy transfer to or from chlorophyll, carotenoids play an important role in protecting photosynthetic organisms from damage resulting from the photochemical generation of oxygen radicals (Sandmann et al. 1993). As we discussed briefly, the photon absorption by chlorophylls can lead to generation of a chlorophyll triplet that has a relatively long lifetime. Chlorophyll triplets can react with $O_2$, which is a stable triplet in the ground state (diatomic oxygen is a diradical). The result of such a reaction is the generation of singlet $O_2$, which is

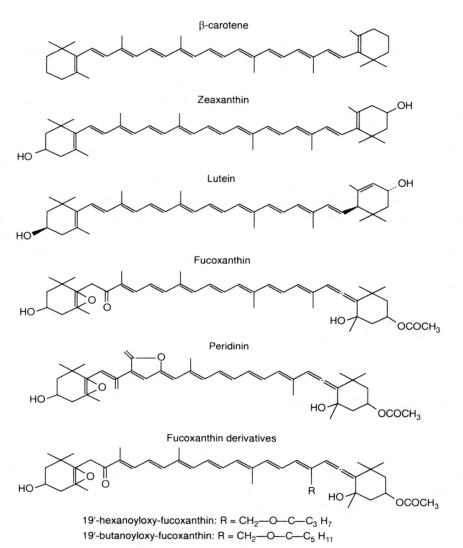

**Figure 2.12** Some structures of the principal carotenoids in algae. The basic structure is a conjugated isoprene backbone with cyclic 6-carbon side groups. Oxygenation of the side groups confers hydrophylicity, and such carotenoids are called *xanthophylls*. There are myriad xanthophylls and carotenoids in nature, and most are brightly colored. Zeaxanthin and lutein are yellow, fucoxanthin is yellow-green, peridinin is orange-red, and β-carotene is orange. Note that the opposing ring systems may be in either a *trans* position (as shown for the β-carotene here) or in a *cis* configuration as shown for fucoxanthin and peridinin. The configuration of the rings can vary. In vivo in algae, over half of the β-carotene is normally in a *cis* configuration.

highly reactive and can oxidize pigments, lipids, and nucleic acids. Carotenoids form excited state triplets via energy transfer from an excited triplet state of chlorophyll, thereby preventing the formation of singlet $O_2$. The resulting deactivation of the carotenoid triplet leads to the generation of heat. Let us now examine in some detail de-excitation pathways for excited states.

## De-excitation Pathways

There are three possible de-excitation pathways from an excited state. One of these, as we have mentioned, is reradiation by either fluorescence or luminescence. A second is the kinetic transfer and dissipation of the energy to the environment in the form of heat. The third, and most important in photosynthesis, is the coupling of the excited state energy dissipation to a chemical reaction as, for example, in the oxidation of a molecule. This latter process is called photochemistry.

Now imagine that the only de-excitation pathway is via fluorescence. The ratio of photon absorption to emission is called the quantum yield of fluorescence, $\phi_f$. A plot of intensity of the absorption spectrum of the $Q_y$ of chlorophyll in the frequency (or wavenumber) domain is, in effect, a distribution of the population of the electrons occupying the lowest singlet excited state orbital of the molecule. Integration of the area under this curve gives the total singlet state population (N). If each of these singlets decays to the ground state via fluorescence, which can be described by a first-order rate constant, $k_f$, the decay of the singlet state population can then be described simply as

$$dN/dt = -k_f N \tag{2.11}$$

and the total population of excited state molecules can be obtained by integrating Equation 2.11; thus,

$$N = N_0 e^{-k_f t} \tag{2.12}$$

The rate constant can be expressed in reciprocal time units of $1/\tau_0$, allowing us to rewrite Equation 2.12 as

$$N = N e^{-(t/\tau_0)} \tag{2.13}$$

where $\tau_0$ is called the *intrinsic* or *natural* lifetime and corresponds to the time required for the population of excited states to decay to $1/e$ of the initial level.

Absorption bands of single transitions in molecules follow Gaussian distributions. This distribution reflects the fact that the probability of a transition from a lower to a higher excited state is proportional to a transition from a higher to a lower excited state, thus,

$$k_f = 1/\tau_0 = C \int \epsilon \, d\kappa \tag{2.14}$$

where $\epsilon$ is the extinction coefficient and $\kappa$ is the wavenumber corresponding to the excited state. The solution to this equation can be approximated by:

$$1/\tau_0 = 3 \times 10^{-9} \kappa_m^2 \Delta\kappa \, \epsilon_m \tag{2.15}$$

where $\kappa_m$ is the wavenumber of the absorption maximum (in $cm^{-1}$), $\Delta\kappa$ is the bandwidth of the absorption at half-maximum (in $cm^{-1}$), and $\epsilon_m$ is the extinction coefficient at the absorption maximum (in $M^{-1} cm^{-1}$). A typical absorption maximum for chlorophyll *a* in acetone is 665 nm, which corresponds to 15,037.6 $cm^{-1}$; the half-bandwidth is about 30 nm, or 735 $cm^{-1}$, and $\epsilon_m$ is $8 \times 10^4 M^{-1} cm^{-1}$. Based on Equation 2.15, we would expect that the lifetime of the excited state would be about 25 ns.

Using a fast-pulsed laser it is possible to instantaneously populate the excited state, and to measure the *actual* decay of chlorophyll fluorescence. Experimentally this is achieved by exciting the molecules with a single laser pulse of <1 ns duration and following the exponential decay of the fluorescence detected with a fast-responding photomultiplier tube or some similar device (e.g., a solid state detector). The measured time constant, $t_m$, for the decay of chlorophyll fluorescence in acetone is about 5 ns. The measured lifetime is always less than the natural because fluorescence is not the only possible de-excitation pathway; the molecule can also dissipate excitation energy by heat. Thus, the ratio $t_m/\tau_0$ is a quantitative measure of the fraction of the singlet excited states that decay via fluorescence. The fraction is the quantum yield of fluorescence, $\phi_f$, thus:

$$\phi_f = t_m/\tau_0 = 5/25 \text{ or } 20\% \tag{2.16}$$

Thus in acetone, where no photochemical reactions occur, approximately 20% of the absorbed photons return to the ground state via fluorescence, while 80% decays of the molecules return to the ground state by dissipating the excitation energy as heat. This example of the calculation of fluorescence provides at least three pieces of information relevant to photosynthesis. First, a change in the quantum yield of fluorescence denotes a change in fluorescence lifetime. This is easily seen by rearranging Equation 2.16:

$$t_m = \tau_0 \, \phi_f \tag{2.17}$$

Second, as the majority of energy dissipated from the excited state does not appear as fluorescence, the rate constant for thermal deactivation must be larger than that for fluorescence. Third, in order to successfully utilize absorbed excitation energy in a photochemical reaction, the rate constant for the photochemical reaction must be greater than that for fluorescence or thermal deactivation.

We shall return to fluorescence in the next chapter when we will discuss photochemical reactions, and in Chapter 9 where we discuss the effects of nutrient limitation on excitation trapping efficiency.

## Excitation Energy Transfer

If each individual pigment molecule in a cell absorbed light and produced a photochemical reaction by itself without transferring the excitation to neighboring molecules, photosynthesis would be a very inefficient process. Let us consider the photon flux density from the sun. On a cloudless day at local noon, this flux is on the order of 100 quanta $nm^{-2} s^{-1}$. Recall that we can measure the absorption cross-section of a chlorophyll molecule in vitro or in vivo. These cross-sections, which are spectrally dependent, can be averaged between 400 and 700 nm. When so done, the spectrally averaged, optical absorption cross-section in vivo for a single chlorophyll molecule is about 3 to $0.5 \text{Å}^2$. Note that the spectrally averaged cross-section is lower than that at 440 nm because chlorophyll molecules only weakly absorb light between approximately 460 and 630 nm. Based on the rate of photon flux from the sun and the spectrally averaged optical absorption cross-section of chlorophyll *a*, it can be deduced that at noon each pigment molecule absorbs a photon on the order of 5 to 30 times per second. These rates of absorption are one to two orders of magnitude slower than that required to maximize photosynthetic electron transport. On a cloudy day or under lower irradiance conditions (such as those found below the surface of an aquatic condition), the absorption rate is typically one to two orders of magnitude smaller than that at the surface at noon on a sunny day.

In order to increase the probability of photon interception (and ultimately, electron transport), photosynthetic pigments work together as an ensemble. By working together, we mean that excitation energy absorbed by one pigment molecule can be transferred to another molecule. The concept of excitation energy transfer has been theoretically approached using both quantum mechanics and solid state physics (Clayton 1980), but let us consider the problem from a phenomenological perspective.

One manifestation of energy transfer can be deduced from fluorescence excitation and emission spectra. If one measures the spectrum of emission of fluorescence from a typical alga excited with monochromatic light that is absorbed in the Soret region at room temperature, the peak of the emitted light is observed at 685 nm. When plotted as a function of the frequency, the fluorescence emission spectrum is a mirror image of the absorption spectrum of chlorophyll *a*, but is shifted about 10 nm to the red (Color Plate 1). The spectral shift is a consequence of energy (vibrational heat) losses during the de-excitation of the excited singlet of chlorophyll *a* and is called the *Stokes shift*.

In all photoautotrophic cells there are numerous pigments other than chlorophyll *a* that can absorb light. If the fluorescence detector is set to monitor the emission wavelength while the excitation wavelengths are scanned, the excitation spectrum is obtained. The excitation spectrum corresponds qualitatively to the absorption spectrum because many of the absorption bands that correspond to alternative pigments appear to contribute their absorbed energy to the fluorescence emission of chlorophyll *a*. If the pigments are extracted in an organic solvent, fluorescence emission from the individual accessory chlorophylls (e.g., chlorophylls *c* or *b*) can be readily detected. These bands are not detectable in vivo. Thus, a physical mixture of the pigments in solution does not promote energy transfer from one molecule to another, but something in the organization of the pigments in the thylakoid membranes allows this transfer to occur.

All the photosynthetic pigments in vivo are associated with proteins. The proteins act as a scaffolding, ensuring the proper orientation of the pigments within or on membranes, and optimizing light harvesting and energy transfer. This orientation is essential for efficient excitation energy transfer.

The mechanism of transfer of excitation energy can be thought of as occurring as a result of resonance overlap between the emission and absorption spectra of the singlet excited states of two molecules. For example, as previously mentioned the fluorescence emission of chlorophyll *c* overlaps the $Q_y$ absorption band of chlorophyll *a*. The overlap of the emission and absorption wavefunctions allows the excitation energy to be transferred by a process called *resonance*. This process is sometimes described as analogous to the harmonic transfer of energy between two pendulums. Thus, the energy available when a chlorophyll *c* molecule relaxes from its lowest excited singlet state to the ground state leads to a process that induces chlorophyll *a* to undergo a transition from the ground state to the lowest singlet excited state. In the concept of resonance energy transfer—described in 1948 by a German physical chemist named T Förster, and sometimes called "Förster transfer" (Förster 1948)—a photon never actually physically leaves the donor molecule to the acceptor as fluorescence, but the excitation energy migrates as an *exciton*.[14] The excitation is thought to migrate or "hop" from molecule to molecule within the pigment matrix, randomly following interacting, coupled pigment molecules that alternate between the excited and ground state. Ultimately the energy of the absorbed photon decays as heat, is reemitted as fluorescence, or finds an acceptor with a high probability of inducing a charge separation.

The simplest mechanism for energy transfer might be envisioned by emission of light energy per se by a donor that subsequently is reabsorbed by an acceptor. This so-called radiative transfer mechanism can be described by:

$$D* \rightarrow D + h\nu \tag{2.18}$$

$$h\nu + A \rightarrow A* \tag{2.19}$$

Where $D*$ and $A*$ are the excited states of the donor and acceptor molecules, D and A, respectively. In this process, the efficiency of energy transfer is critically dependent on the quantum yield of emission by the donor, the number of acceptor molecules in the path of the emitted light, the extinction coefficient of the acceptor, and the overlap between the emission spectrum of the donor and absorption spectrum of the acceptor. The latter is quantified by the spectral overlap integral, J, defined as:

$$J = \int I_D E_A \, d\nu \tag{2.20}$$

where $I_D$ is the emission spectrum of $D*$, $E_A$ is the absorption spectrum of A, both plotted in the frequency domain and normalized so that a complete overlap corresponds to $J = 1.00$.

Radiative energy transfer does not explain the rate and efficiency of excitation transfer between pigments in photosynthetic organisms. For example, consider the heterogeneous pair of molecules, chlorophylls *a* and *c*. Let us assume that chlorophyll *c*, possessing a lowest singlet excited state at shorter wavelengths than the $Q_y$ band of chlorophyll *a*, transfers excitation energy to the latter pigment in vivo via the radiative mechanism. The emission band of chlorophyll *c* does not completely overlap the absorption band of chlorophyll *a*, therefore $J < 1.00$. Under such conditions, we would expect to see some radiative losses (i.e., fluorescence) originating from the excited state of chlorophyll *c* in the in vivo fluorescence emission spectra. This is not the case; yet if the Soret bands of chlorophyll *c* are excited, fluorescence emission from chlorophyll *a* is observed. Thus, chlorophyll *c* transfers excitation

---

14. The concept of an *exciton* is borrowed from solid-state physics. In this concept, an electron in an excited state has formed an empty electronic shell (i.e., a lower unoccupied orbital) in a lattice of molecules. In the process of decay of the electron to the lower state, the energy of the excited state is conserved by allowing *another* electron, that is at a lower energy state, to occupy the higher energy state. Thus energy can migrate as excitons "hop" from atom to atom, or molecule to molecule, within the matrix.

energy to chlorophyll *a* without the direct emission of light energy per se, i.e., by "radiationless" energy transfer.

Two basic radiationless energy transfer mechanisms can be described: the Förster mechanism and exchange coupling, which is also known as the Dexter mechanism (Turro 1978). The former appears to account for many aspects of the experimental results in heterogeneous chlorophyll excitation transfer processes and between homogeneous chlorophyll molecules, whereas the latter is often more appropriate to describe the transfer between carotenoids and chlorophylls. Let us first consider the Förster mechanism.

As we have briefly discussed, atoms or molecules possess charge density distributions that can be thought of (in the simplest case) as an oscillating dipole. The frequency of the oscillation is $\nu$, and the maximal value of the dipole moment is $\mu_0$. The instantaneous dipole moment, $\mu$, can be calculated:

$$\mu = \mu_0 \cos 2\pi\nu t \tag{2.21}$$

In a molecular sense, the oscillation of the dipole moment reflects the motion of the excited-state electron in D*, causing electromagnetic forces to be exerted on neighboring molecules.

Now consider two electric dipoles, one for donor $\mu_D$, and one for the acceptor $\mu_A$. The oscillator strengths are related to the radiative transitions D* $\leftrightarrow$ D and A $\leftrightarrow$ A*, which are experimentally measurable. The interactive energy between the two dipoles is related to

$$E \propto \frac{\mu_D \mu_A}{R_{DA}^3} \tag{2.22}$$

where $R_{DA}$ is the distance between D* and A. Förster showed that the rate constant for the transfer of energy ($K_{ET}$) between the dipoles is related to $E^2$,

$$K_{ET} \propto E^2 \sim \left( \frac{\mu_D \mu_A}{R_{DA}^3} \right)^2 = \frac{\mu_D^2 \mu_A^2}{R_{DA}^6} \tag{2.23}$$

Thus, energy transfer is proportional to the square of the dipole moment but inversely falls as the sixth power of the distance between the D* and A.

In exchange transfer, the probability of the transfer of excitation energy is related to electron orbital overlap between the donor and acceptor molecules. In this process, as the separation between D* and A increases, energy transfer decreases exponentially.

$$K_{ET} = K J e^{(-2R_{DA}/L)} \tag{2.24}$$

where K is related to the specific orbital interactions, J is the spectral overlap between the emission and absorption bands, $R_{DA}$ is the D-A separation relative to the atomic or molecular radius, L.

The major differences between Förster and exchange energy transfers are:

**1.** The rate of energy transfer in the Förster mechanism is critically dependent on the dipole strength; in the exchange transfer mechanism it is important where there is no dipole (or higher multipole) moment present.

**2.** Förster energy transfer is almost always "downhill," from a higher to lower energy level; direct exchange transfer can be energetically coupled in either direction.

**3.** Because the exchange transfer mechanism requires orbital overlap, the rate constant for energy transfer only occurs when donor or acceptor molecules are extremely close to each other physically; Förster transfer will proceed, albeit with decreased efficiency, over relatively large intermolecular distances.

The resonant energy transfer process highlights the role of the $Q_y$ absorption bands of chlorophyll *a*. The probability of energy transfer is much greater for a downhill transition, where the energy difference between the ground state and lowest excited state of the donor molecule is larger than that of the acceptor molecule. Spectroscopically this is manifested by the donor molecule having a red absorption band at shorter wavelengths (i.e., higher energy) than those of the acceptor. In vivo, chlorophyll *a* has a $Q_y$ absorption maximum at 675 nm, while that of chlorophyll *c* is at 630 nm, and that for chlorophyll *b* is at 655 nm. Both of the latter two chlorophylls have major Soret bands at longer wavelengths than that of chlorophyll *a*, which would preclude direct energy transfer from these higher excited states to chlorophyll *a* via the Soret bands of the latter pigment. In aquatic systems red light is attenuated very rapidly as a consequence of absorption by water itself and by scattering. *Thus, the $Q_y$ bands of the chlorophylls play a negligible role in direct light harvesting but are essential for energy transfer.*

Depending on their structure, carotenoids can both donate and accept excitation energy from chlorophyll *a*. Three important carotenoids in energy donation are fucoxanthin, peridinin, and violaxanthin. Fucoxanthin is found in brown algae, diatoms, and chrysophytes; peridinin is found in dinoflagellates; and violaxanthin is found in numerous green algae (Jeffrey 1980; Jeffrey, Hallegraeff 1987; Larkum, Barrett 1983). Unlike chlorophylls, carotenoids do not have a $Q_y$ absorption band, and the transfer of excitation energy is facilitated via the higher excited states. Thus, carotenoids with an excited state at a shorter wavelength than the lowest blue band absorption of chlorophyll can potentially donate excitation energy to chlorophyll, while those with longer wavelengths can receive excitation energy from chlorophyll. Because the lifetime of the higher excited states of chlorophyll is very short, about 10–15 ps ($1 ps = 1 \times 10^{-12}$ s), the transfer of excitation energy is extremely rapid and probably occurs at very small distances, as a consequence of the Dexter mechanism.

In cyanobacteria and rhodophytes, the phycobilipigments are bound to proteins to form macromolecular, water-soluble structures called *phycobilisomes* (we will discuss the structure of phycobilisomes in Chapter 6). In freshwater cyanobacteria a red pigment, phycoerythrin, absorbs green light and fluoresces orange. In most marine cyanobacteria the analogous pigment is phycourobilin, which absorbs and emits at shorter wavelengths. Some marine cyanobacteria contain both phycoerythrin and phycourobilin. The transfer of excitation energy from phycourobilin or phycoerythrin to chlorophyll *a* is facilitated by two other phycobilipigments, phycocyanin and allophycocyanin. The former absorbs in the orange and fluoresces in the orange-red, while the latter absorbs in the orange-red and fluoresces in the red. The fluorescence emission band of phycoerythrin overlaps the absorption band of phycocyanin, and the fluorescence emission band of the latter overlaps the absorption band of allophycocyanin so that finally a cascade of excitation energy can be funneled into chlorophyll *a*. This light-harvesting system is highly efficient, and allows cyanobacteria to absorb and transfer green light to chlorophyll (Fujita, Shimura 1975; Gantt 1981).

The absorption of light by photosynthetic pigments in vivo, whether by chlorophylls, carotenoids, or phycobilipigments, differs from the absorption of light by most nonphotosynthetic organisms because energy can be transferred from one molecule to another. Thus, in photosynthetic systems absorbed excitation energy is not a property of a single molecule, but instead becomes the collective property of an ensemble of pigments. The concept of an ensemble of pigments that can share and transfer excitation energy from higher to lower excited states is called an *antenna* or *pigment bed*. It is important to understand that the energy absorbed within an antenna has not yet been converted to chemical energy, and thus has not been "trapped" by a photochemical process.

# 3

# The Photosynthetic Light Reactions

The absorption of light by photosynthetic pigments does not, in and of itself, lead to a chemical reaction; cooked spinach is green but quite photochemically dead. The search for the mechanism of the photochemical reactions has been and remains a major focus of research in photosynthesis, and we will present these ideas from conceptual as well as historical perspectives. Before doing so, however, let us first briefly define the term *light reaction*.

A chemical reaction transforms one or more substrates to one or more products by altering electronic bonding configurations within atoms or molecules. Changes in bonding configurations usually are accompanied by changes in free-energy states. In photochemical reactions, the changes in the electronic states are induced by the energy of light (Hader, Tevini 1987). The energy of light is used to produce excited states that ultimately lead to a redistribution of electrons between molecules. Specifically, in photosynthesis, the energy of absorbed photons is used to modify the electronic structure of pigment molecules to the extent that an electron can be physically transferred from a donor to an acceptor. Thus, the light reactions in photosynthesis are photochemically catalyzed oxidation–reduction reactions.

As we briefly discussed in Chapter 1, the addition of an electron to (or the removal of oxygen from) a molecule is called reduction; this process requires an electron source, namely another molecule that donates its electron, and is oxidized. Therefore, oxidation–reduction reactions require pairs of substrates, and can be described by a pair of partial reaction, or half-cells:

$$A_{ox} + n(e^-) \rightleftharpoons A_{red} \tag{3.1a}$$

$$B_{red} - n(e^-) \rightleftharpoons B_{ox} \tag{3.1b}$$

The tendency for a molecule to accept or release an electron is therefore relative to some other molecule being capable of conversely releasing or binding an electron. Chemists scale this tendency, called the *redox potential*, E, relative to the reaction:

$$H_2 \rightleftharpoons 2H^+ + 2e^- \tag{3.2}$$

which is arbitrarily assigned an E of 0 at pH 0 and is designated $E_0$. (Recall that by definition pH is a shorthand notation for "power of hydrogen" and is defined as the negative $\log_{10} [H^+]$; thus, pH 0 = 1 M $H^+$.) It is more useful (and experimentally practical) to define $E_0$ at pH 7 and 298 K (i.e., room temperature) at 1 atmosphere pressure (= 101.3 kPa). When so defined, the redox potential is denoted by the symbols $E_0'$ or sometimes $E_{m7}$. The $E_0'$ for a standard hydrogen electrode is –420 mV.

The reference of a redox couple to the hydrogen half-cell is often designated by the term $E_h$.

Oxidation–reduction reactions result in a change in free energy. This change in free energy can be related to the electrical potential for each half reaction using the Nernst equation:

$$E = \left(E_0 + 2.3RT\right) \big/ \left(nF \ \log_{10}\left[A_{ox}\right]\big/\left[A_{red}\right]\right) \tag{3.3}$$

where E is the redox potential (in volts, or more typically in biological systems, millivolts), $E_0$ is an arbitrarily accepted standard redox potential, F is Faraday's constant (= 96,487 coulombs $\equiv$ 1 mole of electrons), n is the number of moles of electrons (Faradays) transferred in the half-cell reaction, R is the Boltzmann gas constant, T is temperature in Kelvin, and $A_{ox}$ and $A_{red}$ are the activities (or more commonly, the concentrations) of the oxidized and reduced forms of the molecules, respectively. At room temperature (298 K or 25 °C), the value of 2.3 RT/F is 59 mV. A useful form of the Nernst equation for the two half-cells in a reaction is therefore:

$$\Delta E_h = \left(\Delta E_0' + 59\right) \big/ \left(n \log_{10}\left[A_{ox}\right]\left[B_{red}\right]\big/\left[A_{red}\right]\left[B_{ox}\right]\right) \tag{3.4}$$

where $\Delta E_h$ and $\Delta E_0'$ are the differences between $E_h$ and $E_0'$ for the two half-cells, respectively. The sign of the redox potential refers to the electrophilicity of the substrate; a molecule that is more electrochemically negative relative to another can donate electrons to the latter, thereby becoming oxidized. The Nernst equation describes an *equilibrium* condition for both electronic and ionic processes and is frequently used in biophysics to calculate the electrical potential across a membrane given the concentration (or more correctly, the activity) of ions on both sides of the membrane (Cramer, Knaff 1990).

From an experimental viewpoint, biochemical redox reactions are usually measured by following a chemical reaction (for example in a spectrophotometer) and measuring the potential with an electrode made from some inert element, usually of platinum or gold. The potential difference is measured relative to a reference electrode, such as a silver/silver chloride (calomel) half-cell. The reactions are carried out under anaerobic conditions, and the rate of the reaction is measured as a function of potential (Fig 3.1). Because proteins and other biological molecules (especially those in membranes) do not interact directly with the measuring electrode (and hence their "true" potential is not faithfully recorded), small molecules of known redox potential are usually added to the solution to mediate the reaction. By using a mixture of such mediators, it is possible to fix or "poise" the redox potential at a given value and measure the reaction of the desired molecule (e.g., from changes in absorption). The redox state is then altered by the addition of a desired mediator and the reaction measured again. The continuation of this titration results in a curve of, for example, a change in absorption versus redox potential. A log transformation of the curve can be used to deduce the midpoint potential of the reaction; the slope of the log-transformed curve is directly proportional to the number of electrons transferred (see Fig 3.1b).

Ideally, redox titrations should be independent of the concentration of the mediators. By this means it is experimentally possible to assign relative midpoint poten-

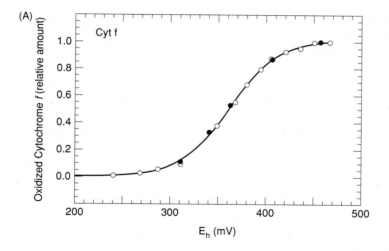

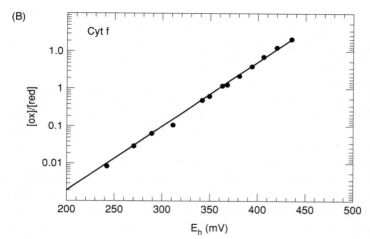

**Figure 3.1** An example of a potentiometric titration of a photosynthetic electron carrier, cytochrome *f*. In this example, the fraction of oxidized cytochrome was deduced from measurements of the change in absorption. The potentiometric titrations were done with a platinum electrode in combination with a calomel reference electrode. The redox state was adjusted with a "cocktail" buffer, consisting of 2-anthraquinone sulfonate ($E_{m7}$ = −225 mV), hydroquinone ($E_{m7}$ = +280 mV), duroquinone ($E_{m7}$ = +68 mV), ε-hydroxy-1,4-naphthoquinone ($E_{m7}$ = −139 mV), 1,4 -napthoquinone ($E_{m7}$ = +60 mV), and 1,2-naphthoquinone ($E_{m7}$ = +135 mV). The data points are measured values; the curve is the fit of the data to the Nernst equation (Eq 3.3). From these data it can be seen that the midpoint potential (i.e., the potential where half of the cytochrome is oxidized and half is reduced) is +362 mV. In (B), the data are plotted in a log transform by deriving the ratios of oxidized to reduced cytochrome at each midpoint potential. From this graph, it can be seen that the slope of the fit is 60 mV per decade of change in [ox]/[red] cytochrome. Based on Eq 3.4, this slope corresponds n = 1. Thus, based on this type of analysis, we can deduce that the oxidation or reduction of cytochrome *f* is a one electron transfer with a midpoint potential at pH 7.0 of +362 mV. (Data courtesy of John Whitmarsh and Sabine Metzger)

tials to electron carriers in a series. It should be noted that in practice, redox titrations are often more difficult to obtain than might first appear. Many of the electron carriers in photosynthetic systems have oxidized minus reduced absorption bands that overlap those of chlorophylls and carotenoids and, hence, are not easily measured by spectrophotometric means. To overcome this problem, absorption bands are usually chosen far away from the Soret absorption region; however, the alternative absorption bands are often characterized by relatively low extinction coefficients, thus relatively high concentrations of biological material and a sensitive spectrophotometer are required. Relatively few redox titrations of electron carriers in the photosynthetic apparatus have been made with aquatic photosynthetic organisms, and it is often assumed that the midpoint potentials measured from one species are the same for all. It should be noted, however, that redox reactions cannot be measured in vivo in intact cells, and the reactions measured in vitro do not necessarily correspond to the reaction potentials in vivo, as the microenvironment of protein or carrier may (and usually does) differ significantly between the two conditions. Additionally, midpoint potentials reflect equilibrium conditions that are not necessarily applicable in vivo, especially when a large fraction of donor or acceptor molecules are reduced or oxidized. Thus, while redox titrations are extremely helpful in giving strong clues as to energetic relationships between electron carriers in vivo, in and of themselves such measurements do not necessarily provide an accurate picture of electron transfer processes.

In the search for the mechanisms of the light reactions, biophysicists postulated or provided kinetic evidence for the existence of various oxidants and reductants in the photosynthetic machinery. In many cases the electron carrier was not chemically well characterized and was simply referred to by a letter or a letter followed by a number. The letter is often an abbreviation such as D [for electron "donor"], A [for electron "acceptor"], "Q" [for "quencher"], and the number usually designated the wavelength at which oxidation–reduction has a maximal absorption difference or the sequence in a chain of carriers. Sometimes the same electron carrier was described by two or more investigators working on different aspects of electron transport and thus some components have numerous appellations, which can be confusing. Before describing the electron transport systems and the redox potentials of individual components constituting the systems, however, let us examine the phenomenology of reaction centers.

## THE PHOTOSYNTHETIC UNIT AND THE DISCOVERY OF REACTION CENTERS

By the early part of the 20th century, it was assumed that all oxygenic photosynthetic organisms contain chlorophyll *a*, and that somehow the pigment is involved in the photochemical consumption of carbon dioxide or evolution of oxygen. As it is not necessary to create or destroy the pigment in order for the reaction to occur, it was further assumed that the pigment is not itself a substrate, but rather a catalyst. It was thought that when each chlorophyll molecule absorbs a photon, it somehow produces $O_2$ or fixes $CO_2$.

By the late 1920s, the search for the photochemical reaction of photosynthesis was well under way. To measure the rate of the photochemical reaction and the stoichiometry of chlorophyll to $O_2$ evolution or $CO_2$ consumption, physical chemists tried to synchronize the reaction; that is, they sought to make all the reactions occur simultaneously. Synchronization permits derivation of kinetic rate constants, which are often important in deducing reaction pathways and limiting steps. When a photosynthetic organism, such as an alga, is exposed to continuous light, photons are delivered to and absorbed by chlorophyll molecules in a random fashion. Under such conditions, some chlorophylls are busy absorbing photons while others may be waiting for photons to arrive; it is difficult under such conditions to count the number of chlorophyll molecules that are working at a given moment and consequently difficult to measure the rate of the true photochemical reactions as distinct from the other reactions that may also occur in the process of oxygen evolution or carbon dioxide fixation.

In 1932, two biophysicists, Robert Emerson and William Arnold, devised an experiment to synchronize the photosynthetic reactions by delivering light in discrete, short pulses (Emerson, Arnold 1932a). The pulsed-light system permitted them to expose cells to very short bursts of light separated by dark periods. They engineered a flash system with a commutator coupled to a dozen automobile ignition points, a 2200 volt discharge capacitor, and a flash tube. By varying the speed of the commutator rotation, they could deliver high intensity pulses of light with only about 20 μs duration, separated by a dark period that could be varied from 35 to 425 ms. They used this system to illuminate cultures of the green alga *Chlorella* in a Warburg manometer (the state-of-the-art device at the time) and measured oxygen evolution. *Chlorella* was chosen because it was easy to grow and hardy. By varying temperature, the duration of light and dark periods, or the flash frequency, they found that they could kinetically identify two distinct processes (Emerson, Arnold 1932b). They observed that if a sufficiently long dark period was allowed between flashes, the yield of $O_2$ per flash was independent of temperature. This result implied that evolution of $O_2$ was a truly photochemical reaction. However, at 25 °C, the time required for the completion of the dark reactions was about 20 ms (Fig 3.2), while at 1 °C the half-time for completion of the dark reaction was on the order of 100 ms. The temperature dependence of the dark reaction implied enzymatic processes were involved.

Emerson and Arnold's results suggested that the photochemical reaction (i.e., the reaction that occurred during the light pulse) occurred very rapidly but was closely tied to the evolution of $O_2$, while the rate-limiting steps, which could be required to regenerate the substrate for the light reaction or to remove a product of the reaction, occurred in the dark (the period between flashes) and required enzymes. Most importantly, they reported that if the interval between flashes was sufficiently long so that the chlorophyll molecules had time to complete the dark reaction before the next flash, and the flashes were sufficiently bright so as to saturate the process, then the ratio of the number of moles of chlorophyll molecules apparently required for the evolution of a mole of $O_2$ or the reduction of a mole of $CO_2$ in *Chlorella pyrenoidosa* was remarkably constant, averaging about 2500 chlorophyll/$O_2$. Thus, the now-classic Emerson and Arnold experiments established

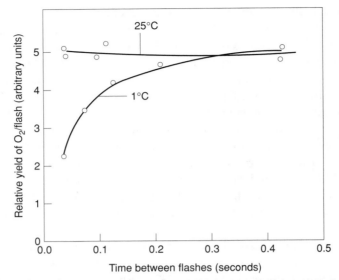

**Figure 3.2** The effect of temperature on oxygen flash yields in the unicellular green alga *Chlorella pyrenoidosa*, as reported by Emerson and Arnold in 1932. At low temperature, the flash yields were lower as the interval betwen flashes decreased; however, the maximum yield of oxygen was independent of temperature. These results implied that one of the reactions involved in oxygen evolution was temperature dependent but not light dependent, while the light-dependent reaction was not temperature dependent.

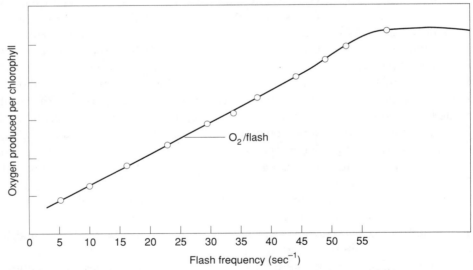

**Figure 3.3** The relationship between the frequency of flashes and the yield of oxygen. This relationship is linear up to some maximum flash frequency, at which point the evolution of oxygen becomes limited by process(es) other than light. The slope of the line in the linear portion is the oxygen flash yield (i.e., the oxygen evolved per single flash).

that: (a) photosynthesis consisted of light and dark reactions, (b) at high light, the dark reaction(s) was rate limiting, and (c) many chlorophyll molecules simultaneously participated, or cooperated, in the evolution of $O_2$.

The latter experimental results were met with skepticism at the time, but were interpreted by Gaffron and Wohl (1936) to mean that photosynthetic pigments were part of an entity called a *photosynthetic unit*, which they defined as "the mechanism which must undergo the photochemical reaction to produce one molecule of oxygen or reduce one molecule of carbon dioxide." At that time it was widely believed, based on experiments by Warburg and Negelein (Warburg et al. 1923), that four quanta were absorbed for each molecule of carbon dioxide assimilated, and that the oxygen evolved came from carbon dioxide. Note that the concept of a photosynthetic unit was that of a mechanism, not necessarily a physical entity. This concept is one of the most useful yet misunderstood notions in photosynthesis (Myers 1994).

Over the decades, numerous measurements of the ratio of chlorophyll/$O_2$ have been made with a wide variety of algae using the same basic approach employed by Emerson and Arnold. Contemporary experimental protocols usually provide light from xenon flash tubes as short (<10µs) pulses, and the oxygen is usually detected with a polarographic electrode. A plot of the evolution of oxygen as a function of flash frequency is linear between about 5 and 50 flashes per second; the slope of the curve is the oxygen production per flash (Fig 3.3). Simultaneous measurements of chlorophyll permit the calculation of the "size" of the photosynthetic unit, as chlorophyll/$O_2$ (also called Emerson–Arnold number). This ratio varies somewhat between algal species and with growth conditions; values between 1500 and 2500 chlorophyll/$O_2$ are generally reported for eukaryotic algae (Falkowski et al. 1980; Falkowski, Dubinsky, Santostefano 1985; Fujita et al. 1988; Myers, Graham 1971). In phycobilisome-containing classes, the Emerson–Arnold number is significantly lower, on the order of 1000 chlorophyll/$O_2$.

The realization that all of the individual chlorophyll molecules do not participate directly in the photochemical processes of photosynthesis stimulated further searches for the mechanism of the light reaction. Three basic approaches, which are complementary, were adopted. The first was directed toward elucidating the spectral response function (i.e., the wavelength dependence or "action spectrum") of the photosynthetic reactions. The second was directed toward measuring the maximum quantum yield of oxygen evolution. The third was to deduce the effective absorption cross-section (i.e., "size") of the photochemical target.

## ACTION SPECTRA AND THE EVIDENCE FOR TWO PHOTOSYSTEMS

If the absorption of light by chlorophyll *a* was essential for oxygen evolution, then what are the other pigments, such as carotenoids or phycobilins, doing? If these accessory pigments contributed to the photochemical production of oxygen, then the wavelength dependence of oxygen evolution should closely follow that of the absorption spectrum for pigments. The wavelength dependence of a photochemical reaction is called an *action spectrum*, and the ratio of the product formed per unit

## ❏ OXYGEN ELECTRODES

*An oxygen electrode electrochemically reduces $O_2$ to $H_2O$ and/or $OH^-$. The reaction is accomplished by establishing an electrical potential between a cathode, usually made of platinum, and a silver/silver chloride anode. At voltages of $-0.65V$ or less (i.e., more negative), the following reactions occur at the cathode:*

$$O_2 + 4H^+ + 4e^- \rightarrow 2(H_2O) \qquad (3.5a)$$

*which is coupled to*

$$4Ag \rightarrow 4Ag^+ + 4e^- \qquad (3.5b)$$

*at the anode.*

*The silver is regenerated by the electrolyte, KCl, by the reaction*

$$Ag^+ + Cl^- \rightarrow AgCl \qquad (3.6)$$

*A constant potential is maintained between the cathode and anode; the electrode is said to be "polarized." The electrical signal detected by a polarographic oxygen electrode is proportional to the flux (not concentration) of $O_2$:*

$$I = nFAJ_{O_2} \qquad (3.7)$$

*where I is current (in amperes), n $(= 4)$ is the number of electrons used to reduce each $O_2$, F is Faraday's constant, A is the surface area of the cathode, and $J_{O_2}$ is the flux of oxygen (Gnaiger, Forstner 1983). Because $O_2$ is continuously consumed at the cathode, and the current output is directly proportional to the surface area of the cathode, there is an inevitable compromise between sensitivity and autoconsumption of $O_2$. In a Clark-type electrode the sample is separated from the cathode by a membrane, usually made of Teflon® or polytetrafluoroethylene; these materials allow the diffusion of $O_2$ but not ions. The diffusion of $O_2$ is often facilitated by stirring, which introduces "noise" to the signal and consequently constrains the use of such electrodes to samples with relatively high absolute rates of oxygen consumption or evolution. This problem can be overcome by operating the electrode in a pulsed mode, where the polarization potential is switched on briefly and the rate of oxygen consumption is recorded, or by using thin silicone membranes, which have high diffusivities for $O_2$. In either case, however, as the diffusivity for $O_2$ across the membranes ranges from $10^{-11}$ to $10^{-13} m^2/s$, depending on their thickness, the time constant for the measurement of $O_2$ in a Clark-type electrode is relatively long, on the order of 0.01 to 0.1s; this time constant is much too long for measurements from single turnover flashes of light.*

*An alternative electrode design, developed by Blinks and Skow (1938) and subsequently improved on by Haxo and Blinks (1950), allowed the placement of the sample directly on the platinum cathode (Fig 3.4). The sample was separated from the anode by an ion-permeable membrane, such as cellulose (a candy wrapper will do in a pinch), and medium continuously flows over and perfuses the sample. Oxygen produced by the sample is immediately consumed on the electrode surface, and the current produced is directly proportional to the rate of oxygen consumption. Hence the "Blinks electrode" (or bare-platinum electrode as it is sometimes called) directly measures the oxygen production. Because the sample rests directly on the cathode, the time constant for the Blinks electrode can be extremely rapid, on the order of 10ms, and the current generated is often high (milliamps). The rate electrode permits the detection of oxygen from a single flash; however, because the signal is directly proportional to the number of cells that are in direct contact with the cathode (a condition that is virtually impossible to reproduce from preparation to preparation), the absolute rate of oxygen flux cannot be accurately determined. In summary, in a Clark electrode, the absolute rates of oxygen evolution can be accurately determined, but the design limits the sensitivity and rate of the measurement. In a Blinks electrode, the sensitivity and rate of measurement are increased by several orders of magnitude, but the absolute value of the rate of oxygen production or consumption is not accessible; all measurements are relative.*

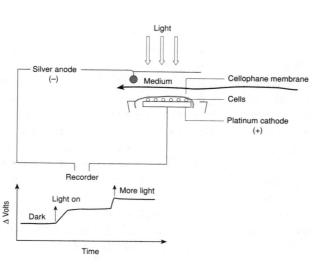

**Figure 3.4** A schematic cross-section of an oxygen rate electrode. The cells, thallus, or leaf blade sits directly on a platinum button and is covered by a permeable membrane, such as cellophane. Medium continuously flows over the membrane, supplying the cells with nutrients and carbon dioxide. A silver ring is in contact with the medium, and a voltage potential of about 0.7 V is applied between the platinum cathode and silver anode. Oxygen produced by the cells is immediately consumed by the cathode, hence the current produced by the electrode is directly proportional to the rate of oxygen evolved. An example of a recorder trace from such an electrode is also shown.

light absorbed is called a *quantum yield*. If a pigment contributed to production of oxygen, then the quantum yield would be high in the wavelengths corresponding to the absorption bands of the pigment.

In 1942 and 1943, Emerson[1] and Lewis reported that the quantum yield for oxygen evolution declined by about 25% between approximately 470 and 550 nm in *Chlorella*, suggesting that the absorption of light by carotenoids was less efficient in oxygen evolution than that of chlorophyll (Emerson, Arnold 1942; Emerson, Lewis 1943). The experimental protocol used by Emerson in the 1930s and 1940s required the use of manometers and high densities of algae, making the measure-

---

1. Robert Emerson was a Quaker and not drafted during World War II (Jack Myers, personal communication).

ment of oxygen evolution tedious and slow. In the late 1940s Lawrence Blinks and his student Francis Haxo, at the Hopkins Marine Laboratory, developed a sensitive oxygen electrode that could directly measure the rate of oxygen evolution (Haxo, Blinks 1950). The oxygen rate electrode consisted of a platinum button that served as a cathode, upon which a monolayer of cells or a thin piece of macrophyte algal tissue was placed. The sample was capped by a cellophane membrane, which allowed the free diffusion of media, gases and water, and a silver/silver chloride anode was placed over the cap. After exposure to light, oxygen produced by the cells was consumed by the cathode, generating an electrical current that was directly proportional to the rate of oxygen evolution.

Using a specially constructed monochromator to provide continuous illumination at defined wavelengths, Haxo and Blinks (1950) measured the wavelength dependency of oxygen evolution in a variety of marine macrophytes. They were interested in determining the ability of carotenoids and other pigments to "sensitize" $O_2$ production—how much oxygen is evolved per unit light absorbed? They observed that in most algal classes, the wavelength dependence of oxygen evolution approximated the absorption spectrum of the organism, and concluded that, in general, the absorption of light by carotenoids was less efficiently used to drive photosynthetic $O_2$ production than that absorbed by chlorophyll (Fig 3.5). However, in the four species of red algae examined, they observed that the light absorbed by the phycobilipigment, phycoerythrin, sensitized the evolution of oxygen, but that the light absorbed by chlorophyll *a* and carotenoids was relatively ineffective in producing oxygen. They concluded,

> The striking result of these investigations is not so much the participation of phycoerythrin and phycocyanin in photosynthesis in red algae (this had been fairly clear before), but rather the relative *inactivity* of chlorophyll and carotenoids. Apparently light absorbed by the latter pigments is only very slightly used in the process of oxygen production.

The results of Haxo and Blinks raised the question, "What does the chlorophyll in a red alga do?"

In 1943, Emerson and Lewis noted that while blue, orange, and short-wavelength red light (<660 nm), which are absorbed primarily by chlorophyll *a*, stimulated the production of oxygen, long-wavelength red light (>700 nm), which is also absorbed by the pigment, is relatively ineffective in oxygen evolution (Emerson, Lewis 1943). This effect came to be known as the *red drop* (Fig 3.6a). The red drop is simply a jargon term meaning that the quantum yield of $O_2$ is lower at long wavelengths of red light. Moreover, Emerson observed that if a shorter wavelength of light was simultaneously added to the long wavelength, the quantum yield for oxygen evolution could be restored (Fig 3.6b). In fact, the quantum yield with both long and short wavelengths was greater than the sum of the oxygen evolved by each wavelength of the same intensity when presented individually. This effect, called *enhancement*, increased the quantum yield for oxygen evolution in far-red light, offsetting the red drop (Myers 1971). The red drop and enhancement phenomena provided strong evidence that there were *two* independent light reactions sensitized by two separate antenna systems. This result ran counter to the then-accepted dogma of a single photochemical process in oxygenic photosynthesis.

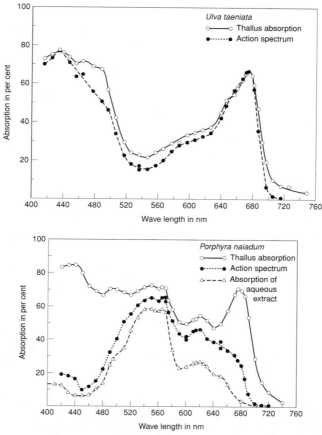

**Figure 3.5** The absorption and photosynthetic action spectra for the green alga *Ulva taeniata* (top), and the red alga *Porphyra naiadum* (bottom). The action spectra were obtained with an oxygen rate electrode (see Fig. 3.4), in conjuction with a monochromator that selected light at specific wavelengths. For *Ulva*, the spectra were normalized at the chlorophyll *a* $Q_y$ band at 675 nm. (Courtesy of Francis Haxo, with permission)

Interestingly, Blinks, working at about the same time as Emerson, was unable to experimentally reproduce the setup needed to observe the enhancement effect. Instead, Blinks used sequential inputs of light of different wavelengths and showed that the constructive interactions between two wavelengths could occur even when a dark period of milliseconds to a second was interspersed. These results strongly implied that the interaction between the two light reactions was mediated by chemical products rather than by an excited state of a pigment.

Using the state-of-the-art spectrophotometers of the day, Duysens worked with photosynthetic (anaerobic) bacteria and observed that upon illumination there was a small decrease in absorbance in intact cells at about 425 nm (Duysens 1954a). This pattern could be observed in such organisms because the Soret bands of bacteriochlorophyll do not have an overlapping absorption in this (blue) region of the

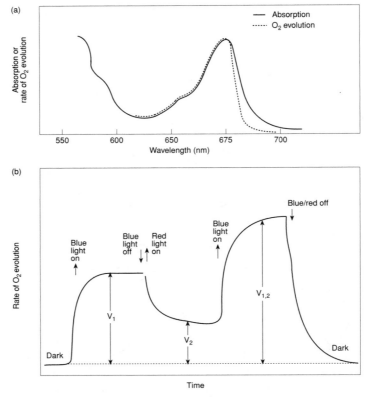

**Figure 3.6** (a) An example of the "red drop." A careful comparison of the absorption and action spectra (see Fig 3.5) in the red and far red portion region revealed that the quantum yield of oxygen evolution was lower than expected (i.e., the absorption of light by chlorophyll *a* in the far red region did not lead to a proportional production of oxygen). (b) Enhancement. Using an oxygen rate electrode (Fig 3.4), the rate of oxygen evolution is measured at two wavelengths. In the classical experiment with *Chlorella pyrenoidosa*, the two wavelengths selected were 645 nm and 700 nm. The former corresponds to a chlorophyll *b* absorption band, while the latter to a long wavelength region of chlorophyll *a*. Let us denote the two rates as $V_1$ and $V_2$, respectively. The rate of oxygen evolution observed when both wavelengths of light are given simultaneously, $V_{1,2}$, is greater than the sum of the two rates, $V_1 + V_2$. This effect is called *enhancement*, and can be quantified as $V_{1,2}/V_1 + V_2$.

spectrum.[2] He hypothesized that this photochemical reaction was due to a light-induced oxidation of a cytochrome, and he searched for a similar pattern in oxygenic cells. In that same year he reported that red light induced a reversible absorption change in the green alga *Chlorella* at about 525 nm (Duysens 1954b; Fig 3.7). Bessel Kok observed a similar light-dependent decrease in absorption at 700 nm in *Chlorella*, which he attributed to the oxidation of a special chlorophyll molecule (Kok 1957). Kok subsequently identified the target, or "reaction center," by EPR spectroscopy as a special pigment molecule(s) within the photosynthetic

---

2. The Soret bands of bacteriochlorophyll absorb in the near ultraviolet, around 360 nm. As the $Q_y$ band of the pigment is in the far red (i.e., around 820 to 900 nm), bacteriochlorophyll has no visible absorption to the human eye. The orange color of extracted bacteriochlorophyll-protein complexes from purple photosynthetic bacteria is due to the presence of carotenoids that transfer excitation energy to the bacteriochlorophyll.

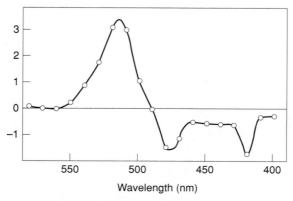

**Figure 3.7** The change in the absorption spectrum of a *Chlorella* suspension upon irradiation with red light (from Duysens 1954, with permission). See Figure 3.8 for an explanation of how this measurement is made.

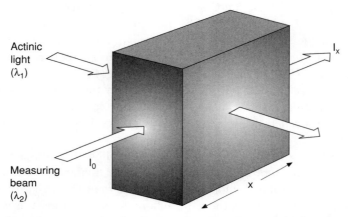

**Figure 3.8** A schematic representation showing how the effect of an "actinic" (i.e., photochemically sensitizing) light is measured in a spectrophotometer. A suspension of cells, chloroplasts, or membranes is placed in a spectrophotometer normal to a measuring beam, $I_0$. The absorption of light is detected as described in Figure 2.11. At each measuring wavelength, the sample is illuminated from the side by a second, strong light source, at a specified wavelength, $\lambda_1$. Changes in absorption induced by the cross illumination are determined at a variety of wavelengths. A methodical analysis of such absorption changes can be used to infer the photochemical "targets" (e.g., Fig. 3.7).

unit that is capable of photochemically transferring an electron (i.e., it formed a radical) (Kok, Beinert 1962). Duysens and Kok's observations provided independent biophysical evidence that the target for the light reaction in photosynthesis contained a photochemical receptor different from the majority of the chlorophyll molecules (Fig 3.8).

A second line of evidence for two reaction centers in photosynthetic light reactions was inferred from fluorescence patterns in algae. The quantum yield of fluorescence (defined as the ratio of light emitted as fluorescence to light absorbed) for chlorophyll extracted in an organic solvent, or of most isolated chlorophyll proteins, is constant. In contrast, the quantum yield of fluorescence of chlorophyll in vivo undergoes repeatable variations in response to changes in irradiance.

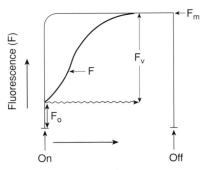

**Figure 3.9** A fluorescence induction, or "Kautsky" curve. Immediately (within picoseconds) upon illumination by an actinic light, fluorescence from chlorophyll *a* can be detected. The initial fluorescence level observed is designated $F_0$. As the sample continues to absorb photons, fluorescence rises to a maximum value, $F_m$. The difference between these two states, $F_m - F_0$, is called variable fluorescence, $F_v$.

At room temperature algae fluoresce with a peak emission at about 685 nm. Upon illumination fluorescence quickly rises from a nil to a low constant level, designated $F_0$. If the illumination is strong enough, the fluorescence will increase from the $F_0$ level to a maximum value, $F_m$. The difference between the $F_m$ and $F_0$ fluorescence levels is called the variable fluorescence, $F_v$ (Fig 3.9). The changes in fluorescence in intact leaves were first described in the 1930s by Kautsky, who observed the variations with his naked eye; the time course of changes in fluorescence is sometimes called the *Kautsky effect* (Kautsky, Hisrsh 1931; Kautsky et al. 1960).

If a dilute culture of algal cells is exposed to blue light, the emission of red light is generally so faint as to be barely perceptible to the human eye. Thus, in vivo the quantum yield of chlorophyll fluorescence is lower than that in vitro; the fluorescence is said to be *quenched*. As the natural fluorescence lifetime $\tau_0$ is constant, the observed fluorescence lifetime must be shorter in vivo than in vitro (Chapter 2). This phenomenon can only occur by allowing competing pathways for the de-excitation of the excited singlet state in vivo. Two of these pathways are photochemistry and heat, and we shall denote the rate constants for these processes as $k_p$ and $k_d$ respectively. Let the rate of de-excitation of the singlet excited state to fluorescence be denoted by $k_f$. Thus, the quantum yield for fluorescence ($\phi_f$; defined as the ratio of light emitted as fluorescence to light absorbed) can be related to the rate constants for the three processes as:

$$\phi_f = k_f / \left( k_f + k_d + k_p \right) \tag{3.8}$$

The action spectra for oxygen evolution and in vivo fluorescence at room temperature are remarkably similar (Neori et al. 1988; Fig. 3.10). The correspondence between these two phenomena suggests that they share a common photochemical reaction. Moreover, in any algal preparation, the quantum yield of variable fluorescence is inversely related to oxygen evolution (Bonaventura, Myers 1969). That is, when variable fluorescence is large, oxygen evolution is small, and conversely when oxygen evolution is large, variable fluorescence is small. To account for the relationship between oxygen evolution and fluorescence, Duysens and Sweers

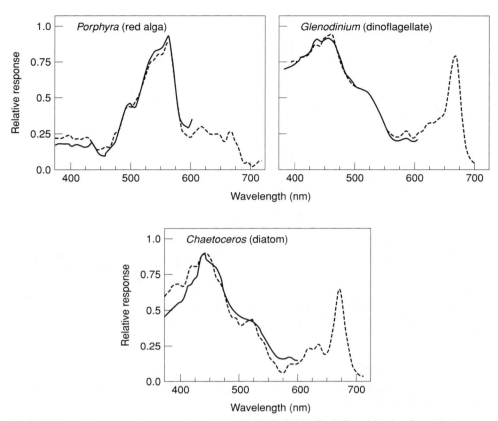

**Figure 3.10** Action spectra for oxygen evolution (solid line) (see Fig 3.5) and in vivo fluorescence excitation spectra (dashed line) in a red alga, *Porphyra perforata*, a dinoflagellate, *Glenodinium* sp, and a diatom, *Chaetoceros gracilis*. To make the fluorescence measurements, the cells were illuminated with light of selected wavelengths, and the fluorescence of chlorophyll *a* was measured. The fluorescence measurements were made in the presence of the inhibitor, DCMU, and correspond to the $F_m$ state (see Fig 3.9). Note the close correspondence between the two spectra. (From Neori et al. 1986, with permission)

(1963) postulated the existence of a fluorescence quencher, "Q." When a reaction center absorbs a photon it becomes oxidized and transfers its electron to Q, forming $Q^-$. In this process some of the energy of the photon has been used to chemically reduce Q. We say that a reaction center is *open* when it can use the energy of an absorbed photon to drive an electron to Q. Under these conditions fluorescence is quenched. We say that a reaction center is *closed* when the quencher is in the reduced state, $Q^-$. Photons arriving at the closed reaction center cannot be used for photochemistry until the reaction center is rereduced by an electron extracted from some donor and $Q^-$ is reoxidized by some acceptor. When the reaction center is closed, the probability is high that incoming photons will be reemitted as fluorescence. It follows that the maximum quantum yield for photochemistry occurs when all Q molecules are oxidized (Fig 3.11), and the maximum quantum yield for fluorescence occurs when all Q molecules are reduced. Thus, to a first order, the quantum yields of photochemistry and fluorescence are inversely related to each other (Butler 1972; Butler, Kitajima 1975b).

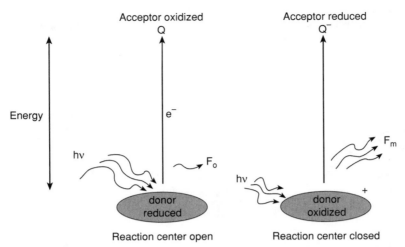

**Figure 3.11** A schematic representation of Duysen and Sweer's 1963 model of variable fluorescence (see Fig 3.9). The model posulates an electron donor and acceptor. The latter is a fluorescence quencher, Q. In the dark, the donor is reduced, Q is oxidized, and the fluorescence yield is low (i.e., the $F_0$ state). The reaction center in this condition is said to be "open"; i.e., it is capable of moving an electron from the donor to Q. Upon absorption of a photon, Q becomes reduced and the donor becomes transiently oxidized. Absorbed photons have a higher probability of being reemitted and fluorescence rises to the $F_m$ state.

It was apparent that the two basic lines of evidence for reaction centers in eukaryotic algae and higher plants (e.g., the light-dependent oxidation of chlorophyll *a* at 700 nm and the change in fluorescence yield upon illumination) were not due to the same reaction. The change in fluorescence yield is inversely correlated with the evolution of oxygen, while the oxidation of the pigment that absorbs at 700 nm (called $P_{700}$) is not related to fluorescence changes. Moreover, the wavelength dependency of the absorption difference at 700 nm clearly differs from those for oxygen evolution (Fig 3.12). The photochemical process that was responsible for the bleaching of $P_{700}$ is called *photosystem I* (PSI); the process correlated with changes in variable fluorescence and oxygen evolution is called *photosystem II* (PSII). These two photosystems consist of photochemical *reaction centers* that are energetically coupled to *antennae*, which serve to harvest the light energy and transfer that energy to the reaction center. The pigment composition of the antenna differs for each photosystem and between species, sometimes giving rise to distinctive action spectra for PSI and PSII.

Compared with PSII, relatively few PSI action spectra have been reported for algae. Based on a comparison of the published action spectra, it is clear that the antenna systems serving the two photosystems differ in green algae and cyanobacteria, while in diatoms and prochlorophytes the antenna systems seem to be spectrally similar. In *Chlorella*, oxygen evolution is greater at shorter wavelengths of light and receives excitation energy from such accessory pigments as chlorophyll *b*, whereas the effective absorption cross-section of $P_{700}$ is greater at longer wavelengths and receives excitation energy primarily from chlorophyll *a* (Myers 1971). In cyanobacteria and red algae, excitation energy absorbed by the phycobilisomes is transferred almost exclusively to PSII. In diatoms and prochlorophytes, the

## ❏ PSI Action Spectra

*The absorption difference coefficient for $P_{700}$ at 700 nm is $60\,mM^{-1}\,cm^{-1}$. When $P_{700}$ is oxidized, the absorption at 700 nm decreases relative to that in the reduced state (Fig 3.13). The difference between reduced and oxidized absorption is quantitatively related to the number of $P_{700}$ molecules in the sample. The ratio of total chlorophyll to $P_{700}$ in algae typically ranges from 300 to 3000; that is, >0.5% of the total pigment is $P_{700}$ (Falkowski, Owens 1980; Perry et al. 1981). A sensitive spectrophotometer is capable of detecting absorption differences of about 0.0002 with an acceptable signal-to-noise ratio. Thus, to measure $P_{700}$ in a sample, one needs at least 3 mg of chlorophyll. In practice, the absorption changes associated with PSI are often made at 820 nm because light scattering at longer wavelengths is much smaller. At that wavelength, the photo-oxidation of PSI results in an increase in absorptivity; however, at 820 nm the absorption difference coefficient is an order of magnitude smaller than at 700 nm. Thus, precise measurements require a proportionately larger sample size. This often poses practical problems, especially with microalgae, in obtaining sufficient material for measurement.*

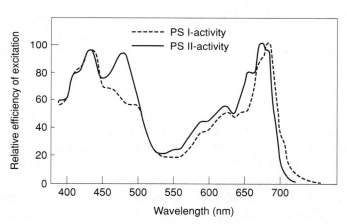

**Figure 3.12** Action spectra for photosystems I and II in *Chlorella*. Note that PSI is much less sensitive than PSII to excitation between 450 and 500 nm, and between 650 and 675 nm. These two absorption bands correspond to chlorophyll *b*. Hence, we might infer that chlorophyll *b* does not play a major role in harvesting light for PSI in this organism. Note also that PSI is more sensitive than PSII to wavelengths above about 700 nm.

antenna systems transfer excitation energy to both PSII and PSI with comparable efficiency. The spectral distinctions between the photosystems have evolved into a shorthand nomenclature of "PSI" and "PSII light"; however, it must be kept in mind that these distinctions depend on the organism under investigation. A PSI light for *Chlorella* may be a fine excitation source for PSII in a diatom (Owens, Wold 1986).

## THE MAXIMUM QUANTUM YIELD OF PHOTOSYNTHESIS

The accurate measurement of the maximum quantum yield of photosynthesis has occupied many researchers for a variety of reasons. From the viewpoint of a bio-

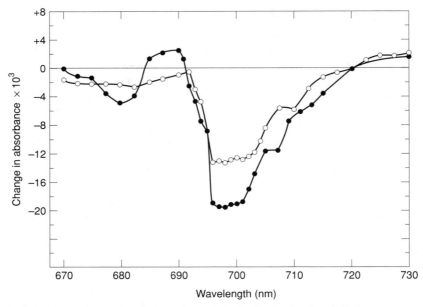

**Figure 3.13** Oxidized minus reduced absorption spectra for P$_{700}$ in the diatom *Skeletonema costatum* (○), and the green alga *Dunaliella tertiolecta* (●). These measurements were made as shown in Fig 3.8 with a blue actinic light. There is no change in absorption at 720 nm, hence this wavelength is used as a reference or "isosbestic" point. Maximum changes in absorption are observed between about 695 and 703 nm.

physicist attempting to understand the mechanisms of the photochemical reactions, the maximum quantum yield, while not necessarily providing a mechanism, limits the possibilities. From the viewpoint of a physiologist, the maximum quantum yield is useful in understanding the inevitable inefficiencies that arise in coupling photosynthesis to growth. From an ecological perspective, the maximum quantum yield has been (mis)applied to calculate how much solar energy can be converted to fixed carbon. We will discuss the latter two viewpoints in subsequent chapters; for now let us focus on the biophysical aspects.

What is the maximum quantum yield of photosynthesis and why do we care? Let us begin with the definition. A *quantum yield* (usually designated by the symbol ϕ) is the ratio of moles of product formed or substrate consumed to the moles of photons absorbed in a photochemical reaction. The inverse of a quantum yield (1/ϕ) is called a *quantum requirement* (i.e., moles photons absorbed per mole product formed or substrate consumed). The ratio of the *energy* stored in the product to the *energy* absorbed as light is called a *quantum efficiency*. As the energy of photons is wavelength dependent, so too is a quantum efficiency. Because all the photochemical reactions in photosynthesis proceed from the lowest energy singlet excited state of chlorophyll (Chapter 2), it is immaterial for the calculation of the quantum yield whether the absorbed quantum was blue or red; the quantum efficiency for the former will inevitably be smaller than that calculated for the latter. It should be pointed out that quantum yields (or efficiencies) must be related to a specific product or substrate. Thus, a quantum yield for $O_2$ evolution is not necessarily (and in fact, seldom is) the same as that for $CO_2$ fixation (Myers 1980). The differences are primarily due to the level to which $CO_2$ and alternative electron acceptors are reduced.

The maximum quantum yield is a measure of the largest quantity of product formed or substrate consumed to the smallest number of photons absorbed. For this measurement, a subjective judgment call must be made. The maximum yield is not an average value (Myers 1980). Consider the following analogy: In a foot race, the fastest runner is the winner of the race, but not necessarily the record-holder. Only one runner can hold the record at one time; the best time in the race is immaterial to the record if the runner did not run faster than the record-holder. Similarly, the maximum quantum yield is not the best quantum yield, nor is it necessarily the steady-state quantum yield. It is the maximum value derived under any physiological condition that gives the highest value; i.e., it is the "record holder."

As briefly mentioned, the maximum quantum yield of photosynthesis had been measured in the early 1920s by Otto Warburg (and co-workers in Berlin) who won the Nobel Prize in 1931 for his work on the coupled oxidation–reduction reactions in mitochondrial respiration. Warburg liked to work with very dense cultures of $CO_2$-starved *Chlorella*. This avoided two problems: First, because the cultures were dense, it could be assumed for all practical purposes that all the incident light was absorbed. Second, he reasoned that in a $CO_2$-starved state, the initial products of photosynthesis would not lead to any repressive (i.e., negative) feedback on photosynthesis; therefore he would measure the *maximum* quantum yield. He used a series of short-term illumination periods, interspersed by dark periods and found that the maximum quantum yield for $CO_2$ fixation was 0.25; that is, that for each $CO_2$ fixed, four photons were absorbed. As Warburg was well respected, perhaps even slightly feared (who argues with one of the most famous Nobel laureates?), few openly doubted, or had reason to doubt, his measurements. Lower values for the quantum yield could be dismissed as reflecting poor measurements or physiological feedbacks rather than the "true" chemical mechanism. As it was understood that the evolution of oxygen required four single-electron transfers, the Warburg measurements suggested that there was a single photochemical reaction that operated four times in series or in parallel. This measurement delayed the interpretation of the action spectra and red drop in the context of two photosystems by more than two decades.

In the 1950s, Emerson, who had previously worked in Warburg's lab, carefully reexamined the maximum quantum yield in *Chlorella* and reported maximum values of between 0.12 and 0.10 quanta/$O_2$ (Emerson 1943; Emerson et al. 1957). Warburg and Emerson worked together in Emerson's lab in 1952 but failed to resolve the discrepancy. Independent measurements from other laboratories, such as those of Bessel Kok and Jack Myers, emerged supporting Emerson's lower value, and those are generally accepted today (Myers 1980). Given that four electrons must be extracted from $H_2O$ to produce each molecule of $O_2$, a minimum quantum requirement for $O_2$ of eight photons suggests that at least two photons are absorbed for each electron transferred. While measurements of the maximum quantum yield did not directly lead to the deduction of two photosystems, the measurements supported the hypothesis that the photochemical mechanism included two photo-chemical reactions.

## EFFECTIVE ABSORPTION CROSS-SECTIONS

Let us now consider the "size" of the target that absorbs light and transfers the excitation energy to a reaction center. In order to demonstrate that the flash intensities they used were saturating for evolution of oxygen, Emerson and Arnold (1932b) measured oxygen flash yields as a function of flash intensity. As flash energy was increased, the yield of oxygen increased, ultimately reaching a plateau. The resulting "killing curve" was an exponential (Fig 3.14). Subsequently, Ley and Mauzerall (1982) showed that if the absolute number of photons in each flash is known, Y can be quantitatively related to flash intensity by a cumulative one-hit Poisson function:

$$\frac{Y}{Y_{max}} = 1 - e^{-\sigma E} \tag{3.9}$$

where Y is the flash yield of $O_2$ evolved or $CO_2$ fixed at flash energy E, $Y_{max}$ is the maximum flash yield, and $\sigma$ is the slope of the exponential curve. The left-hand side of Equation 3.9 is a value from zero to unity and defines a probability of a photon hitting a target capable of evolving oxygen or reducing carbon dioxide. The probability is related to the number of molecules that make up the antenna for the photochemical target and to the efficiency of energy transfer to the target. We shall call $\sigma$ the "effective" or the "functional" absorption cross-section. Note that if the flash energy is dimensionalized as quanta/nm², $\sigma$ has dimensions of nm²/quanta; that is,

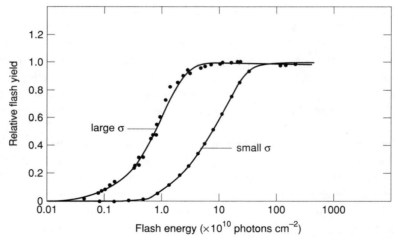

**Figure 3.14** The light intensity saturation profiles for oxygen flash yields in *Chlorella vulgaris*. Oxygen flash yields were induced with pulses from a laser light source at 596 nm. As the intensity of the laser source is increased, the oxygen evolved per flash increases, up to some saturation level. The data are fit to a cumulative one-hit Poisson function. Cells with large functional absorption cross-sections for PSII ($\sigma_{O2}$) saturate at lower excitation energy than cells with small absorption cross-sections. (Modified from Ley, Mauzerall 1982, with permission)

### ❏ POISSON

*This is the second time so far in this book that we encounter a Poisson distribution; the first is found in the Chapter 1 description of the molecular clock. A few words about Poisson are relevant to students of aquatic photosynthesis. Siméon-Denis Poisson (1781–1840) was a student of two giants of mathematics and physics, Lagrange and Laplace, at the École Polytechnique, located near the Panthéon on the Left Bank in Paris. Poisson was interested in physics and physical chemistry, and he developed theories on electrostatics, electromagnetic phenomena, and the stability of planetary orbits. In the area of statistics, Poisson developed a theory of very large numbers, compactly expressed in Equation 3.9.*

*One apparently apocryphal motivation for the development of this equation is sometimes suggested to be a military application. During the reign of Napoleon Bonaparte, the École Polytechnique served as a center for basic and applied research for the military (a role that the institute continues to this day). Cavalry officers wished to estimate more precisely their losses when charging an infantry in a fixed position. If the number of rounds fired by the infantry is known (a trained English infantry soldier could fire three rounds per minute), and the duration of exposure to the shots (i.e., how fast a horse can run and how far it has to go) are known, the Poisson distribution can be used to calculate the "hit" rate. This application, which is the literal basis of so-called "target theory," can be extended to any physical process in which hits or encounters are absolutely stochastic and there are large numbers of events per unit target. In Chapter 7 we shall see another variation on a Poisson function, used to describe a photosynthesis-irradiance curve.*

*One of Poisson's most famous students was Gustave-Gaspard Coriolis, who did his doctoral thesis on the effects of the Earth's rotation on the motion of geophysical fluids. Poisson thought Coriolis was a "solid, but not brilliant," student.*

---

this cross-section is referenced to the probability of using a photon at a specific wavelength for a photochemical reaction. By *effective* cross-section we mean the target size as inferred indirectly from its interactions with photons of a specific frequency; we did not actually measure the physical dimensions of the light-absorbing system, but inferred the probability of the absorption of photons based on ability to detect a photochemical response. A neutron capture cross-section or X-ray inactivation cross-section could similarly be described for a photosystem (and such cross-sections often provide clues as to the structure and properties of the photosystems; e.g., Whitmarsh et al. 1993).

The abstract concept of effective absorption cross-section is useful in developing a quantitative understanding of photosynthesis and many other processes involving interactions of particles with targets (Mauzerall 1978). Consider the following analogy: The antenna on a roof has an absorption cross-section with respect to the radiowaves emitted by a radio station. The physical cross-section of the antenna is the length of its arms. When the antenna is perpendicular to the radiowave there is a high probability that the arms of the antenna will intercept the signal. In this state, the reception of the signal is strong and the effective absorption cross-section of the antenna is large. As the antenna is rotated about an axis, the reception will decrease and reach a minimum when the radiowaves are parallel to the antenna arms. Thus, while the physical cross-section of the antenna does not change, the probability of the antennae intercepting the radiowaves changes. The ratio of the physical cross-section to the effective cross-section of the antenna is a measure of the efficiency by which the antenna receives the signal from the radio station, i.e., it is the quantum efficiency of the antenna.

Similarly, on a molecular level the physical target of the photosynthetic system may be constant; however, the effective absorption cross-section can vary. Variations can be induced, for example, by adding a carotenoid to the antenna which may absorb excitation but not transfer it to chlorophyll *a*, or conversely by removing excitation from an excited chlorophyll *a* molecule before it can be transferred to a reaction center. Thus, while the light is absorbed, it may be more or less effective in producing a photochemical response. The concept of the effective cross-section includes an implicit quantum yield for the transfer of excitation from the antenna to a photochemical reaction center and is useful for describing the wavelength dependence of a photochemical response. In green algae, for example, the effective absorption cross-section for oxygen evolution will be large in the blue and red but small in the green. Similarly, in red and blue-green algae that contain phycoerythrin, the apparent absorption cross-section is large in the green but smaller in the blue due to the lack of chlorophyll *b*.

### The Relationship Between the Effective Absorption Cross-Section and the Maximum Quantum Yield

Recall that we can define the absorption of light by molecules in terms of an *optical cross-section* (Chapter 2). If one measures the absorption of light by a whole cell at a given wavelength, and references that absorption (which can be due to a variety of contributing pigments) to the concentration of chlorophyll *a*, it is possible to derive a chlorophyll-specific optical cross-section, $\sigma_{chl}(\lambda)$, in units $nm^2$/Chl *a*. This cross-section, which is not a constant, describes the tendency for interaction (i.e., absorption) of all the absorbers at a certain wavelength, but "assigns" that absorption to chlorophyll *a*.

Now consider a photosynthetic unit. Each photosynthetic unit contains PSII and PSI reaction centers. We should note that the ratio of these two reaction centers does not have to be unity. Let us designate $X$ numbers of PSIIs and $Y$ numbers of PSIs (where $X$ and $Y$ are integers) and the photosynthetic unit contains (for example) 2500 chlorophyll *a* + *b* molecules with a chlorophyll *a/b* ratio of 3; there are then $3/4 \times 2500 = 1875$ chlorophyll *a* molecules per photosynthetic unit.

At wavelength $\lambda$, the *optical* absorption cross-section of a photosynthetic unit ($\sigma_{PSU}$) is given by:

$$\sigma_{PSU(\lambda)} = \sigma_{chl(\lambda)}\left(Chl/O_2\right) \qquad (3.10)$$

where $\sigma_{chl}$ is the optical absorption cross-section of chlorophyll *a* at wavelength $\lambda$ (see Chapter 2) and Chl/$O_2$ is the "size" of the photosynthetic unit. Chl/$O_2$ is the same as the Emerson–Arnold ratio; that is, it is the ratio of chlorophyll per oxygen produced by a single turnover flash. The term $\sigma_{PSU}$ has dimensions $nm^2$/$O_2$. This

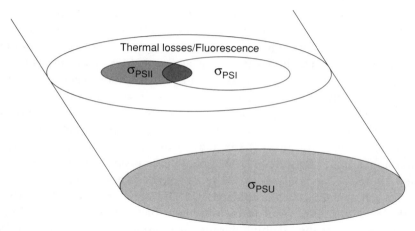

**Figure 3.15** A schematic representation of the quantum yield of photosynthesis in relation to the effective and optical absorption cross-sections of the photosynthetic apparatus. The large elliptical area represents the optical absorption cross-section of a photosynthetic unit, i.e., the total light-harvesting area. A fraction of the absorbed light leads to oxygen evolution. That fraction corresponds to the effective absorption cross-section of PSII (see Fig 3.14), and is designated $\sigma_{PSII}$. The ratio $\sigma_{PSII}/\sigma_{PSU}$ is the quantum yield for oxygen evolution. An analogous effective absorption cross-section exists for PSI, and could be measured, for example, by following the flash intensity saturation curve for $P_{700}$ absorption changes (e.g., see Fig 3.13b). Loss processes, such as heat and fluorescence, are represented by the difference $[\sigma_{PSU} - (\sigma_{PSII} + \sigma_{PSI})]$. (After Dubinsky 1992, with permission)

cross-section implicitly includes the light absorbed by *both* PSI and PSII reaction centers.

Recall now that we could measure and calculate a functional absorption cross-section for PSII alone from the flash-intensity saturation curve for oxygen evolution at wavelength $\lambda$ (Eq 3.9). The ratio of that cross-section, $\sigma_{PSII}$ (with dimensions $nm^2$/quanta) to $\sigma_{PSU}$, gives:

$$\phi_{max} = \sigma_{PSII}/\sigma_{PSU} \tag{3.11}$$

This ratio has dimensions $O_2$/quanta absorbed; that is, it is the maximum *quantum yield for oxygen evolution*. Thus, the quantum yield of oxygen evolution can be thought of as the ratio of the optical absorption cross-sections of PSII + PSI to the effective absorption cross-section of PSII. Simply put, the optical absorption cross-section for a photosynthetic unit describes the ability of the "unit" to absorb light at a given wavelength. The effective absorption cross-section describes the ability of light of the same wavelength to promote a photochemical reaction. The ratio of these two processes is a quantum yield (Fig 3.15). If the ratio of PSII to PSI reaction centers is known, the functional absorption cross-section of PSI can be calculated by difference (Dubinsky et al. 1986; Greene et al. 1991; Ley, Mauzerall 1982).

**Variable Chlorophyll Fluorescence**

A fluorescence-based technique for estimating reaction centers was described by Malkin and Kok (1966). In this approach, it is assumed that the photochemical quencher of fluorescence in PSII (i.e., Q) is stoichiometrically identical to the reaction center. Given that assumption, if a photosynthetic system is exposed to an actinic (i.e., a photochemically stimulating) light,[3] the rate of rise in fluorescence will be a product of the intensity of the actinic light and the effective absorption cross-section of PSII and the quantum yield of fluorescence. If a quencher (i.e., a reaction center) is present and open, it can absorb photons from the actinic source for photochemistry, and these would then be unavailable for fluorescence. Moreover, if, and only if, the reaction center undergoes a single photochemical reaction (i.e., a single "turnover"), the number of photons used for photochemistry (i.e., not appearing as fluorescence) will be directly proportional to the number of reaction centers. This condition can be satisfied by poisoning the cell with an inhibitor such as 3′-(3,4-dichlorophenyl)-1′,1′-dimethyl urea (DCMU), which prevents the oxidation of Q prior to measurement of the kinetic changes in fluorescence. The area over the resulting fluorescence induction curve is proportional to Q, and can be quantitatively related to it if the effective absorption cross-section is also known.

It is possible to obtain the same information without using DCMU by illuminating the sample with an actinic flash so intense that the fluorescence signal rises much more rapidly than the oxidation of Q. This can be technically achieved using brief flashes to cumulatively saturate the reaction center within a single turnover. One such technique is based on the so-called pump-and-probe method in which the change in the quantum yield of a weak probe flash, measured prior to and following the pump flash, can be used to infer the photochemical efficiency (Fig 3.16). This basic technique was first applied to the analysis of variable chlorophyll fluorescence

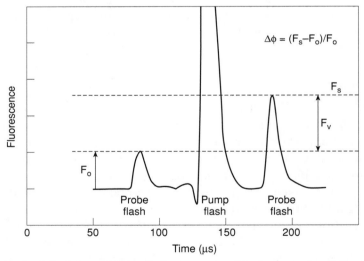

**Figure 3.16** A schematic diagram showing the basic concept of the "pump and probe" technique for measuring variable fluorescence. The fluorescence induced by a weak "probe" flash is recorded as $F_0$. At some time, the sample is exposed to an actinic "pump" flash followed by a second weak probe flash of the same intensity as the first. The change in fluorescence between the first and second probe flashes is a measure of variable fluorescence.

---

3. The term *actinic* means that the light induces some photochemical effect.

by Mauzerall (1972) who, by varying the time delay of the pump and probe flash, observed that in the green alga *Chlorella* the fluorescence yield rose to a maximum within about 10 μs, and after 100 μs began to decay with relatively complex kinetics (Fig 3.17). Butler (1972) interpreted these data within the context of photochemical charge separation in PSII. Subsequently, fluorescence decay was used to infer the kinetics of the electron transfer reactions on the acceptor side of PSII (which we will discuss in Chapter 4). Thus, measurements of maximal variable fluorescence in this time domain (<500 μs) represent the fraction of reducible Q. This notion was supported by the observation that the change in the quantum yield of fluorescence induced by a saturating pump flash and measured 80 μs later was identical with or without DCMU.

By changing the intensity of the actinic flash while maintaining a constant time delay between the pump and probe flashes (i.e., between 10 and 100 μs), a flash-intensity saturation curve of variable fluorescence is obtained (Falkowski, Wyman et al. 1986). The slope of the curve describes the effective absorption cross-section of PSII (i.e., $\sigma_{PSII}$) (Eq 3.9; Fig 3.18). It must be stressed that, unlike a fluorescence induction curve, the pump-and-probe method flash induces a single turnover of PSII and hence $\sigma_{PSII}$ is not complicated by the turnover of Q, which if it occurs can give the false impression of multiple cross-sections. Multiple PSII cross-sections, which have been hypothesized for PSII (Melis, Thielsen 1980), would be manifested as the weighted sum of the individual cross-sections.

It should be clear now that the apparent "size" of a photosystem based on the ratio of chlorophyll and/or accessory pigments to a reaction center (as, for example, estimated from the Emerson–Arnold number) does not predict the rate of light absorption by a reaction center. The measurement of bulk chlorophyll does not differentiate between the two reaction centers, nor does it directly relate to the effec-

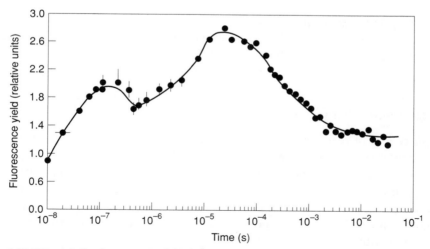

**Figure 3.17** Chlorophyll *a* fluorescence yield changes in the dark-adapted cells of the green alga *Chlorella* after a saturating nanosecond laser flash. The rise near 20 ns was ascribed by Butler (1972) to the reduction of the quencher $P_{680}^{+}$ by Z; the rise in the microsecond range is due to the disappearance of the carotenoid triplets; the decrease in fluorescence yield in the 10 μs to millisecond range is due to the electron transfer from $Q_A^-$ to $Q_B$ and $Q_B^-$. (Data from Mauzerall 1972)

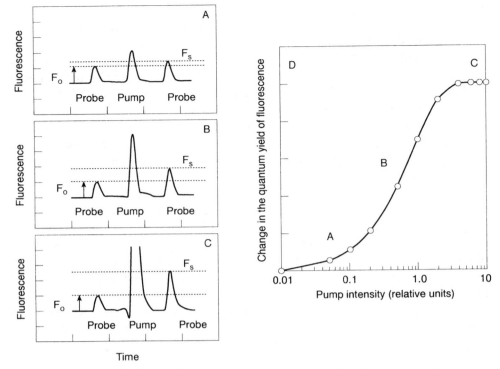

**Figure 3.18** A schematic diagram showing how the pump-and-probe technique can be used to measure the effective absorption cross-section of PSII. In this application, the pump flash intensity is altered, and the change in the quantum yield of fluorescence is measured as described in Fig. 3.16. As the pump flash intensity is increased from a low level (A) to a moderate level (B), it finally becomes saturated at some level (C). The relationship between the change in the quantum yield of fluorescence and flash energy can be described by a cumulative one-hit Poisson function (D) (see Fig 3.14).

tive absorption cross-section of a photochemical reaction. The meaningful construct should be based on the number of reaction centers and their respective effective absorption cross-sections (Falkowski et al. 1981).

## Energy Transfer Between Reaction Centers

The discovery of reaction centers and the realization that most of the pigments in photosynthetic apparatus were not directly involved in photochemical reactions led to the development of conceptual models where most of the pigments harvest light energy and transfer the energy from one pigment molecule to another until it reaches a reaction center. Once a photon is absorbed and a singlet excited state of a pigment molecule is attained, how is the excitation energy transferred to the reaction center with relatively high efficiency?

As excitation energy is preferentially transferred "downhill" (from higher to lower energy states), the $Q_y$ absorption bands of the reaction center should be at a longer wavelength than that of the primary antenna for efficient trapping (Chapter 2). In PSII the wavelength difference is small; the red peak for the lowest singlet excited state of chlorophyll *a* in most antenna systems is around 675 nm in vivo, while the major absorption band for the reaction center pigments is at 680 nm. Because this difference is so small, PSII is said to be a "shallow trap"; excitation energy can escape from the reaction center back to the pigment bed. Fluorescence at room temperature is one manifestation of this relatively inefficient trapping. In fact, excitation energy may "visit" a trap numerous times before it is absorbed and used in a photochemical process; the notion of a "trap" for PSII is somewhat of a misconception. In contrast, the absorption maximum for PSI is 25 nm red-shifted relative to its antenna and hence excitation energy has a lower probability of reentering the antenna once it is absorbed by the reaction center; PSI has virtually no fluorescence at room temperature.

Does each reaction center have its own, local antenna system, or is the excitation absorbed anywhere within a common pigment system available to any reaction center? The concept of energy sharing is controversial but essential to understanding the effective absorption cross-section (Joliot et al. 1973; Ley, Mauzerall 1986). Let us reconsider the flash-intensity saturation curve for PSII (see Fig 3.14). A saturation curve for photosystem II does not have to be based on oxygen but can also be obtained for variable fluorescence. Using the pump-and-probe technique, the fluorescence yield of a weak probe flash is measured prior to and following an actinic pump flash of varying intensity. As in the case of the flash intensity saturation curve for oxygen, the flash-intensity saturation curve for the change in fluorescence closely follows a cumulative one-hit Poisson function. By measuring both oxygen and fluorescence saturation profiles on the same sample simultaneously and normalizing each variable to the maximum (i.e., saturated) value, the effective absorption cross-sections for both processes can be directly compared.

Experimentally, both saturation curves are extremely similar, which indicates that the phenomenon that gives rise to both signals has a common origin, or "target." However, closer inspection usually reveals that fluorescence saturation curves often lag a true cumulative one-hit Poisson function at low flash intensities, and then rise more steeply at higher flash intensities. Simply put, less energy is dissipated at low flash intensities. Where did the energy go? The deviation between the two saturation profiles can be reconciled by postulating excitation transfer between reaction centers. If the exciton (see Chapter 2) encounters a "closed" reaction center, might it not escape and wander about in the antenna until it finds another reaction center? In such a case, the energy of the photon would be absorbed (and hence not emitted as fluorescence), and be capable of performing photochemistry (evolving oxygen). If we arbitrarily assign a value of 1 to a condition when all reaction centers are open, and designate A as a fraction of closed reaction centers, the difference $(1 - A)$ is the fraction of open reaction centers at any given flash intensity. As the flash intensity increases, more and more reaction centers become closed and the probability of finding an open reaction center will decrease; the fluorescence yield increases. The probability, P (0 to 1), of energy transfer between reaction centers can be calculated by plotting normalized values of the two cross-sections against each other; the deviation from linearity can be directly related to P. P varies from about 0.2 to 0.6 in algae.

## THE EFFICIENCY OF PHOTOCHEMISTRY

The ratio of variable fluorescence ($F_v$) to the maximum fluorescence ($F_m$) can be quantitatively related to the efficiency of photochemistry. By definition, when all reaction centers are open the probability of excitation escape is low and fluorescence is minimal, at the $F_0$ level. When the reaction centers become closed, absorbed excitation energy cannot be directed to photochemistry (i.e., no charge transfer occurs) and thus $k_p$ in Equation 3.8 is zero. Under such conditions, fluorescence rises to a maximum value, $F_m$. The quantum yield of photochemistry in photosystem II, $\phi_p$, is therefore related to the change in fluorescence by:

$$\phi_p = k_p/(k_f + k_d + k_p) = (F_m - F_0)/F_m = (F_v/F_m) \tag{3.12}$$

Thus, the ratio of the quantum yields for fully open and fully closed reaction centers normalized to $F_m$ is a measure of the quantum yield of photochemistry in PSII. This efficiency should not be confused with the quantum yield of photosynthesis, which is the ratio of $O_2$ evolved or $CO_2$ fixed per unit light absorbed; rather, it reflects the probability of PSII reaction centers to use the available excitation energy for photochemistry.

### Measuring the Efficiency of Photochemistry with Photoacoustics

An alternative measurement of photochemical efficiency can be derived from the heat budget. Consider any absorber of visible radiation—for example, a piece of black paper. Place a disk of the paper in a clear, sealed vessel (such as one made of Plexiglas) with a small volume of air such that the air cannot escape. Let us now place a small microphone (such as the kind that is used in a hearing aid) in the chamber. If we now flash a light on the chamber, the black paper will absorb the light and (by definition) convert it to heat. The production of heat will result in an expansion of the air and a pressure wave will ensue, which can be detected by the microphone. The difference between the pressure wave using a disk of white paper and a disk of black paper can be used to determine the efficiency of heat conversion. If photochemistry occurs, some of the absorbed energy will not be reradiated as heat. The chemically stored energy (ES) can be quantitatively defined as:

$$ES = \phi_p(\Delta E)/h\nu \tag{3.13}$$

where $\phi_p$ is the quantum yield of photochemistry, $\Delta E$ is the energy difference (measured as the change in heat) between a nonabsorbing process and the photochemical process per absorbed photon, and $h\nu$ represents the energy of the absorbed photons.

In measurements of photochemical efficiency in algae, a sample (which may be filtered onto a filter disk) is placed in a gas-tight chamber in the dark and the time-integrated pressure wave is recorded from a flash of light. The sample is then exposed to a strong, continuous background light. The pressure wave from the flash superimposed on the continuous light is recorded. The difference between the pressure waves in the dark (when all reaction centers are open, and hence energy storage from the flash is maximal) and that under strong continuous light (when all the reaction centers are closed and energy storage from the flash is minimal) is a direct measure of the photochemical energy storage (Malkin, Canaani 1994). By selecting specific wavelengths for the flash and by using inhibitors, the efficiency of PSII and PSI can be separately determined (Berges et al. 1996). It should be stressed that the efficiency is a function of the wavelength of the flash; higher efficiencies will be obtained for red rather than blue flash excitation. The maximal photochemical energy conversion efficiency for photochemistry (including both PSII and PSI) is about 35%. The loss of absorbed excitation as fluorescence varies between 2 and 5%. The difference is heat.

## Primary Photochemical Reactions in Photosystem II

When a photon is absorbed by PSII an excited state of a chlorophyll *a* molecule is formed in the reaction center. Some fraction of these excited state chlorophyll molecules may become oxidized, resulting in a charge separation. This charge separation is very rapid (on the order of about 150 ps; $1\,ps = 1 \times 10^{-12}\,s$). As excitation energy from the antenna is used for photochemistry, less excitation energy is available for fluorescence. This effect can be kinetically observed in the picosecond time domain by observing the fluorescence decay following a single flash induced by a laser. When all the reaction centers are open, a short lifetime on the order of 150 ps is the major component of the fluorescence decay (Holzwarth 1986). Upon closure of the reaction center, this lifetime disappears, and fluorescence is emitted at longer lifetimes. Thus, when a reaction center is open, it greatly enhances the probability of trapping the excitation before it is lost as fluorescence. This trapping must take place faster than the competing loss processes.

## Primary Photochemical Reactions in Photosystem I

The room-temperature fluorescence emanating from PSI is very low, and in most eukaryotic algae is strongly contaminated at wavelengths <700 nm by the fluorescence from PSII. At cryogenic temperatures of liquid $N_2$ (77 K) or He (4.2 K), PSI fluoresces between 730 to 750 nm, and the signal can usually be discriminated from the contributions of PSII, which are at shorter wavelengths (Ley 1980). A simple interpretation of the relatively low fluorescence yield is that the rate constants for photochemistry and nonradiative losses are so fast that they effectively outcompete radiative losses (Fig 3.19). At cryogenic temperatures the possibility of electron transfer reactions is greatly reduced, and therefore $k_p$ (Eq 3.8) is effectively zero. Hence, the rate of fluorescence emission for PSII and PSI is increased. Laser-induced absorption difference spectra of PSI suggest that the electron transfer occurs on a time scale of about 20 ps, and fluorescence lifetime analyses suggest that the time required to trap the excitation energy in the bed is comparably short.

One way of detecting $P_{700}$ is by EPR spectroscopy (Kok, Beiner 1962; Weaver, Weaver 1969). Upon illumination, $P_{700}$ photo-oxidation produces a radical that is easily detectable (in fact, it is hard to see any other radical because the signal from $P_{700}$ is so strong). The EPR signal is split into two harmonics, indicating a symmetry

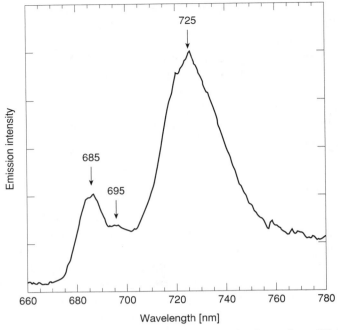

**Figure 3.19** A low-temperature fluorescence emission spectrum showing peaks at 685, 695, and 725 nm. The first two emission bands correspond to pigments associated with PSII, while the latter corresponds to PSI. At room temperature, typically only one major band is observed, which in optically thin samples is centered at 685 nm.

in the radical formation. The Landé *g*-factor for oxidized $P_{700}$ is 2.023, which further indicates a radical. Based on these observations, it was proposed that the PSI reaction center consists of two chlorophyll molecules, which are called a "special pair." The red shift in the absorption spectra of the $Q_y$ band of PSI can be explained by molecular orbital model calculations in which opposing faces of the conjugated ring systems of two chlorophyll molecules are brought so close their π bonds interact. The overlap of the π bonds occurs within a spatial distance of about 0.3 nm. A similar structure has been postulated for the reaction center of PSII and appears likely based on analogy with the deduced structure of the ancestral bacterial reaction center. In PSI, the absorption of excitation energy by one of the chlorophyll *a* molecules constituting the special pair leads to its ionization, forming a cation. The electron is transiently donated to the second chlorophyll *a* molecule, forming an anion radical. This initial charge separation is extremely rapid, and the electron is subsequently donated to a secondary acceptor at a lower potential energy level, thereby reducing the possibility of a backreaction.

### Electron Tunneling

The actual photochemical electron transfer reaction in the photosynthetic reaction centers occurs by a quantum mechanical process called *tunneling*. The tunneling phenomenon, developed from theoretical arguments in physics in the mid-1920s, allows a subatomic particle to move through an energy barrier even if its energy is less than the height of the barrier. In this construct, particles are postulated to have wavelike behavior, comparable to that of light. The wavelength is inversely proportional to the particle's mass. Particles with small mass, such as electrons, have wavelengths as large as or larger than those of atoms. Electrons normally are prevented from leaving an atom or molecule by a potential energy barrier. We can imagine, however, that when electrons strike the energy barrier, not all are reflected, but rather some penetrate into the barrier as a wave whose amplitude decreases very rapidly with distance from the atom or molecule. When it reaches the other side of the barrier (i.e., as it approaches an acceptor), the amplitude of the waveform has not died down completely, and the electron appears on the opposite side with a very small amplitude but the same frequency. To quote DeVault (1980), "Thus, they [the electrons] can easily ooze through and around atoms and molecules."

In most bimolecular chemical reactions, electron transfer reactions are permitted only at the intersecting potential energy surface between the substrate and the product. This surface is dependent on internuclear coordinates (a function of intermolecular distance); the coordinates can be deduced from the structural analyses of the oxidized and reduced forms of the bimolecular reaction. Nuclear vibrations are much slower than electronic oscillations, and hence the probability of the intersection of internuclear coordinates becomes kinetically limiting. In the tunneling process, the electron can pass from the donor to acceptor as a wavefunction, without a loss of energy.[4] The process is temperature independent. The energy barrier (e.g., a voltage potential), effectively "screens" transfers without reducing the energy of the particle, much the way a neutral density filter (like gray sunglasses) attenuates a photon flux but not the energy of the individual photons (which is determined by their frequency). In electron tunneling, the rate of electron transfer can (actually, must) be extremely rapid, on the order of picoseconds. This time is shorter than that required for internuclear distances to adjust (this is called the *Frank–Condon principle*), and therefore the donor and acceptor nuclei are not at an energetic equilibrium. The electrostatic adjustments that subsequently are made to accommodate the electron transfer lead to a change in the volume of the reaction center. Thus, photosynthetic reaction centers literally expand and contract with each electron transfer.

The generation of electrons by reaction centers is the initial step in a series of coupled electron transfer reactions that ultimately lead to the production of useful chemical energy and reductant. Let us now examine the basic functions and processes in the photosynthetic electron transport chain.

---

4. This process is comparable to that of energy transfer as discussed in Chapter 2.

# 4

# Photosynthetic Electron Transport and Photophosphorylation

The main role of the photosynthetic electron transport chain is to provide chemical reductants used to assimilate inorganic carbon and chemical energy to sustain all the activity of the organism. While the reaction centers are the engines of the photosynthetic apparatus, the drive train consists of a highly organized structure that mediates the transfer of electrons and protons. In converting the energy of light to chemical energy, the electrons extracted from water are used to transiently reduce molecules in the electron transport chain. The protons produced in the photochemical oxidation of water and transported by other reactions represent a gain in free energy within the thylakoids that is ultimately coupled to ATP synthesis in the chloroplast. Photochemistry also provides an excess of free energy that forces electrons onto molecules that do not welcome them. The electrons subsequently move down electrochemical gradients toward less electronegative components. Ultimately, some of these electrons are accepted by $CO_2$, where the excess of negative charge is neutralized by protons.

Three basic tools have been used to identify the components in the photosynthetic electron transport chain and assign functions to them. First, many of the electron transfer components have been identified from the analysis of mutants, especially of the green alga *Chlamydomonas* sp, and in some cyanobacteria in which molecular genetic systems have been developed (Levine, Ebersold 1960; Vermaas 1993). Second, biochemical isolation of some of the components has permitted biophysical and structural investigations of functions and organization of the photosynthetic apparatus (Barber J 1992). Third, many inhibitors of specific electron transfer reactions have been synthesized and/or isolated from natural sources and have been used to selectively block specific portions of pathways. Inhibitors have served very useful roles, especially in kinetic analyses and in mutant selection (Badour 1978; Trebst 1980).

## THE Z-SCHEME

In the early 1950s, Robin Hill and his colleagues (Davenport 1952) in England discovered two cytochromes in chloroplasts. One was called cytochrome $b_6$, and the other, cytochrome $f$. The midpoint redox potential ($E_{m7}$) for the former was 0.0 volts; for the latter it was approximately +0.35 volts (see Fig 3.1). Thus, in principle, reduced cytochrome $b_6$ could be oxidized by cytochrome $f$.

Recognizing that the photochemical evidence provided by Emerson, Duysens, Kok, and others strongly suggested the existence of two photochemical reactions,

Hill and Bendall (1960) proposed that the two cytochromes acted to transfer electrons from one photosystem to the other in vivo. Their hypothesis was supported by experimental data provided first by Duysens, who observed that cytochrome *f* was oxidized by long wavelength light in *Chlorella* (Duysens 1954a). At that time, it was understood that the short wavelength light promoted oxygen evolution reaction whereas the long wavelength light sensitized the oxidation of $P_{700}$ (Kok 1957). Hill and Bendall proposed that the two photoreactions operate in series, with cytochromes acting as electron carriers between them. Photons absorbed by one photosystem oxidize water and produce a weak reductant that can reduce cytochrome *f*. Photons absorbed by the other photosystem oxidize the reductant formed by the first photochemical reaction and produce a second, stronger reductant. A schematic representation of the connection between the two photosystems, based on the apparent redox potentials of the two reaction centers and the cytochromes, resembled the letter Z, and hence the concept of two light reactions connected by an electron transport chain came to be called the *Z-scheme* (Fig 4.1).

Based on the Z-scheme, the photosynthetic electron transport chain can be divided into three segments: (a) the donor side of PSII, which includes the reactions responsible for the injection of electrons into PSII from water, (b) the intersystem electron transport chain, which includes all the carriers between PSII and PSI, and (c) the acceptor side of PSI, in which the primary reducing agent, NADPH, is formed and exported for carbon fixation.

## THE DONOR SIDE OF PHOTOSYSTEM II: DISCOVERY OF THE S STATES

Working with a modified version of the Blinks oxygen rate electrode, Pierre Joliot and Bessel Kok independently reported that the yield of oxygen obtained during the first few saturating flashes oscillated in a curious fashion (Joliot 1993; Kok et al. 1970). Inspection of the data revealed that the oxygen flash yield was maximal on the third flash and on every fourth flash thereafter. The oscillation of the oxygen flash yield with four-flash periodicity was damped with increasing numbers of flashes. To explain the data, Kok hypothesized five oxidation states for a water-splitting process (which were called "S" states). With each flash one electron was removed from some molecule(s) called "S." Only after four electrons were removed from S could two water molecules be oxidized and an $O_2$ molecule be evolved.

$$S_0 \underset{\longleftarrow}{\xrightarrow{hv}} S_1 \underset{\longleftarrow}{\xrightarrow{hv}} S_2 \underset{\longleftarrow}{\xrightarrow{hv}} S_3 \xrightarrow{hv} S_4 \qquad (4.1)$$

$$O_2$$

Each flash could advance the system by one oxidation state. Thus, if no electrons were removed from the molecule(s) involved in water splitting (i.e., the idealized starting condition), the sample would be at $S_0$. After one flash one electron is removed from $S_0$, forming $S_1$. A second flash removes a second electron and advances the system by one electron equivalent. This process is repeated four times

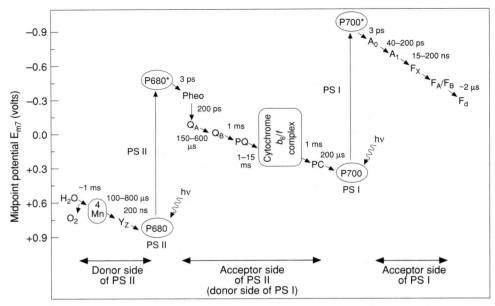

**Figure 4.1** The "Z-scheme" for photosynthetic electron transport. In this schematic representation, the photosynthetic electron carriers are placed in series on a scale of midpoint potentials. The $E_{m7}$ for the oxidation of water by a one-electron reaction is +0.8 V. Thus, in order to photo-oxidize water, an electrical potential must be minimally of that value. The oxidation of the primary electron donor in PSII, $P_{680}$, leads to a charge separation of about 1.2 V. This charge separation occurs within about 1 ps, and the formation of a reduced phaeophytin anion intermediate follows within about 3 ps. The electron hole in $P_{680}^{+}$ is filled in by the oxidation of the amino acid tyrosine, $Y_z$, which obtains electrons in turn from Mn atoms. The time scale for the reduction of $Y_z$ varies, depending on the "S" state (see text). The Mn atoms obtain electrons from water. Hence, like a front-wheel drive in a car, electrons are "pulled" from water via the photochemical oxidation of $P_{680}$. The reactions leading to the rereduction of $P_{680}^{+}$ from water are designated to be on the "donor side" of PSII. The phaeophytin anion reduces the "primary" acceptor, $Q_A$, which is a quinone bound to a protein. This reaction leads to a change in the midpoint potential of about +0.2 V, which helps to stabilize the electron and reduces the probability of a useless backreaction between the phaeophytin anion and $P_{680}^{+}$ (note that it takes five orders of magnitude longer to reduce $P_{680}^{+}$ from $Y_z$ than it takes to reduce phaeophytin; hence in the absence of the electron transfer to $Q_A$, the probability of a backreaction is very high). Two electrons are sequentially transferred from $Q_A$ to the secondary acceptor, $Q_B$; the time constants for these electron transfers are dependent on the level of reduction of $Q_B$. Upon receiving two electrons, $Q_B$, which, like $Q_A$, is a plastoquinone (PQ) molecule, dissociates from its "binding pocket" and diffuses within the thylakoid membrane until it reaches the cytochrome $b_6/f$ complex. Reduced plastoquinone is oxidized by cytochrome $b_6$, which is in turn oxidized by cytochrome $f$. The oxidation of plastoquinol is typically the slowest reaction overall in the photosynthetic electron transport pathway. Cytochrome $f$ delivers electrons to either a copper-containing protein, plastocyanin (PCy), in the case of most chlorophyte algae, or an iron-containing protein, cytochrome $c_6$, in the case of chromophytes. In either case, this electron carrier ferries electrons to the reaction center of PSI, $P_{700}$, by diffusion in the thylakoid lumen. All the reactions between phaeophytin and $P_{700}$ are on the "acceptor side" of PSII or the "donor side" of PSI, depending on the reaction center of reference. In the PSI reaction center, the absorption of a second photon leads to the generation of a second photochemical charge separation, with a midpoint potential difference of about 1.7 V. The electron is rapidly passed through a series of electron carriers, $A_o$, a chlorophyll monomer, $A_1$, phylloquinone (also called vitamin K), $F_x$, an iron sulfur cluster, $F_A$ and/or $F_B$, which are iron-containing proteins, and then to Fd, a molecule of ferredoxin. The reactions from $P_{700}^{+}$ to ferredoxin are on the "acceptor side" of PSI. This basic scheme was proposed by Robin Hill in the 1950s. Twenty years earlier Hill provided the first demonstration of photochemical activity in isolated chloroplasts by showing that light-dependent reduction of an artificial electron acceptor (methemoglobin, in which the chemical reduction of iron could be detected by a hand-held spectroscope) could be coupled to the evolution of oxygen. This PSII reaction came to be called the *Hill reaction*. (Courtesy of J Whitmarsh and Govindjee)

## ❑ ANAEROBIC PHOTOSYNTHETIC ELECTRON TRANSPORT IN BACTERIA

*As we mentioned in Chapter 1, there are two major groups of anaerobic photosynthetic bacteria, namely those utilizing a quinone and those utilizing an iron-sulfur complex in the photosynthetic electron transport scheme. The former pathway is found in Chromatiaceae (purple sulfur bacteria) and Rhodospirillaceae (purple nonsulfur bacteria), while the latter is found in Chlorobiaceae (green sulfur bacteria). In the purple bacteria, the Soret bands of the bacteriochlorophylls absorb in the ultraviolet and the $Q_y$ band is in the infrared, hence the purified pigment is invisible to the human eye. However, the pigment is bound to a protein in vivo that also binds carotenoids, such that when the complex is isolated it appears orange, red, or purple, depending on the species (McDermott et al. 1995). Bacteriochlorophylls from green photosynthetic bacteria have Soret bands in the violet and indigo regions of the spectrum, and $Q_y$ bands in the infrared; consequently, the purified pigment would appear yellow/orange when purified. It should be noted that in both groups, because the $Q_y$ band is in the infrared, the corresponding energy levels are too small to facilitate water splitting.*

*Electron transport in photosynthetic bacteria can be either cyclic or noncyclic, depending on the metabolic needs of the cell (Fig 4.2). When operating in a cycle, protons are pumped (at the expense of light energy) from the N side to the P side of the membrane and are used to generate ATP (see text). In noncyclic electron transport in green bacteria, the reaction center photo-oxidizes a substrate, such as sulfur or succinate, and generates NADH, which can be used to fix $CO_2$ into pyruvate, reduced ferredoxin, and 2-oxoglutarate.*

---

and on the fourth flash $S_3$ is converted to $S_4$, two $H_2O$ molecules are oxidized, one molecule of $O_2$ is evolved, and $S_4$ converted back to $S_0$, thereby allowing the cycle to be repeated (Fig 4.3). The amplitude of the oscillation of the oxygen flash yield was small when the sample was preilluminated with continuous light prior to the flash sequence. These results suggested that in the steady state the relative amount of the S states was constant and that each step has the same quantum yield. In this model each step requires only one quantum per electron. The fact that the oxygen flash yield oscillates suggests that each oxygen-evolving center accumulates charges independently; that is, the individual units do not share electrons (Joliot 1993).

To account for the high yield of oxygen on the third flash in the experimental data, Kok postulated that for some reason the dark condition is not populated primarily with $S_0$, but with the $S_1$ state. The exact reason why the dark condition is advanced one oxidation state has never been fully explained. That the $S_2$ and $S_3$ states are not stable indefinitely can be demonstrated by preilluminating with one or two flashes, and waiting for some period before measuring oxygen evolution on the subsequent flash. At 25 °C, the $S_3$ state decays with a half-time of about 15 seconds in *Chlorella* (Fig 4.4). The damping of the four-flash periodicity could be accounted for by assuming that some fraction of the targets underwent a backreaction between flashes (a "miss") and so did not advance an S state, and some other fraction of the traps

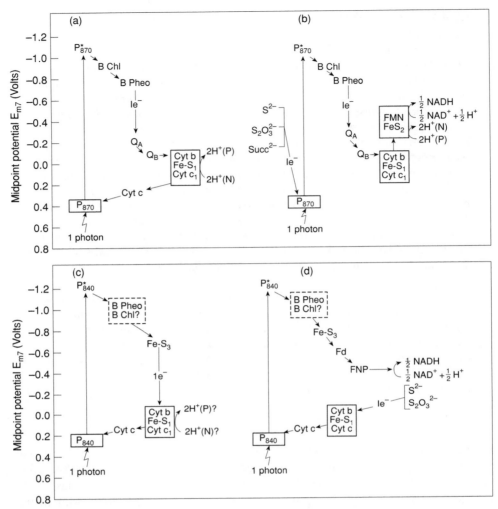

**Figure 4.2** The bacterial photosynthetic electron transport pathways. (a) Cyclic electron transport in Chromatiaceae and Rhodospirillaceae. $P_{870}$—reaction center BChl; BChl—Bacteriochlorophyll; BPheo—Bacteriopheophytin; $Q_A$—primary acceptor quinone; $Q_B$—secondary acceptor quinone; Cyt b—cytochrome $b$; Fe-S$_1$—iron-sulfur protein; Cyt $c_A$—cytochrome $c_1$; Cyt c—Cytochrome $c$; H$^+$ (N)—H$^+$ in N phase; M$^+$ (P)—M$^+$ in P phase. (b) Noncyclic electron transport in Chromatiaceae and Rhodospirillaceae. Fe-S$_2$—iron-sulfur protein 2; FMN—flavin mononucleotide. (c) Cyclic electron transport in Chlorobiaceae. $P_{840}$—reaction center BChl; Fe-S$_3$—iron-sulfur protein 3. (d) Noncyclic electron transport in Chlorobiaceae. The primary photochemistry of the Chloroflexaceae resembles that of the Chromatiaceae and Rhodospirillaceae, while that of the Heliobacteriaceae resembles that of the Chlorobiaceae. The reaction center BChl in the Heliobacteriaceae is $P_{798}$. The homology of the photoreaction of the Chromatiaceae and Rhodospirillaceae with photosystem II of O$_2$-evolving organisms, and of the photoreaction of the Chlorobiaceae with photosystem I of the O$_2$-evolving organisms, is discussed in Chapters 1 and 6.

absorbed two or more photons (i.e., a double hit) and advanced more than one S state. In this way, a continuous, long train of flashes leads to randomization of the S states. In continuous light, the S states are completely randomized.

Using Kok's model we can see that the oxygen flash yields measured by Emerson

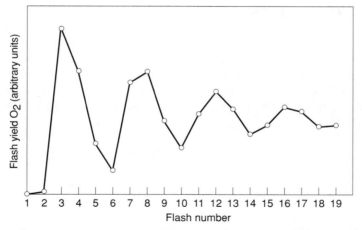

**Figure 4.3** The effect of successive single-turnover flashes on oxygen flash yields. Note that the flash yield is initially low on the first flash, and is highest on the third flash. The oscillation has a four-flash periodicity, the amplitude of which dampens over time with a series of successive flashes.

and Arnold are a measure of the conversion of $S_3$ to $S_4$; that is, that the oxygen produced by a flash "counts" the number of PSII reaction centers in the $S_3$ state. Assuming that in a long train of flashes the S states are scrambled, and the rates of misses and double hits are equal, the number of PSII reaction centers can be derived from the oxygen flash yields by multiplying the latter by four; the oxygen evolved at any given flash represents 25% of the total number of PSII reaction centers.

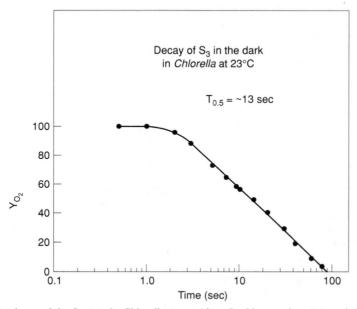

**Figure 4.4** The decay of the $S_3$ state in *Chlorella pyrenoidosa*. In this experiment, two single turnover flashes were rapidly given, to populate the $S_3$ state. This protocol was followed by a third flash with some increasing time delay. The oxygen flash yield induced by the third flash was measured at each time point. The results suggest that the $S_3$ state decays with a half-time of about 13 seconds.

## ❏ ELECTRON TRANSFER

*It must be noted that some components of the photosynthetic electron transport chain, such as the cytochromes, transfer electrons without a concomitant exchange of protons; however, the electron transfer in other carriers, such as plastoquinone, is accompanied by proton transfers. Protons carry an electrical charge, and the number of protons transferred may differ from the number of electrons in a half-cell reaction. This process can be generalized by the expression*

$$[A_{ox}] + [ne^-] + m[H^+] \rightleftharpoons [A_{red}] \qquad (4.2)$$

*where* m *is the number of protons involved in the reduction of* $A_{ox}$. *The redox potential for this reaction can be calculated by:*

$$E = E_{m7} + 59/n \, log\left([A_{red}]/[A_{ox}][H^+]^m\right) \qquad (4.3)$$

*which can be rewritten as:*

$$E = E_{m7} + 59/n \, log([A_{red}]/[A_{ox}]) + 59(m/n)pH \qquad (4.4)$$

*Thus, by measuring E as a function of pH and the concentrations of* $A_{ox}$ *and* $A_{red}$, *it is possible to determine* $E_{m7}$, n, *and* m. *Some commonly used redox mediators, their potentials, and their values for* m *and* n *are shown in Table 4.1.*

**Table 4.1** Mid-point potentials for some common electron carriers in photosynthesis research

| | ox + n(e⁻) + m(H⁺) $\rightleftharpoons$ red | | | Change in $E_m$(mV) when pH increased by 1 unit |
|---|---|---|---|---|
| | n | m | $E_{m7}$(mV) | |
| Dithionite ox/red | 1 | 0 | −610 | 0 |
| Methyl viologen ox/red | 1 | 0 | −450 | 0 |
| $CO_2/CH_2O$ | 2 | 2 | −430 | −60 |
| Ferredoxin ox/red | 1 | 0 | −430 | 0 |
| $H^+/^1/_2H_2$($H_2$ 1 atm) | 1 | 1 | −420 | −60 |
| $NAD^+/NADH$ | 2 | 1 | −320 | −30 |
| $NADP^+/NADPH$ | 2 | 1 | −320 | −30 |
| Menaquinone/menaquinol | 2 | 2 | −74 | −60 |
| Plastoquinone/plastoquinol | 2 | 2 | ~0 | −60 |
| Fumarate/succinate | 2 | 2 | +30 | −60 |
| Ubiquinone/ubiquinol | 2 | 2 | +40 | −60 |
| Ascorbate ox/red | 2 | 1 | +60 | −30 |
| PMS ox/red | 2 | 1 | +80 | −30 |
| $DCPIP/DCPIPH_2$ | 2 | 2 | +220 | −60 |
| TMPD ox/red | 1 | 0 | +260 | 0 |
| $DAD/DADH_2$ | 2 | 2 | +275 | −60 |
| Cytochrome $f$ (ox/red) | 1 | 0 | +350 | 0 |
| Cytochrome $c_{553}$ (ox/red) | 1 | 0 | +370 | 0 |
| Plastocyanin (ox/red) | 1 | 0 | +380 | 0 |
| Ferricyanide ox/red | 1 | 0 | +420 | 0 |
| $P_{700}/P_{700}^+$ | 1 | 0 | +480 | 0 |
| $O_2$(1 atm)/2$H_2O$(55 M) | 4 | 4 | +840 | −60 |
| $P_{680}/P_{680}^+$ | 1 | 0 | +1100 | 0 |

DAD is 2,3,5,6-tetramethylphenylene diamine; PMS is phenazine methosulphate; TPMD is N,N,N′,N′-tetramethyl-p-phenylene diamine; DCPIP is 2,6-dichlorophenolindophenol. (Adapted from Nicholls DG and Ferguson SJ, *Bioenergetics*. London: Academic Press, 1992)

The discovery of the S states stimulated considerable effort to elucidate the biochemical mechanism responsible for the water-splitting reaction. A number of investigators found EPR signals in isolated chloroplasts and thylakoid membranes that closely corresponded to Mn(III) and Mn(IV), and oscillated with a four-flash periodicity, exactly in phase with the S states (Babcock et al. 1989; Babcock, Sauer 1973; Rutherford 1989). Mn is a rather unusual transition metal in that it can exist in a wide range of oxidation states, from +2 to +7. Chemical analysis of PSII complexes isolated from thylakoid membranes established that for each PSII reaction center there are four Mn atoms, and a loss of one of these leads to a total loss of oxygen evolution. Based on a variety of spectroscopic investigations and biochemical data, it appears that the four Mn atoms, acting as an ensemble, sequentially lose electrons (Fig 4.5), such that one $O_2$ is released from the oxidation of $2H_2O$. In the initial condition, three of the Mn are oxidized to Mn(III) and one is oxidized to Mn(IV). The photo-oxidation of Mn leads to a sequential oxidation of the Mn "cluster" to give three Mn(IV) and one Mn(V). The release of $O_2$ occurs in one fell swoop on the $S_3 \rightarrow S_4$ conversion.

While the four electron transfer reactions in the water-splitting process are sequential, each driven by the absorption of a photon by the PSII reaction center (hence the quantum yield for each electron transfer is unity), the protons released often follow a 0, 1, 1, 2 pattern, although other patterns may be observed. The major point here is that the protons are not "stored" on some amino acids or other molecules, but rather are released into the thylakoid lumen prior to the evolution of oxygen. The primary consequence of the proton release is the acidification of the lumenal side of the thylakoid membrane (Junge 1977).

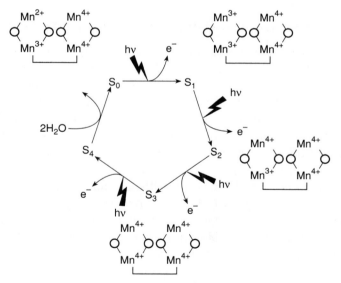

**Figure 4.5** The Mn "clock." Each of the S states for oxygen evolution in PSII leads to the different oxidation state of Mn. There are numerous schemes to account for the oxidation states. In this scheme, two of the four Mn atoms participate in electron transfer reactions. One by one, the absorption of photons by $P_{680}$ leads to the accumulation of four positive charges in the Mn cluster, at which point four electrons are removed, in one fell swoop, from two molecules of water to produce one molecule of $O_2$.

Using nonionic detergents such as digitonin and Triton X-100, it is possible to solubilize thylakoid membranes and, by using artificial electron acceptors, maintain the oxygen-evolving ability of the photosynthetic apparatus. The actual site for water splitting probably occurs in one of the proteins that constitute the reaction center of PSII; the four Mn atoms appear to be located at the PSII reaction center protein designated D1 (discussed in Chapter 6) (Debus 1992). Oxygen evolution is facilitated by peripheral proteins called the oxygen-evolving enhancers (or OEEs). Two of the OEE proteins, one of apparent molecular mass between 22 and 24 kDa and the other between 16 and 18 kDa, can be easily removed from the membranes by washing with NaCl. These two proteins are not found in cyanobacteria. One protein with a molecular mass of 33 kDa is bound to the lumenal side of the thylakoid membrane. This latter protein is ubiquitous, and can be removed from the membrane by washing with Tris or $CaCl_2$. The ease with which the three OEE proteins can be removed suggests that they are extrinsic—loosely bound to the surface of the membrane. Removal of the 33 kDa protein leads to a marked reduction of oxygen evolution but does not prevent photochemical oxidation of the PSII reaction center. Cyanobacterial mutants lacking the 33 kDa protein are still capable of evolving oxygen, albeit at lower rates. Hence, the 33 kDa protein appears to be essential for efficient water oxidation. In both cyanobacteria and eukaryotic algae, the 33 kDa protein occurs in a 1:1 stoichiometry with PSII reaction centers. The functional role of the 33 kDa protein can be replaced by $Cl^-$ ions in vitro. $Cl^-$ is suggested to be essential in transiently stabilizing protons released in the water oxidization process.

## THE FORMATION OF A RADICAL PAIR IN PHOTOSYSTEM II

Using isolated thylakoid membranes, or even better, parts of membranes enriched in PSII, it is possible to keep the primary donor and acceptor artificially oxidized and reduced, respectively, with chemical mediators. For example, the addition of hydroxylamine ($NH_2OH$) competitively blocks electron flow from water to the reaction center (thereby preventing the rereduction of the donor), and dithionate, a reducing agent, keeps the acceptor reduced. Following illumination, EPR spectra reveal the formation of an anion radical, and optical spectra identify the acceptor as phaeophytin *a* (a chlorophyll *a* molecule lacking Mg) (Klimov et al. 1979). The electron donor is a chlorophyll *a* molecule with an oxidized–reduced absorption difference maximum near 680 nm, which thus is often called $P_{680}$. Calculated values for the charge separation gives a midpoint potential, $E_{m7}$, of $P_{680}^+$ of +1.1 volts (Renger 1992); this is the strongest known biological oxidant. The oxidation of water requires about 0.8 volts. Thus, in the oxidation of water the net energy efficiency is about 0.8/1.1, or about 73%.

The photochemical oxidation of $P_{680}$ leaves an electron "hole" that is temporarily filled by the oxidation of an intermediate donor molecule. That donor molecule, identified by both EPR spectra and confirmed by a specific (i.e., site-directed[1]) muta-

---

1. *Site-directed mutations* are those in which specific amino acids are altered in a protein sequence.

tion in cyanobacteria, is the amino acid tyrosine, located in a specific protein that constitutes part of the reaction center. The single letter code for tyrosine is Y, hence the donor is called $Y_z$. The electron transfer from $Y_z$ to $P_{680}^+$ takes between 20 and 300 ns, with the longer times found at higher S states. This reaction oxidizes $Y_z$, making it strongly electrophilic. The $Y_z^+$ appetite for electrons is sated by oxidizing Mn, leading in turn to the oxidation of water. Thus $P_{680}$ does not oxidize water directly, but pulls electrons from a neighboring electron donor, creating a cascade of electron holes which leads to the oxidation of water. Depending on the S state, the oxidation of Mn takes between 30 and 500 µs, with shorter times found for lower S states. At very high continuous photon fluence rates, when PSII reaction centers are photochemically turning over rapidly, electron donation from water can potentially limit photosynthesis. This limitation can lead to unfilled electron holes in donor molecules. Such holes can potentially lead, in turn, to the generation of free radicals that can oxidize or destroy pigments and proteins within the reaction center. This donor side limitation is postulated to be a cause of *photoinhibition* in PSII (Aro et al. 1993; Baker, Bowyer 1994; Prasil et al. 1992).

The phaeophytin *a* anion radical has a midpoint electrical potential of about −0.5 volts, and is very short lived (about 3 ps). Its electron is rapidly passed on to a secondary electron acceptor, $Q_A$, which is a bound quinone, where it can reside[2] for between about 150 and 600 µs. $Q_A$ is identical to the fluorescence quencher, Q, postulated by Duysens and Sweers (1963)[3] (see Chapter 3). The midpoint potential difference between $P_{680}^+$ (+1.1 V) phaeophytin anion radical (−0.5 V) amounts to 1.6 volts. If $P_{680}^+$ absorbs a photon at 680 nm (=1.8 eV), the energy conserved in the primary charge separation is approximately 1.6/1.8 (=89%).

In the reduction of $Q_A$, the electron drops to a midpoint potential of about 0.1 volt, a difference of −0.5 volts. As $Q_A$ has a higher midpoint potential (i.e., is more positive) than phaeophytin *a*, the rapid transfer of the electron to $Q_A$ reduces the probability of charge recombination between $P_{680}^+$ and the phaeophytin anion radical (i.e., a backreaction). Because the lifetime of the phaeophytin *a* anion radical is so short, it is called an *intermediate acceptor* and is often designated by the letter I, whereas $Q_A$ is often called the first "stable" electron acceptor. The photochemical charge separation reactions described are summarized as follows:

$$Y_z P_{680} I Q_A \underset{\substack{3ps \\ h\nu}}{\rightleftarrows} Y_z P_{680}^+ I^- Q_A \underset{\sim 150ps}{\rightleftarrows} Y_z P_{680}^+ I Q_A^- \underset{\sim 100ns}{\rightleftarrows} Y_z^+ P_{680} I Q_A^-$$
(4.5)

The reduction of $Q_A$ is completed within about 300 ps after the absorption of the excitation energy. Note that the backreaction predicts the emission of a photon.

While the electron transfer from phaeophytin *a* to $Q_A$ reduces the possibility of a backreaction, or charge recombination between $P_{680}^+$ and $I^-$, a backreaction between the acceptor and donor sides of PSII can, and does, occur. The manifestation of a backreaction can be demonstrated by exposing cells to a light and then placing them in darkness. As the charges of radical pairs recombine, a luminescence

---

2. By "reside" we mean that 1/e of the electrons leave the acceptor during this period.
3. It is coincidental the Q and $Q_A$ have similar symbols. $Q_A$ is used to designate the first (i.e., the "Ath") quinone in PSII.

(sometimes called *delayed light emission*) is given off at the same wavelength as chlorophyll fluorescence in vivo, around 685 nm. The backreaction primarily occurs from charge recombination between $Y_z^+$ and $Q_A^-$, and the half-time for the decay of this luminescence is on the order of 4 seconds (Fig 4.6). This backreaction can occur because the rate of rereduction of $Y_z^+$ from electrons donated by the Mn cluster is much slower (several hundred microseconds) than the rate of rereduction of $P_{680}^+$ (hence the "direct" backreaction between $Q_A^-$ and $P_{680}^+$ is very rare). The quantum yield for the recombination luminescence between $Q_A^-$ and $Y_z^+$ is about 0.001 (Lavorel 1975).

In addition to a backreaction, there is evidence of an electron cycle around PSII. This evidence is based on the observation that simultaneous measurements of oxygen flash yields and variable fluorescence are sometimes uncoupled, especially under high continuous background irradiance levels (Fig 4.7). Under such conditions, variable fluorescence may be higher than oxygen flash yields. As variable fluorescence is a measure of the reduction level of $Q_A$, while oxygen flash yields are a

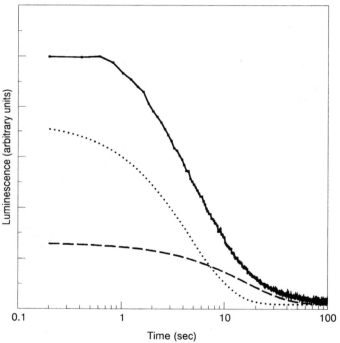

**Figure 4.6** The decay of luminescence in *Chlorella pyrenoidosa*. When an oxygenic photoautotroph is taken from the light to darkness, some small number of reaction centers are trapped with a reduced $Q_A$ and/or $Q_B$ pool (see Fig. 4.1). In the absence of light, the electrons on these acceptors cannot advance to PSI, but they can back react with electron "holes" on the donor side of PSII. Even though there is a potential energy barrier that prevents this backreaction, it still can occur. The backreaction leads to the emission of photons, the intensity of which decays over a period of a few seconds (solid line). In the specific example shown, the sample was preilluminated with two flashes, thereby advancing the S states from $S_1$ to $S_3$. Deconvolution of the luminescence decay reveals a component that decays with a half-time of 3.2 s (dotted line), and one that decays with a half-time of 12 s (dashed line). The former is a consequence of $S_3Q_B^-$ recombinations, while the latter is due to the charge recombination from $S_2Q_B^-$. (Data courtesy of Ondrej Prasil)

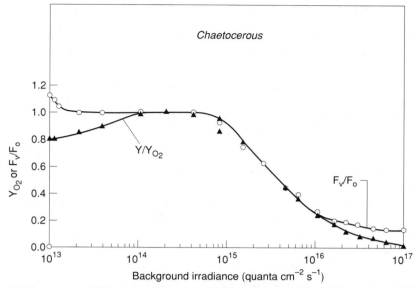

**Figure 4.7** Changes in variable fluorescence and oxygen flash yields as a function of background light. These two variables provide information on the fraction of open/closed reaction centers as perceived from the donor side and acceptor side of PSII. At very low background irradiance, oxygen flash yields are lower than maximum because the time interval between "hits" is not sufficient to keep the $S_3$ state populated to its maximum level (see Fig 4.4). Variable fluorescence, measured with a pump and probe method (see Fig 3.16), often decreases upon exposure to very low light, presumably because some reaction centers contain a small fraction of reduced $Q_A$. As light intensity is increased, a plateau in both variable fluorescence and oxygen flash yields is encountered. This plateau corresponds to a region of irradiance when statistically "all" reaction centers are open and functional at any moment in time, i.e., light absorption limits electron transport. At higher irradiance levels, both yields decrease reflecting an increased probability of encountering a closed reaction center. At very high irradiance, fluorescence yields may remain higher than oxygen flash yields, suggesting some small fraction of electrons can cycle around PSII.

measure of the fraction of reaction centers in the $S_3$ state, the uncoupling indicates that $Q_A$ can be photochemically reduced but the electron that reduced $Q_A$ did not originate from water. This cyclic reaction is similar to a backreaction, but it is much faster than that of the direct backreaction between $Y_z^+$ and $Q_A^-$. It has been suggested that the cycle is mediated by cytochrome $b_{559}$, an electron carrier found in all PSII reaction centers that has no known role in direct forward or backward electron transfer reactions (Falkowski, Fujita et al. 1986; Heber et al. 1979; Prasil 1996).

It should be noted that all the prosthetic groups in PSII (and PSI, for that matter) are bound to specific proteins. In PSII, two proteins in particular, designated D1 and D2, provide scaffolding for the Mn in the water-splitting complex and contain $Y_z$, $P_{680}$, phaeophytin $a$, $Q_A$, and the $Q_B$ binding site (which we shall discuss shortly). Although we examine these proteins in more detail in Chapter 6, it should be recognized that they are essential for orientation and positioning all of the electron transport components in the reaction center (Murphy 1986).

## THE ACCEPTOR SIDE OF PHOTOSYSTEM II

For photosynthetic electron transport to proceed, the reduction of $Q_A$ must be followed by its oxidation. $Q_A^-$ transfers electrons one at a time to a second quinone, designated $Q_B$. The nonheme Fe does not appear to be essential in this electron transfer process. Isolated $Q_A$ and $Q_B$ are identical plastoquinone molecules; however, in vivo the two electron carriers have different characteristics, which are conferred by their association with different proteins. $Q_A$ is chemically bound to its specific protein, whereas $Q_B$ can be removed with mild solvents. The electron transfer between $Q_A$ and $Q_B$ can be monitored by following fluorescence decay on the microsecond time scale using a pump-and-probe technique (Crofts, Wright 1983; see Chapter 3).

By varying the time between the pump flash and the probe flash, the decay in fluorescence is found to be proportional to the rate of oxidation of $Q_A^-$ (Fig 4.8). If a single pump flash is used, fluorescence decays with a half-time on the order of 150 μs. Following two pump flashes, it decays with a half-time of ~600 μs. The fluorescence decay of a third flash is comparable to the first, while that of a fourth flash is comparable to the second. Thus, the kinetics of fluorescence decay follow a binary oscillation. This periodicity is explained by showing that $Q_B$ sequentially accumulates two electrons and two protons; the first electron transfer is rapid, the second is slower. These kinetics are described by the reaction sequence as follows:

$$Q_A + e^- \quad \overset{h\nu}{\rightleftharpoons} \quad Q_A^-$$
$$Q_A^- + Q_B \quad \rightleftharpoons \quad Q_A + Q_B^-$$
$$Q_A + e^- + Q_B^- \quad \overset{h\nu}{\rightleftharpoons} \quad Q_A^- + Q_B^-$$
$$Q_A^- + Q_B^- \quad \rightleftharpoons \quad Q_A + Q_B^{2-}$$
$$Q_B^{2-} + 2H^+ \quad \rightarrow \quad Q_BH_2$$

This portion of the photosynthetic electron transfer chain is often called the *two-electron gate*.

The proton and electron transfers from $Q_A$ to $Q_B$ are competitively inhibited by atrazine and substituted urea compounds, of which 3'(3,4-dichlorophenyl)1', 1'-dimethyl urea (DCMU) is the most commonly used (Table 4.2). DCMU binds competitively with $Q_B$ to one of the proteins constituting the reaction center. This protein, referred to as D1, is also called the "herbicide-binding protein." Upon the addition of DCMU or atrazine and subsequent exposure to light, $Q_A$ becomes reduced and cannot be oxidized efficiently by $Q_B$, hence PSII reaction centers become closed and fluorescence becomes high. Over a period of time in darkness, however, $Q_A$ can become reoxidized by the backreaction. These results experimentally confirmed the basic hypothesis put forth by Duysens and Sweers (1963) that the change in fluorescence yield of chlorophyll in vivo is primarily a consequence of the oxidation level of a quencher on the acceptor side of the reaction center.

The reduction of $Q_B$ is virtually isoenergetic with the oxidation of $Q_A^-$, the difference only being about 0.1 V. The equilibrium constant for the first electron transfer is about 25, favoring the reduction of $Q_B$, while that for the second electron is only about 5. To prevent the equilibrium rereduction of $Q_A$ with reduced $Q_B$ from

**Table 4.2** Common inhibitors of photosynthesis and their mechanism of action

| Compound | Structure | Concentration Typically Used | Inhibits | Mechanism |
|---|---|---|---|---|
| Antimycin A | Antimycin $A_1$; R = n-hexyl<br>Antimycin $A_3$; R = n-butyl | 0.1–50µM | Cyclic electron transfer around PSI | Unknown, blocks electron transfer from Fe-S carriers |
| Ammonia | $NH_3$ (not $NH_4^+$) | 0.5–10mM (The activity of $NH_3$ required is ~100µM.) | Electroneutral uncoupler | $NH_3$ transported with $H^+$ to lumen, converted to $NH_4^+$; $NH_4^+$ exported to stroma via $K^+$ channels |
| Atrazine | 2-Chloro-4-ethylamino-6-isopropylamine-s-triazine; Gesaprim | 1–20µM | Electron transfer on the acceptor side of PSII | Binds to $Q_B$ pocket in PSII, substitutes for plastoquinone |
| CCCP | Carbonylcyanide m-chloro phenyl-hydrazone | 1–2µM* for ΔpH dissipation<br>100–300µM* for ΔΨ | Uncoupler; Collapses both ΔΨ and ΔpH | Proton uniporter; lipid soluble anionic form enters lumen; neutral form leaves. Can also oxidize cytochrome $b_{559}$ at high concentrations |
| DBMIB | 2,5-Dibromo-3-methyl-6-isopropyl-p-benzoquinone; dibromothymoquinone | 1–10µM | Reoxidation of $PQH_2$ by cytochrome $b_6$ | Blocks plastoquinol binding site of cytochrome $b_6$ |

**Table 4.2** *Continued*

| Compound | Structure | Concentration Typically Used | Inhibits | Mechanism |
|---|---|---|---|---|
| DCMU | 3'-(3,4-Dichlorophenyl)-1,1'-dimethylurea; DCMU; Diuron | 1–20μM | Electron transfer on the acceptor side of PSII | Binds to $Q_B$ pocket in PSII, substitutes for plastoquinone |
| FCCP | Carbonylcyanide $p$-trifluoromethoxy-phenylhydrazone | 1–10μM | Uncoupler; Protonophore, collapses $\Delta\Psi$ and $\Delta pH$ | See CCCP |
| Gramicidin | HCO-L-Val-Gly-L-Ala-D-Leu-L-Ala—D-Val—L-Trp-D-Leu-L-Trp-D-Val-L-Val—D-Leu-L-Trp-D-Leu-L-Trp—HO—CH$_2$—CH$_2$—NH<br>Gramicidin A | 1–20μM* | Uncoupler; Collapses both $\Delta\Psi$ and $\Delta pH$ | Forms channels in the thylakoid membrane that permits movement of Na$^+$, K$^+$, Cl$^+$, H$^+$ |
| HOQNO, NOQNO | 2-$n$-Heptyl-4-hydroxy-quinoline-$N$-oxide HOQNO 2-$n$-Nonyl-4-hydroxy-quinoline-$N$-oxide NOQNO | 10–20μM | Inhibits cytochrome $b_6f$ function | Binds to PQ docking site on cytochrome $b_6f$ complex |

| Compound | Structure | Concentration | | |
|---|---|---|---|---|
| Hydroxylamine hydrochloride | $NH_2OH \cdot HCl$ | 1–10mM | PSII oxygen evolving complex | Competes with $H_2O$ for binding to Mn complex |
| Methylamine | $CH_3NH_2$ | 1–10mM | Uncoupler, electroneutral | (See ammonia) |
| Nigericin | | 1–5μM* | Uncoupler, collapses ΔpH | Antiporter of $H^+$ at the expense of $K^+$ |
| Methyl Viologen (Paraquat) | | 0.05–1mM | Nonselective destruction of chloroplast | Competes with ferredoxin for electrons from PSI, reduced MV generates superoxide anion $O_2^{-}$ |
| Tris | Tris-(hydroxymethyl)-methylamine | 10–100mM | PSII oxygen evolving complex | Washes OEE proteins from the thylakoid membrane |
| Valinomycin | | 0.5–1μM* | Ionophore, dissipates ΔΨ but not ΔpH across thylakoid membrane | Catalyzes uniport of $K^+$ across thylakoid, but not $H^+$ |

*Typical concentration used with 30μM chlorophyll.

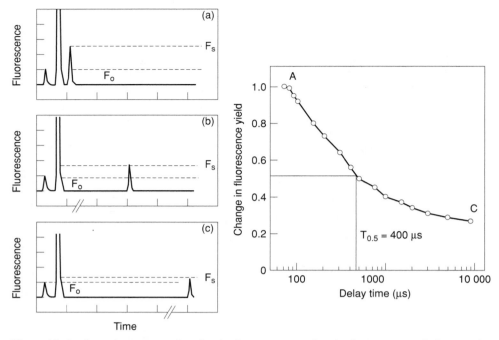

**Figure 4.8** A schematic representation showing how a pump-and-probe fluorescence technique can be used to follow the oxidation of $Q_A^-$. By increasing the interval between the pump and second probe flash, it is possible to follow the kinetics of decay of fluorescence. That decay is proportional to the oxidation of $Q_A^-$.

becoming a significant impediment to further electron transport, the doubly reduced $Q_B$ (which has accumulated two negative charges) extracts $2H^+$ from the stromal fluid; it dissociates from its binding site to become part of the plastoquinone (PQ) pool, leaving an empty "pocket" to be filled by an oxidized plastoquinone.

Free (i.e., unbound) plastoquinol[4] is a highly hydrophobic molecule (Fig 4.9). It diffuses throughout the center of the lipid bilayer that constitutes the thylakoid membranes; the diffusion coefficient is on the order of $10^{-9} cm^2 s^{-1}$. The size of the plastoquinone pool in vivo can be estimated from the difference in the fluorescence induction curves with and without DCMU. The area over the induction curve in the presence of DCMU is proportional to the number of electron equivalents represented by oxidized $Q_A$ (see Chapter 3). In the absence of DCMU, $Q_A$ can turn over repeatedly, but if the actinic light is strong enough the fluorescence will rise to the same level as that obtained with the herbicide. The area over the nonpoisoned fluorescence induction curve represents the number of electrons that have passed through $Q_A$ to the plastoquinone pool before the latter becomes completely reduced. The difference between the areas reflects the number of electron equivalents required to reduce the plastoquinone pool. This number is twice the plasto-

---

4. The terms *plastoquinone, plastosemiquinone,* and *plastoquinol* correspond to fully oxidized, partly reduced (one electron and one proton), and fully reduced (two electrons and two protons) forms of the same molecule.

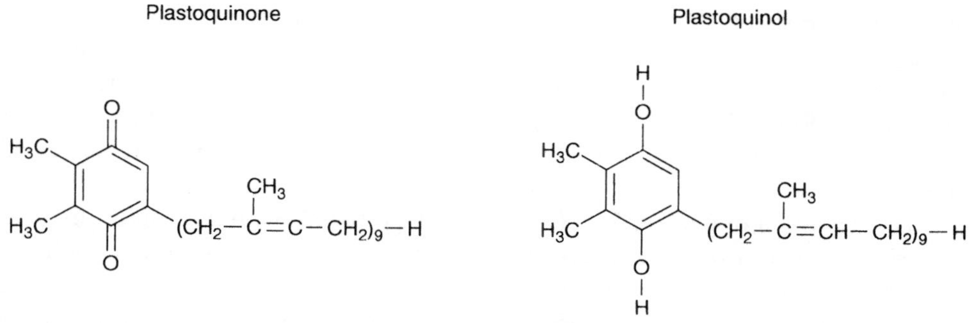

Plastoquinone                                    Plastoquinol

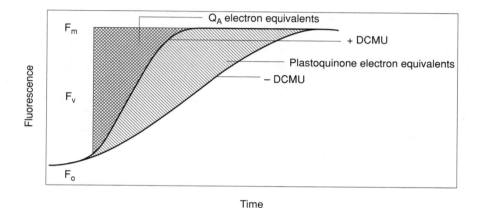

**Figure 4.9** The structures of plastoquinone and plastoquinol.

**Figure 4.10** The analysis of fluorescence induction curves to derive the relative fraction of $Q_A$ and plastoquinone. If a fluorescence induction curve is obtained in the presence of DCMU, it can be assumed for all practical purposes that, once it becomes reduced, $Q_A$ does not undergo reoxidation within the time of the measurement. Under such conditions, the rate of rise will be proportional to the effective absorption cross-section of PSII, and the area over the induction curve will be proportional to the number of electrons transferred to $Q_A$. As $Q_A$ can only accept one electron, this area is a measure of the relative number of reducible $Q_A$ molecules. If the same measurement is made in the absence of DCMU, but with a sufficiently strong actinic light, $Q_A^-$ will reduce plastoquinone. This process will continue until the plastoquinone pool is fully reduced. The area over the induction curve in this case is proportional to the sum of plastoquinone and $Q_A$ in the system.

quinone pool size (each plastoquinone-reduced accepted two electrons, but each $Q_A^-$ turnover represents a single electron transfer). Assuming a stoichiometry of $Q_A$ to $P_{680}$ of 1, the ratio of plastoquinone to PSII reaction centers varies from about 5:1 to 20:1; consequently, this plastoquinone is called the *plastoquinone pool* (Fig 4.10).

The total plastoquinone pool size can also be assayed spectrophotometrically. Plastoquinone can be extracted with organic solvents such as acetone or methanol and, following fractionation with organic solvents, can be oxidized with ferricyanide and reduced with sodium borohydride. The oxidized-minus-reduced difference spectra can be used to calculate the total quinone pool size.

$PQH_2$ is oxidized by cytochrome $b_6/f$, a protein complex containing two cytochrome $b_6$ molecules with a molecular mass of 25 kDa, one cytochrome $f$ molecule with a mass of 33 kDa, an iron-sulfur protein of 20 kDa, and an 18 kDa protein called subunit IV. Subunit IV is thought to interact with the iron-sulfur protein and cytochrome $b_6$ to form a pocket where plastoquinol "docks" to the complex. The overall complex is thought to be a dimer with an apparent molecular mass of about 210 kDa and is an integral part of the photosynthetic membrane (Cramer et al. 1996).

The oxidation of plastoquinol ($PQH_2$) by the cytochrome $b_6/f$ complex involves two single-electron transfer reactions and can be measured using a spectrophotometric technique called *flash photolysis*.[5] In this method the change in absorption of a molecule is measured following a flash. The time course of the flash kinetics can be used to deduce the oxidation rate of the donor. This technique can be used to follow the oxidation of $PQH_2$ by measuring the kinetics of the reduction of cytochrome $b_6/f$. This reduction occurs on the order of 1 to 10 ms, or about 2- to 50-fold slower than the reduction of PQ (i.e., $Q_B$) by $Q_A$. The oxidation can be inhibited by some substituted artificial quinones, especially 2,5 dibromo-3-methyl-6-isopropyl-*p*-benozoquinone (DBMIB). Whereas the application of DCMU prevents the reduction of PQ, the application of DBMIB prevents its oxidation. Thus, the use of the inhibitors DCMU and DBMIB allows the redox state of the plastoquinone pool to be artificially modified.

In the oxidation of $PQH_2$, two electrons are passed sequentially (i.e., one at a time) from the iron-sulfur (nonheme) protein to cytochrome *f* within the cytochrome $b_6/f$ complex. The oxidation of $PQH_2$ is the slowest step in electron transfer in the photosynthetic electron transport chain, but this should not be construed as the overall slowest step in photosynthesis—at light saturation, it is ultimately limited by carbon fixation. Because the oxidation of $PQH_2$ is so slow, however, under moderate light over 90% of the PQ pool can be reduced while the cytochrome $b_6/f$ complex is oxidized. Moreover each $PQH_2$ molecule does not pass its electrons and protons to another PQ in "bucket brigade" fashion, but rather must diffuse laterally through the membrane to the cytochrome $b_6/f$ protein complex. The potential for accumulation of electrons in the PQ pool effectively makes the pool an electrical capacitor, temporarily storing reducing equivalents.

The oxidation of each $PQH_2$ is accompanied by the release of two protons into the fluids bathing the inner side of the thylakoid membrane (i.e., the lumen). The thylakoid membrane in vivo is not especially permeable to the passive diffusion of protons, and thus the transport of protons from the outer (i.e., stromal) side of the thylakoid membrane to the inner side produces both an electrical and a pH gradient which together constitute an electrochemical gradient. The electrical gradient is a consequence of the +1 charge carried by the proton (Cramer 1982).

The proton gradient represents a considerable storage of free energy. This potential energy can be calculated from

$$\Delta p = \Delta \psi - 2.303(RT/F)\Delta pH \tag{4.6}$$

$$= \Delta \psi - 59\Delta pH \tag{4.7}$$

---

5. Flash photolysis was a technique developed by Sir George Porter, who won the Nobel Prize for chemistry for the elucidation of fast photochemical reaction mechanisms.

## ❑ THE CYTOCHROMES

*The nomenclature of cytochromes is based on their absorption bands. Like all hemes, cytochromes have a blue Soret absorption band, called the γ band, that is spectroscopically obscured by that of the chlorophylls in vivo. A second absorption band, the β band, is found between 515 and 530 nm and is also common to all cytochromes; it is not, therefore, useful for distinguishing among them. The third band, the α band, is found in the orange-red region, or about 600 nm for a-type cytochromes; at about 560 nm for b-type cytochromes; and at or near 550 nm for c-type cytochromes. Thus, cytochrome $b_6$ has an absorption maximum at 563 nm, whereas cytochrome f (which is a c-type cytochrome—the "f" designation comes from the Latin,* folium, *meaning "leaf") has an absorption difference maximum at 554 nm. Coupled with relatively low extinction coefficients of about $17 mM^{-1} cm^{-1}$, the overlap of absorption bands often complicates the determination of cytochromes by spectrophotometric methods, especially in vivo. In vitro, redox mediators are often used to discriminate among cytochromes, taking advantage of their often different midpoint potentials (Fig 4.11). Alternatively, other methods, such as EPR spectroscopy, can be used to assay cytochromes as the oxidized $Fe^{3+}$ in the heme is paramagnetic.*

---

where Δp is the proton motive force in volts, Δψ is the electrical potential difference across the membrane (P-phase – N-phase) in volts, and ΔpH is the pH gradient across the membrane (P-phase (lumen) – N-phase (stroma)). The electrical

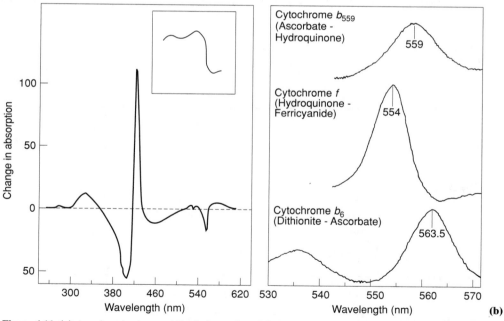

**(a)**                    **(b)**

**Figure 4.11** (a) A reduced minus oxidized absorption difference spectrum for cytochrome *f*. The major absorption difference peak at 420 nm is obscured in vivo by the Soret band of chlorophyll *a*, hence the absorption band at 554 nm is usually measured (see inset). The oxidized spectrum is made in the presence of excess potassium ferricyanide while the reduced spectrum is made in the presence of ascorbate. (b) A detail of the oxidized minus reduced difference spectra of three major cytochromes found in thylakoid membranes, namely cytochrome $b_{559}$, cytochrome *f*, and cytochrome $b_6$. Note that the oxidized minus reduced spectra for the three are obtained with different redox mediators.

gradient can sometimes be measured by neutral microelectrodes, or by using the distribution of ions which are intrinsically able to penetrate the membrane ($SCN^-$; triphenylmethylphosphonium$^+$) or are allowed to equilibrate by added ionophores ($^{86}Rb^+$ in conjunction with valinomycin). The pH gradient can be indirectly inferred by following the quenching of fluorescence of an artificial dye such as 9-aminoacridine. These methods do not work particularly well in intact cells. An alternative method, which is applicable in vivo, is based on the change in absorption of a thylakoid-membrane–bound carotenoid, β-carotene, within PSII reaction centers. Empirically, the transthylakoid electrochemical gradient affects the absorption spectrum of the carotenoid with an absorption change at 518 nm—the larger the gradient the larger the absorption change. The absorption difference is linearly proportional to the gradient. This so-called *electrochromic shift* takes advantage of a Stark-like effect (Chapter 2) and can be used to quantify the electrical gradients either transiently following a flash, or under steady-state conditions (Buchel, Garab 1995; Gottfried et al. 1991; Paillotin, Breton 1977). Under steady light conditions, Δp reaches a value of about 0.18 V.

The $H^+$ fluxes observed during the oxidation of $PQH_2$ by the cytochrome $b_6/f$ complex are larger than the electron flow predicted by the linear oxidation of the $PQH_2$ pool. Linear oxidation gives an expected $H^+/e^-$ ratio of 1, while the measured values are closer to 2. To account for this apparent discrepancy, one of the electrons donated by $PQH_2$ to cytochrome $b_6/f$ cycles back to PQ (which now has lost it protons). In the cycle, electrons from a semi-oxidized $PQH_2$ reduced cytochrome $f$ can reduce one of the two cytochrome $b_6$ molecules, and release $2 H^+$ into the lumen

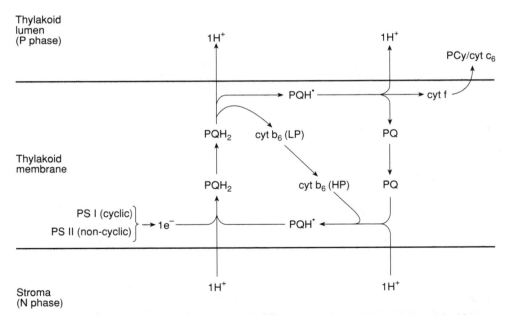

**Figure 4.12** The proton-motive Q cycle according to Mitchell (1975). In this cycle, plastoquinol is oxidized by a low potential cytochrome $b_6$, and protons carried by the molecule are deposited in the thylakoid lumen. The plastoquinone can then cycle back to the stromal side and accept an electron from a high potential cytochrome $b_6$, and extract protons from the stromal phase.

(Fig 4.12). The reduced cytochrome $b_6$ can, in turn, transfer its electrons to the second $b_6$ molecule, which, after two turnovers, rereduces PQ to $PQ^{2-}$. The negatively charged $PQ^{2-}$ can accept more protons from the stromal side to form $PQH_2$, and release the protons into the lumen. This so-called *Q cycle*, or cytochrome cycle, effectively doubles the stoichiometry of protons translocated per electron translocated; that is, two $H^+$ are moved per net electron transferred from plastoquinol to cytochrome $b_6/f$. Note that the Q cycle does not require the absorption of additional excitation energy by a reaction center, and therefore does not affect the maximum quantum yield for oxygen evolution. This type of cycle was postulated by Peter Mitchell (who won the Nobel Prize for the theory of the coupling of ATP to electrochemical and proton gradients) for the cytochrome $bc_1$ complex in mitochondria, a complex that has structural analogies to the cytochrome $b_6/f$ complex in chloroplasts (Mitchell 1975).

The Q cycle is a nebulous and unresolved area of photosynthetic electron transport. The two hemes in the cytochrome $b_6$ protein have slightly different redox potentials, and are spaced within the protein at opposite sides of the thylakoid membrane. One of these is located closer to the lumenal side or P side (see Chapter 1) and sometimes called the low-potential heme, while the second is closer to the stromal or N face, and is sometimes called the high-potential heme. The measured $E_{m7}$ values for the two hemes are somewhat variable. The low-potential heme is generally thought to have an $E_{m7}$ of about −0.05 to −0.08 V, while the high-potential heme is +0.16 V. Thus the $\Delta E_{m7}$ between the two hemes is about 0.21 to 0.24 V. While this potential difference can favor the electron transfer from the high-potential cytochrome $b_6$ to PQ, the kinetics of the electron transfer are not well resolved in vivo (see Cramer et al. 1996, for a review).

To derive the overall stoichiometry of $H^+$ transport from stroma to lumen per electron flowing from water to (ultimately) $CO_2$, we need to also consider the protons deposited in the lumen of the thylakoid for each electron extracted from $H_2O$ by the photochemical oxidation of $P_{680}$. This is balanced by protons taken up on the stromal side of the membrane during the reduction of $CO_2$ to $CH_2O$, using (ultimately) an electron obtained from PSI. If the Q cycle is operating, the overall stoichiometry of $H^+$ moved from the stroma to the lumen per electron transferred from $H_2O$ to $CO_2$ (i.e., the so-called $H^+/e^-$ ratio) is three, whereas it is two if the Q cycle is not operative (Kobayashi et al. 1995).

## PHOTOPHOSPHORYLATION

The protons removed from the stroma and deposited in the lumen store up to 18 kJ per mole $H^+$ transported as an electrochemical gradient (this energy difference is largely as a $\Delta pH$ [Eq 4.7] and is equivalent to a pH gradient of 3 units). The circuit is completed by the movement of $H^+$ from the lumen back to the stroma through the ATP synthase complex (Nelson 1980). ATP synthase is a multiprotein complex with an average molecular mass of 500 kDa. It consists of a 200 kDa $CF_0$ (CF is the abbreviation for "coupling factor") integral membrane protein and a 390 kDa $CF_1$ peripheral protein attached to $CF_0$ on the stromal side. Isolated $CF_0$ components

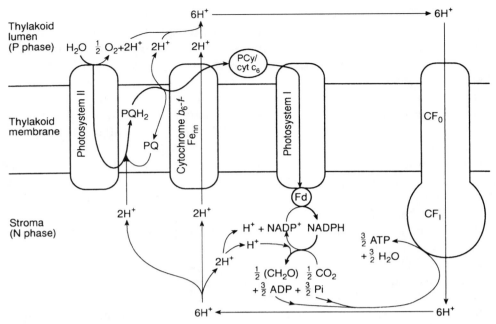

**Figure 4.13** An overall scheme for electron and proton transport in the photosynthetic membrane. The orientation of the two photosystems is critical. The water-splitting side of PSII faces the thylakoid lumen, and the protons extracted from water are deposited there. Additional protons are added as a consequence of the oxidation of plastoquinol. The proton gradient is dissipated through the $CF_0$ $CF_1$ ATPase, leading to the formation of ATP in the stroma. Moreover, the reducing side of PSI faces the stroma, and provides reductant in the form of NADPH through reduced ferredoxin via the enzyme ferredoxin – $NADP^+$ reductase.

act as an $H^+$ channel, allowing the equilibration of the proton gradient across the thylakoid membrane (Fig. 4.13). Under appropriate conditions, the $CF_1$ complex acts as an ATPase, capable of hydrolyzing ATP to ADP and orthophosphate. In combination, the $CF_0CF_1$ supercomplex couples the vectorial movement of $H^+$ across the membrane (lumen to stroma) to the scalar synthesis of ATP. The process is freely reversible and the direction of the reaction is determined by the equilibrium of the substrates. Given a high ATP level and a low pH gradient, the complex will operate in "reverse," pumping $H^+$ across the membrane (stroma to lumen) by hydrolyzing ATP. However, under the normal conditions in the light, when a pH gradient is established and ATP is consumed by anabolic processes, the $CF_0CF_1$ complex couples the free energy available from the translocation of 4 moles of $H^+$ from lumen to stroma to the phosphorylation of ADP to produce 1 mole of ATP (Berry, Rumberg 1996; Kobayashi et al. 1996). The energy conserved in each γ-phosphate bond of ATP is equal to 0.34 eV. With 18 kJ per mole protons of energy in the pH gradient and not more than 45 kJ per mole needed to phosphorylate ADP in the stroma in the light, the ATP synthase conserves approximately 63% of the energy in the proton gradient.

Interestingly, there was a reluctance to accept the concept of ATP formation resulting from a pH gradient established by photochemical reactions in a chloro-

## ❏ ATP HYDROLYSIS

*How much energy is available from the hydrolysis of the terminal phosphate bond in ATP? The energy of hydrolysis of ATP can be measured as heat production. The actual amount of energy released is dependent on the relative concentrations of the products and substrates of the reaction, and is quantified by the change in free energy, ΔG. In classic biochemical texts, the free energy of hydrolysis of ATP to ADP and Pi (inorganic phosphate) is usually calculated under "standard conditions" assuming 1 mole per liter for the substrate and products at 25 °C. Under these conditions, the standard free energy, ΔG°, is given as:*

$$\Delta G° = RT \ln[ATP]/[ADP][Pi] \tag{4.8}$$

*and is equal to about −29 kJ per mole, where the minus sign signifies that the reaction is exergonic. It is important to understand that this value is for an equilibrium reaction, where an equilibrium constant, K, is defined as:*

$$K = [ATP]/[ADP][Pi] \tag{4.9}$$

*In vivo, however, the rate of formation of ATP is generally extremely high relative to the pool for ADP. The condition in a living cell is far from equilibrium, and [ATP]/[[ADP] ratios are high but also variable; hence the ΔG for the hydrolysis of ATP is higher than that calculated for standard conditions and is not constant. It ranges from about −45 to about −55 kJ per mole (Alberts et al. 1983). By maintaining a large disequilibrium between ATP and its primary hydrolysis products, the cell is able to direct biosynthetic reactions without major backreactions.*

---

plast. Before the 1950s the biological phosphorylation of ADP to produce ATP had been associated with water-soluble proteins in "substrate-level phosphorylation" and with mitochondrial and bacterial membranes as "oxidative phosphorylation." In the early 1950s some in vivo indications were obtained for whole cells of unicellular green microalgae and submerged vascular plants (Kandler 1950; Simonis, Grube 1952; Wassink et al. 1951) that were consistent with a light-dependent phosphorylation of ADP. This work showed a light-dependent decrease in intracellular inorganic phosphate, and a light-stimulated rate of ATP-dependent glucose assimilation and of [32]P-inorganic phosphate assimilation under anaerobic conditions. However, this work fell short of the unequivocal demonstration of a process other than glycolytic or mitochondrial ADP phosphorylation involved in the light-dependent phosphorylations. Even under anoxia, it was reasonably argued that illuminated photosynthetic cells could produce $O_2$ and thus permit mitochondrial as well as glycolytic phosphorylations.

At the same time, the work by Melvin Calvin, Andrew Benson, and their collaborators showed that the intermediates of $CO_2$ fixation pathways were phosphorylated (see Calvin, Bassham 1962; Chapter 5). This work indicated the need for large, light-stimulated (if not light-dependent) phosphorylation processes as a major metabolic pathway to supply the required ATP. Based on the rate of fixation of $CO_2$

and the concomitant consumption of ATP, it became clear that the rate of ATP synthesis in the light must be at least five times that in the dark.

Breakthroughs in demonstrating light-dependent phosphorylation came in the early 1950s from work on subcellular systems, namely chromatophores of photosynthetic bacteria (Frenkel 1954) and "chloroplasts" of higher land plants (Arnon et al. 1954). It is now known that the "chromatophores" of purple photosynthetic bacteria are invaginations of the plasmalemma, while the chloroplasts used in these early experiments had damaged envelope membranes that fortuitously permitted access of redox mediators and of substrates and cofactors of phosphorylation to the thylakoid membranes where ADP phosphorylation occurs. The work on chloroplasts in particular was criticized at the time because of the need for added redox mediators, the low rates of phosphorylation obtained, and the problems of eliminating mitochondrial contamination. All of these problems were overcome by Daniel Arnon and his collaborators (e.g., Arnon et al. 1954), and by other research groups, who demonstrated not only the light dependence of ADP phosphorylation but also that light energized the ATP production without the need for light-dependent $CO_2$ fixation. There are still difficulties in directly demonstrating ADP photophosphorylation in vivo at the rates required to sustain the observed magnitude of $CO_2$ fixation. Estimates of *net* ATP production can be undertaken only at light–dark and dark–light transients, where induction effects on ATP production and consumption confound matters. Estimates of ATP *turnover* in steady-state illumination involve $^{32}P$-inorganic phosphate incubations. These measurements are complicated by slow equilibration of the extracellular and intracellular inorganic phosphate pools relative to the rate of incorporation of intracellular phosphate in ADP phosphorylation.

Early work on the mechanism of photophosphorylation was greatly influenced by work on oxidative phosphorylation. The role of the membrane in oxidative and photosynthetic phosphorylation was perceived as a means of organizing the catalysts and intermediates in two dimensions (as opposed to three dimensions for substrate-level phosphorylation in the soluble phase, such as occurs in glycolysis) and of permitting the occurrence of lipid-soluble intermediates. A revolution in our understanding of much of bioenergetics, including photophosphorylation, came from the insight of Mitchell (1961). His *chemiosmotic coupling hypothesis* was soon seen to be readily accommodated in the Z-scheme of Hill and Bendall for $O_2$ evolution and $NADP^+$ reduction in thylakoids, granted certain vectorial dispositions of reactions. Indeed, work from Andre Jagendorf's laboratory testing the chemiosmotic hypothesis showed that $H^+$ gradients across the thylakoid membrane were most likely obligate intermediates in photophosphorylation, rather than merely being in equilibrium with the "real" lipid-soluble high-energy intermediate (Jagendorf, Margulies 1960).

Thylakoids were to prove an ideal test-bed for the chemiosmotic hypothesis. One advantage was that an energy supply from light was much more readily regulated than an energy supply from a chemical reductant. Another important advantage of thylakoids is that the $H^+$ electrochemical gradient in thylakoids is largely present as a pH gradient rather than an electrical potential difference. The expected result of a transmembrane electrogenic $H^+$ flux is a change in electrical potential difference rather than production of a pH difference as a result of the relative values of electrical capacitance and of $H^+$ buffer capacity per unit membrane area. In mitochondria and bacterial chromatophores the conductances to $K^+$, $Mg^{2+}$, and $Cl^-$ are low, hence the $H^+$ electrochemical potential gradient is maintained mainly as an electrical potential difference. Thylakoid membranes have higher conductances to $K^+$, $Mg^{2+}$, and $Cl^-$ so that the electrical potential difference component of the $H^+$ electrochemical difference ($\Delta\psi$) is largely exchanged via $Cl^-$ influx and $K^+$ or $Mg^{2+}$ efflux into a pH gradient. Essentially, continued net $H^+$ influx was permitted as the inside-positive (lumenal) electrical potential difference ($\Delta p$) was dissipated by $K^+$, $Cl^-$, and $Mg^{2+}$ fluxes.

The domination of the $H^+$ electrochemical potential difference by a pH gradient in thylakoids facilitates a number of tests of the chemiosmotic hypothesis. One is that illumination of thylakoids in the absence of phosphorylation results in buildup of a large $H^+$ gradient (mole $H^+$ per $m^2$ membrane area). Darkening plus addition of all phosphorylation prerequisites ($Mg^{2+}$, inorganic phosphate, ADP) yields an $H^+$-flux–dependent ADP phosphorylation. Another important test of chemiosmosis was the acid-bath technique, in which the thylakoid lumen was transiently rinsed in a low-pH buffer and subsequently transferred to a high-pH medium. This process generated an $H^+$ gradient and permitted phosphorylation (provided the ATP synthetase was activated). These results established chemiosmosis as a probable mechanism of photophosphorylation and were important in suggesting to a skeptical biochemical audience that chemiosmosis was a possible mechanism for membrane-associated phosphorylations. Transmembrane pH differences were more acceptable to most biochemists as a driving force for phosphorylation than was the (then nebulous) concept of transmembrane electrical potential differences.

The formation of ATP is *coupled* to the $H^+$ and electrochemical potential gradients (mainly present as the $\Delta pH$ component) established across the thylakoid membrane by the light reactions. A series of inhibitors are known to "uncouple" these processes, and in so doing ATP synthesis is abolished but electron transport proceeds, often at a faster rate. There are different types of uncouplers that can be used to examine, for example, the relative importance of the pH gradient or electrochemical potential to the synthesis of ATP. Any agent that can disrupt membrane permeability—as can detergents (including household detergents) for example, as well as solvents and hydrophilic hydrocarbons—can act as uncouplers. Many of these are components of anthropogenic pollution, especially in freshwater ecosystems. In biochemical and biophysical investigations, however, three types of uncouplers are especially useful in understanding some of the mechanisms of photophosphorylation in secondary processes (e.g., protein synthesis or membrane transport). Carbonyl cyanide *m*-chlorophenylhydrazone (CCCP) and its fluoro-analogue (FCCP) can cross the cell membranes in their dissociated (anionic) and undissociated form and abolish both the pH and electrochemical gradients. Ionophores such as nigericin and valinomycin also act as uncouplers; the former collapses the pH gradient but not the electrical gradient while the latter does the opposite. Neither of these (or any other ionophore) is specific for thylakoid membranes; they can operate as carriers or shuttles for protons or other ions in any membrane, including the plasmalemma. Thus, although their application to studies of photosynthesis in intact cells is limited, they are extremely useful in studies on isolated thylakoids. Finally, weak bases can act as uncouplers by becoming reversibly protonated. Of occasional interest here is ammonium because in some aquatic systems its concentration may become appreciable. It should be noted, however, that the concentration of $NH_4^+$ required to uncouple must be sufficiently high to develop a transthylakoid flux of $NH_4^+$ greater than that for $H^+$. The calculated values for inhibition are on the order of $50\,mM\ NH_4^+$, a concentration that is so high as to be irrelevant under most conceivable aquatic conditions (even in most high-rate oxidation ponds). Thus, while $NH_4^+$ and other weak bases (e.g., methylamine) can act as uncouplers in vitro, they are not normally present in sufficient concentrations in aquatic environments to inhibit ATP formation. However, this is not to say these compounds at high concentrations may not have other effects.

## ELECTRON TRANSFER FROM THE CYTOCHROME $b_6/f$ COMPLEX TO PHOTOSYSTEM I

After receiving and manipulating electrons from $PQH_2$, the cytochrome $b_6/f$ complex is reoxidized by one of two small water-soluble molecules that diffuse in the thylakoid lumen to the reaction center of PSI. This electron transfer proceeds from cytochrome $f$ to either a copper-containing protein, plastocyanin, or a soluble $c$-type cytochrome (cytochrome $c_6$), or by both of these in some cyanobacteria and eukaryotic algae. Plastocyanin is a polymeric protein containing four identical subunits of about 10 kDa, each with a copper atom bound to the imidazole nitrogens of two histidines and two sulfur atoms from cysteine; its redox midpoint potential is $+370\,mV$. Oxidized plastocyanin, like many other copper-containing organic molecules, is blue. Cytochrome $c_6$ (sometimes called cytochrome $c_{553}$) is a heme protein with a molecular mass of about 10 kDa and a midpoint redox potential of $+350\,mV$. Both molecules appear to have similar reactivities with their reductant and oxidants in vivo. The reduction of PSI by either cytochrome $c_6$ or plastocyanin occurs with a half-time of about $500\,\mu s$. On a molar basis there is approximately one plastocyanin or cytochrome $c_6$ per PSI reaction center.

## THE ACCEPTOR SIDE OF PHOTOSYSTEM I

Electrons delivered to PSI reduce the oxidized chlorophyll $a$ dimer $P_{700}^+$. The absorption of a photon leads to the oxidation of $P_{700}$ to $P_{700}^+$. The immediate electron acceptor from $P_{700}^+$ is a chlorophyll $a$ molecule, designated $A_0$. The electron transfer for the primary donor, $P_{700}$, poised at about 0.5 volts, to $A_0$ poised at $-1.10$ volts, occurs about 10 ps and is followed by the transfer of the electron to a phylloquinone (vitamin $K_1$) molecule, designated $A_1$. The half-time for this second electron transfer is about 35 ps. From $A_1$, the electron is passed to an iron-sulfur complex, $F_x$, within about 200 ps (Chitnis 1996). $F_x$ is oxidized by a second iron-sulfur complex, $F_B/F_A$, that ultimately transfers the electron to a nonheme iron protein, ferredoxin. This entire cascade of electron transfer events occurs in $<100\,\mu s$. Ferredoxin has a mid-

## ❏ DISTINCTION BETWEEN CYTOCHROME $c_6$ AND CYTOCHROME $f$

*Soluble photosynthetic cytochrome c in algae and cyanobacteria has been mistaken for cytochrome f in the cytochrome $b_6/f$ complex, which makes some of the older photosynthetic literature confusing. The situation was clarified by Wood (Wood 1976; Wood 1977), who clearly distinguished between these two c-type cytochromes based on careful redox titrations and biochemical characterizations. The water-soluble cytochrome $c_6$ has been found in all members of the Chromista, Euglenophyta, Rhodophyta, and Cyanobacteria that have been examined (Sandmann et al. 1983; Wood 1976; Wood 1977). It was also found in 11 of the 15 strains of Chlorophyta examined (Sandmann et al. 1983), but in none of the "higher" Viridiplantae. Plastocyanin is absent from all members of the Chromista, Euglenophyta, and Rhodophyta examined and from 4 of the 15 strains of cyanobacteria examined by Sandmann (1986). Plastocyanin appears to be present in all of the Viridiplantae and is the only electron carrier described linking the photosynthetic electron transport from cytochrome $b_6/f$ to PSI in most texts on photosynthesis.*

*Where plastocyanin and cytochrome c can both be produced, their relative levels can be altered by the availability of exogenous copper relative to iron (Sandmann 1986 and references therein). Generally it is easier to manipulate copper because this metal is incorporated into few enzymes and proteins compared with Fe, and so its deficiency has fewer obvious adverse effects other than a suppression of plastocyanin relative to cytochrome $c_6$.*

---

point potential ($E_{m7}$) of about −0.5 volts, has a molecular weight of about 11,000, and does not diffuse easily across the thylakoid membrane. Through the action of the membrane-based enzyme ferredoxin-NADP$^+$ reductase (FNR), ferredoxin reduces the readily diffusible, low molecular weight molecule NADP$^+$, producing NADPH which is used as a source of electrons and protons for the reduction of carbon dioxide. Some fraction of the reduced ferredoxin is used as a cofactor for enzymes responsible for the reduction of $NO_2^-$ to $NH_4^+$, and $SO_3^{2-}$ to the level of sulfhydryl (—SH). In the absence of sufficient iron, many aquatic photoautotrophs synthesize a flavin-based electron transport component, flavodoxin, that serves in place of ferredoxin (LaRoche et al. 1995).

In the light, electrons from reduced ferredoxin may also be used to reduce a small, 12 kDa, water-soluble protein called thioredoxin. The electron transfer is mediated by an iron-sulfur–containing enzyme, ferredoxin-thioredoxin reductase, located in the thylakoid stroma. Thioredoxin contains one disulfide (i.e., S—S) bond per peptide. The reduction of the disulfide leads to the formation of two sulfhydryl (i.e., S—H) groups, which in the dark are reoxidized back to a disulfide bridge.

Thioredoxin activates a number of enzymes in the photosynthetic carbon fixation pathway (Chapter 5) by reducing the disulfide groups in the enzymes. This activation is one mechanism by which the photosynthetic electron transport chain communicates with the dark reactions of photosynthesis. The redox regulation of thioredoxin is also critical in regulating the rate of expression of some chloroplast-encoded genes (Chapter 6).

## CYCLIC ELECTRON FLOW AROUND PHOTOSYSTEM I

Although the Z-scheme appeared to account for the apparent oxidation–reduction kinetics of the cytochrome $b_6/f$ complex, the proposal that there were two photosystems connected in series by an electron transport chain was not immediately nor universally accepted. One objection to the scheme was based on the observation by Arnon that the light-dependent formation of ATP in isolated chloroplasts could occur without the concomitant evolution of molecular oxygen (Arnon et al. 1965). Thus, one of the light reactions (PSI) could operate independently of the other. This did not exclude the Z-scheme, but it did complicate its interpretation.

To explain the results, Arnon proposed that electrons could cycle around PSI. The cycle takes electrons from ferredoxin back to the cytochrome $b_6/f$ complex through the NADPH-plastoquinone oxidoreductase and plastoquinone, and thus via plastocyanin or cytochrome $c_6$ back to $P_{700}$. This pathway allows for the generation of ATP without the oxidation of water or the reduction of carbon dioxide (and without the formation of NADPH that can be used to reduce $CO_2$). The fraction of electrons cycling around PSI is poorly quantified in steady-state photosynthesis. However, as the minimum measured quantum requirement for oxygen evolution is usually about 10 quanta/$O_2$, while the Z-scheme predicts 8, it suggests that about 20% of the photons absorbed could contribute to such a cycle *under light-limiting conditions*. Cyclic electron flow around PSI is an important source of ATP in nitrogen-fixing cyanobacteria, and is the only photochemical reaction that occurs in heterocysts (specialized cells found in some nitrogen-fixing cyanobacteria that contain the nitrogen-fixing pathway; see Chapter 8) and appears to be important in eukaryotic cells under nutrient limitation.

Because of the observation that PSI could operate independently of PSII, Arnon was not convinced that the two photosystems were really connected in vivo by an electron transport scheme, as envisaged by Hill and co-workers. Compelling evidence that the evolution of oxygen required an electron transport system that connected the two photosystems in series came from analyses of mutants, particularly of *Chlamydomonas reinhardtii*. Mutants were developed that were incapable of photosynthetic oxygen evolution; the organism required a source of reduced carbon. By using artificial oxidants or reductants applied to isolated, broken chloroplasts, it was possible to characterize the component(s) of the electron transport chain that was affected by the mutation. In this way, Paul Levine and colleagues showed that a mutant lacking cytochrome $c_6$ (which was called cytochrome $c_{553}$ at that time) was unable to evolve oxygen (Levine et al. 1960). Analyses of this and other mutants helped establish the Z-scheme as essential for photosynthetic oxygen evolution, while accommodating a cycle of electrons around PSI. Subsequently, a great many photosynthetic mutants of *Chlamydomonas* and cyanobacteria have been characterized, and such analyses have proven invaluable in elucidating the function of specific components in the photosynthetic apparatus.

It has been suggested that *Chlamydomonas* mutants purportedly lacking PSI reaction center proteins (and hence, persumably not having any PSI photochemical activity) can still be coaxed into fixing $CO_2$ and oxidizing water (Greenbaum et al. 1995). This photosynthetic pathway was suggested to operate solely by the photochemical activity of PSII, which appears to permit the reduction of NADPH directly from cytochrome $b_6$. The overall pathway is theoretically permitted as the energy contained in a single quantum of red light exceeds that for the generation of the reductant. However, the mutants appear to contain small amounts of PSI and the maximum quantum yield for $CO_2$ fixation is not different from the wild-type cell in which both photosystems are presumed to operate in series.

## THE MEHLER REACTION

A suite of veiled redox reactions that also can generate ATP at the expense of light energy is called the *Mehler reaction*, sometimes called *pseudocyclic electron transport*. This process involves the electron transport sequence from the donor side of PSII to the reducing side of PSI, where the $O_2$ generated by the oxidation of water is reduced (Fig 4.14), ultimately leading to the production of $H_2O$. Thus, there is no *net* $O_2$ exchange as a result of this process; however, the electron transport pathway is not truly cyclic. The Mehler reaction can be detected, however, by studying the uptake of the stable isotope $^{18}O_2$. Oxygen consumption by the Mehler reaction can be distinguished from the other in vivo $O_2$-uptake processes by differences in their $O_2$ affinities and by isotopic discrimination between $^{18}O_2$ and the more common isotope, $^{16}O_4$.

As with cyclic electron flow around PSI and phosphorylation, some 20% of absorbed photons in low light could be used in the Mehler reaction. This can be coupled to the phosphorylation of ADP. It should be noted, however, that the same

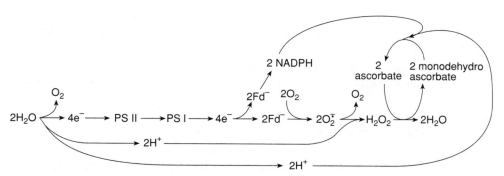

**Figure 4.14** The Mehler reaction. The Mehler reaction involves a stoichiometric $O_2$ evolution and $O_2$ uptake involving electron flow through both photosystems and generation of a transthylakoid $H^+$ gradient. Superoxide and $H_2O_2$ are intermediates in the reduction of $O_2$ to $H_2O_2$, and superoxidase dimutase and peroxidases such as ascorbate peroxidase may be involved in the reduction of $O_2$ to $H_2O_2$.

photons cannot be used for both truly cyclic and pseudocyclic processes. An unresolved question is the extent of the coupling of electron transport in the Mehler reaction to ADP phosphorylation. An optimal allocation of photons among the photosystems with a Q cycle for $H^+$ pumping yields 0.375 ATP per absorbed photon for the Mehler reaction, assuming two photons are used to move one electron, three $H^+$ are pumped per electron moved, and four $H^+$ are required to generate one ATP. If the rate of electron flow through the Mehler reaction exceeds the demand for ATP when the Q cycle is engaged, then the ATP/electron ratio could be decreased by one-third by disengaging the Q cycle. Further reductions in ATP/electron ratios could be achieved by further dissipation of the $H^+$ gradient (other than via the ATP synthase). A possible reason for the Mehler reaction is the photochemical utilization of absorbed light in excess of what is required to reduce $CO_2$, $NO_3^-$, $SO_4^{2-}$. This can, in principle, alleviate the potentially damaging effects of high rates of photon absorption by PSII, provided its rate is not constrained by coupling to ADP phosphorylation. The Mehler reaction, by increasing the ATP/NADPH ratio, may be used in powering the energy-dependent transport of solutes such as inorganic carbon (see Chapter 5). An optimal allocation of photons among the photosystems with a Q cycle for $H^+$ pumping yields 0.5 ATP per absorbed photon for the Mehler reaction and 0.67 ATP per absorbed photon for cyclic electron transport around photosystem I.

## REGULATION OF THE FLUXES OF ATP AND REDUCTANT

The two basic products of the photosynthetic electron transport chain are ATP and reductant, especially NADPH. These two products are used for different purposes. In addition to its role in the Calvin–Benson cycle (which we will discuss in Chapter 5), ATP is essential for polymerization reactions in the synthesis of macromolecules, for translocation of many ions and solutes, as well as for the activation of substrates in metabolic pathways. NADPH is used in carbon assimilation to reduce carbonyl bonds (i.e., to saturate double bonds) and in nitrogen assimilation. The ratio of the fluxes of ATP/NADPH is partially dependent on the ratio of PSII/PSI reaction centers, as this ratio influences the relative importance of linear and cyclic electron transport. Modification of the electron traffic is also achieved by feedbacks from the metabolic pathway.

It might be assumed that the Z-scheme predicts that the ratio of numbers of PSII/PSI is unity, but in fact that is not necessarily the case. In chromophytes the PSII/PSI ratio is often two or more. The deviation of the ratio to values greater than one is presumably accommodated by increased rates of electron turnover of PSI relative to PSII. In chlorophytes and prochlorophytes, the ratio is close to unity, while in cyanobacteria and rhodophytes it is generally 0.5 to 0.25. In the latter groups, a fraction PSI is assumed to operate in vivo to provide ATP via cyclic electron flow around PSI.

In summary, the two light reactions in oxygenic photosynthesis are coupled via an electron transport chain. The photochemical reactions in PSII generate an oxidant that is strong enough to oxidize water. The electrons from water produce a reductant in PSI that is strong enough to reduce carbon dioxide. Although PSII is thermodynamically capable of carrying out the entire process independently of PSI, all known oxygenic photoautotrophs contain both photosystems. In the next chapter we examine how the products of the light reactions are used to reduce inorganic carbon.

# 5

# Carbon Acquisition and Assimilation

The NADPH and ATP generated by the electron transport chain in the thylakoid membranes couple the light reactions to carbon fixation and, ultimately, to cell growth. For a microalga growing photoautotrophically, approximately 95% of the NADPH and more than 60% of the photosynthetically generated ATP are used to assimilate and reduce inorganic carbon. The pathway for inorganic carbon fixation invariably involves the enzyme ribulose-1,5-bisphosphate carboxylase/oxygenase (Rubisco). As we shall explain shortly, Rubisco can only use $CO_2$ as a substrate. Hence, inorganic carbon uptake must ultimately lead to the formation of $CO_2$ in the chloroplast stroma. Here we first examine the problems related to carbon availability in aquatic systems and then address the biochemical pathways for the assimilation of inorganic carbon.

## THE PHYSICS AND CHEMISTRY OF INORGANIC CARBON IN AQUATIC ENVIRONMENTS AND ORGANISMS

$CO_2$ is found in the atmosphere as a gas. The molecule is linear and uncharged. Molecular orbital calculations for $CO_2$ suggest that the bonding between the carbon and two oxygen molecules involves both s and p orbitals, where the former contribute to $\sigma$ bonds and the latter to $\pi$ bonds. In most terrestrial plant photosynthesis, $CO_2$ is acquired as a gas from the atmosphere by diffusion into the gaseous interstices of the leaves via specialized cells, called *guard cells*, that reversibly control the size of pores, called *stomata*. The diffusive flux between the leaf cell walls and atmosphere is controlled by the concentration gradient.

$CO_2$ is a unique gas, however. In aqueous solution it can undergo nucleophilic displacement from a water molecule, leading to the formation of an extended $\pi$ bond structure. The subsequent deprotonation of $H_2CO_3$ leads to the formation of bicarbonate and carbonate anions, as described by the following equations:

$$H_2O + CO_2 \rightleftharpoons H_2CO_3 \rightleftharpoons H^+ + HCO_3^- \rightleftharpoons 2H^+ + CO_3^{2-} \tag{5.1}$$

The equilibrium reactions are shifted toward the right at high pH and toward the left at low pH. Specifically, in seawater at 20°C, the $pK$[1] for the first deprotonation reaction is about 6, and for the second deprotonation is about 9. Thus, in the

---

1. The equilibrium constant $K$ for the first deprotonation reaction is defined as $K = [H_2CO_3]/[H^+]$ $[HCO_3^-]$. The $pK$ is $-\log_{10} K$ and is the pH at which equal amounts of substrate and products exist (see Fig 5.1).

ocean, with an average pH of approximately 8.2, virtually all (>95%) of the inorganic carbon is present in the form of bicarbonate (Fig 5.1). Free $CO_2$ is found only rarely as the primary species of inorganic carbon in aquatic systems. This form of inorganic carbon is predominant in acidic lakes, whereas carbonate is the predominant form of carbon in alkaline lakes.

The chemical equilibrium reactions between inorganic carbon and protons form a buffering system. Indeed, in seawater the inorganic carbon equilibrium is the major determinant of pH; hence, pH cannot be regarded as an independent variable.

The ionic forms of $CO_2$ do not contribute to the vapor pressure of the gaseous form, thus the concentration of the sum of all the dissolved inorganic carbon ($T_{CO_2}$) can greatly exceed the atmosphere/water equilibrium concentration of gaseous $CO_2$ ($pCO_2$). The vapor pressure is predicted from Henry's law:

$$[CO_2] = K_H pCO_2 \qquad (5.2)$$

where $[CO_2]$ is the concentration of $CO_2$ in moles/liter, $K_H$ is the Henry's law constant of about $10^{-1.5}$ and is a weak function of temperature and ionic strength, and $pCO_2$ is the partial pressure of the gas in atmospheres. In the surface ocean, for example, total dissolved inorganic carbon (i.e., $T_{CO_2}$) is approximately 2mM, while $[CO_2]$ is only about 10μM. This $[CO_2]$ is close to that of the atmosphere (corresponding to approximately 360μmoles/moles total gas). Thus, there is approximately a 50-fold higher concentration of dissolved inorganic carbon in the ocean than of $CO_2$ in the atmosphere[2] (Table 5.1). Although it is common and convenient to express dissolved $[CO_2]$ in ocean surface waters in terms of $pCO_2$, this can be misleading unless it is borne in mind that this reverses causality. It would appear, rather, that sea-surface dissolved $[CO_2]$ determines atmospheric $CO_2$ concentration (Broecker et al. 1980).

In fact, on time scales of thousands of years, atmospheric $CO_2$ partial pressure is determined by oceanic processes that control the dissolved $CO_2$ concentrations in surface waters. Besides controlling dissolved $CO_2$ concentrations (and pH), these processes also determine the burial of $CaCO_3$ in the sediments of the ocean, the continental weathering of silicates, carbonates, and organic matter, and volcanic and metamorphic outgassing of $CO_2$ (Berner 1990; Berner et al. 1993; Spivack et al. 1993).

The inorganic carbon system in aquatic environments has very little chance to reach equilibrium with adjacent gas and solid phases. At the left side of Equation 5.1, $CO_2$ in solution *tends* to equilibrate with the gas phase (i.e., the $CO_2$ in the overlying atmosphere under natural conditions). At the right side of the equation the $CO_3^{2-}$ *tends* to equilibrate with the solid phase of $CaCO_3$ or $MgCa(CO_3)_2$. Furthermore, the equilibrium constants for the various inorganic carbon reactions are

---

2. Henry's law is dependent on the partial pressure of the gas under consideration. At sea level, the total atmospheric pressure is ~101 kPa. As the volume concentration of $CO_2$ in the atmosphere is about 0.036%, the partial pressure of the gas corresponds to about 36 Pa. At higher elevations, as would be found for Alpine lake conditions for example, the equilibrium concentration of dissolved $CO_2$ would be necessarily lower than that at sea level due to the lower overall total atmospheric pressure.

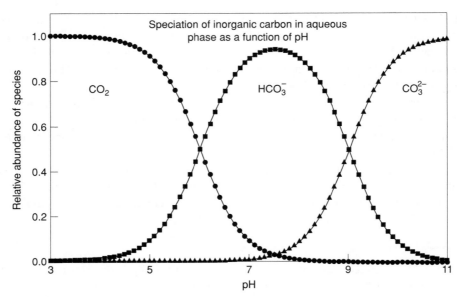

**Figure 5.1** The distribution of the three inorganic carbon species as a function of pH.

**Table 5.1** Carbon pools in the major reservoirs on Earth

| Pools | Quantity ($\times 10^{15}$ g) |
|---|---|
| Atmosphere | 720 |
| Oceans | 38,400 |
|     Total inorganic | 37,400 |
|     Surface layer | 670 |
|     Deep layer | 36,730 |
|     Total organic | 1,000 |
| Lithosphere | |
|     Sedimentary carbonates | >60,000,000 |
|     Kerogens | 15,000,000 |
| Terrestrial biosphere (total) | 2,000 |
|     Living biomass | 600–1,000 |
|     Dead biomass | 1,200 |
| Aquatic biosphere | 1–2 |
| Fossil fuels | 4,130 |
|     Coal | 3,510 |
|     Oil | 230 |
|     Gas | 140 |
|     Other (peat) | 250 |

temperature and salinity dependent. The partitioning of $CO_2$ between aqueous solution and gas phase increasingly favors the gas phase as temperature or salinity increases. (One way to remember this is to recall that warm soda water tends to outgas $CO_2$ more rapidly than cold soda; adding salt to the soda will accelerate the outgassing.)

The imbalance between the species of inorganic carbon in aquatic systems is primarily related to the slowness of the uncatalyzed equilibration of dissolved $CO_2$ and the hydrated forms $H_2CO_3$. and $HCO_3^-$. The association-dissociation reactions,

$$H_2CO_3 \rightleftharpoons H^+ + HCO_3^- \tag{5.3a}$$

and

$$HCO_3^- \rightleftharpoons H^+ + CO_3^{2-} \tag{5.3b}$$

are very rapid relative to biological interactions with the inorganic carbon system.[3] However, the hydration (hydroxylation)-dehydration (dehydroxylation) reactions,

$$H_2O + CO_2 \rightleftharpoons H_2CO_3 \tag{5.4a}$$

and

$$OH^- + CO_2 \rightleftharpoons HCO_3^- \tag{5.4b}$$

are much slower than some key biological interactions in carbon assimilation (Table 5.2). Accordingly, in some cases the maximum rates of carbon fixation can only be maintained if these slow reactions are catalyzed. The enzyme, carbonic anhydrase, performs this function (Stumm, Morgan 1981).

In the ocean, $Ca^{2+}$ and $CO_3^{2-}$ are generally present in excess of the concentrations in equilibrium with $CaCO_3$, meaning that the solution is supersaturated. Disequilibrium between dissolved inorganic carbon and solid $CaCO_3$ is common in natural waters. This condition is a consequence of inorganic or organic phosphates that inhibit the nucleation of $CaCO_3$ crystal formation and/or crystal growth. Most aquatic phototrophs manipulate these inhibitors in a manner that prevents $CaCO_3$ precipitation on their surface even when $CaCO_3$ in solution is well above saturation.

The presence of $CaCO_3$ in marine sediments and sedimentary and metamorphic rocks (e.g., marble) is primarily a consequence of biologically catalyzed precipitation. The biochemical pathway leading to the formation of $CaCO_3$ is unknown. In photosynthetic organisms, such as coccolithophorids and crustose red algae, calcification (the deposition of $CaCO_3$) appears to be metabolically coupled to photosynthetic reactions. In the crustose red algae, $CaCO_3$ is precipitated extracellularly. In coccolithophorids, a glycoprotein matrix is formed in the Golgi apparatus; $CaCO_3$ crystal growth in that intracellular secretory system creates calcified plates, or coccoliths, which are extruded to the cell surface.

Calcification leads to a loss of one $Ca^{2+}$ for each atom of carbon precipitated (refer to Eq 1.10). The loss of $Ca^{2+}$ is compensated by the formation of $H^+$, which shifts the equilibrium of the inorganic carbon system, described in Equation 5.1, to the left. Thus, calcification potentiates the formation of $CO_2$, leading to higher $pCO_2$ while simultaneously reducing the concentration of total dissolved inorganic carbon. It should be noted that although the biological formation of $CaCO_3$ requires metabolic energy, the energy is not stored in the chemical bonds of the product; that is, calcification is not a chemical reduction of $CO_2$. Rather, the energy is used to reduce the entropy in formation of the crystalline carbonate.

---

3. For our purposes here, the rate constant, $K$, can be thought of as the exponential rate of change of reactant(s) to product(s). The reactions described in Equations 5.3 and 5.4 can be represented by so-called first order reactions, where the time to complete one-half of the reaction is $t_{1/2} = 0.693/K$. Rate constants are listed in Table 5.2.

**Table 5.2** Some physicochemical attributes of carbon dioxide and other inorganic carbon species relevant to photosynthesis by aquatic photolithotrophs

| Parameter | Value in freshwater | Value in seawater (35 kg salts per m$^3$) |
|---|---|---|
| Concentration of $CO_2$ in equilibrium with 35 Pa | 22.4 (5 °C) 16.0 (15 °C) | 18.8 (5 °C) 13.5 (15 °C) |
| $CO_2$ in the gas phase/mmol m$^{-3}$ | 11.9 (25 °C) 9.3 (35 °C) | 10.2 (25 °C) 8.1 (35 °C) |
| pK$_{a1}$, of carbonic acid $$= -\log_{10}\frac{[HCO_3^-]}{[CO_2 + H_2CO_3]}$$ | 6.25 (5 °C) 6.42 (5 °C) 6.35 (25 °C) 6.31 (35 °C) | 6.11 (5 °C) 6.05 (15 °C) 6.00 (25 °C) 5.97 (35 °C) |
| pK$_{a2}$, of carbonic acid $$= -\log_{10}\frac{[CO_3^{2-}]}{[HCO_3^-]}$$ | 10.55 (5 °C) 10.43 (15 °C) 10.33 (25 °C) 10.25 (35 °C) | 9.34 (5 °C) 9.23 (15 °C) 9.10 (25 °C) 8.95 (35 °C) |
| $D_{CO_2}$/m$^2$ s$^{-1}$ | $0.95 \cdot 10^{-9}$ (0 °C) $1.94 \cdot 10^{-9}$ (25 °C) in gas phase, $1.04 \cdot 10^{-5}$ (25 °C) | |
| $D_{HCO_3^-}$/m$^2$ s$^{-1}$ | $0.52 \cdot 10^{-9}$ (0 °C) $1.09 \cdot 1^{-9}$ (25 °C) | |
| $D_{CO_3^{2-}}$/m$^2$ s$^{-1}$ | $0.41 \cdot 10^{-9}$ (0 °C) $0.80 \cdot 10^{-9}$ (25 °C) | |
| Rate constant for $CO_2 + H_2O \rightarrow H_2CO_3$/m$^3$ mol$^{-1}$ s$^{-1}$ | $9.4 \cdot 10^{-7}$ (25 °C) | $9.4 \cdot 10^{-7}$ (25 °C) |
| Rate constant for $CO_2 + OH^- \rightarrow HCO_3^-$/s$^{-1}$ | 8.5 (25 °C) 0.03 | 14.1 (25 °C) 0.03 |
| Rate constant for $H_2CO_3 \rightarrow CO_2 + H_2O$/s$^{-1}$ | 14 (25°C) | 8 (25°C) |
| Rate constant for $HCO_3^- \rightarrow CO_2 + OH^-$/s$^{-1}$ | $1.9 \cdot 10^{-4}$ (25 °C) | $15 \cdot 10^{-4}$ (25 °C) |

## Stable Isotopes of Carbon

A final aspect of the physics and chemistry of inorganic carbon is the occurrence of stable isotopes, and the factors determining their distribution among the various global pools. The most common form of carbon is $^{12}$C, which constitutes some 98.9% of the natural carbon in the world. The remaining 1.1% is in the form of $^{13}$C. (The natural abundance of $^{14}$C is <0.0001%.) The molecular collision frequency (which determines the rate of reaction in a binuclear chemical process) of the lighter isotope is greater than that of the heavier isotope. Thus, in a chemical process involving carbon, $^{12}$C is usually more likely to undergo a reaction than $^{13}$C. This tendency is called *isotope fractionation* and leads to different $^{13}$C/$^{12}$C ratios in different natural C pools. The natural abundance ratios of isotopes are usually expressed relative to an arbitrary, but precisely defined, standard. In the case of carbon, the standard usually used is a Cretaceous sedimentary Belemnite carbonate from the Peedee deposit in South Carolina (called the PDB standard). The isotope fractionation is generally expressed as the difference (in parts per thousand, ‰) between the sample

## ❑ UREY AND THE GEOCHEMICAL PROCESSES

*During World War II, the thermodynamic theory of isotope fractionation was applied to the separation of the highly fissionable $^{235}U$ from the relatively inert $^{238}U$, thereby facilitating the production of atomic weapons. Interestingly, during the war Urey, who was a professor in the chemistry department at Columbia University in Manhattan (the atomic bomb production project was code-named the Manhattan Project), co-authored a paper with a graduate student on the isotope fractionation of $^{13/12}CO_2$ in seawater (Reid, Urey 1943). This paper, which was a model system for isotope fractionation of other (more militarily important) elements, paved the way for the use of stable isotope fractionation measurements in understanding the sources and rates of fixation of inorganic carbon in aquatic photosynthetic organisms (Degens et al. 1968; Wong, Sackett 1978). Following the war, Urey moved to the Scripps Institution of Oceanography where he pursued the investigation of natural and radioactive isotopes. He and his colleagues developed interests in mechanisms of fractionation of other natural stable isotopes, especially $^{18}O$. Urey hypothesized that the isotopic fractionation of $^{18/17/16}O$ in carbonates in marine sediments was primarily controlled by the temperature of the ocean at the time of the precipitation of the $CaCO_3$. This hypothesis ultimately led to the use of $^{18/16}O$ ratios in marine carbonate sediments to reconstruct the temperature of the ocean over geological time. This inference is sometimes called paleothermometry. Similarly, the ratio of $^{13/12}C$ in carbonates reflects the availability of soluble inorganic carbon at the time of precipitation of the calcium carbonate; hence this isotope ratio can be used to reconstruct the approximate concentration of $CO_2$ in the ocean over geological time.*

---

and the standard in the δ notation, thus:

$$\delta^{13}C = \left\{ \left[ \frac{\left(^{13}C/^{12}C\right)_{sample}}{\left(^{13}C/^{12}C\right)_{PDB}} \right] - 1 \right\} \times 1000 \tag{5.5}$$

The PDB standard is at the high $^{13}C/^{12}C$ end of the natural range, hence the $\delta^{13}C$ values for atmospheric and dissolved $CO_2$ and for organic carbon are almost always negative.

Our understanding of the physical-chemical basis of isotope fractionation was largely an outgrowth of the discovery of radioactive isotopes during the early part of the 20th century. It was realized that certain species of atoms had identical chemical properties but different physical properties. By the late 1920s, Harold Urey isolated deuterium from hydrogen by distillation, and demonstrated differences in vapor pressure among $H_2O^{16}$, $D_2O^{16}$, and $H_2O^{18}$. Vapor pressure is related to the *intrinsic* vibrational frequency of the nucleus of an atom, and hence the principle of the fractionation was effectively based on the *thermodynamic* properties of the isotopes (Urey 1947). The stable hydrogen isotope, deuterium, was identified by its emission spectra, and Urey went on to show that the isotopic fractionation could be predicted from knowledge of the energy states of the atoms and their moments of inertia (i.e., "statistical mechanics"). He won the Nobel Prize for chemistry in 1934.

*Thermodynamic* or *equilibrium fractionation* can be thought of as an intramolecular phenomenon that occurs for reactions at equilibrium. For example, in

**Table 5.3** Value of α′ (equilibrium fractionation) for partial processes involved in oxygen and carbon solubilization and in the assimilation of inorganic carbon into marine phytoplankton organic material*

| Process | α′ | Temperature |
|---|---|---|
| $CO_2(aq) + H_2O \rightleftharpoons HCO_3^- + H^+$ | 1.00900 | 25 °C |
| $CO_2(aq) + H_2O \rightleftharpoons HCO_3^- + H^+$ | 1.01070 | 10 °C |
| $CO_2(aq) + RH \rightleftharpoons RCO_2^- + H^+$ | 1.00300 | 25 °C |
| $CO_2(g) \rightleftharpoons CO^2(aq)$ | 0.99894 | 25 °C |
| $CO_2(g) \rightleftharpoons CO_2(aq)$ | 0.99887 | 10 °C |
| $O_2(g) \rightleftharpoons O_2(aq)$ | 1.00073 | 2 °C |

* A value in excess of 1 indicates accumulation of $^{13}C$ (or $^{18}O$) on the right side of the equation.

the case of $CO_2$, a fractionation occurs between the atmosphere and aqueous phases because of differences in vapor pressures of $^{13}[C]CO_2$ and $^{12}[C]CO_2$. At the same thermal energy, the lighter isotope undergoes a higher rate of collision, simply as a consequence of its smaller mass. A second, and biologically important, isotope fractionation mechanism can also occur. That process, based on the collision frequency when the system is not in equilibrium, is called *kinetic fractionation*. If the reaction is kinetically catalyzed by, for example, an enzyme and the concentration of the substrate molecules is relatively high so that the reaction is not limited by the rate of supply of substrate, the product formed often will have a different isotopic composition from the substrate. Kinetic fractionation relates to the more rapid reaction of one isotope (almost invariably the lighter) than of the other in a unidirectional reaction. For example, kinetic fractionation occurs in the formation of organic carbon in the photosynthetic pathway and leads to a much greater depletion of $^{13}C$ in the product than does the precipitation of carbonate.

When considering a specific chemical reaction, it is often useful to reference the change in isotopic composition to the substrates (sub) and products (prod) of that reaction. This equilibrium fractionation factor can be written as:

$$\alpha' = \frac{\left[ ^{13}C/^{12}C \right]_{sub}}{\left[ ^{13}C/^{12}C \right]_{prod}} \tag{5.6}$$

The equilibrium isotope ratio of dissolved $^{12/13}CO_2$ ($\delta^{13}CO_2$) in seawater ranges from about −10 to −7‰ relative to the dissolved bicarbonate ions. (The minus sign indicates that dissolved $CO_2$ is isotopically lighter than dissolved bicarbonate.) The differences are inversely proportional to temperature, and are a consequence of the temperature effects on the rates of hydration and dehydration reactions (Table 5.3). The uptake and incorporation of inorganic carbon in photosynthetic organisms lead to a further fractionation, resulting in a depletion of $^{13}C$ in aquatic photoautotrophs. The extent of the depletion is highly variable and is a function of carbon availability and of the transport processes for inorganic carbon into the cells, as well as the carboxylation pathway. The overall effect of photosynthesis is the enrichment of the inorganic carbon pool in $^{13}C$, while the organic carbon produced is enriched in $^{12}C$.

## Carbonic Anhydrase

The slow kinetic equilibration between $CO_2$ and $H_2CO_3$, described by the reaction

$$CO_2 + H_2O \rightleftharpoons H_2CO_3 \qquad\qquad (5.7)$$

has a rate constant of $\sim 0.03\ s^{-1}$ at $25\,^{\circ}C$. This reaction rate is slow relative to many physiological requirements, and can be rapidly catalyzed by the enzyme carbonic anhydrase. Carbonic anhydrase is actually a group of phylogenetically unrelated enzymes (Badger, Price 1994), all of which use hydroxylated Zn in their active site (Silverman 1991). However, under Zn limitation, other elements may substitute for Zn in vitro and, apparently, in vivo (Morel et al. 1994). Carbonic anhydrase is one of the most catalytically active enzymes known—a turnover rate of $600{,}000\,s^{-1}$ is not uncommon. The half-saturation constant for the enzyme (i.e., the $K_m$) with respect to $HCO_3^-$ ranges from about 5 to 10 mM (see the discussion of enzyme kinetics later in this chapter). The reactions catalyzed by the enzyme, however, are not coupled to exergonic reactions. Thus, the enzyme cannot bring about a *disequilibrium* between $CO_2$ and $H_2CO_3/HCO_3^-$, meaning that it cannot bring about a higher concentration of $CO_2$ in comparison with $HCO_3^-$ than would ultimately be obtained by uncatalyzed $HCO_3^-$ to $CO_2$ conversion. Rather, these enzymes function to supply $CO_2$ to a $CO_2$-specific enzyme such as a carboxylase, and facilitate the diffusive transport of inorganic carbon into cells. The latter role is especially important in the ocean where free $CO_2$ concentrations are so low but the concentration of $HCO_3^-$ is large.

Carbonic anhydrase activity is often found on the plasmalemma and as an extracellular, soluble enzyme. The lipid component of the plasmalemma and envelope membranes of aquatic plants are impermeable to the charged $HCO_3^-$ and $CO_3^{2-}$ ion, but relatively permeable to uncharged $CO_2$. The diffusion of $CO_2$ may limit the rate of carbon fixation, whereas carbonic anhydrase can facilitate diffusion by accelerating the formation of $CO_2$ at or near the cell surface. In addition, carbonic anhydrase is found at various intracellular locations, where it helps to supply the appropriate form of inorganic carbon to carboxylases.

## The Uptake of Inorganic Carbon

Photosynthesis requires net transport of inorganic carbon from the bulk medium into the cell. As the site of carbon fixation in a eukaryotic cell is in the chloroplast stroma, which is surrounded by two to four membranes and contained in a cell surrounded by a plasma membrane and often a cell wall, it is a wonder that the inorganic carbon transport does not limit the rate of carbon fixation. Or does it?

In some cases diffusion is the sole means by which inorganic carbon crosses the membranes. As only $CO_2$ can freely cross the plasmalemma or chloroplast envelope membranes, the gas must dissolve in the membrane lipid phases, diffuse across the membrane, and dissolve back into the aqueous phase at the other side. Diffusion occurs from high to low concentrations of the diffusing solute. The diffusion transport across a plane can be described by Fick's law:

$$J_{bs} = D\,dC/dl \qquad\qquad (5.8a)$$

where $J_{bs}$ is the flux of the diffusing molecule $C$ through the plane. $J$ has dimensions $mol\ m^{-2}\ s^{-1}$ and $C$ has dimensions $mol\ m^{-3}$, $D$ is the diffusion coefficient with dimensions $m^{-2}\ s^{-1}$, and l is the boundary layer with dimensions of length (m). The concentration gradient is *dC/dl*. This differential equation is often solved using the finite difference form:

$$J_{bs} = \frac{D(C_b - C_s)}{1}$$    (5.8b)

where $C_b$ is the bulk phase concentration of the diffusing molecule, and $C_s$ is the concentration of the molecule at the surface of the plane (Fig 5.2). Similar equations describe diffusion to a cylindrical or spherical surface, or among membranes within cells, allowing a formal, mathematical description of the flux with values of $D$ and $C$ adjusted for water-lipid partition coefficients. Organisms with purely diffusive inorganic carbon supply include some freshwater and marine macrophytes (Maberly et al. 1992; MacFarlane, Raven 1990; Madsen 1991).

## Boundary Layers

The diffusion boundary layer is the layer of fluid around all solid objects within which molecules are diffusively translocated in a direction normal to the surface of the object. The effective thickness is determined by a phase transition between a well-mixed bulk medium and an unmixed boundary layer. The diffusion boundary layer thickness depends on the size of the object, the relative velocity of the object and fluid medium, and the viscosity of the fluid. For spherical phytoplankton cells ≤50 µm in diameter, the diffusion boundary layer is effectively equal to the radius of the cell and is little affected by movement of the cells relative to water at any attainable velocity. For attached macrophytes the diffusion boundary layer thick-

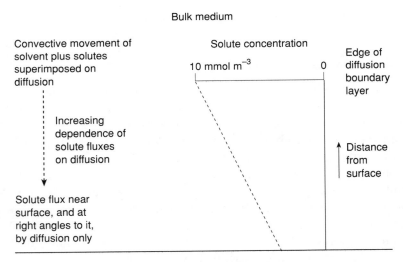

**Figure 5.2** A conceptual diagram of a boundary layer. The concentration gradient from the bulk fluid phase to the surface of the photosynthetic organism is assumed to be linear. The diffusion boundary layer, l, is an abstraction that permits calculation of the diffusion gradient using Eq 5.8b. In reality, the boundary layer between convective and diffusive domains is not as sharp as shown.

ness depends on the size and shape of the organism and the rate at which water flows over them. Even under conditions of rapid water movement over the surface of an attached macrophyte, with $D = 1.5.10^{-5} m^2 s^{-1}$, the calculated diffusion boundary layer of $15 \mu m$ permits a maximum $CO_2$ flux of $2.6 \mu mol \, CO_2 \, m^{-2} \, s^{-1}$.

The boundary layer thickness can be estimated from hydrodynamic first principles (Pasciak, Gavis 1974; Vogel 1981) or measured from models of the organism that undergo diffusion-limited losses under in situ conditions.[4] The intracellular diffusion pathlength is estimated from electron micrographs assuming molecular diffusion coefficients. Restrictions of $CO_2$ diffusion within a cell, for example as a result of impedance by membranes, are often assumed to be offset by carbonic anhydrase in the cytosol and chloroplast stroma. This enzyme facilitates the diffusion of $HCO_3^-$ in parallel with $CO_2$ (Badger et al. 1994). Finally, $\delta^{13}C$ measurements can be used in conjunction with measurements of photosynthesis to estimate the total pathlength of diffusion (MacFarlane, Raven 1990; Maberly et al. 1992).

The measured rates of carbon fixation in the majority of aquatic plants can only be supported by actively transporting inorganic carbon from the medium into the cells. Estimates of steady-state intracellular inorganic carbon concentrations during photosynthesis, as well as estimates of intracellular free $CO_2$ concentrations (which are based on intracellular inorganic carbon and pH measurements), strongly suggest that inorganic carbon is actively transported. These two lines of evidence hold for cyanobacteria and freshwater microalgae grown at their normal in situ inorganic carbon concentrations. The postulated inorganic carbon pump has been called the *carbon-concentrating mechanism*. In marine species, there is also evidence for active transport of inorganic carbon (Fig 5.3), although in some unicellular algae and macrophytes (Johnston et al. 1992; Maberly et al. 1992; Raven et al. 1995) the rates of diffusive fluxes of $CO_2$ appear adequate to support photosynthetic demands.

The location and identification of the carbon-concentrating mechanisms remain somewhat elusive. In cyanobacteria, the only possible location of the active inorganic carbon pump is the plasmalemma. In eukaryotes there is evidence consistent with active inorganic carbon transport at the plasmalemma in some cases and at the inner envelope membrane of plastids in others. There has been considerable effort to establish the molecular basis of active transport of inorganic carbon, but no structural gene encoding an inorganic carbon transporter has thus far been identified although some potential proteins have been described to fill this role (Ramazanov et al. 1993; Rotatore et al. 1992). Semi-crystalline arrays of Rubisco, with precisely regulated carbonic anhydrase activity, appear to be involved in the carbon-concentrating mechanism. In cyanobacteria, the enzymes occur in the carboxysome; in eukaryotes they occur within the chloroplast in a structure called the pyrenoid (Fig 5.4).

---

4. For example, an organism or model particle can be coated with a substance such as benzoic acid. The diffusion-limited dissolution of the coating over time leads to a loss of mass of the organism or particle. By rearranging Equation 5.7, the change in weight (i.e., the flux $J$) can be related to $l$ through the diffusion coefficient of benzoic acid.

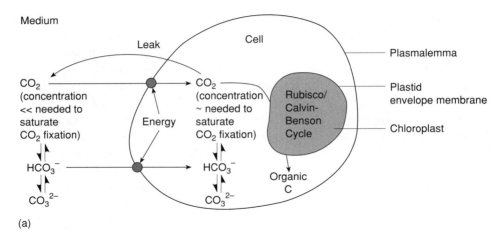

(a)

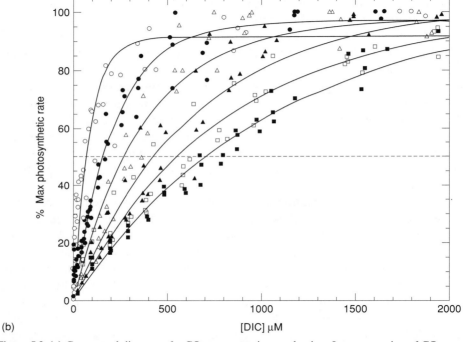

(b)

**Figure 5.3** (a) Conceptual diagram of a $CO_2$-concentrating mechanism. Interconversion of $CO_2$ and $HCO_3^-$ at the cell surface is frequently catalyzed by carbonic anhydrase. Carbonic anhydrase is invariably involved in $HCO_3^-$ to $CO_2$ conversion near the site of Rubisco. In eukaryotes the active transport step must occur at one or more of the non-porin-containing membranes between the medium and Rubisco (plasmalemma and inner envelope membrane in green algae). (b) Experimental data showing the evidence for a carbon concentrating mechanism in a marine diatom. The rate of photosynthesis in *Thalassiosira pseudonana* was measured as oxygen evolution for cultures grown under different levels of total dissolved inorganic carbon (DIC). Cultures were grown at 250 (○), 700 (●), 1250 (△), 1730 (▲), 2000 (□), and 2300 (■) µM DIC. The average DIC concentration in seawater in the upper ocean is about 2000 µm. The results show that the affinity for DIC increases as the ambient concentration of DIC decreases. Presumably this phenomenon occurs as a consequence of the induction of a carbon concentrating mechanism. (Courtesy of Anthony Fielding, Paul J. Harrison, and David Turpin)

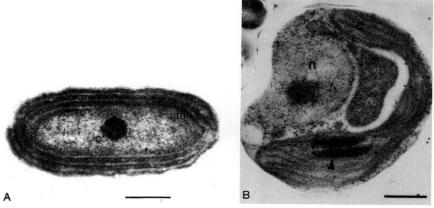

**Figure 5.4** Transmission electron micrographs showing (A) the carboxysome in the freshwater cyanobacterium *Synechoccus* labeled with a colloidal gold antibody probe to large subunit of Rubisco, and (B) a section through the marine diatom *Phaeodactylum tricornutum*, showing a pyrenoid within the chloroplast (arrow), also labeled with a probe directed against Rubisco. The probes are made with an electron dense colloidal gold "tag," approximately 5 nm in diameter. Where the antibody binds, electrons from the microscope are scattered by the gold, leaving a small black dot. Only a small fraction of antibody cross-reacts with its target molecule. Hence, the label shows the location, but not the concentration of Rubisco. Scale bars = 0.5µm (Courtesy of Michael McKay)

## THE CALVIN–BENSON OR PHOTOSYNTHETIC CARBON REDUCTION CYCLE

The uptake of inorganic carbon into a cell is but the first step in the photosynthetic assimilation of carbon. All oxygenic photoautotrophs incorporate $CO_2$ into organic matter by adding four electrons and four protons to the carbon atom, effectively forming carbohydrate. The net reaction for carbon fixation may be summarized as:

$$CO_2 + 2H_2O + 8 \text{ photons} \rightarrow CH_2O + H_2O + O_2 \qquad (5.9)$$

This reaction can be more explicitly described by including the reductant NADPH and need for ATP as follows:

$$CO_2 + 2NADPH + 2H^+ + 3ATP$$
$$\rightarrow (CH_2O) + H_2O + 2NADP^+ + 3ADP + 3Pi \qquad (5.10)$$

where ATP and NADPH were generated by the photosynthetic electron transport chain (Chapter 4) with the following stoichiometry:

$$2H_2O + 2NADP^+ + 3ADP + 3Pi + 8 \text{ photons}$$
$$\rightarrow O_2 + 2NADPH + 2H^+ + 3ATP \qquad (5.11)$$

The primary metabolic pathway responsible for carbon reduction is the photosynthetic carbon reduction cycle (PCRC), alternatively called the C3 pathway or sometimes the Calvin–Benson cycle after Melvin Calvin and Andrew Benson, who led the research team that elucidated the cycle (Fig 5.5). In eukaryotic algae, these reactions occur in the water-soluble phase of the chloroplast stroma.

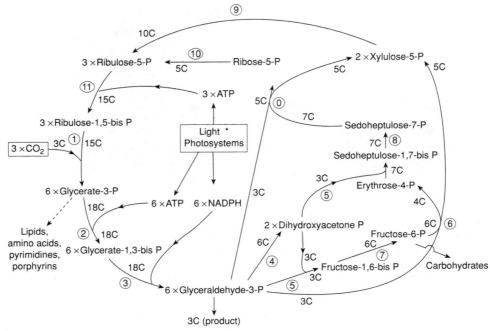

**Figure 5.5** The photosynthetic carbon reduction (Calvin–Benson) cycle. This representation does not indicate any oxygenase activity of Rubisco, i.e., it assumes a very high ratio of carbon dioxide to oxygen, which favors carboxylase and suppresses oxygenase. The ratio of carbon dioxide fixed to ATP and NADPH used is 1CO$_2$:3ATP:2NADPH. Number of C atoms involved in each reaction (per 3C fixed) is given in uncircled numbers beside the reaction arrows. The enzymes of the cycle (circled numbers) are (1) ribulose biphosphate carboxylase (regulated enzyme) (E.C.4.1.1.39); (2) 3-phosphoglycerate kinase (E.C.2.7.2.3); (3) 3-phosphoglyceraldehyde dehydrogenase, NADP-linked (regulated enzyme) (E.C.1.2.1.13); (4) phosphotriose isomerase (E.C.5.3.1.1); (5) aldolase (E.C.4.1.2.13); (6) transketolase (E.C.2.2.1.1); (7) fructose-1,6-biphosphate-1-phosphatase (regulated enzyme) (E.C.3.1.3.11); (8) sedoheptulose-1,7-biphosphate-1-phosphatase (regulated enzyme) (E.C.3.1.3.37); (9) phosphopentose epimerase (E.C.5.1.3.1); (10) phosphoribose isomerase (E.C.5.3.1.6); (11) phosphoribulokinase (regulated enzyme) (E.C.2.7.1.19); (*) catalytic role of CO$_2$.

In the early 1950s, Calvin and co-workers used radioactively labeled carbon, as $^{14}$CO$_2$, to trace the pathway of intermediates of carbon assimilation in the unicellular green alga, *Chlorella*. $^{14}$C had been available to biologists for about a decade before Calvin's group used it (Calvin, Bassham 1962). $^{14}$C is a convenient tracer which enables the time course of labeling of organic compounds from $^{14}$CO$_2$ to be determined. The rationale is that the first compound formed with the highest specific activity (i.e., largest fraction of radioactively labeled carbon atoms relative to total carbon atoms) in the shortest time-interval practicable is the primary product of the carboxylation reaction. Subsequent compounds in the reaction chain are labeled sequentially and will necessarily have lower specific activities. Using the then new technique of two-dimensional paper chromatography, followed by autoradiography, the group purified and identified a variety of low molecular weight compounds that were radioactively labeled at various time points. A system was developed where, on addition of labeled inorganic carbon, the cells were killed vir-

## ❏ RADIOACTIVE TRACERS

*The use of radioactive tracers to study metabolic pathways became a major focus of nuclear chemistry immediately before and following World War II. The first radioactive isotope of carbon that could be conveniently produced was $^{11}C$, which has a 20-minute half-life. This isotope was produced by neutron bombardment of nitrogen compounds in a cyclotron (which had been invented in 1929 by E. Lawrence) and decays by emission of a positron (i.e., a positively charged particle with the same mass as an electron). The positron emission can be easily detected as the interaction of the particle with an electron leads to annihilation and the subsequent emission of a gamma ray; the gamma radiation can be detected by a Geiger counter and also can be detected with a photomultiplier as Cherenkov[5] photon emission. The isotope is relatively easy to make, but because it has such a short half-life, its utilization requires close access to a cyclotron. This limited its practical application in photosynthesis research to a few laboratories, primarily (in the early 1950s) Lawrence Berkeley Laboratory and Brookhaven National Laboratory.*

*It was predicted that a second isotope with a long half-life, $^{14}C$, could also be produced by neutron bombardment of nitrogen, and it was identified in small quantities in the mid-1940s. The initial discovery of $^{14}C$ sparked interest in elucidating its half-life and its distribution, all the more so because the detonation of atomic weapons in the post-war era led to a large enrichment of the atmosphere with $^{14}C$ (so-called "bomb carbon"). The natural production of $^{14}C$ as $^{14}[C]CO$ comes about by cosmic (neutron) radiation bombardment of $N_2$ in the upper atmosphere (the stratosphere). This process leads to the ejection of a proton, forming $^{14}C$ which is subsequently oxidized to $^{14}[C]CO_2$. This radioactive isotope decays with a low energy electron (a beta particle) that is difficult to detect with a conventional Geiger counter. Willard Libby, a physical chemist at the University of Chicago, developed a modified Geiger counter for measuring low energy radioactivity decays. He first detected natural levels of $^{14}C$ in methane collected from sewage taken from Baltimore harbor in Maryland. The half-life of the isotope, originally calculated from analysis of wood samples provided to Libby by an archeologist working on Egyptian artifacts, was determined to be 5730 years. Libby won the Nobel Prize for chemistry in 1960 for the development of radiocarbon dating.*

*$^{14}C$ is commercially prepared by bombardment of aluminum nitride (AlN) or beryllium nitride ($Be_2N_2$) with neutrons in a nuclear reactor. In commercial production, tens of grams of substrate are irradiated for up to two years to produce sufficient yields. Because of the length of time required for its production, $^{14}C$ is a relatively expensive isotope to manufacture.*

---

tually instantaneously by dripping them into hot alcohol. The labeled compounds were quantitatively degraded to enable their identification. The first labeled product formed was a three-carbon molecule, subsequently identified as 3-phosphoglyceric acid.

By determining which of the individual carbon atoms in each of the products was labeled, it emerged that only $\frac{1}{6}$ of the carbon was used to form an end product.

---

5. Cherenkov radiation is a phenomenon that occurs when a charged particle travels faster than the speed of light in a specific medium, leading to emission of visible (blue) photons.

Most ($^5/_6$) of the label incorporated from $^{14}CO_2$ was recycled to form a new acceptor for fixation of more $CO_2$. The net effect was that labeled carbon rapidly traversed the cycle and reappeared (with newly fixed $^{14}C$) in the initial $^{14}CO_2$-fixation product. The cyclic movement of label meant that the $^{14}C$ location within the molecules was crucial for deciphering the precursor-product relationships. The data showed that the first product (in 2–5 s) of $^{14}CO_2$ fixation was 3-phosphoglyceric acid (3-PGA) with the $^{14}C$ label in the carboxyl group. The label then spread into $C_3$, $C_4$, $C_5$, $C_6$, and $C_7$ sugar monophosphates and $C_5$, $C_6$, and $C_7$ sugar bisphosphates, then sucrose and starch. In parallel, the label was found in small amounts in organic and amino acids that did not contain a phosphate ester (Fig 5.6).

The deduced cycle identified $C_3$, $C_4$, $C_6$, and $C_7$ phosphorylated sugars as intermediates in the formation of a $C_5$ compound that is used as a substrate for further $CO_2$ fixation. The exact nature of the $C_5$ acceptor was unknown, and ultimately was deduced by isotope equilibrium labeling studies. Under such conditions, the radioactivity in each compound reflects the pool size rather than the labeling rate. By start-

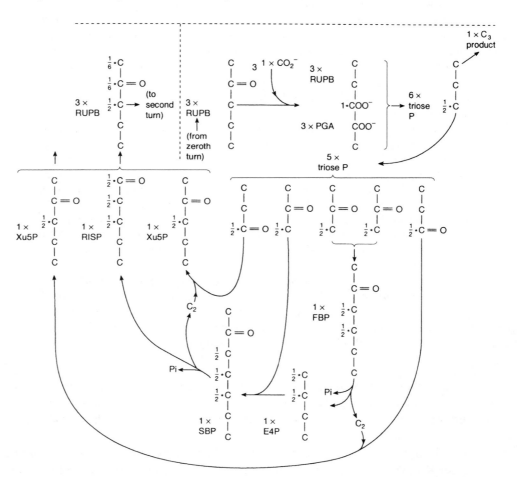

**Figure 5.6** Intramolecular labeling pattern of intermediates in the Calvin–Benson cycle during the first turn of the cycle following a pulse of radioactive $CO_2$. (—C=O, aldehyde or ketone group; —COO⁻, carboxyl anion; remaining groups are either primary or secondary alcohols.)

ing with illuminated cells, labeled with $^{14}CO_2$ to equilibrium, and decreasing the concentration of $^{14}CO_2$ supplied to the cells, it was possible to deduce the substrate for carboxylation. As $CO_2$ becomes limiting, the rate of carboxylation must decrease while the pool size of the acceptor substrate increases. The $C_5$ substrate identified in this way was ribulose-1,5-bisphosphate (RuBP). The stoichiometry of RuBP increase and PGA decrease was 1:2; that is, for each RuBP that accumulated as a result of formation reactions exceeding the carboxylation rate, two molecules of 3PGA were lost as a result of consumption reactions. The deduced carboxylation reaction was

$$RuBP + CO_2 + H_2O \rightarrow 2 \times 3PGA \tag{5.12}$$

This reaction was later confirmed by the identification of the enzyme carboxy-dismutase, which was subsequently called ribulose-1,5-bisphosphate carboxylase/oxygenase, or Rubisco. It should be noted that this carboxylation reaction is *not* reductive—no electrons or hydrogen atoms have been added to carboxyl carbon (Fig 5.7).

The phosphorylation of the carboxyl carbon on 3PGA to form 1,3-bisPGA permits the reduction of the one carbon with the NADPH to form glyceraldehyde 3P (G3P). *This is the only chemical reductive step in the entire Calvin–Benson cycle.* Glyceraldehyde 3P can be isomerized to dihydroxyacetone phosphate (DHAP). These latter two compounds are collectively called *triose phosphates*. The reduction of the carboxyl group on 3PGA to an aldehyde would not be possible with NADPH alone, were not the 3PGA phosphorylated to 1,3-bisPGA. Whereas the direct reduc-

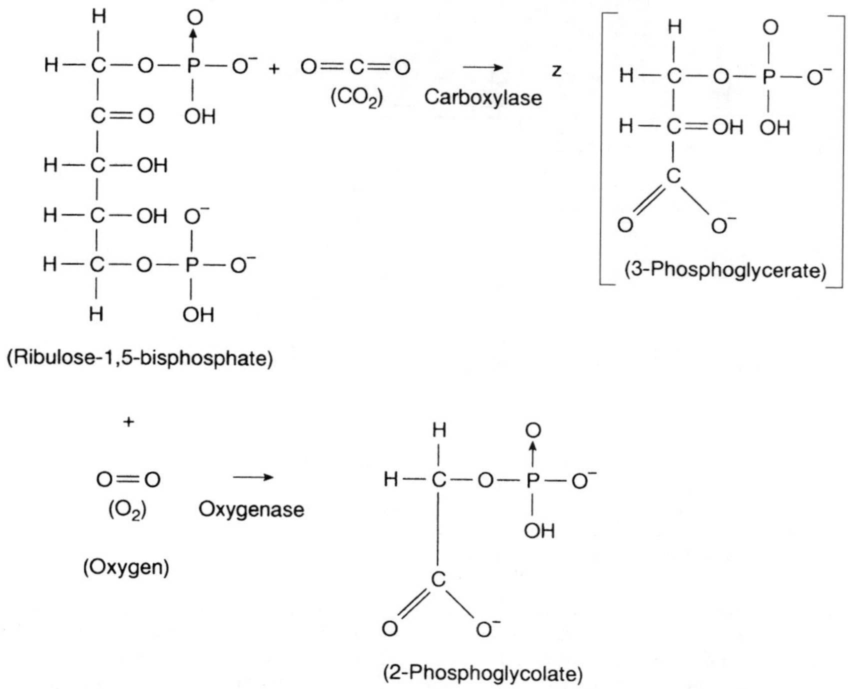

**Figure 5.7** Structures of substrates and products of reactions catalyzed by Rubisco.

## ❏ GLYCEROL SYNTHESIS

*In some microalgae, such as species of the halotolerant chlorophyte* Dunaliella, *and in the symbiotic dinoflagellate* Symbiodinium microadriaticum *(also called zooxanthellae), a major product of photosynthetic carbon fixation is the 3-carbon polyalcohol, glycerol (Fig 5.8). Glycerol is produced from a side reaction of DHAP. In this pathway DHAP is reduced in the chloroplast by DHAP-reductase to glycerol 3P. The enzyme uses NADPH in* Dunaliella *and NADH in zooxanthellae. Glycerol 3P is exported from the chloroplast and dephosphorylated via the action of a specific phosphatase to yield glycerol. Glycerol can be converted back to DHAP. The backreaction goes through DHA via the action of glycerol dehydrogenase, followed by phosphorylation via DHA kinase. The glycerol cycle is regulated in vivo by external osmolarity. The molecular basis of the signal transduction appears to be keyed to the plasma membrane.*

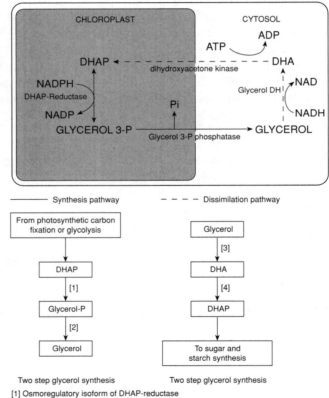

**Figure 5.8** The glycerol cycle in the green unicellular marine alga *Dunaliella*. Dihydroxyacetone phosphate, synthesized in the Calvin–Benson cycle (see Fig 5.5), can be converted to glycerol 3-P via DHAP reductase. Glycerol 3-P is exported from the chloroplast to the cytosol and dephosphorylated via glycerol 3-P phosphatase. Glycerol can be converted back to DHAP via the action of glycerol dehydrogenase and dihydroxyacetone kinase. (Courtesy of Arun Goyal)

tion of an unmodified carboxyl group is thermodynamically permitted with ferredoxin (or flavodoxin) as a reductant, these are not the substrates for the reduction in vivo.

The subsequent reactions in the Calvin–Benson cycle basically serve to regenerate RuBP (see Fig 5.6). The regeneration sequence converts $5/6$ of the triose phosphates, produced by the reaction of $CO_2$ with RuBP, into ribulose-5-P (Ru5P) and hence more RuBP. One-sixth of the triose phosphates are removed from the cycle and are available for storage, synthesis, or energy transformations. The overall regeneration process can be described by the equation

$$3(G3P) + 2DHAP \rightarrow 3Ru5P \tag{5.13}$$

This balanced equation contains 15 carbon atoms on both sides.

The first reaction in the sequence converting $5C_3$ compounds into $3C_5$ compounds leads to the formation of the six-carbon sugar phosphate fructose-1,6-bisphosphate (FBP) through the condensation of one molecule each of G3P and DHAP. The reaction is catalyzed by the enzyme aldolase. Carbon atom 1 in FBP is dephosphorylated to form fructose-6-phosphate (F6P) via the action of FBPase. This is essentially an irreversible reaction. The first two carbon atoms of F6P are transferred to a second molecule of G3P to form the five-carbon compound, xylulose-5-phosphate. The remaining four carbons of the F6P become erythrose-4-phosphate (E4P). This reaction is catalyzed by transketolase. The E4P is condensed with DHAP to form seduheptulose-1,7-bisphosphate (SBP). This reaction is directed by the same aldolase that led to the formation of FBP from G3P and DHAP. The dephosphorylation of SBP to S7P, facilitated by the corresponding phosphatase (SBPase), is another essentially irreversible reaction in the sequence. The S7P is then acted on by the aforementioned transketolase, leading to the transfer of the first two carbons from the S7P to a third molecule of G3P to form xylulose 5P (X5P). The remaining five carbons ($C_3$ to $C_7$) of the S7P form ribose-5P (R5P). The three five-carbon sugar phosphates produced in the regeneration sequence consist of one molecule of R5P and two of X5P. The final two enzyme-catalyzed reactions in the cycle convert these two compounds to ribulose-5P (Ru5P). These reactions are catalyzed by ribose phosphate isomerase and phosphopentose epimerase, respectively.

The stoichiometry of the reactions in the Calvin–Benson cycle is interesting. For each three turnovers of Rubisco, the cycle needs six turnovers of PGA kinase and G3P dehydrogenase; three of phosphoribulokinase; two each of triose phosphate isomerase, aldolase, and phosphopentose epimerase; and one each of the two phosphatases and ribulose-5P phosphate isomerase. Thus, the required activity for each of the enzymes in the cycle can vary by sixfold.

The reactions leading from PGA to FBP are effectively the reverse of glycolysis, with NADPH/NADP⁺ used instead of NADH/NAD⁺. Thus, overall, two ATPs and two NADPHs are used per $CO_2$ fixed. A third ATP is needed to convert Ru5P to RuBP using the enzyme phosphoribulokinase. The reactions that convert triose-3-P to FBP to Ru5P (with the exception of SBPase) are common to the oxidative pentose phosphate pathway in respiration (which we will discuss in Chapter 8).

## Regulation of the Calvin–Benson Cycle

The reactions in the Calvin–Benson cycle can be classified into three basic categories. The first group consumes either ATP or NADPH, which are generated by the photosynthetic electron transport chain in the thylakoid membranes. This group consists of three enzymes, namely PGA kinase, G3P dehydrogenase, and phosphoribulokinase. A second group of enzymes catalyzes irreversible reactions. This group also is composed of three enzymes: Rubisco and the two phosphatases. The third group consists of enzymes directing reactions that are reversible and do not consume ATP or reductant. As might be expected, the activity of the last group is virtually unaffected by light or darkness; however, the activities of the first two groups are greatly reduced in the dark. In the first group, the loss of activity is not only a consequence of reduction in the supply of the essential substrates ATP and NADPH, but is also due to allosteric[6] interactions. The reactions do not continue at the expense of ATP and NADPH that might be generated by respiratory pathways. Even if they did, they would constitute a futile cycle with no net $CO_2$ fixation. In the second case, the loss of activity in darkness prevents the concentration of substrates from falling to zero; such a condition would effectively lead to an initial reduction in the efficiency of the cycle in the light.

The regulation of the six enzymes that constitute the first two groups is basically understood, at least in a general sense (MacDonald, Buchanan 1990). Increases in light intensity in the environment are transduced to the stroma by the activity of the photosynthetic electron transport chain as increases in pH, decreases in free $Mg^{2+}$ activity, and an increase in the level of reduction of thioredoxin (Chapter 4). Specifically, by reducing the disulfide groups in the target enzyme, thioredoxin activates FBPase, SBPase, and phosphoglycerate kinase. Additionally, increased light intensity can lead to an increase in the steady-state ratios of ATP/ADP and NADPH/NADP$^+$. The magnitude of these latter changes is not necessarily great, and any regulatory effect on enzyme activity afforded by changes in ATP/ADP and NADPH/NADP$^+$ ratios is likely to be indirect. In contrast, pH, free $Mg^{2+}$ activity and thioredoxin reduction levels are major regulatory signals. Most of the signals (and hence, enzyme activity) reach maximal levels at photon fluence rates considerably lower than those required to saturate $CO_2$ fixation.

These considerations of the regulation of the enzymes in the Calvin–Benson cycle do not directly reveal the rate-limiting step in the pathway. Let us consider three sets of conditions, namely photosynthesis at (1) low (i.e., limiting) inorganic carbon levels, (2) saturating inorganic carbon but light that is not saturating the photosynthetic electron transport chain, and (3) saturating inorganic carbon and light. Strong inferences can be made concerning rate-limiting steps in a metabolic pathway by examining not only the activities of the enzymes in the pathway, but also the concentrations of substrates and products. For example, when $CO_2$ is limiting, Rubisco activity becomes limited by the supply of inorganic carbon. Under such conditions, the other substrate for Rubisco, RuBP, increases while the product

---

6. Allosteric interactions are modifications in the activity of an enzyme by the action of a molecule other than a substrate that changes either the binding affinity for the substrate or the maximal activity of the enzyme.

## ❏ Pool Sizes and Fluxes

*In the analyses of metabolic pathways and other multicomponent systems, it is important to distinguish between pool sizes and fluxes. A pool size is the quantity of a reactant or product of a reaction; it has units of mass per cell or mass per chlorophyll. A flux is the rate at which matter passes through a linear pathway or around a cyclic pathway; it has units of mass per cell (or chlorophyll) per time.*

*At a given steady-state flux, under defined, invariant external conditions and activities of enzymes, the pool sizes of all the intermediates in the pathway are time invariant. This condition (which cannot occur in a photosynthetic organism in nature) comes about because the fluxes of substrates for each reaction are equal to the fluxes of products of each reaction in the pathway.*

*In the overall photosynthetic process, where the Calvin–Benson cycle is coupled to photosynthetic electron transport chain, a perturbation of the system by (for example) a decrease in incident light will lead to an immediate reduction in the fluxes of materials through the light-dependent reactions, that is, in the flux of electrons through the photosystems. Reducing the $CO_2$ supply will reduce the flux of materials through the immediately $CO_2$-dependent reactions, such as Rubisco.*

*In the case of the light reactions, the fluxes of electrons and protons are regulated by the redox state of the electron carriers. For these oxidation–reduction reactions, the total pool size of an intermediate (oxidized plus reduced) component is modified only by net synthesis or net breakdown of the electron transport components. This generally occurs on time scales of many minutes to hours. On increasing the rate of a light reaction, the electron donors to that reaction become more oxidized while the acceptors become more reduced. It is important to understand that though the donors and acceptors are analogous to substrates and products in an enzyme-catalyzed pathway, unlike in enzyme reactions the electron carriers in the electron transport chain are not consumed or synthesized in these reactions.*

*In the Calvin–Benson cycle, the intermediates of the pathways are substrates and products that are continuously produced and consumed. In other words, the pool size of the intermediates is free to vary independently of the level of enzymes that produce or consume them. The changes in pool size can be dramatic (an order of magnitude) and rapid (milliseconds to minutes). For example, the pool size of RuBP decreases when the supply of $CO_2$ increases, leading to a lower rate of resynthesis of the RuBP regenerating reactions in the cycle. On longer time scales (tens of minutes) the activities of the enzymes in the pathway may adjust via allosteric effects which can further moderate the pool sizes of intermediates.*

---

of the enzyme activity, PGA, decreases. When light is limiting, the overall effect is to shift the limitation from Rubisco to the preceding and succeeding reactions that consume ATP and NADPH. Consequently, under such conditions RuBP levels are lower and PGA levels are higher than those under $CO_2$ limitation.

The question as to what is the overall limiting step in the Calvin–Benson cycle when $CO_2$ is saturating Rubisco activity and light is not limiting photosynthetic electron transport remains somewhat open. A compelling argument can be made that, under such conditions, the rate-limiting step is Rubisco activity itself. The evidence for Rubisco as a limiting step is based on correlation and molecular genetic manipulation of the level of expression of the enzyme (Stitt 1986). We will consider this situation further in the context of photosynthesis in continuous light in Chapter 7, but first, let us examine the properties of the enzyme in some detail.

### Rubisco

Rubisco may constitute from 5% to perhaps as much as 50% of the soluble protein in algal cells and is sometimes said to be the single most abundant enzyme in the world. In cyanobacteria, the enzyme is localized in a hexagonal crystalline form surrounded by a protein membrane to form structures called *carboxysomes*. Carboxysomes appear to be virtually pure Rubisco, and are the site of carbon fixation (McKay et al. 1993). In some eukaryotic algae, high concentrations of Rubisco are localized within the stroma in bodies called *pyrenoids* (McKay, Gibbs 1991). Pyrenoids do not appear to be bound by a membrane.

By taking advantage of the long time required for equilibration of $CO_2$ with $HCO_3^-$, Cooper and co-workers (1969) used $^{14}CO_2$ and $H^{14}CO_3^-$ to demonstrate that $CO_2$ rather than $HCO_3^-$ is the substrate for Rubisco (Fig 5.9). In addition to catalysis of a carboxylase reaction Rubisco also catalyzes an oxygenase reaction. These two reactions can be summarized as follows (Andrews et al. 1973; Lorimer 1981):

Carboxylase activity of Rubisco

$$RuBP + CO_2 + H_2O \rightarrow 2[3P\text{-glycerate}] \tag{5.14a}$$

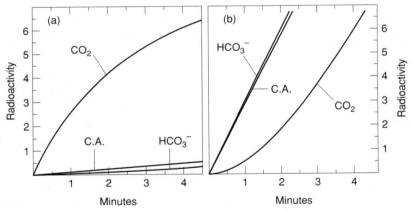

**Figure 5.9** The isotope disequilibrium technique to determine the active species used in carboxylation reactions. Radioactivity refers to the stable organic carbon product obtained following the addition of radioactive $CO_2$ (a) or $HCO_3^-$ (b). The lines designated $CO_2$ are for the situation when the added $CO_2$ is radioactive and the $HCO_3^-$ is unlabeled. Those lines designated $HCO_3^-$ describe the condition when the added $HCO_3^-$ is radioactive and $CO_2$ is unlabeled. Lines designated C.A. pertain to the instance when either member is radioactive and the other is unlabeled in the presence of carbonic anhydrase. The calculations are based on the assumption that the rate of $^{14}C$ incorporation into stable organic carbon is directly proportionate to the concentration of the active species at pH 8.0 at 10°C. (From Cooper et al. 1969)

Oxygenase activity of Rubisco

$$RuBP + O_2 \rightarrow 1[3P\text{-glycerate}] + 1[2P\text{-glycolate}] \tag{5.14b}$$

$CO_2$ and $O_2$ are kinetically competitive (see Fig 5.7). The oxygenase reaction can be quantitatively significant when Rubisco is functioning in high oxygen environments such as air. The oxygenase activity is phenomenologically manifested as a light-dependent consumption of $O_2$. This reaction, together with downstream reactions that are involved in glycolate metabolism, is called *photorespiration*. The oxygenase activity is competitively inhibited by $CO_2$.

Rubisco can be inhibited by the naturally occurring 2-carboxy-D-arabinitol-1-phosphate (CA1P), which competitively blocks the active site for carboxylation on the large subunit (Hartman, Harpel 1994). An artificial substrate analogue, 2-carboxy-D-arabinitol-1,5-bisphosphate (CABP), which can be synthetically made as a [14]C-labeled compound, has a very high affinity for Rubisco and [14]C-labeled CABP is sometimes used to quantify Rubisco.

With an optimal supply of cofactors and carboxylation substrates, the maximum specific reaction rate ($V_{max}$) of Rubisco at 25 °C does not exceed ~60 mol $CO_2$ mol$^{-1}$ enzyme s$^{-1}$. This is low relative to that determined for many other enzymes and, when combined with its relatively high molecular mass, means that the rate of $CO_2$ fixation (mol s$^{-1}$) expressed *per unit mass of protein* is very low relative to the rates at which many other enzymes handle their substrates. The low catalytic efficiency of Rubisco explains why it is such a large fraction of the soluble protein in photosynthetic cells.

There is a considerable range in the affinity of isolated Rubisco for $CO_2$ among the various taxa of photosynthetic organisms. Half-saturation constants ($K_m$'s) range from about 10 to 200 μM. Generally organisms with $CO_2$ pumps, or that normally live in environments with $CO_2$ concentrations well above air-equilibrium values (such as occurs in many freshwater environments), have Rubiscos with relatively high $K_m$ values (Table 5.3). Rubiscos with the highest affinity for $CO_2$ are found in terrestrial vascular $C_3$ plants that rely on $CO_2$ diffusion from the present-day atmosphere (Table 5.3; Read, Tabita 1994).

In addition to the $K_m$ and $V_{max}$ for carboxylation, an important pair of kinetic parameters in the overall function of Rubisco are the $K_m$ and $V_{max}$ for $O_2$ in the oxygenase reaction. A selectivity factor, τ, can be defined that indicates the rates of $CO_2$ fixation relative to $O_2$ fixation when both $CO_2$ and $O_2$ are at limiting concentrations. τ is given by

$$\tau = \frac{V_{maxCO_2} K_{mO_2}}{V_{maxO_2} K_{mCO_2}} \tag{5.15}$$

where $V_{maxO_2}$ is the maximum velocity of the oxygenase activity of Rubisco (mol $O_2$ assimilated per mol enzyme per second), $V_{maxCO_2}$ is the maximum velocity of the carboxylase activity of Rubisco (mol $CO_2$ assimilated per mol enzyme per second), $K_{mO_2}$ is the half-saturation constant for $O_2$ in the oxygenase activity, and $K_{mCO_2}$ is the half-saturation constant for $CO_2$ in the carboxylase activity. The τ values can be used to compute the ratio of oxygenase activity ($v_0$) to carboxylase activity ($v_c$) of

## ❑ ENZYME KINETICS

*An enzyme (E), being a catalyst, lowers the energy barrier between substrates (S) and products (P) and is not itself consumed in the reaction. In so doing, enzymes direct the formation of specific products from specific substrates. The reaction rate is linearly proportional to the concentration of enzyme. The kinetic parameters for enzyme-catalyzed reactions were formulated in 1913 by Michaelis and Menten and serve as the basis for the analysis of many experimental kinetic processes, including the uptake of nutrients by aquatic plants (Dugdale 1967). In the original assumption of Michaelis and Menten, an enzyme reaction could be generalized by the expression*

$$E + S \underset{k_{-1}}{\overset{k_{+1}}{\rightleftharpoons}} ES \xrightarrow{k_{+2}} E + P \qquad (5.16)$$

*The change in concentration of the enzyme-substrate complex (ES) with time is*

$$\frac{d[ES]}{dt} = (k_{+1})[E][S] - (k_1 + k_2)[ES] \qquad (5.17)$$

*where K's are the respective rate constants for the reactions. At steady state, the rate of change of ES is zero, and the overall rate constant for the reaction, $K_m$, is calculated*

$$K_m = \frac{[E][S]}{[ES]} = \frac{k_{-1} + k_{+2}}{k_{+1}} \qquad (5.18)$$

*The velocity, V, of decomposition of ES to the product, is*

$$V = k_{+2} \frac{[E][S]}{K_m + [S]} \qquad (5.19)$$

*At maximum velocity, E = ES, and therefore,*

$$V_{max} = k_{+2}[ES] = k_{+2}[E] \qquad (5.20)$$

*By substitution for $K_{+2}$ [E] in Equation 5.19, we obtain*

$$V = \frac{V_{max}[S]}{K_m + [S]} \qquad (5.21)$$

*Equation 5.21 is the usual representation of the Michaelis–Menten equation and describes a hyberbolic curve between substrate concentration and rate of reaction. The lower the value of $K_m$, the higher the affinity of the enzyme for the substrate, and vice versa.*

*Inhibition of enzyme activity can be broadly categorized as either competitive or noncompetitive. A competitive inhibitor reacts with the enzyme to form an enzyme-inhibitor complex; the reaction proceeds in parallel to the formation of the normal enzyme-substrate complex. The net result is an apparent decrease in the affinity of the enzyme for substrate (i.e., an increase in $K_m$), without altering $V_{max}$. In noncompetitive inhibition, part of the enzyme activity is lost, usually by the irreversible complexation of the enzyme or enzyme-substrate complex with a chemical. A typical example of a noncompetitive inhibitor is $Hg^{2+}$, which binds tightly to sulfhydryl groups. In so doing, part of the enzyme activity is irreversibly lost, resulting in a lowering of $V_{max}$; however, the affinity of the remaining, functional enzyme for its substrates remains unchanged.*

*In the specific case of Rubisco, the $K_m$ for $CO_2$ was, for a long period, over-estimated for in vitro enzyme assays as a result of incomplete activation of the enzyme. Additionally, the maximum activity in vitro was sometimes underestimated by noncompetitive inhibition of the enzyme with impurities (trace metals) in commercial preparations of RuBP. In vivo activity is sometimes markedly reduced compared with that of the fully activated enzyme in vitro as a consequence of both naturally formed competitive and noncompetitive inhibitors in vivo. Thus, the in vivo activity may not truly reflect full activity of the total enzyme concentration.*

———————

the various Rubiscos in air-equilibrium solutions at 25 °C (see Table 5.3). The higher the value of $\tau$, the higher the affinity for $CO_2$ relative to $O_2$.

Values of $\tau$ vary significantly between algal classes. Thermodynamic models of the conformational states of Rubisco suggest that the difference in activation energy between the highest and lowest affinity enzymes is about 4.2 kJ/mole, the equivalent of a single hydrogen bond. Such a change in activation energy is extremely small in such a large molecule, and suggests that very subtle changes in amino acid sequences can produce large effects in substrate affinity. Such subtle changes can be induced by a single amino acid substitution outside of the active site. Based on molecular phylogenetic data, Rubisco in eukaryotic cells appears to have two ancestors. One ancestral form can be traced to β-proteobacteria and is found in Rhodophyceae and chromophytes. A second Rubisco can be traced to cyanobacteria and is found in the plastids of green algae and higher plants. In general, the highest values of $\tau$ are found in eukaryotes with plastids whose Rubisco was derived from β-proteobacteria (Table 5.4), whereas the lowest values are found in cyanobacteria and green algae. A third form, containing only two large subunits and called form II Rubisco, is derived from α-proteobacteria and is found in the Dinophyta (Morse et al. 1995; Whitney et al. 1995); the kinetic properties of that enzyme are not well characterized.

## Photorespiration

The relative amount of oxygenase activity of Rubisco in vivo depends on the intrinsic kinetics of the Rubisco in the organism and the steady-state $CO_2$ and $O_2$ concentrations. Many aquatic plants under natural conditions have an in vivo $O_2/CO_2$ ratio that is less than that found at air equilibrium due to $CO_2$ enrichment of the medium or the $CO_2$ concentrating mechanism. This means that the ratio of oxygenase to carboxylase activity in vivo is usually much less than the ratio in air-equilibrium solution (Raven 1984; Yokota et al. 1987). However, even if the rate of oxygenase activity is low, the photorespiratory production of phosphoglycolate cannot continue indefinitely as it is a sink for phosphorus. Thus, there is an urgent need to metabolize the phosphoglycolate, if only to recycle phosphorus. The first step is hydrolysis to produce inorganic phosphate and glycolate. Some of the glycolate is lost to the outside world as an excreted product. Thus, glycolate excretion is a reflection of photorespiration (i.e., oxygenase activity of Rubisco).

**Table 5.4** Values of $K_{mCO_2}$ (= $K_{1/2(CO_2)}$), $\tau$, $v_0/v_c$ (rate of oxygenase activity [$v_0$] relative to rate of carboxylase activity [$v_c$] by Rubisco in air-equilibrium solution) and $CO_2$ compensation concentration for a P-glycolate metabolic pathway that produces 0.5 $CO_2$ for each 1 $CO_2$ consumed in Rubisco oxygenase. All data are for the $L_8S_8$ form of the enzyme, unless otherwise indicated

| Organisms | $K_c$ (= $K_{1/2}$ $CO_2$) | $\tau$ | $v_0/v_c$ | [$CO_2$]comp $n$/mmol m$^{-3}$ |
|---|---|---|---|---|
| *Rhodospirillum rubrum* ($L_2$) | 89 | $15 \pm 1$ | 1.32 | 7.87 |
| *Rhodopseudomonas sphaeroides* | | | | |
| ($L_2$) | 80 | $9 \pm 1$ | 2.20 | 13.1 |
| ($L_8S_8$) | 36 | $62 \pm 4$ | 0.320 | 1.90 |
| *Synechococcus* sp | 240 | $41 \pm 4.4$ | 0.561 | 2.88–3.55 |
| *Aphanizomenon flosaquae* | 105 | $48 \pm 2$ | 0.413 | 2.45 |
| *Aphanizomenon alpicula* | 80 | $48 \pm 2$ | 0.413 | 2.45 |
| *Coccochloris peniocystis* | 121 | $47 \pm 2$ | 0.437 | 2.60 |
| *Plectonema boryanum* | 100 | $54 \pm 2$ | 0.366 | 2.19 |
| *Chlamydomonas reinhardtii* | 29 | $61 \pm 5$ | 0.324 | 1.93 |
| *Scenedesmus oliquus* | 38 | $63 \pm 2$ | 0.317 | 1.89 |
| *Euglena gracilis* | 25 | $54 \pm 2$ | 0.366 | 2.18 |
| *Polypodium aureum* (fern) | 16 | 82 | 0.241 | 1.44 |
| Mean of 9 terrestrial $C_3$ vascular (flowering) plants | 12 | 79 | 0.251 | 1.49 |
| Mean of 6 terrestrial $C_4$ vascular (flowering) plants | 75 | 75 | 0.269 | 1.57 |
| *Panicum milioides* ($C_3$/$C_4$ intermediate flowering plants) | 76 | 76 | 0.261 | 1.55 |
| *Cylindrotheca* $N_1$ | $105.6 \pm 605$ | $105.6 \pm 6.5$ | 0.187 | 1.11 |
| *Cylindrotheca fusiformis* | $110.8 \pm 9.0$ | $110.8 \pm 9.0$ | 0.179 | 1.06 |
| *Olisthodiscus luteus* (Heterosigma carterae) | $110.5 \pm 58$ | $110.5 \pm 58$ | 0.197 | 1.17 |
| *Porphyridium cruentum* | $128.8 \pm 7.55$ | $128.8 \pm 7.55$ | 0.154 | 0.915 |

However, the excretion rate is not a quantitative index of photorespiration as the majority of the glycolate is further metabolized rather than excreted. The pathways of glycolate metabolism involve the release of between 0.25 and 1.0 carbon atoms per carbon from glycolate that is metabolized, leaving 0 to 0.75 of the remaining carbon from glycolate that can be used for biosynthesis (Raven 1984; Raven 1993). When glycolate is completely oxidized to $CO_2$ some of the energy, but none of the organic carbon, is recovered by the photorespiring organism. The best characterized pathway of glycolate metabolism is that found in higher plants and some green algae (Fig 5.10).

A purely diffusive exchange of $CO_2$ and $O_2$ between the medium, Rubisco, and the sites of $O_2$ evolution would give competitive kinetics for the effects of varied external $O_2$ and $CO_2$ concentrations on the rate of $CO_2$ fixation. In terrestrial $C_3$ plants, which rely purely on diffusive $CO_2$ supply to Rubisco, photorespiratory consumption of $O_2$ can easily be 25% of the activity of the enzyme in vivo (see Raven 1984). In contrast, most aquatic plants have significantly less $O_2$ inhibition of photosynthesis than predicted from Rubisco kinetics (Raven 1984); that is, photorespiration in aquatic plants is usually low.

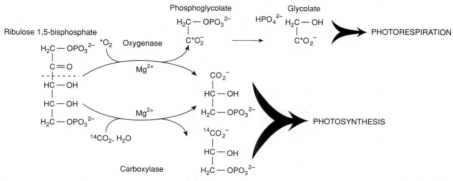

**Figure 5.10** The photorespiratory pathway. If Rubisco oxygenates rather than carboxylates RuBP, a primary product is 2-phosphoglycolate. The product can be dephosphorylated, leading to the formation of glycolate, and subsequently, via amination, to produce glycine and serine (see Lawlor 1993 for more details on this pathway).

## β-Carboxylation

All organisms (including human beings) fix $CO_2$ and/or $HCO_3^-$ in the dark (Table 5.5). Dark carbon fixation was noted in the earliest work using $^{14}CO_2$ to trace the pathways of incorporation of inorganic carbon by Calvin and co-workers (and was largely ignored by them). It is also observed in measurements of macrophyte and phytoplankton primary productivity.

Dark carbon fixation is required to replenish intermediates in metabolic cycles, such as the tricarboxylic acid cycle, when the intermediates are withdrawn for anabolism, or to allow two otherwise competing pathways (e.g., glycolysis and glu-coneogenesis) to operate simultaneously in a cell. Frequently the alternative pathway involves the carboxylation of a substrate. The replacements, or *anaplerotic carboxylations*, thus provide essential compounds for growth that cannot be produced from the Calvin cycle (Dennis, Turpin 1990). Among these are several essential amino acids, tetrapyrroles, pyrimidines, purines, and lipids. The rate of synthesis of these metabolites is generally higher in the light than in the dark (Raven 1976a), so anaplerotic carbon fixation is generally higher in the light. The major anaplerotic carboxylation reactions are catalyzed by phosphoenolpyruvate carboxylase (PEPC), phosphoenolpyruvate carboxykinase (PEPCK), and pyruvate carboxylase (PC). We will discuss these reactions in the context of cell synthesis in Chapter 8. These enzymes catalyze the carboxylation of the β-carbon of 3C substrates, and hence their activity is often called *β-carboxylation*.

The incorporation of inorganic $^{14}C$ in the dark largely reflects β-carboxylation reactions, and has been used as a test for N-limitation of natural phytoplankton assemblages. The rate of β-carboxylation increases following the addition of $NH_4^+$ to N-deficient but not N-replete cells (Guy et al. 1989; Morris et al. 1971). The stimulation, if any, of β-carboxylation induced by the added $NH_4^+$ reflects the anaplerotic formation of amino acids.

Although the predominant short-term (2–10 s) products of inorganic carbon fixation in aquatic plants are three-carbon compounds, approximately 10% of the inorganic carbon can be found in 4C dicarboxylic acids such as malate, aspartate, and

**Table 5.5** Some properties of carboxylases*

| Enzyme | Reaction | Source | $K_{mCO_2}$ (μM) | Molecular Mass | Specific Reaction Rate (sec⁻¹) under Optimal Conditions (25°C) | Role in Aquatic Plants |
|---|---|---|---|---|---|---|
| Rubisco | RuBP + $CO_2$ + $H_2O$ → 2PGA | *Synechococcus* sp | 167–240 (pH 8.3) | 550,000 | 27–29 | Sole carboxylase that converts $CO_2$ into ($CH_2O$), lipids, etc. |
| | | *Chlamydomonas* sp | 29–55 (pH 8.0–8.2) | 15–53 | | |
| Phosphoenol pyruvate carboxylase | PEP + $HCO_3^-$ → OAA + Pi | *Zea mays* | 2 | 400,000 | ≥167 | Anaplerotic role in producing $C_4$ dicarboxylates needed in synthesis of amino acids, porphyrins, pyrimidines; $C_4$ photosynthesis in *Hydrilla* |
| | | *Coccochloris peniocystis* | 8 | ? | | |
| Phosphoenol pyruvate carboxykinase | PEP + $CO_2$ + ADP → OAA + ATP | *Ascophyllum nodosum* | 0.48 (pH 8.0) | (440,000?) | 242 | Probably anaplerotic role as for PEPC; "$C_4$" photosynthesis in *Udotea*. Also operates as decarboxylase |
| Pyruvate carboxylase | pyruvate + $HCO_3^-$ + ATP → OAA + ADP + Pi | *Rattus* | 49 (pH 8) | 700,000 | 208 | Probable anaplerotic role as for PEPC |
| Malic enzyme | pyruvate + NADPH + $H^+$ + $CO_2$ ⇌ malate + Pi | *Solanum tuberosum* | 230 (pH 7.6) | ? | ? | Mainly as decarboxylase |

| Enzyme | Reaction | Organism | | | | Function |
|---|---|---|---|---|---|---|
| Carbamyl phosphate synthetase | $NH_4^+ + HCO_3^- + 2ATP \rightarrow NH_2COOP + 2ADP + Pi$ (affinity for glutamine as N source 50–100× that for $NH_4^+$) | *Pisum sativum* | 16 (pH 8.1) | — | — | Synthesis of arginine, pyrimidines |
| Acetyl CoA carboxylase | acetyl CoA + $HCO_3^-$ + ATP → malonyl CoA + ADP + Pi | *Isochrysis galbana* *Cyclotella cryptica* | 15 (pH 7.9) 6 (pH 8.2) | 700 700 | — 180 | Lipid synthesis (other than fermentative was ester synthesis in *Euglena*) |
| Methylcrotonyl CoA carboxylase | methylcrotonyl CoA + $HCO_3^-$ + ATP → 3-methylglutaconyl CoA + ADP + Pi | *Pisum sativum*, *Solenam tuberosus* | 4–11 | (133×) | — | Catabolism of isoleucine, valine, threonine, methionine, odd-numbered fatty acids |
| Propionyl CoA carboxylase | propionyl CoA + $HCO_3^-$ + ATP → succinyl CoA + ADP + Pi | *Suus* (pig) heart | 49 (pH 8.0) | 700,000 | 252 | Catabolism of leucine; mevalorate shunt |
| Urea amido lyase | Urea + $HCO_3^-$ + ATP → allophanate + ADP + Pi (allophanate → $2NH_4^+$ + $2CO_2$) | — | — | — | — | Conversion of urea to $NH_4^+$ and $HCO_3^-$ in organisms lacking urease |
| 5 amino ribonucleotide carboxylase | 5-aminoimidazole ribonucleotide + $CO_2$ → 5-aminoimidazole-4-carboxylic acid ribonucleotide | — | — | — | — | Purine synthesis |

*Where available, the data are for the enzymes from aquatic photoautotrophs.

oxaloacetate, as well as in the amino acids arginine and citrulline. Radioactive label-ing studies strongly indicate that the four-carbon dicarboxylic acids are primary products, that the initially labeled carbon has not been derived from previously formed three-carbon substrates. The production of oxaloacetate and malate impli-cates PEPC, PC, and/or PEPCK as the enzymes involved in the fixation. PEPC and PC use $HCO_3^-$ (Cooper, Wood 1971), whereas each PEPCK uses $CO_2$ as the inor-ganic carbon substrates (Table 5.5). None of these enzymes displays oxygenase activity. In unicellular algae, these three soluble enzymes are apparently located in the cytoplasm. Like Rubisco, the β-carboxylation reactions do not lead to a bio-chemical reduction of inorganic carbon—no electrons with or without protons have been added.

One carboxylation reaction that is not usually detected in these experiments is acetyl CoA carboxylase (ACC), an enzyme essential in lipid elongation (Fig 5.11). In the latter case, the turnover of $H^{14}CO_3^-$-derived carbon in malonyl-CoA is very rapidly lost (as $^{14}CO_2$) when each two-carbon acetyl unit is added to the growing fatty acid. As each two-carbon unit incorporated into a lipid involves a single inor-ganic carbon fixed by ACC, and half of the total organic carbon produced in net

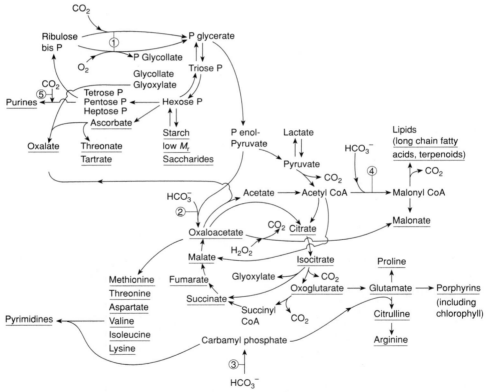

**Figure 5.11** Carboxylation reactions related to biosynthesis in photosynthetic organisms using phosphoenolpyruvate carboxylase (PEPC) as the primary carboxylating enzyme. (1) Rubisco (carboxylase and oxygenase activities), (2) PEPC, (3) carbamyl phosphate synthase (CPS), (4) acetyl CoA carboxylase and (5) 5′-aminomidazole ribonucleotide carboxylase (AIRC). End products of carboxylation reactions are underlined. Not all of the compounds underlined are end-products in all organisms.

productivity can be lipids in diatoms, the required rate of ACC action is $1/4$ of the rate of net carbon fixation on a 24-hour basis (Raven 1995).

In two groups of higher plants, β-carboxylations are exploited to increase carbon fixation efficiency and/or minimize water loss. For example, many succulents (such as *Kalanchoe*, *Sedum*) have developed a metabolic pathway whereby net $CO_2$ (as $HCO_3^-$) fixation occurs at night, forming malic acid. During the day, the malate is decarboxylated by malic enzyme and the $CO_2$ released is fixed by Rubisco. This so-called Crassulacean[7] Acid Metabolism (CAM) reduces water loss by transpiration because stomata only need be open at night when solar energy input to provide the latent heat of evaporation of water is absent. In classic $C_4$ plants, such as sugar cane and many other tropical grasses, the Calvin–Benson cycle is found only in specialized cells, those of the bundle sheath. These cells are surrounded by a mesophyll that contains the β-carboxylation enzymes. This specialized arrangement of cells is known as *Kranz anatomy*. Carbon fixed by the mesophyll leads to the formation of malate or aspartate by the carboxylation of phosphoenolpyruvate through oxaloacetate. The malate or aspartate is then transported to the bundle sheath where it is decarboxylated by malic enzyme or PEPCK. The $CO_2$ so generated is refixed by Rubisco. This process essentially elevates $CO_2$ concentrations in the bundle sheath, leading to a higher ratio of carboxylation/oxygenation for Rubisco. Hence, photorespiratory losses in $C_4$ plants are low relative to $C_3$ plants. In both CAM and $C_4$ plants, the β-carboxylation reactions are the major route of entry of inorganic carbon into photosynthetic carbon fixation; in these plants $C_4$ acids are the major initial-labeled products. *The major point in understanding the potential role of β-carboxylation reactions in the overall net carbon economy of a photosynthetic organism is that these reactions must be segregated either temporally or spatially from the Calvin–Benson cycle*. If such a segregation does not occur, the two reactions are competitive and the decarboxylation of $C_4$ acids cannot lead to a net increase in overall carbon fixation.

In summary, while β-carboxylation reactions are essential for cell metabolism, these pathways are not critically important to the *net* carbon fixation of most aquatic photoautotrophs. Although $C_4$ acids are sometimes identified as the first major labeled product (even in *Chlorella* during acclimation from high to low $CO_2$ conditions; see Graham, Whittingham 1968), these pathways have not been convincingly demonstrated to be a significant source of $CO_2$ for Rubisco in any microalga or cyanobacterium (Kerby, Raven 1985). There is, however, good evidence for both $C_4$-like and CAM pathways in submerged aquatic macrophytes. The only known marine macrophyte with a $C_4$ pathway is the macroalga *Udotea fabellum*, which uses PEPCK as the initial carboxylase (Reiskind, Bowes 1991). In freshwater, some aquatic vascular plants that were primarily $C_4$ or CAM terrestrial plants and reinvaded aquatic environments (so-called secondary aquatic plants) retain their $C_4$ or CAM characteristics when growing submerged (Keeley 1990).

---

7. Named after a family of higher terrestrial plants, the Crassulaceae.

## ❏ ISOTOPE FRACTIONATION IN PHYTOPLANKTON AND HIGHER PLANTS

*Recall that earlier we mentioned that in the fixation of $CO_2$, Rubisco kinetically discriminates against the heavier isotope $^{13}C$, leading to an isotopic fractionation of approximately –25 to –30‰ (Farquhar et al. 1989; Park, Epstein 1961). In the fixation of $HCO_3^-$, PEPC discriminates against $^{13}C$ by only about 3‰ to 5‰. In part, the reduced discrimination for bicarbonate is a consequence of its larger molecular weight; $^{13}CO_2$ is 2.2% heavier than $^{12}CO_2$ while $H^{13}CO_3^-$ is only 1.6% heavier than its $^{12}C$ counterpart. Consequently, plants that use the Calvin–Benson pathway exclusively (i.e., $C_3$ plants) are isotopically enriched in $^{12}C$ relative to plants that utilize β-carboxylation pathways (Table 5.6). In terrestrial plant systems, the two pathways are clearly demarked by their isotopic composition; $C_3$ plants are 10‰ to 15‰ more enriched in $^{12}C$ than are $C_4$ plants. In aquatic systems, however, isotope fractionation patterns appear to be much more complicated and blurred. To a first order, as the Calvin–Benson pathway is predominant, the variations in isotopic composition are strongly influenced by the availability of inorganic carbon in relation to the concentration of $CO_2$ in the water, the diffusion boundary layer, and the rate of photosynthesis (Osmond et al. 1987; Raven et al. 1990). For example, as inorganic carbon becomes limiting, the ability of the organism to discriminate between the two isotopes is reduced. Consequently, the incorporation of $^{13}C$ increases (Zohary et al. 1994). In marine planktonic systems, the isotopic fractionation of carbon leads to formation of organic material with $\delta^{13}C$ of about –18‰ to –22‰, primarily due to an isotopic discrimination at the initial carboxylation reaction of Rubisco. However, the $\delta^{13}C$ of organic carbon in marine macrophytes in "normal" seawater can vary up to 30‰ (–5‰ to –35‰) (Raven et al. 1995). There can be even larger variability in freshwater ecosystems, where there are large variations in inorganic carbon source $\delta^{13}C$ values (Raven et al. 1994).[8] Interspecific variations, the effect of temperature, the occurrence of boundary layers, and the concentration and isotopic composition of the source $CO_2$ and $HCO_3^-$ (not, alas, measured in all data sets) can all lead to different degrees of isotope fractionation (see Falkowski 1991; Rau 1988; Raven et al. 1994; Raven et al. 1995; Thompson, Calvert 1994). It would therefore appear that there is a close inverse correlation between specific growth rate and $\delta^{13}C$ between the medium and the organism in microalgae and macrophytes provided that the specific growth rate is not limited by dissolved inorganic carbon (Laws et al. 1995; Raven et al. 1995).*

### Spatial and Chemical Allocation of the Reduced Carbon Products of the Photosynthetic Carbon Fixation

Products can be removed from the Calvin–Benson cycle as phosphorylated $C_3$, $C_4$, $C_5$, $C_6$, and $C_7$ sugars and as 3PGA, as long as the number of reduced carbon atoms

---

8. Because the $\delta^{13}C$ of the external inorganic carbon can vary markedly in aquatic ecosystems, it is more convenient to report the relative isotope discrimination between an organism and the external source carbon. To this end, a factor, $\varepsilon_p$, can be defined: $\varepsilon_p = 1000(\delta_e - \delta_p)/(1000 + \delta_p)$ where $\delta_e$ and $\delta_p$ are the $\delta^{13}C$ of the external inorganic carbon and the organism's organic carbon, respectively. Laws et al. (1995) showed that for a marine diatom, the relationship between the ratio of the specific growth rate per mole of external $CO_2$ was inversely and linearly proportional to $\varepsilon_p$. Note that $\varepsilon_p = \alpha - 1$ (see Table 5.6).

**Table 5.6** Values of α (kinetic fractionation) for partial processes involved in the assimilation of inorganic carbon and of reactions of oxygen into marine phytoplankton organic material (~25 °C). α is defined as the ratio of the rate constant for a molecule containing the lighter isotope to that for a molecule containing the heavier isotope

| Processes Involving Carbon | α |
|---|---|
| Gaseous $CO_2$ → dissolved $CO_2$ | 1.0010 |
| Dissolved $CO_2$ diffusion in solution | 1.0007 |
|  | 1.0009 |
| Dissolved $CO_2$ or $HCO_3^-$ flux through membranes | 1.00? |
| Uncatalyzed dissolved $CO_2$ → $HCO_3^-$ | 1.013 |
| Uncatalyzed $HCO_3^-$ dissolved $CO_2$ | 1.022 |
| Dissolved $CO_2$ → $HCO_3^-$ catalyzed by carbonic anhydrase | 1.0001 |
| $HCO_3^-$ → $CO_2$ catalyzed by carbonic anhydrase | 1.0101 |
| Fixation of dissolved $CO_2$ by eukaryotic Rubisco | 1.029 |
| Fixation of dissolved $CO_2$ by cyanobacterial Rubisco | 1.022 |
|  | 1.025 |
| Fixation of dissolved $CO_2$ by β-proteobacterial Rubisco | 1.018 |
| Fixation of $HCO_3^-$, expressed in terms of dissolved $CO_2$, by PEPC | 1.0047 |
| Fixation of $HCO_3^-$, expressed in terms of dissolved $CO_2$, by CPS | 1.001? |
| Fixation of dissolved $CO_2$ by PEPCK | 1.024–1.040 |
| Carboxylation reactions ("intrinsic" isotope effects) | ~1.060 |
| Decarboxylation reactions ("intrinsic" isotope effects) | 1.06 |
| Enzymatic decarboxylations (9 examples of $RCOO^-$ H+ → RH $CO_2$) | 0.9989–1.032 |
| **Processes Involving Oxygen** |  |
| Gaseous $O_2$ → dissolved $O_2$ | 1.0028 |
| Conversion of $H_2O$ to $O_2$ by photosystem II | 0.9997 |
| $O_2$ uptake by cytochrome oxidase | 1.0204 |
| $O_2$ uptake by the alternate oxidase | 1.0306 |
| $O_2$ uptake by the oxygenase activity of Rubisco | 1.0208 |
| $O_2$ uptake by glycolate oxidase | 1.0222 |
| $O_2$ uptake by Mehler reaction | 1.0151 |

(Modified from Raven 1997b)

removed is balanced by fixation. In cyanobacteria, the photosynthetic products are freely available for storage and biosynthetic reactions anywhere in the cell. With the exception of the Viridiplantae, all other taxa store their "reserve" polysaccharide outside the chloroplasts, so a smaller fraction of the total cell carbon is present in the chloroplasts (see Chapter 8). In eukaryotes, however, the products of the cycle are only freely available if these are exported from the plastids. In unicellular algae, chloroplasts typically contain at least half of the total cellular complement of carbon and nitrogen, so at least half of the carbon fixed is retained in the chloroplast. However, well over half of the reduced carbon must leave the chloroplast even if the reduced carbon atoms subsequently return in a different chemical form.

## DOES INORGANIC CARBON SUPPLY LIMIT PHOTOSYNTHESIS AND GROWTH IN NATURE?

Investigations of short-term photosynthetic responses to changes in inorganic carbon supply for organisms grown under their "natural" conditions suggest that most of the marine phytoplankton are not carbon limited. In general, aquatic photoautotrophs that can actively transport inorganic carbon suppress the oxygenase and stimulate the carboxylase activities of Rubisco. In these organisms, photosynthesis is saturated with respect to inorganic carbon at the levels normally found in seawater. One possible exception is the coccolithophorid *Emiliana huxleyi* and probably other coccolithophorids (Merrett 1991; Raven, Johnston 1991). In *Emiliana*, the inorganic carbon pump does not appear to influence the behavior of Rubisco to the extent that occurs in diatoms, and the cells appear to be undersaturated with respect to dissolved inorganic carbon at the concentrations typical of seawater (Nielsen 1995), although growth seems to be inorganic carbon–saturated in seawater (Paasche et al. 1996). The phytoplankton in general appear to be able to acclimate physiologically their inorganic carbon acquisition mechanisms such that when transferred from high to low inorganic carbon concentrations, they develop a higher affinity for inorganic carbon. Riebesell and co-workers (1993) suggested that the growth of many diatoms is close to or actually limited by inorganic $CO_2$ in the present-day ocean, but this remains an open question. However, if the diatoms and cyanobacteria showing extensive acclimation (Raven 1991a; Raven 1993) are typical of marine phytoplankton, then photosynthesis would have been saturated with inorganic carbon even in the relatively low $CO_2$ environments that appear to have been characteristic of glacial times.

The effect of inorganic carbon limitation on photosynthesis can be further inferred from measurement of the *compensation concentration of $CO_2$*. When an organism relying on diffusive $CO_2$ entry is illuminated in a closed system it will come to the compensation concentration. This is the $CO_2$ concentration in the medium at which $CO_2$ uptake by Rubisco (plus other anaplerotic carboxylases operating in parallel with it) is equal to $CO_2$ production by all respiratory pathways. For the Rubisco-related processes the $CO_2$ and $O_2$ uptake rates are $V_c$ and $V_o$ respectively, and the $CO_2$ evolution rate via photorespiration pathway is $0.5\,V_o$. At the $CO_2$ compensation concentration ($[CO_2]_{comp}$), $V_o/V_c = 2$.

$$\text{Because} \quad \frac{V_o}{V_c} = \frac{[O_2]}{[CO_2] \cdot \tau} \tag{5.22a}$$

$$\text{and} \quad \frac{[O_2]}{[CO_2]_{comp} \cdot \tau} = 2 \tag{5.22b}$$

$$\text{thus} \quad [CO_2]_{comp} = \frac{[O_2]}{2\tau} \tag{5.22c}$$

The computed values for $[CO_2]_{comp}$ range from 2.45–3.55 mmol m$^{-3}$ for cyanobacteria down to 0.915 mmol m$^{-3}$ for the red alga *Porphyridium* (see Table 5.3). As $CO_2$ fixation by anaplerotic carboxylases is less than $CO_2$ production for "dark" respiration in the light, these computed $[CO_2]_{comp}$ values are minimal estimates for $[CO_2]_{comp}$ in vivo (Brooks, Faraquhar 1985). Accordingly, any measured value for $[CO_2]_{comp}$ in vivo that is less than the computed $[CO_2]_{comp}$ value suggests the presence of a $CO_2$-concentrating mechanism, and moreover, suggests that the presence of such a mechanism markedly reduces the potential limitation of photosynthesis by the availability of inorganic carbon.

The relationship between carbon assimilation rates (i.e., photosynthesis) in vivo and the concentration of $CO_2$ can be described by a hyperbolic function comparable to that for enzyme kinetics. In general, however, the half-saturation constant for the uptake of $CO_2$ for photosynthesis (often called the $K_{s(CO_2)}$) is lower than the $K_{mCO_2}$ for isolated Rubisco. Before we can use this as an indication that the $CO_2$ supply is other than by $CO_2$ diffusion, the potential for light- and $CO_2$-saturated photosynthesis in vivo must be compared with the Rubisco carboxylase activity from that organism when the enzyme is fully activated and has optimal substrate and cofactor supply. Such a comparison must, of course, be normalized to equal biomasses from the two measurements. A twofold "excess" of in vitro Rubisco activity over the in vivo rate of inorganic carbon acquisition at light and $CO_2$ saturation could then account for $K_s$ with respect to $CO_2$ that was half of that of the $K_m$ for Rubisco in vitro. Many of the discrepancies between $K_s$ and $K_m$ values are much larger than this, and it is unlikely that the excess of Rubisco activity in vitro can account for them (Raven 1984; Sukenik et al. 1987b). Furthermore, variations in $K_{s(CO_2)}$ with changes in the external inorganic carbon supply are not paralleled by changes in Rubisco catalytic capacity in vivo (e.g., Raven 1991a, 1993).

Macrophytes with high affinities for inorganic carbon are mainly found in high-light intertidal habitats, and have light-saturated photosynthetic rates that are saturated by seawater levels of inorganic carbon. The organisms that are not saturated with inorganic carbon in high light are more commonly found in lower irradiance environments when synthetic rates may be light, rather than carbon, limited. In marine macrophytes that rely on a diffusive $CO_2$ supply to Rubisco, photosynthesis is saturated with $CO_2$ under conditions of high light. However, photosynthesis is usually saturated with inorganic carbon in their normal, low-photon flux density habitats (Johnston et al. 1992; Maberly et al. 1992).

Freshwater environments have a much greater range of inorganic carbon concentrations and speciation (as previously discussed) and generalizations about the extent of inorganic carbon limitation are very difficult to sustain. For phytoplankton, large lakes (e.g., the Great Lakes of North America) may be insulated by their size from the impact of changes in inorganic carbon concentrations. Smaller water bodies frequently have free $CO_2$ concentrations in excess of air-equilibrium concentrations. Saline lakes often have $CO_2/HCO_3^-$ as their major anions. $CO_2$ in such lakes is often close to air-equilibrium levels. Generally, phytoplankton photosynthesis in lakes is saturated by inorganic carbon. However, if (nonsaline) lakes are nutrient-rich, inorganic carbon may be depleted as phytoplankton assimilate inorganic carbon, nitrogen, and phosphorus (Chapter 8). Some of the algae in such lakes apparently have $CO_2$-concentrating mechanisms as they can acclimate to lower inorganic carbon concentrations by increasing their affinity for inorganic carbon without significantly decreasing their saturated rate of photosynthesis.

Freshwater macrophytes have a wide range of mechanisms for inorganic carbon acquisition (Raven 1984). This will be considered later in the context of their evolutionary origins, and particularly multiple origins of freshwater tracheophytes and bryophytes from several terrestrial ancestors. The various means of direct or indirect uptake of $HCO_3^-$, acquisition of $CO_2$ directly from the high-$CO_2$ root environment, and CAM all help to offset the inorganic carbon limitation that would occur in organisms relying on a diffusive $CO_2$ supply to Rubisco. These various mechanisms may not always prevent $CO_2$ limitation at light-saturated photosynthesis under natural conditions. However, they are typically sufficient to allow inorganic C-saturated photosynthesis under lower photon fluence rate, typically found in natural aquatic ecosystems. A number of freshwater macrophytes use $HCO_3^-$ and have been shown to acclimate to lower inorganic carbon concentrations by increasing the expression of carbon-concentrating processes (Raven, Johnston 1993). Organisms with a diffusive $CO_2$ supply to Rubisco do not show acclimation of inorganic carbon affinity to changed external inorganic carbon concentrations (Madsen 1993).

Overall, inorganic carbon probably does not limit photosynthesis in most aquatic photoautotrophs. It is potentially limiting in some freshwater phytoplankton, macrophytes, seagrasses, and perhaps some marine phytoplankton (as suggested earlier in the case of *Emiliana*). Regardless, dissolved inorganic carbon is likely to be even less frequently limiting for growth (Raven et al. 1993), despite significant photosynthetic drawdown of inorganic carbon in nature, including the open ocean under bloom conditions (Codispoti et al. 1982).

In the next chapter, we will examine the molecular architecture of the photosynthetic machinery and some aspects of how the synthesis of the components is regulated.

# 6

# The Molecular Structure of the Photosynthetic Apparatus

As described in the preceding chapters, photosynthesis involves light harvesting, primary charge separation in PSII and PSI, electron transport, ATP and NADPH formation, carbon fixation, and regeneration of substrates in the Calvin–Benson cycle. The biophysical and biochemical integration of photosynthetic processes requires the synthesis and coordinated assembly of numerous proteins, lipids, prosthetic groups, and cofactors. The synthesis and assembly of all of the molecules that make up the photosynthetic apparatus are controlled and directed by the genetic machinery of the organism. Significant advances in understanding photosynthetic processes, evolutionary relationships, and trends among photosynthetic organisms, as well as the mechanisms and regulation of response to environmental cues, have emerged from studies of the molecular genetics and structure of key components of the photosynthetic apparatus. These studies have particularly helped in testing biophysical and biochemical models and hypotheses for the mechanisms and control of partial photosynthetic reactions. Here we examine some of the basic elements related to the molecular biology and structure of the photosynthetic apparatus. We will primarily focus on the light-harvesting systems, the two reaction centers, the ATP synthase complex, and Rubisco.

## THE LOCATION AND MAPS OF THE PHOTOSYNTHETIC GENES

In all eukaryotic photosynthetic cells, the photosynthetic genes are distributed between two distinct genetic compartments, namely the nucleus and the chloroplast. The genes encoded in the nucleus are transcribed there, and the messenger RNA is translated in the cytoplasm on 80S ribosomes. The resulting proteins are imported into the chloroplast and directed to specific locations (for example, the thylakoid membrane). The nuclear-encoded proteins are frequently modified in the chloroplast by specific proteases that cleave a signal or transit peptide. These signal or transit sequences contain molecular "addresses" that facilitate transport across organellar membranes and direct the protein to specific macromolecular complexes (Anderson, Gray 1991; Apt et al. 1994; Bustos, Golden 1991; Franzen et al. 1990).

The chloroplast-encoded genes are transcribed in the chloroplasts and the mRNAs are translated on 70S ribosomes within the organelle. Chloroplast-encoded genes, which are maternally inherited in oogamous aquatic plants, are generally far more conserved (less variable) than nuclear-encoded genes. Hence, much of the photosynthetic apparatus, such as the key reaction center proteins, the catalytic subunit of Rubisco, parts of the ATP synthase, and the cytochrome $b_6/f$ complex, are encoded in the chloroplast genome, and the molecular sequence and structure of these proteins are relatively conserved from the most ancient cyanobacteria to macrophytes and higher plants (Barber J 1992; Bryant 1994; Morden, Golden 1987). In contrast, nuclear-encoded genes, such as the light-harvesting pigment proteins, usually display far more variation, reflecting a higher degree of evolutionary selection and possibly mutation (Reith 1995).

## Gene Nomenclature

A system of nomenclature exists for photosynthetic genes. For example, genes encoding proteins for a specific photosystem are denoted as psa or psb, where ps is shorthand notation for "photosystem" and the "a" refers to PSI and "b" to PSII. Specific genes are assigned to the respective ps by a capital letter starting from A in accordance with the sequence of their discovery. For example, psbA was the first gene identified for PSII, and codes for the reaction center protein D1. The second gene identified, psbB, codes for a protein designated CP47, a chlorophyll-binding protein that serves to transfer excitation energy from the main light-harvesting antenna to the reaction center. Similarly, psaA is a gene encoding one of the two major proteins that make up the PSI reaction center, and so on. Nuclear-encoded genes are indicated by a capital letter in the first letter of the gene name (e.g., Lhca1, Lhcb4); plastid-encoded genes are not capitalized (e.g., pcbA).

A list of the basic genes and their products is given in Table 6.1. Similar nomenclatures are prescribed for the cytochrome $b_6/f$ complex, where the *p*hotosynthetic *e*lectron *t*ransport (i.e., pet) genes encode for the proteins that make up the complex. The ATPase or coupling factor genes are designated by atpA to atpI. Rubisco is composed of two proteins of different molecular mass: a small subunit encoded by a gene designated rbcS in red algae and chromophytes (Rbcs in Viridiplantae) and a large subunit encoded by rbcL. The names for the genes encoding light-harvesting chlorophyll proteins were originally derived from a nomenclature from higher plant genetics, where the *c*hlorophyll *a*, *b* genes (i.e., cab) were first identified. Subsequently, cab genes have been renamed *l*ight-*h*arvesting *c*hlorophyll genes, or Lhc, with photosystem designation denoted by a or b. Thus, Lhcb1 is a nuclear gene encoding for a light-harvesting chlorophyll protein that binds chlorophylls *a* and *b* and is associated primarily with photosystem II. As most algal classes do not contain chlorophyll *b*, the genes are usually named according to the chromophore bound to the protein. For example, the fucoxanthin chlorophyll proteins in chromophytes (FCPs), the peridinin chlorophyll proteins (PCPs) of dinoflagellates, and the phycobiliproteins of the cyanobacteria and cryptomonads are major groups of light-harvesting complexes; found uniquely in algae, their proteins are encoded by unique genes with common elements within the three groups (Green, Durnford 1996).

The expression of genes can be, and usually is, controlled at a number of levels, and the level of control is often dependent on the gene location and its product. It

**Table 6.1** Major photosynthetic genes identified in aquatic oxygenic photoautotrophs

| Gene[a] | Function | Organism | Total Codons[b] |
|---|---|---|---|
| petA | cytochrome *f* | *C. reinhardtii* | 316 |
| | | *C. reinhardtii* (strain 137c) | 317 |
| | | *C. reinhardtii* (strain cw-15) | 317 |
| | | *Synechocystis* sp (PCC 6803) | 328 |
| petB | cytochrome $b_6$ | *C. reinhardtii* (strain 137c) | 215 |
| | | *Chlorella protothecoides* (strain 211-7A) | 215 |
| | | *Synechocystis* sp (PCC 6803) | 222 |
| | | *Prochlorothrix hollandica* | 222 |
| | | *Synechococcus* (PCC 7942) | 215 |
| PetC | Reiske Fe-S polypeptide, subunit III | *Synechocystis* (PCC 6803) | 192 |
| | | *Synechocystis* (PCC 6803) | 180 |
| petD | cytochrome $b_6$-*f* complex, subunit IV | *C. reinhardtii* | 160 |
| | Rieske Fe-S polypeptide, subunit IV | *Chlorella protothecoides* (strain 211-7A) | 160 |
| | | *Prochlorothrix hollandica* | 160 |
| | | *Synechococcus* (PCC 7942) | 160 |
| | | *C. reinhardtii* (strain 2137 mt⁺) | 160 |
| | | *Chlamydomonas eugametos* | 160 |
| | | *Synechocystis* sp (PCC 6803) | 160 |
| PetE | plastocyanin | *Synechocystis* sp (PCC 6803) | 126 |
| | | *Prochlorothrix hollandica* | 131 |
| | | *Synechococcus lividus* | 125 |
| PetF | ferredoxin I | *Synechococcus* sp | 97 |
| | | *Anabaena* sp | 99 |
| | | *Anacystis nidulans* | 99 |
| petG | cytochrome $b_6$-*f* complex, subunit V | *Chlamydomonas eugametos* | 37 |
| | | *Chlamydomonas reinhardtii* | 37 |
| PetH | ferredoxin-NADPH reductase | *Anabaena* sp | 440 |
| | | *Synechococcus* sp | 402 |
| PetI (IsiB) | flavodoxin | *Synechococcus* sp | 170 |
| | | *Anacystis nidulans* | 170 |
| | | *Synechocystis* sp | 170 |
| PetJ | cytochromes $c_{553}$, $c_6$ | *Synechocystis* sp | 120 |
| PetK | cytochrome $c_{550}$ | *Synechocystis* sp | 407 |
| PetL | cytochrome $b_6$-*f* complex, 3.5 kDa subunit | None reported for cyanobacteria or algae | 28 |
| PetM | cytochrome $b_6$-*f* complex, 4 kDa subunit cytochrome $b_6$-*f*, subunit VII PetM protein | *Chlamydomonas reinhardtii* | 100 |
| psaA | P700-Chla protein, subunit la | *Anabaena variabilis* | 752 |
| | | *Synechocystis* sp (PCC 6803) | 751 |
| | | *Synechococcus* sp | 755 |
| | | *Synechococcus vulcanus* | 755 |
| psaB | P700-Chla protein, subunit lb | *Anabaena variabilis* | 741 |
| | | *Synechocystis* sp (PCC 6803) | 731 |
| | | *Synechococcus* sp | 741 |
| | | *Synechococcus vulcanus* | 741 |
| psaC | 8 kDa 2(4Fe-4S) protein; binds iron-sulfur clusters that are terminal electron acceptors in PSI | *Synechococcus vulcanus* | 81 |
| | | *Anabaena* sp | 81 |
| | | *Synechococcus* sp | 81 |
| | | *Synechocystis* sp (PCC 6803) | 81 |
| | | *Chlamydomonas reinhardtii* | 81 |
| PsaD | ferredoxin docking protein | *C. reinhardtii* | 196 |
| | | *Synechococcus* sp | 139 |
| | | *Synechocystis* sp | 141 |
| PsbP | 23 kDa oxygen evolving protein of photosystem II | None reported for cyanobacteria or algae | 258 Higher plants |
| PsbQ | 16 kDa PSII protein | None reported for cyanobacteria or algae | 149 Higher plants |
| PsbR | 10 kDa PSII protein | None reported for cyanobacteria or algae | 99 Higher plants |
| PsbS | 22 kDa PSII protein, CP24 | None reported for cyanobacteria or algae | 274 Higher plants |
| PsbT | PSII subunit | None reported for cyanobacteria or algae | 31 |
| PsbU | Not reported in GENBANK | None reported for cyanobacteria or algae | |

**Table 6.1** *Continued*

| Gene[a] | Function | Organism | Total Codons[b] |
|---|---|---|---|
| PsbV | cytochrome c-550 signal peptide | *Synechocystis* sp (PCC 6803) | 160 |
| PsbW | 6.1 kDa PSII protein | None reported for cyanobacteria or algae | 137 Higher plants |
| PsbX | 23 kDa PSII protein | None reported for cyanobacteria or algae | 258 Higher plants |
| Psb1 | oxygen evolving enhancer 1 (OEE1), precursor protein | *Chlamydomonas reinhardtii* | 291 |
| Psb2 | oxygen evolving enhancer 2 (OEE2), | *Chlamydomonas reinhardtii* | 245 |
| Psb3 | oxygen evolving enhancer 3 (OEE3), precursor protein | *Chlamydomonas reinhardtii* | 199 |
| Fcp | fucoxanthin-chlorophyll binding protein | *Macrocystis pyrifera* | 217 |
|  |  | *Isochrysis galbana* | 201 |
| FcpA | fucoxanthin-chlorophyll binding protein | *Phaeodactylum tricornutum* | 196 |
| FcpB | fucoxanthin-chlorophyll binding protein | *Odontella sinensis* | 203 |
|  |  | *Phaeodactylum tricornutum* | 198 |
| FcpC | fucoxanthin-chlorophyll binding protein | *Phaeodactylum tricornutum* | 197 |
| FcpD | fucoxanthin-chlorophyll binding protein | *Phaeodactylum tricornutum* | 197 |
| FcpE | fucoxanthin-chlorophyll binding protein | *Phaeodactylum tricornutum* | 197 |
| FcpF | fucoxanthin-chlorophyll binding protein | *Phaeodactylum tricornutum* | 197 |
| Lhcb1 | 28.5 kDa LHCII apoprotein | *Dunaliella tertiolecta* | 253 Mature peptide |
| pcb | 35 kDa Chlorophyll a/b binding protein | *Prochlorococcus marinus* | 352 Mature peptide |
| cpcA | phycocyanin, α-subunit | *Pseudanabaena* sp | 162 |
|  |  | *Synechocystis* sp (PCC 6803) | 162 |
| cpcB | phycocyanin, β-subunit | *Pseudanabaena* sp | 172 |
|  |  | *Synechocystis* sp (PCC 6803) | 172 |
| cpeA | phycoerythrin, α-subunit | *Pseudanabaena* sp | 164 |
| cpeB | phycoerythrin, β-subunit | *Pseudanabaena* sp | 185 |
| Pcp | peridinin chlorophyll protein | *Amphidinium carterae* (CS-21) | 369 |
|  |  | *Symbiodinium* sp | 365 |
| atpA | ATP synthase, CF1 alpha subunit | *Chlamydomonas reinhardtii* | 454 |
|  |  | *Synechocystis* sp (PCC 6803) | 504 |
|  |  | *Anabaena* sp | 506 |
| atpB | ATP synthase, CF1 beta subunit | *Chlamydomonas reinhardtii* | 574 |
|  |  | *Chlamydomonas reinhardtii* | 491 |
|  |  | *Anabaena* sp | 471 |
|  |  | *Prochloron didemni* | 483 |
|  |  | *Synechocystis* sp (PCC 6803) | 483 |
| AtpC | ATP synthase, CF1 gamma subunit | *Phaeodactylum tricornutum* | 370 |
|  |  | *Synechocystis* sp (PCC 6803) | 314 |
|  |  | *Anabaena* sp | 315 |
| AtpD | ATP synthase, CF1 delta subunit | *Synechocystis* sp (PCC 6803) | 185 |
|  |  | *Anabaena* sp | 183 |
| PsaE | PSI-subunit IV, role in cyclic electron transport? | *Synechococcus* sp | 70 |
|  |  | *Synechococcus* sp (PCC 6301) | 75 |
|  |  | *Synechococcus* sp | 76 |
|  |  | *Synechocystis* sp | 74 |
| PsaF | plastocyanin docking protein | *Synechococcus* sp | 164 |
|  |  | *Synechocystis* sp | 165 |
|  |  | *Synechocystis* sp (PCC 6803) | 165 |
| PsaG | PSI, 10 kDa subunit (polypeptide 35) | *Chlamydomonas reinhardtii* | 126 |
| PsaH | PSI, 11 kDa subunit (polypeptide 28) | *C. reinhardtii* (WT 137c) | 130 |
| PsaI | PSI, small subunit (subunit XIII) | *Synechocystis* sp (PCC 6803) | 130 |
|  |  | *Synechococcus* sp | 38 |
| PsaJ | PSI subunit | *Synechococcus* sp | 41 |
|  |  | *Synechocystis* sp | 40 |
| PsaK | PSI subunit X, polypeptide 37 precursor, 8.4 kDa | *C. reinhardtii* (WT 137c) | 114 |
|  |  | *Synechococcus* sp | 83 |
| PsaL | PSI, large subunit (subunit XI) | *Synechocystis* sp (PCC 6803) | 69 |
|  |  | *Synechococcus* sp | 149 |
| psbA | 32 kDa Qb protein, D1 (herbicide binding protein) | *Prochlorothrix hollandica* | 353 |
|  |  | *Prochlorococcus marinus* | 360 |
|  |  | *Synechococcus elongatus* | 360 |
|  |  | *Synechocystis* sp (PCC 6803) | 360 |
|  |  | *Synechocystis* 6714 | 360 |

**Table 6.1** *Continued*

| Gene[a] | Function | Organism | Total Codons[b] |
|---------|----------|----------|-----------------|
| psbB | 47 kDa Chla protein, CP47 | *Prochlorothrix hollandica* | 514 |
| | | *Synechococcus* sp | 508 |
| | | *Synechocystis* sp | 507 |
| | | *Chlamydomonas reinhardtii* | 508 |
| psbC | 43 kDa Chla protein, CP43 | *Chlamydomonas reinhardtii* | 461 |
| | | *Synechococcus* sp | 461 |
| psbD | 34 kDa protein, D2 | *Chlamydomonas reinhardtii* | 352 |
| psbE | 9 kDa cytochrome b-559, β-Subunit | *Chlamydomonas reinhardtii* (CC-125) | 82 |
| | | *Synechocystis* sp (PCC 6803) | 81 |
| psbF | 4 kDa cytochrome b-559, α-Subunit | *Synechocystis* sp (PCC 6803) | 44 |
| | | *Chlamydomonas reinhardtii* | 44 |
| | | *Chlamydomonas eugametos* | 44 |
| psbG | PSII-G protein, 24 kDa polypeptide | *Synechocystis* sp (PCC 6803) | 248 |
| psbG2? | possible NAD(P)H dehydrogenase subunit | *Synechocystis* sp (PCC 6803) | 219 |
| psbH | PSII Reaction center, 10 kDa phosphoprotein | *Chlamydomonas reinhardtii* | 88 |
| | | *Synechocystis* sp (PCC 6803) | 64 |
| psbH | open reading frame 1 | *Prochlorothrix hollandica* | 90 |
| psbH | open reading frame 2 | *Prochlorothrix hollandica* | 64 |
| psbI | PSII-I polypeptide | *Anacystis nidulans* | 39 |
| psbJ | cytochrome b-559 apoprotein | None reported for cyanobacteria or algae | 40 |
| psbK | PSII-K polypeptide, 4 kDa | *Synechocystis* sp (PCC 6803) | 37 Mature peptide |
| | | *Chlamydomonas reinhardtii* | 37 Mature peptide |
| | | *Anacystis nidulans* | 35 Mature peptide |
| psbL | PSII-L polypeptide, photoelectron transport | *Chlamydomonas eugametos* | 38 |
| | | *Chlamydomonas reinhardtii* | 44 |
| psbM | PSII-M polypeptide | None reported for cyanobacteria or algae | 34 Higher plants |
| psbN | PSII-N polypeptide | *Synechocystis* (PCC 6803) | 43 |
| | | *Chlamydomonas reinhardtii* | 44 |
| psbO | PSII-O polypeptide, Mn-stabilizing protein | *Synechococcus elongatus* | 102 |
| atpE | ATP synthase, CF1 epsilon subunit | *Chlamydomonas reinhardtii* | 141 |
| | | *Chlorella ellipsoidea* | 134 |
| | | *Anabaena* sp | 137 |
| | | *Synechocystis* sp (PCC 6803) | 136 |
| | | *Synechococcus* sp | 137 |
| atpF | ATP synthase, CF0, b subunit | *Synechocystis* sp (PCC 6803) | 179 |
| | | *Anabaena* sp | 187 |
| atpG | ATP synthase, CF0, b′ subunit | *Synechocystis* sp (PCC 6803) | 143 |
| | | *Anabaena* sp | 163 |
| atpH | ATP synthase, CF0, c subunit | *Chlamydomonas reinhardtii* | 82 |
| | | *Synechocystis* sp (PCC 6803) | 81 |
| | | *Anabaena* sp | 81 |
| atpI | ATP synthase, CF0, a subunit | *Synechocystis* sp (PCC 6803) | 276 |
| | | *Anabaena* sp | 251 |
| rbcL | RUBISCO, large subunit | *Anabaena* sp | 476 |
| | | *Prochlorothrix hollandica* | 470 |
| | | *Cylindrotheca* sp | 490 |
| | | *Pleurochrysis carterae* | 488 |
| | | *Synechococcus* sp | 474 |
| rbcS[c] | RUBISCO, small subunit | *Anabaena* sp | 110 |
| | | *Prochlorothrix hollandica* | 109 |
| | | *Chlamydomonas moewusii* | 140 Mature peptide |
| | | *Cylindrotheca* sp | 140 |
| | | *Pleurochrysis carterae* | 139 |
| | | *Synechococcus* sp | 118 |

[a] First letter of chloroplast gene is lower case; nuclear gene is upper case.
[b] The total codons approximately correspond to the number of amino acids in the gene product. The approximate molecular mass (in daltons) of the gene product can be estimated by multiplying the number of codons by 110.
[c] Nuclear encoded for chlorophytes; chloroplast encoded for chromophytes.

is not our purpose or intention to review the molecular basis of gene expression here, but rather discuss salient points that will help convey key concepts in gene expression in algal cells, especially in relation to the assembly, function, and repair of the photosynthetic apparatus.

## ❏ CODONS AND CODON USAGE

*Each primary amino acid is "encoded" by three nucleotides that collectively are referred to as a* codon. *As there are four nucleotides, the number of possible codons is $4^3 = 64$. There are 20 primary amino acids. Thus, some amino acids may have more than one codon (Fig 6.1). Because of this degeneracy of information, it is not possible to absolutely predict the nucleotide (e.g., DNA) sequence from an amino acid sequence, although the converse is straightforward. In practice, the third-base position in a codon is much more variable than the first two, and some organisms use codons enriched in G and C in the third position, while others favor A and T. For example, some Viridiplantae, such as the green algae* Chlamydomonas *sp or* Dunaliella *sp, have high G/C codon usage in the third position, while Bacillariophyceae appear to be generally more skewed toward A/T (Grossman et al. 1990; LaRoche et al. 1990). In theory, a G/C bias might be expected to confer thermal stability to the double helix structure of DNA as this base pairing leads to three hydrogen bonds, where the A-T base pair has only two hydrogen bonds. However, thermophilic organisms appear to equally use G/C and A/T in the third position, and no specific reason that explains the advantage for a specific codon usage has emerged.*

---

### Regulation of Gene Expression

All genes can be roughly divided into two parts: (1) a coding region consisting of nucleotides that contain codons for specific amino acids that constitute the gene product, and (2) a noncoding, control region that is usually oriented 5' to the coding region.[1] The control region contains the promotor elements, where RNA polymerase binds to DNA and initiates transcription (Alberts et al. 1983).

Transcriptional control is based on the ability to regulate the rate of synthesis of mRNA for a specific gene product. This is usually achieved by altering the affinity of specific areas in the control region of the gene to bind DNA-dependent RNA polymerase. In prokaryotic cells RNA polymerase binding is regulated by a specific peptide that is an integral part of the enzyme (Houmard 1994). The subunit structure of RNA polymerase contains a series of core polypeptides, designated α, β, β', and γ, and a variable polypeptide region is designated σ. The binding of the polymerase to DNA is determined largely by the σ region. These so-called σ factors are elements that recognize a DNA sequence as being a binding site for RNA polymerase and help the enzyme to initiate transcription properly. Similar sequences have been identified in chloroplasts; however, as they are not identical to prokaryotic σ factors, they are called sigma-like factors (SLF). In the nucleus of eukaryotic cells, the binding of RNA is directed by multiple control factors; however, a specific binding region, approximately 25 bases upstream (i.e., 5') to the coding region, contains the nucleotide sequence TAAAAT, which is a consensus recognition site. Many

---

1. The orientation of DNA is specified on the basis of the orientation of the bound deoxyribose. The 5' end of the sugar is covalently bound to a phosphate ester, whereas the 3' end contains a hydroxyl group. In the replication of DNA, the DNA polymerase adds nucleotides from the 5' to the 3' end. Hence, nucleotides 5' to a coding region are "upstream," meaning in front of the coding region.

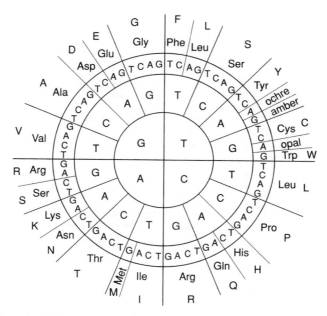

**Figure 6.1** The codon wheel. Each primary amino acid found in protein is encoded by at least one set of three nucleotide bases, or codon, in DNA. The code for each of the 20 amino acids is shown here, along with the single letter abbreviation for each of the amino acids. The three codons, ochre, amber and opal, are "stop" codons, i.e., they indicate a termination of translation.

other motifs[2] have been identified in the control region, which may be several hundred bases long. These motifs contain regions that bind specific proteins (transcription elements) and in so doing promote or repress the transcription of mRNA (Blowers et al. 1990; Donald et al. 1990; Grossman et al. 1993a,b).

There are potentially many levels of control of gene expression within a cell. As briefly discussed, the rate of *transcription* is one level (Fig 6.2). The stability of transcripts can vary as specific RNAs are employed to remove the message. The rate of protein synthesis can be regulated at a number of levels, as can the activity or stability of the protein. These processes—transcriptional, post-transcriptional, translational, and post-translational control—are not mutually exclusive, and frequently expression is regulated at more than one level. A general rule, that is not absolutely upheld but is nonetheless a useful guide, is that cyanobacterial and eukaryotic nuclear-encoded genes are controlled at the level of transcription. This is to say that the correspondence between variations in the level of proteins is often a consequence of the rate of transcription of mRNA, and the pool size of mRNA is correlated with the pool size of protein (Rochaix et al. 1989). Thus, variations in environmental signals that affect the accumulation of proteins in cyanobacteria or nuclear-encoded proteins are often related to factors that affect RNA polymerase binding and RNA synthesis (Houmard 1994). As we will shortly describe, the transduction of these signals is often complex.

---

2. A *motif* is a usually small, highly conserved sequence of DNA or protein that is used for some common function. For example, the sequence GGTTAA is a so-called G-box motif, as it is often found in nuclear-encoded promoter sequences as a binding site for transcription factors.

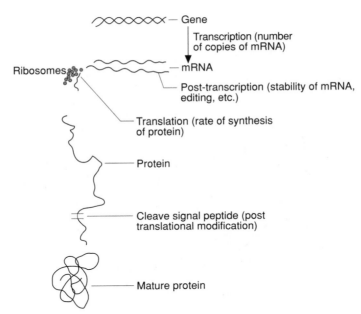

**Figure 6.2** Level of control of gene products. Each polypeptide is encoded by a single gene. Each gene is transcribed to form one or more copies of messenger RNA, via the action of the enzyme RNA polymerase. The number of copies of mRNA is regulated by noncoding regions of the gene, called promotor sequences. Once mRNA is formed, it must be translated on rRNA to form the protein. Regulation at this level may be achieved by causing the mRNA to break down, by blocking rRNA docking sites, by reducing the number of amino acids available, etc. Control of protein synthesis at this level is called transcriptional or post-transcriptional. Once formed, the protein may have signal or transit peptide sequences that must be removed before the protein is functional. This step may require one or more specific proteases, and control of gene expression at this level is called post-translational.

A second level of control is via the *post-transcriptional processing* of mRNA. In eukaryotic cells the coding region is often interspersed with noncoding sequences called *introns* that are similarly transcribed by the RNA polymerase. The mRNA sequences corresponding to introns are removed by enzymatically splicing the mRNA in the nucleus prior to export to the cytoplasm. The splicing is directed by specific nucleotide sequences in the mRNA. This post-transcriptional "maturation" of mRNA leads to the synthesis of smaller transcripts. *Splicing* is one mechanism for post-transcriptional control of gene expression. A second mechanism is via *mRNA degradation*. Mature mRNA molecules are enzymatically degraded. The degradation rate is specific for the transcript and the lifetime of mRNAs can vary in algal cells from a few minutes to a few hours (Mullet 1993; Mullet 1987; Sakamoto et al. 1993). RNA degradation can be assessed by inhibiting mRNA synthesis with antibiotics and following the levels of specific RNAs. A third level of post-transcriptional control is so-called *RNA editing*. In this situation, for example, a cytosine in the mRNA may be replaced with a uracil, leading to the coding for a different amino acid than that predicted from the DNA sequence. Such an apparent inconsistency in the universality of the genetic code is found in reaction center protein D1, and is a consequence of mRNA editing. Post-transcriptional control of gene expression is a common feature of many chloroplast-encoded genes.

A third level of control of gene expression is at the level of *translation*. Messenger RNA is translated to proteins on ribosomes. Each mRNA molecule can in principle be used numerous times, and hence is a potential source of amplification for a gene. Translation is dependent on many factors: the availability of processed mRNA; the availability of ribosomes that is commensurate with the demand for protein synthesis; the availability of amino acids, including the availability of tRNA molecules that are "charged" with their specific amino acid; and the availability of ATP. There are potentially numerous examples of translational control. Depression of cell growth by limiting nutrients often can be attributed to a reduction in translation rates. For example, in heterotrophic prokaryotic cells, growth rates in chemostat cultures are usually highly correlated with the abundance of ribosomal RNA (Lee, Kemp 1994). Transient inhibitor studies in such cases suggest that protein synthesis is limited by the rate of translation of mRNA. In eukaryotic cells, similar effects of translational limitation can be found, especially when nitrogen or carbon is a limiting element (Herzig, Falkowski 1989).

Synthesized proteins do not necessarily partake in cell functions immediately following translation; frequently, they are modified. *Post-translational modification* permits a level of feedback between the gene product, the level of transcription, and often in sensing metabolic processes. Two post-translational modifications that are important in the function and assembly of the photosynthetic apparatus are the *cleavage of leader sequences* and *protein phosphorylation* (Bennett 1991; Flugge 1990).

Two basic categories of leader sequences can be distinguished, namely signal sequences and transit sequences. *Signal sequences* are leading portions of a nuclear-encoded protein that are targeted to the endoplasmic reticulum. In chromophyte algae, where the chloroplast is encapsulated by four membranes, the outer membrane appears to be derived from the endoplasmic reticulum and is contiguous with that structure around the nucleus (Chapter 1; Apt et al. 1994; Bassham et al. 1991; Grossman et al. 1990). Hence, nuclear-encoded proteins that are imported into the chloroplast, such as the fucoxanthin-chlorophyll proteins, contain a leader sequence that facilitates transport of the protein into the chloroplast. This sequence contains a positively charged residue in the first four amino acids followed by a hydrophobic domain. As the protein *transits* across the chloroplast membranes, the signal sequence is spliced, leaving a smaller, mature protein. In the chlorophytes, the leader sequence is a 33-36 amino acid portion of the protein at the N-terminus that facilitates transport of the nuclear-encoded proteins across a simpler, two-membrane envelope. The transit peptide directs the protein toward its locus within the chloroplast and is cleaved within the organelle to form the mature protein (Flugge 1990; Kavanagh et al. 1988; Mayfield et al. 1989). The cleavage of signal or transit sequences is a form of post-translational control process essential for the synthesis and assembly of light-harvesting chlorophyll proteins in eukaryotes, as well as in the integration of the small subunit of Rubisco in chlorophyte algae (Ellis 1990).

*Protein phosphorylation* and dephosphorylation are mediated by a series of protein kinases and phosphatases, respectively. The phosphorylation reactions are keyed to specific amino acids, most commonly serine, threonine, and histidine. Phosphorylation is ATP dependent and ATP consuming[3] and is usually keyed to specific metabolic steps. Many thylakoid proteins including the light-harvesting chlorophyll proteins, phycobiliproteins, D1, and D2 are phosphorylated (Bennett 1984; Bennett 1991). For these proteins, phosphorylation is triggered by the redox state of the plastoquinone pool (Allen et al. 1981); the kinase appears to sense the status of the pool through an interaction with the cytochrome $b_6/f$ complex (Frid et al. 1992). Thus, as the plastoquinone pool becomes reduced, a protein kinase is activated and a number of proteins in the thylakoid membrane become phosphorylated (Race, Hind 1996).

Many other proteins, such as nitrate reductase and enzymes in the Calvin cycle, may also be phosphorylated (Huber et al. 1992). Phosphorylation often alters the specific activity of the target enzyme and may alter its affinity for specific binding sites. Soluble proteins may be reversibly phosphorylated and bind to control regions of specific genes, thereby providing a feedback control between metabolism and gene expression. In such cases, the kinase often utilizes GTP rather than ATP as the substrate and G proteins (i.e., GTP-binding) are common vehicles for transducing environmental signals to chemical cues (Danon, Mayfield 1991; Eskins et al. 1991; Johanningmeier, Howell 1984; Rodriguez-Rosales et al. 1991; Sasaki et al. 1991).

The removal of phosphate groups from proteins is achieved through the action of specific phosphatases. Some microalgal toxins are highly tuned to inhibit phosphatases in the cytoplasm or nucleus (not in the chloroplast) and in doing so can cause severe illness or even death in humans. Two such toxins are okadaic acid and microcystin. Okadaic acid is a lipid soluble protein phosphatase inhibitor produced by some dinoflagellates and is responsible for diarrhetic shellfish poisoning. Microcystin is a cyclic eight amino acid polypeptide with a variable sequence region. The microcystins, so called because they are produced by the cyanobacterium *Microcystis aeruginosa*, are water-soluble protein phosphatase inhibitors. Often these and other phosphatase and kinase inhibitors are used to assess the pathways of control and effect of phosphorylation of proteins or small peptides (Cohen et al. 1990; MacKintosh et al. 1990).

With this brief primer on control of gene expression, let us examine some of the processes required for the assembly and organization of the photosynthetic apparatus. We begin with the light-harvesting chlorophyll-protein complexes.

## LIGHT-HARVESTING PIGMENT-PROTEIN COMPLEXES

Light-harvesting pigment-protein complexes are a diverse group of proteins that bind pigments and transfer absorbed excitation energy to a photosynthetic reaction center. Broadly speaking, two major classes of pigment-protein complexes can be identified. The first are chlorophyll-protein complexes that are usually, but not always, hydrophobic molecules that invariably contain some carotenoids (Green, Durnford 1996; Hiller et al. 1991; Jeffrey 1980; Larkum and Barrett 1983). The second are the phycobiliproteins, which are water-soluble molecules found in cyanobacteria, cryptomonads, and Rhodophyceae (Gantt 1981; Grossman et al.

---

3. This is the definition of a kinase.

1993b). Both types of complexes confer the observable colors to algal cells and the chlorophyll-protein complexes contain >95% of the cell chlorophyll. Light-harvesting chlorophyll proteins are encoded in both the nucleus and chloroplast, although the typical pigment of eukaryotic algal classes is a consequence of only nuclear-encoded genes. We first examine some of the elements of phycobiliproteins.

In the phycobiliprotein-containing algae, the pigments are organized in large, water-soluble structures that can be resolved by electron microscopy (Fig 6.3a). The pigments are a series of modified linear tetrapyrroles that are covalently bound via one or two thioether bonds to cysteine on the apoproteins (Fig 6.3b). The light absorption properties of the pigments are a consequence of extended conjugated double bonds in the linear tetrapyrroles. This structure is called a *chromophore*. The number of chromophores found per unit of protein varies between species. The pigments can be removed only by relatively harsh treatments such as acid hydrolysis, not by organic solvent extraction. The phycobiliproteins consist of two subunits, designated $\alpha$ and $\beta$, that form multimeric complexes. The molecular masses of both subunits are similar, ranging between 17 and 22 kDa depending on the specific phycobiliprotein and species. In freshwater cyanobacteria, the phycobiliproteins aggregate into a disk-shaped trimer $(\alpha\beta)_3$ approximately 11 nm in diameter and 3 nm thick. These structures can be resolved by electron microscopy. In marine cyanobacteria, the unit structure appears to be a dimer $(\alpha\beta)_2$.

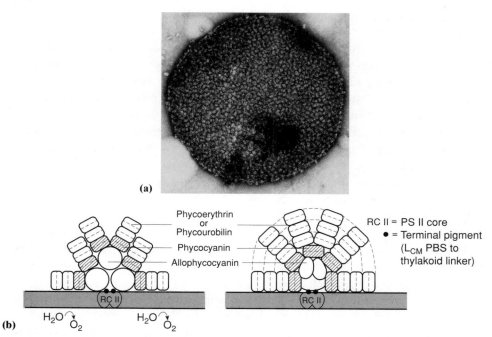

**Figure 6.3** (a) A transmission electron micrograph showing the basic structure of phycobilisomes. (b) A schematic diagram of a phycobilisome. The basic structure is hemidiscoidal with a three-member core containing allophycocyanin. Six "rods" are normally bound to the core. Phycocyanin is always located closest to the core. The core itself is energetically coupled to the reaction center of photosystem II. The more distal regions of the rods contain either phycocyanin, phycoerythrin, or phycourobilin bound to proteins, depending on the species, light intensity, and the color of the light in which the organism is grown. (Courtesy of Elisabeth Gantt)

In all cyanobacteria the genes encoding the phycobiliproteins are arranged on an operon, together with genes encoding small linker proteins that serve to organize the disks into phycobilisomes. These structures consist of a rod extending radially from a core (Bryant 1994; Zuber 1986). The rods consist of stacked disks; at the distal end the green-light–absorbing phycoerythrobilin (in freshwater species) and phycourobilin (in marine species) are connected to the orange-wavelength–absorbing phycocyanobilin. In some cyanobacteria species, phycoerythrin is lacking and the rod contains only phycocyanobilin. The core structure contains a series of stacked disks; at the distal end the green-light–absorbing phycoerythrobilin (in freshwater species) and phycourobilin (in marine species) are connected to the orange-wavelength–absorbing phycocyanobilin. In some species of cyanobacteria, phycoerythrin is lacking and the rod contains only phycocyanobilin (Swanson et al. 1991). The core structure contains a series of stacked disks of allophycocyanobilin. The fluorescence emission spectra of this red-orange–absorbing pigment-protein complex overlaps the $Q_y$ absorption band of chlorophyll *a*. The excitons captured at the distal end of the rods migrate by resonance energy transfer (the Förster mechanism; see Chapter 2) to the core, where they are delivered directly to chlorophyll proteins associated with PSII reaction centers (Glazer 1984). One phycobilisome serves two PSII reaction centers. Overall energy transfer efficiency from the phycobilisomes to the reaction center is about 90%. The energy transfer is via a cascade, from shorter-wavelength–absorbing chromophores to longer-wavelength–absorbing chromophores. The energy is ultimately coupled to the lowest singlet excited state of chlorophyll *a*.

As cyanobacteria have no major chlorophyll-protein complex serving PSII, the optical absorption cross-section for the reaction center is basically determined by the absorption spectra of the phycobilisomes (Fujita et al. 1985; Ley, Butler 1977). In contrast, PSI is primarily served by chlorophyll-protein complexes, and hence, in cyanobacteria and Rhodophyceae, the two photosystems have distinctly different action spectra (Mörschel, Rhiel 1987). In cryptophyceae, phycoerythrin is localized in the thylakoid lumen and transfers excitation energy to PSII via chlorophyll *c* as an intermediate.

In the light-harvesting chlorophyll-protein complexes, pigments are noncovalently bound to the proteins by hydrophobic interactions, and the complexes can be disrupted by a solvent with a low dipole moment relative to water; commonly used solvents are acetone and low molecular weight alcohols. This disruption facilitates the quantitative extraction of photosynthetic pigments, but the relative ease with which the pigments are removed from the complexes has hampered their biochemical and structural characterization (Thornber 1986).

Intact light-harvesting chlorophyll-protein complexes have been isolated from a variety of algae using detergents that solubilize the thylakoid membranes while being gentle enough to prevent the dissociation of the pigments from the protein (Green, Durnford 1996). Such nonionic or zwitterionic detergents as Triton X-100, and β-octylgluoside and digitonin are commonly used to solubilize intact pigment-protein complexes. Following solubilization, the complexes may be isolated by sucrose-density gradient centrifugation and further fractionated by electrophoresis under mild conditions without significant denaturation (so-called "green gels"). The integrity of the pigment-protein complex can be assessed by analyzing the transfer of excitation energy from the accessory chlorophylls (*b* or *c*) to chlorophyll *a* by means of fluorescence excitation/emission spectroscopy (Sukenik et al. 1989). For example, if a detergent disrupts energy transfer, excitation of chlorophyll *b* leads to autofluorescence of chlorophyll *b*; whereas if energy transfer is not disrupted, excitation of chlorophyll *b* is manifested by fluorescence emission by chlorophyll *a*. Further characterization of the complex is obtained by a variety of absorption spectroscopies, including visible wavelengths, and with polarized light to infer orientation of the pigments in relation to each other. In this context, circularly polarized or linearly polarized light can be used to assess the orientation of absorption dipoles relative to each other (Garab et al. 1987). This form of spectroscopy can be used to infer the orientation of $\pi$ bonds in chlorophyll molecules within the pigment-protein complexes. These spectroscopic analyses are usually conducted in conjunction with biochemical analyses and structural studies.

Some of the light-harvesting chlorophyll proteins are highly conserved across phylogenetic lines. Chief among these are CP43 and CP47, two chloroplast-encoded proteins (Alfanso et al. 1994; Pakrasi et al. 1985). These two complexes bind only chlorophyll *a* and both are highly fluorescent at room temperature (actually, in room light these complexes, when isolated, are red rather than green). At the temperature of liquid nitrogen (77 K), CP43 is observed by an emission band at 684 nm whereas CP47 emits at 695 nm (Chapter 3; Eaton Rye, Vermaas 1991). These two pigment-protein complexes are thought to serve as "core" antennae to PSII; that is, they absorb energy from the major light-harvesting pigment-protein complexes and transfer the energy directly to the reaction center (Vermaas 1993).

The peripheral antennae consist of the major, nuclear-encoded, light-harvesting chlorophyll-protein complexes that often bind accessory chlorophylls. The genes are usually found in multiple, closely related but not identical, forms called *gene families*. In chlorophytes these complexes bind chlorophylls *a* and *b* as well as oxygenated carotenoids (xanthophylls) such as lutein (and are called the *light-harvesting* chlorophyll proteins, LHCs). A group of light-harvesting chlorophyll-protein complexes, LHCII, serves PSII; a second, immunologically and biochemically different group, LHCI, serves PSI. The LHCs are a large number of closely related pigment-protein complexes (Green et al. 1991; Green, Kühlbrandt 1995). LHCII and LHCI are closely related to each other from a phylogenetic perspective; however, LHCII generally has a chlorophyll *a/b* ratio averaging between 1.1 and 3, whereas in the LHCI the ratio is >5. Hence, in chlorophytes, absorption of light by chlorophyll *b* preferentially excites PSII. The apoproteins of LHCs range in size from about 20 to 30 kDa, and often multiple genes are expressed in an organism (Sukenik et al. 1987b).

In chromophyte algae, there may be 10 to 15 genes for antenna proteins (Grossman et al. 1990). In diatoms and other algae containing the carotenoid fucoxanthin, the major light-harvesting chlorophyll-protein complexes bind fucoxanthin and chlorophylls *a* and *c* (the *fucoxanthin-chlorophyll proteins*, FCPs) (Boczar, Prèzelin 1989). In many dinoflagellates, a water-soluble pigment-protein complex containing the red xanthophyll carotenoid peridinin is found bound to a protein containing chlorophyll *a* with or without chlorophyll *c* (Jovine et al. 1995). The peridinin chlorophyll proteins (PCPs and ACPs) are distinct from a second complex found in some dinoflagellates that contains chlorophylls *a* and *c*, but apparently not peridinin.

The amino acid sequences for a number of eukaryotic LHCs and FCPs have been deduced from their gene sequences or cDNA clones (i.e., DNA libraries made from mRNA templates). All sequences obtained thus far have some similarities. Based on their hydropathy plots,[4] LHCs have three transmembrane-spanning regions, the first and third of which are relatively highly conserved (Fig 6.4) (Green, Pichersky 1994). The apoproteins are translated with a transit or leader sequence (depending on the taxon) in the cytosol and transported across the chloroplast envelope where the leader is cleaved. Thus, the post-translational modification produces a mature apoprotein that becomes incorporated in the thylakoids. This apoprotein is smaller than that predicted from the nucleotide sequence owing to the presence of a signal sequence in the precursor molecule. The mature apoprotein binds chlorophylls and carotenoids, which are synthesized in the chloroplast (Chitnis, Thornber 1988). In a number of species, it appears that if chlorophyll biosynthesis is reduced or inhibited, the apoprotein is specifically degraded, leading to the suggestion that chlorophyll is essential to stabilize the apoprotein (Klein et al. 1988; Michel et al. 1983). In some species, however, it would appear that this second post-translational control mechanism is not present, as stable apoprotein can be found in the membranes even when chlorophyll biosynthesis is totally blocked (Mortain-Bertrand et al. 1990).

The structure of an LHC from pea has been deduced from electron diffraction patterns of two-dimensional crystals (Kuhlbrandt et al. 1994). This structure gives a trimer of three identical subunits, each thought to bind seven chlorophyll *a* molecules, five chlorophyll *b* molecules, and two molecules of lutein. The intermolecular distance between chlorophyll *b* and the closest chlorophyll *a* averages about 0.4 nm. This short distance is essential to maintaining the subpicosecond transfer of excitation from the former to the latter pigment. The carotenoids are assumed to quench chlorophyll triplets by exchanging electrons in higher excited states. This exchange reduces the possibility of forming a singlet $O_2$ (Chapter 2), which is a highly reactive species and, if formed in a photosynthetic reaction center for example, can cause irreversible damage (Prasil et al. 1992).

In addition to LHC, a high-resolution structure of the peridinin-chlorophyll-protein complex from dinoflagellates has also been elucidated (Hiller et al., 1996). The structure reveals close proximity between the π bonds of the carotenoid, peridinin, and chlorophyll *c*, thereby facilitating a higher efficiency of energy transfer from the former to the latter pigment.

---

4. A *hydropathy plot* is a projection of the relative hydrophobicity or hydrophylicity of amino acids in a protein sequence. A sequence of 7 to 10 hydrophobic amino acids is capable of spanning a membrane. Hence hydropathy plots are often used to provide clues as to the number of potential transmembranes spanning regions in a protein.

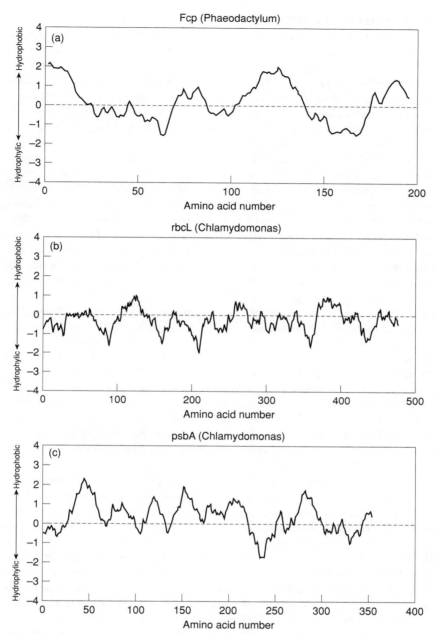

**Figure 6.4** An example of the hydropathy plots of three proteins: the fucoxanthin chlorophyll *a,c* binding protein from the marine diatom *Phaeodactylum tricornutum*, the large subunit of ribulose 1,5-bisphosphate carboxylase/oxygenase from *Chlamydomonas reinhardtii*, and reaction center protein, D1, from *Chlamydomonas*. Numbers greater than zero indicate hydrophobic domains in the protein, while numbers less than zero indicate hydrophilic regions.

## ❏ CHLOROPHYLL BIOSYNTHESIS

*All chlorophyll molecules in vivo are bound to proteins via hydrophobic interactions, a category of noncovalent bonds. A variety of amino acids appear to be used to bind the pigments to the apoproteins, including histidine, glutamate, and glutamine (Hiller et al. 1993; Kohorn 1990; Kuhlbrandt et al. 1994). Subtle changes in the binding of chlorophylls can lead to changes in the probabilities of populating the higher excited states, and hence in absorption and fluorescence properties of the pigments. The rules governing these changes are poorly understood.*

*The synthesis of chlorophyll occurs in the chloroplast. For all nuclear-encoded light-harvesting chlorophyll proteins, the assembly of the pigment-protein complex occurs after the proteins have been imported into the chloroplast but probably before insertion into the thylakoid membranes (Beale, Weinstein 1991). Chlorophyll biosynthesis is highly regulated and is initiated from the five-carbon amino acid, glutamate (Fig 6.5a) (Beale, Weinstein 1990). Glutamate serves as a key branchpoint in nitrogen metabolism (which we will discuss in Chapter 8), and the synthesis of chlorophyll competes with protein synthesis in chloroplasts (Precali, Falkowski 1983). In a rather unusual biochemical reaction, a glutamyl-tRNA is used with NADPH to form glutamate-1-semialdehyde, which subsequently undergoes a transfer of the amino nitrogen from carbon-2 to carbon-1, to produce the amino acid δ-aminolevulinic acid (ALA) (Beale, Castelfranco 1974). ALA is not used in protein synthesis (i.e., it is not a "primary" amino acid and hence has no codon), but is the common precursor of hemes and chlorins (Jordan 1991). It should be noted that in older texts, ALA synthesis occurs as a condensation of succinyl CoA and glycine, rather than from gluta-mate (Meeks 1974). This pathway was identified from studies on heme synthesis in animal systems and is not valid for chlorophylls or hemes in algae (except for hemes in* Euglena*). The formation of ALA is highly regulated by light in plant cells, and the pool sizes of ALA are extremely small (on the order of $10^{-15} M$) (Beale 1976; Owens et al. 1978).*

*In the continuation of chlorin synthesis, two molecules of ALA condense to form porphobilinogen, and four molecules of porphobilinogen are used to form the tetrapyrrole, uroporphyrinogen III (Fig 6.5b). The latter undergoes a series of decarboxylation and reduction reactions, followed by the insertion of Mg into the ring, and condensation to form a fifth ring to produce protochlorophyllide (Jordan 1991). Chlorophyll c forms in a branched pathway prior to the synthe-sis of protochlorophyllide (Jeffrey 1980). In most higher plants, the reduction of protochlorophyllide (a yellow pigment) to chlorophyllide (a green pigment) is catalyzed by light; however, in many algae, if not most, chlorophyll synthesis can occur in the dark, at least for a short period of time (a day or so).*

*In the synthesis of chlorophylls a and b, a phytol chain formed from ger-anylgeraniol in the chloroplast, is added to ring 4 in an esterification reaction. The synthesis of geranylgeraniol is common to both phytol and carotenoid syn-thesis, and phytol synthesis can be thought of as a branchpoint in the formation of carotenoids. Chlorophyll b is formed from chlorophyll a (Schoch et al. 1977; Shlyk 1970). The phytol group confers a high degree of hydrophobicity to chloro-phylls a and b compared with chlorophyll c (with one exception—see Nelson, Wakeham 1989), and hence the former pigments are not water soluble.*

*A number of inhibitors of chlorophyll synthesis are available, and are useful in studies of the pathway, the post-translational stabilization of the chlorophyll-binding proteins by the pigments, and the relationships and feedbacks between chlorophyll biosynthesis and apoprotein biosynthesis. Gabaculene is a fungal compound that inhibits the formation of ALA synthesis specifically in the chlorophyll biosynthetic pathway (i.e., it has no large effect on heme synthesis). When chlorophyll synthesis is blocked with gabaculene, Lhcb (formerly called cab) mRNA is still transcribed and translated (LaRoche et al. 1991).*

## Regulation of LHC Expression

There are numerous nucleotide motifs in the control regions of light-harvesting pigment-protein complexes that permit regulation of gene expression. The levels of control of expression of the complexes are often multiple and interactive. The expression of complexes is nonlinearly dependent on light intensity, spectral quality, temperature, and nutrient regime. Of these, the responses to spectral irradiance (quantity and quality) are the most studied and often the most dynamic. In cyanobacteria when cells are grown under green light, which is preferentially

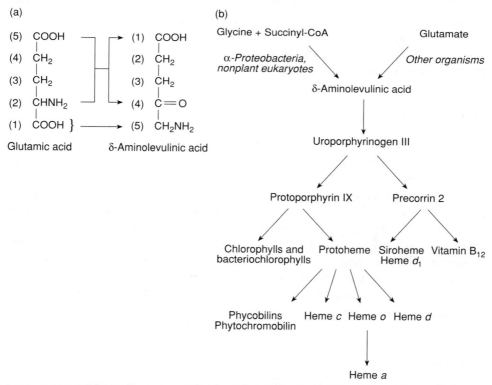

**Figure 6.5** (a) The pathway for the formation of δ-aminolevulinic acid. This amino acid is a precursor for linear tetrapyrroles such as the phycobilipigments as well as for cyclic tetrapyrroles such as porphyrins and chlorins. This secondary amino acid is formed in algae including cyanobacteria and higher plants, from the transamination of glutamic acid. In bacteria and nonphotosynthetic organisms, and for porphyrins in *Euglena*, it is formed from the condensation of glycine and succinyl Co-A. (b) The pathway leading from δ-aminolevulinic acid to chlorophylls (chlorins) and hemes (porphyrins).

absorbed by phycoerythrin and hence favors the excitation of PSII, the cells increase the synthesis of chlorophyll-protein complexes, thus helping to supply excitation energy to PSI (Fujita et al. 1987; Myers 1986). Conversely, differential stimulation of PSI with blue or red light leads to the synthesis of phycoerythrin. This process, called complementary chromatic adaptation (more strictly it is an acclimation process), is primarily a consequence of differential stimulation of mRNA synthesis in response to changes in spectral irradiance; that is, it is transcriptionally regulated (Houmard 1994). The acclimation process has been suggested to be keyed to the photosynthetic electron transport chain at the level of cyt $b_6/f$; that is, when the cytochrome $f$ is oxidized, transcription of phycobiliproteins is increased (Fujita et al. 1994). The specific signal transduction mechanism is unclear, but is thought to be mediated via a post-translational phosphorylation of a DNA-binding protein that interacts with the control region of the gene (Houmard 1994).

Acclimation to light intensity is commonly reflected by increased levels of chlorophyll proteins at lower photon fluxes, and vice versa (Falkowski 1980; Falkowski, LaRoche 1991; Richardson et al. 1983). This process is also transcriptionally and post-translationally modified by the redox status of the intersystem electron transport chain through a post-translationally regulated phosphorylation cascade (Escoubas et al. 1995). This regulation permits cells to increase or decrease the rate of synthesis of chlorophyll-protein complexes in response to irradiance levels. The response may or may not be coupled to the synthesis of reaction centers, and requires a molecular mechanism for integration of the signals between multiple genes in different compartments of the cell.

## THE REACTION CENTERS

For decades before the application of molecular biology and structural biology to photosynthesis research, the concept of what exactly constituted a reaction center was vague and defined primarily from biophysical data. Phenomenologically, a reaction center is the site where the excitation energy of light is converted to photochemical energy. The biophysical abstractions can be related to molecular structures.

The reaction center proteins are associated with or span the thylakoid membranes; this is permitted by their hydrophobicity (Vermaas et al. 1988). Isolation protocols for the reaction centers usually require detergents for solubilization of the proteins and removal of the complexes from the membrane lipids (Berthold et al. 1981). Once added, detergents are difficult to remove and this poses a challenge for crystallization and subsequent structural studies.

### Photosystem II

Many of the early advances in understanding photosynthetic reaction centers came from work with anaerobic photosynthetic bacteria. Bacterial reaction centers were first isolated (by accident) by Roderick Clayton, and subsequent biophysical and biochemical analyses of the crystallized proteins stimulated considerable interest in these organisms (Blankenship et al. 1995). Bacterial photosynthetic reaction centers fall into two major types. The first is characterized by purple and some green bacteria, in which a quinone is the first stable electron acceptor (see Chapter 4). The redox potential generated by these organisms is only mildly reducing, and the organisms cannot generate reduced pyridine nucleotides (e.g., NADPH) directly, but must couple the reduction to an electron transport system. In other, green sulfur bacteria, the first stable electron acceptor is an iron-sulfur complex, which is highly reducing. These organisms can form reduced pyridine nucleotides directly. There are striking homologies between these two types of bacterial reaction centers and PSII and PSI reaction centers, respectively.

By the mid-1980s high resolution X-ray diffraction patterns of the reaction center from the purple bacteria *Rhodopseudomonas sphaeroides* had been elucidated (Michel and Deisenhofer 1986). The structure (Fig 6.6) revealed two protein subunits, designated L and M, forming a heterodimer. The reaction center pigments were noncovalently bound to these subunits through the imidazole nitrogen of histidine. This linkage between histidine and tetrapyrroles is common; it is found in myoglobin, hemoglobin, and apparently in the bacterial reaction center. From the orientation of the pigments and proteins in the crystal, it became clear that a special pair of bacteriochlorophyll molecules, $P_{870}$, long hypothesized from biophysical evidence, formed the initial charge-separating unit, and the electrons photochemically driven from the special pair moved on to bacterial phaeophytin and subsequently

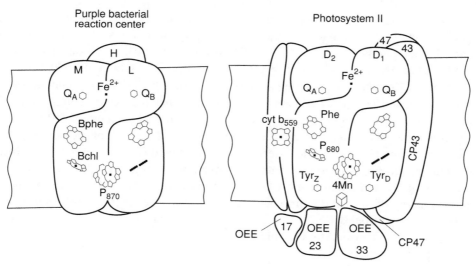

**Figure 6.6** (Left) A schematic diagram showing the structural homology between the photosynthetic reaction center from purple bacteria and that from photosystem II of oxygenic photoautotrophs. The L, M, and H proteins are abbreviations for "light," "medium," and "heavy," based on the apparent molecular masses from polyacrylamide gel electrophoresis. The L subunit has strong sequence homology with D1, while the M subunit is homologous to D2. There is no structural analog of cytochrome $b_{559}$ in purple bacteria or of the M protein in oxygenic photoautotrophs. (Right) A diagram showing a face-on view of PSII reaction centers. The reaction centers are thought to aggregate as dimers, loosely attached to each other through the core antenna complexes, CP43 and/or CP47. The light-harvesting complexes of PSII form trimers, and in chlorophytes are thought to be energetically coupled to the reaction center through minor, nuclear-encoded chlorophyll protein complexes, CP24, CP26, and CP29.

on to a quinone (see Fig 4.2; Michel, Deisenhofer 1988). Every amino acid in the structure was known from the gene sequences.

Prior to the elucidation of the structure of the bacterial reaction center (which ultimately led to a Nobel Prize for the researchers), it was generally assumed that the reaction center for PSII was located on either CP47 or CP43, two chloroplast-encoded, chlorophyll-containing proteins (Steinback et al. 1985). However, two other chloroplast-encoded proteins designated D1 and D2,[5] which are the psbA and psbD gene products, have striking sequence homology to the L and M subunits, respectively, of the bacterial reaction center (Michel et al. 1988). Based on the homology, it was suggested that D1 and D2 must make up the PSII reaction center. By the late 1980s, Nanba and Satoh (1987) had isolated a core complex containing D1 and D2 and cytochrome $b_{559}$. This complex, which lacked quinones but contained chlorophyll $a$ and phaeophytin $a$, could undergo photochemical charge separation, providing that an artificial electron donor and acceptor were available. The notion that CP47 or CP43 constituted the reaction center was abandoned, and it was generally accepted that the reaction center of PSII contains D1, D2, and cytochrome $b_{559}$ (which consists of two protein subunits) (Fig 6.7). CP43 and CP47 were assigned to roles of core antennae responsible for directing excitation energy from the major light-harvesting chlorophyll pigment-protein complexes to the reaction center (Barber J 1987). Although X-ray diffraction patterns of PSII reaction centers have been obtained, they do not reveal the structure in sufficient detail to provide a clear molecular model of the photochemical process (Ford et al. 1995).

The nucleotide sequence of psbA has been described for a large number of species, including cyanobacteria and prochlorophytes, diatoms, chlorophytes, and many higher plants (Avni et al. 1994; Bouyoub et al. 1993; Erickson et al. 1984; Golden et al. 1986; Karabin et al. 1984; Kloos et al. 1993; Metz et al. 1990; Morden and Golden 1989; Nixon et al. 1991; Smart and Mcintosh 1991; Svensson et al. 1991; Winhauer et al. 1991). The deduced amino acid sequence predicts a protein with 352 or 353 amino acids, depending on species, giving a molecular mass of 39 kDa. The apparent molecular mass of D1 protein, as revealed by gel electrophoresis, is 32 kDa, and eight amino acids from the C-terminus are removed from the precursor before the mature protein is inserted into the thylakoid membrane. The amino acid sequence of D1 is among the most highly conserved of any photosynthetic protein; approximately 85% of the amino acids are conserved between cyanobacteria and higher plants (Barber J 1992). This conservation of primary structure is presumed to be related to conservation of function. Hydropathy analysis suggests that the mature protein has five transmembrane spanning regions.

Based both on analogy with the bacterial reaction center protein L and on mutation studies with cyanobacteria and the chlorophyte *Chlamydomonas,* D1 contains the plastoquinone-binding site $Q_B$, the donor tyrosine $Y_Z$, and binding sites for chlorophyll $a$ and phaeophytin $a$. The quinone-binding site has been of special inter-

---

5. When these proteins are radioactively labeled with [35]S they appear as broad, *diffuse* bands on an autoradiogram following polyacrylamide gel electrophoresis and fluorography, hence the names D1 and D2 (i.e., diffuse band 1, etc.).

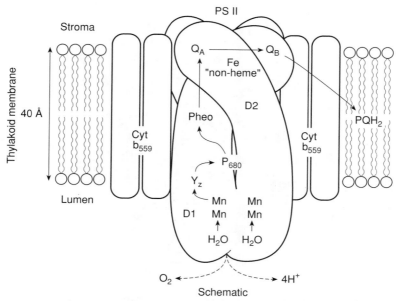

**Figure 6.7** A schematic diagram showing the path of electron transfer reactions within the PSII reaction center. The water-splitting complex, represented by the 4 Mn atoms, is contained within D1 and D2, and electrons are transferred from Mn to tyrosine $Y_Z$ to the chlorophyll molecule $P_{680}$. The photochemical oxidation of $P_{680}$ leads to the transient reduction of a phaeophytin intermediate, which reduces $Q_A$. Note that $Q_A$ is thought to reside on the stromal side of the reaction center. $Q_A$ passes its electrons to $Q_B$, which, upon receiving a pair of electrons, dissociates from its binding site on D1 to diffuse as plastoquinol in the interstices of the thylakoid membrane lipids. There is no proven role for cytochrome $b_{559}$, although it is thought that when plastoquinone is largely reduced, this cytochrome can facilitate electron transfer from $Q_B$ to $Y_Z$ or Mn, thereby engaging a cycle of electrons around PSII.

est to molecular biologists because it is also the site for binding of herbicides such as DCMU and atrazine. Consequently, single amino acid substitutions in this region can produce herbicide resistance and such resistance is often desired in commercial production of crop cultivars.

It is possible to radioactively label D1 and other proteins by incorporating substrates in vivo. Most plant physiologists and researchers using freshwater algae use $^{35}$S-labeled methionine for this purpose (Ohad et al. 1985). This substrate is convenient as it maintains high specific activity and hence allows easy detection on an autoradiogram. In marine eukaryotic algae, however, methionine is often not taken up from the medium. It is possible to provide $^{35}$S as sulfate; however, given the high concentration of background sulfate in seawater (25 mM), this approach requires very high levels of radioactivity (Mortain-Bertrand et al. 1990). It is therefore more convenient to label the proteins with $^{14}$C, which, while not specificallly incorporated into protein, permits relatively high levels of radioactivity to become detected in protein (Friedman, Alberte 1986; Greene et al. 1992).

When a pulse of radioactivity is given to an alga in vivo and is subsequently chased with nonradioactive substrate, it is possible to observe the biochemical turnover of the proteins (Fig 6.8). Using this pulse-chase method, Ohad, Kyle, and Arntzen (1984) observed that D1 appears to turn over very rapidly, on the order of

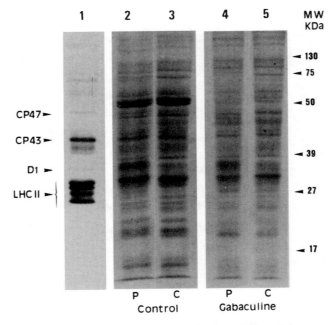

**Figure 6.8** The turnover of D1. Cells of the chlorophyte alga *Dunaliella tertiolecta* were labeled with radioactive sulfate, which becomes incorporated into the amino acids cysteine and methionine. After some period, the label is "chased" with excess nonradioactive sulfate. The thylakoid membranes were isolated and the proteins were separated by polyacrylamide gel electrophoresis. The first lane shows positions of some of the membrane components as visualized with antibodies and a reporter chemical. The second and third lanes show autoradiographs of the radioactively labeled proteins before and one hour after a chase. Note the large loss of radioactivity in the D1 protein. This loss is indicative of rapid degradation. However, as the total amount of D1 remained virtually constant, protein synthesis must have occurred simultaneously. From such types of experiments, it has been shown that D1, and to a lesser extent D2, turn over rapidly in vivo.

30 min in *Chlamydomonas*. Subsequently, it became clear that rapid D1 turnover was characteristic in many organisms, and that the rate of D1 turnover could be manipulated by light intensity. Specifically, if a cell or plant is placed in high light, D1 lost its label much more rapidly, and in fact there was a net loss of the protein; so the synthesis rate was not sufficiently high to keep pace with the rate of degradation. Ohad and colleagues (1990) proposed that D1 degradation was the primary cause of photoinhibition. Interestingly, if photosynthetic electron transport is blocked by DCMU, D1 does not rapidly degrade, even under high light.

D2, encoded in the chloroplast by psbD, is a protein of 352 to 353 amino acid residues, and like D1 appears to have five transmembrane-spanning helices (Svensson et al. 1991; Trebst 1987). The overall homology between D1 and D2 is only 28%, but localized regions are much higher. The amino acid sequences are 86% homologous between cyanobacteria and higher plants. The protein contains the binding site for $Q_A$, the tyrosine $D(Y_D)$, and histidines which are proposed to bind the reaction center chlorophyll and phaeophytin (Vermaas 1993). Like D1, D2 also turns over in vivo, although the rate of turnover is significantly lower.

The two reaction center proteins D1 and D2 are held together by a nonheme iron atom that straddles between them (Diner et al. 1991). The role of this iron is

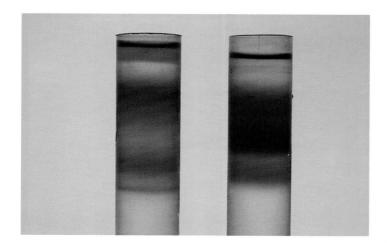

**Color Plate 1** Isolation of individual chlorophyll protein complexes by centrifugation on a sucrose-density gradient following solubilization in a mild detergent. The image on the top is taken with an incandescent light and shows the major green band corresponding to a light-harvesting pigment-protein complex associated primarily with photosystem II. The orange band at the top of the tube is almost pure carotene, the bulk of which is not associated with a protein in vivo. The figure on the bottom is that of the same sample illuminated with a blue background light. The red fluorescence emission from the chlorophyll protein complexes is clearly visible. In vivo the intensity of the fluorescence emission would be much weaker as the excitons would be transferred to the reaction centers.

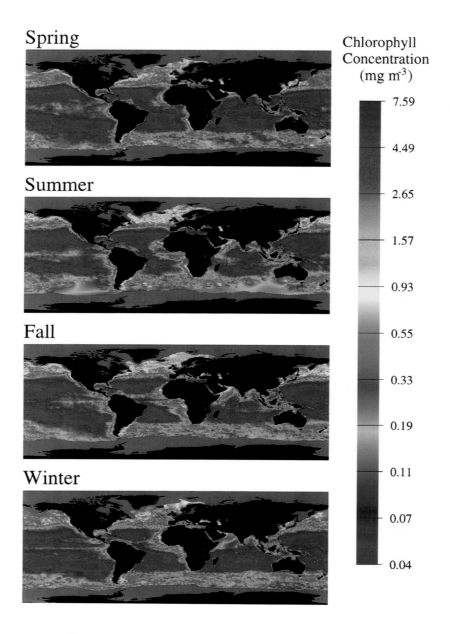

**Color Plate 2** The seasonally averaged upper ocean chlorophyll *a* concentrations derived from global maps of satellite measurements of ocean color. The data were calculated using algorithms such as that represented in Figure 10.6 and are based on the Coastal Zone Color Scanner data set obtained between 1978 and 1986.

**SPRING**

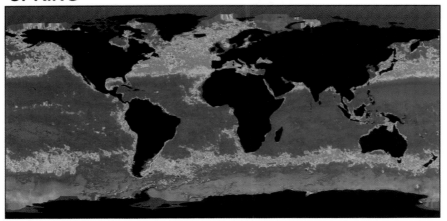

**SUMMER**

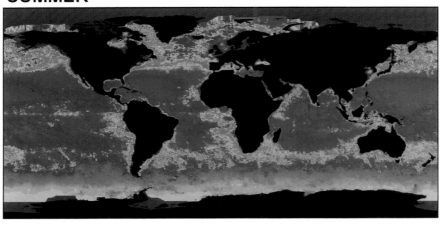

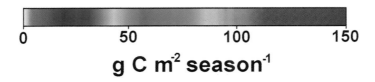

**Color Plates 3 and 4** Global maps of the seasonal variations in vertically integrated net primary production derived from the global maps of upper ocean chlorophyll (Color Plate 2) and a depth-integrated model as given in Equation 10.9. Variations between chlorophyll distributions and net primary production are primarily a consequence of temperature as it affects $P^B_{opt}$. (Courtesy of Michael Behrenfeld)

**FALL**

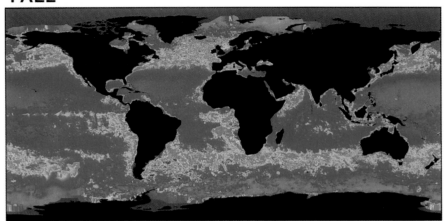

**WINTER**

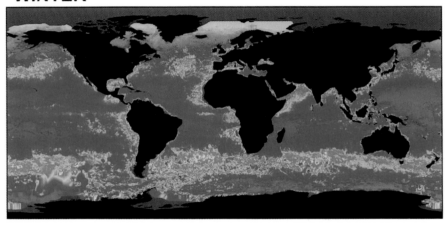

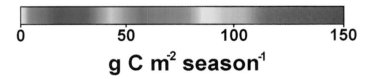

0  50  100  150

g C m$^{-2}$ season$^{-1}$

not completely understood. In bacterial reaction centers the nonheme iron can be replaced by other transition metals such as vanadium without any noticeable change in photochemical activity; this does not appear to be the case in PSII reaction centers (Blankenship et al. 1995). The iron can be oxidized to form Fe III at potentials above 400 mV. The oxidized iron is capable of oxidizing $Q_A^-$ within 50 μs, although it is not clear that this occurs in vivo (Vermaas et al. 1994). The absorption shifts associated with this redox titration led to the appellation of the nonheme iron as $Q_{400}$ in the biophysical literature.

The assembly of the PSII reaction center requires the synthesis of cytochrome $b_{559}$. This cytochrome consists of two proteins that have electrophoretic migration rates corresponding to relative molecular masses of 4 and 9 kDa, respectively (Tae, Cramer 1994). Both subunits appear to have one transmembrane-spanning region. The genes for these proteins are encoded by the adjacent chloroplast-encoded genes, psbE and psbF, respectively. Deletion of either of these genes inhibits the accumulation of D2; consequently, functional reaction centers are not formed. Thus, cytochrome $b_{559}$ appears to be critically important for the assembly and function of PSII reaction centers (Vermaas 1993; Whitmarsh et al. 1994). Cytochrome $b_{559}$ has been hypothesized to facilitate cyclic electron transfer around PSII (Prasil et al. 1996).

## Photosystem I

The reaction center of photosystem I was isolated and biochemically characterized before that of PSII (Kok 1961). The core complex of PSI is a heterodimer, containing two proteins of molecular mass 83 and 82 kDa, encoded by two chloroplast genes designated psaA and psaB, respectively (Golbeck, Bryant 1991). The two proteins are about 45% identical in amino acid sequence and both are highly hydrophobic. Hydropathy plots suggest that each protein may span the thylakoid membrane as many as 11 times. Like PSII, the amino acid sequences for PSI are highly conserved, and approximately 90% of the residues are identical (or substituted with a conservative replacement) between cyanobacteria and higher plants. A high resolution crystal structure of the PSI reaction center has not yet been obtained, but the complex has been crystallized and low resolution X-ray diffraction patterns have been developed (Almog et al. 1992).

The two core proteins are bound together by hydrophobic interactions. The complex contains approximately 100 chlorophyll *a* molecules; 12 to 15 β-carotenes; the primary electron donor $P_{700}$ (which is a dimer of chlorophyll *a*); the primary electron acceptor, designated $A_0$ (which is a chlorophyll *a* molecule); a secondary electron acceptor $A_1$, which is phylloquinone (vitamin $K_1$; 2-methyl-3-phytyl-1,4-naphthoquinone); and a tertiary electron acceptor $F_x$, which is an iron-sulfur complex (4Fe–4S) (Golbeck, Bryant 1991; Mullet et al. 1980; Fig 6.9). Two other iron-sulfur complex acceptors, designated $F_a$ and $F_b$, are found on a 9 kDa protein encoded by a chloroplast-encoded gene psbC. Biophysical evidence, including a splitting of the EPR signal for the $P_{700}^+$ and "hole burning," suggest that $P_{700}$ is a chlorophyll dimer, which is comparable to that of *Chlorobium* reaction centers

(Setif 1992). In this model, the π bonds of two chlorophyll *a* molecules are closely opposed to each other and held in this orientation by the proteins. The resulting electronic configuration leads to a formation of lower energy excited states, resulting in the spectral shifting of the absorption maxima to longer wavelengths (Golbeck, Bryant 1991).

## Cytochrome $b_6/f$

Electron transport between PSII and PSI is linked via the cytochrome $b_6/f$ complex. This complex consists of four different proteins, namely one cytochrome *f*, one cytochrome $b_6$ subunit containing two hemes, an iron-sulfur protein, and a protein denoted subunit IV (Malkin 1992). In algae the cytochrome *f*, $b_6$, and subunit IV proteins are encoded in the chloroplast by petA, -B, and -D genes, respectively, while the gene for the iron-sulfur component, PetC, is localized in the nucleus. The petB and -D genes are co-transcribed and are part of an operon. Subunit IV contains a highly conserved amino acid sequence consisting of Pro-Glu-Trp-Tyr, that is presumed to form a plastoquinol-binding region; mutant analysis indicates that this subunit, together with part of the cytochrome $b_6$, forms a pocket where plastoquinol docks to the complex (Cramer et al. 1991; Cramer et al. 1994). The assembly of the subunits to form the complex occurs in a 1:1:1:1 stoichiometry and is dependent on a supply of heme. The latter is synthesized by enzymes encoded in the nucleus. The synthesis of heme is dependent on the availability of assimilable iron (Geider, LaRoche 1994). Iron limitation can limit heme synthesis and thus impair the func-

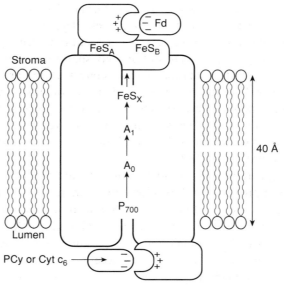

**Figure 6.9** A schematic diagram showing the basic organization of PSI. Plastocyanin or cytochrome $c_6$, depending on taxa, docks to a binding protein on lumenal side of the thylakoid and donates its electron to $P_{700}$. The major protein component of the reaction center contains two large chlorophyll-binding proteins, in which the electron transfer components $P_{700}$, $A_0$, $A_1$ and an iron sulfur cluster are found. Electrons exit from the reaction center on the stromal side, reducing ferredoxin.

## ❏ HOLE BURNING

*If, in a population of molecules, a small fraction of the molecules is irradiated with an intense beam of monochromatic light (i.e., a laser) at low temperature, the rate of production of the excited states can exceed the rate constants for de-excitation. In such a case, a spectral "hole" is produced in the absorption or fluorescence emission band. This process is called hole burning. The width of the hole in the frequency domain is related to the lifetime of the excited state (Chapter 3). From analyses of hole widths, inferences about the rate of energy transfer can be made within a subpopulation of chlorophyll-protein complexes (Renger 1992).*

---

tion of cytochrome $b_6/f$ in the photosynthetic electron transport chain (Greene et al. 1992).

### ATP Synthase/ATPase Complex

The $CF_0CF_1$ ATP synthetase complex consists of nine different polypeptides (Ort, Oxborough 1992). The $CF_1$ component is a peripheral complex on the stromal side of the thylakoid membranes with a total apparent molecular mass of about 250 kDa and has five subunits designated $\alpha$, $\beta$, $\gamma$, $\delta$, and $\varepsilon$. The stoichiometry of the subunits is 3:3:1:1:1, respectively (Glaser, Norling 1991; Ivashchenko et al. 1991; Labahn et al. 1990; Pancic et al. 1992). The $\alpha$ and $\beta$ subunits alternate in a ring, with the $\gamma$, $\delta$, and $\varepsilon$ and components asymmetrically adjoining the membrane side of the complex (Fig 6.10). The $CF_0$ component is an integral membrane complex with a molecular mass of about 200 kDa; has four subunits, designated I, II, III, and IV; and is found in a stoichiometry of 1:1:12:1. Subunits I and II have hydrophilic domains that appear to project into the stroma, while subunits I and III appear to interact with the $\alpha$ subunit of $CF_1$.

The genes encoding subunits are designated atpA to atpE, while subunits I to IV are encoded by aptF-atpI. In Heterokonta, and Rhodophyta all of the subunits, except the AtpG subunit of $CF_1$, are encoded in the chloroplast (Pancic et al. 1992; Pancic, Strotmann 1993; Reith, Manholland 1993). In the Heterokonta, the nuclear-encoded AtpG gene includes a leader sequence that appears to target the protein to the endoplasmic reticulum, permitting the polypeptide to cross the endoplasmic reticulum surrounding the chloroplasts of these algae. In Viridiplantae and Euglenophyta, the ATP synthetase genes, AtpC, AtpD, and AtpG, are nuclear-encoded. The structure of the ATP synthase complex has been determined from mitochondria, and as the sequence homology at the amino acid level is closely related to that of the chloroplast complex, it is likely that the chloroplast structure is similar. The $CF_1$ component of the complex interacts with ATP, ADP, and inorganic phosphate; $CF_0$ acts as a proton channel. The ATP synthase complex can operate either as a synthesizer of ATP if the proton gradient is thermodynamically favorable for such, or as an ATPase, in which case protons are actively transported from the stroma to the lumenal side of the thylakoid at the expense of ATP hydrolysis. In the formation of ATP, two of the subunits act as catalytic sites, where the dehydration reaction,

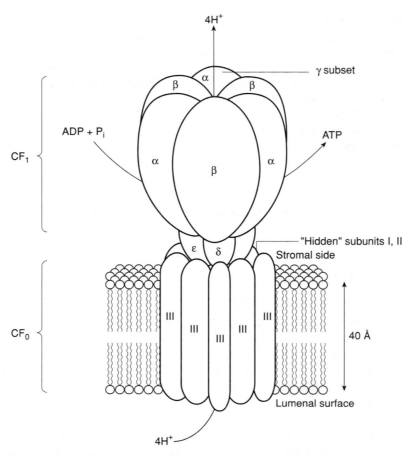

**Figure 6.10** A schematic diagram showing the basic structure of the proton ATPase, or ATP synthetic machinery found in photosynthetic membranes. The $CF_1$ structure sticks into the stromal fluid, where it binds ADP and inorganic phosphate. It is attached to the $CF_0$ complex, embedded in the thylakoid, via a series of small coupling polypeptides. Protons accumulated in the lumen pass through to the stroma through the core of the complex, and in the process, lead to the formation of ATP. The process is reversible, that is, excess ATP can be hydrolyzed and the energy is coupled to the pumping of protons from the stroma to the lumen.

ATP $\rightleftharpoons$ ADP + Pi, at each site is close to equilibrium and the ATP produced is tightly bound to the complex (Ort et al. 1992). The energy input from the proton gradient is used to release the ATP to produce soluble ATP, which is very far from thermodynamic equilibrium with the existing ADP and inorganic phosphate. A large electrochemical potential is required to activate and maintain catalytic activity of the complex; this gradient amounts to at least 50 kJ, and more likely 72 kJ, per mol ATP and is provided by 4 mol of $H^+$. The gradient can be maintained at very low photon fluxes at the expense of linear electron transport; however, in darkness the enzyme becomes inactivated and ATP synthesis ceases within a few seconds. The mechanism of altering ATP affinity appears to involve the translocation of a proton in $CF_0$. This translocation changes the affinity of subunit III of $CF_0$ with the $\varepsilon$ subunit of $CF_1$. This leads in turn to a change in the conformational state of $CF_0$ and alters the nucleotide affinity of the $\beta$ subunits. This mechanism allows a "long distance" interaction between the proton channel and the ATP-binding domains of the complex.

The $CF_0CF_1$ complex in vivo is subject to a hierarchy of regulatory processes including the electrochemical gradient across the thylakoid membrane, the oxidation state of a cystine bridge on the γ subunit of $CF_1$, and the interactive binding of ATP, ADP, and inorganic phosphate to $CF_1$. The reduction of the cystine sulfide bridge leads to an order of magnitude increase in catalytic activity. This reduction is activated by light, presumably through an endogenous donor such as thioredoxin, a small protein that contains a redox-activated dithiol/disulfide center (Chapter 4). Thioredoxin is reduced by reduced ferredoxin in PSI through the action of an enzyme, ferredoxin:thioredoxin oxidoreductase. This enzyme is post-transcriptionally controlled by the redox state of the electron transport chain and appears to affect the rate of transcription of a variety of chloroplast-encoded genes, especially psbA (Danon, Mayfield 1994).

Specifically, reduced thioredoxin can activate mRNA binding to an activator of translation within the chloroplast. The binding of the translational activator to the mRNA facilitates the translation of the message. Hence, in the light, when photosynthetic electron transport occurs, thioredoxin becomes chemically reduced. Reduced thioredoxin stimulates the translation of psbA and mRNA, leading to increased synthesis of D1 protein. This is an example of redox regulation of gene expression in photoautotrophs (Allen et al. 1995). We shall discuss the regulation of LHCII by light intensity via the redox status of the plastoquinone pool in Chapter 7.

### Ribulose-1,5-Bisphosphate Carboxylase/Oxygenase

Rubisco is a hydrophilic protein complex containing two subunits (Hartman, Harpel 1994). The large subunit, of approximately 53 kDa, is encoded by the rbcL gene, whereas the small subunit, of 14 kDa, is encoded by the RbcS (or rbcS) gene. The protein can account for up to 25% of the total cell protein in algae, and the two subunits are generally easily identified on stained polyacrylamide gels (Fig 6.11).

In vivo, the functional enzyme complex is a multimer of eight small and eight large subunits. In prokaryotes, heterokonts, haptophytes, cryptophytes, and rhodophytes, the large and small subunits are encoded on adjacent genes in the same genome. Thus, in prokaryotes, rbcL and rbcS are closely spaced on adjacent genes, and in the aforementioned eukaryotes both subunits are encoded in the chloroplast genome. In the euglenoids, chlorophyte algae, and higher plants, rbcL is localized in the chloroplast, whereas RbcS is nuclear-encoded (Freyssinet, Sailland 1991; Martin et al. 1992). Structural analysis of the crystalline protein complex reveals that the eight large subunits are arranged in a circular array while the eight small subunits form a lower node around the larger subunits (Fig 6.12). The active site of Rubisco is on the large subunit; consequently, that portion of the enzyme is relatively highly conserved at the amino acid level (Lorimer 1981). A specific N-terminal domain on one of the large subunits appears to interact sterically with sequences from the C-terminus of the adjacent large subunit. Thus, there are eight active sites per enzyme molecule.

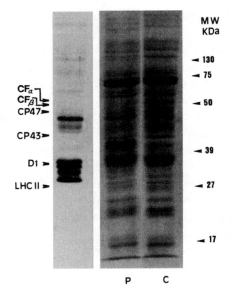

**Figure 6.11** Proteins on a polyacrylamide gel following electrophoretic separation showing the relative abundance of Rubisco. The large subunit forms a highly visible band at 55 kDa.

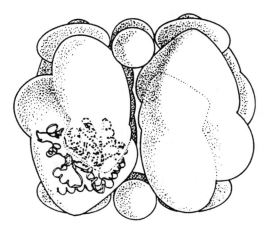

**Figure 6.12** A molecular diagram of the architecture of assembled Rubisco. Four dimers of the large subunits are arranged around a 4-fold (i.e., cross) axis, to build up the core of the molecule. Clusters of four small subunits bind at each end. The active sites for the enzyme are contained in the large subunits; one of these is shown on the left front dimer. (Adapted from Knight et al. J Mol Biol 1990, 215:113–160)

Control of expression of Rubisco activity in aquatic plants occurs at multiple levels and is related to the supply of $CO_2$ and other nutrients, but usually not light (Glover 1989). Whereas in higher plants, rbcS is transcriptionally controlled by irradiance level, in algae this environmental cue generally has little effect on the Rubisco level (Fisher et al. 1989; Sukenik et al. 1987b; but see Orellana, Perry 1992). There is some indication of transcriptional control of rbcL in some eukaryotes, but generally the enzyme is constitutively expressed. In cyanobacteria the level of rbcL transcripts may be entrained in a circadian rhythm, but is not a light-intensity–dependent gene. In *Chlamydomonas*, a decrease in ambient $CO_2$ has no effect on the steady-state level of mRNA of either rbcL or RbcS, but the protein level decreases (Portis et al. 1986). This effect appears to be a consequence of translational regulation. In chlorophyte algae, post-translational modification of Rubisco involves the removal of the N-terminal signal sequence from the small subunit following import of the unprocessed protein into the chloroplast. In all eukaryotes a further, essential post-translational modification requires conformational changes (i.e., proper "folding") aided by a specific protein called a *molecular chaperone* (Ellis 1990). The chaperone may in turn be regulated by environmental factors such as temperature and light (Roy 1992).

In vivo, Rubisco *enzyme activity* is highly regulated by light at a post-transcriptional level. That is, the enzyme levels do not necessarily reflect enzyme activity. Post-transcriptional regulation involves the reversible reaction of $CO_2$ with a lysine residue in the large subunit to form a carbamate intermediate form of the enzyme (Hartman et al. 1994). This intermediate is stabilized by the addition of $Mg^{2+}$. The carbamylation site differs from the catalytic site and the $CO_2$ used to form the carbamate intermediate is different from that used to carboxylate substrate ribulose-1,5-bisphosphate. The carbamylation site has a relatively low affinity for $CO_2$, and in vivo the enzyme would be largely inactive were it not for the presence of another enzyme that catalyzed the carbamylation. In vivo activation is mediated by Rubisco activase, a nuclear-encoded enzyme that is post-transcriptionally controlled (Portis et al. 1986). The activation requires ATP, RuBP, $CO_2$, and $Mg^{2+}$. The activase lowers the $CO_2$ concentration for full activation of Rubisco from $23\,\mu M$ (the concentration required for spontaneous activation) to $4\,\mu M$. The activase further prevents the inhibition of activation of Rubisco by RuBP. The light requirement for activation is related to the supply of ATP, which is a required substrate for the activase. The likely source of the ATP is via cyclic electron flow around PSI. As the light intensity is increased, the ATP supply is increased, and the rate of activation of Rubisco increases (Ogren 1984).

Catalysis by Rubisco involves the conversion of enzyme-bound RuBP to an enediolate which then can react with either $CO_2$ or $O_2$ to form anionic adducts. The ultimate formation of two moles of phosphoglycerate from the 3-keto-2-carboxy intermediate involves the reaction with a molecule of water. The oxygenase activity occurs when a hydroperoxy intermediate is formed and the subsequent disproportionation of RuBP results in the removal of a molecule of water to form one mole each of 2-phosphoglycolate and 3-phosphoglycerate (Hartman et al. 1994). This reaction is not unique to Rubisco, but can occur in other enzymes that have a carbanion intermediate. The oxygenase reaction is not the only side reaction that can occur. In approximately 1 out of 400 turnovers of the Calvin–Benson cycle, RuBP is converted to xylulose-1,5-bisphosphate and there is a similar frequency of production of an $\alpha$-keto intermediate (probably 3-keto-arabinitol-1,5-bisphosphate). Both of these "false" intermediates are potent inhibitors of Rubisco activity and contribute to the decline of enzyme activity in vitro with time. Their removal in vivo by metabolic processes may be a further important function of Rubisco activase.

## OVERALL REGULATION OF
## THE PHOTOSYNTHETIC APPARATUS

A useful, but by no means universal, rule of thumb concerning the regulation of the synthesis of components of the photosynthetic apparatus is that the genes coding for proteins involved in light-harvesting and photosynthetic electron transport are regulated by light while the genes coding for proteins in the Calvin–Benson cycle are not (Gruerson, Covey 1988). This means that light intensity more often affects the relative abundance of components of the electron transport chain than the enzymes involved in carbon fixation (Sukenik et al. 1987b). The regulation processes involve many genes not discussed here, including those responsible for lipid biosynthesis (Cho, Thompson 1989; Gombos, Murata 1991; Gombos et al. 1991; Hirayama, Inamura 1991; Horvath et al. 1987; Jones, Harwood 1993; Somerville, Browse 1991). It must be remembered that the structural organization of the photosynthetic apparatus requires that the electron transport chain be organized in membranes while the carbon fixation enzymes are soluble proteins. In Chapter 7 we examine how this machinery operates in continuous light.

# 7

# Photosynthesis in Continuous Light

Ultimately, the complex web of reactions that leads to photosynthetic carbon fixation must function in a coordinated fashion. Among other things, coordination means that light absorption by PSII and PSI is balanced so that electron transport between the two photosystems is optimized, the flux of reductant and ATP generated by the electron transport system is provided in the proper ratios and is sufficient to support the maximum rate of carbon fixation for a given light environment, and excess excitation energy is dissipated to prevent or minimize damage to the photosynthetic apparatus. As solar radiation is broad-band, continuous, and continuously changing, this coordination is dynamic and regulated at a number of levels to accommodate, insofar as possible, the changes in spectral irradiance regimes (Falkowski 1992). These include adjustments in the absorption cross-sections of the antenna systems, changes in the numbers of reaction centers and electron transport components and their relative proportions, and biochemical feedback and feedforward changes in the Calvin–Benson cycle, as well as changes in the levels of enzymes involved in carbon metabolism. Here we explore first the factors determining the photosynthesis-irradiance response, and then causes and consequences of their variations.

## THE PHOTOSYNTHESIS-IRRADIANCE CURVE

When a photosynthetic organism is confined in an enclosed volume, there is a net exchange of $CO_2$ and $O_2$ between the organism and the media. This exchange is light dependent. In darkness, there is a net consumption of $O_2$ and evolution of $CO_2$ due to respiratory processes (which we will discuss in Chapter 8). As the organisms are exposed to light, $O_2$ ultimately is evolved and $CO_2$ is consumed as a result of photosynthesis.

The rate of photosynthesis is controlled by the efficiency of light utilization to drive the ensemble of photosynthetic reactions from water splitting to carbon fixation. To a first order, the light dependency can be described as:

$$P_E = E_a \phi_E \tag{7.1}$$

where $P_E$ is a photosynthetic rate at any incident irradiance $E$, $E_a$ is the light absorbed by the organism (in quanta m$^{-2}$ time$^{-1}$), and $\phi_E$ is a quantum yield at irradiance $E$ (Bannister 1974). The absorbed light is measured or calculated from the incident spectral irradiance $E_{o(\lambda)}$ in conjunction with the spectrally averaged optical absorption cross-section, $a^*$:

$$E_a = E_{o(\lambda)}\, a^* \tag{7.2}$$

The in vivo, spectrally averaged optical absorption cross-sections are derived from measurements of the absorption spectra of cells (or a blade or leaf of a macrophyte) in a spectrophotometer, taking care to reduce or eliminate artifacts of light scattering (Dubinsky 1980; Kirk 1975; Morel 1991b). In this approach, the optical absorption cross-section is measured at each wavelength ($\lambda$) and normalized to chlorophyll *a*, thus:

$$a^*_{(\lambda)} = \frac{-\ln\left[E_{(\lambda)}\big/E_{o(\lambda)}\right]2.3}{\text{chlorophyll } a} \tag{7.3a}$$

where $E_{(\lambda)}$ is the transmitted irradiance for wavelength, and $E_{o(\lambda)}$ is the incident irradiance. The values of $a^*_{(\lambda)}$ can then be spectrally integrated over the range of photosynthetically available radiation (typically 400 to 700 nm):

$$\bar{a}^* = \int_{400}^{700} a^*_{(\lambda)} d_{(\lambda)} \tag{7.3b}$$

where $d_{(\lambda)}$ is the first derivative of absorbed irradiance with respect to $\lambda$. This calculation integrates all pigment absorption bands whether they be from carotenoids, phycobilipigments, accessory chlorophylls, or wherever and "assigns" them to chlorophyll *a* (Dubinsky et al. 1984). There is no implicit assumption about energy transfer in Equation 7.3b. The optical cross-section, $a^*$, describes the spectrally averaged target for the absorption of photons by all pigments in the photosynthetic

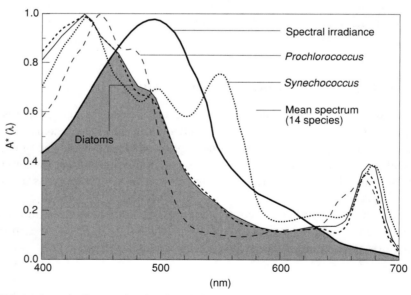

**Figure 7.1** A schematic diagram showing the relationship between the optical absorption cross-section and spectral irradiance. The typical optical absorption cross-sections normalized to chlorophyll *a* for diatoms, the cyanobacteria *Synechococcus* and *Prochlorococcus*, and an "average phytoplankton" are shown. Downwelling spectral irradiance at some depth, z, in a hypothetical water column is also represented. The area intersected by the absorption and spectral irradiance gives the spectrally averaged optical absorption cross-section (shaded for the case of the average phytoplankton).

apparatus (and other pigments outside of the photosynthetic apparatus, for that matter) (Fig 7.1). The numerical value of $\bar{a}^*$ is dependent on the spectral quality of the incident irradiance and will be different for different light sources or for different positions in a water column (Kirk 1994b). The value of $\bar{a}^*$ is independent of photon-flux densities.

As we discussed in Chapter 3, the quantum yield must be specifically related to a product of the photochemical reaction. For oxygenic photoautotrophs, usually this is oxygen evolved or carbon dioxide fixed; hence the units for the quantum yield are normally moles $O_2$ evolved or $CO_2$ fixed/moles photons absorbed. In practice, aquatic photosynthesis-irradiance relationships are usually based on the light-dependent changes in radioactive carbon incorporated into acid stable organic matter or changes in dissolved oxygen in the bulk fluid. It should be understood that exchanges of oxygen represent net fluxes, and are directly influenced by respiration (Geider, Osborne 1992). In contrast, measurements of the incorporation of radiocarbon into organic material are initially blind to the respiratory losses of carbon because the respired carbon is not radioactively labeled (Geider et al. 1986; Geider, Osborne 1989; Li, Goldman 1981; Pring, Jeusor 1992). Because of its sensitivity, the radiocarbon method is by far the most commonly used method to measure photosynthesis in natural phytoplankton communities. The isotope can be conveniently detected by scintillation counting, a highly sensitive and precise method. However, depending on the length of the incubation and the rate of growth of the cells, the method gives an ambiguous measurement of something between true net and true gross photosynthetic rates (we will discuss this in Chapter 9). Alternatively, changes in dissolved oxygen can be measured with an oxygen electrode, or by chemical titration using the Winkler method (see Geider, Osborne 1992 for a discussion of methods for measuring algal photosynthesis). Changes in oxygen concentration can be positive (net evolution) or negative (net consumption). Moreover, the measurement of oxygen evolution can be related to light reactions of photosynthesis, and specifically to PSII.

Unfortunately, most oxygen electrodes are relatively insensitive and often "noisy." Their use requires either considerable amounts of photosynthetic material, or averaging over relatively long periods of time. Hence, they are seldom used in the field (Bender et al. 1987). A "pulsed" electrode is more sensitive; the Winkler-based titrations are labor intensive, and, though they can be made with relatively high precision, good measurements require considerable care (Williams, Jenkinson 1982).

The photosynthesis-irradiance ($P$ vs. $E$)[1] response typically can be divided into three distinct regions, namely a light-limited region, a light-saturated region, and a

---

1. Irradiance is denoted by optical physicists by the symbol $E$ (not to be confused with the same symbol used in quantum mechanics to denote an energy level). Irradiance is the flux of radiant energy on an infinitesimally small element of a surface, divided by the area of that element. In some ways, this definition is internally inconsistent, in that an infinitesimally small area is a point, which does not have a surface area. Nonetheless, this formal definition yields empirically to instruments that measure irradiance with a defined surface area, and the commonly used units are in W m² or mol quanta $m^{-2}$ $s^{-1}$. The symbol $I$, which is sometimes used to denote irradiance, has been abandoned because it has been adopted to denote radiation intensity, which is the flux of radiant energy per unit solid angle in a specified direction (Kirk 1994). Radiant intensity, $I$, has units W (or mol quanta $s^{-1}$) steradian$^{-1}$.

photoinhibited region (Fig 7.2). At low irradiance levels, photosynthetic rates are linearly proportional to irradiance; a doubling of light intensity produces (almost) a doubling of photosynthetic rate. In this region of the *P* vs. *E* curve, the rate of photon absorption determines the rate of steady-state electron transport from water to $CO_2$, and thus it is called the light-limited region. If photosynthesis is measured as the change in $O_2$ concentration, then at low irradiance levels the rate of oxygen consumption will be greater than the rate of oxygen evolution; hence net oxygen evolution will be negative. At *very* low irradiance levels, which are often not experimentally resolved, the rate of $O_2$ evolution is sometimes lower than expected based on an extrapolation from slightly higher light levels (Kromer 1995). The deviation from linearity, first noted in 1949 by Bessel Kok (who noted the "S" states; see Chapter 4), is due to oxygen consumption in the thylakoids, a process often called *chlororespiration*. This phenomenon is especially pronounced in cyanobacteria, where the photosynthetic and respiratory metabolisms share common electron carriers, especially plastoquinone (Scherer 1990).

The light intensity at which photosynthesis balances respiration is called the *compensation light intensity, $E_c$*. It should be noted that the compensation light intensity measured at some point in time only equals the daily compensation light intensity if light is constant—a condition that occurs only in a laboratory. If the photosynthesis-irradiance curve is measured by following the incorporation of radioactive carbon into the cells, the time course of uptake is always positive and the compensation light intensity appears to be very close to zero (i.e., darkness). The initial slope of the photosynthesis-irradiance curve is proportional to the maximum quantum yield of photosynthesis (Kok 1948). This slope is not necessarily (in fact, seldom is) exactly the same for oxygen evolution and carbon fixation (Myers 1980).

In the aquatic sciences literature, the initial slope of the photosynthesis irradiance curve is often denoted by the symbol α (Jassby, Platt 1976). The slope can be

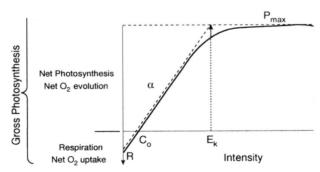

**Figure 7.2** An example of a typical photosynthesis vs. irradiance curve. This curve could be derived from measurements of net oxygen exchange between the organism and the bulk fluid. In the dark, there is a net consumption of oxygen as a consequence of respiration. Dark respiration, R, is generally assumed to remain constant in the light (see Chapter 8). At low irradiance levels, the evolution of oxygen is approximately a linear function of irradiance, and the ratio between photosynthesis and irradiance in this portion of the photosynthesis–irradiance profile is often denoted by the symbol α. At some irradiance level, photosynthetic rates reach a plateau. The light-saturated rate is denoted $P_{max}$. The saturation irradiance, $E_k$, is given as intercept between α and $P_{max}$. At supra-optimal irradiance levels, photosynthetic rates frequently decline from the light-saturated value. The rate of decline, β, is analogous to the intial slope, α, but with an opposite sign.

normalized to chlorophyll biomass and, if so, a superscript "B" is added to denote this normalization, thus, $\alpha^B$. The units for $\alpha^B$ are ($O_2$ evolved or $CO_2$ fixed per unit chlorophyll)/(quanta per unit area). Note that there is no dimension of time in the initial slope and that the irradiance term is for incident light ($E_o$), not absorbed light ($E_a$). The initial slope of the photosynthesis irradiance curve is not a photosynthetic rate, rather it is related to the *maximum* quantum yield, $\phi_m$, of photosynthesis through light absorption (Herron, Mauzerall 1971). This can be understood in the context of Equation 7.1, where the limit quantum yield is conditionally defined:

$$\phi_m = dP_E / dE_a$$
$$\text{as } E_o \to \text{zero(lim)} \tag{7.4}$$

If the initial slope is measured on a leaf or blade of a highly absorbing tissue, or in a culture of cells so dense that for all practical purposes all the photosynthetically active radiation is absorbed, the slope measured in incident light ($dO_2/E_o$ or $dCO_2/dE_o$) is approximately the same as that measured for absorbed light ($dO_2/E_a$ or $dCO_2/E_a$); thus the slope can be (and usually is) taken as a direct measure of the maximum quantum yield of photosynthesis (Lawlor 1993). This situation is approximated in higher plants, macrophyte algae, and extremely dense microalgal cultures where a relatively small fraction of the incident light (<10%) is lost by reflection or transmission (Ramus 1990). In fact, higher plant physiological ecologists often view the entire photosynthesis-irradiance response as a direct measure of the quantum yield of photosynthesis (Evans, Caemmerer 1988; Long et al. 1994; Osmond, Chow 1988). In natural phytoplankton communities or optically thin cultures, however, light absorption is a small fraction of the incident light and the initial slope is *not* a measure of the quantum yield (Falkowski, Dubinsky, Wyman 1985). To quantitatively relate the initial slope to the maximum quantum yield, the fraction of incident light that is absorbed must be measured (Eq 7.2). As measurements of light absorption in photosynthetic material are difficult, especially in natural samples, accurate measurements of the absolute maximum quantum yield of photosynthesis in natural phytoplankton communities are rare (Babin et al. 1995; Bidigare et al. 1992; Cleveland et al. 1989; Dubinsky et al. 1984).

One means of deriving the maximum quantum yield from $\alpha^B$ is to measure the spectral irradiance and the spectrally averaged optical absorption cross-section normalized to chlorophyll *a*, *a\**. The convolution of these two parameters, which gives the optical absorption cross-section for all of the pigments in the cell (Chapter 2), can be normalized to chlorophyll *a*. This normalization is convenient as it permits calculation of the absorbed light from measurements of chlorophyll *a* and incident spectral irradiance, both of which are technically feasible. From knowledge of $\bar{a}*$, the maximum quantum yield can be calculated thus:

$$\phi_m = \alpha^B / \bar{a}* \tag{7.5}$$

We can reframe Equation 7.5 to expand the terms. Let us assume that the pigments that absorb light are associated with the photosynthetic process and are related either to PSII or PSI. The ensemble of these pigments therefore is related to photosynthetic units, containing *x*PSII reaction centers + *y*PSI reaction centers. The *optical* absorption cross-section, $\bar{a}*$ (with units $m^2$ per unit chlorophyll *a*), can be rewritten as the product of the number, *n*, of functional photosynthetic units (with dimensions $O_2$/Chl $a$), and the *optical* absorption cross-section (see Chapter 3) of a photosynthetic unit, $\sigma_{PSU}$ (with dimensions $m^2/O_2$), thus:

$$a^* = n\sigma_{PSU} \tag{7.6}$$

Note that $n$ is the inverse of the Emerson–Arnold number (see Chapter 3); that is, it is the maximum number of oxygen molecules evolved in a single electron turnover of PSII and PSI normalized to chlorophyll $a$, while $\sigma_{PSU}$ describes the rate at which photons can be absorbed to *effectively* promote oxygen evolution (i.e., $m^2$ per $O_2$; see Chapter 3). From Equations 7.5 and 7.6, it can be shown that:

$$\alpha^B = n\sigma_{PSU}\phi_m \tag{7.7}$$

Equation 7.7 relates changes in $\alpha^B$ to the product of three terms: $n$, $\sigma_{PSU}$, and $\phi_m$ (Falkowski 1980; Herron et al. 1971). Note that because $\sigma_{PSU}$ is an absorption cross-section, it is wavelength dependent; consequently, $\alpha^B$ is wavelength dependent as well. In other words, measurements of $\alpha^B$ obtained with broad-band light sources will depend on the spectral quality of the light source. Thus, measurements of $\alpha^B$ (like $a^*$ or $\sigma_{PSU}$) values obtained with a quartz halogen light, which is relatively rich in the red portion of the spectrum, are not directly comparable to those obtained with a fluorescent light source or under natural solar radiation (Kirk 1992; Laws et al. 1990). To overcome this problem, $a^*$ is sometimes defined for the light source (Eq 7.5) in the measuring system or for a "white" light condition; the quantum yields thus calculated are directly comparable irrespective of the spectral quality of the light source.

It is possible to modify further Equation 7.7 and consider $\alpha^B$ from another viewpoint. Recall (Chapter 3) that the maximum quantum yield of photosynthesis can be related to the ratio of the absorption cross-section of the photosynthetic unit ($\sigma_{PSU}$) to that of the *functional* absorption cross-section of PSII ($\sigma_{PSII}$) (with dimension of $m^2$/quanta) (Chapter 3):

$$\phi_m = \sigma_{PSII}/\sigma_{PSU} \tag{3.11}$$

Substitution for $\phi_m$ in Equation 7.7 gives:

$$\alpha^B = n\sigma_{PSII} \tag{7.8}$$

Equation 7.8 reveals that the initial slope of the $P$ vs. $E$ curve is directly proportional to the *functional* absorption cross-section of PSII ($\sigma_{PSII}$) and the numbers ($n$) of photosynthetic units (Falkowski 1992), and is *not* a direct measure of $\phi_m$.[2]

## Light-Saturated Photosynthesis

As irradiance increases, photosynthetic rates become increasingly nonlinear and rise to a saturation level, $P_{max}$. By definition, at light saturation, the rate of photon

---

2. In this regard, because for most practical purposes all photosynthetically active radiation incident on a leaf is absorbed (the optical density of a leaf is about 3 or 4; that is, less than 10% of the light passes through from one side of a leaf to the other), the initial slope of the $P$ vs. $E$ curve in higher plants *is* directly proportional to $\phi_m$.

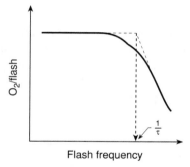

**Figure 7.3** A conceptual diagram showing the meaning of the rate-limiting reaction of photosynthesis. When oxygen evolution per flash is plotted as a function of flash frequency, the yield is constant at low flash rates. As flash frequency increases, however, the oxygen flash yield will fall off as processes other than light absorption become rate limiting. The intercept between the constant yield and the declining yield corresponds to the rate of the limiting reaction(s), denoted $1/\tau$. Note that this is another way of presenting the data shown in Figure 3.3.

absorption exceeds the rate of steady-state electron transport from water to $CO_2$. Unlike $\alpha^B$, light-saturated photosynthesis explicitly incorporates time in its dimensions (e.g., $O_2$ evolved or $CO_2$ fixed per unit chlorophyll per unit time), and is independent of either the optical or functional absorption cross-section of the photosynthetic apparatus. Consequently, $P_{max}$ *cannot be derived directly from knowledge of light absorption.* Instead, the maximum photosynthetic rate is related to the number of photosynthetic units ($n$) and their maximum turnover rate ($1/\tau$):[3]

$$P^B_{max} = n(1/\tau) \tag{7.9}$$

At light saturation, $1/\tau$ is the maximum rate at which electrons are transferred from $H_2O$ to the terminal electron acceptors (e.g., $CO_2$) in the steady state (Myers, Graham 1971). Conceptually, $1/\tau$ can be directly measured by following the oxygen evolution induced by a saturating flash as a function of flash frequency. At some flash frequency, oxygen evolution will become saturated (Fig 7.3a); that frequency corresponds to $1/\tau$ (Kok 1956). In practice, however, such an experiment is technically complicated by the nature of flash systems. Flash systems use energy stored in large capacitors. As the flash rate increases, it becomes difficult to recharge the capacitors fully and the light energy per flash decreases. The flash rates needed to reach $1/\tau$ are typically between 200 and $1000\,s^{-1}$; and it is difficult to maintain flash intensities sufficient to saturate oxygen evolution at such rates. However, rearrangement of Equation 7.9 (i.e., solving the equation for $1/\tau$) reveals that $1/\tau$ is the ratio of the maximum rate of steady-state photosynthesis under continuous light and the photosynthetic unit size (i.e., the Emerson–Arnold number); these latter two parameters can be measured relatively easily in the laboratory, and $1/\tau$ is usually derived from them rather than directly measured.

What causes the curvature in the steady-state photosynthesis irradiance curve? It is convenient to consider the intersection of $\alpha$ and $P_{max}$ (see Fig 7.2). This abstract

---

3. The $\tau$ used in Equation 7.9 is a unit of time and should not be confused with the same symbol ascribed to the $CO_2/O_2$ selectivity factor for Rubisco in Chapter 5.

## ❏ CALCULATING $1/\tau$

*The calculation of $1/\tau$ from measurements of oxygen evolution in continuous saturating light and the oxygen flash yields was first described by Myers and Graham (1971) for* Chlorella. *The rationale for the calculation can be described as follows: Imagine that the frequency of single-turnover saturating flashes was increased infinitely, until the light became continuous. The oxygen evolution supported by continuous saturating light (i.e., $P^B_{max}$) is expressed as moles $O_2$ per unit chlorophyll per unit time. The oxygen evolved per single-turnover flash corresponds to an instant in time; in principle the same amount of oxygen will be evolved for a flash lasting 1 microsecond or 1 nanosecond. Thus, oxygen flash yields have dimensions of moles $O_2$ per mole chlorophyll. If the reciprocal of the Emerson–Arnold number (i.e., $O_2$/chlorophyll) is multiplied by $P^B_{max}$, the result is a rate corresponding to the maximum steady-state rate of photosynthetic electron transport.*

point on the photosynthesis-irradiance curve, which is never actually measured, is often called the light-saturation parameter, denoted by $E_k$ in the aquatic sciences literature[4] (Talling 1957). $E_k$ represents an optimum on the photosynthesis irradiance curve. At irradiance levels lower than $E_k$, the rate of photon absorption is less than $1/\tau$ and the quantum yield of photosynthesis is higher but absolute photosynthetic rates are less than maximal. At higher irradiance levels, the rate of photon absorption exceeds $1/\tau$, and the quantum yield of photosynthesis decreases but nothing can be gained (and potentially much can be lost) by increasing light absorption without simultaneously increasing $1/\tau$.

$E_k$ can be defined as:

$$E_k = P_{max}/\alpha \tag{7.10}$$

$E_k$ is independent of whether $P_{max}$ and $\alpha$ are normalized to chlorophyll, cell volume, or so on, as long as both parameters are normalized to the same variable. Substitution for $\alpha$ and $P_{max}$ in Equations 7.9 and 7.10 reveals that

$$E_k = 1/(\sigma_{PSII}\tau) \tag{7.11a}$$

Thus, $E_k$ is directly proportional to the reciprocal of both $\sigma_{PSII}$ and $\tau$ (Falkowski 1992). Because $E_k$ is determined in part by $\sigma_{PSII}$, and $\sigma_{PSII}$ is wavelength dependent (Eq 3.11), $E_k$, like $\alpha$, is wavelength dependent and will vary as an inverse function of the photosynthetic action spectrum of PSII; that is, as the quantum yield for photosynthesis increases at a given wavelength, $E_k$ will be lower. It should be noted that $E_k$ is a special point on the photosynthesis-irradiance curve. By simply rearranging Equation 7.11a, it is clear that

$$E_k\sigma_{PSII} = 1/\tau \tag{7.11b}$$

---

4. Curiously, the concept of $E_k$ apparently did not transcend the aquatic sciences literature to higher plant physiology. Nor, for that matter, has the term $\alpha$. Rather, higher plant physiologists have, for the most part, assumed that because the optics of leaves are so complicated, the mathematical representation of $P$ vs. $E$ curves is empirical (Leverenz 1992); generally, they have been more concerned with assessing the factors limiting the maximum quantum yield and the light-saturated rate of photosynthesis (Farquhar et al. 1980), rather than describing the shape of the curve.

The left side of Equation 7.11b describes the rate of photochemistry at steady-state irradiance level $E_k$, whereas the right side is the maximum rate of photosynthetic electron transport. These two processes are equal only at one irradiance level, namely $E_k$. At irradiances less than $E_k$, electron transport capacity exceeds the rate at which photons are absorbed and delivered to PSII, and at irradiance levels greater than $E_k$ the converse is true. Hence, the optimum photosynthetic rate is achieved at $E_k$ even though the *quantum yield of photosynthesis at that irradiance may not be maximal.*

**Supraoptimal Irradiance**

Further increases in irradiance beyond light saturation can lead to a reduction in photosynthetic rate from the maximum saturation level (Baker, Bowyer 1994). This reduction, which is dependent on both the intensity of the light and the duration of exposure, is often called *photoinhibition* in the aquatic sciences literature, although more formally, *photoinhibition is the light-dependent, slowly reversible retardation of photosynthesis, independent of any developmental change* (Long et al. 1994; Neale 1987). Such a definition indicates that photoinhibition can occur at suboptimal irradiance levels and would be manifested as a hysteresis[5] in the $P$ vs. $E$ curve; that is, the photosynthetic rates as a function of light intensity would depend on whether the $P$ vs. $E$ curve is measured for increasing or decreasing light intensity (Osmond 1994).

Photoinhibition can be thought of as a modification of $P_{max}$ by either a reduction in the number of photosynthetic units or by an increase in the maximum turnover rate (Eq 7.9). It is rather simple to demonstrate that the reduction in the photosynthetic rate is primarily a consequence of the increase in turnover time by exposing the organism to a supraoptimal irradiance level and then measuring either the oxygen flash yield or maximum variable fluorescence yield in the dark (Long et al. 1994; Neale 1987). Invariably, photoinhibition results in a reduction in both of these parameters, which implies that photoinhibition leads to a reduction in the photochemical efficiency of PSII (Falk et al. 1992; Falkowski et al. 1994; Giersch, Krause 1991; Jones, Kok 1966; Matorin et al. 1992; Öquist et al. 1992; Samuelsson, Richardson 1982; Steemann-Nielsen 1952; Vincent et al. 1984). Thus, photoinhibition effectively leads to a reduction in the population of functional ($O_2$-evolving) reaction centers.

We have seen that the basic features of the photosynthesis-irradiance curve—the initial slope, the maximum photosynthetic rate, and the light saturation parameter and photoinhibition—can be related to three parameters, namely $n$, $\sigma_{PSII}$, and $1/\tau$. It follows that variations in $P$ vs. $E$ curves are a consequence of variations in one or more of these biophysical parameters. Let us now examine how these parameters vary in vivo, and the causes of their variation.

---

5. A hysteresis produces a lag in a process in relation to its driving force. For example, photosynthetic electron transport may be lower for a given irradiance when measured when samples are exposed to light in succcessively decreasing irradiance levels compared with that measured when exposed to successively increasing irradiance levels.

## VARIATIONS IN $n$, $\sigma_{PSII}$, AND $1/\tau$ IN CONTINUOUS LIGHT

Changes in the biophysical parameters that determine the photosynthetic response in continuous light can be measured with an oxygen rate electrode and/or by following changes in the quantum yield of fluorescence. Let us first consider an optically thin, homogeneous, monolayer sample of cells on a bare platinum oxygen rate electrode (see Chapter 3), illuminated by a uniform beam of white light. A photosynthetic response can be elicited by exposing the sample to a continuous light, and the photosynthesis-irradiance curve can be derived by varying its intensity. If a single-turnover saturating flash is superimposed on the continuous background light, the oxygen evolved in response to the actinic flash can be simultaneously detected. The oxygen flash yield will be indicative of the fraction of the total number of PSII reaction centers in the $S_3$ state at that moment. By varying the intensity of the actinic flash it is possible to quantitatively measure the absorption cross-section of PSII under a continuous background irradiance by determining the flash intensity saturation profile for oxygen. Moreover, by following the change in the quantum yield of fluorescence preceding and succeeding the actinic "pump" flash, it is possible to follow the oxidation of $Q_A^-$ simultaneously from the decay of variable fluorescence (see Fig 4.8; Falkowski, Wyman et al. 1986).

The oxygen flash yield behavior elicited by saturating single-turnover flashes is markedly different under continuous background light than in darkness. While in darkness, the oxygen flash yield is maximum on the third flash and subsequently follows a four-flash periodicity (see Fig 4.3); in continuous background light, flash yields are independent of flash number from the very outset (Joliot 1993). This difference reveals that the S states are randomly distributed, even at very low continuous irradiance levels. The randomization of the S states in continuous light simplifies the interpretation of oxygen flash yields, as under such conditions it follows that 25% of the PSII reaction centers are in the $S_3$ state at any instant of time (Myers, Graham 1971; Falkowski et al. 1981).

The yields of oxygen induced by a saturating flash are markedly affected by continuous background irradiance levels. If the sample is exposed to *very low* irradiance levels and the flash rate is less than about $1\,s^{-1}$, the oxygen produced by the flash will be 50% to 75% of the maximum value observed at a slightly higher flash rate or continuous irradiance levels. The decline in flash yield under such conditions (i.e., with background irradiance levels comparable to that of the light of the moon, or about $0.1\,\mu mol\,quanta\,m^{-2}s^{-1}$) is a consequence of the decay of the $S_3$ state to lower S states (see Fig 4.4; Ley, Mauzerall 1982). From knowledge of the effective absorption cross-section of PSII and the lifetime of $S_3$, we can calculate the lower limit of gross oxygen evolution. A typical value of $\sigma_{PSII}$ at 475 nm is approximately 4 to 5 $nm^2$/quanta. To maintain $O_2$ evolution and a maximum steady-state population of $S_3$, each PSII reaction center must receive a minimum of 1 quanta/s. Thus, the minimum irradiance required to maintain this photosynthetic rate is about $2 \times 10^{13}\,quanta\,cm^{-2}s^{-1}$ ($\sim 0.33\,\mu mol\,quanta\,m^{-2}s^{-1}$); this corresponds to approximately 0.02% of the maximum solar irradiance incident on the Earth's surface at local noon. Indeed, some red algae appear to be able to grow photoautotrophically at such very low photon flux densities (Littler et al. 1985). Importantly, even under such low irradiance conditions a pH gradient across the thylakoid membranes is established, as proton pumping is primarily the consequence not of the action of single reaction centers, but of the ensemble of reaction centers in the chloroplast (Raven 1984a). However, the intrinsic permeability of the lipid bilayer to protons places constraint on the efficiency of photosynthesis at very low photon flux densities, due to leakage of $H^+$ across the thylakoids as well as to decay of the S states (Raven, Beardall 1981b, 1982).

As continuous background irradiance increases slightly, oxygen flash yields reach a maximum and remain at a relative plateau over some range of irradiances (Ley, Mauzerall 1982). This region corresponds to $\alpha$, the region of the photosynthesis-irradiance curve where the quantum yield of oxygen evolution is maximum. The plateau of the flash yields indicates that *the probability of an exciton encountering an open reaction center is constant*; this is another definition for $\alpha$.

A further increase in irradiance induces a sharp decline in oxygen flash yields. The inflection corresponds to $E_k$, a region when reaction centers start to become closed by the background light (Kolber, Falkowski 1993). The flash yields continue to decline asymptotically to zero as background light intensity approaches saturation. It should be noted that, even at light saturation (indeed, even at supraoptimal light), there is a finite probability of finding an open reaction center at any given moment in time (Falkowski, Wyman et al. 1986; Ley, Mauzerall 1982).

It is possible to simultaneously measure the fluorescence parameters, $F_0$, $F_m$, and the maximum change in variable fluorescence along with the oxygen flash yields. $F_v$ and the components of fluorescence are indicative of the redox state of $Q_A$ and fluorescence quenching behavior is a function of irradiance. At the very lowest irradiance levels, while the oxygen flash yield is rising, variable fluorescence yields decline slightly (Falkowski et al. 1986). The reason for this decline is unclear; however, it is often correlated with a small increase in $F_0$, suggesting a closure of PSII reaction centers. This phenomenon may be due to the reduction of $Q_A$ in a small fraction of reaction centers that have a low turnover time (the so-called "$\beta$-centers"; see Melis, Anderson 1983). It has also been interpreted as a change in the intrinsic quantum yield of chlorophyll fluorescence induced by an electrochemical potential that is established across the thylakoid membrane at low irradiance levels (Crofts, Yerkes 1994; Falkowski, Wyman et al. 1986; Ley, Mauzerall 1982).

The decline in variable fluorescence ceases at the same irradiance at which oxygen flash yields plateau (Falkowski et al. 1988). If the two indices of PSII activity are normalized at this point, the subsequent behavior of variable fluorescence and oxygen flash yields is identical up until light saturation. As light becomes saturating, the relative values of variable fluorescence are typically 10% to 15% higher than those for oxygen flash yields. This mismatch between variable fluorescence and oxygen flash yields implies that at light saturation PSII reaction centers appear to be relatively more closed on the donor side (i.e., they form little $S_3$), than the acceptor side (there is still variable fluorescence, indicating a pool of oxidized $Q_A$). The uncoupling between variable fluorescence and oxygen flash yields suggests cycling of electrons around PSII at high irradiance levels, which supports 10% to 15% of the electron flow (Falkowski, Fujita et al. 1986; Prasil et al. 1996). This cycle effectively dissipates "excess" light, and may be a mechanism for photoprotection.

As we have seen, the maximum quantum yield of photosynthesis can be expressed as the ratio of the effective absorption cross-section of PSII to that of the photosynthetic unit (Eq 3.11). Photosynthetic organisms have developed mechanisms for adjusting both of these cross-sections to optimize light absorption by either PSII or PSI, or to reduce total photon absorption at high irradiance levels. Far more is known about the adjustment of PSII cross-sections than for PSI because changes in the former are relatively easy to monitor from changes in fluorescence or oxygen evolution (Bonaventura, Myers 1969; Falkowski, Fujita 1987; Falkowski et al. 1994; Fujita et al. 1994; Genty et al. 1990; Ley 1980; Zipfel, Owens 1991). These changes in fluorescence yields and oxygen evolution indicate that the functional absorption cross-section of PSII varies as a function of background irradiance. The variations occur on a variety of time scales and can profoundly influence the photosynthesis-irradiance response (Falkowski et al. 1994; Olaizola et al. 1994). We will consider three types of adjustments, namely the state transitions, nonphotochemical quenching resulting from xanthophyll cycling, and photoacclimation.

## State Transitions

The distribution of excitation energy between PSII and PSI may profoundly influence the rate of electron flow from water to NADPH. If more excitation energy is absorbed by PSII than by PSI, the electron carriers on the acceptor side of PSII (e.g., plastoquinone) could become quickly reduced, resulting in decreased photosynthetic rates. Such a condition reduces the quantum yield of photosynthesis, especially at subsaturating light. To reduce the effect of unbalanced excitation energy, plants have evolved a variety of mechanisms that allow for the redistribution of excitation energy between the photosystems.

In 1969, Bonaventura and Myers, working with a bare platinum oxygen rate electrode, observed that when the unicellular green alga *Chlorella* was exposed to light at 645 nm, which is preferentially absorbed by chlorophyll *b* and transfers the excitation energy more to PSII than to PSI (which they knew from the action spectra for $O_2$), chlorophyll fluorescence decreased and oxygen evolution increased over a period of about 5 to 10 minutes to a new steady state. When cells were subsequently exposed to light at 680 nm, which was preferentially absorbed by chlorophyll *a* and was linked more to PSI than to PSII, fluorescence increased and oxygen evolution decreased over a period of 5 to 10 minutes to a new steady state. They called the 645 nm light, Light 2, and the 680 nm light, Light 1; and correspondingly, the conditions induced by each of the respective lights were called State II and State I. Murata (1970b), working with a red alga with which it was easier to selectively excite PSII and PSI because the phycobilisomes primarily direct absorbed excitation to the former photosystem, observed a similar response. Because the time for the transition from State I to State II and vice versa was much too long to be attributable to the Emerson enhancement, it was clear that the two states were a consequence of another phenomenon.

Bonaventura and Myers suggested that the state transitions were brought about by complementary changes in the functional absorption cross-sections of PSII and

PSI (i.e., $\sigma_{PSII}$ and $\sigma_{PSI}$). Thus, when cells are initially exposed to Light 1, relatively more photons are absorbed by PSI than PSII and initially the quantum yield for oxygen evolution is low. Somehow, over a period of a few minutes, the effective absorption cross-section for the light-harvesting antennae serving PSII increased, leading to an increase in the quantum yield for oxygen evolution. Interestingly, the fluorescence yield acted in a complementary fashion: when oxygen evolution was high, fluorescence was low and vice versa. The process was readily reversible such that if cells were exposed to Light 2, the effective absorption cross-section of PSII somehow decreased. Bonaventura and Myers suggested that the cross-section lost by one or the other photosystem was gained by the complementary photosystem such that an optimum quantum yield for photosynthesis could be maintained. This hypothesis has been experimentally verified by simultaneous measurements of the changes in PSII and PSI cross-sections during state transitions (Samson, Bruce 1995). Alternatively, Murata (1970b) suggested that excitation absorbed by one photosystem could directly "spill over" to the other photosystem, assuming that the light-harvesting systems were shared by both photosystems. Experimental evidence for the spillover model has been provided in cyanobacteria (Fujita et al. 1994).

In the early 1980s, it was discovered that if thylakoid membranes were exposed to $\gamma$-$^{32}$P-labeled ATP, some proteins became labeled with the phosphate (Bennett 1980). One of the most prominent proteins to become phosphorylated was the light-harvesting chlorophyll-protein complex which is primarily associated with PSII (LHCII). When cells were exposed to Light 2, the light-harvesting chlorophyll proteins became labeled with $^{32}$P, while the LHC proteins in cells exposed to Light 1 did not become phosphorylated (Allen et al. 1981; Bennett 1984). The phosphorylation of the light-harvesting chlorophyll *a*/*b* proteins could be related to the redox state of the plastoquinone pool. When the reduction of the plastoquinone pool was blocked with DCMU, the light-harvesting pigment-protein complexes were not phosphorylated. However, if the oxidation of plastoquinol by the cytochrome $b_6/f$ complex was inhibited with DCMIB, phosphorylation was greatly enhanced. Thus, the state transitions observed by Bonaventura and Myers were phenomenologically related to the phosphorylation of the light-harvesting chlorophyll-protein complex, and the redox status of the plastoquinone pool appeared to control both the phosphorylation of the light-harvesting complex and the state transitions (Bennett 1991).

Subsequent to the discoveries of the state transitions and redox-dependent phosphorylation of light-harvesting complexes, considerable effort was exerted both to understand how the effective absorption cross-sections of PSII and PSI were related to phosphorylation, and to isolate and characterize the kinases and phosphatases responsible for the reversible reactions. Phosphorylation of light-harvesting complexes is almost universal; it is found not only in the chlorophyll *a*/*b* pigment-protein complexes of green algae and higher plants, but also in the phycobilisomes of cyanobacteria and the chlorophyll *a*/*c* complexes of chromophyte algae (Allen 1992; Fork et al. 1991; Fujita et al. 1994). In the chlorophyll *a*/*b* proteins the amino acids phosphorylated are either serine or threonine and are close to the N-terminus. Phosphorylation adds negative charge to the protein and, though the overall change in charge density may be small, it appears to be locally significant enough to induce a detachment of some fraction of the pigment-protein complex from PSII. Does the detached light-harvesting complex migrate to the complementary photosystem? It would appear so. Careful studies of the simultaneous changes in the complementary effective absorption cross-sections of PSII and PSI in both eukaryotic algae and cyanobacteria suggest that the state transitions lead to changes in PSII cross-sections on the order of about 10% and simultaneously affect PSI cross-sections in the opposite way (Allen 1992).

Do state transitions occur in nature? And if so, how important are they? The original discovery of the state transitions, based on changes in spectral quality, obscured the ecophysiological aspects of the response. In most aquatic systems, red and far-red light is rapidly attenuated with depth in the water column (an exception is algal mats, when far-red light can penetrate into the inner layer), while blue and/or blue-green irradiance has the greatest penetration. A cell in the upper portion of the water column, exposed to increased red and far-red light, would be in a Light 1 state and have a high PSII cross-section. As the absolute irradiance in this portion of the water column is also high, such a physiological condition would be counterproductive; the absorption of light by the cell, especially the absorption of light by PSII, is not rate limiting and could actually reduce the quantum yield of photosynthesis by overexcitation of the reaction center. Cells deeper in the water column, exposed to a higher proportion of blue and blue-green light, would be predisposed to a Light 2 state and be unable to increase light absorption for PSII at low photon flux densities. This would also be counterproductive as the cells would be reducing the functional absorption cross-section of PSII when they are starved for light.

The state transitions probably do occur as a first line of regulation to small changes in irradiance level (Falkowski et al. 1994). The state transitions are not so much dependent on the wavelength of excitation as the reduction level of the plastoquinone pool. In this context, cells at high irradiance, which tend to have a reduced PQ pool, would also tend to promote phosphorylation of the light-harvesting pigment-proteins serving PSII. This effect would thereby reduce the effective absorption cross-section of PSII and excitation delivery for that photosystem. Cells deeper in the water column, with a largely oxidized PQ pool, would tend to dephosphorylate the light-harvesting pigment-protein complex and thereby increase the absorption cross-section and light-harvesting ability of PSII. The changes in the absorption cross-section of PSII afforded by the state transitions are on the order of 10% to 20%. Such changes are relatively small, but perhaps are important at lower irradiance levels. Such changes would produce a corresponding shift in $E_k$ and thus help to balance light absorption with electron transport. However, such an effect is much too small to significantly optimize light utilization at high irradiance levels.

It is important to recognize, however, that while the magnitude of the change afforded by state transitions is relatively modest, the response is relatively rapid (Ley 1980). The rapidity with which an organism may adjust the absorption cross-section of PSII at low irradiance allows for adjustment in light utilization to match the scale of the passage of clouds across the sky and the changes in irradiance received by the understory of canopies in kelp forests.

## Nonphotochemical Quenching—The Xanthophyll Cycle

The state transitions alter the effective absorption cross-sections of the photosystems by physically coupling and decoupling the light-harvesting antennae of chlorophyll-protein complexes with the reaction centers. An alternative mechanism for dynamically altering the effective absorption cross-section of the antennae is to dissipate absorbed excitation energy thermally. Evidence for such a dissipation can be found by following the quenching of in vivo fluorescence.

In vivo chlorophyll fluorescence was introduced in the 1960s as a means of estimating phytoplankton chlorophyll without extracting pigments (Lorenzen 1966). Literally tens of thousands of profiles of fluorescence have been made in the oceans using a variety of commercial instruments. Early on researchers noted that the quantum yield of in vivo fluorescence was highly variable, and was light dependent (Abbott et al. 1982; Slovacek, Hannan 1977; Yentsch, Ryther 1967). This light dependency of fluorescence yields can be seen in Figure 7.4 where at high irradiance levels both $F_0$ and $F_m$ decline markedly. The variability in fluorescence was a source of frustration to oceanographers who desired to establish simple regression relationships between in vivo and extracted chlorophyll fluorescence (Slovacek, Hannan 1977).

According to an early interpretation, changes in chlorophyll fluorescence yields were related to the oxidation state of $Q_A$ (recall that "Q" was first used as an abbreviation for the "quencher" of fluorescence). When a photosynthetic organism is taken from light to darkness, $Q_A^-$ becomes oxidized relatively rapidly, on the time scale of milliseconds, and hence fluorescence should return to preillumination values. When DCMU is added in the light, all $Q_A$ should become reduced and variable fluorescence should be eliminated. Under such conditions, the quantum yield of fluorescence should be constant, but this does not occur—DCMU-poisoned cells still display a light dependency of fluorescence yield. Much more commonly, after exposure to bright light chlorophyll fluorescence yields in the dark are relatively low for an extended period, sometimes for many minutes (Bates 1985). This phenomenon cannot be attributed to quenching by the photochemical reduction of $Q_A$, and hence is called *nonphotochemical fluorescence quenching* (Falkowski, Kiefer 1985; Falkowski, Wyman et al. 1986; Schreiber et al. 1986).

The question of the origin of nonphotochemical quenching is related to the photobiological function of the quenching process(es). If quenching occurs only in the pigment bed, it should be associated with a change in the effective absorption cross-section of PSII. This effect is independent of any effect on the quantum yield of photochemistry within the reaction center. Thus, a reduction in variable fluorescence must have origins in the reaction center. To resolve this problem we consider the following model. A loss of quantum efficiency in photochemistry of PSII, resulting from an increase in nonphotochemical quenching within the reaction center, would lead to a reduction in the saturation level of a flash-intensity saturation curve for variable fluorescence (or oxygen evolution), without invoking any change in the effective absorption cross-section of PSII. In contrast, thermal dissipation in the antennae competes with the reaction center for excitation energy (Chapter 3) and would be reflected by a decrease in the effective

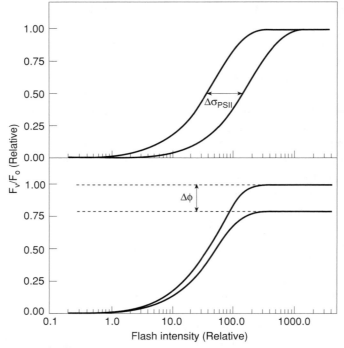

**Figure 7.4** The effect of nonphotochemical quenching on the effective absorption cross-section of PSII. An increase in nonphotochemical quenching in the antenna leads to a reduction in the effective absorption cross-section without necessarily a loss in the maximum quantum yield of photochemistry. If nonphotochemical quenching occurs in the reaction center, however, there would be a reduction in photochemical efficiency without a concomitant loss of effective absorption cross-section.

absorption cross-section of PSII (Genty et al. 1990; Olaizola et al. 1994; Vassiliev et al. 1994).

If one measures both the minimum and maximum quantum yields of fluorescence simultaneously as a function of background irradiance, nonphotochemical quenching of both fluorescence components is readily detectable at higher irradiance levels. Simultaneous and proportional decreases in the $F_0$ and $F_m$ signals should therefore correspond to a decrease in the absorption cross-section of PSII (Falkowski et al. 1994; Krause, Weis 1991). Thus, if the origin of nonphotochemical quenching is in the antenna of PSII, we would expect to find a significant reduction in the effective absorption cross-section of PSII at high irradiance levels. That is exactly what is observed (Fig 7.4). The change in PSII absorption cross-section afforded by the nonphotochemical quenching can approach 50%, thus implying a corresponding decrease in excitation delivery to PSII reaction centers (Kolber et al. 1993; Olaizola et al. 1994). Such a decrease in absorption cross-section is significant, and will shift $E_k$ to correspondingly higher values (Eq 7.11a).

What causes antenna quenching? In the mid-1960s, Harry Yamamoto, working with higher plants, observed that three oxygenated carotenoids (i.e., the xanthophylls), namely zeaxanthin, antheroxanthin, and violaxanthin,[6] could be intercon-

---

6. It should be noted that violaxanthin is an important light-harvesting pigment in eustimatophytes, which are commonly found in coastal waters (Sukenik et al. 1992).

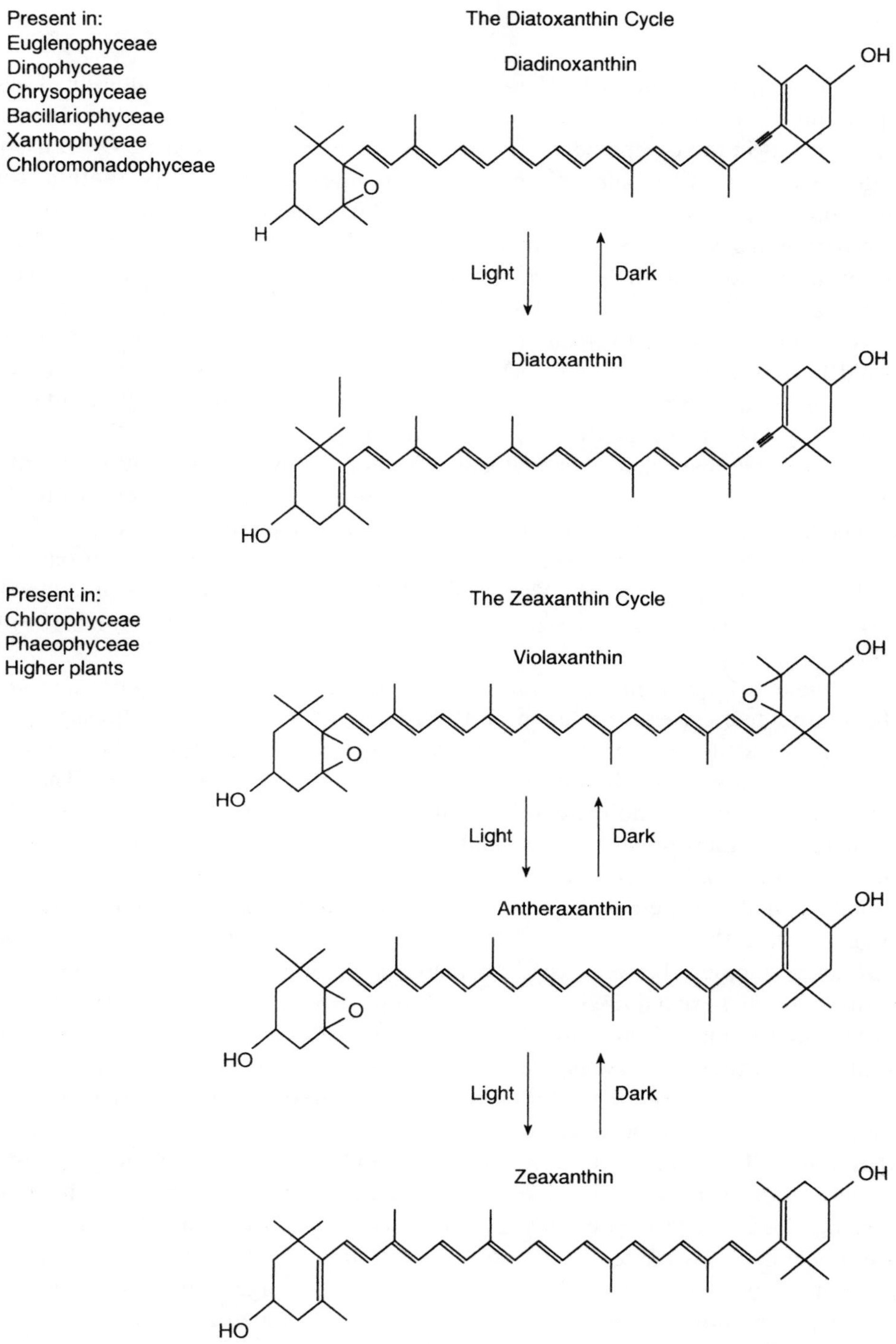

**Figure 7.5** The xanthophyll cycles. In chromophyte algae, the epoxidated xanthophyll, diadinoxanthin, is enzymatically de-epoxidated and converted to diatoxanthin in the light. The backreaction is enzymatically catalyzed in the dark. Diatoxanthin appears to be a quencher of excitation energy within the antenna, and its formation leads to a reduction in the effective absorption cross-section of PSII. In chlorophyte algae, the xanthophyll cycle involves the sequential de-epoxidation of violaxanthin, through antheroxanthin to zeaxanthin. The accumulation of zeaxanthin and antheroxanthin is correlated with an increase in nonphotochemical quenching in the antenna of PSII.

verted (Yamamoto et al. 1963). These three compounds differ by the addition of one or two epoxide groups on the flanking rings (Fig 7.5). At high light most of the xanthophyll was in the de-epoxidated form, zeaxanthin, while in darkness the zeaxanthin was converted to violaxanthin through the intermediate antheroxanthin. The interconversion was rapid, on the order of 30 minutes, and stoichiometric. In microalgae this conversion rate can be an order of magnitude faster. For each mole of zeaxanthin formed, one mole of violaxanthin plus antheroxanthin was lost. Tracer analysis with $^{18}O_2$ revealed that the source of the oxygen for the epoxidation was molecular $O_2$, not water (Yamamoto, Chichester 1965). The de-epoxidation reaction could be blocked with a thiol, such as dithiothreitol (Yamamoto, Kamite 1972). These three xanthophylls are found in all higher plants and chlorophytes (and have been purported to be in the phaeophytes) (Hagar, Stransky 1970; Siefermann-Harms 1985). Subsequently, an analogous xanthophyll cycle was found in chromophyte algae in which the monoepoxide diadinoxanthin is converted to the de-epoxidated form diatoxanthin in high light, and the backreaction occurs in darkness (Hagar, Stansky 1970). Dithiothreitol also blocks the de-epoxidation reaction in the chromophytes (Olaizola, Yamamoto 1993). No xanthophyll cycle or analogue has been discovered in phycobilisome-containing organisms (Siefermann-Harms 1985) or in the prochlorophytes.

In the mid-1980s, Demmig-Adams correlated nonphotochemical quenching with the xanthophyll cycle (Demmig et al. 1987; Demmig-Adams 1990). She suggested that somehow the de-epoxidated xanthophylls quenched chlorophyll fluorescence, and that this process was important in protecting PSII from overexcitation. The correlation between nonphotochemical quenching and the formation of diatoxanthin in diatoms further implicated the xanthophylls in thermal deactivation (Olaizola, Yamamoto 1993). Normally, photosynthetic carotenoids transfer excitation energy to chlorophylls. In the case of nonphotochemical quenching in the antennae, it is suggested that the reverse occurs (Ting, Owens 1993). This process can result from resonance coupling between the epoxidated xanthophylls, zeaxanthin and diatoxanthin, and the excited singlet states of chlorophyll *a*, which favors the deactivation of the singlet state of chlorophyll (Frank, Cogdell 1996). In these two epoxidated xanthophylls, there is a singlet excited state with an absorption band with a slightly lower energy level than that of a higher singlet excited state of chlorophyll *a*. The formation of these carotenoids in the antennae tends to facilitate the loss of excitation in the bed via radiationless decay (i.e., heat). The resonance energy transfer requires a very close physical proximity of the chlorophylls and xanthophylls (Frank, Cogdell 1996). Alternatively, it has been suggested that the formation of xanthophylls is correlated with the aggregation of light-harvesting chlorophyll protein complexes serving PSII (Horton 1992); such an aggregation would lead to a decrease in fluorescence yield and a reduction in the functional absorption cross-section of PSII.

**Photoacclimation**

The state transitions and nonphotochemical quenching mechanisms operate to adjust the absorption cross-section of PSII on time scales of minutes, but when a photosynthetic organism is placed for a long period of time in a given light regime it acclimates to that regime within the limits of its genetic potential and environmental constraints. This long-term acclimation to irradiance, called *photoacclimation*, is relatively easy to observe in unicellular algae and macrophytes, where chlorophyll per cell or per unit surface area can increase five- to tenfold as irradiance decreases (Falkowski 1980; Prezelin, Matlick 1980; Ramus 1990; Richardson et al. 1983). The response is not a linear function of irradiance; rather, at extremely low light levels, cells often become a bit chlorotic, and on exposure to slightly higher (but still low) irradiance, chlorophyll reaches a maximum (Fig 7.6) (Falkowski, Owens 1980). Increases in irradiance lead to a decrease in the cellular complement of chlorophyll, until a minimum value is reached. The absolute irradiance levels that induce these effects are species specific, and the chlorotic response is not universal (Geider et al. 1986).

The changes in pigmentation resulting from photoacclimation have two profound consequences for light absorption properties of the cells. First, cells acclimated to high irradiance levels generally have relatively high carotenoid concentrations relative to chlorophyll *a*. Carotenoids such as β-carotene and zeaxanthin do not transfer excitation energy to the reaction center and consequently act to screen the cell from excess light (Siefermann-Harms 1985). Some xanthophylls, such as lutein, transfer excitation energy but with reduced efficiency, and therefore effectively reduce the functional absorption cross-section of the associated photosystem (Sukenik, Bennett et al. 1987). Because these carotenoids absorb light without a concomitant increase in the functional absorption cross-section of PSII, organisms acclimated to high irradiance levels often have lower maximum quantum yields for photosynthetic oxygen evolution.

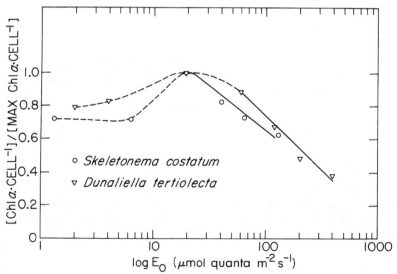

**Figure 7.6** The change in cellular chlorophyll *a* concentration in two species of unicellular algae grown at different irradiance levels. At very low irradiances, chlorophyll *a*/cell is often slightly depressed, rising to a maximum value at some low to moderate light level, and thence decreasing as a log-normal with increased irradiances.

Second, when cells acclimate to low irradiance levels, the subsequent increase in pigmentation is associated with an decrease in the optical absorption cross-section normalized to chlorophyll ($a_\lambda^*$) (Falkowski, Dubinsky, Wyman 1985; Morel, Ahn 1990). This effect is due primarily to the self-shading of the chromophores between layers of thylakoid membranes, and is an inverse function of the number of membranes in the chloroplast (Fig 7.7)—the more membranes, the lower the optical absorption cross-section (Berner et al. 1989). Thus, as cells accumulate chlorophyll, each chlorophyll molecule becomes less effective in light absorption.

The light absorbed by a cell can be described by:

$$E_{a(\lambda)}\big/\text{cell} = E_{o(\lambda)}a_{(\lambda)}^*\big(\text{Chl/cell}\big) \tag{7.12}$$

where $E_{o(\lambda)}$ is the incident irradiation at wavelength $\lambda$. A doubling of cellular chlorophyll does not produce a doubling in the rate of light absorption (Dubinsky et al. 1986). The reduction in the chlorophyll-specific optical absorption cross-section can

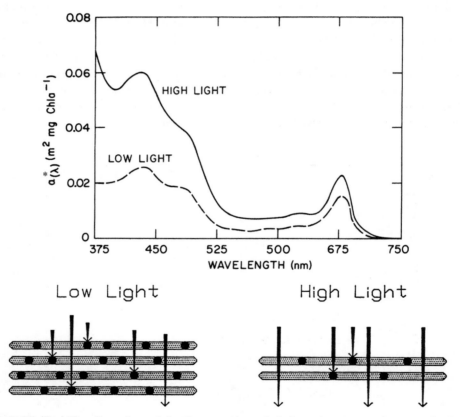

**Figure 7.7** (Top) The effect of growth irradiance on the optical absorption cross-section normalized to chlorophyll *a*. Cells grown at high light have less cellular chlorophyll (see Fig 7.8) and generally have fewer thylakoid membranes or membrane stacks within the chloroplast. Hence, there is less chance of self-shading in cell (bottom). The optical consequences of these changes in chloroplast ultrastructure are an increased optical absorption cross-section for cells with lower chlorophyll content.

## ❑ NONPHOTOSYNTHETICALLY ACTIVE PIGMENTS IN AQUATIC PLANTS

*There are many examples of pigments in algae that do not transfer excitation energy to either PSII or PSI. Some of these pigments have commercial value. For example, there are species of chlorophytes that can be found in alpine snow banks (Kawecka, Eloranta 1986). There, algae are frequently bright red due to the presence of the xanthophyll astaxanthin (Fig 7.8), which is found in the cytoplasm of these cells (Droop 1955; Goodwin 1980; Lee, Ding 1991). In natural aquatic systems, astaxanthin occurs in trace amounts in a variety of planktonic chlorophytes, and due to its accumulation in higher trophic levels, tends to give a reddish-pink color to the meat of salmon and trout (Al-Khalifa, Simpson 1988). In commercial aquaculture of these fish where a fishmeal based on higher crop plants is used to raise the fingerlings, the resulting color of the fish flesh is grayish-white. As grayish-white salmon are viewed as less desirable than reddish-pink salmon (and fetch less money for the producers), commercial salmon farms feed the salmon astaxanthin-enriched foods obtained from commercial algal producers in order to color the fish flesh a reddish-pink prior to harvesting.*

*In another chlorophyte alga,* Dunaliella bardawil, *up to 5% of the dry weight of the cell is due to the carotenoid β-carotene (Avron, Ben-Amotz 1992). This carotenoid is a precursor of vitamin A, and is used as a food supplement in many human food manufacturing processes. In vivo, β-carotene is thought to screen out excess light; the "extra" β-carotene is physically separated from the thylakoids and does not transfer excitation energy to either photosystem (Ben-Amotz, Avron 1983; Ben-Amotz et al. 1989). The commercial value of β-carotene production in 1994 was approximately US$40 million per annum.*

*The xanthophyll, lutein, can transfer some excitation energy to PSII, albeit with low efficiency. This carotenoid is commercially used as feed for chickens. The xanthophyll is absorbed into egg yolks, conferring a yellow-orange color that is viewed by many consumers as attractive (Borowitzka, Borowitzka 1988).*

*One final example of a nonphotosynthetic pigment is zeaxanthin, which in cyanobacteria is bound to water-soluble proteins. In the prochlorophyte* Prochlorothrix hollandia, *the pigment is found in a periplasmic space between the cell wall and plasma membrane. In all cyanobacteria, zeaxanthin proteins appear to accumulate when cells are grown at high light, and undoubtedly the pigment helps to absorb excess excitation, thereby reducing the rate of photoinhibition (Post et al. 1993; van der Staay 1992).*

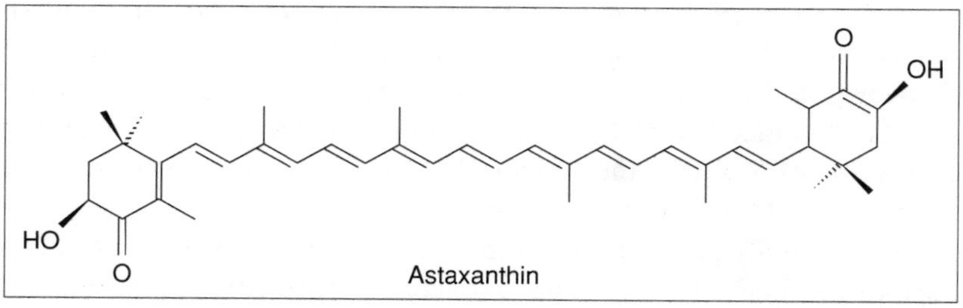

**Figure 7.8** The structure of astaxanthin, a carotenoid that transfers excitation energy efficiently to chlorophyll *a*.

be visualized by considering the fate of photons incident on two stacks of thylakoid membranes: one is a thin stack from a cell acclimated to high irradiance levels, and the second is a thick stack from a cell acclimated to low irradiance levels. The probability of a photon passing through a thick stack of membranes without being absorbed is small compared with a thin stack. This process can be demonstrated by taking a few coins and laying them on a light box. If the coins are placed so that they do not touch each other, the light absorbed will be the sum of the geometric cross-sections of the coins. If, however, the coins are overlapping in layers, the same number of coins will absorb less light; they will have a smaller optical absorption cross-section per coin. This so-called *package effect* reduces the effectiveness of increased pigmentation in harvesting light (Berner et al. 1989; Dubinsky et al. 1986; Kirk 1994b) and has important implications for the "capital costs" (Chapter 8) of light harvesting (Raven 1986). The diminution in the optical absorption cross-section with increased chlorophyll is also a function of cell size: the larger the cell the more important this effect (Morel 1991b). At some point a cell is, for most practical purposes, optically black, and further increases in pigment levels confer no advantage in light absorption.

There are two basic photoacclimation responses in algae. In one, acclimation is accomplished primarily by changes in the number of photosynthetic reaction centers, while the effective absorption cross-section of the reaction centers remains relatively constant. The second is characterized by relatively large changes in the functional size of the antennae serving the reaction centers, while the number of reaction centers remains relatively constant (Falkowski et al. 1980). Complementary changes in either of these responses produce the same effect on the initial slope of the photosynthesis-irradiance curve (Eq 7.8). As the functional size of the antennae serving PSII, and not the number of reaction centers, determines $E_k$, organisms that vary the cross-section would tend to have more control over the light-saturation parameter, as long as $\tau$ remains constant (Falkowski et al. 1981).

### What Controls $1/\tau$?

The maximum turnover rate of a photosynthetic unit is determined by the slowest electron transfer reaction from water to $CO_2$ in the steady state. This rate can vary from about $1000s^{-1}$ to less than $20s^{-1}$. The rate-limiting step in the overall pathway has been the subject of significant discussion and debate (Falkowski 1981; Haehnel 1977; Myers, Graham 1971; Steemann-Nielsen 1975; Stitt 1986). The slowest step in the intersystem electron transport is the reoxidation of plastoquinol (Haehnel 1977). However, a number of studies of the rate-limiting steps in photosynthesis suggest that carbon fixation itself, or some process controlling the fixation such as the regeneration of RuBP in the Calvin–Benson cycle (Chapter 5), is rate limiting (Stitt, Sonnewald 1995). How can this issue be resolved?

It is experimentally possible to manipulate $1/\tau$ in algae by growing cells under a wide range of irradiance levels in nutrient-saturated conditions (Falkowski, Dubinsky, Wyman 1985; Myers, Graham 1971; Stitt, Sonnewald 1995). When growth is limited only by irradiance (which is accomplished with a turbidostat), $1/\tau$ increases with increasing growth irradiance levels. Using this experimental manipulation, Sukenik and co-workers (1987) followed changes in the pool sizes of a number of electron transport components and Rubisco in the marine chlorophyte *Dunaliella tertiolecta*. They found that $1/\tau$ varied by over a factor of 4, from $75\,s^{-1}$ in low-light–grown cells to almost $300\,s^{-1}$ in cells grown at high light, but the stoichiometry of PSII:PQ:cyt $b_6/f$:PSI remained remarkably constant. This stoichiometry was 1 RCII:30 PQ:1.5 cyt $b_6/f$:1.5 RC I.[7] The constancy in this stoichiometry suggested that the oxidation of PQ by cyt $b_6/f$ was not rate limiting. They called the statistical entity with the fixed stoichiometric ratio an *electron transport chain*. However, the oxidation of plastoquinol could still be rate limiting for overall photosynthesis. This oxidation step, which can take up to 10 ms, appears to be limited by the diffusion of plastoquinol within the lipid bilayer of the thylakoid membranes. The diffusion of PQ can be modeled as a random walk. As the molecule moves in search of its docking site on the cytochrome $b_6/f$ complex, it may bump into other membrane-spanning proteins and have to go around. The effective diffusion coefficient for plastoquinol within the thylakoid membranes is on the order of $1 \times 10^{-9}\,cm^2/s$. If the density of cytochrome $b_6/f$ on the thylakoid membranes increased with increasing growth irradiance, the rate of oxidation of plastoquinol could be facilitated without a need to invoke an increase in the ratio of cytochrome $b_6/f$ to plastoquinol. Quantitative analysis of the thylakoid membrane surface area, deduced from transmission electron micrographs, revealed that the concentration of electron transfer components was, on average, two times larger in cells grown at low irradiance than at high irradiance. The thylakoid surface density was $4.4 \times 10^5\,cm^2/cm^3$ for low-light–adapted cells, and $2.2 \times 10^5\,cm^2/cm^3$ for high-light–adapted cells. Assuming that the distribution of reaction centers and other proteins on the membranes is homogeneous (which is reasonable in this organism), they used the Einstein diffusion equation to estimate the average time for diffusion of plastoquinol:

$$d^2 = Dt \tag{7.13}$$

where $d$ is the distance between RCII and the cytochrome $b_6/f$ complex, $D$ is the diffusion coefficient, and $t$ is time. The calculated times were 2.4 and 1.1 ms for high-light– and low-light–adapted cells, respectively. The calculated values of $\tau$ for whole system electron transport were 3.2 and 14 ms for the high-light– and low-light–adapted cells, respectively. These results strongly suggest that neither the diffusion nor the oxidation of plastoquinol determines the maximum rate of photosynthetic electron flow at light saturation.

In the same experiment, the ratio of the electron transport components to Rubisco varied significantly, from 1.2 to 4.6 moles of Rubisco per PSII, increasing at higher growth irradiance levels. A plot of the ratio of Rubisco to electron transport chains versus $1/\tau$ is linear (Fig 7.9). These results suggest that dark reactions, and possibly carboxylation per se, are the overall limiting step of photosynthesis at light saturation. This situation may occur as a result of the compartmentalization of Rubisco within the stromal fluids, while all the electron transport components are

7. It should be noted that the proportions of PSII:PSI can vary widely among different algal classes, and even within classes. The values given here are an example, and should not be considered a paradigm.

## ❏ TURBIDOSTAT

*A turbidostat is a device used to control the growth of an organism to maintain a constant population level. In photosynthetic investigations, this device can only be used for microalgae or small colonies of cells that are relatively small and can be diluted. The device usually is a cylindrical tube, about 10 to 20 cm in diameter, in which the algae grow. The tube is surrounded by banks of lights. As the cells grow, light in the growth vessel is attenuated. A detector, either within the vessel or more frequently outside the vessel, monitors the culture density from the attenuation of light. At a selected density, an electronic signal activates a pump to dilute the culture with fresh medium while simultaneously removing an equal volume of old culture. The volume of added medium is recorded and a steady-state growth rate is reached that is identical to the dilution rate. In photosynthesis studies, it is important that the density of the culture in the turbidostat be kept optically thin. ("Optically thin" is an operational term that can be determined by seeing if an object, such as a hand, placed on the opposite side of the culture vessel is clearly visible.) The growth rate can be manipulated by (for example) changing the irradiance level or temperature. Cells grown in a turbidostat are not nutrient limited and are in a constant, definable, and reproducible physiological state. The device is convenient to have, but difficult to build and maintain.*

---

localized on membranes. The surface area of the thylakoid membranes increases over twofold as cells grow at low irradiance levels; however, the volume of the chloroplast containing the Calvin–Benson cycle enzymes only increases by 30%. As the Calvin–Benson cycle depends on reductant and ATP generated on the membranes, effectively the higher surface area to volume ratio in the chloroplasts from low-light–grown cells compared with that from high-light–grown cells imposes a substrate (ATP and NADPH) limitation on the Calvin–Benson cycle.

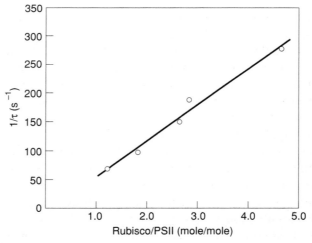

**Figure 7.9** The relationship between $1/\tau$ and the ratio of Rubisco/PSII in the chlorophyte alga *Dunaliella tertiolecta*, grown under nutrient-replete conditions at different growth irradiance levels in a turbidostat. The ratio of PSII to other electron transport components remains constant. (Courtesy of Sukenik et al., with permission)

These results point to an apparent paradox in photoacclimation, namely that acclimation to low irradiance levels via an increase in the numbers of photosynthetic units often leads to a corresponding reduction in the maximum rate of whole chain electron transport from water to $CO_2$. This paradox limits the utilization of light in dense algal systems; as the culture becomes denser the cells become more shade adapted and the light-saturated rate of photosynthesis decreases. The reduction in photosynthetic capacity in shade-adapted cells is a significant limitation of production in algal mass cultures where high biomass density is desirable. Optimization models have been developed to increase production rates (Burlew 1953; Sukenik et al. 1991).

The inverse relationship between $n$ and $\tau$ can be used to estimate the maximum photosynthetic rate achievable. Empirical regression of cellular chlorophyll levels and $\tau$ for a number of species predicts a minimum $\tau$ of 1 ms (recall from Chapter 3 that the oxidation rate of $Q_A^-$ is about 0.5 ms under steady-state continuous irradiances). Assuming that the Emerson–Arnold number is 2000 chlorophylls/$O_2$, then for a chlorophyll concentration of 1µg/l, there are $3.3 \times 10^{11}$ $O_2$-evolving centers turning over 1000 times per second. This rate of photosynthetic electron transport would support 2.0µmoles $O_2$/hour, which is equal to a carbon-fixation rate of 24µg C µg$^{-1}$ chlorophyll $a$ hour$^{-1}$, which is a very high rate indeed (Falkowski 1981). Shade-adapted cells necessarily have lower maximum photosynthetic rates. It should be pointed out that this rate of photosynthesis is limited by intrinsic processes; it would require a change in the kinetics of electron transport or the structure of the photosynthetic apparatus to give higher rates.

### Kinetics and Mechanisms of Photoacclimation

Photoacclimation is most often related to changes in the abundance and composition of the photosynthetic pigments, but it also affects carbon fixation, respiration rates, and chemical composition of the organism, as well as cell volume. The kinetics of the changes in cellular chlorophyll have been studied in a number of species (Falkowski 1984; Post et al. 1984; Steemann-Nielsen 1964). In the experimentally contrived situation where light is provided continuously over a 24-hour day, the responses following a shift from high to low irradiance or vice versa basically follow first-order kinetics. Thus, for example, the half-time for acclimation to low light in the chlorophyte *Dunaliella tertiolecta* is on the order of about 13 hours (i.e., comparable to the generation time), while in the diatom *Thalassiosira weisflogii* it is about 100 hours. In the real world, however, the response to intensity is confounded with a response to day-night cycles, and it is necessary to distinguish between light-intensity regulation and light–dark responses (Post et al. 1984). When a light–dark cycle is superimposed on a change in light intensity the algae become entrained in a circadian rhythm keyed to the light–dark cycle, but acclimate to the mean light levels to which they are exposed during the photoperiod (Fig 7.10). While chlorophyll per cell may increase during the middle of the scotophase (see Chapter 6), the algae do not shade-adapt at night, but rather acclimate to the mean irradiance level to which they are exposed during the day.

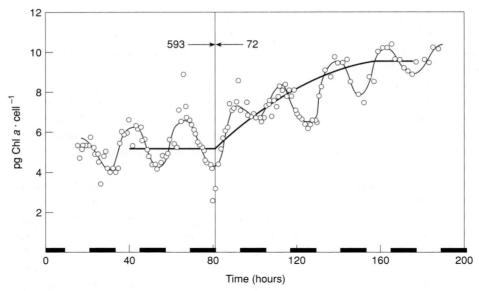

**Figure 7.10** The effect of a light-dark cycle superimposed on a change in irradiance on cellular chlorophyll *a* content in the marine diatom *Thalassiosira weisflogii*. Cells entrained in a 12:12 hr light–dark cycle undergo a diel increase and decrease in cellular chlorophyll content, in which chlorophyll *a* is highest in the middle of the photophase and begins to decrease before the dark period, reaching a minimum in the dark and increasing before the light period. Cells to the left side of the 80 hr mark were grown with a photon flux of about 600 μmol quanta $^{-2}$s$^{-1}$ but "woke up" to a low light of about 70 μmol quanta m$^{-2}$s$^{-1}$ at the 80th hour. From that point on, the cells acclimated to the low light with an overall increase in cellular chlorophyll *a* content, but maintaining a diel cycle. (From Post et al. 1984)

Careful kinetic studies of photoacclimation in *D. tertiolecta* have provided considerable insight into the process and its regulation (Falkowski 1984; Sukenik et al. 1990). On transfer from high to low irradiance, the first observable response is an increase in the abundance of the messenger RNA encoding the light-harvesting chlorophyll proteins (LaRoche et al. 1991). This response can be detected within 2 hours following the light shift, and the mRNA level reaches a maximum within 12 hours. Changes in transcription of reaction center genes are not observed until later. The messenger RNA for the light-harvesting chlorophylls is translated and the pigments are incorporated, resulting in the production of a larger antenna for PSII. Over a period of a few hours, there is an increase in the synthesis of reaction centers, and subsequently, of membranes, such that over a period of a day there is a large increase in the stacks of thylakoid membranes within the cell (Sukenik et al. 1990). The increase in pigmentation is not accompanied by an increase in Rubisco; the level of this enzyme per cell is relatively independent of irradiance in this species (Sukenik, Bennett et al. 1987).

The light-harvesting chlorophyll-protein complex often contains a number of individual, related but not identical proteins that migrate at slightly different apparent molecular masses on a denaturing polyacrylamide gel (i.e., electrophoresis). As cells acclimate to various irradiance levels the relative abundance of each of the individual proteins that constitute the ensemble of the complex can vary (Sukenik et al. 1988). The variations appear to correspond to changes in pigmentation within the light-harvesting chlorophyll-protein complex itself, such that it can be envisioned that individual proteins preferentially bind specific pigments. Thus, cells acclimated to high irradiance may differentially express a component of the light-harvesting complex with a low accessory chlorophyll content and high carotenoid content. This component can be repressed at low light and replaced by a component with high accessory pigmentation and low carotenoid levels. This phenomenon requires feedback between photosynthetic electron transport and the nucleus where the genes for the light-harvesting pigment-proteins are encoded.

A similar phenomenon implicating photosynthetic electron transport in photoacclimation occurs in cyanobacteria. In these organisms, the stoichiometry between PSII and PSI can be markedly altered by spectral irradiance (Fujita et al. 1990; Fujita et al. 1994). The phycobilisomes, which serve as the light-harvesting antennae for PSII, have relatively large optical absorption cross-sections, while PSI, which is excited by chlorophyll *a*, has a relatively small absorption cross-section. To balance electron flow between PSII and PSI, cyanobacteria generally have more PSI reaction centers relative to PSII; however the ratio between the reaction centers can be altered both by light intensity and the spectral distribution of irradiance. When cells are grown under low irradiance levels or orange light, both of which favor excitation of PSII, PSI/PSII ratios increase. This effect can be reversed by high irradiance or red light, both of which increase the excitation energy delivered to PSI.

The effect of acclimation to low irradiance can be simulated in both eukaryotic cells and cyanobacteria by blocking the reduction of the plastoquinone pool with sublethal concentrations of DCMU (Beale 1970; Escoubas et al. 1995; Koenig 1990). Cells maintained at high light with $10^{-7}$ M DCMU accumulate chlorophyll *a*, thereby mimicking the acclimation to low light. If, however, the oxidation of plastoquinol is blocked with DBMIB, no increase in chlorophyll *a* is observed. Thus, the photoacclimation state of the cell appears, like the state transitions, to be regulated by the redox state of the plastoquinone pool (Escoubas et al. 1995). Moreover, if the dephosphorylation of proteins is inhibited with 1 nM okadaic acid,[8] cells transferred from high to low irradiance do not acclimate. This phenomenon can be interpreted by hypothesizing that under high irradiance levels, when the plastoquinone pool is largely reduced, a kinase is activated that phosphorylates a protein and either directly or through one or more intermediates binds to the regulatory region of the genes encoding the light-harvesting chlorophyll-protein complexes and suppresses the transcription of the gene. Under low irradiance levels, when the plastoquinone pool is more oxidized, a phosphatase dephosphorylates the signal protein and derepresses the gene(s), leading to the synthesis of the light-harvesting chlorophyll-protein complexes (Fig 7.11).

In cyanobacteria the intersystem redox state also appears to direct the transcription of PSII and PSI reaction centers (Fujita et al. 1988). Thus, the state transitions can be viewed as a short-term response to the redox state of the plastoquinone pool, and photoacclimation can be viewed as a long-term response

---

8. Okadaic acid is a polyether lipid, isolated from dinoflagellates, that very specifically blocks serine and threonine phosphatases (MacKintosh et al. 1991).

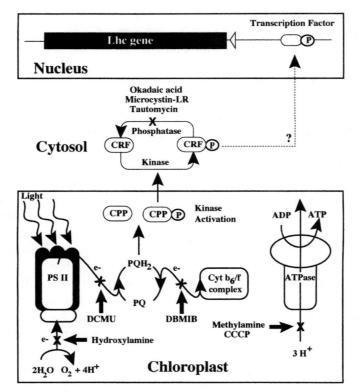

**Figure 7.11** A schematic diagram showing the basic regulation of nuclear genes by irradiance. In the specific case shown here, the target gene is that encoding for the light-harvesting chlorophyll protein serving as the antenna for PSII. Irradiance levels are detected from changes in the redox status of the plastoquinone pool. As light intensity increases, the pool becomes increasingly reduced, and a protein kinase, coupled to the redox state of plastoquinone, phosphorylates a chloroplast protein (CPP). Phosphorylated CPP is transported from the chloroplast to a secondary kinase in the cytosol, where a chlorophyll protein repressor factor (CRF) is phosphorylated and binds to transcription control region of the target gene, thereby reducing the level of transcription. The process is reversed when the plastoquinone pool becomes oxidized and a protein phosphatase dephosphorylates CRF. The dephosphorylation of CRF can be inhibited with such phosphatase inhibitors as okadaic acid, microcystin, and tautomycin. The effect of low light can be pharmacologically mimicked by the addition of the electron transport inhibitor, DCMU, while that of high light can be mimicked by the application of DBMIB. Uncouplers of electron flow, such as methylamine and CCCP, have no effect, nor does the disruption of water splitting on the donor side of PSII. (From Escoubas et al. 1995)

to the same control mechanism. In effect, the redox state of the plastoquinone pool is a biological light meter that can signal the status of intersystem electron traffic and effect feedback responses in the light-harvesting systems.

### The Effect of Temperature

As photosynthetic carbon assimilation is enzymically controlled, it is a temperature-dependent process. Classically, because enzyme-catalyzed reactions are dependent on intermolecular collisions, their temperature sensitivity can be described by the Arrhenius equation:

$$k = Ae^{-E_a/RT} \qquad\qquad (7.14)$$

where $k$ is the first-order reaction rate constant, $A$ is the concentration of substrate, $E_a$ is the energy of activation (i.e., the minimum energy required for the reaction), $R$ is the Boltzmann gas constant, and $T$ is temperature in Kelvin. The integrated form (with respect to temperature) of the Arrhenius equation is

$$\log k_1/k_2 = E_a/(2.3R)\left[T_2 - T_1/T_2 T_1\right] \qquad\qquad (7.15)$$

where $k_1$ and $k_2$ are reaction rate constants at temperatures $T_1$ and $T_2$, respectively. The ratio of the rate constants for a 10 °C interval (called the $Q_{10}$) is often used as a convenient description of the effect of temperature. The temperature effect is not linear over very wide ranges; except for thermophilic species, temperatures above 30 to 35 °C generally lead to decreases in activity (and at even lower temperatures for some organisms, e.g., those from polar regions). Typically, if an aquatic photosynthetic organism undergoes a rapid change in temperature (on the order of minutes) within the linear portion of the temperature response function, the maximum photosynthetic rate at light saturation will alter by a factor of approximately two for a 10 °C change (Davison 1991).

A true photochemical reaction is not dependent on intermolecular collisions and hence is temperature independent. Thus, it is often erroneously assumed that the light-dependent portion of the photosynthetic response is temperature independent. Photosynthetic electron transport is temperature dependent for a number of reasons (Raven, Geider 1988). First, being associated with membranes, some of the electron transfer processes are dependent on membrane fluidity. Biological membranes behave as liquid crystals—at some critical temperature they "freeze," meaning that the viscosity increases to a level that prevents independent movement of components associated with the membranes. One way of observing this behavior is to monitor the electron spin resonance of a suitably labeled lipid molecule in the membrane as a function of temperature. At high, but still physiological, temperatures the labeled lipid has an opportunity to move freely and the EPR signal is isotropic (Barnett, Grisham 1972). As the membrane is cooled and reaches the lower critical freezing temperature, the label's movements are constrained to a more ordered motion, dictated by its exact position within the membrane, and the EPR signals reflect this ordered motion. In the absence of modifying molecules like cholesterol, the critical temperature is often reflected by a sharp discontinuity in the Arrhenius relationship, where the change in activation energy ($\Delta E_a$) represents the energy barrier imposed by the increase in membrane viscosity (Fig 7.12). In general, critical temperature is approximately 10 °C below the optimal growth temperature. The critical temperature is largely determined by the length of the hydrocarbon chain composing the lipids, and the degree of saturation; the longer and more saturated the chain, the higher the critical temperature.

A second effect of temperature in the electron transport system is related to thermal effects on intermolecular collision processes, independent of any effect on membrane fluidity per se. The diffusion of electron carriers, such as plastoquinone and plastocyanin, is temperature dependent. Given a decrease in temperature, we can expect that the electrochemical turnover time of these components will increase.

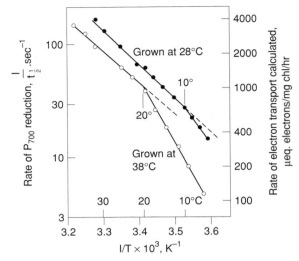

**Figure 7.12** The effect of temperature on the activity of a thylakoid membrane component. In the specific example shown, the rate of PSI reduction in intact cells of the cyanobacterium *Anacystis* is plotted as a function of reciprocal temperature (i.e., an Arrhenius plot). The slope of the lines is directly proportional to the energy of activation of the process. The break in the slope indicates the temperature at which the membrane undergoes a change from a liquid crystal structure to a more "frozen" state. Cells grown at 28 °C have a break in slope at approximately 10 °C, while those grown at 38 °C show a break at approximately 20 °C. (From Norio Murata, with permission)

Overall, the effect of short-term changes in temperature on the initial slope of the photosynthesis-irradiance relationship is relatively minor (Malone, Neale 1981; Tilzer et al. 1986). This small temperature effect suggests that the rate-limiting processes in the light-limited region of the $P$ vs. $E$ curve are light absorption and primary charge separation, not intersystem electron transport. However, as the light-saturated rate of photosynthesis is strongly affected by temperature, there is a reduction in $E_k$ at decreased temperatures (Cote, Platt 1984; Cota et al. 1994). This reduction is further reflected in the rate of reduction in $Q_A$ (Maxwell et al. 1995), and leads to a propensity for overexcitation of PSII at relatively low irradiance levels. Phenomenologically, the effects of a reduction in temperature are comparable to those due to increased irradiance (Davison 1991).

## MATHEMATICAL REPRESENTATIONS OF THE PHOTOSYNTHESIS-IRRADIANCE RESPONSE

As we have seen, the relationship between photosynthesis and irradiance is dynamic; that is, it varies in response to variations in irradiance. As such, therefore, the concept of a $P$ vs. $E$ curve is artificial. Nonetheless, there has been considerable effort directed toward developing mathematical representations of $P$ vs. $E$ curves in aquatic sciences, and we can identify two motivations for this activity. The first is a desire to relate short-term, small-scale photosynthetic rates to long-term, large-scale processes. For example, biological oceanographers and limnologists frequently

## ❏ TEMPERATURE ACCLIMATION

*In many aquatic photoautotrophs, the photosynthetic apparatus physiologically acclimates to changes in temperature in a comparable fashion to that of photoacclimation. At low temperatures, there tends to be a reduction in chlorophyll/cell or, in macrophytes, per unit blade area, and an increase in carboxylation activity (e.g., Rubisco levels are elevated) (Davison 1991). These alterations lead to a reduction in light absorption capacity while increasing photosynthetic capacity. The effect is that light-saturated photosynthetic rates per unit carbon biomass can often be maintained at decreased temperatures, while simultaneously reducing the propensity of the cell or organism to photoinhibition. The molecular basis for these responses appears to be comparable (or identical) to that described for photoacclimation (Maxwell et al. 1994). A reduction in temperature tends to lead to an increase in the reduction status of plastoquinone, which in turn leads to a redox-mediated feedback on cab gene expression. The effect is that the decrease in temperature is signaled by the redox state of the plastoquinone pool.*

---

attempt to extrapolate measurements of photosynthesis at fixed irradiance levels to daily integrated primary production. Such an extrapolation requires an empirical mathematical model; such models usually are based on a description of the photosynthesis-irradiance response (Jassby et al. 1976; Smith 1936; Talling 1957). A second motivation is to understand the feedback and feedforward controls of photosynthesis in relationship to irradiance (Farquhar et al. 1980; Geider et al. 1996). This application usually results in a model structure consisting of coupled differential equations that allow for exploration of the effects of kinetics and effectors on partial reactions. We shall discuss both model types in general, and some of the assumptions made in their application.

The basic description of a *P* vs. *E* curve requires a nonlinear mathematical function to account for the light-saturation effect. Quite a few such functions have been employed, with varying degrees of success. Two early formulations were a rectangular hyperbolic function, such as a Michaelis–Menten formulation (Table 7.1 and

**Table 7.1** Examples of some equations used to model photosynthesis-irradiance relationships

| | |
|---|---|
| $P = P_m\left(\dfrac{\alpha E}{P_m + \alpha E}\right)$ | Rectangular hyperbola |
| $P = P_m\left(\dfrac{\alpha E}{\sqrt{P_m^2 + (\alpha I)^2}}\right)$ | Quadratic |
| $P = P_m\left(1 - e^{-\alpha E/P_m}\right)$ | Exponential |
| $P = P_m\left(1 - e^{-\sigma_{PSII}\tau E}\right)$ | Exponential |
| $P = P_m\tanh\left(\dfrac{\alpha E}{P_m}\right)$ | Hyperbolic tangent |

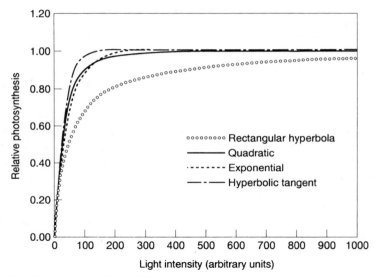

**Figure 7.13** Graphical representations of the four photosynthesis-irradiance equations given in Table 7.1. Note the similarity of responses for the hyperbolic tangent, exponential, and quadratic functions. The curves are modeled results assuming no photoinhibition.

Fig 7.13), and an inverse power function, introduced by Smith (1936). The former function generally does not fit $P$ vs. $E$ curves adequately; the curves bend too slowly and the saturation effect is poorly described (Bannister 1974). The latter function, used by Talling in 1957 to deduce $E_k$, is often acceptable but has not been widely adopted. In the mid-1970s, Jassby and Platt introduced the hyperbolic tangent function. This function often appears to fit experimental data with a high degree of fidelity, especially if a coefficient for photoinhibition is included (Platt et al. 1980). The hyperbolic tangent function is often used in limnology and oceanography, but has not been adopted by higher plant physiologists. The latter favor use of an empirical index of "curvature," based on light-saturation profiles for leaves (Leverenz 1992). This type of model has been applied in systems with very high extinction coefficients (such as a leaf), that results in heterogeneous light absorption. A mathematical analogue was introduced to aquatic sciences by Bannister (1979), but was not widely adopted as the physiological interpretation of the curvature coefficient is obscure.

In 1986, Dubinsky and co-workers suggested that because the relationship between oxygen evolution obtained with a single turnover flash closely follows a cumulative one-hit Poisson function, a similar formulation could be applied to a photosynthesis-irradiance curve. The cumulative one-hit Poisson function assumes that each flash promotes one, and only one, turnover of PSII and that the quantum yield for oxygen evolution in the open reaction centers is constant and independent of flash energy. To account for the multiple turnovers of PSII in continuous light, Dubinsky added a turnover time to the exponential expression, thus

$$P = P_{max}\left[1 - \left(e^{-\sigma_{PSII} \cdot \tau \cdot E}\right)\right] \tag{7.16}$$

where $\tau$ is identical to that for whole chain electron transport (Eq 7.9).

By substitution, using Equation 7.11a it can be shown that Equation 7.16 is identical with:

$$P = P_{max}\left[1 - \left(e^{-\alpha E/P_{max}}\right)\right] \tag{7.17}$$

which was used by Webb and colleagues (1974) to describe $P$ vs. $E$ curves (Webb, Burley 1965). Dubinsky and colleagues (1986) found that measured rates of $O_2$ evolution fit Equation 7.17 with reasonable correlation, and used the equation to calculate the average $\sigma_{PSII}$ for broad-band spectral irradiance.

The application of an exponential function to the analysis of the photosynthesis-irradiance relationship has distinct advantages in mathematically simplifying an apparently complex process, but the function has implicit assumptions. Differentiation of Equation 7.16 with respect to irradiance leads to a linear approximation:

$$\lim E \to 0, \quad P \approx \sigma_{PSII}\,\tau\,P_{max}E \tag{7.18}$$

where the right-hand side of the approximation is identical to $\alpha^B E$. The exponential curve implicitly assumes that the average time that a PSII reaction center remains closed following the absorption of an exciton is the same in saturating continuous light as it is at subsaturating light. Recall that $\tau$ is the turnover time for whole chain electron transport from water to $CO_2$; it is independent of the absorption cross-section of PSII and is experimentally derived from $P_{max}$ and oxygen flash yields using Equation 7.16. Equation 7.16 suggests that $\tau$ could be calculated at any irradiance $E$:

$$\tau_E = \left(P_E\right)\big/\left(Y_E\right)^{-1} \tag{7.19}$$

where $P_E$ is the steady-state photosynthetic rate and $Y_E$ is the oxygen flash yield at backround irradiance $E$. If both the oxygen flash yield and the photosynthetic rates in continuous light follow a cumulative one-hit Poisson function and $\sigma_{PSII}$ is independent of irradiance, then $\tau$ must be a constant for a given species at a given physiological state, which seems highly unlikely (Baumert 1996). Although the exponential function may adequately describe a $P$ vs. $E$ curve from a statistically acceptable and empirical viewpoint, it does not account for multiple limiting steps or changes in the absorption cross-section of PSII. It is difficult to use integrated processes such as $P$ vs. $E$ curves to establish rate-limiting steps; therefore, determining the validity of particular models is problematic.

## The Problem of Determining Rate-Limiting Steps

In mathematically describing $P$ vs. $E$ curves, an implicit assumption is made concerning rate-limiting steps. In the cumulative one-hit Poisson function, for example, both $\sigma_{PSII}$ and $\tau$ are assumed to remain constant. Such an assumption implies that the rate of whole-chain electron transport is limiting throughout the entire photosynthesis-irradiance curve. Although $\tau$ is related to the ratio of electron transport chains to Rubisco, and this ratio in turn sets an upper limit to photosynthetic electron transport, this does not mean that intersystem electron transport is never rate limited. In the experiment describing the behavior of variable fluorescence as a function of background light, for example, it is clear that $Q_A$ becomes increasingly reduced at higher irradiance levels. It is relatively straightforward to calculate the rate at which electrons enter the intersystem transport system from knowledge of the incident irradiance, the absorption cross-section of PSII, and the quantum yield of photochemistry:

$$e/t = E_o \sigma_{PSII(E)} \phi_{PSII(E)} \tag{7.20}$$

where $e/t$ is the rate of election transport. As electrons enter the chain on the acceptor side of PSII, they reduce PQ. The redox state of the pool can be assessed by measuring the rate of reduction of cytochrome $b_6/f$ from absorption difference spectra following a flash. Cytochrome $f$ has an absorption difference maximum at 554 nm; when the cytochrome is reduced it absorbs more strongly at this wavelength (see Chapter 4). When a brief saturating flash is superimposed on a background light, if the cytochrome is oxidized then little change in the absorption difference spectra will be observed (Haehnel 1977). Moreover, by following the kinetics of reduction of the cytochrome, it is possible to infer the rate of oxidation of $PQH_2$.

The minimum half-time for the $PQH_2$ is about 1 ms (Cramer et al. 1991). This step is approximately four to five times slower than the maximum steady-state reduction rate of PQ. The latter corresponds to the oxidation of $Q_A^-$, which in the steady state has a half-time of about 500 μs (Crofts, Wright 1983). Thus, when the rate of electron flow out of PSII exceeds 1 electron per ms, PQ reduction will be greater than oxidation, and the PQ pool will become progressively reduced. For example, assuming a spectrally averaged absorption cross-section for PSII of about 20 nm², this rate will be reached at an average irradiance of (1000 s⁻¹ × 1/20 nm² quanta⁻¹ × 10²⁰ nm²/m²) = 5 × 10²⁰ quanta m⁻² s⁻¹ or about 830 μmoles of quanta m⁻² s⁻¹. This irradiance level is approximately that of 40% of the full solar irradiance at noon at the equator.

While $PQH_2$ may become progressively reduced at high irradiance levels, the overall rate of electron transport is not necessarily limited by $PQH_2$ oxidation. This can intuitively be described by imagining going to the movies and standing in line to buy a ticket, and then having to stand in line again to have the ticket collected by an usher. Two rate-limiting steps exist in this simple chain. Ticket sales become limiting when the rate of arrival of patrons (electrons) exceeds the rate of sales ($PQH_2$ oxidation). The usher (Rubisco activity) becomes rate limiting when he or she cannot keep up with the rate of sales. The oxidation of the plastoquinone pool can be rate limiting for electron traffic between PSII and PSI, but the rate of utilization of reductant on the acceptor side of PSI can also be rate limiting, and can in fact control the maximum rate of plastoquinol oxidation. The modification of the rate of oxidation of $PQH_2$ by the dark reactions is comparable to the issues addressed by "queuing theories," in which a set of coupled differential equations is used to describe a multistep process with possible switches in rate-limiting steps (Baumert 1996). The multiple limitations of photosynthesis depending on irradiance greatly complicate the mathematical representation of the photosynthesis-irradiance response.

Having now examined some aspects of photosynthetic responses in continuous light, in Chapter 8 we examine how these processes are integrated with the rest of the cellular machinery to create new cells.

# 8

# Making Cells

The principal products of the photosynthetic reactions are sugars, reductant, ATP, and molecular $O_2$. In all photoautotrophs, these products are themselves substrates for biosynthetic reactions. The synthesis of many essential cellular components, such as amino and nucleic acids, requires elements other than carbon, hydrogen, and oxygen. For example, oxidized (and environmentally more stable) forms of nitrogen (usually $NO_3^-$) or sulfur (as sulfate, $SO_4^{2-}$) must be reduced to the level of ammonium ($NH_4^+$) or sulfide (–SH) to serve the purposes of most biosynthetic reactions. These reductions come at the expense of photosynthetically generated electrons, and hence influence the quantum yield for carbon fixation. Additional elements, such as phosphorus and trace metals, are required to form nucleic acids, lipids, prosthetic groups for enzymes, porphyrins, and chlorins required for the syntheses of photosynthetic pigments and electron carriers, and the other myriad molecules that make up the organism. The acquisition and incorporation of these elements are tied to carbon fixation.

Biosynthetic processes occur both inside and outside of the chloroplast, and often involve oxidation reactions that require respiratory pathways. Because the respiratory pathways effectively operate as the inverse of photosynthetic reactions, the two processes are invariably coupled within the cell. Coupling is achieved via fluxes of common carbon products and substrates, and by the rate of production of reductant and energy relative to demands for growth and maintenance of the organism (Geider, Osborne 1989; Raven 1976b).

Here we address some of the concepts and mechanisms required for the understanding of how photosynthesis is related to the making of cells. We begin with a discussion of the elemental and biochemical composition of aquatic photoautotrophs, examine how some key elements are assimilated, discuss the critical role of respiration in the biosynthetic pathways of aquatic autotrophs, and finally explore how photosynthetic processes are related to overall growth efficiencies.

## THE CHEMICAL COMPOSITION OF AQUATIC PHOTOSYNTHETIC ORGANISMS

Knowledge of the elemental and biochemical composition of a photoautotroph is essential to relating nutrient supply to growth and for interpreting physiological variability and its causation.

Measurement of the elemental composition of marine organisms dates virtually to the beginning of the formal study of marine biology, late in the 19th century (Mills

1989). Chemists had determined the elemental composition of a wide variety of organisms, and by the dawn of the 20th century, a significant focus on the role of marine organisms in the nitrogen cycle of the oceans was emerging. The inextricable relationship between the chemistry of the environment and that of organisms is exemplified by the so-called *Redfield ratio*, named after the marine chemist Alfred Redfield, who (following a suggestion of the British marine biologist HW Harvey) determined that the bulk elemental composition of particulate organic material in the ocean is remarkably constrained and similar to the concentration of the major elements in seawater (Redfield 1934). The commonly taken proportion of the major elements is 106 C:16 N:1 P (by atoms). This elemental composition (i.e., the Redfield ratio), is generally regarded as representative of the *average* elemental composition of marine phytoplankton.

As is true for most averages, there are deviations from the Redfield ratios. Based on the Redfield ratios, an average phytoplankton would have a C:N ratio of 106/16 (i.e., 6.6). Variations in C:N ratios are related to cell-wall composition of different taxa, as well as growth conditions (which we will discuss in Chapter 10). For example, dinoflagellates with cellulose cell walls typically have C:N ratios slightly higher than the Redfield ratio (between 8 and 10), while cyanobacteria, which can contain relatively large amounts of protein, often have lower C:N ratios (between 5 and 6). C:N ratios less than 4 and greater than 40 have been reported for natural marine particulate materials; however, in general the variability in algae in the oceans is relatively small (Geider 1987).

Atkinson and Smith (1983) reviewed the C:N:P ratios of marine macrophytes, and found that the mean value C:N ratio of 14 and C:P ratio of 550 are common. The data were obtained from organisms collected in the field, and hence had a poorly defined nutritional history. (However, the same could be said of phytoplankton, which often appear to have chemical compositions conforming to the typical Redfield values.) The biochemical basis for the high C:N and C:P ratios in aquatic macrophytes is related to the greater fraction of extracellular carbon devoted to the structure of the organisms. These structural components are primarily used to make cell walls and are composed mainly of polysaccharides that contain very little nitrogen or phosphorus.[1] One of the roles of these materials in the cell walls is to maintain turgor pressure. Additionally, the physical properties of the polysaccharides permit dissipation of the energy of breaking waves and energy storage in elastic extension of the plants (Raven, Johnston 1993). These physical properties of macrophyte polysaccharides enable large organisms to withstand the mechanical stresses of high-energy littoral zones, while simultaneously permitting the organisms to take advantage of the reduced boundary layer thickness in such turbulent environments (Raven 1984a).

The relatively low C:N ratio for phytoplankton reveals two general features of

---

1. In marine macrophytes, some of the cell-wall polysaccharides often contain a covalently bound sulfate group, whereas others (e.g., alginates) have carboxyl groups. These natural compounds, such as carageenans, alginates, and agars, are relatively inert and have highly desirable chemical properties as gels and emulsifiers. They are used commercially in the food and chemical industry as stabilizers, thickeners, and bulking agents; in microbiology as substrates to grow bacteria and microalgae; and in molecular biology as a matrix for electrophoresis and macromolecule purification.

**Table 8.1** Proximate analysis of algal cells

| Species | Metabolites (percentage dry weight of cells) | | | | | |
| | Protein* | Carbohydrate | Fat | Total pigment** | Ash | Total |
|---|---|---|---|---|---|---|
| CHLOROPHYTA | | | | | | |
| *Tetraselmis maculata* | 52 | 15.0 | 2.9 | 2.1 | 23.8 | 96 |
| *Dunaliella salina* | 57 | 31.6 | 6.4 | 3.0 | 7.6 | 106 |
| HAPTOPHYTA | | | | | | |
| *Monochrysis lutheri* | 49 | 31.4 | 11.6 | 0.8 | 6.4 | 99 |
| *Syracosphaera carterae* | 56 | 17.8 | 4.6 | 1.1 | 36.5 | 116 |
| BACILLARIOPHYCEAE | | | | | | |
| *Chaetoceros* sp | 35 | 6.6 | 6.9 | 1.5 | 28.0 | 78 |
| *Skeletonema costatum* | 37 | 20.8 | 4.7 | 1.8 | 39.0 | 103 |
| *Coscinodiscus* sp | 17 | 4.1 | 1.8 | 0.5 | 57.0 | 81 |
| *Phaeodactylum* | | | | | | |
| *tricornutum* | 33 | 24.0 | 6.6 | 2.9 | 7.6 | 73 |
| DYNOPHYCEAE | | | | | | |
| *Amphidinium carteri* | 28 | 30.5 | 18.0 | 2.4 | 14.1 | 93 |
| *Exuviella* sp | 31 | 37.0 | 15.0 | 1.1 | 8.3 | 92 |
| CYANOBACTERIA | | | | | | |
| *Agmenellum* | | | | | | |
| *quadruplicatum* | 36 | 31.5 | 12.8 | 1.5 | 10.7 | 93 |

Source: Parsons et al. (1961).
*Nitrogen × 6.25.
**Chlorophylls and carotenoids (sum of mg and MSPU/100 mg dry weight).

unicellular photoautotrophs, namely (a) they contain a relatively large proportion of organic nitrogen, which is primarily in the form of protein, and (b) they have no large "sinks" for organic carbon within the organism. Typically, marine phytoplankton are 30% to 50% protein (Table 8.1) by weight (Hitchcock 1977; Parsons et al. 1961; Sakshaug 1973). The average C:N ratio of protein is 3.5. The remaining 50% to 70% of the cell carbon is primarily contained in carbohydrate and lipid (Parsons et al. 1961). By comparison with algal macrophytes or higher plants, unicellular algae have very little capacity to accumulate fixed carbon. While the excretion of dissolved organic carbon is effectively a carbon sink for unicellular algae, such sinks are small compared with those of algal macrophytes or higher plants.

Redfield recognized that the elemental composition of organisms was related to their biochemical composition (Redfield 1934). Because of the relatively high nitrogen and phosphorus requirements of microalgae, he considered nitrogen and phosphorus the elements most likely to limit the rate and extent of phytoplankton growth in the sea (Redfield 1958). These elements, which are seldom in excess of a few micromolar, are called *macronutrients* (as opposed to essential trace elements, such as iron or zinc, which are present in nanomolar or lower concentrations and are called *micronutrients*). We will discuss nutrient limitation in Chapter 10; in the present chapter we will examine how these elements are assimilated and how that assimilation affects and is affected by photosynthesis.

## Nutrient Assimilation

The synthesis of amino acids requires the incorporation of nitrogen in the form of ammonium ($NH_4^+$) into carbon skeletons (Syrett 1981). Two essential amino acids as well as some lipids require reduced sulfur. Nucleic acids and the nucleotides require phosphate and nitrogen. Thus, in addition to carbon there are three other essential macronutrients required for cell growth: N, P, and S. In addition, some microalgae, especially diatoms, require Si. We will now briefly consider some aspects of these elements in relation to biosynthesis and photosynthesis.

## Nitrogen

In natural aquatic ecosystems, the predominant form of nitrogen is $N_2$, which is not directly accessible to most oxygenic organisms. $N_2$ can be reduced to $NH_3$ at high temperatures (above approx. 500 °C). This reaction,

$$N_2 + 3H_2 \rightarrow 2NH_3 \tag{8.1}$$

was discovered in 1865, and commercially developed by Haber in Germany.[2] The reaction described by Equation 8.1 is exergonic, yielding 72 kJ/mole of $NH_3$, but at atmospheric pressures and physiological temperatures the reaction is slow. Moreover, as $H_2$ is a relatively rare gas in aerobic environments, the source of reductant to facilitate the reaction described in Equation 8.1 is accommodated by alternative substrates in vivo (Postgate 1984).

Biological $N_2$ fixation is catalyzed by the multimeric enzyme nitrogenase, a highly conserved enzyme that is found in some species of heterotrophic and symbiotic bacteria as well as photoautotrophic cyanobacteria (Carpenter, Capone 1983). In biological systems, nitrogen fixation is energetically coupled to ATP, and is an endergonic reaction, requiring the equivalent of 12 to 15 moles of ATP per mole of N fixed. The primary reductant in vivo appears to be ferredoxin, which derives its electrons in turn from the oxidation of organic substrates (Postgate 1984).

Nitrogenase is highly sensitive to molecular oxygen, and is irreversibly inhibited by exposure to $O_2$ in vitro. Thus, the photosynthetic production of oxygen and the enzymatic reduction of $N_2$ necessarily require some spatial and/or temporal separation of the two pathways. In most freshwater filamentous cyanobacteria, the separation is primarily spatial (Haselkorn, Buikema 1992; Wolk 1973). When the filaments grow in the absence of an alternative nitrogen source other than $N_2$, specialized cells called *heterocysts* are formed at intervals between vegetative cells (Fig 8.1). Heterocyst development is a primitive form of cell differentiation. In the process, all PSII activity is lost, and the proteins involved in oxygenic photosynthesis are degraded, while PSI activity is maintained. Simultaneously, the genes encoding the nitrogenase proteins (the *nif* genes) undergo a rearrangement and form an operon leading to the production of active enzyme (Haselkorn 1992; Zehr et al. 1991). Nitrogen fixation is localized specifically in heterocysts, and light is used for cyclic electron flow around PSI to maintain a supply of ATP for the process. The primary organic nitrogen product (glutamate) is exported to adjacent vegetative (and photo-oxygenic) cells, while carbon skeletons, formed by the respiratory and photosynthetic processes in the latter cells, are translocated to the heterocysts (Flores, Herrero 1994).

---

2. To this day, the Haber reaction remains the primary commercial process used to manufacture nitrogen-based fertilizers.

**(A)**

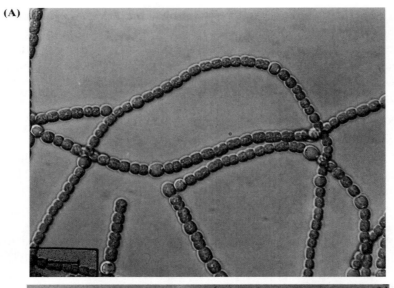

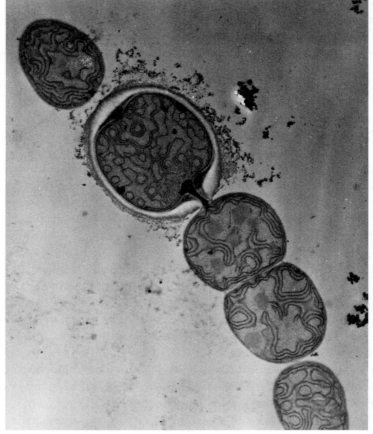

**(B)**

In some nonheterocystous cyanobacteria, the separation between oxygenic photosynthesis and nitrogen fixation is temporal; cells evolve oxygen and reduce carbon during the day, and fix nitrogen and oxidize carbon at night (Fay 1992; Mitusi et al. 1986). In such cells, the temporal uncoupling between carbon fixation and nitrogen fixation leads to large diel oscillations in carbohydrate and protein pools in the cells.

The most common nitrogen-fixing cyanobacteria in marine environments are filamentous, nonheterocystic cells belonging to the genus *Trichodesmium* (Carpenter, Capone 1992). In *Trichodesmium*, nitrogen fixation and oxygenic photosynthesis operate simultaneously; in fact, nitrogen fixation requires light, presumably to provide a source of ATP and reductant from photosynthetic pathways. The mechanism by which nitrogenase is protected from damage by $O_2$ in these organisms remains enigmatic (Carpenter, Price 1976; Carpenter et al. 1990).

For all eukaryotic photoautotrophs, the only forms of inorganic nitrogen that are directly assimilable are nitrate ($NO_3^-$), nitrite ($NO_2^-$), and ammonium ($NH_4^+$). The more highly oxidized form, nitrate, is the most thermodynamically stable form in oxidized aquatic environments, and hence is the predominant form of fixed nitrogen in most aquatic ecosystems (although not necessarily the most readily available form). Following translocation across the plasmalemma (which is an energy-dependent process), the assimilation of $NO_3^-$ requires chemical reduction to $NH_4^+$ (Fig 8.2). This process is mediated by two enzymes, namely, nitrate reductase and nitrite reductase (Berges, Harrison 1995; Eppley 1978; Falkowski 1983a; Morris, Syrett 1965). Nitrate reductase is located in the cytosol and uses NAD(P)H to catalyze the two-electron transfer:

$$NO_3^- + 2e^- + 2H^+ \rightarrow NO_2^- + H_2O \qquad (8.2)$$

In cyanobacteria, nitrate reductase is coupled to the oxidation of ferredoxin rather than a pyridine nucleotide (Flores, Herrero 1994). The nitrite formed by nitrate reductase is reduced in a six-electron transfer reaction:

$$NO_2^- + 6e^- + 8H^+ \rightarrow NH_4^+ + 2H_2O \qquad (8.3)$$

Nitrite reductase utilizes ferredoxin in both cyanobacteria and eukaryotic algae; in the latter the enzyme is localized in the chloroplast. In both cyanobacteria and eukaryotic algae, photosynthetic electron flow is an important source of reduced ferredoxin for nitrite reduction (Raven 1976a).

The overall stoichiometry for the reduction of nitrate to ammonium can be written as:

$$NO_3^- + 8e^- + 10H^+ \rightarrow NH_4^+ + 3H_2O \qquad (8.4)$$

---

**Figure 8.1** (A) A Nomarski differential contrast image of *Anabaena* sp grown for 24 hours in medium lacking fixed inorganic nitrogen. The heterocysts are the slightly larger, rounder cells with prominent refractile polar granules. (Photo by William J. Buikema) (B) Transmission electron micrograph showing a lateral section through a heterocyst. Only one of the two polar granules was caught in the section, stained deep black. The granule is made of cyanophycin. Closest to the granule external to the outer membrane of the vegetative cell wall is a lamellar glycolipid layer outside which a polysaccharide is seen as both a white mass and hairy fringes. (Courtesy of Kristin Black and Robert Haselkorn)

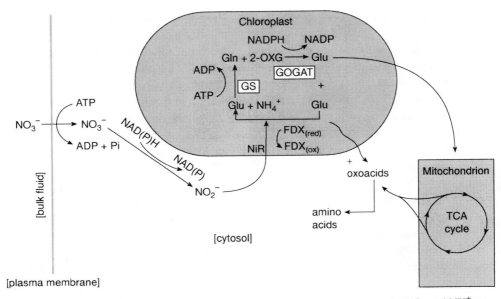

**Figure 8.2** Pathway of nitrogen assimilation in aquatic, eukaryotic photoautotrophs. $NO_3^-$ and $NH_4^+$ are actively transported from the environment across the plasma membrane into the cytoplasm, and can be stored within the vacuole of the cell. When amino acid synthesis is required, $NO_3^-$ is reduced to $NO_2^-$ by nitrate reductase (NR), a cytoplasmic enzyme that uses either NADH or NADPH. $NO_2^-$ is reduced to $NH_4^+$ in the chloroplast by nitrite reductase (NiR), an enzyme that uses reduced ferredoxin. $NH_4^+$ is incorporated into glutamic acid to form glutamine via the action of glutamine synthetase (GS); the process leads to a stoichiometric hydrolysis of ATP to ADP. The amido nitrogen of glutamine is subsequently transferred to 2-oxoglutarate (2-OXG) via the activity of NADPH-dependent glutamine 2-oxoglutarate aminotransferase (GOGAT); this reaction yields two molecules of glutamate. One of the glutamate molecules reenters the assimilation pathway as a substrate for GS, thereby forming a cycle. The second molecule of glutamate is exported to the cytoplasm where it undergoes transamination reactions with α-keto acids produced in tricarboxylic acid cycle (TCA) in the mitochondria.

Assuming all the electrons for this reduction originate from water, the free energy change of this process requires 288 kJ per mole $NH_4^+$ formed.

The incorporation of ammonium into amino acids is primarily brought about by the sequential action of glutamine synthetase (GS) and glutamine 2-oxoglutarate aminotransferase (GOGAT) (Falkowski, Rivkin 1976; Lea, Miflin 1974; Zehr, Falkowski 1988). Ammonium assimilation by GS requires glutamate as a substrate and ATP, and catalyzes the irreversible reaction:

$$\text{glutamate} + NH_4^+ + ATP \rightarrow \text{glutamine} + ADP + Pi \qquad (8.5)$$

The amido nitrogen of glutamine is subsequently transferred to 2-oxoglutarate (produced by the Krebs cycle, which we will discuss presently), and reduced, forming two moles of glutamate:

$$2\text{-oxoglutarate} + \text{glutamine} + NADPH \rightarrow 2\big[\text{glutamate}\big] + NADP^+ \qquad (8.6)$$

In some species of algae and higher plants this reductive reaction is coupled to ferredoxin rather than pyridine nucleotide. Both GS and GOGAT are found in chloroplasts, although isozymes of both enzymes may also be localized in the

## ❑ NITRATE REDUCTASE

*Nitrate reductase is a highly regulated enzyme in aquatic photoautotrophs (Guerrero et al. 1981). The enzyme is encoded in the nucleus, and in microalgae the levels of catalytic activity closely follow levels of the enzyme protein. When cells are entrained in a light–dark cycle, nitrate reductase reaches a plateau around the middle of the photophase, and is minimal in the scotophase (Fig 8.3) (Eppley et al. 1969; Packard 1973). The level of enzyme activity is, to a first order, transcriptionally regulated; the activity levels are related to the rate of synthesis of the mRNA for the protein (Ramalho et al. 1995; Smith et al. 1992). The cycle of activity appears keyed to the level of intracellular carbohydrate (J Vergara, personal communication). When the end products of photosynthesis begin to accumulate in surplus, nitrate reductase mRNA transcription is suspended; conversely, when levels of intracellular carbohydrates are depleted, nitrate reductase expression is enhanced. Nitrate reductase levels often vary inversely with light-harvesting chlorophyll protein, suggesting they have common signal transduction pathways, i.e., the redox state of the photosynthetic electron transport system.*

*In higher plants there is evidence of strong post-translational regulation of nitrate reductase activity via reversible protein phosphorylation (Campbell 1996; Kaiser, Huber 1994). Nitrate reductase may be phosphorylated in aquatic photoautotrophs, but it would appear that this process plays a relatively minor role in regulation of the enzyme's activity in these organisms.*

cytosol. Whatever the location of the enzymes, however, glutamate must be exported from the chloroplast to the cytosol where transamination reactions can proceed, thereby facilitating the syntheses of other amino acids.

As we have attempted to illustrate, the basic assimilatory pathways for inorganic

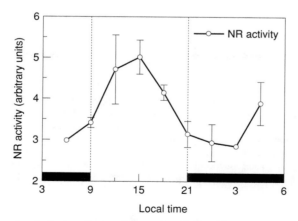

**Figure 8.3** The diel cycle of nitrate reductase in a marine diatom. The enzymatic activity of nitrate reductase often is a rate-determining step in the assimilation of nitrate by aquatic photoautotrophs. The activity of the enzyme is highly regulated at a transcriptional level, and undergoes a diel cycle with a maximum peaking at mid-day and minimum during the dark period. The data shown are from *Thalassiosira weisflogii*. (Courtesy of Juan Vergara and John Berges)

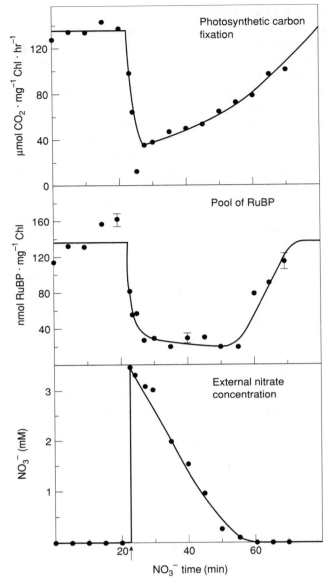

**Figure 8.4** The interaction between photosynthesis and nitrogen assimilation. When the freshwater chlorophyte *Selenastrum minutum* is grown with limiting concentrations of nitrate, and subsequently supplied with nitrate, photosynthetic carbon fixation is markedly depressed while nitrate is assimilated. This phenomenon arises because nitrate assimilation uses reductants and ATP supplied by photosynthetic pathways (see Fig 8.2), hence there is competition for these substrates in the Calvin–Benson pathways. The reduction in the pool size of RuBP reflects a temporary diversion of ATP and reductant to nitrogen assimilation pathways. (Data courtesy of Ivor Elrifi)

nitrogen are inextricably dependent on organic carbon substrates, reductants, and ATP that are supplied by both photosynthetic and respiratory pathways (Turpin 1991). However, this dependency is not a one-way street; when nitrogen is limiting, photosynthesis and respiratory processes are affected (Fig 8.4) (Morris et al. 1971;

Turpin, Bruce 1990). Let us first examine this feedback in the context of photosynthesis.

When the rate of supply of inorganic nitrogen is lower than that required for maximum biosynthetic capacity of a cell, the element becomes limiting for growth. For unicellular algae, this type of limitation can be conveniently contrived by means of a chemostat, where experimental control over the degree of limitation is possible (Caperon 1968; Herzig, Falkowski 1989). On a biochemical or molecular biological level, nitrogen limitation can be thought of as a form of translational control, where the supply of amino acids limits the translation of mRNA and hence reduces the rate of protein synthesis (Falkowski et al. 1989). This is readily demonstrated by assaying the rate of protein synthesis and cellular concentrations of the free amino acids in nitrogen-limited cells in comparison with nitrogen-replete cells (Table 8.2) (Flynn et al. 1989; Zehr et al. 1988). The reduction in free amino acids is further reflected in lower overall levels of cellular protein, and usually by a concomitant increase in carbohydrate or lipid contents. On a bulk chemical level, these changes are often seen as an increase in the organic carbon to organic nitrogen ratio of the whole organism (Goldman 1980).

The effects of nitrogen limitation are further reflected in photosynthetic processes at a biophysical level. The maximum change in the quantum yield of photochemistry of PSII, as inferred from chlorophyll fluorescence yields (Chapter 3), increases as a hyperbolic function of the rate of nitrogen supply in chemostat cultures (Kolber et al. 1988). The decreased photochemical efficiency in PSII under nitrogen-limited conditions is primarily a consequence of nonradiative (i.e., thermal) dissipation of absorbed excitation energy in the pigment bed. This decrease in photochemical efficiency is reflected in both an increase in the lifetimes of the excited states and an increase in the steady-state yield of fluorescence at low temperatures. The lesion appears, in large part, to be due to a decrease in the number

**Table 8.2** Free amino acid concentration (fmol cell$^{-1}$) in cultures of *Thalassiosira pseudonana* grown under N-limited and N-replete conditions

|  | N-limited | N-replete | Replete/Limited |
|---|---|---|---|
| Aspartate | 0.19 | 0.96 | 5.1 |
| Glutamate | 0.38 | 2.6 | 6.8 |
| Asparagine | 0.02 | 0.55 | 34 |
| Glutamine | 0.05 | 1.43 | 31 |
| Lysine | 0.04 | 0.25 | 5.8 |
| Arginine | 0.03 | 0.15 | 4.5 |
| Threonine | 0.07 | 0.12 | 1.8 |
| Serine | 0.19 | 0.36 | 1.9 |
| Tyrosine | 0.02 | 0.05 | 3.3 |
| Glycine | 0.14 | 0.30 | 2.2 |
| Alanine | 0.10 | 0.43 | 4.3 |
| Valine | 0.03 | 0.13 | 4.2 |
| Leucine | 0.03 | 0.10 | 3.1 |
| Isoleucine | 0.03 | 0.06 | 2.4 |
| Phenylalanine | 0.01 | 0.05 | 3.6 |
| Methionine/tryptophan | 0.02 | 0.19 | 11.2 |
| Total | 1.3 | 7.7 | 5.8 |

Source: Zehr et al. (1988).

of functional PSII reaction centers relative to the antennae (Falkowski 1992). Based on immunological analyses, the chloroplast-encoded proteins, D1, CP43, and CP47, are markedly reduced relative to the nuclear-encoded, light-harvesting chlorophyll proteins (Falkowski et al. 1989; Kolber et al. 1988). Moreover, the functional absorption cross-section of PSII increases under nitrogen-limiting conditions, while the probability of energy transfer between PSII reaction centers decreases. From a structural viewpoint, the reaction centers behave as if they were energetically isolated with a significant portion of the light-harvesting antenna disconnected from the photochemical processes (Vassiliev et al. 1995).

The effect of nitrogen limitation on PSII photochemistry is further reflected in the photosynthetic responses in continuous light. The maximum rate of electron transport from water to $CO_2$ decreases, while the minimum quantum requirement for $O_2$ evolution increases (Chalup, Laws 1990; Herzig, Falkowski 1989; Laws, Bannister 1980). Thus, as cells become increasingly nitrogen deficient, the efficiency with which absorbed light is used for photochemistry decreases. The reduction in photosynthetic energy conversion in nitrogen-limited eukaryotic cells appears to be related to the compartmentalization of amino acid biosynthetic processes. As the export of glutamate from the chloroplast leads to the formation of amino acids in the cytosol, tRNAs in the cytosol are likely to become charged with their respective amino acids more readily than the counterpart tRNAs in the chloroplast (Falkowski et al. 1989; Kolber et al. 1988). It would appear likely that this differential distribution of amino acids between the plastid and cytosol leads to a higher rate of translation of nuclear-encoded proteins relative to those encoded in the plastid.

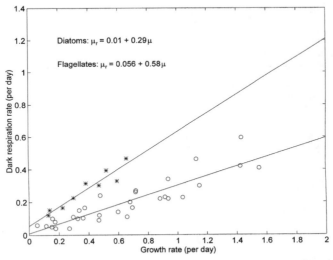

**Figure 8.5** Two examples of the relationship between dark respiration and growth rate. Stars are data from two flagellates: the marine chrysophyte *Pavolova lutheri* and the chlorophyte *Dunaliella tertiolecta*. Circles are data from the marine diatoms *Thalassiosira weisflogii* and *T. allenii*. In all cases cells were grown in nitrogen-limited chemostats under 12 hr:12 hr light–dark cycles. The intercept of respiration at zero growth rate is that required for maintenance. The data show that maintenance respiration for diatoms can be virtually nil, while that for flagellates is significantly higher. (Courtesy of Edward Laws)

Nitrogen limitation also affects the rate of respiration. As nitrogen limitation leads to a reduction in growth and photosynthetic rates, so it leads to a reduction in respiratory rates. The relationship between the specific growth rate and specific respiration rate is linear (Geider 1992; Geider et al. 1986) with a positive intercept at zero growth; this intercept is called *maintenance respiration* (Fig 8.5). As we will later examine, the relationship between photosynthesis and specific growth rate is nonlinear in nitrogen-limited chemostats, hence the ratio between the maximum rate of photosynthesis and respiration decreases as cells become increasingly limited (Herzig, Falkowski 1989). The molecular basis of the alterations in respiratory rates is unclear; however, the demands for carbon skeletons and ATP, two of the major products of the respiratory pathways, are markedly reduced if protein synthesis is depressed (Raven 1984a; Raven, Farquhar 1990; Turpin 1991).

## Phosphorus

In aquatic environments soluble inorganic phosphorus primarily occurs in the form of orthophosphate anions. In marine systems the overwhelming ionic state is $HPO_4^{2-}$, and to a smaller degree $PO_4^{3-}$ (Stumm, Morgan 1981). A variable source of soluble phosphorus is also found in soluble organic molecules; the element can be made accessible for assimilation by photoautotrophs through the action of extra-cellular and membrane-bound phosphatases that nonspecifically hydrolyze the phosphate group (Perry, Eppley 1981; Rivkin, Swift 1979). Regardless of its source, phosphate can be directly incorporated into nucleic acid precursors and carbohydrate and hydrocarbon skeletons without electron transfer reactions. Thus, phosphorus metabolism is primarily a study of the chemistry of hydrolytic and dehydration reactions rather than redox reactions.

The limitation of photosynthesis by phosphorus can be at least twofold. First, there is limitation of nucleic acid synthesis. This limitation can be at the level of genome replication, or at the level of RNA synthesis (i.e., a form of transcriptional control). It can affect photosynthetic energy conversion by reducing the rate of synthesis of proteins in the photosynthetic apparatus. This is effectively a negative feedback on photosynthesis. Secondly, a more immediate response to phosphorus limitation is on the rate of synthesis and regeneration of substrates in the Calvin–Benson cycle, thereby reducing the rate of light utilization for carbon fixation (Woodrow, Berry 1988).

## Sulfate

Sulfur is required for the synthesis of two amino acids, cysteine and methionine, and for the synthesis of certain sulfur-containing lipids that account for about 10% of the thylakoid lipid. To incorporate the element into carbon skeletons, sulfate must be reduced in vivo. The uptake of sulfate is an ATP-dependent process and the reduction of the molecule is catalyzed by a series of enzymes in the chloroplast that utilize both NADH and NADPH (Schmidt, Jager 1992). Normally sulfate reduction accounts for only about 1% of the total photosynthetic electron flow; hence, it is not a significant sink for reductant in algae (Raven 1993).

Sulfate is the second most abundant anion after chloride in the ocean, and is never limiting for the cell growth of marine phytoplankton or macrophytes. For rooted seagrasses, reduced sulfate as hydrogen sulfide in anaerobic sediments can provide a source of sulfur for the organisms. In freshwater ecosystems, however, the concentration of inorganic sulfur is about 100-fold lower than that in marine environments. Moreover, in freshwater systems the anaerobic reduction of sulfate to hydrogen sulfide can lead to losses of the element to the atmosphere. Consequently, on occasion sulfate may become limiting to protein synthesis in some freshwater systems, and some freshwater photoautotrophs induce high affinity transport systems to help acquire sulfate at very low external concentrations (Grossman et al. 1994). Sulfate limitation leads to a loss of photosynthetic pigments and enzymes, and to a general reduction in photosynthetic activity. In cyanobacteria, sulfur deficiency elicits the synthesis of alternative phycobiliproteins with less sulfur per molecule (Mazel, Marliere 1989).

As we have briefly discussed, the assimilation of the three macronutrients requires carbon skeletons. Some of these skeletons can be produced in the chloroplast, but most are generated by respiratory pathways in the mitochondria. Let us now examine the role of respiration in making cells and in coupling photosynthesis to growth.

## THE ESSENTIAL ROLE OF RESPIRATION IN BIOSYNTHESIS

Respiration is the sum of metabolic processes that consume $O_2$ and evolve $CO_2$. In defining respiration, we will focus on those processes that are related to the oxidation of organic carbon to provide substrates for cell growth. In so doing, we include both dark respiration and photorespiration.

When a photosynthetic organism is taken from the light to darkness, photosynthesis ceases and there is a net consumption of $O_2$. This phenomenon is commonly called *dark respiration*, and is responsible for the light-independent production of $CO_2$. There are four basic components of dark respiration. The primary pathway leading from carbohydrates to smaller, more oxidized molecules is *glycolysis*. This pathway is one of the most primitive respiratory metabolic processes. It is found in most prokaryotic, and all eukaryotic, cells. In glycolysis, hexose is oxidized to pyruvate, and the oxidation is coupled to the reduction of $NAD^+$. Some of the energy of the phosphorylated intermediates in the glycolytic pathway (which were phosphorylated at the expense of ATP) is conserved in the *substrate phosphorylation* of ADP (Fig 8.6). The major role of glycolysis is to provide substrates for further respiratory oxidative processes. In eukaryotic green algae, portions of the glycolytic pathway may be found in the cytoplasm, and some of the reactions may be found in the chloroplast stroma (Raven, Beardall 1981a). The extent to which the complete sequence occurs in each of these compartments is extremely variable. Very few data are available on the location of glycolytic reductions in nonchlorophyte algae (Raven 1984a; Raven 1976a; Raven 1976b; Raven, Beardall 1981a).

A second reaction sequence that consumes hexose is the *oxidative pentose phosphate pathway*, sometimes called the *pentose phosphate shunt* (Fig 8.7). This pathway

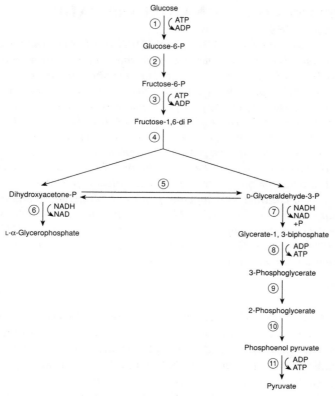

**Figure 8.6** Glycolysis, or the Embden–Meyerhof pathway for fermentative oxidation of glucose. The enzymes in the pathway are: (1) hexokinase; (2) glucosephosphate isomerase; (3) phosphofructokinase; (4) aldoase; (5) triosephosphate isomerase; (6) glycerophosphate dehydrogenase; (7) glyceraldehyde 3-phosphate dehydrogenase; (8) 3-phosphoglycerate kinase; (9) phosphoglyceromutase; (10) 2-phosphoglycerate; (11) pyruvate kinase. These reactions occur in the cytosol and/or stroma of eukaryotic cells.

phosphorylates and subsequently oxidizes hexose to produce NADPH, $CO_2$, and pentose phosphate. The latter is converted via heptulose and tetrose phosphates to hexose phosphate and triose phosphate. The hexose and triose phosphates can be recycled or fed into glycolytic reactions. In chlorophyte algae, the complete reaction sequence of the oxidative pentose phosphate pathway is found in both the cytosol and the chloroplasts. For other algae, it seems that reactions specific to the oxidative pentose phosphate pathways are absent from chloroplasts (Raven 1984a). The major role of this pathway is to provide a nonphotosynthetic source of NADPH (via ferredoxin reduction), which is essential for lipid biosynthesis and $NO_2^-$ reduction in the dark.

A third reaction sequence involved in dark respiration is the *Krebs cycle*, sometimes known as the *tricarboxylic acid* or *citric acid cycle* (Fig 8.8). The reactions of the Krebs cycle in eukaryotic photosynthesis are mainly located in the mitochondrial matrix; that is, they are not associated with the mitochondrial membranes (Fig 8.9). In the Krebs cycle, the pyruvate produced in glycolysis is aerobically oxidized to $CO_2$ by a sequence of single electron transfer reactions. These oxidations are

## ❏ DIFFERENT ROLES OF NADPH AND NADH
## IN EUKARYOTES

*While the two cofactors, NADH and NADPH, are thermodynamically isoenergetic and can serve similar functions, the formation and utilization of NADH and NADPH are distinctly different in eukaryotic photoautotrophs. NADPH is formed in the chloroplast from photosynthetic electron transport and in the cytosol primarily via the pentose phosphate pathway. The reductant is not transported directly out of the chloroplast and is not directly converted to NADH (Table 8.3). Substrates, such as triose phosphates, can be exported from the chloroplast and oxidized to form NADH in respiratory reactions, and this process is a form of energetic coupling between photosynthesis and respiration (Table 8.1). The distinction or specificity of reductant cofactor potentially allows functionally identical enzymes in competing pathways to operate simultaneously in opposite directions. For example, lipid biosynthesis requires NADPH as a reductant, while the oxidation of lipids is coupled to the formation of NADH (Dennis, Turpin 1990; Lawlor 1993). Similar competing pathways occur in glycolysis and gluconeogenesis and are separated by cofactor specificity.*

---

mediated by $NAD^+$ and FAD. Intermediates in the Krebs cycle are withdrawn to form carbon skeletons for amino acids, lipids, tetrapyrroles, and other biosynthetic processes. The oxidation of pyruvate is coupled to the reduction of $NAD^+$, and ultimately $O_2$, leading to the formation of NADH and $H_2O$. In the absence of $O_2$, the pyruvate formed from glycolysis can be anaerobically oxidized to lactate or, via pyruvate decarboxylase, to acetaldehyde and ethanol. These breakdown products would be produced in the degradation of cells in natural aquatic environments.

The fourth component of dark respiration is *respiratory electron transport* in the inner mitochondrial membrane and its associated proton pumping. This process, which is coupled to the Krebs cycle, leads to the phosphorylation of ADP via a proton flux through the ATP synthase complex, similar to that found in the chloroplast (Fig 8.9). The mitochondrial electron transport chain is by far the largest source of ATP in respiratory processes. The NADH in the mitochondrial matrix is oxidized by dehydrogenases associated with a respiratory electron transport chain located

**Table 8.3** Permeability of molecules into higher plant chloroplast envelope (after Heber 1974); the generalization of this information to non-green plastids is not established

| Relative Rate of Permeation | Substrate/Product |
|---|---|
| Very rapid | $Cl^-$, $NH_4^+$, $NO_3^-$, $O_2$, glycerol, triose phosphate, orthophosphate |
| Rapid | 3-phosphoglycerate, neutral amino acids, glycolate, dicarboxylic amino acids and keto acids (malate, oxaloacetate, aspartate, glutamate) |
| Slow | ATP, organic anions, bicarbonate ions, $H^+$ |
| Very slow | cations, $Mg^{2+}$, $K^+$, serine, alanine, hexose monophosphates, hexose, pentose sugars, glycine |
| Extremely slow | NAD(P), NAD(P)H, ADP, GTP, pyrophosphate, sucrose, glucose, sorbitol, mannitol |

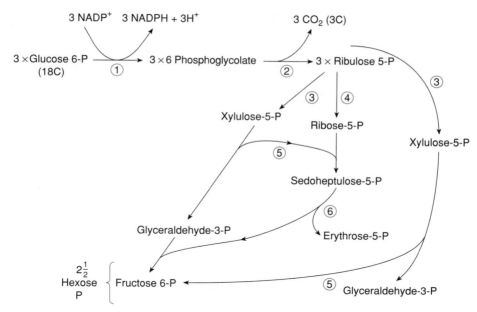

**Figure 8.7** The oxidative pentose phosphate pathway. The enzymes in this pathway are (1) glucose 6-phosphate dehydrogenase; (2) 6-phosphogluconase dehydrogenase; (3) phosphopentose mutase; (4) phosphopentose isomerase; (5) transketolase; (6) transaldolase. The stoichiometry of carbon in the pathway is shown; for every 18 carbon atoms entering the pathway (a total of 3 glucose-6-phosphate molecules), 3 leave as $CO_2$ in the formation of ribulose 5-phosphate, which ultimately is used to synthesize 2.5 molecules of a six-carbon sugar. These reactions occur in the cytosol and (in the Viridiplantae) in the stroma.

on the inner mitochondrial membrane. The coupling among redox reactions, proton fluxes, and ATP production can be disrupted by uncoupling reagents that affect the electrochemical potential across the inner mitochondrial membrane (e.g., see Ahmad, Morris 1967). The mitochondrial ATP synthase is structurally similar to the chloroplast $CF_0CF_1$ complex; however, a major difference between chloroplastic and mitochondrial systems is that the pH gradient dominates the electrochemical gradient in the former, whereas in the latter, the electrical potential difference is much more important. The mitochondrial respiratory electron transport system oxidizes most of the NADH generated in the Krebs cycle, and produces virtually all of the ATP supplied by the organelle (Raven 1976a).

Most of the electron traffic in the mitochondrial respiratory chain goes through a cytochrome oxidase to molecular oxygen. This electron transfer can be noncompetitively inhibited by cyanide. In some algal and higher plant mitochondria a second, cyanide-insensitive pathway exists, whereby electrons can be diverted to an alternative electron acceptor, quinol oxidoreductase, that transfers electrons from a quinol to $O_2$ (Grant, Hommersand 1974; Laties 1982). The pathway is not found in prokaryotic organisms. In microalgae, the alternative oxidase pathway can be induced or stimulated by the addition of cyanide (Heldt-Hansen et al. 1983). Alternative oxidase can be inhibited by substituted hydroxamic acids such as salicylhydroxamic acid (SHAM) and *m*-chlorobenzhydroxamic acid (CLAM). In higher plants and presumably in algae, the role of the alternative oxidase appears to be

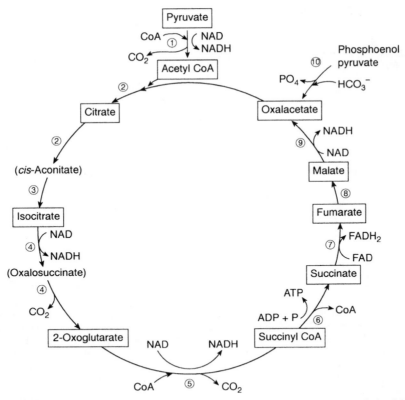

**Figure 8.8** The tricarboxylic acid cycle. The initial substrate for the cycle is pyruvate, derived from glycolysis (see Fig 8.6), which is decarboxylated via the activity of pyruvate decarboxylase (1) to form acetyl co-enzyme A. The subsequent enzymes in the pathway are: (2) citrate synthase; (3) aconitase; (4) isocitrate dehydrogenase; (5) α-ketoglutarate (= 2-oxoglutarate) dehydrogenase; (6) succinate thiokinase (this pathway occurs in the mitochondrial matrix); (7) succinate dehydrogenase; (8) fumarase; (9) malate dehydrogenase. Phosphoenolpyruvate can enter the cycle anaplerotically by conversion to oxaloacetate via the activity of phosphoenolpyruvate carboxylase (10) or other, taxon-specific carboxylases (see Fig 8.10).

dissipation of excess energy through a nonproductive pathway (Siedow, Umbach 1995). At high light levels, the photosynthetic electron transport system can generate so much ATP that it represses glycolysis via allosteric interactions. The alternative oxidase permits the glycolysis and the kinetic cycle sequence to proceed without producing as much ATP as would occur with the same biosynthetic carbon flux using only cytochrome oxidase (Dennis, Turpin 1990).

The synthesis of a very wide range of biosynthetic intermediates depends on the removal of compounds from the Krebs cycle. The key intermediates removed are oxaloacetate and 2-oxoglutarate (also called α-ketoglutarate). Removal of intermediates from the cycle would cause the cycle to cease to function unless there is an alternative supply of the substrate to the cycle. The replenishing reactions are called *anaplerotic* processes (Fig 8.10). Before discussing these reactions, let us first consider the use of oxaloacetate and 2-oxoglutarate in making cells.

Both oxaloacetate and 2-oxoglutarate possess a ketone group on the α-carbon. This feature of the structure facilitates transamination reactions. 2-Oxoglutarate

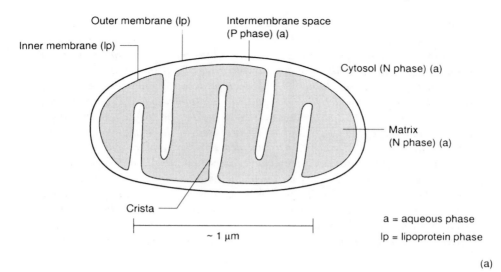

(a)

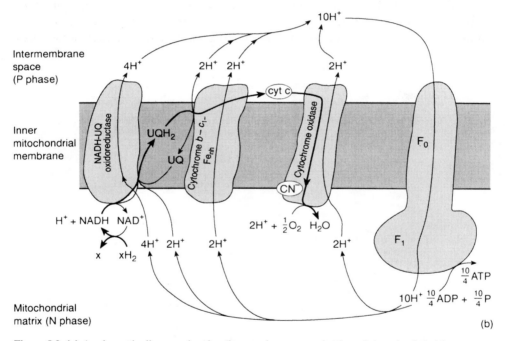

(b)

**Figure 8.9** (a) A schematic diagram showing the membrane organization of the mitochondrion. Aqueous phases and lipoprotein phases are denoted, as are the relative electrical potentials (see Fig 1.1). (b) The mitochondrial electron transport pathway, located on the inner mitochondrial membrane, showing the stoichiometry of proton pumping and ATP formation. Cyanide blocks the electron transfer from cytochrome oxidase to oxygen. In eukaryotic photoautotrophs, an alternative, cyanide-insensitive oxidase permits electron transfer to oxygen, albeit usually at lower rates. $F_0$ and $F_1$ are coupling factors analogous to the ATP synthase complex in the chloroplast (see Chapters 4 and 6).

forms the carbon skeleton of glutamate. The amino group comes from the glutamine synthetase–glutamate synthase pathway. Glutamate is often the most abundant free amino acid in algae, and plays a key role in amino acid synthesis by supplying the carbon skeleton and α-amino nitrogen to a number of oxyacids. The

## ❏ ATP

*The energy of hydrolysis of the phosphate bonds of ATP is essential in macromolecule syntheses. Polymerization reactions, which are required to form proteins from amino acids, complex carbohydrates from sugars, or lipids from oxidized precursors (see Table 5.5), all require dehydration steps. The energy required to catalyze the dehydration reactions is supplied by ATP. For example, in protein synthesis, ATP hydrolysis is used to assemble a tRNA with its appropriate amino acid, and additional ATPs are used in the elongation reactions directed by the mRNA and rRNA molecules. For each amino acid added to a protein, three ATP molecules are hydrolyzed; this investment in energy does not include the ATP used in the synthesis of the amino acids or in corrections of errors (Bouma et al. 1994). Recall that in the absence of photorespiration, the Calvin–Benson cycle consumes three ATPs and two NADPHs for each $CO_2$ fixed; the energy and reductant are required to regenerate ribulose-1,5-bisphosphate and generate the reduced carbon product (Chapter 5).*

---

amino acids derived from glutamate are arginine, proline, and hydroxyproline. In addition, the synthesis of tetrapyrroles such as chlorins and porphyrins in all photoautotrophs (with the exception of mitochondrial porphyrins in euglenoids) uses

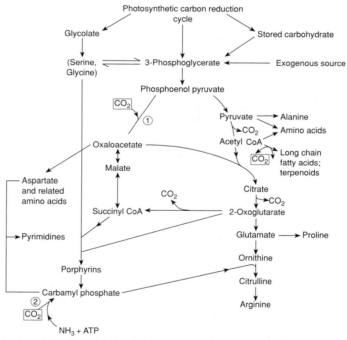

**Figure 8.10** Relation of $CO_2$ ($HCO_3^-$) fixation by reactions other than the carboxylation of ribulose bisphosphate to the synthesis of essential metabolites. Reaction 1: carboxylation of pyruvate (by pyruvate carboxylase) or phosphoenolpyruvate (by phosphoenolpyruvate carboxylase or phosphoenolpyruvate carboxykinase) ("$C_3 + C_1$ Carboxylation"). Reaction 2: carbamyl phosphate synthetase. Reaction 3: acetyl CoA carboxylase (the carboxyl group introduced in this reaction is "catalytic" in that decarboxylation occurs in the chain elongation reaction in fatty acid and terpenoid synthesis).

the carbon skeleton and half of the nitrogen of glutamate. The reaction sequence involves an interesting intermolecular rearrangement of glutamate attached to a glutamyl tRNA to yield δ-aminolevulinic acid, eight molecules of which are required for the synthesis of one molecule of tetrapyrrole (Von Wettstein et al. 1995).

Oxaloacetate is the starting point for the synthesis of the aspartate, and hence the aspartate family of amino acids as well as of pyrimidines. It is thus vital for synthesis of proteins and nucleic acids. Aspartate is formed from oxaloacetate by transamination from glutamate. The amino acids derived from carbon skeleton and/or amino group of aspartate are threonine, isoleucine, methionine, and lysine.

As mentioned, the removal of carbon skeletons from the Krebs cycle requires anaplerotic reactions to maintain the supply of the intermediates in the cycle. The oxaloacetate is supplied by carboxylation reactions that add $CO_2$ or $HCO_3^-$ to a three-carbon compound, either pyruvate or phosphoenolpyruvate. In the case of pyruvate, the carboxylation is catalyzed by pyruvate carboxylase, an enzyme that contains biotin as a bound cofactor. In the case of phosphoenol pyruvate, the carboxylation can be catalyzed either by phosphoenol-pyruvate carboxylase or phosphoenolpyruvate carboxykinase. These anaplerotic carboxylation reactions can operate in the dark, and are part of the dark carbon fixation processes described in Chapter 5 (see Table 5.4 and Table 5.6).

The fraction of anaplerotic carbon fixation required to sustain the flux of aspartate, glutamate, and their derivatives can be computed as a fraction of total carbon fixed and retained in the cells. This amounts to approximately 0.33 mole carbon per mole organic nitrogen. Thus, for a cell with a C:N ratio of 6.6, anaplerotic carbon fixation accounts for about 5% of the fixed carbon in the organism (Raven et al. 1990; Raven and Farquhar 1990; Turpin 1991). This fraction is even less if expressed in terms of gross $CO_2$ fixation because a greater fraction of carbon fixed by the Calvin–Benson cycle is respired than for carbon fixed via anaplerotic pathways. For a macrophyte with a C:N ratio of 13.7, the maximum contribution of anaplerotic carboxylations to overall carbon assimilation is 2.4%. Other anaplerotic carboxylases are listed in Table 5.5. These are all essential for biosynthesis, but together contribute much less to total carbon assimilation than the β-carboxylases discussed above. The exception, in quantitative terms, is acetyl CoA carboxylase (Raven 1995); however, the inorganic carbon fixed by this enzyme is not retained by the organism for more than a second or two.

All the other amino acids and purines required by the cell are produced by reactions that do *not* consume carbon skeletons from the Krebs cycle. Instead, the carbon skeletons for these intermediates are derived from glycolysis and the oxidative pentose phosphate cycle, *without* necessarily involving any oxidation–reduction or net $CO_2$ exchange reactions. Accordingly, removal of 3-phosphoglyceric acid, phosphoenolpyruvate, pyruvate, or acetyl CoA from the glycolytic pathway, or erythrose-4-P or ribose-5-P from the pentose phosphate pathway, does not require anaplerotic replenishment. These carbon skeletons can all be derived from either hexose or triose phosphates.

The respiratory processes depicted in Figures 8.6 to 8.8 can account for all biosynthesis of carbon skeletons required for making cells. These pathways are coupled to photosynthesis through the metabolism of hexose (or its polymeric forms) and the reductant and energy stored in the chemical bonds that constitute hexose. The rate of hexose synthesis is directly related to the photosynthetic process, whereas the utilization of hexose for biosynthesis and energy is directly related to respiratory processes. Because of this coupling, as we will shortly explain, respiration rates are generally proportional to growth rates.

## Respiratory and Photosynthetic Quotients

A useful concept in plant metabolism is that of photosynthetic and respiratory quotients. The photosynthetic quotient is defined as mole $O_2$ produced per mole $CO_2$ assimilated. For the production of carbohydrate ($CH_2O$), the photosynthetic quotient is 1.0:

$$CO_2 + 2H_2O + 8 \text{ photons} \rightarrow (CH_2O) + H_2O + O_2 \tag{8.7}$$

The respiratory quotient is defined as mole $CO_2$ produced per mole $O_2$ consumed. For the complete oxidation of carbohydrate, the respiratory quotient is 1.0:

$$(CH_2O) + O_2 + H_2O + 6ADP + 6Pi \rightarrow CO_2 + 2H_2O + 6ATP + 6H_2O \tag{8.8}$$

The actual photosynthetic or respiratory quotient is critically dependent on the reduction level of the primary product or substrate. In respiratory pathways, the reduction level is formally defined as the reciprocal of the respiratory quotient. Let us consider some examples.

All nitrogen in organic material is reduced to the level of ammonium ($NH_4^+$). In natural aquatic ecosystems, nitrogen is frequently supplied as nitrate ($NO_3^-$). To borrow from the adage that there is no such thing as a free lunch, the eight electrons required for the reduction of nitrate to ammonium come from the respiratory oxidation of carbohydrate and from the photosynthetic oxidation of water. Whatever the source of the electrons, they reduce nitrate at the expense of $CO_2$ reduction. In the simple case where carbon is reduced to the level of carbohydrate, the reduction of nitrate to ammonium follows a general equation:

$$nCO_2 + (n+1)H_2O + HNO_3 \rightarrow (CH_2O)_n NH_3 + (n+2)O_2 \tag{8.9}$$

where $n$ is the C:N ratio (by atoms) of the cell. The photosynthetic quotient therefore is $[(n+2)/n]$; that is, it is nonlinearly proportional to the C:N ratio. If a cell had a C:N ratio of 7, and its organic carbon were reduced, on average, to the level of carbohydrate, and the sole source of nitrogen for the cell were nitrate, the photosynthetic quotient would be 9:7, or about 1.3. Thus, under identical conditions, carbon fixation rates would be 30% higher for a cell growing with ammonium as the nitrogen source than for the same cell growing with nitrate as the nitrogen source, but the rate of photosynthetic oxygen evolution would be identical. Experimental data support this hypothetical difference (Myers 1980).

More complicated scenarios develop when considering the actual reduction level of carbon. Assume that a cell starts with carbohydrate as its storage product and needs to synthesize proteins and other macromolecules. Carbon in proteins and lipids is more reduced than carbohydrate. Consider the same cell as above (with a C:N ratio of 7 by atoms), using $NH_4^+$ as its inorganic nitrogen source; a balanced equation can be written as follows:

$$1.38(CH_2O) + 0.14NH_4^+ + 0.33O_2 + 1.38H_2O$$
$$\rightarrow (CH_{1.86}N_{0.14}O_{0.12}) + 0.38CO_2 + 0.14H^+ + 2.52H_2O \qquad (8.10)$$

This scenario results in a respiratory quotient of 1.15. If we combine this respiratory quotient with a photosynthetic quotient of 1.0,

$$1.38CO_2 + 2.76H_2O + 0.14NH_4^+ + 0.33O_2$$
$$\rightarrow (CH_{1.86}N_{0.14}O_{0.62}) + 0.38CO_2 + 0.14H^+ + 2.04H_2O + 1.38O_2 \qquad (8.11)$$

we obtain an overall ratio of $CO_2$ assimilated by the cell for growth to $O_2$ evolved by photosynthesis of 1.05.

Photosynthetic quotients are critically important for relating photosynthetic electron flow, obtained from measurements of oxygen evolution, to carbon fixation. Respiratory quotients can provide information on the level of reduction of respired carbon.

It should be pointed out that the form of nitrogen assimilated can affect photosynthetic electron transport. The reduction of $NO_3^-$ to $NH_4^+$ requires reductant but not ATP, whereas $NH_4^+$ assimilation into amino acids requires ATP and reductant. In *Chlamydomonas* at low irradiance levels, up to 40% of the photosynthetically produced reductant is used for the reduction of $NO_3^-$; this fraction declines to about 10% at saturating irradiance levels. Thus, at low irradiance levels $NO_3^-$ assimilation may temporarily out-compete $CO_2$ fixation for reductant, leading to a suppression of $CO_2$ fixation (but not $O_2$ evolution). Moreover, some algae apparently can modulate the production of ATP and NADPH by controlling the relative activities of cyclic electron flow around PSI as opposed to linear electron transport from water to NADPH. Turpin and Bruce (1990) have proposed that this modulation is achieved via state transitions (Chapter 7). They suggest that $NO_3^-$-assimilating cells increase the effective absorption cross-section of PSII, thereby encouraging linear electron transport, whereas cells that assimilate $NH_4^+$ increase the relative absorption cross-section of PSI, thereby encouraging cyclic electron flow around PSI (and hence ATP production). It should be noted that the nutrient-dependent state transitions are effective only at subsaturating irradiance levels.

### Measurements of Rates of Dark Respiration as a Function of Rates of Growth

As we have stressed, respiration is not simply an oxidative process that produces (as do thylakoid reactions of photosynthesis) ATP and reductant, but also unique carbon skeletons for biosynthesis. Respiration is therefore essential for cell growth. If the biosynthetic processes are prerequisite for growth, then a plot of specific respiration rate against specific growth rate should be linear with a positive slope and a positive intercept on the specific respiration rate axis (see Fig 8.5). Indeed, data from carefully executed experiments in microalgae show a linear relation between specific rate of dark respiration and specific growth rate (Geider 1992; Laws 1975). The slope of the line gives the respired carbon per unit carbon assimilated, while the intercept gives the specific rate of maintenance respiration.

Maintenance respiration corresponds to the minimum oxidative metabolism required to maintain cell viability at zero growth. Such basic processes as repair of damaged proteins (i.e., protein turnover), nucleic acid turnover, and recouping leaked solutes must be supported whether a cell is growing or not. These processes are energy consuming, and hence some fraction of the cell metabolism is apportioned to them. Maintenance respiration rates are variable between species and are positively correlated with the compensation point (Langdon 1988). On average, maintenance respiration accounts for the consumption of about 1% of the cell organic carbon per day at 25 °C (Geider, Osborne 1989). An alternative means of estimating the rate maintenance metabolism is by extrapolating the specific growth rate versus incident photon flux density to zero photon flux density. A negative intercept on the specific growth rate axis yields an estimate of the specific maintenance rate.

## Allometry

Respiration rates are also a function of the size of an organism. This phenomenon is well documented in heterotrophs, especially endothermic animals (Schmidt-Nielson 1970), but in the case of unicellular photoautotrophs the relationship is more nebulous (Banse 1976; Chisholm 1992; Fenchel 1974). The study of the correlation between processes and the size of an organism is called *allometry*, and the relationships scale nonlinearly, taking the form:

$$R = a W^{(b)} \tag{8.12}$$

where $R$ is respiration rate[3] per unit biomass, $W$ is the cell or organism mass, and $a$ and $b$ are dimensionless coefficients. The coefficient $b$ has a value of about $-0.25$ and appears to be extremely constant for phytoplankton (Banse 1976; Laws 1975) when examined over several orders of magnitude of $W$. The intercept $a$ ranges from about 0.2 to about 0.4. Over small ranges in $W$, interspecific variability dominates $R$, and the allometric relationships are often obscured.

Allometric relationships offer an empirical estimate of respiration (or growth rates) based on size. The intrinsic biological basis of the relationships is not well understood, although the ratio of mitochondrial activity to cell volume may be a critical determinant. Cytosol volume and mitochondrial surface area do not necessarily scale proportionately, and neither is strictly scaled to the surface area of the organism. Thus, large organisms with low surface-to-volume ratios and reduced mitochondrial volume fraction often have reduced volume-based respiratory electron transport rates compared with small organisms.

---

3. Note that $R$ is the *specific* respiration rate, which, like specific growth rate, has dimensions of time$^{-1}$.

## Respiration Rates in the Light and Dark

As respiration and photosynthesis lead to opposing fluxes of $O_2$ and $CO_2$, the rate of dark respiration in the light cannot be readily ascertained. If a cell or organism is grown at a constant light intensity, dark respiration is commonly taken as the rate of oxygen consumption immediately on placing the organism or cells in the dark. Over a period of several hours, this respiratory rate declines, as the pools of carbohydrate within the cell slowly become depleted and proteins begin to accumulate. If a cell or organism is grown at an irradiance level that is subsaturating for photosynthesis, and subsequently is exposed to higher light levels thereby accelerating photosynthetic rates, the respiratory rate will accelerate. This phenomenon can be observed by taking the cells from the higher irradiance level to darkness; the initial respiratory rate is significantly higher than that found several tens of minutes later (Fig 8.11). This phenomenon, called *enhanced post-illumination respiration*, has been observed in cyanobacteria (Brown, Webster 1953), eukaryotic algae (Beardall et al. 1994; Falkowski, Owens 1978; Falkowski, Dubinsky, Santostefano 1985), and higher plants (Decker 1955; Heichel 1970; Kromer 1995).

It is possible, using the stable isotope $^{18}O_2$ as a tracer, to determine respiration in the light and to distinguish this consumption of oxygen from the simultaneous photosynthetic generation of $O_2$. The rationale for the use of this tracer is as follows. Photosynthetic $O_2$ originates from water. The naturally more abundant isotope of $O_2$ is $^{16}O$. Thus, photosynthetic oxygen evolution would lead to the production of $^{16}O_2$ from $H_2{}^{16}O$. If $^{18}O_2$ is added to a closed chamber, the respiratory consumption of the gas can be measured as depletion of the heavy isotope, while the increase in $^{16}O_2$ estimates gross photosynthesis. Net changes of $O_2$ ($^{18}O_2$ plus $^{16}O_2$) in the light give a measure of net photosynthesis. Using this technique, Weger and colleagues (1989) identified mitochondrial respiration as responsible for the enhanced post-illumination respiration, but moreover found that the enhanced respiration was

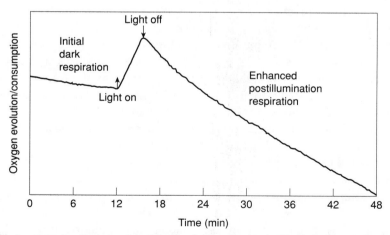

**Figure 8.11** An example of enhanced postillumination respiration in *Thalassiosira weisflogii*. After establishing the initial dark respiration rate, cells were exposed to an intense beam ($1200\,\mu E\cdot m^{-2}\cdot s^{-1}$) for 5 min. Following illumination, the respiration rates are initially elevated compared with the preillumination rates, and decline slowly over a period of approximately 1 hour.

observed in the light as well as in the period immediately following the transfer from the light to darkness.

## BALANCED AND UNBALANCED GROWTH

Because of variations in light in nature, photosynthesis and respiratory rates change continuously throughout the day. These changes are reflected in the biochemical composition, and the variations reflect the mobilization and allocation of specific constituents in response to environmental cues. Before discussing these variations, however, let us consider the growth of a homogeneous population in a steady state.

The steady-state growth rate of population of organisms can be described by:

$$\mu = dN/dt \left( 1/N \right) \tag{8.13}$$

where $\mu$ is the specific growth rate (with units of 1/time), $N$ is the number of organisms, and $t$ is time. The specific growth rate of a cell can also be related to its constituents, and described by the general exponential equation as shown for numbers of organisms. For example, in the case of carbon we can calculate a carbon-specific growth rate, $\mu_C$, as:

$$\mu_C = dC/dt \left( 1/C \right) \tag{8.14}$$

and identical expressions could be used for DNA, phosphorus, nitrogen, and so on.

Aquatic plants growing under constant conditions reach a steady-state biochemical composition, and under such conditions, normally, the rate of growth of any cell constituent is identical if *averaged over one generation*. This condition is called *balanced growth*, and the assumption of balanced growth is often implicit in the calculation of population growth rates from the time-dependent rate of incorporation of an element (such as carbon) into the organic material of the organism (Eppley 1980). The condition that the process is averaged over a generation is often difficult to meet in a practical sense (Eppley 1981).

In nature, the variations in irradiance and other external, environmental processes necessitate a buffering between photosynthesis and cell growth. Carbohydrates usually serve this role. For example, short-term variations in irradiance may be reflected at the level of the photochemical reactions by the fraction of reaction centers that are statistically open. The photochemical processes are related to the rate of injection of electrons into the Calvin–Benson cycle, and hence in carbon fixation. As the products of the Calvin–Benson cycle accumulate, however, they form a reserve that dampens short-term variations in the environment from affecting the rate at which the products are utilized in biosynthetic pathways. An analogy can be made to a bank account and the rate of earning and spending. If one has lots of money in a bank account, then small, short-term withdrawals and deposits are barely reflected in the long-term size of the account. The larger the bank account, the smaller will be the impact of short-term fluctuations. Similarly, if a cell has large stores of carbohydrate relative to photosynthetic supply or respiratory demands, short-term variations in environmental processes are not perceptible at the level of growth; the organism's growth responds to the average environmental status.

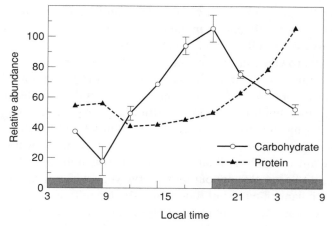

**Figure 8.12** Changes in the relative abundance of carbohydrate and protein in the diatom *Thalassiosira weisflogii* grown on a 12 hr:12 hr light-dark cycle.

One example of the buffering capacity of carbohydrates is diel[4] oscillation of chemical composition of photoautotrophic unicellular algae in response to the photoperiod. When cells are entrained on a light–dark cycle comparable to that found in nature, photosynthetic carbon fixation leads to the accumulation of carbohydrate during the photophase (Fig 8.12). At night a fraction of the carbohydrate is respired with the resulting synthesis of protein (Cuhel et al. 1984; Post et al. 1985). Thus, within a day, protein and carbohydrate pool sizes oscillate, and consequently are not, at a given instant in time, in steady state.

Light limitation of photosynthesis has relatively little effect on overall composition, although there is often a tendency to accumulate more carbohydrate at higher irradiance levels (Falkowski, Owens 1980). Nutrient limitation (which we will discuss in Chapters 9 and 10) can also lead to changes in gross protein abundance in relation to carbohydrate and/or lipid. Nitrogen limitation, for example, leads to elevated relative abundance of carbohydrate or lipid, and often can result in unbalanced growth. One example of the compromises between the phasing of nutrient acquisition and photosynthesis in cell growth is found in the diel migration patterns of some dinoflagellates. In highly stratified aquatic environments, dinoflagellates may ascend to the nutrient-deficient, upper portion of the water column during the day, where they take advantage of the incident solar radiation for photosynthesis. At night, the organisms often descend to nutrient-replete layers in or below the density gradient (usually the thermocline), where they assimilate inorganic nitrogen and phosphate (Raven, Richardson 1984). This type of migration pattern has also been observed for diatoms in the Sargasso Sea, where the buoyancy of these nonmotile cells appears to be regulated by ion composition and levels within the cells (Villareal, Lipshultz 1995). This migration pattern is expected to lead to large diel changes in cell composition, such that cells are high in carbohydrate and low in

---

4. *Diel* means a cycle that includes a full 24-hour day, as opposed to *diurnal*, which means during the day, and *nocturnal*, which means during the night.

protein during the day and low in carbohydrate and high in protein at night. This condition is not necessarily one of unbalanced growth, as the net production of all cell constituents over a cell division remains constant.

Unbalanced growth can occur under certain circumstances, however. One example is the annual cycle in chemical composition found in some macrophytes. In kelps such as *Laminaria* that live in temperate waters the establishment of a thermocline in the spring limits the supply of nutrients to the plants growing in the upper mixed layer. During the stratified periods, the plants build up stores of carbohydrates, mostly mannitol, and consume this carbohydrate in the winter when nutrients are abundant but light is limited (Fig 8.13). This unbalanced growth pattern enables the kelp to grow throughout most of the year, which would not be the case if growth were balanced on a diel time scale. The magnitude of such stores is such that the observed specific growth rate of kelps is 2 to 3 doublings per year in nature. Similar storage capacities can be found for inorganic nutrients such as nitrate and phosphate. Many species of algae can accumulate reserves of inorganic nutrients such that division continues during periods of external nutrient limitation. The surplus uptake of nutrients, called *luxury consumption*, permits one to two divisions in both microalgae and macrophytes.

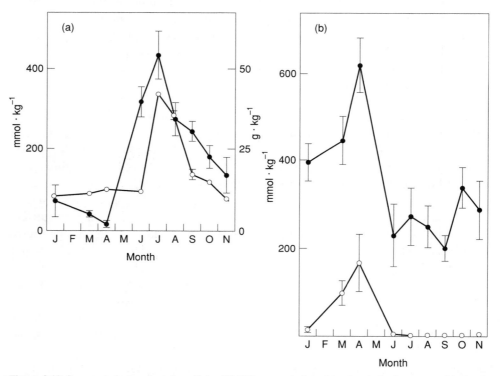

**Figure 8.13** Seasonal changes in intracellular $K^+$, $NO_3^-$, mannitol, and laminarin in the mature blade of the perennial brown marine macroalga *Laminaria digitata* from Arbroath, Scotland. $NO_3^-$ is more readily available in the winter months, light energy in the summer. (a) Seasonal changes in the intracellular concentration of mannitol (mmol·kg$^{-1}$ cellwater; closed circles) and laminarin (g·k$^{-1}$ fresh weight, open circles). (b) Seasonal changes in the concentration (mmol·kg$^{-1}$ cellwater) of $NO_3^-$ (open circles) and of $K^+$ (the counter ion for $NO_3^-$; closed circles). Vertical bars denote 95% confidence limits. Reproduced with permission from Davison and Reed (1985).

**Storage Compounds**

In all aquatic plants, some fraction of the fixed carbon is allowed to accumulate and is used to support growth or maintenance. The form of stored carbon is highly variable between algal classes, and the quantity of carbon is highly dependent on environmental conditions.

The synthesis and use of storage products can be *deterministic*, that is, the result of an evolutionary response to predictable, periodic shortages of the product stored. For example, in most photoautotrophs, carbon is often stored during the photoperiod in the form of polysaccharides or lipids. At night, a part of these carbon reserves is consumed to synthesize amino acids and other nitrogen-containing compounds. Over longer periods at high latitudes, perennial seaweeds often accumulate carbohydrates as energy reserves in the summer and use these reserves in the winter (see Chapter 9).

The production and consumption of storage products can also be an evolutionary response to *stochastic* events. Natural selection presumably favors species whose members carry sufficient energy reserves to deal with most unpredictable but potentially survivable energy shortages. For example, diatoms can accumulate large lipid reserves at high light, and these cells are commonly found in high-nutrient regions such as upwelling zones. Diatoms also survive for extended periods in darkness, slowly consuming their lipid reserves. A strategy such as that adopted by diatoms facilitates outbursts of rapid growth, followed by sinking and upwelling months later.

The diversity of organic carbon reserves closely follows taxonomic lines. Glucose-based polysaccharide reserves are found in all aerobic autotrophs. The standard type ($\alpha$-1,4-glucan, with or without $\alpha$-1,6 branchpoints) is characteristic of cyanobacteria, Chlorophyta, Rhodophyta, Dinophyta, Cryptophyta, and higher plants. In the eukaryotic algae, with the exception of the Chlorophyta, $\alpha$-1,4-glucans are found in the cytosol. In the Chlorophyta and higher plants this storage product is localized in the plastid. All of the other algae produce $\beta$-1,3-glucans and the polymerized products are found in the cytosol. These carbon reserves have been given names such as laminarin, chrysolaminarin, leucosin, and paramylon. Some green marine microalgae in the Chlorophyta also store soluble (vacuolar) polyfructan.

The extent to which the low molecular mass soluble sugars and sugar alcohols function as energy and organic carbon reserves varies between organisms. Compounds such as sucrose, mannitol, glycerol, trehalose, and galactosyl glycerols are sometimes specific to higher or lower taxa, and invariably fit the definition of "compatible solutes." This means that they can contribute to the osmotic potential of "N" phases (see Fig 1.1a,b) without resulting in changes to protein structure and function that would be caused by osmotic solutes such as inorganic ions. The levels of the organic compounds, especially in microalgae, are largely a function of the external osmolarity. One striking example is the accumulation of glycerol in the halotolerant unicellular marine chlorophyte, *Dunaliella* sp. When the external osmolarity is increased, these organisms rapidly synthesize glycerol to compensate for the change in osmotic pressure (Ben-Amotz, Avron 1973). In fact, the intracellular concentration of glycerol is proportional to the extracellular osmolarity. In this manner, *Dunaliella* sp can survive and even thrive in brines with concentrations of salt tenfold higher than seawater.

An example of an additional role of a comparable solute is seen in the brown macroalga *Laminaria* where mannitol varies seasonally. In this case, the variations are not associated with changes in osmolarity in the environment, but rather are related to the relative availability of light or nitrate (see Chapter 9).

Neutral lipids (triglycerides) are storage forms of carbon that are found primarily in diatoms, eustimatophytes, and some chlorophytes. Despite the low density of neutral lipids, the absence of hydroxyl groups, and hence of water hydration, permits a high fraction of stored chemical bond energy per unit mass. Neutral lipids are readily used as a source of ATP via Krebs cycle oxidation, but these forms of carbon are less flexible than sugar-based energy stores in terms of providing carbon skeletons for biosynthetic reactions (see later in this chapter). Triglycerides are typically stored in the cytosol.

Resources other than organic carbon are also stored by photoautotrophs. Inorganic nitrogen can be stored as $NO_3^-$ in the vacuoles of eukaryotic microalgae and macrophytes. $NH_4^+$ is much less commonly stored. Cyanobacteria can store nitrogen in the aspartate-arginine copolymer called cyanophycin. Organic nitrogen storage also occurs as an additional role for some proteins, such as Rubisco and phycobilins, but not light-harvesting integral membrane proteins of chlorophytes and chromophytes.

Phosphorus can be stored as inorganic orthophosphate in vacuoles of all aquatic plants and as polyphosphates in vacuoles of the cytosol of cyanobacteria and algae. Storage of organic phosphate is not common in aquatic autotrophs, but probably occurs as phytic acid (phosphate esterified with inositol) in seeds of aquatic flowering plants.

The size of the storage pool should be considered in relationship to the maximum specific growth rate of the organism. For example, macrophytes often appear to have a large capacity to store nitrogen and other elements, but there is often little difference between microphytes and macrophytes when growth rates are considered. In most cases, the maximum storage capacity for nitrogen is sufficient to provide one doubling of the plant biomass, and in the case of phosphorus, sufficient to sustain approximately three doublings (Raven 1984a).

## Balanced Growth and the Cell Cycle

In a strict sense, the concept of balanced growth is only applicable to a nonsynchronized population of cells, not to a single cell. In all eukaryotic cells, a division cycle can be inferred. This cycle usually consists of four phases, namely an S phase in which DNA is replicated, an M phase when mitosis occurs, and two G phases, or *gaps*, one called G1 occurring between the M and S phase and a second, designated G2, occurring between the S and M phases (Fig 8.14). In nature, the synchronization of the cell cycle is usually keyed to the light–dark cycle, although the entrainment is the consequence of an endogenous clock. Thus, cells that are synchronized

## ❑ ZOOXANTHELLAE: A CASE STUDY IN UNBALANCED GROWTH

*An extreme example of unbalanced growth is found in the case of symbiotic algae in corals. The algae, called zooxanthellae, are dinoflagellates living within the cells of an invertebrate host. The specific growth rate of the cells can be estimated from the frequency of dividing cells (i.e., the mitotic index) based on microscopic examination. Such measurements suggest that the specific growth rate of the algae is about 0.01 per day, corresponding to a division time of between 50 to 75 days, depending on growth irradiance. Simultaneous measurements of photosynthetic rates and zooxanthellae biomass reveal a carbon-specific growth rate of between 0.3 and 1.3 per day. Put simply, the photosynthetic carbon fixation is on the order of 100-fold greater than that required to produce new cells. Where does all the excess carbon go?*

*The primary form of fixed carbon in zooxanthellae is glycerol, produced from the dephosphorylation and reduction of dihydroxyacetone phosphate (see Chapter 5). Glycerol is excreted from the alga into the animal. Being devoid of any organic nitrogen, glycerol is primarily an energy source and is simply respired by the animal host. In this case, the symbiotic association is critically dependent on a permanently unbalanced growth condition of the algal partner. If excess inorganic nitrogen is added to the coral, the zooxanthellae tend to synthesize protein rather than glycerol. In such a situation, the zooxanthellae tend to use fixed nitrogen and carbon for growth of their population within the host, and proportionately less photosynthetically fixed carbon is translocated to the host. Thus, glycerol is synthesized and translocated from zooxanthellae to the animal host as a consequence of near-permanent nitrogen limitation (Falkowski et al. 1993).*

*In free-living phytoplankton, a comparable excretion of organic carbon into the surrounding water often occurs with the onset of nutrient limitation. In some extreme cases, cells continue to fix carbon but are unable to divide. For example, in the freshwater dinoflagellate* Peridinium gatunese, *when nutrients become limiting at the end of a seasonal bloom, the cells continue to synthesize cell walls, which they shed into the water column. In effect, cell wall synthesis is a carbon sink that, in the absence of nutrients, allows photosynthetic electron flow to continue without requiring the cell to sustain balanced growth.*

*Thus, while it is often assumed that, especially in the case of phytoplankton, growth is balanced, such assumptions are highly simplified and dependent on the time scale of the measurements and nutrient status of the cells.*

---

frequently display phased cell division for some time after being taken from a light–dark cycle into a constant light environment. Phased cell division occurs in prokaryotes as well as eukaryotes, although the extent of the phasing is highly class or division specific. For example, diatoms can be entrained in a division cycle, but the extent of the G2 phase is highly variable and sometimes difficult to identify. In chlorophytes and dinoflagellates, however, phased cell division is often very pronounced (Ronneberg 1996).

The specific growth rate of a single-celled organism can be inferred from knowledge of the frequency of dividing cells and the duration of division (McDuff, Chisholm 1982). If a time-course is made over a day of the relative fraction ($f$) of

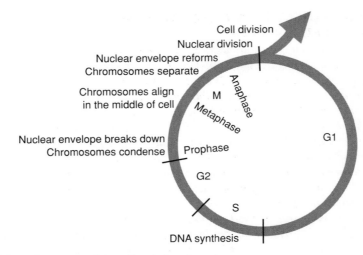

**Figure 8.14** Some key events of the cell cycle in eukaryotes.

cells undergoing cytokinesis (i.e., paired or "doublet" cells, which is equivalent to the M phase in the division cycle), and the duration of division ($t_d$) is known, the specific growth rate can be calculated as:

$$\mu = 1/t_d \ln(1+f) \tag{8.15}$$

This approach, which can be tedious, is highly valuable in determining specific growth rates of cells of a particular species. The efficiency of the approach can be increased by automated flow cytometers that rapidly measure the size of cells from the scattering of light. It should be noted that the calculated $\mu$ is sensitive to the duration of division. One could imagine a $t_d$ of 1 second, in which case if 2% of the cells appeared to be dividing at the moment of observation, then the specific growth rate would be 1710 per day; if it takes a cell 1 hour to divide, the specific growth rate will be only 0.46 per day.

An alternative to counting the number of dividing cells is based on the synthesis of specific proteins keyed to phases of the cell cycle (Lin, Carpenter 1995). In this approach, immunological techniques are used to visualize the occurrence of a nonhistone protein, denoted a proliferating cell nuclear antigen, that is synthesized during the S phase. The occurrence of this apparently ubiquitous protein can be detected using epifluorescence microscopy, and from knowledge of the duration of the S phase the division rate can be calculated using Equation 8.15.

## Models of Phytoplankton Growth

There is an extensive literature describing both growth rates and the chemical composition of phytoplankton in culture, and these data have been used to develop mathematical models that describe growth rate as a function of irradiance, cellular composition, size, and so on. One such model was proposed by Shuter (1979) in which a balanced growth model is developed for sets of environmental conditions. The model permits changes in the allocation of carbon to the photosynthetic apparatus, to structural components (e.g., cell walls), and to the synthetic apparatus (e.g., ribosomes, mitochondria, etc.). The model predicts cell size, doubling times, and crude chemical composition under a variety of scenarios, and was the first use of the so-called "principle of optimal design" (Rosen 1967) in the modeling of phytoplankton. This principle basically holds that cells will allocate resources to optimize growth under all conditions; hence biochemical composition is related to growth rate. For example, in the Shuter model, storage reserves are specifically represented such that fluctuations in nutrients are buffered in the representation of growth rates. A major deficiency of the model is the lack of any explicit photosynthetic process.

At approximately the same time as Shuter was developing his model, a number of researchers began to examine how cell growth is related to photon absorption (Falkowski, Dubinsky, Wyman 1985; Kiefer, Mitchell 1983; Langdon 1988; Laws, Bannister 1980; Sakshaug et al. 1989). These efforts led to the development of growth-irradiance models that attempted to account for the differences in growth rates between species that are held at the same growth conditions. Let us examine the motivation for and outcome of these growth-irradiance models.

The relationship between growth, photosynthesis, and irradiance is not simply linear. As cells grow at each irradiance they can physiologically acclimate to the irradiance, thereby altering the photosynthetic rate. Thus, a simple extrapolation from a photosynthesis-irradiance curve to a growth-irradiance curve will be highly misleading. A large number of experimental observations reveal that different species of photosynthetic organisms grow at different rates, even under optimum conditions for the given species. For example, under the same conditions of temperature, irradiance, and nutrient supply, diatoms frequently grow faster than dinoflagellates (Tang 1996). What accounts for the differences?

There are five basic hypotheses that can be advanced to account for the differences in growth rates between species. First, different species have different light-harvesting properties. Thus, under a given condition some cells may be able to absorb photosynthetically available radiation more effectively than other cells. Second, we might consider variations in the photosynthetic apparatus that affect the quantum yields for photosynthetic carbon fixation. For example, if a cell has a high ratio of PSI/PSII, it might divert more of the absorbed excitation energy toward cyclic electron flow around PSI, rather than in linear electron transport that leads to carbon reduction. Third, we might expect that photosynthesis–respiration ratios of different species are different. Some cells, for example, are motile and consume a portion of their photosynthetically fixed carbon maintaining an energy supply via respiratory activity to support flagellar motion. Such cells might be expected to have a lower quantum yield for growth than cells that do not have such an energy sink. Fourth, we might consider that if some species excrete or secrete a significant fraction of photosynthetically fixed carbon concentration, less carbon is used for cell growth. As briefly described, such a situation occurs in zooxanthellae, with a concomitant reduction in cell growth. Finally, we might consider that if there are large differences in C:N ratios or the level of reduction of organic carbon between species, then differences in photosynthetic quotients might account for significant differences in growth rates.

Let us consider these hypotheses with the context of a model for growth, choosing for simplicity a unicellular alga. Assuming that the organism is wholly photoautotrophic, its net rate of carbon assimilation, $G_c$, with dimensions of carbon fixed per unit chlorophyll per unit time can be described by the difference between photosynthetic carbon assimilation $P$, and the losses of organic carbon due to respiration $R$, and excretion $L$, thus:

$$G_c = P^B - (R + L) \tag{8.16}$$

Now let us consider the three terms on the right side of Equation 8.16 separately. Let the rate of photosynthesis per unit chlorophyll be measured as carbon fixed per unit time as a product of the chlorophyll-specific optical absorption cross-section $a^*$, the incident spectral irradiance (recall that the product of these two variables is the rate of light absorption per unit chlorophyll) $E_o$, and the quantum yield of photosynthesis $\phi_p$, referenced to either oxygen evolution or carbon fixation, thus:

$$P^B = a^* E_o \phi_p \tag{8.17}$$

Note that $\phi_p$ is *not the maximum* quantum yield but the *actual* quantum yield of photosynthesis at irradiance $E_o$. If we wish to express growth as a specific growth rate, $\mu$, then $P$ should have dimensions of time$^{-1}$ (i.e., it is the specific gross photosynthetic rate, $\mu_p$). If $\phi_p$ is the quantum yield for carbon fixation, the specific photosynthetic rate can be derived by multiplying the right side of Equation 8.17 by the chlorophyll–carbon ratio of the cell:

$$\mu_p = a^* E_o \phi_p [\text{Chl}:\text{C}] \tag{8.18}$$

If $\phi_p$ is referenced to oxygen evolution, the photosynthetic quotient must be included. Depending on the nitrogen source, this can be approximated as described by Equations 8.16 or 8.17. Considering these factors, the expanded version of Equation 8.18 then becomes:

$$\mu = \left[ a^* E_\mu (\text{Chl}:\text{C}) \phi_p \right] \left[ 1 - (R + L) / P_\mu \right] M \tag{8.19}$$

where $R$ is the respiration rate, $L$ is the excretion rate of dissolved organic carbon, $P_\mu$ is the photosynthetic rate at the growth irradiance, $E_\mu$, and $M$ is the inverse of the photosynthetic quotient, i.e., $CO_2$ fixed per $O_2$ evolved. $P_\mu$, $R$, and $L$ can be expressed in either carbon or oxygen equivalents, but the ratios $r/P_\mu$ and $E/P_\mu$ must be dimensionless. The photosynthetic carbon gains by a cell are described by the first four variables on the right side of Equation 8.19. Of these variables, $a^*$, $\phi_p$, and Chl:C are related to the physiology of the cell and change as the cell adapts to variations in irradiance, nutrients, or temperature. It should be pointed out that the product of $a^*$ and the Chl/C ratio gives a carbon-specific absorption cross-section, $\sigma_c$, which mathematically represents the fraction of the cellular carbon that "absorbs" light. Losses or inefficiencies in photosynthetic processes are described by the remaining four variables, which also change as the cells acclimate.

The respiration term will be a function of growth rate and cell size, and must be measured directly. Similarly, the excretion term is empirically determined by the intrinsic physiological state. Both terms can be normalized to cell biomass and hence become specific respiration, $\mu_R$ and specific excretion, $\mu_E$. If the specific rates are used, Equation 8.19 can be rewritten as:

$$\mu = \left(a * E_o \, \phi_p [\text{Chl} : \text{C}]\right) - \left(\mu_R + \mu_L\right) \tag{8.20}$$

Additionally, the efficiency of growth (NGE) can be calculated from:

$$\text{NGE} = 1 - \left(\mu_r / \mu + \mu_r\right) \tag{8.21}$$

Net growth efficiency is basically the ratio of the increase in cell organic carbon to the photosynthetic rate of carbon fixation. It is a measure of how much of the photosynthetically fixed carbon is lost in relationship to that used for building new cells. The net growth efficiency is highly variable between species; however, within a species it is relatively insensitive to the growth irradiance and nutrient limitation (Herzig, Falkowski 1989). Thus, as irradiance increases, growth and respiration tend to increase proportionately. As nutrients become limiting, growth and respiration tend to decrease proportionately.

In analyzing experimental data from continuous cultures, a number of interesting features emerge. First, we can consider the rate of photon absorption relative to the rate of electron transport under each growth condition. From measurements of the functional absorption cross-section of PSII (Chapter 3) and the growth irradiance, it is possible to calculate the average interval between photons absorbed by PSII. When this interval is less than $\tau$ for steady-state electron transport (ref. Eq 7.9), then the rate of excitation is in excess of photosynthetic capacity. It emerges that one of the strategies of acclimation to irradiance in effect results in a balance between these two processes. The strategies are based largely on a reduction in the rate of light absorption at high-growth irradiance levels, coupled with a decrease in $\tau$. The reduction in the rate of excitation is achieved primarily via a decrease in pigmentation, while the decrease in $\tau$ is achieved via an increase in the ratio of reaction centers to Rubisco. The net result of this balance is that the quantum yield for growth remains remarkably constant over a wide range of irradiance or nutrient levels (Herzig, Falkowski 1989). In experiments with phytoplankton in continuous culture, little interspecific variation in growth can be attributed to differences in quantum yields, excretion, or photosynthetic quotients. Rather, the greatest source of variation between species growth rates is largely due to variations in the chlorophyll/carbon ratios and, to a lesser extent, to $a*$ (primarily as it affects $\sigma_C$) (Falkowski, Dubinsky, Wyman 1985; Langdon 1988). What is the biological meaning of this analysis?

Earlier we made the analogy between the storage reserves of carbohydrates and a bank account. The economic analogy can be extended to the cost of making cells. These costs can be divided into two major categories, namely *running costs* and *capital costs* (Raven, Beardall 1981).

Running costs may be defined as the direct and indirect energy costs associated with cell growth. For a photosynthetic organism these costs include the energy absorbed from light to reduce carbon, nitrogen, and sulfate; the energy required for acquisition and translocation of these substrates; and the regeneration of intermediates in the various metabolic pathways. Capital costs are investments in the physical structures of the organism required for the metabolic processes. These include the costs of forming cell proteins, pigments, and lipids that are used to make cells.

Capital costs may be viewed as the physical machinery of the cell, while running costs are more akin to the payroll and investments that are made to reproduce and replace depreciated machinery (e.g., the repair or turnover of damaged proteins or nucleic acids).

If we consider the simple growth model expressed in Equation 8.19, the capital cost terms are contained in the chlorophyll–carbon ratio. This ratio describes the extent of photosynthetic light-absorbing capability allocated by a cell relative to its overall organic carbon pools. This ratio is a shorthand notation (and an inexact approximation) for the ratio of chloroplasts to cytoplasm. Some aquatic photosynthetic organisms, such as many dinoflagellates, have relatively low chlorophyll–carbon ratios, while other species, such as diatoms, have relatively high chlorophyll–carbon ratios (Falkowski et al. 1981; Langdon 1988). The running costs for maintaining cytosol functions are generally not widely variable. Thus, in cells that have allocated fewer capital resources to the photosynthetic apparatus relative to nonphotosynthetic portions of cell function, the maximum specific growth rates are often relatively low, while the converse is true for cells that have allocated large portions of the cell to the photosynthetic machinery. However, the latter condition often leads to a faster rate of light-saturated photosynthesis. It should be clear that mechanisms that control the rate of expression of the photosynthetic machinery under given conditions are regulated by feedback controls via photosynthetic pathways (Geider et al. 1996). For example, the rate of expression of PSII reaction centers appears to be regulated via light by signals from thioredoxin redox levels, whereas the light-harvesting proteins are regulated via signals from the plastoquinone redox levels. Thus, there is an integration of photosynthesis and growth rate that permits acclimation of the photosynthetic apparatus to given growth conditions, and optimizes the efficiency by which the products of photosynthetic carbon fixation are used to make new cells.

Given some of these basic concepts in cell synthesis and the role of respiration therein, in Chapter 9 we examine how the photosynthesis process acclimates to change in natural aquatic ecosystems.

# 9

## Photosynthesis and Primary Production in Nature

The natural world is never truly in steady state. Sometimes, however, patterns or cycles in some environmental variables emerge, leading to a degree of predictability (Powell, Steele 1995). One of the more obvious examples is solar irradiance. To a first order, the light reaching the surface of the Earth is given by the path of the sun as it crosses the sky. This path determines the total number of hours of daylight and the maximum incident solar radiation for each point on the globe. Superimposed on this astronomically predictable pattern are chaotic and stochastic variations in light related to meteorological conditions, such as cloud cover and optical thickness, atmospheric aerosol levels and composition, and so forth.[1] Moreover, as light enters aquatic systems it is further modified by the absorption and scattering of the water itself, and of dissolved organic materials and particles, including photosynthetic organisms. Thus, for such a critical variable to photosynthesis as irradiance, there is an element of predictable variability and an element of unpredictable variability. The variability is such that no two minutes, days, weeks, months, years, decades, centuries, or epochs are identical, yet patterns emerge.

One of the wonders of life is the perception and adjustment of biological processes to changes in the external environment. In nature, photosynthetic processes are constantly modified. There are a great number of temporal variations in photosynthetic responses that occur on both short and long time scales. By "short time scale" we mean the physical, biochemical, and physiological responses within the life span of an individual organism or assemblage of organisms. These responses are collectively called *acclimations*. By "long time scale" we refer to ecological and evolutionary *adaptation* by assemblages through selection of phenotypic traits. Physiological acclimations are invariably nonlinearly related to temporal variations in irradiance, temperature, and nutrients. On longer time scales, changes in community structure can significantly affect photosynthetic rates and influence the chemistry of the system. Quantitative understanding of the bases and patterns of the environmental modification of photosynthesis has become a grail for which many aquatic ecologists search, while the qualitative aspects of the phenomena that give rise to these modifications are often overlooked.

---

1. It is important to distinguish between stochastic and chaotic processes in nature, though sometimes it is not easy to do so. *Stochastic* processes are truly random, and are not influenced by previous events. For example, the probability that a tossed coin will land head or tail side up is not dependent on a previous toss. The injection of aerosols into the atmosphere by the eruption of a volcano is an example of a stochastic process in nature. By *chaotic* we mean dynamically nonlinear behavior. In chaotic processes prior events affect subsequent events. In the context of atmospheric conditions, for example, we might assume that the formation and passage of clouds across the sky obey some nonrandom rules that can be mathematically described as "chaotic" (Lorenz 1993).

We strive here to examine the phenomenology of the short-term photosynthetic responses to variations in the aquatic environment. In the following chapter we examine the long-term changes and biogeochemical feedbacks that involve aquatic photosynthetic organisms. Let us begin with a brief look at how aquatic ecologists measure photosynthesis in nature, and then consider acclimation responses within the framework of what we have learned in the earlier chapters.

## ESTIMATING PHOTOSYNTHESIS IN AQUATIC ECOSYSTEMS

Plant physiologists define the term *gross photosynthesis*, $P_g$, as the light-dependent rate of electron flow from water to terminal electron acceptors (e.g., $CO_2$) in the absence of any respiratory losses (Lawlor 1993). It follows that this definition of $P_g$ is directly proportional to linear photosynthetic electron transport and hence, gross oxygen evolution.[2] Gross photosynthesis accounts for all photosynthetic carbon fixation, whether or not the organic carbon formed becomes part of the organism or is excreted or secreted into the environment as organic carbon or $CO_2$; however, the relationship between gross oxygen evolution and $CO_2$ fixation will be modified by the photosynthetic quotient (see Chapter 8).

Respiratory losses in *photosynthetic organism(s)*, $R_P$, can be defined as the rate of electron flow from organic carbon to $O_2$ (or, in the case of anaerobic photosynthetic bacteria, to another electron acceptor) with the concomitant production of $CO_2$. This definition includes all metabolic processes that contribute to the oxidation of organic carbon to $CO_2$, including photorespiration. By definition, photosynthesis only occurs in the light. Respiratory losses in the light, $R_l$, reduce the gross photosynthetic rate.

The difference, $P_g - R_l$, is called *net photosynthesis*, $P_n$

$$P_n = P_g - R_l \tag{9.1}$$

The three terms in Equation 9.1 are all rates; that is, they describe the rate of change of time-dependent processes (Fig 9.1).

Ecologists use the terms *gross* and *net primary production*. Gross primary production is the total amount of electron equivalents originating from the photochemical oxidation of water. It is identical to gross photosynthesis. Net primary production,[3] however, denotes the organic carbon that has been produced by photosynthetic processes within a specified time period of (presumably) ecological rel-

---

2. It should be noted that gross photosynthesis should be defined on the basis of oxygen evolution rather than carbon fixation. This difference is critical, especially if photorespiratory rates are high. In terrestrial $C_3$ plants, for example, as much as 25% of Rubisco activity is oxygenase in the present-day atmosphere and, hence, the quantum yield for carbon fixation is markedly lower than that for oxygen evolution. In marine environments, the photorespiratory components are assumed to be relatively small; however, a large fraction of photosynthetically generated electrons are often used to reduce nitrate because the C:N ratio of the cells is generally close to Redfield's average value of 6.6 by atoms (Chapter 8).

3. The terms primary productivity and primary production are frequently confused. *Productivity* is, strictly speaking, a time-dependent process; it is a rate with dimensions of mass/time. *Production* is a quantity, with dimensions of mass. Productivity describes a rate of change with respect to time; it has dimensions of mass/time. Production is a quantity with dimensions of mass. In aquatic systems, primary production is generally reported in relation to a duration of time and hence can be related to productivity.

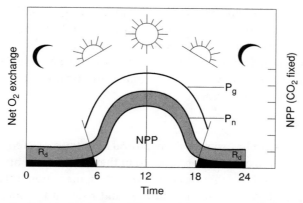

**Figure 9.1** A schematic diagram showing the differences between gross photosynthesis ($P_g$), net photosynthesis ($P_n$), and net primary productivity (NPP) over the period of day. At night (indicated by the dark bar on the abscissa), respiration of the photoautotrophs ($R_d$) leads to a net consumption of oxygen. During the day, respiration is masked by net photosynthetic oxygen evolution, $P_n$. The sum of the respiratory losses with net photosynthesis *in the light* is gross photosynthesis. The sum of dark respiratory losses of the photoautotrophs with net photosynthesis is net primary production.

evance (e.g., daily primary production, annual primary production, etc.) (Williams 1993), which is subsequently made available to other trophic levels (Lindeman 1942). Net primary production (NPP) is related to net photosynthesis by the dark respiration of the photoautotrophs, $R_d$:

$$\text{NPP} = P_n - R_d. \tag{9.2}$$

Net photosynthesis, as defined in Equation 9.1, is the net organic carbon production in the light. Net primary production can (and usually does) include a dark period with an associated respiratory loss of carbon.

In natural aquatic environments, direct measurements of net primary production are virtually impossible to obtain because it is difficult to determine the contribution of algal respiration to total respiratory losses (Li, Maestrini 1993). In fact, although net primary production values are frequently reported in the literature, these are often confused with net photosynthesis. Respiratory losses, when measured, include the metabolic contributions of myriad heterotrophs, and therefore reflect total *community respiration, $R_c$*.

## MEASUREMENTS OF RATES OF GAS EXCHANGE

Almost all measurements of photosynthesis for planktonic organisms in aquatic ecosystems are based on time-dependent rates of change in either oxygen or inorganic carbon (Geider, Osborne 1992). Oxygen does not have a long-lived radio-isotope,[4] and its rate of production is usually quantified from chemical methods. Because the absolute changes in oxygen concentration are usually very small and the background concentration of the gas is usually large, precise measurements are relatively difficult to obtain from a technical standpoint, and are relatively rarely done (Williams, Jenkinson 1982). Moreover, even if done precisely, the evolution of

---

4. The longest-lived radioactive isotope of oxygen, $^{15}O$, has a half-life of 2 minutes.

oxygen in the light represents net community photosynthesis, and fluxes of oxygen in the light and dark include the total community respiration (Bender et al. 1987). Adding dark respiratory losses to the light-dependent oxygen evolution gives a measure of gross photosynthesis. Thus, gross photosynthesis (= gross primary productivity) can be inferred from the measurement of apparent net primary production and community respiration:

$$P_g = \text{NPP} + R_c \tag{9.3}$$

Hence, estimates of net photosynthesis in natural aquatic ecosystems based on measurements of oxygen fluxes are more uncertain than measurements of gross photosynthesis. In the case of benthic primary producers, measurements of net oxygen exchange can be used to infer photosynthesis and respiratory rates of the benthic community (Jahnke, Jackson 1992; Pamatmat, Banse 1969; Rowe, Haedrich 1979). In some cases these measurements are conducted with the aid of enclosures that reduce uncertainties in the sources and sinks of $O_2$ related to physical mixing of waters in the benthic boundary layer.

## The $^{18}O$ Method

An alternative method for measuring photosynthesis in aquatic ecosystems is based on the stable isotope $^{18}O$. The natural abundance of this isotope of oxygen is about 0.200%. A tracer addition of water labeled with $^{18}O$ will lead to the light-dependent production of $O_2$ labeled with the stable isotope (Bender et al. 1987). Alternatively, $^{18}O_2$ can be injected into the head space of an enclosed bottle. In either case, the changes in the isotope abundance can be followed with an isotope ratio mass spectrometer. This technique allows a relatively precise measurement of gross photosynthesis; however, the method is tedious, requires a (bulky and expensive) mass spectrometer, and hence has not been widely used in studies of aquatic photosynthesis in nature.

## The $^{14}C$ Method

By far the most commonly used method is based on the rate of incorporation of radioactive $^{14}C$ in the form of inorganic carbon into acid-stable (usually particulate) organic carbon. This method was introduced to oceanography by the Danish botanist Einar Steemann-Nielsen in 1952, and is, in principle, relatively straightforward (Steemann-Nielsen 1952). If we consider that over some finite time period, the change in concentration of total dissolved inorganic carbon in the bulk water is small relative to the photosynthetic rate of the cells, and the addition of a small amount of radioactively labeled inorganic carbon does not perturb the concentration of the total dissolved inorganic carbon, then the rate of incorporation of radioactivity into organic material obeys the rules of tracer analysis (Chase, Rabinowitz 1967). These conditions are easily met in most marine environments, where the total concentration of inorganic carbon is relatively high (about 2 mM) and the drawdown by photosynthesis is negligible (a few micromoles per hour). In freshwater ecosystems, however, much more care must be taken to determine the ratio of radioactively labeled inorganic carbon to the total inorganic carbon (i.e., the specific activity), as well as the total concentration of inorganic carbon.

The rationale for the $^{14}$C-based tracer method is that the light-dependent rate of incorporation of the radioactively labeled carbon into organic material is quantitatively proportional to the rate of incorporation of nonradioactive inorganic carbon. In laboratory cultures, this process can be verified and it can be shown that the basic assumptions hold (Carpenter, Lively 1980; Li, Goldman 1981). Over short periods of time, before a significant fraction of organic carbon becomes labeled, the radiocarbon method gives a reasonable approximation of gross photosynthetic rate. As the time of exposure to radioactive carbon continues, the organic carbon pool becomes increasingly labeled, ultimately reaching equilibrium with the isotopic ratio of carbon in the bulk water (Dring, Jewson 1982; Li, Goldman 1981). As the label approaches equilibrium, a fraction of the labeled organic carbon is respired, and the rate of incorporation of the tracer begins to approximate the rate of net photosynthesis. At equilibrium, the assimilation of the radioactivity into the organic pool is a measure of net photosynthesis (Morris 1981; Smith, Horner 1981). It should be noted that because $^{14}$C is heavier than the stable natural isotope $^{12}$C, there is an isotopic discrimination against the radioactive isotope during carbon fixation. The commonly accepted discrimination factor is taken as about 5%, and this factor is taken into account in the calculation of the fixation of total inorganic carbon (Strickland, Parsons 1972).

The rate at which equilibrium labeling is approached is dependent on the growth rate of the organism; the faster the growth rate, the faster equilibrium labeling will occur. Thus, the interpretation of radioactive carbon incorporation as gross or net photosynthesis is generally somewhat ambiguous, and is complicated by the duration of incubation in relation to the growth rate. In nature, the latter parameter is usually unknown and numerous discussions have emerged concerning the validity, accuracy, and interpretation of the method (Bender et al. 1987; Carpenter et al. 1980; Eppley 1980; Grande et al. 1989; Li, Goldman 1981; Malone 1982; Morris 1981; Williams 1993).

One of the major problems associated with both the net oxygen exchange measurement and the radiocarbon tracer method is that of integrity and representation of the sample and the incubation of samples in a confined volume. Both methods require incubation of a sample in an enclosed container. Unless extreme care is taken, sampling devices introduce minute concentrations of trace metals, such as zinc or copper, that have been empirically demonstrated to rapidly and often markedly inhibit photosynthetic rates (Carpenter et al. 1980; Fitzwater et al. 1982; Williams, Robertson 1989). The problem appears to be most pronounced in extremely oligotrophic areas of the open ocean, where the environmental concentrations of trace metals are generally extremely low (picomolar). As this problem was not identified until late in the 1970s, virtually all radiocarbon measurements of phytoplankton photosynthesis made prior to that period, and even many succeeding that period, are assumed to have been contaminated by trace metals and are generally considered to be underestimates of the "truer" photosynthetic rates (Martin 1992). The underestimates can be significant, but also variable, so that it is

## ❏ SCINTILLATION COUNTERS

*The use of $^{14}C$ to measure photosynthetic rates has almost exclusively been relegated to aquatic systems and was greatly facilitated by the development of liquid scintillation counting machines. Prior to scintillation counters, the radioactivity incorporated into acid-stable material was measured with a window Geiger counter (Strickland et al. 1972). In the Geiger counter, a set of electrodes was surrounded by a gas at low pressure (usually argon with a small amount of ethanol vapor). The electrode chamber was kept isolated from the atmosphere by a very thin window of mica. $\beta^-$ particles emitted by the radioactive decay of $^{14}C$ passed through the mica and, as they approached the positively charged cathode, created an electrical pulse of up to a few volts. The efficiency of the detecting systems was rather low, as only the $\beta^-$ directly incident on the mica window could be detected (thus eliminating at least half of the radioactive decays from being detected). Some of the particles were scattered by the mica, and in reality the efficiency of counting was <30% and difficult to determine accurately. Hence, some of the historical radiocarbon measurements in the aquatic sciences literature are internally consistent but the absolute values of the calculated photosynthetic rates are inconceivably low.*

*In a scintillation counting machine, the $\beta^-$ particles interact with an organic molecule in solution. The interaction induces an excited state in the organic molecule, which, upon returning to the ground state, leads to the emission of a photon by fluorescence. The photon is detected by a photomultiplier tube. The sensitivity of the instruments is extraordinarily high, and their precision and efficiency are also high. Typically, more than 90% of the radioactive decays of $^{14}C$ can be detected by a liquid scintillation counter. This technique offers unparalleled precision and sensitivity of photosynthetic fixation of inorganic carbon; such precision and sensitivity are essential in aquatic systems where the photosynthetic rate can be very low.*

---

not possible to simply "correct" the problem by multiplying historical values by a constant factor.

Another aspect of the sampling problem is associated with the artificially contrived conditions that accompany enclosure of an aquatic sample in a container (Eppley 1980). Even if no trace metal contaminant is introduced, the sample in a bottle contains, in addition to phytoplankton, bacteria, microzooplankton, and sometimes macrozooplankton. This small-scale food web allows myriad possible exchanges of carbon between the medium and organisms, as well as the potential net loss of phytoplankton during the course of the incubation. It is virtually impossible to account for, let alone measure, these fluxes, yet they are presumed to lead generally to a reduction in measured photosynthetic rates. These so-called "bottle effects" are further exacerbated by uncertainty in reproducing the light environment experienced by the cells. Simulating all of these variations in incubations is impossible. One approach taken is to incubate samples in bottles at discrete depths within the water column (Dandonneau 1993). This approach permits natural time and depth-dependent attenuation of light and this so-called "in situ" method can be used to generate a time-integrated measure of net carbon assimilation through the water column.

It should be noted that although measurements of net oxygen exchange can be used to estimate respiratory losses in the dark from the ensemble of organisms that constitute a planktonic community, radiocarbon measurements are virtually devoid of information related to respiration (Steemann-Nielsen, Hansen 1959). As the radiocarbon method has been used so extensively for measuring photosynthesis in aquatic environments, there is a lack of quantitative understanding of the role of community respiration to net photosynthetic rates in nature (Langdon 1993).

## INTEGRATED WATER-COLUMN PHOTOSYNTHESIS

Let us now consider photosynthesis in a planktonic system. An imaginary construct, called in aquatic sciences a *water column*, is a planar representation of a surface area, usually a square meter, projected to a depth, $z$. Light incident on the water column is attenuated with depth, approximately following an exponential function. The attenuation, which is a consequence of both scattering and absorption, is spectrally dependent. It is convenient to define the attenuation for the spectrally integrated light in terms of an optical depth $\xi$,[5] which is given by:

$$\xi = K_d z \tag{9.4}$$

where $K_d$ is the spectrally averaged vertical attenuation coefficient (in $m^{-1}$) for downwelling light, given by:

$$K_d = \frac{-ln(E_o/E_z)}{z} \tag{9.5}$$

The 1% light depth corresponds to $\xi = 4.6$. Note that $K_d$ and $\xi$ are independent of the absolute surface irradiance; that is, the 1% light depth does not vary with solar irradiance.

Optical depths are independent of physical depths. It is often convenient to relate vertical profiles of photosynthesis in aquatic systems to optical depth rather than physical depth. In so doing, vertical profiles are related to the rate of attenuation of light; such examination frequently reduces much of the variance between profiles (Morel 1988).

We define a special depth, $z_e$, which is the base of the euphotic zone. The *euphotic zone* is the portion of the water column supporting net primary production. The base of the euphotic zone is the *compensation depth*, defined as the depth where gross daily photosynthetic carbon fixation balances phytoplankton respiratory losses over a day. Above the compensation depth, net, daily photosynthesis is positive, below this depth it is negative. The average compensation depth is frequently taken as depth corresponding to 1% of the photosynthetically active radiation at the surface; however, the actual compensation depth is dependent on $E_o$ and probably variable (Falkowski, Owens 1978; Platt et al. 1990; Ryther 1954).

In Figure 9.2, we present an idealized, daily integrated profile of radiocarbon assimilation from the surface to the base of the euphotic zone. Let us assume that

---

5. Strictly speaking, $\xi$ only applies to a defined wavelength $\lambda$, not for broad-band photosynthetically active radiation.

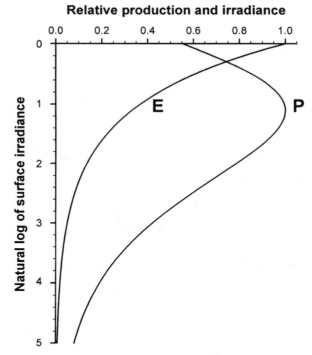

**Relative production and irradiance**

**Figure 9.2** A schematic diagram showing the vertical profile of photosynthesis in a water column and the attenuation of irradiance. The vertical axis is presented as the natural logarithm of irradiance (i.e., the optical depth; see Eq 9.4). The position in the water column corresponding to 1% of the surface irradiance is at an ln of −4.6. It is assumed that the vertical distribution of photoautotrophic biomass is uniform throughout the water column.

the distribution of algal biomass is homogeneous, and therefore immaterial to the shape of the curve. At the surface, photosynthetic rates are typically depressed and rise to a maximum value lower in the water column. From the maximum, the rate declines monotonically. The depression of photosynthesis in the upper portion of the water column is a manifestation of photoinhibition (Long et al. 1994; Neale 1987). Were it not for this effect, the maximum value for the time-integrated photosynthetic rate would always be expected to be at the surface. The maximum, time-integrated photosynthetic rate in situ is not equivalent to that obtained by time-integrating $P_{max}$ values obtained from a photosynthesis-irradiance curve (Chapter 7), because the cells are necessarily at subsaturating irradiance during some part of the day (e.g., at sunrise and sunset) and are often moving vertically, thereby altering their position relative to the light field (Fig 9.3). Rather this maximum value in situ represents a compromise between the irradiance-dependent rate of inhibition higher in the water column and the irradiance-dependent rate of increase in photosynthesis lower in the water column. In fact, the maximum value for photosynthesis in the water column is really an optimum, rather than truly a maximum, and is designated $P_{opt}$ (Wright 1959).

The monotonic decay in photosynthetic rate represents the (low) irradiance-dependent region of the photosynthesis-irradiance curve, convoluted with time and depth-dependent changes in spectral quality. The latter effect is critical to the deter-

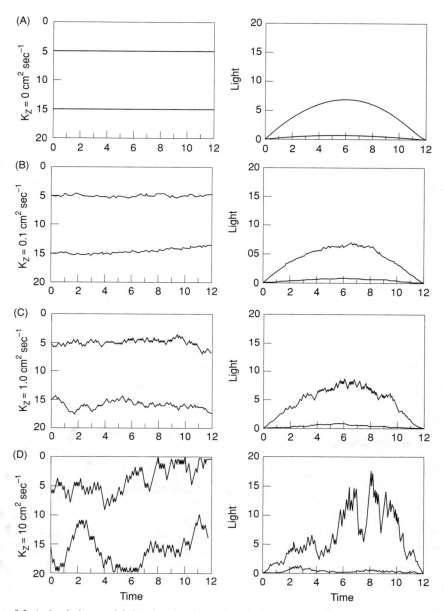

**Figure 9.3** A simulation model showing the effect of vertical motions on the light environment for two imaginary phytoplankton cells, one at 5 m depth and the other at 15 m below the surface. The four panels on the left side are the random walks for cells in water columns with (A), a vertical diffusion coefficient ($K_Z$) of $0 \, cm^2 s^{-1}$; (B) $0.1 \, cm^2 s^{-1}$; (C) $1 \, cm^2 s^{-1}$; and (D) $10 \, cm^2 s^{-1}$. The four panels on the right side show the convolution of solar elevation throughout the day with the position of the cell in the water column. The cell motions were simulated by a Monte Carlo random walk model described in Falkowski and Wirick (1981).

mination of the effective optical cross-section of both photosystems, and hence to the realized quantum yield of net photosynthesis (Laws et al. 1990).

The shape of the photosynthesis versus depth curve can be expressed non-dimensionally as:

$$P/P_{opt} = \left[1 - e^{\left(-E\xi/E_{max}\right)}\right] e^{\left(-\beta dE\xi\right)} \qquad (9.6)$$

where $\xi$ is the optical depth (= 1/e of PAR attenuation), $\beta$ is the sensitivity of the cells to photoinhibition, and $E_{max}$ is the maximum irradiance at the sea surface (adapted from McBride 1992; Platt et al. 1980).

## Phytoplankton Respiration

The biggest problem in the determination of the compensation depth is the accurate measurement of phytoplankton respiration. Traditionally, respiration of the photoautotrophs has been assumed to be 10% of the maximum photosynthetic rate, and independent of irradiance (Ryther 1954). While a good theoretical case can be made that overall respiratory processes are a constant fraction of the growth rate, maintenance respiration should increase as a fraction of gross photosynthesis at low specific growth rates (see Chapter 8). Direct measurements of oxygen consumption, as well as measurements of stable isotopes used as tracers, indicate that respiratory losses relative to the maximum photosynthetic rate are variable (Geider, Osborne 1989). Additionally, in principle the euphotic zone can be influenced by temperature, supraoptimal irradiance levels (which can lead to photoinhibition of photosynthesis near the surface), nutrient limitation (which can reduce the quantum efficiency of photochemistry), the source of nitrogen (as it affects the photosynthetic quotient), and the biochemical composition of the algae (as it affects the respiratory quotient). It is impossible to constrain all of these variables, and consequently the depth of the euphotic zone is easier to define than measure.

The euphotic zone is frequently confused with the critical depth; and though they are related they distinctly differ (Platt et al. 1991). In all aquatic environments, some portion of the surface waters are mixed or easily miscible. This portion is usually identified from thermal or density profiles that reveal an isopycnal (i.e., equal density) layer separated from a lower layer by a gradient called a *pycnocline* (Fig 9.4). The depth of the upper mixed layer is critical to the formation of phytoplankton blooms (Sverdrup 1953). If the upper mixed layer is deeper than the euphotic zone, phytoplankton will spend, on average, more time at low irradiances. Under such conditions, integrated water-column photosynthesis can be less than integrated community respiration and the phytoplankton cannot sustain net positive growth. At some depth, gross primary production, integrated through the water column over a day, will equal the daily water column integrated respiratory rate; this depth is called the *critical depth* (Sverdrup 1953). The critical depth is almost always greater than the compensation depth (Parsons et al. 1984) and can be approximated from:

$$Z_{cr} = E_o/K_D E_c \qquad (9.7)$$

It should be noted that the relevant respiratory costs in the derivation of the critical depth include heterotrophic organisms, such as bacteria and zooplankton (Smetacek, Passow 1990). When the depth of the upper mixed layer is equal to or shallower than the critical depth, net primary production is equal to or exceeds the total respiratory costs within the mixed layer. Under such conditions, in

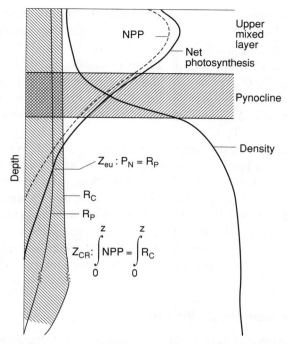

**Figure 9.4** A schematic diagram showing the relationship between the density of the water column, net photosynthesis, net primary production, daily integrated photoautotrophic respiration ($R_p$), daily integrated total community respiration ($R_c$), the depth of the euphotic zone ($Z_{eu}$) and the critical depth $Z_{cr}$. In the case shown, the pycnocline is shallower than the critical depth, and consequently $\Sigma NPP > R_c$ in the upper mixed layer. If the pycnocline is deeper than the critical depth, cells will spend more time at low irradiance levels (see Fig 9.3); consequently $\Sigma NPP < R_c$ and net (positive) growth of the ensemble of the photoautotrophs in the water column cannot be sustained.

principle, as long as nutrients are in excess, net organic carbon in the form of phytoplankton can increase in the upper mixed layer and a phytoplankton bloom can develop.

We can estimate the photosynthetic electron transport rate near the base of the euphotic zone. Let us assume that at the depth corresponding to 1% of the surface irradiance, the photosynthesis–respiration ratio for the photoautotrophs is 1.0 (i.e., it is the compensation depth). Assume that the photosynthetic reaction centers receive sufficient light to drive 1 electron per second; this rate is sufficient to prevent the decay of the $S_3$ state to lower S states and to overcome leaks of $H^+$ through the thylakoid membrane, thereby permitting net ATP synthesis (Raven, Beardall 1982). Let us assume further that the chlorophyll $a$ concentration is 0.5 μg per liter (i.e., about $561 \times 10^{-12}$ moles per liter).

If each photosynthetic unit contains four PSII and four PSI reaction centers, and the average size of the photosynthetic unit is 3000 chlorophyll $a$ molecules per mole $O_2$ evolved, and the unit receives eight quanta per second, then the rate of $O_2$ evolutions is given by:

$$\frac{561 \text{ pmol Chl } a}{3000 \text{ mol Chl } a \text{ mol}^{-1}O_2 \text{ s}^{-1}} = 0.18 \text{ pmol } O_2 \text{ s}^{-1}$$

$$= 670 \text{ pmol } O_2 \text{ l}^{-1} \text{ s}^{-1} \tag{9.8}$$

Assuming a photosynthetic quotient of unity, this photosynthetic rate would lead to the gross photosynthetic fixation of 7.9 ng C per liter per hour. Given a 12-hour photoperiod, we obtain 95 ng C fixed per liter per day or about 0.2 μg C per μg Chl *a* per day. If a sample of water from this depth were incubated in situ for 12 hours with 20 μCi[6] of $NaH^{14}CO_3$, the filter would contain about 17 radioactive counts per minute above background; a very low level indeed. It should be pointed out that the growth rate of the cells at this depth is nil because the respiratory costs consume all of the photosynthetically fixed carbon.

Several thousand vertical profiles of daily integrated carbon fixation have been obtained from many aquatic ecosystems (e.g., Balch et al. 1992). Not surprisingly, the profiles display a high degree of variability. In marine ecosystems, daily integrated photosynthetic rates vary by over two orders of magnitude; and this variance can be higher if kelp forest and seagrass systems are included (Mann 1973; Ramus 1992). In an extremely nutrient-rich region, daily net carbon fixation can reach 10 grams $C/m^2$, while that for an extremely oligotrophic system is more typically 0.1 grams $C/m^2$. What factors contribute to the areal variability on daily time scales?

### The Effect of Photoautotrophic Biomass

To a first order, the major source of variation in areal specific photosynthetic rates in aquatic systems is related to the amount and distribution of photoautotrophic biomass. Simply put, under any irradiance condition photosynthetic electron flow is dependent on the population density of the photosynthetic machinery. The population density of photosynthetic reaction centers is causally related to the concentration of photosynthetic pigments per unit volume or area of aquatic system; hence, normalization of areal photosynthesis to areal pigment should lead to a reduction in variance. It is, from a pragmatic perspective, most convenient to normalize to chlorophyll *a* because that pigment is universally contained by all algal classes (with the exception of some of the marine prochlorophytes that contain divinyl chlorophyll *a*) and aquatic higher plants. Areal photosynthetic rates normalized to areal chlorophyll *a* leads to a reduction of variance by an order of magnitude (Fig 9.5); however, considerable variance remains.

The most ecologically relevant units of plant biomass are organic carbon and nitrogen. In planktonic communities especially, direct measurements of phytoplankton carbon or nitrogen are inextricably complicated by the presence of varying concentrations of nonphytoplankton particulate material (Banse 1977; Eppley, Sloan 1965). As a matter of empirical and operational convenience, therefore, aquatic biologists usually infer the distribution of phytoplankton biomass from the distribution of chlorophyll *a*. The pigment is specific to photoautotrophs and can be measured with ease, rapidity, and sensitivity (Holm-Hanson et al. 1965)—criteria that are important in ecology.

The ratio of organic carbon to chlorophyll in phytoplankton varies from about

6. A *curie* is a unit of radioactive decay. $1\ Ci = 3.7 \times 10^{10}$ disintegrations per second or $2.2 \times 10^{12}$ disintegrations per minute (1 dps is sometimes called a *Becquerel*; thus, $1\ Ci = 3.7 \times 10^{10}\ Bq$).

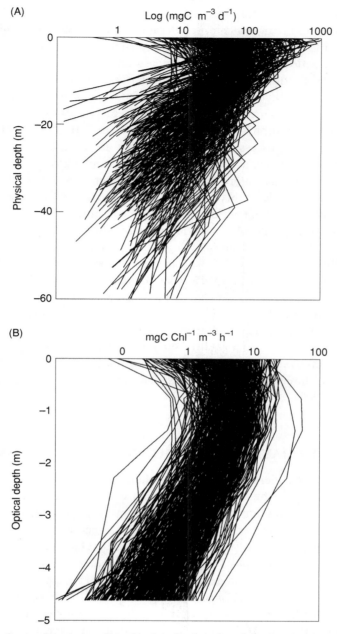

**Figure 9.5** One thousand vertical profiles of carbon fixation plotted as a function of physical depth (A) and (B) normalized to chlorophyll biomass and irradiance and plotted as a function of optical depth. (From Behrenfeld, Falkowski 1997)

10 to more than 200 on a weight/weight basis. The variation in carbon–chlorophyll ratios is determined by genetic and environmental factors. For example, dinoflagellates generally have higher carbon–chlorophyll ratios than diatoms (Tang 1996). Cyanobacteria can also have high carbon–chlorophyll ratios, as in this group of organisms most of the chlorophyll function in light harvesting is replaced by phy-

cobilipigments. Nutrient limitation, especially nitrogen or iron limitation, can lead to marked increases in carbon–chlorophyll ratios. As cells acclimate to different irradiance levels or to different temperatures, carbon–chlorophyll ratios change (Geider 1996). These variations, which are easily measured in laboratory monospecific cultures, are extremely difficult to constrain in natural phytoplankton communities. Numerous species of phytoplankton coexist in the same water mass. Multiple influences, such as light and nutrient limitation, may interact in opposing ways to produce a realized carbon–chlorophyll ratio differing significantly from that which would be produced by a single process alone. Some success has been achieved in deducing the average carbon–chlorophyll ratios in natural phytoplankton by determining the specific activity of purified chlorophyll *a* following incubation with $H^{14}CO_3^-$ (Redalje, Laws 1981). The principle of this technique is that when cells are exposed to radiocarbon for a sufficiently long period to approach equilibrium labeling, by definition the specific activities of all cell components are the same. Hence, the specific activity of chlorophyll *a*, which is measurable, will be proportional to that of the whole cell. The method is tedious and subject to error if there is significant biochemical turnover of chlorophyll (Richards, Thurston 1980; Riper et al. 1979), but its practical application overweighs its disadvantages. Thus, while it is recognized that chlorophyll *a* is an uncertain proxy for more ecologically relevant measures of phytoplankton biomass, such as organic carbon, phytoplankton chlorophyll *a* is accepted as a pragmatic surrogate. It should be stressed that knowledge of the carbon–chlorophyll ratio is not critical to deriving photosynthetic rates, but becomes critical if one is interested in deriving the specific growth rates of cells (Eppley 1972; Eppley, Sloan 1965).

## TEMPORAL VARIATIONS IN LIGHT IN AQUATIC ECOSYSTEMS

For the purposes of understanding photosynthesis in natural aquatic environments, it is desirable to define the underwater irradiance field as the quantity of photons, their wavelength distribution, and, especially for macrophytes and other large photosynthetic organisms, such as symbiotic corals, the direction of the radiation. There is no single set of analytical mathematical equations that has been developed to precisely evaluate these properties. In the field of underwater optics, the specific optical properties that influence the underwater irradiance field are conveniently divided into so-called *inherent* and *apparent* properties (Kirk 1994b; Mobley 1994). The former is independent of the solar zenith angle and includes such properties as absorption and attenuation. The latter is dependent on solar angle, and includes backscatter and reflectance.

Whereas fluctuation scattering by water (Chapter 2) leads to a spectral bias toward the blue, absorption by water itself is superimposed on the scattering process. Water absorbs strongly in the red and infrared. The net effect of both scattering and absorption effectively enriches the penetrating downwelling spectrum in the blue and blue-green wavelengths. Consequently, the $Q_y$ bands of the chlorophylls play negligible roles in harvesting photosynthetically available radiation in aquatic environments; there simply is very little red light for these pigments to absorb. As irradiance penetrates into the water the scattering process increasingly randomizes the angular distribution of light such that the light becomes more diffuse with depth. The depth-dependent diffusion of light is important on sunny days in attenuating the effects of surface waves that alternately focus and defocus the light entering the water. Although defining the underwater light field of an imaginary lake or ocean consisting entirely of water is problematic enough, in nature the underwater light field is further modified by the absorption of selected wavelengths by dissolved organic materials and particles in the water, especially the photosynthetic organisms themselves. Frequently, in coastal waters or in lakes, these modifying optical properties dominate the spectral irradiance characteristics of the water body and shift the maximum penetrating wavelengths from the blue to the green (Kirk 1985; Kirk 1989).

Short-term fluctuations in light intensity, resulting, for example, from the focusing and defocusing of downwelling irradiance by surface waves (Dera, Gordon 1968), can modify photosynthetic activity. This effect arises from a hysteresis in the photosynthesis-irradiance curve, and was first described by Phillips and Myers (1954) for continuous cultures of the chlorophyte *Chlorella*. They found that when cells were grown under flashing light that instantaneously saturated the photochemical reactions, the realized quantum yield for photosynthetic oxygen production and growth was higher than when the cells were grown under continuous light. This flashing light effect is dependent on the frequency and duration of the light and dark periods, and the effect can sometimes be rather dramatic, approaching a 25% enhancement. In kelp forests, water movement leads to movements of the blades, and the resulting flashing light effect has been proposed to enhance photosynthetic rates of such macrophytes (Greene, Gerard 1990; cf. Kübler, Raven 1996).

The physiological basis of the flashing light effect is uncertain. Two candidate processes are likely, namely enhanced post-illumination respiration and disequilibrium between photosynthetic electron transport and the Calvin–Benson cycle. In the first instance, the production of photosynthetically produced storage products will be small when the duration of exposure to a saturating light is short, and the subsequent respiratory rate in the darkened period will be less than it would be if the cells or plants had been exposed to saturating light for a long period. In other words, the enhancement of post-illumination respiration is smaller if cells are exposed to flashing light. In the second instance, under continuous high-light conditions, the photosynthetic electron transport capacity exceeds the maximum rate of utilization of reductant in the Calvin–Benson cycle. In other words, reductant and ATP are produced at a faster rate than they can be consumed (Heber et al. 1990; Stitt 1986). If a dark period is imposed between a light period, carbon fixation processes can "catch up" and consume the reductant and ATP generated by the photosynthetic electron transport chain. Hence, at some optimal flash frequency, the photochemically produced substrates are optimally coupled to the rate of carbon fixation. In fact, the observation of this transient disequilibrium has been argued as evidence that the Calvin–Benson cycle is rate limiting under steady-state illumination (Fisher et al. 1989; Sukenik et al. 1987b).

Whereas the flashing light effect may contribute to an enhancement of photosynthesis under special conditions, a much more ubiquitous and perhaps dramatic effect occurs on diel time scales. Virtually since the introduction of the radiocarbon labeling technique, a mid-day suppression of photosynthesis has been observed in almost all aquatic ecosystems (Lorenzen 1963; Malone 1971; Neale 1987). While this specific phenomenon may be attributable in some instances to photoinhibition (Neale 1987), careful studies of the diel progression of the behavior of the photosynthesis-irradiance relationship typically reveal patterns in the initial slope and the maximum photosynthetic rates that are not readily explained simply by photoinhibition. Rather, it would appear that in many instances, the diel cycles in the photosynthetic parameters are circadian rhythms that continue for some period following exposure of the organisms to continuous light (Harding et al. 1981).

**Diel Cycles and Circadian Rhythms**

One of the major determinants of variability in photosynthetic responses is the diel variation in irradiance. Not only is there a diel variation in cellular chlorophyll content, but both light-saturated and light-limited photosynthetic rates normalized to chlorophyll are generally elevated during the photoperiod compared with the scotophase (Harding et al. 1981). The correlation between these two photosynthetic parameters suggests an increase either in the numbers of active reaction centers during the photoperiod or in their turnover rate ($1/\tau$). Although experimental data proving this is the cause of the variability are scant, there are frequently changes in light-saturated photosynthetic rates through the photoperiod that appear to be related to diel variations in the ratio of Rubisco to reaction centers. Circadian rhythms in photosynthetic responses are not simply due to changes in the stoichiometry of reaction centers or components of the Calvin–Benson cycle, however; they arise from time-dependent changes in the activity of specific components of the photosynthetic apparatus. Presumably regulatory controls from thioredoxin and possibly other redox-sensitive intermediates play important roles in determining the circadian rhythm of maximum photosynthetic rates (see Chapter 5). The causes of variations are related to intrinsic circadian rhythms.

A circadian rhythm is effectively a memory of a photoperiod. In eukaryotic cells, this memory is genetically encoded by a set of nuclear genes called *Per* (i.e., *per*iodicity) genes that appear to be ubiquitous (Takahashi 1992). Cyanobacteria also have genetically regulated circadian rhythms, and can undergo diel cycles in nitrogen fixation and photosynthetic capacity (Flores, Herrero 1994; Mori et al. 1996). The existence of circadian rhythms is demonstrated by observing the behavior of an organism under a normal diel light–dark cycle, followed by exposure to constant conditions (e.g., constant light). If the rhythm is circadian, it will continue for some time in the constant condition and its period compensates for changes in temperature. Circadian rhythmicity is usually expressed for a longer period in continuous darkness than in continuous illumination. The rhythm can be thought of as analogous to the hands of a man-made analogue clock, in which a set of endogenous cues dictates the timing of certain cell processes. The signal transduction appears to be mediated via a protein kinase–phosphatase pathway (Comolli et al. 1996). Such processes as bioluminescence in dinoflagellates, cell division, photosynthetic and respiratory rates, plastid orientation and migration, and chlorophyll biosynthesis all undergo a circadian rhythm (Puiseux-Dao 1981).

Under constant ("free-running") conditions, the clock normally has a period of between 23 and 28 hours, and can be reset by external stimuli. In photoautotrophs the clock is normally set by irradiance (Edmunds, French 1969). Some polar phytoplankton apparently can maintain a circadian rhythm in their photosynthetic response for weeks under constant light (Rivkin, Putt 1987). In such environments the endogenous clock is apparently set via diel variations in light intensity (as opposed to a true day–night cycle).

Most laboratory studies of circadian rhythms in photoautotrophs have employed *synchronous cultures*, meaning cultures in which all cells are at the same state of the cell cycle at a given time. This synchronicity is generally imposed by the transition from dark to light, or by a step change in temperature. Analyses of the composition of cells during the synchronous cycle invariably reveal an increase in the carbon storage reserves, such as polysaccharides or lipids, in the light period with a decrease in the dark period. In some cases the utilization of reserves in the dark is only to maintain cell functions, in other cases the consumption of reserves is additionally coupled to protein synthesis and cell growth (see Chapter 8). Even within a photoperiod the composition of cells can change, reflecting variations in enzyme activities that can, in turn, be traced to differences in the content of individual proteins and the level of transcription (Milos et al. 1990). Nuclear DNA replication often occurs in the light period, while mitosis and cell division commonly occur in the dark period.

In nature, the diel irradiance cycle is the natural synchronizing agent for unicellular algae. Natural synchrony constrains growth rates, especially in eukaryotic cells. If, for example, a cell can divide by binary fission only once in 24 hours, then any excess potential photosynthetic carbon acquisition over and above what is needed to double the cell mass in 24 hours must go unused; otherwise, the cells would not be able to maintain balanced growth. This constraint also applies to a shortfall in nutrient acquisition, in which case binary fission can only occur every 48, 72, 96 hours (or some higher multiple of 24 hours). With strict division synchrony and only one division every 24 hours, the only way to permit more than one binary division in 24 hours is to have multiple fission. This occurs in the Chlorococales and the Volvocales, which are predominantly freshwater orders of the Chlorophyceae. In this case, $2^n$ cells are produced in each synchronous cycle where $n$ can equal 4 or even 5 (Pirson, Lorenzen 1966). Thus, if nutrients and light are in adequate supply, such cells could increase 16- or even 32-fold in 24 hours, as compared with the doubling found in synchronous cultures of organisms such as diatoms which divide by binary fission. In cyanobacteria, cells can divide several times within a 24-hour day, yet maintain a circadian rhythm. Under such conditions, each generation of cells has a different biochemical composition.

The effect of the short-term variations in irradiance due to the combinations of inherent and apparent optical properties of the aquatic environment poses a major difficulty in determining either the optical or effective absorption cross-sections of the photosynthetic apparatus. As both cross-sections are directly dependent on the spectral distribution of irradiance, changes in the cross-section arise simply as a consequence of variations in solar zenith angle as well as depth within the water column (Eqs 9.4 and 9.5). In order to try to account for these variations, a variety of so-called "bio-optical" models have been developed to extrapolate or integrate simulated photosynthesis-irradiance curve results to provide estimates of integrated water column production (Bidigare et al. 1992; Morel 1991a; Platt et al. 1990). Models differ in detail between investigators, but the basic structure is maintained. Let us briefly examine how these models work.

## *P* VS. *E* CURVES AND BIO-OPTICAL MODELS

If we consider the profile of integrated water-column photosynthesis (see Fig 9.2), we can imagine taking slices at every point through the euphotic zone, and at each point the integrated photosynthetic rate represents the summation of photosynthesis-irradiance responses for the period under consideration. This approach summarizes the concept of so-called *bio-optical models*, where samples from discrete depths are incubated at the desired temperature along with an artificial light source over a range of light intensities. A variety of small-scale incubators have been described to optimize this procedure, especially with phytoplankton (Babin et al. 1994; Lewis, Smith 1983). Following the incubation period with $NaH^{14}CO_3$ (which can be from 20 min to a few hours), a series of photosynthesis-irradiance curves are generated for each depth (see Table 7.1). Simultaneously, measurements of the optical absorption cross-section, $a*$, for the ensemble of photosynthetic organisms are made for samples from each depth (Bricaud et al. 1983; Cleveland, Weidemann 1993; Kishino et al. 1985; Michell, Kiefer 1988). Additionally, spectral irradiance is measured in situ as a function of depth, and using numerical, mathematical models, the spectral-irradiance regime is calculated for each depth at any (or all) desired times during the day. The latter gives the photosynthetically available radiation, PAR,[7] at a given time of day (Morel 1978). A convolution of the optical absorption cross-section and spectral distribution of irradiance gives the rate of light absorbed by the organisms at each depth, or the photosynthetically usable radiation, PUR:

$$PUR_{(z,t,\lambda)} = PAR_{(z,t,\lambda)}A*_{\lambda}$$

and

$$PUR_{(z,t)} = \int_{400}^{700} PUR_{(z,t,\lambda)} \tag{9.9}$$

where A* is a normalized optical absorption cross-section that describes the shape of a "typical" algal absorption spectrum (see Fig 9.3).

---

7. Photosynthetically available radiation (PAR) is defined as that portion of the spectrum that, on absorption by a photosynthetic organism, can promote a photochemical charge separation. It is operationally defined as light in the wavelength interval between 350 and 700 nm (Tyler 1966). However, because it is technically difficult to construct detectors that are capable of measuring light between 350 and 400 nm, the wavelength interval for PAR was reduced to 400 to 700 nm. It should be noted that the concept of PAR arose from photosynthetic action spectra (Chapter 3). Early measurements of action spectra neglected wavelengths below about 400 nm, because the light sources used had very little energy in the near ultra violet. Neglecting the near-UV domain does not entail a significant error because the contribution of this radiation in the range to the total is only about 5%.

The photosynthesis-irradiance curves obtained in the artificial light incubator are then "corrected" for the spectral irradiance in situ, and the resulting photosynthetic rates are derived for a given time of the day for a given depth. The latter is sometimes called the photosynthetically stored radiation, PSR. Thus, PAR > PUR > PSR (Morel 1978). Using either measured or modeled data to derive the spectral irradiance throughout the day, hypothetical, time-dependent photosynthetic rates can be calculated through the water column. PAR, PUR, and PSR can all be reduced to common units of energy. In this conversion, PSR is assumed to be in the form of carbohydrate, where $1\,g\,C = 39\,kJ$ (Morel 1991; Platt, Irwin 1973). As the energy of light varies as a function of wavelength, and the latter varies as a function of depth and time in the water column, an empirically derived average energy flux is used where 1 mole of photons (averaged between 400 and 700 nm) is equal to about 240 kJ. On average about 0.13% to 0.16% of PAR incident on the surface of the ocean is stored as energy by the photosynthetic reduction of carbon.

The bio-optical approach, based on analyses of photosynthesis-irradiance curves, is mathematically tedious but gives predictive capability by permitting continuous calculation of photosynthesis based on the rate of light absorbed. There are, however, deficiencies in bio-optical approaches. These include a difficulty in including time-dependent photosynthetic responses, such as a hysteresis induced by photoinhibition, in the idealized representation of the photosynthesis-irradiance curve, as well as the difficulty in accounting for respiratory losses. Summation of a series of short-term measurements of photosynthesis using a bio-optical model and extrapolated to a daily, areally integrated value almost invariably leads to higher estimates of primary production than the measurements based on in situ incubations. Although sources of the discrepancy abound, a major problem is the virtual elimination of dark respiration in the short-term measurements compared with the longer time course of exposure to radiocarbon. Moreover, the predictive capability of the bio-optical approach is much greater in the light-limited portion of the photosynthesis-irradiance curve, but fails to predict, from first principles, the absolute value of the maximum photosynthetic rate (Falkowski 1981). This deficiency reflects more on the difficulty in understanding what controls $P^B_{max}$ than it does on a deficiency of the mathematical treatment per se (Cullen, Yang, MacIntyre 1992).

It is implicitly assumed in bio-optical models based on photosynthesis-irradiance curves that the photosynthesis-irradiance relationship does not depend on the duration of the incubation. That assumption is not true. We have explained that the functional absorption cross-section can, and does, undergo continuous adjustments throughout the day in response to changes in spectral irradiance. Because of feedbacks between photosynthetic rates and irradiances, $P$ vs. $E$ curves constantly change. Recall (Chapter 7) that the optimum position for a cell or organism with respect to photosynthesis-irradiance curve is at $E_k$. As the cell cannot control the irradiance field, there is no option but to adjust either $\sigma_{PSII}$ and/or $\tau$ to attempt to maintain photosynthetic rates at or near $E_k$. Most of the short-term adjustments are achieved via changes in $\sigma_{PSII}$ (Falkowski et al. 1994). These adjustments include state transitions (especially in cyanobacteria and red algae that do not have the option of engaging the xanthophyll cycle to facilitate nonphotochemical quenching), changes in nonphotochemical quenching of excitation energy in the antenna (effectively a reduction in $\sigma_{PSII}$), and photoacclimation via changes in the rates of synthesis of light-harvesting complexes. These options are effectively "nested"; that is, they are all related to changes in the redox state of the plastoquinone pool, but occur on different time scales (Falkowski et al. 1994). The net effect of these adjustments is a continuous irradiance-dependent change in $E_k$ through the water column.

Additional adjustments in the number of functional photosynthetic reaction centers and their maximum electron throughput rates arise as a consequence of metabolic feedback from the Calvin–Benson cycle into the photosynthetic electron transport chain, as well as the potential damage to PSII reaction centers arising from supraoptimal irradiance levels. These dynamic aspects of the photosynthetic apparatus are not readily revealed from any method that requires an incubation and results in a time-integrated measurement over time period longer than the physiological response. Whereas a suppression of photosynthetic rates in mid-day is commonly observed in short-term simulated or in situ incubations, the relevance or even reality of this suppression has not been greatly appreciated without the use of rapid measurement techniques, such as fluorescence (Marra 1978; Vassiliev et al. 1994).

## IN VIVO FLUORESCENCE APPROACHES

One approach that can be used to indirectly probe the biophysical responses of the photosynthetic apparatus in natural aquatic ecosystems is in vivo chlorophyll fluorescence. Fluorescence measurements are extremely sensitive and can be made over a large range of spatial and temporal scales (micrometers to kilometers and microseconds to months), thereby addressing many of the dynamics of aquatic environments.

Let us consider that the rate of photosynthesis in a given volume or area of water is related to the number of photosynthetic reaction centers per unit area or volume of water, their rate of light absorption, and the quantum efficiency of photochemistry. While it is difficult to determine the maximum quantum yields of photosynthesis at limiting irradiance, variations in chlorophyll-specific rates of photosynthesis at light saturation span over an order of magnitude in natural aquatic ecosystems. These variations reflect environmentally and genetically determined changes in the quantum efficiency of photochemistry. These are due, in turn, to variations in the ratio of the optical to functional absorption cross-sections of the photosynthetic apparatus (i.e., variations in the rate of light absorbed or the rate at which the absorbed light is used to drive electron transport), variations in the maximum turnover rate of the photosynthetic electron transport chain, and/or variations in the ratio of PSII/PSI reaction centers (Kolber, Falkowski 1993). How can these phenomena be examined in natural aquatic ecosystems?

Photosynthesis can be expressed as a function of irradiance, in a general form:

$$P^B_{O_2}(E) = f\left(\alpha^B, P^B_n, E\right) \tag{9.10}$$

where $P^B_{O_2}(E)$ is the rate of gross photosynthetic oxygen evolution per unit chlorophyll $a$ (mol $O_2$ evolved [(g Chl $a)^{-1}$ time$^{-1}$], $\alpha^B$ is the initial slope of the photosynthesis-irradiance curve normalized to chlorophyll (Chapter 7). $P_n^B$ is the light-saturated rate, and $E$ is the incident photosynthetically active irradiance (mol photon $m^{-2}$ $time^{-1}$). Equation 9.10 can be rewritten in terms of the functional absorption cross-section and number of PSII reaction centers as follows:

$$P_{O_2}^B(E) = \sigma_{PSII}\ \phi_{RC}\ f\ n_{PSII}\ \phi_P\ E \tag{9.11}$$

where $\sigma_{PSII}$ is the functional absorption cross-section of PSII ($m^2$/quanta), $\phi_{RC}$ is the quantum yield of photochemistry within PSII (i.e., 1 electron/quanta absorbed), $n_{PSII}$ is the ratio of PSII reaction centers to chl $a$ (mol PSII/g chl $a$)$^{-1}$, and $f$ is the fraction of PSII reaction centers that are capable of evolving oxygen (Kolber, Falkowski 1993). $\phi_P$ is the quantum yield of photochemistry for PSII at irradiance $E$. This parameter has two components that can be measured by fluorescence. These are the photochemical quenching coefficient qP (moles electrons transferred per mole photons absorbed by PSII) and the quantum yield of electron transport, $\phi_c$ [mol $O_2$ evolved (mol electron)$^{-1}$ transferred by PSII]. Thus Equation 9.11 can be further modified to:

$$P_{O_2}^B(E) = \sigma_{PSII}\ \phi_{RC}\ f\ n_{PSII}\ q_P(E)\ \phi_c(E)E \tag{9.12}$$

where $q_P$ and $\phi_c$ are irradiance dependent. Equation 9.12 permits calculation of the rate of photosynthetic electron transport through PSII to be derived from knowledge of six variables, $\sigma_{PSII}$, $q_P$, $\phi_c$, $f$, $n_{PSII}$, and $E$. The first five can be estimated from changes in in vivo chlorophyll fluorescence, the last can be directly measured.

As we discussed in Chapter 3, the ratio of the maximum change in variable fluorescence ($F_v$) to the maximum fluorescence yield ($F_m$) in the absence of any background light is a measure of the maximum quantum efficiency of photochemistry in PSII. Consider now a condition where the rate of photon absorption by PSII is faster than the rate of electron transfer from $Q_A$ to $Q_B$. Under such conditions, PSII fluorescence will rise to $F_m$. If the ratio of the rate of photon delivered to that emitted as fluorescence is measured during this period, the resulting fluorescence kinetic curve can be used to derive the functional absorption cross-section of PSII. Taking advantage of this concept, a fluorescence method using rapid, subsaturating pulses of light that cumulatively saturate PSII within one turnover of $Q_A$ has been developed and used to derive vertical profiles of $F_0$, $F_v$, $F_m$, and $\sigma_{PSII}$. The flashlets are each approximately $5\mu s$ in duration, and each is approximately 10% of saturation level. Cumulative saturation of PSII occurs within about $50\mu s$, while the half-time for $Q_A^-$ oxidation requires about $150\mu s$. This so-called *fast repetition rate fluorescence method* allows simultaneous measurements of the quantum yields of photochemistry and the functional absorption cross-section of PSII under ambient irradiance and/or in darkness (Greene et al. 1994; Kolber et al. 1994; Kolber, Falkowski 1992). The difference between the maximum change in variable fluorescence between a sample in ambient light and that in darkness gives a quantitative measure of the fraction of reaction centers that are closed by the background light at that moment. This process can be thought of as a competition to close reaction centers between the ambient background light and the light produced by the fluorometer. In the dark, the only actinic light source is the fluorometer; the fluorescence yield therefore is related to the total fraction of functional (photochemically competent) reac-

## ❑ IN VIVO FLUORESCENCE

*In vivo chlorophyll fluorescence was introduced to biological oceanography by Carl Lorenzen, who simply pumped seawater through a flow-through cuvette in a fluorometer on the deck laboratory of a ship (Lorenzen 1966). Continuous profiling of in vivo chlorophyll fluorescence was simple and extremely valuable in advancing an understanding of spatial and temporal distribution of phytoplankton biomass (Ascioti et al. 1993; Platt 1972). An early, important discovery, based on pumping water from a hose up to a deck-based fluorometer, was the ubiquitous deep-chlorophyll maximum in the thermally stratified waters of the central ocean basins (Cullen, Eppley 1981). This feature was previously poorly defined because it had been undersampled using traditional fixed-depth measurements of extracted pigments. Horizontal sections of in vivo fluorescence often revealed sharp discontinuities across frontal regions. Statistical analyses of the variance in in vivo fluorescence in the frequency domain (so-called "spectral analysis") were used to correlate the distributions of ocean turbulence (i.e., kinetic energy) with phytoplankton (Platt 1972). Such cross-correlations underscored the dominance of physical processes (as opposed to biological processes) in determining the distribution of phytoplankton and have been used to investigate the nonlinear (i.e., "chaotic") dynamics of phytoplankton in aquatic ecosystems (Ascioti et al. 1993).*

*By the mid-1970s, commercial instruments capable of measuring chlorophyll fluorescence in situ became widely available, and continuous vertical profiles at fixed stations were used routinely to infer phytoplankton distributions. Self-contained, battery-powered fluorometers were developed for long-term (months) continuous recording of in vivo fluorescence. Laser-stimulated fluorescence systems, mounted on fixed-wing aircraft (Hoge, Swift 1981) or operated from ships (Chekalyuk, Gorbunov 1992), are used to map large-scale features of phytoplankton chlorophyll. Solar-induced (so-called "passive") fluorescence methods have also been commercially developed to measure the upwelling fluorescence intensity at 685 nm (Chamberlin et al. 1990; Kiefer et al. 1989; Stegmann et al. 1992; Topliss, Platt 1986).*

*Early on in the application of in vivo fluorescence to aquatic ecosystems, it was realized that the quantum yield of fluorescence was variable. For example, fluorescence yields were higher during the day than at night (Owens et al. 1980) and increased during the day with the passage of clouds across the sky (Abbott et al. 1982). The diel rhythms in fluorescence were initially attributed to alternations in cellular chlorophyll concentrations or circadian rhythms (Brand 1982; Owens et al. 1980). Vertical profiles of fluorescence in the upper ocean reveal a high quantum yield at night, whereas during the day the fluorescence becomes increasingly quenched (Falkowski, Kolber 1995). The quenching phenomenon gives the illusion that a chlorophyll maximum has formed in the subsurface, although extracted chlorophyll analysis clearly indicates this is not so (Fig 9.6). These early observations of what subsequently was called nonphotochemical quenching (Schreiber et al. 1986) created considerable confusion and stimulated efforts to reduce the variability in the fluorescence yields. These efforts included, for example, the continuous addition of DCMU to the flow-through cuvette (Slovacek, Hannan 1977), prior exposure of the cells to a bright light (to maximize the quenching in all samples), alteration of the intensity (both increasing and decreasing) of the excitation light, and preincubation with a far-red light to oxidize the plastoquinone pool (Bates 1985). All of these failed to produce a truly*

*linear relationship between in vivo fluorescence and phytoplankton chlorophyll.
The light-intensity–dependent variations in fluorescence yields often reflect short-
term adjustments in the functional absorption cross-section of PSII.*

---

tion centers. Under ambient irradiance, some fraction of reaction centers will be
closed at the instant of the flash by the background light (i.e., the sun). The difference between the fluorescence yields in the light and dark can be used to estimate
the rate of photosynthetic electron transport instantaneously, in situ, without any
need for incubation in a closed container (Kolber, Falkowski 1993).

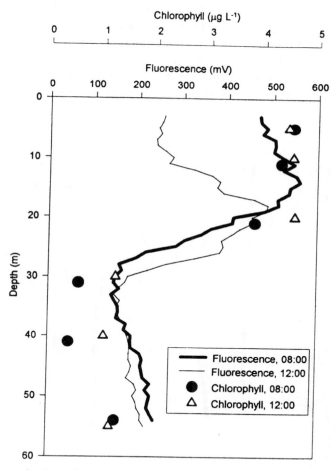

**Figure 9.6** An example of nonphotochemical quenching of in vivo fluorescence in the ocean. An in
situ fluorometer, with a xenon flash excitation source, was lowered from the surface to 55 m at 0800
and 1200 hours local time in the northwestern Atlantic in April. The fluorescence intensity was shown
in real time on the deck of the ship and recorded in engineering units as a voltage. During the vertical
profile, water samples from discrete depths were obtained and the chlorophyll *a* was extracted in 90%
acetone and analyzed independently. A comparison of the in vivo fluorescence profiles between early
morning and midday reveals a sharp decrease in the fluorescence intensity in the upper 20 m that is
not reflected in the extracted chlorophyll analyses.

Three representative vertical profiles of fluorescence signatures acquired with a fast repetition rate fluorometer in situ in an unstratified euphotic zone are shown in Figure 9.7a–c. During the night, profiles of the minimal fluorescence yield induced by the fluorometer ($F_0$ and the maximum yield $F_m$) are parallel and conform to the vertical structure of phytoplankton chlorophyll. Under these conditions, all the reaction centers are presumed to be open at the instant of the flash because the only ambient light is night-sky light. The vertical structure of the functional absorption cross-section is similarly uniform.

A profile recorded early in the morning, during an overcast day, reveals that as the irradiance level increases toward the surface, $F_0$ increases to a value of $F'$, while $F'_m$ remains relatively constant. The functional absorption cross-section of PSII is also lower in the upper portion of the water column. When nutrients are abundant (we will discuss nutrient limitation shortly), the decrease in the functional absorption cross-section at high irradiance reflects nonphotochemical quenching of excitation in the pigment bed due primarily to the xanthophyll cycle and/or physical loss of absorbing pigments (Lee et al. 1990). In phytoplankton, nonphotochemical quenching in the pigment bed relaxes in the dark on the time scale of about 5 to 60 minutes (Olaizola, Yamamoto 1993) and does not affect variable fluorescence, which

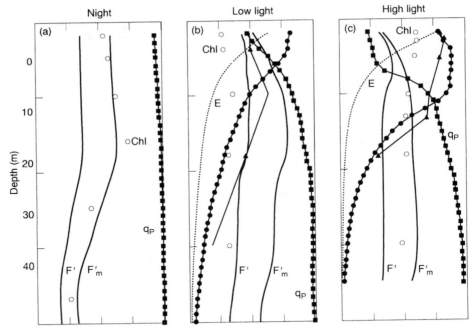

**Figure 9.7** Representative vertical profiles of $F'$, $F'_m$, $q_P$, $P_f^B$ (closed circles, the fluorescence-based estimates of primary production), $P_C^B$ (closed triangles, $^{14}$C-based estimates of primary production), downwelling irradiance (400–700 nm) ($E$), Chl $a$ (open circles). The profiles were taken from a site at 37° 48′ N, 74° 46′ W in the western North Atlantic in March 1989. Profiles (a) at night, when photosynthesis is nil, $F'$ and $F_m$ are parallel and correspond closely to the distribution of Chl; (b) in the early morning of an overcast day, $q_p$ is depressed slightly in the upper portion of the water column; and (c) under high irradiance levels (note the sharp inflection of $q_p$ at approximately 10 m, corresponding to the $E_k$ value in situ).

is a photochemically induced process (Falkowski 1992). Hence, the relative changes in F′ and F′$_m$ are a consequence of the closure of some reaction centers by the ambient light in the upper portion of the water column. This closure is sometimes called *dynamic* quenching.

During a bright, sunny day the effect of the absorbed radiation on the closure of reaction centers is much more pronounced. In the upper portion of the water column the variable fluorescence decreases toward the surface due to the increase in irradiance. This behavior corresponds to the decreased probability of finding an open PSII reaction center at higher photon flux densities. At some irradiance level, typically about 10% of the maximum surface irradiance, variable fluorescence yields reach a steady-state level. From this point downward, the probability of finding an open PSII reaction center is relatively constant. The inflection depth at which variable fluorescence starts to decrease corresponds to $E_k$ in situ. In the bright sun, nonphotochemical quenching is manifested by a reduction in the functional absorption cross-section of PSII, and is usually accompanied by a reduction in the maximum photochemical yields in the dark. If one were to measure $P$ vs. $E$ curves throughout the water column, a systematic decrease in $E_k$ with depth emerges (Fig 9.8), indicative primarily of the increase in the functional absorption cross-section and numbers of PSII reaction centers with depth. The decreases in the maximum quantum yield of photochemistry in the upper portion of the water column reflect photoinhibitory damage—a loss in the number of functional reaction centers (Falkowski 1992).

The application of variable fluorescence methods to natural aquatic ecosystems has provided a basis for understanding short-term acclimations of the photosyn-

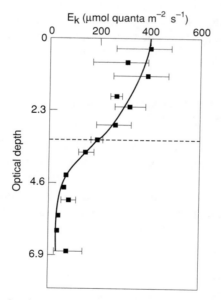

**Figure 9.8** A vertical profile showing changes in $E_k$ values as a function of optical depth. The $E_k$ values were calculated from short-term measurements of photosynthesis-irradiance responses from samples obtained at discrete samples throughout the water column. The photosynthesis-irradiance responses were derived from incubations with $H^{14}CO_3^-$. The station was located in an extremely nutrient poor region of the subtropical North Atlantic Ocean. The horizontal dashed line is the depth of the mixed layer. (Courtesy of Marcel Babin and Andre Morel)

## ❏ NONPHOTOCHEMICAL QUENCHING

*Nonphotochemical quenching of fluorescence can have two origins, namely the antenna and the reaction center. Nonphotochemical quenching in the antenna leads to a decrease in the functional absorption cross-section of PSII. The decrease in absorption cross-section occurs because the quencher in the pigment bed increases the competition with the reaction center for excitation energy. In other words, the antenna now shares more of its absorbed excitation energy between two sinks: the reaction center and the nonphotochemical quencher (which dissipates the excitation energy as heat). In effect, nonphotochemical quenching in the antenna is equivalent to introducing a second trap, albeit one which is not photochemically competent. Consequently, the decrease in functional absorption cross-section in the antenna is directly proportional to the rate of excitation delivery to the reaction center, but does not significantly affect the maximal photochemical efficiency of the reaction center. Thus, excitation energy absorbed by the reaction center has the same probability of promoting an electron transfer with and without nonphotochemical quenching in the antenna; however the probability that an excitation will be absorbed by the reaction center is less in the presence of the quencher.*

---

thetic apparatus in nature. Because the measurements of variable fluorescence can be made in situ under ambient irradiance, do not require an incubation in an enclosed container, and are virtually instantaneous, they can be used to examine how short-term changes in irradiance and nutrients affect photosynthesis. Additionally, transects of variable fluorescence across sections of the ocean or within a lake can be used to understand how geophysical processes, such as vertical mixing, insolation, and nutrient fluxes induce variability in photochemical energy conversion efficiency. We will examine these variations on small and large spatial scales.

## INTEGRATED WATER-COLUMN LIGHT UTILIZATION EFFICIENCY

If we consider that light entering a water body can either be absorbed or not be absorbed by the photosynthetic apparatus, and that the major variation in the areal distribution of the photosynthetic system can be semiquantitatively related to the areal concentration of chlorophyll $a$, then the time-integrated rate of carbon fixation per unit area, normalized to the areal chlorophyll and time-integrated photon flux, is a measure of the light-utilization efficiency of a water column. This efficiency, denoted $\psi$, is defined as:

$$\psi = \frac{\int_{to}^{td}\int_{zo}^{ze} P(t,z)\,dz\,dt}{\int_{zo}^{ze} B(z)\,dz \int_{to}^{td} E_o(\lambda)\,dt\,di} \tag{9.13}$$

where $\int P(t,z)\,dz\,dt$ is primary productivity integrated from the surface to the base of the euphotic zone over a day, $\int B(z)\,dz$ is the chlorophyll-based biomass integrated from the surface to the base of the euphotic zone, and $\int E_o(\lambda)\,dt\,di$ is spectrally integrated, photosynthetically available radiation incident on the surface integrated over a day (Falkowski 1981).

Note that $\psi$ has the same dimensions as the initial slope of the photosynthesis-irradiance curve, and represents the product of the water-column averaged optical absorption cross-section ($m^2 g^{-1}$ chlorophyll $a$) and the water-column averaged quantum yield of photosynthetic carbon fixation ($g C mol^{-1}$ photons). $\psi$ can also be defined as the ratio of the energy of carbon fixed to that of the photon flux. If $E_o$ is given in terms of energy, $\psi$ then has dimensions of $m^2 Chl^{-1}$; thus, it is the water-column averaged functional absorption cross-section for photosynthetic carbon fixation (Morel 1991), designated by the symbol $\psi^*$.

In some regions, $\psi$ appears to be relatively constant throughout the year, and in the mid-1980s it was proposed that this parameter was, in fact, constant in the world oceans, averaging about $0.4 g C g^{-1} Chl\ a\ m^{-2} mol^{-1}$ photons (Platt 1986). In other words, for each mole of photosynthetically active radiation impinging on a square meter of sea surface, each gram of chlorophyll beneath that square meter of sea surface would fix 0.4g of carbon. That analysis was based on the then-extant data sets, which primarily focused on the coastal ocean and nutrient-rich regions of the open ocean. However, closer inspection and analyses revealed that $\psi$ was not constant, but increased as the average daily irradiance decreased (Fig 9.9). Moreover, $\psi$ was lower in low-nutrient regions of the open ocean. Thus, the average, integrated water-column quantum yield for carbon fixation, and/or the average integrated optical absorption cross-section of the photosynthetic organisms are variable in natural aquatic ecosystems. What causes these variations?

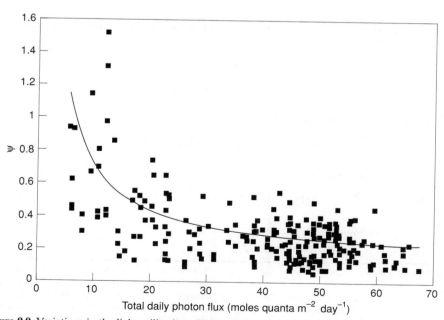

**Figure 9.9** Variations in the light utilization efficiency function, $\psi$ (calculated from Eq 9.9) in relation to total daily incident photosynthetically active radiation. The data are compiled from a large number of $^{14}$C-based measurements of primary production in the world oceans.

## ❏ PRIMARY PRODUCTION MODELS

*There are myriad mathematical models that calculate vertically integrated primary production in aquatic ecosystems. Inspection of the models reveals, however, close relationships or even equivalence, if the differences in notation and representation are taken into account. To this end, we can develop a classification system that accounts for virtually all daily primary production models. The system is based upon implicit levels of integration (Table 9.1).*

## VARIATIONS IN THE QUANTUM YIELD OF PHOTOSYNTHESIS IN NATURAL AQUATIC ENVIRONMENTS

Based on the analyses of photosynthesis-irradiance curves with complementary and corresponding measurements of the chlorophyll-specific optical absorption cross-sections, it is clear that the maximum quantum yield of carbon fixation varies in the ocean. One of the major correlative factors leading to this variation is the availability of inorganic nutrients. In most of the open ocean, the nutrient most often limiting is nitrogen. It must be stressed that the concentration of dissolved fixed inorganic nitrogen per se is not as critical as the flux of nitrogen, as determined by either distance from the nutricline (which often corresponds with the depth of the mixed layer) or the rate of supply of nutrients from lateral sources or internally (Dugdale 1967; Dugdale 1977; Eppley 1981; Goldman, Brewer 1980). The relationship between the distance from the nutricline and the maximum quantum yield for carbon fixation was first noted by Cleveland and co-workers in the Sargasso Sea

**Table 9.1** Classification system for daily net primary productivity (NPP) models based on implicit levels of integration

$$\text{NPP} = \int_{\lambda=400}^{700} \int_{t=sunrise}^{sunset} \int_{z=0}^{Z_{eu}} \Phi(\lambda,z,t) \cdot \text{PAR}(\lambda,t,z) \cdot$$
$$a^*(\lambda,z) \cdot \text{Chl}(z) d\lambda \, dt \, dz - R$$

II. *Wavelength-integrated models*

$$\text{NPP} = \int_{t=sunrise}^{sunset} \int_{z=0}^{Z_{eu}} \varphi(z,t) \cdot \text{PAR}(t,z) \cdot \text{Chl}(z) dt \, dz - R$$

III. *Time-integrated models*

$$\text{NPP} = \int_{z=0}^{Z_{eu}} P^B(z) \cdot \text{PAR}(z) \cdot \text{DL} \cdot \text{Chl}(z) dz$$

IV. *Depth-integrated models*

$$\text{NPP} = P^B_{opt} \cdot \text{PAR}(0) \cdot \text{DL} \cdot \text{Chl} \cdot Z_{eu}$$

Each category includes a photoadaptive variable [i.e., $\varphi$, $\Phi$, $P^B(z)$, $P^B_{opt}$] corresponding to the resolution of the described light field. The variables $\Phi$ and $\varphi$ are chlorophyll-specific quantum yields for absorbed and available photosynthetically active radiation, respectively. Wavelength-resolved models and wavelength-integrated models are parameterized using measurements of net photosynthesis and require subtraction of daily photoautotrophic respiration (R) to calculate NPP. $P^B(z)$ and $P^B_{opt}$ are chlorophyll-specific rates obtained from measurements of daily primary production and thus do not require subtraction of respiration. DL = daylength (hours). (From Behrenfeld, Falkowski 1997b)

(1989), and was subsequently supported by variable fluorescence measurements from the Gulf of Maine that showed a high correspondence between the maximum quantum efficiency of photosystem II and nutrient supply (Kolber et al. 1990). The lateral supply of nutrients also can have a very significant effect on the quantum yield of carbon fixation. For illustrative purposes, we can take as a case in point the variations in the maximum quantum yield for carbon fixation in a nutrient-rich upwelling region off the coast of northwestern Africa in comparison with a highly oligotrophic region in the central subtropical Atlantic (Fig 9.10). Throughout most of the upper portion of the water column in the upwelling region the maximum quantum yield for carbon fixation is $0.06 \, mol \, C \, mol^{-1}$ quanta (i.e., a minimum quantum requirement of about 17). In this vertically mixed environment, the maximum quantum yields remain relatively constant throughout the euphotic zone. In contrast, the maximum quantum yield in the oligotrophic region is about $0.005 \, mol \, C \, mol^{-1}$ quanta (i.e., a quantum requirement of about 200!). Closer to the base of the nutricline the maximum quantum yield increases markedly, and approaches values of about 0.08 (Babin et al. 1996).

The calculated values of the maximum quantum yield of carbon fixation in natural aquatic environments are usually lower than the theoretically achievable yield of about 0.10 (Babin et al. 1996). Part of the difference may be ascribed to methodological problems, especially in the accurate measurement of the chlorophyll-specific optical absorption cross-sections (Bidigare et al. 1992), but much of the discrepancy is attributable to variations in the photosynthetic apparatus. One of these variations is the synthesis and accumulation of nonphotosynthetically active

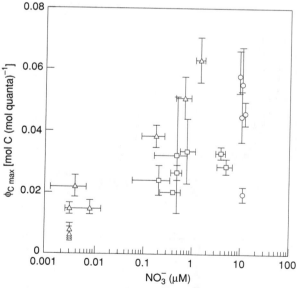

**Figure 9.10** A plot showing the correlation between external nutrient concentration (represented, in this case, by $NO_3^-$) and the maximum quantum yield for photosynthetic carbon fixation. The data were obtained from three regions in the North Atlantic: circles are from an upwelling region off northwest Africa, squares are from a transition region, and triangles are from an oligotrophic region. (Data courtesy of Marcel Babin and Andre Morel)

pigments in cells in high-irradiance, low-nutrient environments. Such pigments include the carotenes and some xanthophylls, such as zeaxanthin, that are associated with the cell walls of cyanobacteria (Fujita et al. 1994). These so-called "photoprotective" pigments contribute to absorption of photosynthetically active radiation but do not transfer absorbed excitation energy to either PSII or PSI; thus, the accumulation of such pigments depresses the maximum quantum yield of photosynthesis (Babin et al. 1996). Additionally, however, a major cause of the depression in the quantum yield is the reduction in photochemically active reaction centers, especially in low-nutrient environments (Falkowski 1992; Falkowski et al. 1989). The decrease in PSII reaction centers can be inferred from nutrient-dependent decreases in variable fluorescence normalized to $F_0$ (Fig 9.11). There is little quantitative information concerning the abundance of PSI reaction centers in natural aquatic photosynthetic organisms; however, the extant data suggest that the ratio of chlorophyll to PSI reaction centers is markedly reduced in low-nutrient regimes. The reduction in PSII reaction centers leads to a greater fluorescence yield of chlorophyll in vivo, as absorbed excitation energy is not as effectively trapped by photochemical reactions (Greene et al. 1994).

As we implied in Figure 9.11, the nutrient-related reduction in the number of photochemically functional reaction centers is mostly confined to the middle and upper portion of the euphotic zone (Kolber, Falkowski 1993). However, in this portion of the water column a loss of photochemically functional reaction centers may also arise as a consequence of photoinhibition.

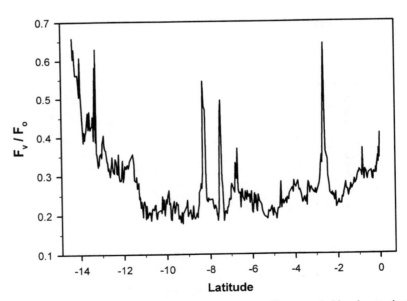

**Figure 9.11** Variations in the quantum efficiency of photosystem II as revealed by changes in the ratio of variable fluorescence to $F_0$. These data were obtained from night-time transects in the South Pacific Ocean, along a line at 140° W, from 15° S to the equator. The "spikes" correspond to eddy-induced turbulence regions in which nutrients are supplied.

## Photoinhibition

There is abundant evidence that photoinhibition occurs in natural phytoplankton communities, although the mechanisms of the phenomenon are complex (Prasil et al. 1992). In natural phytoplankton communities, the near-surface organisms often exhibit mid-day depressions in the quantum efficiency of photochemistry as evidenced by lower values of variable fluorescence normalized to $F_m$. This depression cannot be simply explained by nonphotochemical quenching in the pigment bed, which also occurs. The latter is manifested as a decrease in the functional absorption cross-section of PSII during mid-day, and an increase in the cross-section at night. Nonphotochemical quenching in the reaction center is manifested by a time-dependent increase in $F_v/F_m$ in the dark (i.e., a change in the maximum quantum yield for photochemisty in PSII) (Weis, Berry 1987). This quenching process can be due to either a loss or damage to the proteins within the reaction center, or to the generation of slowly dissipating charged intermediates on the donor or acceptor side of PSII (see Chapter 7). Whatever the origin, slowly reversible, nonphotochemical quenching within the reaction center is usually taken as a measure of photoinhibition, while nonphotochemical quenching within the antenna is not (Olaizola et al. 1994).

The kinetics of relaxation of nonphotochemical fluorescence quenching in the pigment bed and reaction center are independent of each other. The quenching process in the antenna relaxes with a half-time of a few to tens of minutes, is correlated with the change in the functional absorption cross-section of PSII, and has little effect on maximal variable fluorescence. The second component, with a half-time of a few to tens of hours, corresponds with a slow increase in variable fluorescence and is related to the "repair" of PSII reaction centers. Presumably "repair" includes the synthesis of D1 and perhaps other reaction center proteins (Baker, Bowyer 1994). It should be noted that the high-light–induced decrease in the functional absorption cross-section of PSII will lead to a corresponding increase in $E_k$, thereby dynamically altering the functional photosynthesis–irradiance relationship. If cells are exposed to supraoptimal irradiance levels for extended periods, however, the reduction in functional cross-sections may not be sufficient to prevent damage to PSII reaction centers (Falkowski et al. 1994). The damage is largely repaired overnight, on the provision that sufficient nutrient resources are available to provide the substrates for the reparation.

Photoinhibition is a time-dependent phenomenon (Takahashi et al. 1971). Cells or plants exposed to very high irradiance levels for brief periods reveal little or no effect. In contrast, cells exposed for longer periods show a decrease in photochemical energy conversion levels. The time dependence is nonlinear, making it difficult to accommodate the effect in mathematical representations of photosynthetic responses (Falkowski, Wirick 1981). In phytoplankton, the exposure level to supraoptimal irradiance is not only determined by the solar radiative flux, but by the rate of vertical mixing, the depth of the upper mixed layer, and the rate of attenuation of radiation within the mixed layer (Long et al. 1994; Neale 1987). While the latter two variables can be determined from measurements of the vertical profiles of density and light, the rate of vertical mixing is extremely difficult to determine directly. Rather, mixing can be inferred from photosynthetic characteristics of the organisms. For example, if one knows the time dependence of nonphotochemical quenching from laboratory and field studies and measures the vertical profile of nonphotochemical quenching, a minimum rate of mixing can be inferred (Olaizola 1993). Similarly, on longer time scales the rate of photoacclimation can be used to deduce the light history of the phytoplankton, and hence some understanding of when the organisms at or near the base of the euphotic zone were last at or near the surface (Falkowski 1983; Lewis et al. 1984). Empirically, however, even in relatively rapidly mixing water columns with shallow mixed layers and strong attenuation of photosynthetically active radiation, on sunny days there is almost always some evidence of a mid-day depression in the quantum yield of photochemistry in PSII, as inferred from variable fluorescence measurements. This suppression often causes the maximum daily photosynthetic rate to occur at a depth below the surface.

## The Effect of Temperature

It should be recognized that photoinhibition from PAR occurs when the rate of excitation absorption by reaction centers exceeds the rate of photochemistry (Chapter 7). In PSII, the rate of excitation absorption is given by

$$PSII_{(\lambda)} = \sigma_{PSII(\lambda)} E_{(\lambda)} \tag{9.14}$$

where $PSII_{(\lambda)}$ is the rate of PSII photon absorption at wavelength $\lambda$. In nature, $\lambda$ must be spectrally integrated between 400 to 700 nm to give the average PSII absorption cross-section (Falkowski 1983; Lewis et al. 1984). The rate of photochemistry in the steady state is maximally equivalent to $1/\tau$, which defines the rate of electron transport from water to $CO_2$ (Chapter 7). As $1/\tau$ is primarily limited by the ratio of electron transport components to Rubisco, it is temperature dependent. Thus, at low temperatures the maximum rate of electron transport is generally lower, and cells become photoinhibited at lower irradiance levels. The extreme of this phenomenon occurs in algae trapped in the ice in the polar seas. In such cells decreases in the maximum rate of photosynthesis can be observed at 15 μmol quanta $m^{-2}s^{-1}$ (Cota 1985; Platt et al. 1980). Some crustose red algae growing on the seamounts in the Atlantic become photoinhibited at 1 μmol quanta $m^{-2}s^{-1}$; a very low photon fluence rate indeed (Littler et al. 1985). At the other extreme of high temperatures, the maximum rate of electron transport may be greatly accelerated, but elevated temperatures are almost always a consequence of strong vertical stratification that often leads to a reduction in the flux of nutrients into the euphotic zone. As nutrient limitation tends to decrease the number of functional reaction centers, this situation tends to lead to photoinhibitory responses as well, albeit that the effect of temperature in such a situation is indirect, perhaps even correlative, rather than causal (Falkowski et al. 1994).

Because there is a relationship between irradiance and temperature on the maximal rate of photosynthetic electron transport and the ability of cells to repair photoinhibitory damage, the realized effect of temperature on the maximum daily

## ❏ UV-B INHIBITION

*Historically, UV radiation has been divided into three bands, based on empirical biological effects: UV-A is defined as spanning from 320 to 400nm, UV-B ranges from 280 to 320nm, and UV-C is taken from about 200 to 280nm (Hader, Tevini 1987; Seliger, McElroy 1965). Virtually all of the UV-C radiation emitted from the sun is absorbed by gases in the stratosphere.[8] The gases that are responsible for the absorption of UV radiation are molecular oxygen $O_2$, and ozone, $O_3$. The former primarily is responsible for the absorption of UV-C while the latter is particularly important in absorbing UV-B radiation.*

*Ozone is produced by a photochemical reaction in the stratosphere:*

$$O_2 \xrightarrow{h\upsilon} O + O$$

$$\lambda = 234 \ nm$$

$$O + O_2 \rightarrow O_3$$

*The destruction of $O_3$ can be catalyzed by halogens such as chlorine. One source of chlorine is the photo-oxidation of anthropogenically created halocarbons, such as carbon tetrachloride and the chlorofluorocarbons. These reactions can be summarized as:*

$$RCl \xrightarrow{h\upsilon} R + Cl^{\bullet}$$

$$\lambda = 225 \ nm$$

$$Cl^{\bullet} + O_3 \rightarrow ClO + O_2$$

$$ClO^{\bullet} + O \rightarrow Cl^{\bullet} + O_2$$

*where R is an organic molecule. Note that this is a chain reaction that regenerates chlorine radicals; hence a single molecule of the halocarbon can potentially destroy many thousands of molecules of $O_3$ (Molina, Rowland 1974). The net effect of the destruction of stratospheric ozone on the radiation budget of the Earth is to allow a higher flux of UV radiation to impinge on the surface (Ramanathan 1975). Some of this radiation enters aquatic environments, where it is can be absorbed by $O_2$ and by dissolved organic compounds in the water, and to some extent by water itself (Baker, Smith 1982). However, some of the UV radiation can be absorbed by photosynthetic organisms. Two major sites of damage have been identified as a consequence of the absorption of UV radiation, namely the reaction center of PSII (Cullen et al. 1992; Cullen, Neale 1993; Raven 1991b; Roberts et al. 1991) and DNA (Setlow 1974).*

*The photosynthetic pigments typically have minor absorption bands in the UV. For example, there are weak resonant absorption bands of chlorophyll a in the UV-A region, and these are potential targets for UV radiation in reaction centers. Additional targets for UV radiation are found in the UV-B region; these targets include the tyrosine donor to PSII, $Y_Z$, and the PSII acceptor, $Q_A$ (Greenberg et al. 1989; Prasil et al. 1992). It should be noted that absorbed UV radiation is not transferred from the antenna to the reaction center with high efficiency; if it were, we would expect to observe PSII fluorescence emission in vivo when*

---

8. The *stratosphere* is that portion of the Earth's atmosphere that extends from about 10 to 45 km above the surface and is separated from the lower atmosphere (i.e., the *troposphere*) by a thermal gradient, the *tropopause*.

*cells are excited in the UV, but in fact this has seldom been observed (Halldall, Taube 1972). Thus, for UV radiation to damage the reaction center, it must be directly absorbed by the target, either $P_{680}$ (a chlorophyll molecule), the tyrosine donor, or the quinone acceptor. At the surface of the ocean, convolution of all the optical absorption cross-sections for all potential targets in PSII in the UV with the natural photon fluence in this region of the spectrum suggests that the minimum time between direct hits is about 20 to 30 s (Vassiliev et al. 1994). This rate of absorption is three to four orders of magnitude smaller than that for photosynthetically active radiation. Thus, approx. 0.01% of the photons absorbed by PSII are in the UV. Potentially these high-energy photons can ionize molecules and result in irreversible damage to the photochemical processes in the reaction center (Cullen et al. 1993; Tevini, Pfister 1985).*

*One classical approach to identifying photochemical targets is to determine the action spectrum (Hader et al. 1987). In the case of UV radiation, this approach is generally implemented by determining the extent of photoinhibition (e.g., the loss of variable fluorescence or $O_2$ evolution) as a function of wavelength. Action spectra for UV radiation effects on photosynthesis do not reveal clear absorption peaks that would correspond to a specific target molecule, but rather damage per unit photon absorbed increases exponentially at shorter wavelengths (Fig 9.12).*

*The action spectrum for damage to DNA is qualitatively similar to that for photoinhibition. In DNA the target molecules are primarily thymidines, which can dimerize following absorption of a high-energy photon (Wang 1975). The T-T base pair leads to misreads of the coding sequences, and ultimately can lead to mutations unless the damage is repaired. Most organisms have evolved DNA repair systems; however, at high UV fluence rates, repair may not keep pace with the damage.*

*While the primary site of UV-B damage to the photosynthetic apparatus appears to be PSII, the exact mechanism of this damage is contentious. The net effect on photosynthesis reflects a steady-state relationship between the damage and repair systems (Cullen, Neale 1993). It is frequently assumed that the damage includes destruction of D1. As the repair of this protein requires* de novo *synthesis, transcription is requisite. Whether the repair systems are themselves damaged by UV-B remains unclear. Numerous strategies to screen UV-B radiation have evolved in photosynthetic organisms. One of the most common is the production of pigments which absorb the radiation and screen it from the photosynthetic apparatus. Some carotenoids, such as β-carotene, serve this purpose (Dohler, Haas 1995). However, other pigments, such as nonessential, aromatic amino acids, are frequently found in aquatic organisms exposed to high natural UV fluxes. These compounds, first isolated from symbiotic corals in Australia, are relatively ubiquitous, and their extremely high UV-B absorption cross-sections serve to effectively remove UV-B radiation as a photodamaging agent in organisms in which they are found (Dunlap, Chalker 1986; Karentz et al. 1991). However, the increased destruction of stratospheric ozone by anthropogenic halocarbons may lead to enhanced UV-B fluxes, and the potential damage of this radiation to photosynthetic organisms can only be speculated (Smith et al. 1992).*

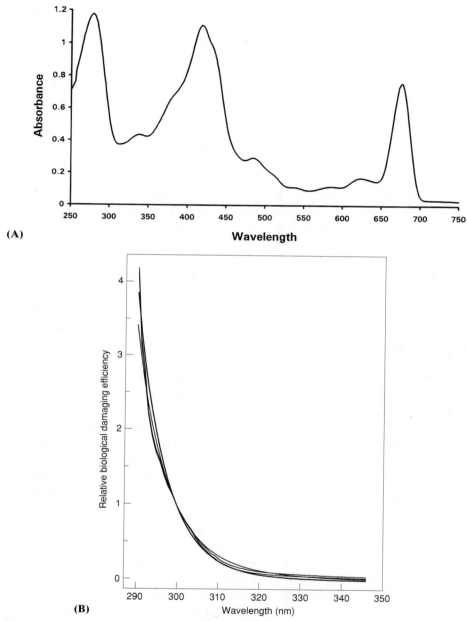

**Figure 9.12** (A) An absorption spectra from 250 to 750 nm for isolated photosystem II reaction centers lacking all light-harvesting complexes, but containing $P_{680}$, the phaeophytin intermediate acceptor, $Q_A$, and the water-splitting Mn cluster. Note the UV-absorption band centered at about 280 nm, which corresponds largely to the absorption of light by $Q_A$. This is a potential target for direct damage from UV-B absorption in all oxygenic photoautotrophs. (Courtesy of Michael Seibert) (B) Relative biological damaging efficiency curves for the inhibition of photosynthesis between 290 nm and 347 nm derived from Behrenfeld et al. (1993), Rundel (1983), and Cullen and Lesser (1991). The latter two correspond to a marine diatom and dinoflagellate, respectively. (Courtesy of Michael Behrenfeld)

photosynthetic rate (i.e., $P_{opt}^B$) does not follow a simple Arrhenius function as might be expected based on the results from laboratory cultures of algae (Chapter 7). Whereas $P_{opt}^B$ increases from near zero temperatures to near 20°C, at temperatures above approximately 20°C, $P_{opt}^B$ declines. The decline appears to be a consequence of the reduction in nutrients in the near-surface waters at the elevated temperatures (Balch et al. 1993; Behrenfeld, Falkowski 1996).

## HORIZONTAL SECTIONS OF PHOTOSYNTHETIC EFFICIENCY

Most of the discussion of short-term variations in photosynthetic responses thus far has focused on vertically controlled processes in the water column. Transects of variable fluorescence measurements across large areas of the ocean and/or a lake reveal large variations in the maximum quantum yield of photochemistry in PSII and in $\sigma_{PSII}$ that cannot be ascribed simply to variations in irradiance or time of day. One of the most apparent causes of the horizontal variability is due to fluxes of nutrients, which are generally correlated with thermal gradients. In aquatic systems, horizontal inhomogeneity in chemical properties can be brought about by physical forces that produce eddies, current meanders, storm-induced mixing, and so on. These chemical gradients are sometimes extremely subtle, but are amplified by their effects on the quantum yield of photochemistry. For example, in a section from the extremely low-nutrient waters of the Sargasso Sea in the western North Atlantic to the nutrient-rich waters on the continental shelf off the eastern coast of the United States, variable fluorescence normalized to $F_m$ increases by a factor of about three. A similar variation in the quantum yield of photochemistry can be observed through an upwelling eddy in the central oligotrophic ocean. Nutrient supplementation experiments with enclosed samples reveal that the quantum yields can be restored by the addition of nutrients within a day or two. These observations reveal that: (1) phytoplankton can rapidly respond, on the time scale of hours to days, to nutrient supplies, (2) that nutrient supplies markedly affect the maximum rate of photosynthetic energy conversion on large spatial scales in aquatic environments, and (3) that physical phenomena that facilitate or retard the flow of nutrients into the euphotic zone determine not only the upper limit of photoautotrophic biomass, but also the photophysiological status of the photoautotrophic organisms. Based on the variations in the quantum efficiency of photochemistry in aquatic ecosystems, it would appear that in nutrient-poor regions, the photoautotrophs are chronically stressed. That is, most of the time the organisms do not obtain sufficient nutrients to synthesize damaged reaction centers, and a larger fraction of the absorbed excitation energy is dissipated as heat and fluorescence, rather than utilized in photochemical reactions in PSII.

Although it is clearly beyond the scope of any treatise to completely examine all the possible short-term acclimation responses of photosynthetic organisms in natural aquatic ecosystems, we have tried here to give the reader an appreciation of "the rules of the game" of how photosynthetic organisms respond on these time scales. These rules include acclimatory changes in the numbers of functional reaction centers, their absorption cross-sections, and their proportion to Calvin cycle enzymes in response to variation in spectral irradiance, nutrient supply, and temperature. In Chapter 10, we turn to an examination of the role of aquatic organisms on longer time scales, and their adaptations and evolutionary selection in relation to biogeochemical cycles.

# 10

## Aquatic Photosynthesis in Biogeochemical Cycles

In 1830, the British geologist Charles Lyell (whom we met in Chapter 1) carefully elaborated on a theory to explain geological formations and the distribution of fossils. That theory, which came to be called *uniformitarianism*, was "an attempt to explain the former changes in the Earth's surface by reference to causes now in operation." Thus, such phenomena as erosion, volcanic eruptions, glaciations, floods, and earthquakes, have, over long periods of time, produced mountains, deltas, outwash plains, and island masses. The theory of uniformitarianism provided, for the first time, a rational framework through which to interpret the geological history of the Earth. The reconstruction of the Earth's history depended heavily on understanding the distribution of fossils, and Lyell was an astute and capable taxonomist. He grasped that the fossil remains found in geological formations corresponded to life-forms that had existed in relict seas that were now mountains, and that many organisms found in the sedimentary record were extinct.

Thirty years after the publication of Lyell's classic text, Darwin[1] proposed that the observed adaptations of extant species were the result of natural phenomena such as competition and stress that resulted in the selection of individual species. Darwin built on the Mathusian concept of populations potentially growing beyond their available resources, and the known occurrence of heritable variation (even in the days before Mendel's work became widespread). These ideas led, in turn, to the theory of natural selection—that is, differential survival of organisms as a function of their genetic potential and the influence of biotic factors such as competition for resources, predators, and pathogenesis, as well as abiotic factors such as climate. Abiotic factors were particularly emphasized by Wallace, who was acknowledged by Darwin as having independently conceived of the theory of evolution by natural selection (and who, by almost scooping him, motivated Darwin to publish the *Origin*

---

1. The first of the three volumes of *Principles of Geology* was published in 1830 and became a hot item among natural scientists (meaning most scientists) in the mid-19th century. Together with copies of the Bible and the works of Alexander von Humbolt, Darwin took a copy of the first volume of *Principles of Geology* with him on the *Beagle* expedition in 1831. He sent letters back to England from Latin America explaining the validity of many of Lyell's concepts, and over the course of the five-year voyage Darwin received the additional volumes in mail packages that caught up with him at ports of call. Darwin was greatly inspired by Lyell, and the two became close colleagues. Darwin was elected to the Royal Society in 1839 for his contributions to the understanding of geology. His theories of evolution, based on natural selection, were not published until almost 30 years later, partly as a consequence of the fear of the furor they would cause with the strong religious fervor gripping England at the time. Incidentally, Lyell himself understood the concept of evolution, but he leaned heavily on the theories of Lamark and Buffon to explain selection mechanisms.

*of Species* earlier than he had originally intended). These ideas underpin the current views of the origin of species and the notion of evolutionary adaptations, i.e., the characteristics of organisms that can be rationalized as consequences of natural selection and which facilitate growth and reproduction in a given environment. Species that cannot adapt to changes in their environment ultimately become extinct.

To paraphrase the late aquatic ecologist G. Evelyn Hutchinson, the ecological theater of the present is only a scene in the ongoing evolutionary drama of the Earth (Hutchinson 1965). Hutchinson's thespian metaphor is an ecological interpretation of uniformitarianism. The genes of every extant species have been transferred from generation to generation, through the eons, mutating and, by natural selection, adapting to the changes in climate and chemistry that have been part of the history of the Earth. The mutations and adaptations can often be inferred from phylogenetic relationships based on molecular techniques (see Chapter 1). Extinctions represent the limitations of physiological acclimation to accommodate the roulette wheel of evolutionary selection. The interpretation of the causes and selection mechanism for the genetic variability has traditionally been viewed in the context of climate and geological processes (Lipps 1993).

Within the context of selection, therefore, the engines of metabolism must also adapt to changes in the environment, and in this regard photosynthesis is no exception. Over the course of time, the photosynthetic activity and associated metabolic processes carried out by aquatic photoautotrophs have fundamentally transformed the chemistry of the Earth, which has, in turn, profoundly influenced the course of biological evolution in both aquatic and terrestrial ecosystems (Kasting 1993). Hence we come to an evolutionary paradox: There is compelling molecular biological evidence that the fundamental processes of photosynthesis, such as photochemical charge separation and the pathways of carbon fixation, are highly conserved, but these processes themselves must be sufficiently plastic to accommodate the environmental changes that have occurred since the origins of oxygenic photoautotrophs.

That cyanobacteria are not only extant in the modern ocean but are exceedingly abundant,[2] and are the evolutionary forerunners via endosymbiosis of eukaryotic photoautotrophs, suggests extraordinary adaptive capacity. For every success story, however, myriad failures can be found in the fossil and sedimentary record. The fossils of extinct species give clues of both cyclic and catastrophic changes in the physical and chemical environment of aquatic systems in times long past. It should be pointed out that success and failure are relative rather than absolute terms; the relic taxa often flourished for tens of millions of years, leading to the accumulation of hundreds of meters of calcified or silicified remains in the sediments (Berger, Herguera 1992). It is largely from the sedimentary record that we can infer previous episodes in the evolutionary drama (Knoll, Bauld 1989) (Fig 10.1).

In this chapter we examine some of the long-term adaptations of aquatic photosynthetic organisms to the environment and the feedbacks between the biotic and

---

2. It is estimated that there are about $10^{27}$ cyanobacteria cells in the modern ocean (P. Tett, personal communication).

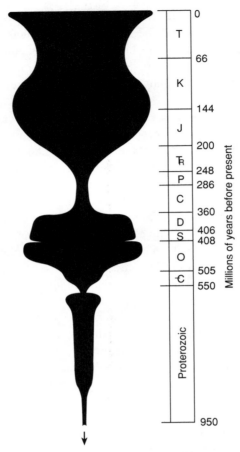

**Figure 10.1** A schematic representation showing the radiations and extinctions of phytoplankton taxa over geological time. The taxonomic richness, or diversity, is inferred from fossil structures. In the Paleozoic period (i.e., the Cambrian through the Permian epochs), the record is basically constructed from prasinophytes and poorly preserved remains, whereas the Triassic and later periods are dominated by dinoflagellate cysts and skeletal remains of coccolithophorids and diatoms. (Modified from Knoll 1989)

abiotic realms. The latter is of special interest as it is essential to understanding how climatic phenomena affect and are affected by aquatic photoautotrophs.

## FORCINGS AND FEEDBACKS IN THE EARTH CLIMATE SYSTEM

All organisms on the Earth must adapt to the planet's climate. The climate of the Earth is "forced" by radiative budgets; that is, the radiative balance of the Earth is dictated, to a first order, by the incident solar energy, its reflection and reradiation back to space by the Earth's surface, and the gas composition of the atmosphere. These terms are quantitatively related by a set of equations.

Consider a hypothetical object, or body, with a coherent mass of material having uniform temperature and composition. The body has a sufficient number of molecules that absorb and emit electromagnetic radiation in all parts of the spectrum so that (1) all incident radiation is completely absorbed (the object is "black") and (2) the maximum possible emission of radiation is realized at all wavelengths in all directions (i.e., it is isotropic). The amount of radiation emitted by a black body ($E_\lambda^*$) is determined by its temperature and described by *Planck's law* as:

$$E_\lambda^* = \left[ \frac{c_2}{\lambda^5 \left[ e^{(c_1/\lambda T)} - 1 \right]} \right] \tag{10.1}$$

where T is absolute temperature, $c_1$ and $c_2$ are constants, and $\lambda$ is the emission wavelength. The *blackbody irradiance* is obtained by integrating Equation 10.1 over all wavelengths. The result is given by:

$$E^* = \sigma T^4 \tag{10.2}$$

where $\sigma$ is a constant (called the *Stefan-Boltzmann constant*) and has a value of 5.67 $\times 10^{-8} W m^{-2} deg^{-4}$. Equation 10.2 is called the *Stefan-Boltzmann law*.

Assuming that the Earth is in radiative equilibrium (i.e., there is no gain or loss of heat as a consequence of radiative processes), then the solar radiation incident on the Earth's surface must be reemitted to space (Budyko 1982; Wallace, Hobbs 1977). We can calculate the equivalent "black body" temperature of the Earth. Assuming an average planetary reflection (or *albedo*), $\alpha_s$, for the Earth of approximately 0.30 (i.e., 30% of the incoming short wavelength radiation from the sun is reflected back to space), from Equation 10.2, the radiative balance is given by:

$$\sigma T^4 = 1/4 S_0 \left(1 - \alpha_s\right) \tag{10.3}$$

where $S_0$ is the incident solar radiative flux at the top of the atmosphere. The value of $S_0$ is about 1373 W m$^{-2}$ (i.e., the solar constant; Chapter 2) and is known with an accuracy of about ±2%. The numerical solution of Equation 10.3 gives an apparent black body temperature for the Earth of 255 K (−18 °C). This is the predicted temperature of the Earth's surface in the absence of an atmosphere. The actual mean temperature of the Earth is presently about 286 K (13 °C). The difference (286 − 255) is 31 K warmer than the calculated black body equilibrium temperature. The increased temperature is a consequence of the reradiation of a portion of the outbound long wavelength radiation back to the Earth's surface from the infrared absorbing gases in the atmosphere. This is commonly called the *greenhouse effect*.

Over geological time, incident solar radiation has varied significantly. The long-term trend has been one of increased solar luminosity since the Archean epoch. Model calculations, based on the measurements of the luminosity of stars of various ages in our galaxy, suggest that solar fluxes increased by approximately 25% over the past 3.5 billion years (Kasting et al. 1988). Superimposed on this trend are short-term variations in orbital trajectories, which can be calculated with reasonable precision (and will be discussed shortly). The albedo of the Earth also has changed. The albedo is driven by a variety of factors, first among these the areal coverage and the optical properties of the clouds. Incoming radiation between about 300 and 1000 nm is considered by atmospheric physicists to be "short wave," while that longer than about 1000 nm is "long wave" (see Fig 2.1). Approximately 45% of the total incident solar energy is short-wave radiation. Clouds can reflect short-wave radiation, thereby cooling the Earth's surface during the day. However, water in the clouds absorbs long-wave radiation and reradiates it back to the Earth's surface. Hence, clouds reduce the loss of heat from the Earth's surface at night. Changes in planetary albedo are also critically dependent on the area of ice cover, the range of terrestrial vegetation, and soil moisture. The oceans reflect about 5% of the total short-wave radiation incident on the surface of the water back to space.

Perhaps the most difficult of the radiative transfer terms to quantify is related to the gas composition of the atmosphere. As just seen for clouds, water is itself a greenhouse gas, and from a climatic perspective, water vapor in the atmosphere is the most important greenhouse gas. The second most important greenhouse gas is $CO_2$. The net absorption of $CO_2$ by photoautotrophs has led to a long and steady drawdown of this radiatively active gas in the Earth's atmosphere; however, there have been cyclic perturbations in atmospheric $CO_2$ that result from *feedbacks* with the climate system.

Feedbacks are processes that enhance or attenuate an initial forcing. For example, if the Earth's climate begins to cool because of a decrease in the incident solar radiation ($S_0$ in Equation 10.3), the atmosphere tends to lose water vapor. The loss of water vapor leads to a reduction in the greenhouse warming and hence produces a positive feedback; the climate would tend to continue to cool. A loss of water vapor and cool temperatures would tend to reduce the absorption of $CO_2$ by terrestrial plants, thereby potentially elevating the atmosphere's $CO_2$ levels. As $CO_2$ is also a greenhouse gas, this effect is potentially a negative feedback that could offset the loss of water vapor. Unraveling the potential cascade of feedbacks is complex and a subject of active study in climate change research (Sellers et al. 1996). It should be noted in this regard that the oceans do not exert a direct physical feedback on the Earth's climate system. The thermal mass of the oceans is vast compared with the atmosphere. The equivalent of the entire heat capacity of the atmosphere is contained in only the upper three meters of the oceans. Hence the major role of the oceans in the heat budget is as a heat sink or source, lagging in time behind the atmosphere.

## THE SUPPLY OF NUTRIENTS

As incident solar radiation is higher at the equator than at the poles, the distribution of heat in aquatic ecosystems is dependent on latitude. In the oceans, solar heating at low latitudes induces a poleward flux of warm waters in the surface that is balanced by an equatorial flux of cold polar water at depth. This so-called thermohaline circulation produces clockwise gyres of circulation in the northern hemisphere and counterclockwise gyres in the southern hemisphere (Pickard, Emery 1990). Moreover, the mid-latitude and lower latitude oceans become thermally stratified, and hence the upper mixed layers are separated from the waters that communicate with the deep ocean (Fig 10.2). The vertical stratification is, on smaller scales, reproduced in lakes as a function of latitude and season. The consequences of the thermal stratification on the distribution of nutrients is profound.

## ❏ CLOUD ALBEDO

The effect of particle size on light scattering has an interesting connection to cloud optical properties and phytoplankton. Clouds are composed largely of water vapor that has condensed on submicroscopic particles, called cloud condensation nuclei (CCN). CCN are composed of submicrometer particles of sulfate salts. As the number of CCN increases, a given amount of water vapor has more nuclei upon which to condense, thereby decreasing the average droplet size and increasing the light-scattering properties of clouds. Thus, for the same amount of water vapor, clouds with more CCN will scatter more solar radiation than those with fewer CCN. The albedo of clouds is important in regulating the heat budget of the Earth.

Some species of phytoplankton, such as the coccolithophores, produce a compound, dimethylsulfoniopropionate $[(CH_3)_2 S^+ CH_2 CH_2 COO^-]$, that hydrolyzes to the volatile gas dimethyl sulfide $[(CH_3)_2 S]$ (DMS). DMS is subsequently oxidized to form aerosol sulfate particles in the lower atmosphere (Kiene et al. 1996). Sulfate is highly hygroscopic and adsorbs water from the atmosphere; the aerosol sulfate particles are an important CCN source. Charlson et al. (1987) suggested that the biological production of DMS by phytoplankton in the ocean could affect low level cloud albedo over the oceans, and thus influence the Earth's heat budget. Interestingly, over spatial scales of hundreds of kilometers there is a remarkably high correlation between the distribution of phytoplankton chlorophyll and marine stratus cloud albedo in the North Atlantic (Falkowski et al. 1992), suggesting that phytoplankton can influence the Earth's heat budget.

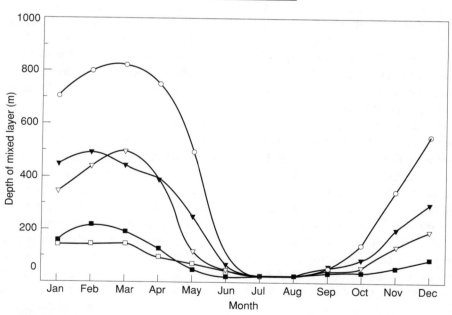

**Figure 10.2** Monthly changes in the average depth of the upper mixed layer of the North Atlantic shown as a function of latitude ($\square$ 33° N, $\blacksquare$ 40° N, $\nabla$ 47° N, $\blacktriangledown$ 54° N, $\bigcirc$ 61° N). Note the extensive depth of the mixed layer in the high latitudes in winter; such dramatic seasonal mixing does not occur elsewhere in the world oceans. Compare the seasonal progression of the mixed layer depth with the seasonal and latitudinal variation in chlorophyll shown in Color Plate 2.

A general feature of aquatic environments is that because the oxidation of organic nutrients to their inorganic forms occurs below the euphotic zone where the competing processes of assimilation of nutrients by photoautotrophs do not occur, the pools of inorganic nutrients are much higher at depth. As the only natural source of photosynthetically active radiation is the sun, the gradients of light and nutrients are from opposite directions. Thermal or salinity differences in the surface layers can produce vertical gradients in density that effectively retard the vertical fluxes of soluble nutrients from depth. Thus, in the surface layers of a stratified water column, nutrients become depleted as the photoautotrophs consume them at rates exceeding their rate of vertical supply (Harrison 1980).

There are two major sources of nutrients in the euphotic zone: (1) the local regeneration of simple forms of combined elements (e.g., $NH_4^+$, $HPO_4^{3-}$, $SO_4^{2-}$) resulting from the metabolic activity of metazoan and microbial degradation; and (2) the influx of distantly produced, "new" nutrients, imported from the deep ocean, the atmosphere (i.e., nitrogen fixation, atmospheric pollution), or terrestrial runoff from streams, rivers, and estuaries. In the open ocean the concept of new and regenerated nutrients (Dugdale, Goering 1967) can be usefully related to the form of inorganic nitrogen assimilated by phytoplankton. Because biological nitrogen fixation is relatively low in the ocean (see below) and nitrification in the upper mixed layer is sluggish relative to the assimilation of nitrogen by photoautotrophs, nitrogen supplied from local regeneration is assimilated before it has a chance to become oxidized. Regenerated nitrogen is primarily in the form of ammonium or urea. In contrast, the fixed inorganic nitrogen in the deep ocean has had sufficient time (hundreds of years) to become oxidized, and hence the major source of new nitrogen is in the form of nitrate. Using $^{15}NH_4$ and $^{15}NO_3$ as tracers, it is possible to estimate the fraction of new nitrogen that fuels phytoplankton production (Dugdale, Wilkerson 1992). This approach provides an estimate of both the upward flux of nitrate required to sustain the $^{15}NO_3^-$-supported production, as well as the downward flux of organic carbon which is required to maintain a steady-state balance (Dugdale et al. 1992; Eppley et al. 1979).

In the steady state, the upward flux and uptake of new nitrogen, which in the open ocean can be assumed to be largely in the form of $NO_3^-$, can be related to the downward flux of organic carbon. The flux of organic carbon from the euphotic zone is often called *export production*, a term coined by Wolfgang Berger. Export production is an important conduit for the exchange of carbon between the upper ocean and the ocean interior (Berger et al. 1987). This conduit depletes the upper ocean of inorganic carbon and other essential nutrients due to photosynthesis and biosynthesis of organic particles. In the central ocean basins, export production is a relatively small fraction of total primary production, amounting to between 5% and 10% of the total carbon fixed per annum (Dugdale, Wilkerson 1992). At high latitudes and in nutrient-rich areas, however, diatoms and other large, heavy cells can form massive blooms and sink rapidly. In such regions, export production can account for 50% of the total carbon fixation (Bienfang 1992; Campbell, Aarup 1992; Sancetta et al. 1991; Walsh 1983). The oxidation and subsequent remineralization of the exported production enriches the ocean interior with inorganic carbon by approximately $300\,\mu M$ in excess of that which would be supported solely by air–sea exchange (Broecker et al. 1980). This enrichment is called the *biological pump* (Sarmiento et al. 1994; Volk, Hoffert 1985). The biological pump is crucial to maintaining the steady-state levels of atmospheric $CO_2$ (Sarmiento et al. 1992; Siegenthaler, Sarmiento 1993).

The concept of new, regenerated, and export production is central to understanding many aspects of the role of aquatic photosynthetic organisms in biogeochemical cycles in the oceans. In the steady state, the globally averaged fluxes of new nutrients must match the losses of the nutrients contained in organic material. If this were not so, there would be a continuous depletion of nutrients in the euphotic zone and photoautotrophic biomass and primary production would slowly decline (Eppley et al. 1979). Thus, in the steady state, the sinking fluxes of organic nitrogen and the production of $N_2$ by denitrifying bacteria must equal the sum of the upward fluxes of inorganic nitrogen, nitrogen fixation, and the atmospheric deposition of fixed nitrogen in the form of aerosols (the latter is produced largely as a consequence of air pollution, and to a lesser extent from lightning).

## THE CONCEPTS OF LIMITATION

In the ecological theater of aquatic ecosystems, the observed photoautotrophic biomass at any moment in time represents a balance between the rate of growth and the rate of removal of that trophic level. For simplicity, we can express the time-dependent change in photoautrophic biomass by a linear differential equation:

$$dB/dt = [B](\mu - m) \tag{10.4}$$

where $[B]$ is photoautrophic biomass (in any convenient unit, e.g., organic carbon, chlorophyll, etc.), $\mu$ is the specific growth rate (units of 1/time), and $m$ is the specific mortality rate (units of 1/time). In this equation, we have lumped all mortality terms, such as grazing, sinking, autocatalytic cell death, and so on, together into one term, although each of these loss processes can be given explicitly (Banse 1994). Two things should be noted regarding Equation 10.4. First, $\mu$ and $m$ are independent variables; that is, changes in $B$ can be independently ascribed to one or the other process. Second, by definition, a steady state exists when $dB/dt$ is zero.

In the Archean and early Proterozoic ocean, oxygen increased in the atmosphere; that is, the global solution to Equation 10.4 must have been > 0. Photoautotrophic biomass could have increased until some element became limiting. Thus, the original feedback between the production of photoautotrophic biomass in the oceans and the atmospheric content of oxygen was determined by an element that limited the crop size of the photoautotrophs in the Archean or Proterozoic ocean. What was that element, and why did it become limiting?

The original notion of limitation in ecology was related to the *yield* of a crop. A limiting factor was the substrate least available relative to the requirement for synthesis of the crop (von Liebig 1840). This concept formed a strong underpinning of agricultural chemistry and was used to design the elemental composition of fertilizers for commercial crops. This concept subsequently was embraced by ecologists and geochemists as a general "law" (Odum 1971).

Nutrients can also limit the *rate* of growth of photoautotrophs (Blackman 1905; Dugdale 1967). Recall that if organisms are in balanced growth (Chapter 8), the rate of uptake of an inorganic nutrient relative to the cellular concentration of the nutrient defines the growth rate (Herbert et al. 1956). The uptake of inorganic nutrients is a hyperbolic function of the nutrient concentration and can be conveniently described by a Michaelis–Menten type (Chapter 5) of expression:

$$V = \left( V_{max}[S] \right) \big/ \left( K_s + [S] \right) \tag{10.5}$$

where $V$ is the instantaneous rate of nutrient uptake, $V_{max}$ is the maximum uptake rate, $[S]$ is the substrate concentration, and $K_s$ is the concentration supporting the half the maximum rate of uptake (Dugdale 1967; Monod 1942). There can be considerable variation between species with regard to $K_s$ and $V_{max}$ values and these variations are potential sources of competitive selection (Eppley et al. 1969). For example, in the oligotrophic open ocean, the $K_s$ values for the uptake of nitrate are frequently $<0.1\,\mu M$, while in coastal waters they are five- to tenfold higher (Garside 1985). Thus, it is sometimes argued that coastal species are at a competitive disadvantage in oligotrophic environments, and are essentially excluded from the latter as a result of inefficient nutrient uptake systems (Kilham, Hecky 1988; Tilman 1982). But it should be noted that since the concentration of dissolved inorganic nitrogen in the upper mixed layer of the central ocean basins is frequently only 5 to 50 nM, even with a $K_s$ of 100 nM, most of the time the uptake systems for nitrogen in cells living in such environments are far from saturated (Harrison et al. 1996). Organisms that thrive in high-nutrient environments, such as diatoms, tend to have higher $V_{max}$ values, and hence can acquire nutrients more rapidly. Thus, when nutrients are supplied in pulses, such as in upwelling conditions or with the passage of an eddy, organisms that have high $V_{max}$ characteristics and can store inorganic nutrients in vacuoles become transiently abundant (McCarthy 1980; Turpin, Harrison 1979).

It should be noted that Liebig's notion of limitation was not related a priori to the intrinsic rate of photosynthesis or growth. For example, photosynthetic rates can be (and often are) limited by light or temperature. These environmental variables are not substantive—they are not part of the plant composition. Assuming light and liquid water are available, ultimately some substance will limit how much of a crop can be produced, although the availability of the substance does not readily predict the rate of crop production (recall the difficulties in relating a pool to a flux as discussed in Chapter 5). Recognizing the distinction between the yield and rate of growth, the British plant physiologist FF Blackman (1905) advanced the notion of rate limitation as a physiological, and hence an ecological concept. The two concepts of limitation (yield and rate) are often confused in the aquatic sciences literature. The former is more relevant to biogeochemical cycles, the latter is more critical to selection of species in ecosystems.

## REDFIELD RATIOS

The average level of chemical reduction of carbon in phytoplankton is equivalent to that of carbohydrate, nitrogen is reduced to the level equivalent of ammonia, and phosphorus is at the oxidation level of phosphate. The oxidation of the phyto-planktonic organic matter can be represented by this balanced equation:

$$(CH_2O)_{106}(NH_3)_{16}H_3PO_4 + 138O_2$$
$$\rightarrow 106CO_2 + 122H_2O + 16NO_3^- + PO_4^{3-} + 19H^+ \tag{10.6}$$

In the deep ocean, where photosynthesis is nil and the flux of organic matter from the surface layer is in biochemical equilibrium with the oxidation and (subsequent) remineralization of the nutrient elements, the proportion of C:N:P in the inorganic nutrient pools approximates (but, as we will soon see, does not exactly equal) that of the particulate organic forms (Chapter 8; Redfield 1958). As Equation 10.6 indicates, the oxidation of the organic material consumes molecular oxygen. As the consumption of oxygen is stoichiometric with the rate of regeneration of nitrate and carbon dioxide from organic sources, the degree of oxygen sub-saturation in a water body, sometimes called the *apparent oxygen utilization*, can be used to calculate the amount of nutrients regenerated below the euphotic zone (Sverdrup et al. 1942). For example, the concentration of $NO_3^-$ in the aphotic zone of the Pacific Ocean is approximately $40\,\mu M$. From Equation 10.6 we can calculate that the oxidation of $40\,\mu M$ $NH_3$ to the molar equivalent of $NO_3^-$ requires $345\,\mu M$ $O_2$. This $O_2$ concentration is approximately that of the air-saturated value for seawater at $0\,°C$.

### Nitrogen or Phosphate Limitation?

Globally, nitrogen and phosphorus are the two elements that immediately limit, in a Liebig sense, the biologically mediated carbon assimilation in the oceans by photoautotrophs. We will discuss the role of iron shortly. It is frequently argued that since $N_2$ is abundant in both the ocean and the atmosphere, and, in principle, can be biologically reduced to the equivalent of $NH_3$ by $N_2$-fixing cyanobacteria (i.e., diazotrophs), nitrogen cannot be limiting on geological time scales (Barber 1992; Broecker et al. 1980; Redfield 1958). Therefore, phosphorus, which has no atmospheric source, must ultimately limit biological productivity. The underlying assumptions of these tenets should, however, be considered within the context of the evolution of biogeochemical cycles and the manifestations of those cycles in contemporary aquatic ecosystems.

Where did the nitrate in the ocean interior come from? The original source of fixed inorganic nitrogen for the oceans was via biological nitrogen fixation (Fig 10.3). Although in the Archean atmosphere, electrical discharge or bolide impacts may have promoted NO formation from reaction between $N_2$ and $CO_2$, the yield for this reaction is low. Moreover, atmospheric $NH_3$ would have been photodissociated by UV radiation (Kasting 1990) while $N_2$ would have been stable (Kasting 1990; Warneck 1988). Biological $N_2$ fixation is a strictly anaerobic process (Postgate 1987), and the sequence of the genes encoding the catalytic subunits for nitrogenase is highly conserved in cyanobacteria and other eubacteria, strongly suggesting a common ancestral origin (Zehr et al. 1995). The antiquity and homology of nitrogen fixation capacity also imply that fixed inorganic nitrogen was scarce prior to the

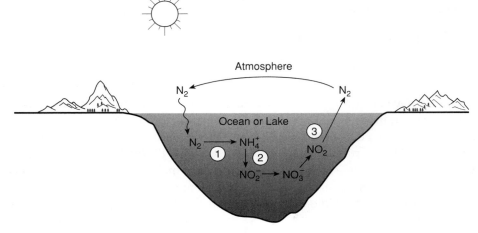

**Figure 10.3** The basic transformations of nitrogen. $N_2$ in the atmosphere is converted to $NH_4^+$, mostly in the upper portion of the water column (1), via the action of prokaryotic nitrogen fixers (primarily cyanobacteria). The $NH_4^+$ is incorporated into photoautotrophs, which sink into the ocean or lake interior. The subsequent heterotrophic oxidation of organic nitrogen provides free $NH_4^+$, which is oxidized through $NO_2^-$ to $NO_3^-$ by nitrifying bacteria (2). This is an oxygen-consuming reaction. $NO_3^-$ can act as electron acceptor for a diverse group of anaerobic bacteria. The reduction of $NO_3^-$ to $NO_2^-$ and subsequently to $N_2O$ and $N_2$ completes the nitrogen cycle (3). Denitrification occurs in suboxic regions with high organic carbon contents, especially continental margins and midwater suboxic regions of the open ocean.

evolution of diazotrophic organisms; that is, there was strong evolutionary selection for nitrogen fixation in the Archean or early Proterozoic periods.

In contrast to fixed inorganic nitrogen, soluble phosphate in the Archean oceans was probably relatively abundant in the mildly reducing environment of the time (Holland 1984; Van Cappellen, Ingall 1996). While apatite and other calcium-based and substituted solid phases of phosphate minerals precipitated in the primary formation of crustal sediments, secondary reactions of phosphate with aluminium and transition metals such as iron are mediated at either low salinity, low pH, or high oxidation states of the cations (Stumm, Morgan 1981). Although these reactions would reduce the overall soluble phosphate concentration, the initial condition of the Archean ocean probably had a very low fixed N:P ratio in the dissolved inorganic phase. As $N_2$ fixation proceeded, that ratio would have increased with a build-up of ammonium in the ocean interior. The accumulation of fixed nitrogen in the oceans would continue until the N:P ratio of the inorganic elements reached equilibrium with the N:P ratio of the sedimenting particulate organic matter (POM). Presumably, the latter ratio would approximate that of extant, nitrogen-fixing marine cyanobacteria, which is 16:1 by atoms (Copin-Montegut, Copin-Montegut 1983; Redfield 1958) or greater (Letelier, Karl 1996) and would ultimately be constrained by the availability of phosphate.

The formation of nitrate from ammonium is sequentially catalyzed through a nitrite intermediate by two groups of aerobic bacteria; one group oxidizes ammonium to nitrite, the second oxidizes nitrite to nitrate. Both processes require molecular oxygen; hence, nitrification must have evolved following the formation of free molecular oxygen in the oceans by oxygenic photoautotrophs. Nitrification also provides reductant for the chemoautotrophic reduction of inorganic carbon, but is thermodynamically much less efficient than photosynthetic carbon fixation (Kaplan 1983). At present, global $CO_2$ fixation by marine nitrifying bacteria only amounts to about $0.2 \, PgC$ per annum (Raven 1996), or <1% of marine photoautotrophic carbon fixation. From a geological perspective, the conversion of ammonium to nitrate probably proceeded rapidly and provided a substrate, $NO_3^-$, that eventually could serve both as a source of nitrogen for photoautotrophs and as an electron acceptor for a diverse group of heterotrophic, anaerobic bacteria, the denitrifiers.

In the sequence of the three major biological processes that constitute the nitrogen cycle, denitrification must have been the last to emerge. This process, which permits the reduction of $NO_3^-$ to (ultimately) $N_2$, occurs in the modern ocean in three major regions, namely, continental margin sediments, areas of restricted circulation such as fjords, and oxygen minima zones of perennially stratified seas (Christensen et al. 1987; Codispoti, Christensen 1985; Devol 1991; Seitzinger 1988). In all cases, the process requires hypoxic environments and is sustained by high sinking fluxes of POM. Denitrification evolved independently several times; the organisms and enzymes responsible for the pathway are highly diverse from a phylogenetic and evolutionary standpoint (Zumpft 1992).

With the emergence of denitrification, the ratio of fixed inorganic N to dissolved inorganic phosphate in the ocean interior could only be depleted in N relative to the sinking flux of the two elements in POM. Indeed, in all of the major basins in the contemporary ocean, the average N:P ratio of the dissolved inorganic nutrients in the ocean interior is conservatively estimated at 14.7 by atoms (Fanning 1992) or less (Anderson, Sarmiento 1994) (Fig 10.4).

There are three major conclusions that may be drawn from the foregoing discussion. First, because the ratio of the sinking flux of particulate organic N and particulate P exceeds the N:P ratio of the dissolved pool of inorganic nutrients in the ocean interior, on average the upward flux of inorganic nutrients must be slightly enriched in P relative to N in relation to the elemental requirements of the photoautotrophs (Gruber, Sarmiento 1997; Redfield 1958). Hence, although there are some exceptions (Krom et al. 1991; Martin 1992), dissolved, inorganic fixed nitrogen generally limits primary production throughout most of the world's oceans (Barber 1992; Dugdale 1967; Eppley, Peterson 1979; McElroy 1983; Ryther, Dunstan 1971). Second, the N:P ratio of the dissolved pool of inorganic nutrients in the ocean interior was established by biological processes, not vice versa (Redfield 1934; Redfield et al. 1963). The elemental composition of marine photoautotrophs has been conserved since the evolution of the eukaryotic phytoplankton (Lipps 1993). The Redfield N:P ratio of 16:1 for particulate organic matter (Copin-Montegut et al. 1983; Redfield 1958) is an *upper bound* that is not observed for the two elements in the dissolved inorganic phase in the ocean interior. The deficit in dissolved inorganic fixed nitrogen relative to soluble phosphate in the ocean implies a slight imbalance between nitrogen fixation and denitrification on time scales of about $10^3$ to $10^4$ years (Codispoti 1995; McElroy 1983; Redfield 1958; Redfield et al. 1963). Finally, if dissolved inorganic nitrogen rather than phosphate limits productivity in

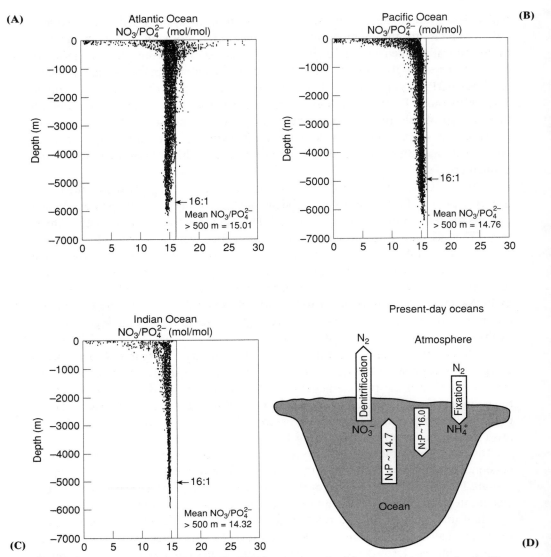

**Figure 10.4** (A–C) Vertical profiles of $NO_3^-/HPO_4^{2-}$ ratios in each of the three major ocean basins. The data were taken from the GEOSECS database. In all three basins, the N:P ratio converges on an average value that is significantly lower than the 16:1 ratio predicted by Redfield. The deficit in N relative to P is presumed to be a result of denitrification. Note that in the upper 500 m of the water column, $NO_3^-/HPO_4^{2-}$ ratios generally decline except in a portion of the Atlantic that corresponds to the eastern Mediterranean. (D) A schematic representation of the discrepancy between the sinking fluxes of nitrogen and phosphate, primarily as particulate organic matter, and the upwelling fluxes of the two elements in the form of inorganic anions.

the oceans, then it follows that the ratio of nitrogen fixation/denitrification plays a critical role in determining the net biologically mediated exchange of $CO_2$ between the atmosphere and ocean (Codispoti 1995).

It should be noted that the Redfield ratios are not generally applicable to estimating nutrient stoichiometries in lakes. Whereas the elemental composition of lacustrian phytoplankton is remarkably similar to that of their marine counterparts, this composition is often not reflected in the chemistry of the inorganic nutrients. Because lakes are relatively small water masses compared with the oceans, are geographically isolated from each other, are markedly influenced by highly variable drainage basins, and are relatively young and short-lived, lake chemistry is far more heterogeneous (Hutchinson 1971; Wetzel 1983). In the northern hemisphere, lakes tend to have inorganic N:P ratios in excess of the Redfield ratio, and hence the biomass of photoautotrophs is frequently limited by phosphate.

The limitation by phosphorus in lacustrine ecosystems is a consequence of two phenomena. First, phosphorus, in its ionic form of phosphate, becomes tightly bound to mineral cations in particulates, thereby forming insoluble phosphate complexes. As, on average, the surface area of particles per unit volume of water is one to three orders of magnitude greater in lakes than in marine environments, the availability of the element in the former environment is low (Froelich 1988). In contrast, the ionic forms of fixed nitrogen (primarily $NH_4^+$ and $NO_3^-$) do not form insoluble complexes, and hence fixed inorganic nitrogen tends to remain dissolved. Second, the numbers of species and population density of nitrogen-fixing cyanobacteria is usually far greater in lakes than in marine environments (Howarth et al. 1988). Thus, as fixed inorganic nitrogen concentrations become low, biological nitrogen fixation is often capable of supplying a sufficient flux of fixed nitrogen to meet photosynthetic demands in many lacustrine ecosystems. Hence, in lacustrine environments nutrients other than nitrogen generally limit biomass of algae, and the concepts of new and regenerated production, while still conceptually valid, are not experimentally as useful as in marine ecosystems.

### The Distribution of Photoautotrophic Biomass

With a few notable exceptions, the spatial and temporal distribution of phytoplankton biomass in the oceans corresponds to the distribution of nutrients, as long as the mixed layer depth is shallower than the critical depth (Chapter 9). The circulation of the major ocean basins is characterized by gyres, which rotate clockwise in the North Atlantic and Pacific, and counterclockwise in the southern hemisphere oceans (Sverdrup et al. 1942). The gyres are primarily a consequence of the poleward fluxes of heat carried by the atmosphere and oceans in the form of winds and currents, superimposed on a rotating Earth. The rotation necessarily produces a Coriolis[3] effect that tends to force fluids in the northern hemisphere to turn to the right of their direction of motion, and vice versa in the southern hemisphere. From an oceanographic standpoint, a major consequence of the rotation of the gyres is to induce upwelling along the edges of the rotating field, which enhances the rate of nutrient flux to the euphotic zone. Thus, in tropical and subtropical regions where

---

3. Recall that Coriolis was a student of Poisson (Chapter 3). He formalized the laws of motion for objects moving on a rotating sphere. Their application to geophysical fluid dynamics is summarized in the equation $F = -2\omega \sin \psi v$, where $\omega$ is the angular velocity of the Earth ($= 0.729 \times 10^{-4} s^{-1}$), $\psi$ is latitude, $v$ is the component of velocity, and F is the Coriolis "force." This force (or more appropriately an effect) quantifies the rate at which an object or fluid in the northern hemisphere will tend to move to the right, while in the southern hemisphere it will move to the left.

the perennial thermocline retards the upward flux of nutrients, phytoplankton biomass is low throughout the year but is enhanced along coastal boundaries where upwelling circulation occurs. In temperate regions, the upper ocean becomes recharged with nutrients following deep convective mixing of the surface waters to depth in the winter. At the onset of stratification in the spring, phytoplankton blooms develop, consuming the surface nutrients. The magnitude of the bloom is limited by the initial nutrient concentration set by the depth of mixing in the preceding winter. The rate of supply of nutrients is a major determinant of the distribution of photoautotrophic biomass in aquatic systems (Yentsch 1980).

The vertical distribution of phytoplankton in the stratified open ocean is characterized by a chlorophyll maximum that closely corresponds to the nutrient gradient (Fig 10.5) (Cullen 1982). Such features represent areas of higher pigment biomass due to the upwelling flux of nutrients. Horizontally, in upwelling regions such as those off the coast of Peru or northwestern Africa, phytoplankton blooms are persistent, whereas in permanently stratified regions of the subtropics phytoplankton biomass is one to two orders of magnitude lower. Similarly, coastal regions of the oceans often have higher photoautotrophic biomass as a consequence of coastal upwelling or riverine fluxes of nutrients (Walsh 1988). Seasonal blooms in temperate latitudes, or in tropical monsoon regions such as the Arabian Sea, are primarily a consequence of increases in nutrient supplies from depth to the euphotic zone. In the former case, the increase is a consequence of deep convective mixing

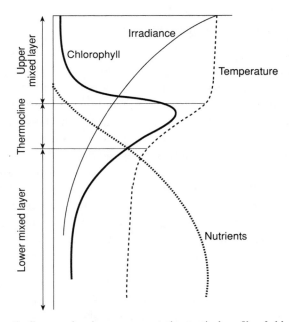

**Figure 10.5** A schematic diagram showing a representative vertical profile of chlorophyll biomass, temperature, irradiance, and nutrients in a stratified water column. The region of greatest vertical stability is that of the thermocline (or pycnocline). Chlorophyll biomass is generally highest in or slightly above the thermocline.

arising from heat exchange between the atmosphere and the water column; in the latter it is a consequence of wind-driven turbulent mixing of and deepening of the upper mixed layer (Mann, Lazier 1991).

The distribution of phytoplankton biomass can be inferred from the concentration of chlorophyll, which, in turn can be conveniently estimated from satellite images of the ocean color. Because of the wavelength dependence of light scattering in water (Chapter 2), the light reflected back to an observer looking down at an imaginary ocean or lake consisting solely of water (with or without dissolved salts) would be blue (Kirk 1994b). The Soret bands of chlorins and the blue-absorbing bands of carotenoids can absorb both the downwelling and upwelling stream of photons, thereby depleting the outbound radiation of blue light. Thus, as photosynthetic pigments increase, the water becomes darker and the ratio of outbound blue to green photons decreases (Fig 10.6).

Empirically, satellite sensors that measure ocean color utilize a number of wavelengths. In addition to the blue and green region, red and far-red spectra are determined to derive corrections for scattering and absorption of the outbound or reflected radiation from the ocean by the atmosphere. In fact, only a small fraction (about 5%) of the light leaving the ocean is observed by a satellite; the vast majority of the photons are scattered or absorbed in the atmosphere. However, based on the ratio of blue–green light that is reflected from the ocean, estimates of photosynthetic pigments are derived. It should be pointed out that the Soret, or blue-

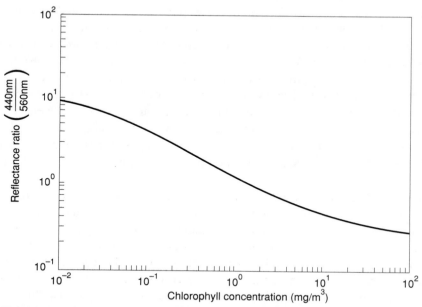

**Figure 10.6** An example of an algorithm relating the ratio of water leaving radiances in the blue (440 nm) and green (560 nm) to the upper ocean "blue-absorbing" pigment concentration. The correlation between "blue-absorbing pigments" and chlorophyll *a* is statistically linear and empirically derived. This type of algorithm is used to derive chlorophyll concentrations from satellite-based measurements of ocean color. (Adapted from Gorden, Morel 1983)

absorbing, region of the spectrum is highly congested; it is virtually impossible to derive the fraction of absorption due solely to chlorophyll *a* as opposed to some other pigment that absorbs blue light (e.g., phaeophytin *a*). The estimation of chlorophyll *a* is based on empirical regression of the concentration of the pigment to the total blue-absorbing pigments (Gordon, Morel 1983). Water-leaving radiances ($L_w$) at specific wavelengths are corrected for atmospheric scattering and absorption, and the concentration of chlorophyll (really the total of all blue-absorbing pigments) is calculated from the ratios of blue and green light reflected from the water body. Examples of two such wavelength ratio algorithms are:

$$Chl = 1.15\left(L_w[443]/L_w[560]\right)^{-1.42} \quad \text{for Chl} < 1 \text{ mg m}^{-3} \tag{10.7}$$

and

$$Chl = 3.64\left(L_w[500]/L_w[560]\right)^{-2.62} \quad \text{for Chl} > 1 \text{ mg m}^{-3} \tag{10.8}$$

Where Chl is chlorophyll *a* in mg/m³. The coefficient of determination for these equations is >0.95 and the relative error is approximately 20% for Equation 10.7 and 30% for Equation 10.8 (Lewis 1992).

One important limitation of satellite images of ocean chlorophyll is that they do not provide information about the vertical distribution of phytoplankton. The water-leaving radiances visible to an observer outside of the ocean are approximately confined to the upper 20% of the euphotic zone. The chlorophyll maximum is almost always located in the lower 20% of the euphotic zone, and thus is not visible to satellite ocean color sensors. A number of numerical models have been developed to estimate the vertical distribution of chlorophyll based on satellite color data (Berthon, Morel 1992; Platt 1986). The models rely on statistical parameterizations and require numerous in situ observations to obtain "typical" profiles for a given area of the world ocean (Morel, Andre 1991; Platt, Sathyendranath 1988). In addition, large quantities of phytoplankton associated with the bottom of ice floes in both the Arctic and Antarctic are not visible to satellite sensors but do contribute significantly to the primary production in the polar seas (Smith, Nelson 1990). Despite these deficiencies, the satellite data allow high-resolution, large-field, synoptic observations of the temporal and spatial changes in phytoplankton chlorophyll in relation to the physical circulation of the atmosphere and ocean on a global scale.

The global, seasonal distribution of phytoplankton chlorophyll in the upper ocean, derived from a compilation of satellite images, is shown in Color Plate 2. To a first order, the images reveal how the horizontal and temporal distribution of phytoplankton is related to the ratio of the fluxes of new and regenerated nutrients and the critical depth. For example, throughout most of the central ocean basins, between 30°N and 30°S, phytoplankton biomass is extremely low, averaging 0.1 to 0.2 mg chlorophyll *a* m⁻³ at the sea surface. In these regions the vertical flux of nutrients is generally extremely low, limited by eddy diffusion through the thermocline. Most of the chlorophyll biomass is associated with the thermocline. Because there is no seasonal convective overturn in this latitude band, there is no seasonal variation in phytoplankton chlorophyll. A slight elevation in chlorophyll is found at the equator in the Pacific and Atlantic Oceans, and south of the equator in the Indian Ocean. In the equatorial regions the thermocline shoals laterally as a result of long-range wind stress at the surface (Pickard, Emery 1990). The wind effectively piles up water along its fetch, thereby inclining the upper mixed layer (Fig 10.7). This results in increased nutrient fluxes, shallower mixed layers, and higher chlorophyll concentrations on the eastern end of the equatorial band, and decreased nutrient fluxes, deeper mixed layers, and lower chlorophyll concentrations on the western end. This effect is most pronounced in the Pacific. The displacement of the band south of the equator in the Indian Ocean is primarily a consequence of basin scale topography.

At latitudes above approximately 30°, a seasonal cycle in chlorophyll can occur. In the northern hemisphere, areas of high chlorophyll are found in open ocean in the North Atlantic in the spring (April–June) and summer (July–September). The southern extent and intensity of the North Atlantic phytoplankton bloom are not found in the North Pacific. In the southern hemisphere, phytoplankton chlorophyll is generally reduced at latitudes symmetrical with the northern hemi-

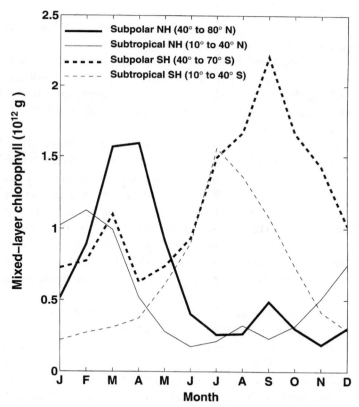

**Figure 10.7** Seasonal variations in the depth-integrated chlorophyll concentrations in the upper mixed layer of the northern (NH) and southern (SH) hemisphere oceans. The seasonal chlorophyll maxima are higher at higher latitudes in both hemispheres. These data, which show the seasonality of phytoplankton biomass in the oceans, were derived from calculations of ocean color images using climatological atlases to infer mixed layer depths. (Courtesy of JA Yoder, KL Howard, and RP Ryan)

sphere in the corresponding austral seasons. For example, in the austral summer (January–March), phytoplankton chlorophyll is slightly lower between 30° S and the Antarctic ice sheets than in the northern hemisphere in July to September (Yoder et al. 1993).

## PRIMARY PRODUCTIVITY IN THE PRESENT OCEAN

Using satellite data of ocean color to estimate upper-ocean chlorophyll concentrations, satellite-based observations of incident solar radiation, atlases of seasonally averaged sea-surface temperature, and a model that incorporates a nonlinear temperature response function for photosynthesis, it is possible to estimate global net photosynthesis in the world oceans (Antoine, Morel 1996; Behrenfeld, Falkowski 1997a; Longhurst et al. 1995). Although estimates vary between models based on how the parameters are derived, for illustrative purposes we use a model based on empirical parameterization of the daily integrated photosynthesis profiles as a function of depth. The model uses the following general equation:

$$PP_{eu} = C_{sat} \cdot Z_{eu} \cdot P_{opt}^{B} \cdot DL \cdot F \qquad (10.9)$$

where $PP_{eu}$ is daily net primary production integrated over the euphotic zone, $C_{sat}$ is the satellite-based (upper water column) chlorophyll concentration, $P_{opt}^{B}$ is the maximum daily photosynthetic rate within the water column, $Z_{eu}$ is the depth of the euphotic zone, $DL$ is the photoperiod (Behrenfeld, Falkowski 1997a), and $F$ is a function describing the shape of the photosynthesis depth profile. This model is similar to others used in both ocean (Behrenfeld, Falkowski 1997b) and lake (Vollenweider 1970) calculations.

Using climatological sea-surface temperatures (Levitus 1982) and satellite-based estimates of incident solar radiation that include the effects of clouds (Bishop 1991), the model predicts that primary production in the world oceans amounts to about 40 Pg per annum (Color Plates 3 & 4). In an imaginary scenario where all clouds are removed from the world, the model predicts that primary production would increase by about 4.5%. The reason for the relatively small increase is that the increased photon flux is offset by increased photoinhibition, especially at low latitudes (Antoine et al. 1996; Behrenfeld, Falkowski 1996). If there were no photoinhibition, the model suggests that primary production would increase in the ocean by about 10%.

The photosynthetically available radiation for the world oceans is $4.5 \times 10^{18}$ moles per annum, which is approximately equal to $9.8 \times 10^{20}$ kJ/yr. The average energy stored by photosynthetic organisms amounts to about 39 kJ per gram of carbon fixed (Platt, Irwin 1973). Given an annual net production of 40 Pg C for phytoplankton, and an estimated production of 4 Pg/yr by benthic photoautotrophs, the photosynthetically stored radiation is equal to about $1.7 \times 10^{18}$ kJ/yr. The fraction of photosynthetically available solar energy conserved by photosynthetic reactions in the world oceans amounts to $1.7 \times 10^{18}/9.8 \times 10^{20} = 0.0017$ or 0.17%. Thus, in the oceans, 0.0007 mol C is fixed on average per mole of incident photons; this is equivalent to an effective quantum requirement of 1400 quanta per $CO_2$ fixed!

The average surface chlorophyll concentration of the world ocean is $0.28\,mg/m^3$ and the average euphotic zone depth is 56 m; thus, the average, integrated chlorophyll concentration is about $22\,mg/m^2$ (Morel 1991). Carbon to chlorophyll ratios of phytoplankton typically range between 40:1 and 100:1 by weight (Banse 1977). Given the total area of the ocean of $3.1 \times 10^8\,km^2$, the total carbon biomass in phytoplankton is between 0.25 to 0.65 Pg. If net primary production is about 40 Pg/yr, and assuming the ocean is in steady state (a condition we will discuss in more detail), the living phytoplankton biomass turns over between 60 and 150 times per year, which is equivalent to a turnover time of 2 to 6 days. In contrast, terrestrial plant biomass amounts to approximately 600 to 800 Pg C, most of which is in the form of wood (Woodwell et al. 1978). Estimates of terrestrial plant net primary production range from about 50 to 65 Pg C per annum, which gives an average turnover time ranging from about 12 to 16 years. Thus, the flux of carbon through aquatic photosynthetic organisms is about a thousandfold faster than terrrestrial ecosystems, while the storage of carbon in the latter is about a thousandfold higher than the former. Moreover, the total photon flux to terrestrial environments amounts to about $2 \times 10^{18}\,mol/yr$, which gives an effective quantum yield of about 0.002. In other words, on average one $CO_2$ molecule is fixed for each 500 incident photons. The results of these calculations suggest that terrestrial vegetation is approximately three times more efficient in utilizing *incident* solar radiation to fix carbon than are aquatic photoautotrophs. This situation arises primarily because of the relative paucity of aquatic photoautotrophs and the fact that they must compete with the medium (water) for light.

## Major Global Biogeochemical Cycles Mediated by Aquatic Photosynthetic Organisms

The present-day atmosphere contains approximately 21% by volume of $O_2$ and only 0.35% by volume of $CO_2$. As photosynthesis and respiration on a global scale are coupled processes, it might be expected that the presence of such a vast quantity of free $O_2$ requires that an equal if not larger amount of photosynthetically derived organic carbon escaped respiratory consumption. Such carbon should be stored as "fossil" organic carbon. Thus, if it is assumed that the original oxygen in the Earth's atmosphere was derived from oxygenic photosynthetic processes in the Archean ocean, the very existence of oxygen in the atmosphere means that globally, respiration and photosynthesis were not always in steady state (Sarmiento, Bender 1994). Indeed this is the case; however, the quantity of fossil organic carbon buried in the crusted sedimentary rocks is far more than predicted based on a 1:1 molar stoichiometry (see Table 5.1). Moreover, fossil oxygen was used to oxidize inorganic substrates, especially iron and sulfur. The oxidation of iron to its common form $Fe^{3+}$, and $S^{2-}$ to $SO_4^{2-}$, resulting from oxygenic photosynthesis, led to major changes in ocean chemistry. The photosynthetic production of oxygen that led to the oxidation of iron in the oceans almost certainly resulted in a negative feedback, whereby photosynthesis became iron limited. In contrast, the concentration of $SO_4^{2-}$ in oceans is second only to chloride in terms of soluble anions, and hence sulfur is never limiting (Redfield 1958). The difference between the sedimentary organic carbon deposits and the sum of the oxidizing equivalents stored in $Fe^{3+}$ and $SO_4^{2-}$ approximately equals the reservoir of total gaseous oxygen (Holland 1984).

Geochemical reconstructions of the concentrations of atmospheric $CO_2$ and $O_2$ suggest significant variations in these two gases have occurred, even following the evolution of early terrestrial higher plants approximately 450 million years ago. A significant determinant of $O_2$ on these time scales has been the global reservoirs of organic carbon and oxidized sulfur and iron at given times (Berner 1990). On the whole, the balance of organic carbon and oxidized sulfur and iron is ultimately determined by tectonic processes that alter rates of burial and exposure of marine sediments. However, the oxidation and reduction processes that lead to the changes in the gaseous composition of the atmosphere are biologically mediated and the geochemical cycles of the major elements are invariably coupled (Williams 1981), meaning that they are interactive. Hence changes in the nitrogen cycle can affect the carbon cycle and alterations in the iron cycle can affect the nitrogen cycle. The interaction of the elements with aquatic photoautotrophs is often a consequence of oxidation-reduction processes, and these processes have greatly affected the distribution of the elements on Earth (Warneck 1988).

Prior to the evolution of oxygenic photosynthesis, the oceans contained high concentrations (about 1 mM) of dissolved iron in the form of $Fe^{2+}$ and manganese (>1 mM) in the form of $Mn^{2+}$, but essentially no copper, as that element would have been precipitated as $Cu_2S$. Thus both Fe and Mn were readily available to the early photoautotrophs, and the availability of these two elements permitted the evolution of the two reaction centers and the oxygen-evolving system that ultimately became the genetic template for all oxygenic photoautotrophs (Blankenship 1992). Hence, the availability of these transition metals, which is largely determined by the oxidation state of the environment, appears to account for their use in photosynthetic reactions.

As photosynthetic oxygen evolution proceeded in the Archean oceans, singlet oxygen ($^1O_2$), peroxide ($H_2O_2$), superoxide anion radicals ($O_2^-$), and hydroxide radicals ($\cdot OH$) were all formed as byproducts (Kasting 1990; Kasting et al. 1988). These oxygen derivatives can oxidize proteins and photosynthetic pigments as well as cause damage to reaction centers (Asada 1994). A range of molecules evolved to scavenge or quench the potentially harmful oxygen byproducts. These molecules include both carotenoids that quench singlet oxygen (see Chapter 2), $\alpha$-tocopherol (and plastoquinol; Hundal et al. 1995), which scavenges lipid-dissolved $\cdot OH$ radicals, and ascorbate which scavenges water-dissolved toxic oxygen species, as well as enzymes such as superoxide dismutase (which converts $O_2^-$ to $O_2$ and $H_2O_2$), peroxidase (which reduces $H_2O_2$ to $H_2O$ by oxidizing an organic cosubstrate for the enzyme), and catalase (which converts $2H_2O_2$ to $H_2O$ and $O_2$). The oldest superoxide dismutases contained Fe and/or Mn, while the peroxidases and catalases contained Fe (Asada et al. 1980). These transition metals facilitate the electron transfer reactions that are at the core of the respective enzyme activity, and their incorporation into the proteins undoubtedly occurred because the metals were readily available (Williams 1981). As $O_2$ production proceeded, the oxidation of $Fe^{2+}$, $Mn^{2+}$, and

$S^{2-}$ eventually led to the virtual depletion of these forms of the elements in the euphotic zone of the oceans. The depletion of these elements had profound consequences on the subsequent evolution of life. In the first instance, a number of enzymes were selected that incorporated alternative transition metals that were available in the oxidized ocean. For example, a superoxide dismutase evolved in the charophyceans, and hence higher plants (and many nonphotosynthetic eukaryotes) that utilized Cu and Zn. Moreover, the presence of $O_2$ permitted the development of aerobic respiration, which is far more efficient (i.e., more $H^+$ are actively transported per electron transferred) than with the previously possible anaerobic pathways that used such substrates as $S^{2-}$ as the terminal electron acceptor (Raven, Beardall 1981a).

Another example of the effect of oxygen evolution on the choice of metals used in the electron transport chain is plastocyanin. Recall from Chapter 4 that, in the absence of copper, cyanobacteria induce the soluble cytochrome $c_6$ ($c_{553}$) that ferries electrons from the cytochrome $b_6/f$ complex to $P_{700}$. Cytochrome $c_6$ appeared earlier in the evolution of photosynthetic organisms than plastocyanin; anaerobic photosynthetic bacteria contain only cytochromes (Blankenship et al. 1995). In the anaerobic Archean ocean, where the availability of Fe was much greater than that of Cu, the utilization of the former metal in this electron transfer reaction was favored. As the oceans became increasingly oxic, copper became increasingly available and was appropriated for this electron transfer step. The terminal oxidase in aerobic respiration, cytochrome oxidase, contains Cu, and the redox status of the metal couples iron-based cytochrome oxidation to molecular $O_2$. The metal ultimately became incorporated into all eukaryotic photoautotrophic mitochondrial $H^+$-pumping electron transport chains.

Despite metal substitutions, some critical photosynthetic electron transfer reactions remained dependent on Fe and Mn, and aquatic photoautotrophs evolved mechanisms to acquire these scarce elements (Morel et al. 1991). These mechanisms often included the formation of extracellular organic complexes that chelated the elements, thereby keeping the oxidized forms in dissolved or colloidal states (Hughes, Poole 1989). It would appear that most of the iron in the aquatic ecosystems is in fact bound to organics.

The build-up of $O_2$ in the atmosphere permitted the formation of stratospheric ozone by the photochemical reaction described in Chapter 9. As the optical absorption cross-section for UV-B radiation by $O_3$ is very large (Crutzen 1988), the flux of UV-B radiation reaching the Earth's surface decreased without a concomitant decrease in photosynthetically available radiation. The decrease in UV-B probably reduced the rate of genetic mutation in aquatic organisms. Simultaneously, however, the presence of $O_2$ permitted the action of a vanadium-containing halogen peroxidase that reacts with organic compounds to form halocarbons. Bromoperoxidase is widespread in algae, and is a significant source of natural halocarbons in the oceans (Gschwend et al. 1985; Manley et al. 1992; Moore, Tokarczyk 1993). The low molecular mass halocarbons evade to the atmosphere where they are oxidized by $OH^{\cdot}$ radicals to form $Cl^{\cdot}$ and $Br^{\cdot}$. These halogen radicals can destroy stratospheric $O_3$ in the same manner as anthropogenically produced halocarbons (Chapter 9). Hence, the evolution of $O_2$ permitted the formation of a UV-B screen in the form of stratospheric $O_3$ and the partial destruction of the screen via the formation of halocarbons (Raven 1997).

Over the past several hundred thousand years, interpretation of the sources and sinks of $O_2$ has been inferred from variations in $^{18}O/^{16}O$ ratios of relict atmospheric $O_2$, obtained, for example, from gaseous bubbles trapped in ice cores in polar regions (Barnola et al. 1987; Bender, Sowers 1994). As $O_2$ originates from the photosynthetic oxidation of water, and the major source of water on Earth is the ocean, isotopic fractionation of atmospheric $O_2$ can reveal the integrated effects of photosynthesis and respiration on long (i.e., geological) time scales. Atmospheric $O_2$ has a higher ratio of $^{18}O_2/^{16}O_2$ than standard mean ocean water (SMOW); the enrichment averages about 24.6%. This fractionation, called the *Dole effect* (Dole et al. 1954), primarily is a consequence of the discrimination against the heavier isotope in respiration; the fractionation by photosynthetic organisms is relatively small (Berry 1992). Analysis of the variations in the Dole effect over the past 150,000 years reveals very small changes, suggesting that globally, photosynthesis and respiration have been largely balanced (Bender, Sowers 1994). Over this period of time, however, there have been two major glacial cycles that have markedly altered the surface area of the open ocean and affected oceanic photosynthetic carbon fixation. Thus, changes in oceanic photosynthesis and respiration were presumably compensated for by terrestrial photosynthesis and respiration to maintain some quasi–steady-state in the isotopic ratio of oxygen in the atmosphere.

## Milankovitch Cycles

Although the isotopic ratio of atmospheric oxygen may have remained relatively constant over the past several hundred thousand years, the concentration of atmospheric $CO_2$ fluctuated between approximately 190 $\mu mol\,mol^{-1}$ (i.e., ppm) and 280 $\mu mol\,mol^{-1}$ (Barnola et al. 1987). These fluctuations occurred on time scales of about 100,000 years, with the last minimum occurring approximately 20,000 years ago (Fig 10.8).

The causes for variations in atmospheric $CO_2$ in glacial–interglacial periods are contentious, but the variations are correlated with variations in the Earth's orbital cycles, which were predicted by a Serbian astronomer, Milutin Milankovitch (1879–1958) (Berger 1988). Based on astronomical observations of the variations in the Earth's orbit, Milankovitch predicted orbital variations due to variations in precession, with a period of about 23,000 years; obliquity, with a period of about 41,000 years; and eccentricity, with a period of about 100,000 years. These orbital variations force changes in the solar "constant" of the Earth (Eq 10.3), presumably triggering periodic glacial and interglacial episodes.

The *Milankovitch cycles* have been highly correlated with changes in a wide variety of marine sedimentary proxy indices of aquatic photosynthesis (Imbrie et al. 1992). One of the most useful of such indicators is the abundance and distribution of calcareous fossilized shells from coccolithophores and foraminifera. The occurrence of cadmium within the calcium carbonate matrices of these fossils is used

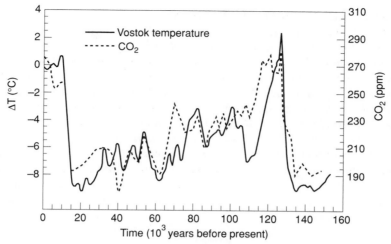

**Figure 10.8** Variations in atmospheric temperature and $CO_2$ as derived from measurements through an ice core taken from the Vostok station in Antarctica. Note that the initial decrease in temperature ca. 110,000 years ago preceded the drawdown in $CO_2$; i.e., the latter was a response to, not a cause of, the climatic variation. For comparison, present-day atmospheric $CO_2$ levels are about 370 ppm. (Adapted from Crowley, North 1991)

to infer the concentration of phosphate in the ocean; empirically, Cd is highly correlated with dissolved $H_2PO_4^{2-}$ in the ocean waters, but once incorporated into the carbonate matrix the metal is not labile (Boyle et al. 1976). The stable isotopic composition of the carbon and oxygen atoms is used to infer $pCO_2$, and the temperature (and indirectly, salinity) of the ocean, respectively, at the time of formation of the shell (Boyle 1986). The concentrations of the constituents in the deposited shells are used to infer export production on geological time scales. These indices suggest that during glacial periods, the surface waters of the open ocean have higher nutrient contents, higher salinity, and apparently higher rates of export production (Berger et al. 1989). The higher rates of export production maintained a relatively low $pCO_2$ at the ocean surface, which presumably may have contributed to a drawdown of atmospheric $CO_2$ (Jasper et al. 1995). What caused the changes in atmospheric $CO_2$?

**High-Nutrient Regions of the Ocean**

In the Quaternary, cyclic oscillations in organic carbon deposition in marine sediments appear to be inversely correlated with atmospheric $CO_2$ (Altabet et al. 1995; Bender, Sowers 1994; Berger et al. 1989; Farrell et al. 1995; Imbrie et al. 1992; Paytan et al. 1996; Raynaud et al. 1993; Schrader 1992). These observations imply that changes in the biological $CO_2$ pump in the oceans have occurred on time scales of $10^3$ to $10^4$ years (Broecker 1982). How could such changes occur?

There are three major areas of the world ocean where inorganic nitrogen and phosphate are in excess throughout the year, yet the mixed layer depth appears to be shallower than the critical depth; these are the eastern equatorial Pacific, the sub-

### ❏ LONG-TERM CLIMATIC FORCING

*The Milankovitch-forced glacial–interglacial cycles can be traced back over the past several million years of the Earth's history. Prior to that period, however, climatic variations in ocean circulation were dramatic. For example, in the mid-Cretaceous epoch, approximately 100 million years ago, the bottom waters of the ocean basins appear to have been approximately 17 °C and were probably anoxic. During this period black shales formed, and such warm periods were followed by glaciations. The causes of the fluctuations in climate can only be speculated (Barron, Washington 1985). To some extent, photosynthetic drawdown of $CO_2$ from the atmosphere was certainly a contributing factor that led to cooling periods. Some cases, for example the transition from the Cretaceous to the Tertiary epoch 60 million years ago (the so-called K-T boundary), appear to have been consequences of the collision with the Earth of an enormous meteorite (Alvarez et al. 1980).*

---

arctic Pacific, and Southern (i.e., Antarctic) Oceans. In the subarctic North Pacific, it has been suggested that there is a tight coupling between phytoplankton production and consumption by zooplankton (Miller et al. 1991). This grazer limited hypothesis is offered to explain why the phytoplankton in the North Pacific do not form massive blooms in the spring and summer like their counterparts in the North Atlantic (Banse 1992). In the mid-1980s, it became increasingly clear that the concentration of trace metals, especially iron, was extremely low in all three of these regions (Martin 1991). Indeed, in the eastern equatorial Pacific, for example, the concentration of soluble iron in the euphotic zone is only 100 to 200 pM. Although iron is the most abundant transition metal in the Earth's crust, in its most commonly occurring form, $Fe^{3+}$, it is virtually insoluble in seawater. The major source of iron to the euphotic zone is aeolian dust, originating from continental deserts. In the three major areas of the world oceans with high inorganic nitrogen in the surface waters and low chlorophyll concentrations, the flux of aeolean iron is extremely low (Duce, Tindale 1991). In experiments in which iron was artificially added on a relatively large scale ($4 \times 4$ km) to the waters in the equatorial Pacific, there were rapid and dramatic increases in photosynthetic energy conversion efficiency and phytoplankton chlorophyll (Behrenfeld et al. 1996; Kolber et al. 1994).

In the iron-limited regions of the oceans, the quantum yields of photosynthesis are also reduced, but the molecular basis of the limitation differs from that of nitrogen limitation. Iron limitation leads to loss of PSI and PSII reaction centers, without a corresponding loss of the antenna pigments. Thus, in iron-limited cells, absorbed excitation energy has a reduced probability of finding a photochemical trap, and correspondingly a higher probability of being reemitted as fluorescence. Indeed, in the iron-limited equatorial Pacific, the quantum yields of photochemistry are approximately one-third that of nutrient replete regions, while the quantum yield of chlorophyll fluorescence (i.e., the ratio of photons emitted to photons absorbed) is up to sixfold higher (Greene et al. 1994). The deficiency in reaction centers appears to be a consequence of an inability to assemble functional electron transfer components in the face of iron limitation (Vassiliev et al. 1995). In addition to affecting the coupling of light harvesting to electron transport, iron limitation can dramatically affect the stoichiometry between PSII and PSI reaction centers. In cyanobacteria, for example, PSI/PSII reaction center ratios are generally much greater than unity, averaging about 3 or 4. Under iron-limiting conditions there is a differential degradation (or lack of synthesis) of PSI reaction centers, such that the ratio of the two photosystems approaches unity. This type of limitation can lead to competitive selection of species that is related to variations in the photosynthetic apparatus. When iron is added to the high nitrate region of the eastern equatorial Pacific, for example, the quantum efficiency of PSII increases rapidly and markedly in the extant *Prochlorococcus* and cyanobacteria community that dominate the phytoplankton (Kolber et al. 1994). However, over a period of a few days, diatoms, which generally have a higher $V_{max}$ (see Eq 10.5) for macronutrients than do the prokaryotes, become dominant. Subsequently, the photosynthetic rate of the diatoms per unit volume of seawater greatly exceeds that of the cyanobacteria, leading to a transient drawdown of $CO_2$ in the euphotic zone. However, if iron were to be supplied continuously the macronutrients would become depleted and the cyanobacteria and prochlorophytes would emerge dominant. In short, nutrient deficiency is a form of stress on photosynthetic energy conversion efficiency that leads to selection of species via competition for a limited resource (Brand 1991).

### Glacial–Interglacial Changes in the Biological $CO_2$ Pump

In an analysis of ice cores from Antarctica, reconstruction of aeolian iron depositions and concurrent atmospheric $CO_2$ concentrations over the past 160,000 years (spanning two glacial cycles) suggests that when iron fluxes were high, $CO_2$ levels were low and vice versa (Martin 1990). Variations in iron fluxes were presumably a consequence of the areal extent of terrestrial deserts and wind vectors. It is hypothesized that increased fluxes of iron to the Southern Ocean stimulated phytoplankton photosynthesis and led to a drawdown of atmospheric $CO_2$. Model calculations suggest that the magnitude of this drawdown could have been cumulatively significant, and accounted for the observed variations in atmospheric $CO_2$ recorded in gases trapped in the ice cores. However, the sedimentary records reveal large glacial fluxes of organic carbon in low- and mid-latitude regions, areas that are presumably nutrient impoverished.

During recent glacial periods, the depression in sea level and corresponding reduction in continental shelf area, combined with a decrease in the intensity of stratification in tropical regions (Herguerra, Berger 1994), appear to have resulted in decreased rates of denitrification relative to nitrogen fixation (Altabet et al. 1995; Ganeshram et al. 1995). Consequently, the ratio of dissolved inorganic nitrogen to phosphate could "catch up" with that of the sinking flux, effectively enhancing the biological $CO_2$ pump. Assuming conservatively a net deficit of dissolved inorganic nitrogen over phosphate in the modern ocean of only 1.3 μmol/kg, the biological pump for $CO_2$ could sequester an additional 300 to 500 Pg C. During glacial periods, this net drawdown would have been further accelerated by eolian transport of minerals to the central ocean basins. The increased flux of iron to the oceans would not only have stimulated the biological pump in the high-nutrient, low-chlorophyll regions (Sarmiento, Orr 1991), but more importantly, would have stimulated $N_2$ fixation in the low-nutrient, low-chlorophyll regions.

The changes in the ratio of $N_2$ fixation relative to denitrification required to produce the inferred changes in atmospheric $CO_2$ are small. The Byrd and Vostok ice core records suggest that atmospheric $CO_2$ declined from approximately $290\,\mu mol\,mol^{-1}$ to $190\,\mu mol\,mol^{-1}$ over a period of ca. 40,000 years between the last interglacial–glacial maximum (Raynaud et al. 1993). Given a C:N ratio of about 6.6 by atoms for the synthesis of new organic matter in the euphotic zone, an equilibrium, three-box model calculation suggests that 2400 Pg of inorganic carbon would have to have been fixed by marine photoautotrophs to account for the change in atmospheric $CO_2$. This amount of carbon is tenfold higher than that released from the cumulative combustion of fossil fuels, which resulted in an increase in $CO_2$. This model accounts for repartitioning of $CO_2$ between the atmosphere and the upper ocean, including internal adjustments in the equilibrium distributions of the major inorganic carbon species (Dickson, Millero 1987). The calculated change in atmospheric $CO_2$ would have required an addition of about 30 Tg fixed N per annum resulting from an increase in biological nitrogen fixation. Biological N fixation in the contemporary ocean is poorly quantified; estimates range from about 20 Tg per annum (Carpenter, Capone 1992) to 32 Tg for the North Atlantic alone (Gruber et al. 1997). Isotopic analysis of $^{15}N/^{14}N$ ratios in marine sediments suggests that the simultaneous reduction in denitrification during glacial periods would have further contributed to the net influx of fixed nitrogen in the oceans (Altabet et al. 1995; Farrell et al. 1995; Ganeshram et al. 1995), requiring even less $N_2$ fixation to achieve the same result.

The enhancement of the effect of the export production (i.e., biological pump) in sequestering atmospheric $CO_2$ in the ocean interior by increasing availability of fixed inorganic nitrogen would have exerted a positive climatic feedback. The initial forcing would have led to increased cooling if atmospheric $CO_2$ were removed by a strengthening of the biological $CO_2$ pump (McElroy 1983). This process is self-limiting; when the N:P ratio of the dissolved inorganic nutrients caught up to that of the sinking flux of particulates, phosphate would be limiting, and the biological $CO_2$ pump would then approach a new steady state. The total primary productivity of the oceans does not have to change markedly between glacial–interglacial periods. During interglacial periods, however, a reduction in eolian fluxes of trace elements would potentially lead to a slight decrease in nitrogen fixation relative to denitrification, and a slow readjustment toward higher atmospheric $CO_2$ levels.

In the modern (i.e., interglacial) ocean, two major factors could similarly affect iron fluxes. First, changes in land-use patterns and climate over the past several thousand years have, and continue to have, marked effects on the areal distribution and extent of deserts. At the height of the Roman empire, some 2000 years ago, vast areas of North Africa were forested, whereas today these same areas are desert. To some extent these changes were possibly climatologically induced, but deforestation was undoubtedly a contributing factor. Similarly, the Gobi Desert in North Central Asia has increased markedly in modern times. The flux of aeolian iron from the Sahara Desert fuels photosynthesis for most of the North Atlantic Ocean; that from the Gobi is deposited over much of the North Pacific (Duce, Tindale 1991).

The primary source of iron for the Southern Ocean is Australia, but the prevailing wind vectors constrain the delivery of the terrestrial dust to the Indian Ocean; consequently, the Southern Ocean is iron limited in the modern epoch (Martin et al. 1990). This leads to the second factor in this climatological feedback. The major wind vectors are driven by atmosphere–ocean heat gradients. Changes in radiative balance of the atmosphere or ocean lead to changes in wind speed and direction. Wind vectors prior to glaciations appear to have supported high fluxes of iron to the Southern Ocean, thereby presumably stimulating phytoplankton production and the export of carbon to depth; the drawdown of atmospheric $CO_2$ appears to have accompanied glaciations in the recent geological past (Berger 1988).

If primary production in the world oceans is limited by nitrogen rather than phosphorus, why are there not more diazotrophs in the ocean in comparison with lacustrine ecosystems (Howarth et al. 1988)? In the oligotrophic open ocean, the major nitrogen-fixing organisms are nonheterocystous cyanobacteria in the genus *Trichodesmium* (Carpenter, Romans 1991). That there are no heterocystous marine cyanobacteria and few other planktonic, free-living marine diazotrophs suggests some factor(s) has limited the abundance and speciation of these organisms, despite the fact that cyanobacteria evolved some 3700 Mybp (Schopf 1993) and diversified more than 2000 Mybp (Knoll 1994; Lipps 1993).

The effect of variations in iron fluxes to the oceans may be less direct, affecting $N_2$ fixation in the low-nutrient, low-chlorophyll regions as well as in high-nutrient, low-chlorophyll regions. Although nitrogenase contains Mo in addition to Fe, experimental incubations with supplemental Mo in the open ocean do not stimulate the growth or development of $N_2$-fixing cyanobacteria, and it is unlikely that Mo is a factor limiting the abundance of these organisms. On the other hand, $N_2$-fixing cyanobacteria, like most cyanobacteria, require relatively high concentrations of iron. The high-iron requirements come about because these organisms generally have high PSI/PSII ratios (Fujita et al. 1988) and much more iron is used in PSI electron transport components than in PSII (Raven 1988). In addition, iron is required to synthesize both subunits of the nitrogenase holoenzyme as well as ferredoxin, an electron carrier that provides the reductant for $N_2$ fixation in vivo. We may speculate that iron availability may limit the abundance and distribution of $N_2$-fixing cyanobacteria in the open ocean, thereby further exacerbating the effect of nitrogen limitation in such environments (Raven 1988). In this regard, *Trichodesmium* is relatively abundant in iron-rich waters of the Arabian and Caribbean Seas as well as the Indian Ocean, and relatively less abundant in iron-deficient regions of the subtropical eastern Pacific. Thus, it would appear that iron or other trace metals, not nitrogen per se, is the factor that ultimately controls primary production and associated biogeochemical cycles in marine environments (Reuter 1982).

It is tempting to speculate that the apparent increased aeolian flux of iron to the oceans during glacial periods may have stimulated nitrogen fixation by cyanobacteria, and hence indirectly provided a significant source of new nitrogen. Such a stimulation would have led to increased photosynthetic carbon fixation, and a drawdown of atmospheric $CO_2$.

An additional deviation from steady-state fluxes of nutrients comes from coasts in the form of eutrophication of rivers due to sewage inputs and agricultural runoff.

Food production requires the use of fertilizer. The consumption of nitrogen in the form of fertilizer in the United States in 1990 was approximately 9 Tg N (1 Tg = $10^{12}$ g); this corresponds to approximately 35 kg per person per year. The global consumption is about 30 Tg. Approximately 50% of the applied nitrogen enters the coastal waters. This source of nutrients is approximately proportional to human population density, and amounts to a net increase of about 50 Tg per annum; that is, each year an additional 50 Tg is added to riverine systems. An additional 25 Tg is added from atmospheric sources as oxides of nitrogen that precipitate over the oceans, primarily in the northern hemisphere. Depending on the effect of denitrification (which is an anaerobic process) (Christensen et al. 1987), in releasing the fixed nitrogen back to the atmosphere, between 0.1 and 0.3 Pg of photosynthetically fixed carbon is added to the ocean carbon inventory each year. Most of this photosynthetically fixed carbon is in the coastal oceans, close to the source of anthropogenically added nitrogen.

## CLIMATE CHANGE AND THE INDUSTRIAL REVOLUTION

Whereas it has been suggested that $CO_2$ may be limiting photosynthesis in marine phytoplankton (Riebesell et al. 1993), this effect, if it occurs, is physiological rather than biogeochemically important (Raven et al. 1993). In that cycles of nutrients internal to the ocean do not lead to large net changes in the fluxes of $CO_2$ with the atmosphere (Sarmiento, Siegenthaler 1992), it follows that for a net change in the flux to occur, nutrients external to the ocean must be added (if there is a net, biologically mediated influx of $CO_2$ from the atmosphere to the oceans) or existing nutrients in the ocean must be removed (if there is a net biologically mediated efflux of $CO_2$ from the ocean to the atmosphere) (Falkowski, Wilson 1992).

As the downward flux of new production contains organic material with a C:N and C:P composition comparable to that predicted by the Redfield relationship, upwelling processes lead not only to nitrogen and phosphorus enrichment of surface waters, but also to a proportional enrichment with dissolved inorganic carbon. Hence, photosynthetic acquisition of carbon in such systems does not require a net exchange of carbon with the overlying atmosphere, and in fact, while the fluxes of $CO_2$ into and out of the ocean are large (on the order of 100 Pg per annum), changes in the biological processes are subtle on the scale of decades (Falkowski et al. 1992).

Between 1850 and 1996, human activities have introduced about 340 Pg of carbon to the atmosphere, of which 220 Pg is a consequence of the burning of fossil fuels and the remainder is a consequence of deforestation and changes in land use. The only fraction of the total that has been measured precisely is the 42% that remains in the atmosphere. Approximately 30% of the total is thought to be taken up by the oceans. The increase in atmospheric $CO_2$ is potentially a climatic forcing. A doubling of atmospheric $CO_2$, from about 350 ppmv to 700 ppmv in the 21st century, would increase the heating rate of the Earth by approximately 4 W/m$^{-2}$. This warming effect was calculated by Arrhenius (1896). It should be noted that a change

## ❏ THE SOUTHERN OCEAN

*From a biogeochemical perspective, the Southern Ocean is interesting and unique. Whereas most recent marine sediments are calcareous, the sediments of the Southern Ocean are primarily siliceous (DeMaster 1979). Silica deposition results from a sedimenting flux of siliceous photoautotrophs; in the Southern Ocean these are diatoms. Diatoms convert orthosilicic acid Si(OH)₄ to opaline silica to form ornate shells, or frustules (Nelson 1976). The major source of orthosilicic acid in the oceans is from the weathering and dissolution of the terrestrial rocks, thus silica concentrations are generally high in fresh waters that have been exposed to such weathering processes. When diatoms or other siliceous organisms (e.g., radiolarians) sink, the silica in their frustules slowly dissolves (Nelson et al. 1995). In the Southern Ocean, however, the flux of diatom frustules is so great that, over geological time, massive sedimentary deposits have formed. This region of the world oceans has been one of the most important in supporting export production (Smith et al. 1990).*

———————————

in the heat flux at the Earth's surface would not be visible from a satellite—the outbound radiation at the top of the atmosphere will remain constant.

The combustion of fossil fuels is, in effect, biogeochemically equivalent to an increase in the respiration of organic carbon. Therefore, increases in atmospheric $CO_2$ are a consequence of a change in the globally averaged ratio of photosynthesis/respiration from a near steady-state condition prior to the industrial revolution, to one that favors respiratory fluxes; that is, *the global carbon cycle is not presently in steady state.* The potential changes in the radiative properties of the Earth's atmosphere brought about by the combustion of fossil fuels represent the first major *biologically* induced alteration in the Earth's climate since the Carboniferous epoch, some 360 million years ago.

The initial reservoir (or "sink" as it is sometimes called) for anthropogenically produced $CO_2$ is the atmosphere, but ultimately atmospheric $CO_2$ comes into chemical equilibrium with the oceans. Of the approximately 7 Pg of $CO_2$ produced in excess each year, some 3 to 4 Pg are removed from the atmosphere (Sarmiento, Sundquist 1992). Of this, approximately 2 Pg diffuse into the ocean, across the air–sea interface, following the concentration gradient. This diffusive flux is independent of photosynthesis. The quantitative role of photosynthetic organisms in the sequestration of anthropogenically produced $CO_2$ is controversial; however, some basic concepts that we have learned can be applied.

In terrestrial ecosystems, especially in C3 plants, the concentration of $CO_2$ in the present-day atmosphere is not sufficient to saturate Rubisco, and, were all else to remain constant, an increase in atmospheric $CO_2$ is expected to stimulate photosynthetic rates (Long, Hallgren 1986). Indeed, for the most part, long-term (in this context, "long term" means a few months to a few years) exposure of terrestrial C3 plants to elevated $CO_2$ does lead to a stimulation of photosynthesis. In some species, however, there is an internal feedback whereby chronic exposure to elevated $CO_2$ leads to a transcriptional repression of Rubsico, so that the stimulatory effect of $CO_2$ is attenuated (Amthor 1995; Long 1991). Nonetheless, interdecadal observations of terrestrial plant vegetation based on satellite images of global leaf area suggest that terrestrial plant biomass stores approximately 0.7 to 1.0 Pg C per annum. It must be emphasized that this is not the steady-state flux. That is, each year, an additional 0.7 to 1.0 Pg is added to the terrestrial plant photosynthetic production, over and above that production of the previous year. This is analogous to compound interest in an investment. However, as the atmospheric $CO_2$ concentration rises, the carboxylation reaction in C3 plants will become increasingly saturated with $CO_2$ until no further increase in photosynthetic rate is achieved. At such a point, the terrestrial photosynthetic sink for atmospheric $CO_2$ will be markedly reduced. The exact level at which $CO_2$ will saturate terrestrial photosynthetic processes is unclear, although C3 plants tend to saturate at approximately 600 to 700 $\mu mol\, mol^{-1}$. If the rates of $CO_2$ accumulation in the atmosphere at the end of the 20th century are extrapolated into the future, saturation of terrestrial plant photosynthesis will occur before the end of the 21st century.

Terrestrial plants markedly differ from their aquatic counterparts in that the basic concepts of Redfield ratios do not apply to the former. Given more inorganic carbon, terrestrial plants can, in principle, store photosynthetic products in wood, roots, or other biological sinks without concomitant stoichiometric investments in nitrogen or phosphorus. The major effect of nitrogen limitation in terrestrial plants is to reduce the formation of leaves. As $CO_2$ is limiting terrestrial C3 photosynthesis, the effect of elevated atmospheric $CO_2$ is direct and proportional to the kinetic saturation profile of Rubisco. In aquatic ecosystems, the effect of elevated $CO_2$ is more indirect, and more subtle, whereas in lakes, the concentration of $pCO_2$ can become extremely small and, potentially, elevated atmospheric $CO_2$ may be somewhat stimulatory. Nonetheless, the *net* flux of organic carbon that can be sequestered in such environments will be dependent on external sources of limiting nutrients. Moreover, as the total photosynthetic production of organic carbon in lacustrine environments is a very small fraction of that in marine ecosystems, the former plays a relatively small role in the net sequestration of anthropogenic carbon.

Clearly it follows that biologically induced variations in atmospheric $CO_2$ are a consequence of processes that lead to deviations from the steady state. These processes must have led to changes in the nutrient reservoirs or fluxes in the ocean.

The foregoing discussion serves to illustrate some important features of biogeochemical cycles and the role of aquatic photoautotrophs therein. First, biogeochemical cycles are coupled. That is, the cycling of carbon through the atmosphere, hydrosphere, and biosphere is often intertwined with the availability of oxygen, iron, nitrogen, phosphorus, and, in the case of terrestrial plants, water. The relationships between the various cycles are complex, nonlinear, and often involve complex feedbacks.

## THE EVOLUTION AND ECOLOGY OF AQUATIC PHOTOAUTOTROPHS

Species diversity is sometimes developed in the context of a "tempo" of evolution; that is, the rate at which phenotypes are selected and maintained in an ecosystem

(Simpson 1944). The observed diversity at some point in time is related to the age and stability of the ecosystem, physiological stresses as they facilitate selection, the degree of genetic isolation of organisms, and the susceptibility to gene transfer and exchange.

By comparison with terrestrial plants, there are relatively few species of aquatic photoautotrophs, though the evolutionary distance between taxa is much greater (Cavalier-Smith 1993a). The exact reason for the relatively small number of species can only be speculated, but presumably it is because there are fewer unoccupied niches in aquatic environments. The concept of a *niche,* which originated in terrestrial ecology, posits that each species is most suitably adapted to a particular, unique multidimensional (and hence abstract) combination of abiotic and biotic environmental factors (Hulburt 1977). A niche amounts to a "job description" for the species, and as the ecological parallel of the Pauli exclusion principle in quantum mechanics, it follows that no two species can occupy the exact same niche simultaneously. Hutchinson suggested that, despite the apparently low absolute diversity of aquatic photoautotrophs, there appear to be relatively few niches and many species in aquatic ecosystems (Hutchinson 1961). The perception of more species than niches has been called the "paradox of the plankton."

The rescue operation for niche theory as applied to phytoplankton has taken two courses. One approach has adopted the route of multiplying the number of niches via such stategems as different optimal ratios of resources (Tilman 1982). The other approach has pointed out the large number (hundreds) of generations needed for competitive exclusion to eliminate the less fit of two species with essentially identical niche requirements in a given fixed environment (MacArthur 1960). This hypothesis then points out that the aquatic environment usually does not remain constant for the required number of generations, so competitive exclusion would not be carried to its conclusion of eliminating one of the species. In reality it is likely that both hypotheses contribute to the resolution of the paradox of the plankton (Anderson 1995).

In temperate and boreal waters, especially coastal and laucustrine environments, rapid variations in the environment are common, and hence steady-state dynamics with respect to competitive exclusion virtually never occur (Powell, Steele 1995; Smayda 1980). In tropical and subtropical environments, however, quasi-stability does occur, and very small differences in species attributes can lead to significant selection. We can further examine the niche selection concept within the construct of nutrient limitation and stress (Sommer 1989).

The effect of long-term nutrient stress on adaptive selection in the photosynthetic apparatus is illustrated by analysis of the light-harvesting complexes of the prochlorophytes and cyanobacteria. When cyanobacteria are limited by iron, not only are PSI reaction centers lost, but a pigment protein complex similar to CP43 is synthesized. The protein, designated CP43′, is encoded by the isiA gene (*iron stress induced*), and binds chlorophyll *a* (Reithman, Sherman 1988; Straus 1994). In cyanobacteria, the pigment-protein complex is not energetically coupled to either PSII or PSI reaction centers, and the light absorbed by the complex is dissipated as fluorescence and heat. The amino acid sequence of CP43′ is similar to the major light-harvesting complex in the three species of prochlorophytes, namely the marine phytoplankter *Prochlorococcus marinus*, the freshwater phytoplankter *Prochlorothrix hollandica*, and the symbiotic alga *Prochloron* sp (LaRoche et al. 1995; van der Staay et al. 1995). In all three organisms, the protein binds either chlorophyll *a* or divinyl chlorophyll *a* and chlorophyll *b* and transfers excitation energy to both reaction centers. Based on sequence analyses of RNA polymerase and other genes, however, it would appear that the three genera of prochlorophytes evolved independently (Palenik, Haselkorn 1992). Moreover, the sequence of CP43′ is completely different from the major light-harvesting proteins (LHCPs) that are found in chlorophytes and higher plants (Green, Kühlbrandt 1995). We can infer therefore that (1) chlorophyll *b* independently arose at least four times in the course of evolution—three times in the prochlorophytes and once in the chlorophytes; (2) the prochlorophytes are not the direct progenitors of eukaryotic chlorophyte chloroplasts; and (3) the origin of the light-harvesting system in prochlorophytes possibly emerged as a consequence of iron limitation of cyanobacteria in the Archean or Proterozoic oceans.

As we have explained, in the surface waters of subtropical and tropical aquatic ecosystems perennial stratification leads to nutrient depletion, which in turn results in loss of photosynthetic energy utilization efficiency. In such environments, very small changes in photosynthetic capability can be positively selected. Hence, high-resolution vertical profiles in such environments can reveal the presence of layered phenotypes of extremely small unicellular phytoplankton with, for example, phycobilisome-containing organisms higher in the water column, followed by prochlorophyte algae that themselves are stratified with increased absorption due to chlorophyll *b* as depth increases (Chisholm 1992). These phenotypes do not appear to be manifestations of physiological acclimation to irradiance, but are the consequence of selection for low-light utilization characterized by high functional absorption cross-sections for prochlorophytes and acclimation to higher irradiance but lower nutrient regimes for the cyanobacteria. In effect, stabilized environments can lead to magnified or amplified niche widths. This "open niche" hypothesis is further illustrated by the dominance of opportunistic species in anthropogenically stressed environments.

There is general correspondence between thermal structure of aquatic ecosystems and nutrient fluxes. Insofar as the upper portion of the water column exchanges heat with the atmosphere, radiant heating and cooling on daily, seasonal, decadal, and especially climatological, time scales has an effect on nutrient fluxes. We can directly observe the changes in thermal structure in an aquatic ecosystem on short time scales of days, seasons, and perhaps even decades, but we can only draw inferences on longer time scales from measurements of proxy variables such as the $^{16/18}O$ ratios in water in ice cores in polar regions. Based on proxy variables, however, it would appear that when atmospheric temperatures were relatively low (i.e., during glacial periods), nutrient fluxes were high, and vice versa (Berger et al. 1992).

The sedimentary record reveals that the diversity of phytoplankton in the oceans has waxed and waned (Bolli et al. 1985). Based on reconstructed records of ocean temperatures, derived from measurements of the isotopic fractionation of $^{18}O/^{16}O$ in $Ca(CO_3)_2$, it would appear that massive extinctions occurred during periods of extensive glaciations. There are five major extinctions in the geological history of the Earth (the "Big Five"):

**1.** The boundary between the Protozeroic and Phanerozoic epochs, about 550 Mybp

**2.** The boundary between the Ordovician and Silurian epochs, about 425 Mybp

**3.** The boundary between the Devonian and Mississippian epochs, about 345 Mybp

**4.** The boundary between the Permian and Triassic epochs, about 230 Mybp

**5.** The boundary between the Cretaceous and Tertiary epochs, about 66 Mybp

The two largest extinctions occurred at the boundary between the Silurian and Ordovician epochs and between the Permian and Triassic epochs. The extinctions were always followed by increased diversity (or "radiations" in the parlance of the paleobotanists) (Lipps 1993). From the Jurassic period onward the evolutionary structure of the phytoplankton can be traced to taxa that are found in the modern ocean.

One of the most critical of these boundaries is that separating the Permian and Triassic. The emergence of the heterokonts, such as diatoms and dinoflagellates, in the Triassic, was accompanied by numerous changes in the photosynthetic apparatus. Two of these were the selection of cytochrome $c_6$ as an electron carrier in the heterokonts in the place of plastocyanin (see Chapter 4) and a general increase in the ratio of PSII:PSI reaction centers. The Permian epoch appeared to abruptly end with mass anoxia in the world oceans, possibly as a result of numerous volcanic eruptions that led to widespread cooling of the upper ocean and large-scale convective overturn (Wignall, Twitchett 1996). The resulting invasion of $CO_2$ and other biologically active gases from the oceans led to the largest extinction recorded in the sedimentary record. The anoxic conditions would have led to an increase in the availability of soluble iron, but a loss of available copper in the upper ocean. This climatically influenced choice of metals continues to be reflected in the extant heterokonts. By comparison with the Ordovician-Silurian or Permian-Triassic extinction, the Cretaceous-Tertiary extinction, which appears to have had such a devastating effect on terrestrial ecosytems, was less catastrophic for phytoplankton (see Fig 10.1; Knoll, Bauld 1989).

The rate of speciation varies significantly from epoch to epoch (Knoll 1994). Divergence and selection can come about from genetic isolation, and indeed, many if not most single-celled aquatic photoautotrophs reproduce asexually. The isolation can lead to a high degree of genetic variability, but is not necessarily selective in that it may not provide an increased fitness, or abililty to carry a gene line forward. Competetive interactions can also be genetically selective, and in this regard, competition for light, nutrients, and competetive exclusion from thermal extremes are bases on which the structure of aquatic photoautrophic communities are interpreted. It should be noted, however, that mutations within one component of the photosynthetic apparatus may not affect fitness. For example, although D1 is highly conserved, mutations within the $Q_B$-binding region of the protein (see Chapter 6) can lead to a threefold decrease in the rate constant for the transfer of an electron from $Q_A$ to $Q_B$. The reduction in electron transport rate may have no effect on whole chain electron transport, unless the mutation materially affects the rate constant $1/\tau$

(see Chapter 7). If, however, the thylakoid membrane lipid structure were to change, the overall electron transport rate could be affected by thermal difference, and species selection would ensue. Such selection apparently restricts the abundance of prochlorophytes from cold, high latitude environments. Hence, a large degree of genotypic variability can be accommodated within the photosynthetic apparatus; however, selection of photosynthetic phenotypes often appears to be a consequence of tolerance of environmental stress.

From the inferred rate of deposition of both organic and inorganic carbon, estimates of both export and total production have been derived, assuming that the relationships between these two processes are similar to that in the modern ocean. From these paleoreconstructions, it would appear that glaciations increased vertical mixing in the upper ocean and enhanced nutrient fluxes to the euphotic zone that stimulated primary production. In such epochs, export production was high, diversity was probably low and vice versa (Lazarus 1983). Thus, we can postulate a general trend: higher phytoplankton diversity is found during periods of low export production. We can infer, based on Hutchinson's concept that the modern ocean is an ecological scene in the ongoing evolutionary drama of the Earth, that when the central oceans are nutrient limited, there is a propensity for phytoplankton to speciate. The speciation and selection are born of physiological stresses in which small alterations in phenotype can presumably confer some adaptive fitness (Mayr 1970). In the modern open ocean or oligotrophic lake, there is generally a diverse phytoplankton community with low export production. Conversely, when nutrients are abundant, a few species become dominant, but productivity increases. Hence there is apparently a tradeoff in aquatic ecosystems between productivity and diversity.

### Relationships Between Speciation and Photosynthesis

Throughout this book we strove to give the reader a feeling that the fundamental concepts of physics and chemistry underpinning mechanistic understanding of photosynthetic processes are overlaid by variations within organisms. The variations in reaction center stoichiometry, light-harvesting capability, Rubisco affinity for $CO_2$ and $O_2$, the organization and structure of the photosynthetic apparatus, and so on are phenotypic manifestations of adaptive variations and selection. To distill these snippets of photosynthetic variability to mathematical parametizations of photosynthesis-irradiance curves ignores the reasons for biological variability, namely natural selection.

Linking an understanding of the genetic variability of functional processes to the ecological performance of photoautrophic organisms is a daunting task. While the overwhelming majority of natural mutations appear to be neutral—that is, they confer no ecological advantage or disadvantage to the ability of the organism to successfully reproduce and compete—it is at present difficult to predict the success, failure, abundance, or distribution of individual species of photoautotrophs in aquatic environments. Some species, such as diatoms, dominate in cold waters of polar seas, while prochlorphyta require the higher temperatures found at lower latitudes. The differences in the success of these organisms are manifested in photosynthetic attributes, yet relating such phenotypic variability to specific genetic differences, such as the fluidity of the thylakoid membranes or the hydrophobic interactions between the reaction center proteins and light-harvesting complexes, remains to be elucidated. It is our hope and challenge that future generations of students of aquatic photosynthesis will help to reveal the plot of the ongoing evolutionary drama in which human behavior is playing an increasingly larger role.

# References

Abbott MR, Richerson PJ, Powell TM. In situ response of phytoplankton fluorescence to rapid variations in light. Limnol Oceanogr 1982, 27:218–225.

Ahmad J, Morris I. Inhibition of nitrate reduction by 2,4 dinitrophenol in *Ankistrodesmus*. Arch Microbiol 1967, 56:219–224.

Al-Khalifa AS, Simpson KL. Metabolism of astaxanthin in the rainbow trout (*Salmo gairdneri*). Comp Biochem Physiol 1988, 91:563–568.

Alberts B, Bray D, Lewis J et al. The molecular biology of the cell. New York: Garland, 1983.

Alfanso M, Montoya G, Cases R et al. Core antenna complexes, CP43 and CP47, of higher plant photosystem II. Spectral properties, pigment stoichiometry, and amino acid composition. Biochemistry 1994, 33: 494–500.

Allen J, Bennett J, Steinback KE, et al. Chloroplast protein phosphorylation couples plastoquinone redox state to distribution of excitation energy between photosystems. Nature 1981, 291:25–29.

Allen JF. Protein phosphorylation in regulation of photosynthesis. Biochim Biophys Acta 1992, 1098:275–335.

Allen JF, Alexciev K, Hakansson G. Regulation by redox signalling. Curr Biol 1995, 5:869–872.

Almog O, Shalom G, Nechushtai R. Photosystem I: composition, organization and structure. In: Barber J, ed. The photosystems: structure, function and molecular biology. Amsterdam: Elsevier 1992:443–469.

Altabet MA, Francois R, Murray DW, Prell WL. Climate-related variations in denitrification in the Arabian Sea from sediment $^{15}N/^{14}N$ ratios. Nature 1995, 373: 506–509.

Alvarez LW, Alvarez W, Asaro F, Michel HV. Extraterrestrial cause for the Cretaceous-Tertiary extinction. Science 1980, 208:1095–1108.

Amthor JS. Terrestrial higher-plant response to increasing atmospheric $[CO_2]$ in relation to the global carbon cycle. Global Change Biol 1995, 1:243–274.

Anderson CM, Gray J. Cleavage of the precursor of pea chloroplast cytochrome-*f* by leader peptidase from *Escherichia-coli*. FEBS Lett 1991, 280:383–386.

Anderson JM, Andersson B. The dynamic photosynthetic membrane and regulation of solar energy conversion. Trends Biochem Sci 1988, 13:351–355.

Anderson LA, Sarmiento JL. Redfield ratios of remineralization determined by nutrient data analysis. Global Biogeochem Cycles 1994, 8:65–80.

Anderson NJ. Temporal scale, phytoplankton ecology and paleolimnology. Freshwater Biol 1995, 34: 367–378.

Andrews TJ, Lorimer GH, Tolbert NE. Ribulose diphosphate oxygenase. I. Synthesis of phosphoglycolate by fraction-1 protein of leaves. Biochemistry 1973, 12:11–17.

Angstrom A. The solar constant and the temperature of the Earth. Prog Oceanogr 1965, 3:1–5.

Antoine D, Andre JM, Morel A. Oceanic primary production 2. Estimation at global-scale from satellite (Coastal Zone Color Scanner) chlorophyll. Global Biogeochem Cycles 1996, 10:57–69.

Antoine D, Morel A. Oceanic primary production 1. Adaptation of a spectral light-photosynthesis model in view of application to satellite chlorophyll observations. Global Biogeochem Cycles 1996, 10:43–55.

Apt KE, Bhaya D, Grossman AR. Characterization of genes encoding the light-harvesting proteins in diatoms: biogenesis of the fucoxanthin chlorophyll *a/c* protein complex. J Applied Phycol 1994, 6:225–230.

Arnon DI, Tsujimo HY, McSwain BD. Photosynthetic phosphorylation and electron transport. Nature 1965, 207:1367–1372.

Arnon DI, Whatley FR, Allen MB. Photosynthesis by isolated chloroplasts. II. Photosynthetic phosphorylation, the conversion of light into phosphate bond energy. J Am Chem Soc 1954, 76:6328–6309.

Aro EM, Virgin I, Anderson B. Photoinhibition of photosystem 2. Inactivation, protein damage and turnover. Biochim Biophys Acta 1993, 1143:113–134.

Arrhenius S. On the influence of the carbonic acid in the air upon the temperature of the ground. Philos Mag 1896, 41:237–275.

Asada K. Mechanisms for scavenging reactive molecules generated in chloroplasts under light stress. In: Baker N, Bowyer J, eds. Photoinhibition of photosynthesis: from molecular mechanisms to the field. Oxford: Bios Scientific, 1994:129–142.

Asada K, Kanematsu S, Okada S, Hayakawa T. Phytogenetic distribution of three types of superoxide dismutases in organisms and cell organelles. In: Bannister JV, Hill HAO, eds. Chemical and biochemical aspects of superoxide dismutase. Amsterdam: Elsevier, 1980:128–135.

Ascioti FA, Beltrami E, Carrol TO, Wirick C. Is there chaos in plankton dynamics? J Plankton Res 1993, 15:603–617.

Atkinson MJ, Smith SV. CNP ratios of benthic marine plants. Limnol Oceanogr 1983, 28:568–574.

Avni A, Mehta RA, Mattoo AK et al. Nucleotide sequence of the *Spirodela oligorrhiza* chloroplast psba gene coding for the D1 (32 kDa) photosystem II protein. Plant Mol Biol 1994, 17:919–921.

Avron M, Ben-Amotz A, eds. *Dunaliella:* physiology, biochemistry and biotechnology. Boca Raton, FL: CRC, 1992.

Babcock GT, Barry BA, Debus RJ et al. Water oxidation in photosystem II: from radical chemistry to multi-electron chemistry. Biochemistry 1989, 28:9557–9565.

Babcock GT, Sauer K. Electron paramagnetic resonance signal II in spinach chloroplasts I. Kinetic analysis for untreated chloroplasts. Biochim Biophys Acta 1973, 325:483–503.

Babin M, Morel A, Claustre H et al. Nitrogen—and irradiance—dependent variations of the maximum quantum yield of carbon fixation in eutrophic, mesotrophic and oligotrophic marine systems. Deep-Sea Res 1996, 43:1241–1272.

Babin M, Morel A, Gagnon R. An incubator designed for extensive and sensitive measurements of phytoplankton photosynthetic parameters. Limnol Oceanogr 1994, 39:496–510.

Babin M, Therriault JC, Legendre L et al. Relationship between the maximum quantum yield of carbon fixation and the Gulf of St. Lawrence. Limnol Oceanogr 1995, 40:956–968.

Badger MR, Price GD. The role of carbonic anhydrase in photosynthesis. Ann Rev Plant Physiol Plant Mol Biol 1994, 45:369–392.

Badour SS. Inhibitors used in studies of algal metabolism. In: Hellebust JA, Cragie JS, eds. Handbook of phycological methods, physiological methods, biochemical methods. Cambridge: Cambridge University, 1978: 479–488.

Baker KS, Smith RC. Bio-optical classification and model of natural waters 2. Limnol Oceanogr 1982, 27: 500–509.

Baker NR, Bowyer JR, eds. Photoinhibition of photosynthesis: from molecular mechanisms to the field. Oxford: Bios Scientific, 1994.

Balch W, Evans R, Brown J et al. The remote sensing of ocean primary productivity: use of a new data compilation to test satellite algorithms. J Geophys Res 1992, 97:2279–2293.

Balch WM, Kilpatrick K, Holligan PM, Cucci T. Coccolith production and detachment by *Emiliania huxleyi* (Prymnesiophyceae). J Phycol 1993, 29:566–575.

Bannister TT. Production equations in terms of chlorophyll concentration, quantum yield and upper limit to production. Limnol Oceanogr 1974, 19:1–12.

Bannister TT. Quantitative description of steady state, nutrient-saturated algal growth, including adaptation. Limnol Oceanogr 1979, 24:76–96.

Banse K. Determining the carbon to chlorophyll ratio of natural phytoplankton. Mar Biol 1977, 41:199–212.

Banse K. Grazing and zooplankton production as key controls of phytoplankton production in the open ocean. Oceanography 1994, 7:13–20.

Banse K. Grazing, temporal changes of phytoplankton concentrations, and the microbial loop in the open sea. In: Falkowski PG, ed. Primary productivity and biogeochemical cycles in the sea. New York: Plenum, 1992:409–440.

Banse K. Rates of growth, respiration, and photosynthesis of unicellular algae as related to cell size—a review. J Phycol 1976, 12:135–140.

Banwell CN, McCash EM. Fundamentals of molecular spectroscopy. London: McGraw-Hill, 1994.

Barber J, ed. The photosystems: structure, function and molecular biology. New York: Elsevier, 1992.

Barber J. Photosynthetic reaction centres: a common link. Trends Biol Sci 1987, 12:321–326.

Barber RT. Geological and climatic time scales of nutrient availability. In: Falkowski PG, Woodhead A, eds. Primary productivity and biogeochemical cycles in the sea. New York: Plenum, 1992:89–106.

Barnett RE, Grisham CM. The interrelationship of membrane and protein structure in the functioning of the (Na+K)-activated ATPase. Biochim Biophys Acta 1972, 266:613–624.

Barnola JM, Raynaud D, Korotkevitch YS, Lorius C. Vostok ice core: a 160,000 year record of atmospheric $CO_2$. Nature 1987, 329:408–414.

Barron EJ, Washington WM. Warm Cretaceous climates: high atmospheric $CO_2$ as a plausible mechanism. In: Sunquist ET, Broeker WS, eds. The carbon cycle and atmospheric $CO_2$: natural variations Archean to present. Washington, DC: American Geophysical Union, 1985:546–553.

Bassham DC, Bartling D, Mould RM et al. Transport of proteins into chloroplasts—delineation of envelope transit and thylakoid transfer signals within the presequences of three imported thylakoid lumen proteins. J Biol Chem 1991, 266:23606–23610.

Bates SS. Sample preconditioning for measurement of fluorescence induction of chlorophyll *a* in marine phytoplankton. J Plankton Res 1985, 7:703–714.

Baumert H. On the theory of photosynthesis and growth in phytoplankton. Part I: Light limitation and constant temperature. Int Rev Ges Hydrobiol 1996, 81: 109–139.

Beale SI. Biosynthesis of the tetrapyrrole pigment precursor 5-aminolevulinic acid, from glutamate. Plant Physiol 1990, 93:1273–1279.

Beale SI. The biosynthesis of δ-aminolaevulinic acid in plants. Phil Trans R Soc Lond B 1976, 273:99–108.

Beale SI. The biosynthesis of aminolevulinic acid in *Chlorella*. Plant Physiol 1970, 45:504–506.

Beale SI, Castelfranco P. The biosynthesis of aminolevulinic acid in higher plants. II. Formation of $^{14}$C-aminolevulinic acid from labeled precursors in greening plant tissue. Plant Physiol 1974, 53:297–303.

Beale SI, Weinstein JD. Biochemistry and regulation of photosynthetic pigment formation in plants and algae. In: Jordan PM, ed. Biosynthesis of tetrapyrroles. New York: Elsevier, 1991:155–235.

Beale SI, Weinstein JD. Tetrapyrrole metabolism in photosynthetic organisms. In: Dailey HA, ed. Biosynthesis of heme and chlorophylls. New York: McGraw-Hill, 1990:287–291.

Beardall J, Burger-Wiersma T, Rijkeboer M et al. Studies on enhanced post-illumination respiration in microalgae. J Plankton Res 1994, 16:1401–1410.

Behrenfeld M, Bale A, Kolber Z, Aiken J, Falkowski PG. Confirmation of iron limitation of phytoplankton photosynthesis in the equatorial Pacific Ocean. Nature 1996, 383:508–511.

Behrenfeld MJ, Chapman JW, Hardy JT, Lee II H. Is there a common response to ultraviolet-B radiation by marine phytoplankton? Mar Ecol Prog Ser 1993, 102:59–58.

Behrenfeld MJ, Falkowski PG. Photosynthetic rates derived from satellite-based chlorophyll concentration. Limnol Oceanogr 1997a, 42:1–20.

Behrenfeld MJ, Falkowski PG. A consumer's guide to phytoplankton primary productivity models. Limnol Oceanogr 1997b (in press).

Ben-Amotz A, Avron M. On the factors which determine massive β-carotene accumulation in the halotolerant alga *Dunaliella bardawil*. Plant Physiol 1983, 72: 593–597.

Ben-Amotz A, Avron M. The role of glycerol in osmotic

regulation of the halophilic alga *Dunaliella parva*. Plant Physiol 1973, 51:875–878.

Ben-Amotz A, Shaish A, Avron M. Mode of action of the massive accumulation β-carotene of *Dunaliella bardawill* in protecting the alga against excess irradiation. Plant Physiol 1989, 91:1040–1043.

Bender M, Grande K, Johnson K et al. A comparison of four methods for determining planktonic community production. Limnol Oceanogr 1987, 32:1085–1098.

Bender M, Sowers T. The Dole effect and its variations during the last 130,000 years as measured in the Vostok ice core. Global Biogeochem Cycles 1994, 8:363–376.

Bennett J. Chloroplast phosphoproteins. Evidence for a thylakoid-bound phosphoprotein phosphatase. Eur J Biochem 1980, 104:85–89.

Bennett J. Chloroplast protein phosphorylation and the regulation of photosynthesis. Physiol Plant 1984, 60:583–590.

Bennett J. Protein phosphorylation in green plant chloroplasts. Ann Rev Plant Physiol 1991, 42:281–311.

Bennett J, Jenkins GI, Hartley MR. Differential regulation of the accumulation of the light-harvesting chlorophyll *a/b* complex and ribulose bisphosphate carboxylase/oxygenase in greening pea leaves. J Cell Biochem 1984, 25:1–13.

Berger A. Milankovitch theory and climate. Rev Geophys 1988, 26:624–657.

Berger WH, Fischer C, Lai C, Wu G. Ocean productivity and organic carbon flux. I. Overview and maps of primary production and export production. Berkeley: Univ of California, 1987.

Berger WH, Herguera JC. Reading the sedimentary record of the ocean's productivity. In: Falkowski PG, ed. Primary productivity and biogeochemical cycles in the sea. New York: Plenum, 1992:455–486.

Berger WH, Smetacek VS, Wefer G, eds. Productivity of the ocean: present and past. New York: Wiley, 1989.

Berges JA, Charlebois DO, Mauzerall DC, Falkowski PG. Differential effects of nitrogen limitation on photosynthetic efficiency of photosystems I and II in microalgae. Plant Physiol 1996, 110:689–696.

Berges JA, Harrison PJ. Relationships between nitrate reductase-activity and rates of growth and nitrate incorporation under steady-state light or nitrate limitation in the marine diatom *Thalassiosira pseudonana* (Bacillariophyceae). J Phycol 1995, 31:85–95.

Berner RA. Atmospheric carbon dioxide levels over phanerozoic time. Science 1990, 249:1382–1386.

Berner RA. Early diagenesis: a theoretical approach. Princeton: Princeton University, 1980.

Berner RA. Palaeozoic atmospheric $CO_2$: importance of solar radiation and plant evolution. Science 1993, 261:68–70.

Berner RA, Canfield DE. A new model for atmospheric oxygen over phanerozoic time. Am J Sci 1989, 289: 333–361.

Berner T, ed. Ultrastructure of microalgae. Boca Raton, FL: CRC, 1993.

Berner T, Baghdasarian G, Muscatine L. Repopulation of a sea anemone with symbiotic dinoflagellates: analysis by in vivo fluorescence. J Exp Mar Biol Ecol 1993, 0:1–14.

Berner T, Dubinsky Z, Wyman K, Falkowski PG. Photoadaptation and the "package" effect in *Dunaliella tertiolecta* (Chlorophyceae). J Phycol 1989, 25:70–78.

Berry JA. Biosphere, atmosphere, ocean interactions: a plant physiologist's perspective. In: Falkowski PG, Woodhead AD, eds. Primary productivity and biogeochemical cycles in the sea. New York: Plenum, 1992:441–454.

Berry S, Rumberg B. $H^+$/ATP coupling ratio of the unmodulated $CF_0CF_1$–ATP synthase determined by proton flux measurements. Biochim Biophys Acta 1996, 1276:51–56.

Berthold DA, Babcock GT, Yocum CF. A highly resolved, oxygen-evolving PSII preparation from spinach thylakoid membranes. FEBS Lett 1981, 134:231–234.

Berthon J-F, Morel A. Validation of a spectral light-photosynthesis model and use of the model in conjunction with remotely sensed pigment observations. Limnol Oceanogr 1992, 37:781–786.

Bhattacharya D, Medlin L, Wainwright PO et al. Algae containing chlorophylls *a* + *c* are polyphyletic: molecular evolutionary analysis of the Chromophyta. Evolution 1992, 46: 1801–1817.

Bidigare RR, Prèzelin BB, Smith RC. Bio-optical models and the problems of scaling. In: Falkowski PG, ed. Primary productivity and biogeochemical cycles in the sea. New York: Plenum, 1992:175–212.

Bienfang PK. The role of coastal high latitude ecosystems in global export production. In: Falkowski PG, Woodhead A, eds. Primary productivity and biogeochemical cycles in the sea. New York: Plenum, 1992:285–297.

Bishop JKB. Spatial and temporal variability of global surface solar irradiance. J Geophys Res 1991, 96: 16839–16858.

Blackman FF. Optima and limiting factors. Ann Bot 1905, 19:281–298.

Blankenship RE. Origin and early evolution of photosynthesis. Photosyn Res 1992, 33:91–111.

Blankenship RE, Madigan MT, Bauer CE, eds. Anoxygenic photosynthetic bacteria. Dordrecht, Netherlands: Kluwer Scientific, 1995.

Blinks LR, Skow RK. The time course of photosystems as shown by rapid electrode method for $O_2$. PNAS 1938, 24:420–427.

Blowers AD, Ellmore GS, Klein U, Bogorad L. Transcriptional analysis of endogenous and foreign genes in chloroplast transformants of *Chlamydomonas*. Plant Cell 1990, 2:1059–1070.

Boczar BA, Prèzelin BB. Organization and comparison of chlorophyll-protein complexes from two fucoxanthin-containing algae: *Nitzschia closterium* (Bacillariophyceae) and *Isochrysis galbana* (Prymnesiophyceae). Plant Cell Physiol 1989, 30:1047–1056.

Bolli HM, Saunders JB, Perch-Nielsen K, eds. Plankton stratigraphy. Cambridge: Cambridge University, 1985.

Bonaventura C, Myers J. Fluorescence and oxygen evolution from *Chlorella pyrenoidosa*. Biochim Biophys Acta 1969, 189:366–383.

Borowitzka MA, Borowitzka LJ, eds. Micro-algal biotechnology. Cambridge: Cambridge University, 1988.

Bouma TJ, Visser RD, Janssen JMUA et al. Respiratory energy requirements and rate of protein turnover in vivo determined by the use of an inhibitor of protein synthesis and a probe to assess its effect. Physiol Plant 1994, 92:585–594.

Boussac A, Rutherford AW. The origin of the split S3 EPR signal in $Ca^{2+}$-depleted photosystem II. Histidine versus tyrosine. Biochemistry 1992, 31:7441–7445.

Bouyoub A, Vernotte C, Astier C. Functional-analysis of the 2 homologous psbA gene copies in *Synechocystis*

PCC-6714 and PCC-6803. Plant Mol Biol 1993, 21: 249–258.

Boyle EA, Sclater FR, Edmond JM. On the marine geochemistry of cadmium. Nature 1976, 263:42–44.

Boyle EA. Paired carbon iosotope and cadmium data from benthic foraminifera: implications for changes in oceanic phosphorus, oceanic circulation and atmospheric carbon dioxide. Geochim Cosmochim Acta 1986, 50:265–276.

Brand LE. Miniumum iron requirements of marine phytoplankton and the implications for the biogeochemical contol of new production. Limnol Oceanogr 1991, 36:1756–1771.

Brand LE. Persistent diel rhythms in the chlorophyll fluorescence of marine phytoplankton species. Mar Biol 1982, 69:253–262.

Branwell CN, McCash EM. Fundamentals of molecular spectroscopy. London: McGraw-Hill, 1994.

Bricaud A, Morel A, Prieur L. Optical efficiency factors of some phytoplankters. Limnol Oceanogr 1983, 28:816–832.

Broecker WS. Glacial to interglacial changes in ocean chemistry. Progr Oceanog 1982, 11:151–197.

Broecker WS, Peng T-H, Engh R. Modeling the carbon system. Radiocarbon 1980, 22:565–598.

Brooks A, Farquhar GD. Effect of temperature on the $CO_2/O_2$ specificity of ribulose-1,5-bisphosphate carboxylase/oxygenase and the rate of respiration in the light. Estimates from gas exchange measurements on spinach. Planta 1985, 165:397–406.

Brown AH, Webster GC. The influence of light on the rate of respiration in the blue-green alga *Anabaena*. Am J Biol 1953, 40:753–758.

Bryant DA, ed. The molecular biology of cyanobacteria. Dordrecht, Netherlands: Kluwer Scientific, 1994.

Buchel C, Garab G. Electrochromic absorbency changes in the chlorophyll-c–containing alga *Pleurochloris-meiringensis* (Xanthophyceae). Photosyn Res 1995, 43:49–56.

Budyko MI. The earth's climate: past and future. New York: Academic, 1982.

Burlew JS. Algal culture from laboratory to pilot plant. Washington, DC: Carnegie Institute, 1953.

Bustos SA, Golden SS. Expression of the psbDII gene in *Synechococcus* sp. strain PCC 7942 requires sequences downstream of the transcription start site. J Bacteriol 1991, 173:7525–7533.

Butler WL. On the primary nature of fluorescence yield changes associated with photosynthesis. Proc Nat Acad Sci USA 1972, 69:3420–3422.

Butler WL, Katajima M. A tripartite model for chloroplast fluorescence. In: Avron M, ed. Third Interm. Congress on Photosynthesis. Amsterdam: Elsevier, 1975a:13–24.

Butler WL, Kitajima M. Fluorescence quenching of photosystem II in chloroplasts. Biochim Biophys Acta 1975b, 376:116–125.

Calvin M, Bassham JA. The photosynthesis of carbon compounds. New York: Benjamin, 1962.

Campbell JW, Aarup T. New production in the North Atlantic derived from the seasonal patterns of surface chlorophyll. Deep-Sea Res 1992, 39:1669–1694.

Campbell WH. Nitrate reductase biochemistry comes of age. Plant Physiol 1996, 111:355–361.

Canfield DE, Teske A. Late Proterozoic rise in atmospheric oxygen concentration inferred from phylogenetic and sulphur isotope studies. Nature 1996, 382:127–132.

Caperon J. Population growth response of *Isochrysis galbana* to nitrate variation at limiting concentrations. Ecology 1968, 49:866–872.

Carpenter EJ, Capone DG. Nitrogen fixation in *Trichodesmium* blooms. In: Carpenter EJ, Capone DG, Rueter JG, eds. Marine pelagic cyanobacteria: *Trichodesmium* and other diazotrophs. Dortecht, Netherlands: Academic, 1992:211–217.

Carpenter EJ, Capone DG, eds. Nitrogen in the marine environment. New York: Academic, 1983.

Carpenter EJ, Chang J, Cottrell M et al. Re-evaluation of nitrogenase oxygen-protective mechanisms in the planktonic marine cyanobacterium *Trichodesmium*. Mar Ecol Prog Ser 1990, 65:151–158.

Carpenter EJ, Lively JS. Review of estimates of algal growth using $^{14}C$ tracer techniques. In: Falkowski PG, ed. Primary productivity in the sea. New York: Plenum, 1980:161–178.

Carpenter EJ, Price CC. Marine *Oscillatoria* (*Trichodesmium*): explanation of aerobic nitrogen fixation without heterocysts. Science 1976, 191:1278–1280.

Carpenter EJ, Romans K. Major role of the cyanobacterium *Trichodesmium* in nutrient cycling in the North Atlantic Ocean. Science 1991, 254:1356–1358.

Cavalier-Smith T. Kingdom protozoa and its 18 phyla. Microbiol Rev 1993a, 57:953–996.

Cavalier-Smith T. The origin, losses and gains of chloroplasts. In: Lewin RA, ed. Origins of plastids. New York: Chapman and Hall, 1993b:291–348.

Chalup MS, Laws EA. A test of the assumptions and predictions of recent growth models with the marine phytoplankter *Pavlova lutherei*. Limnol Oceanogr 1990, 35:583–596.

Chamberlin WS, Booth CR, Kiefer DA et al. Evidence for a simple relationship between natural fluorescence, photosynthesis, and chlorophyll in the sea. Deep-Sea Res 1990, 37:951–973.

Charlson RJ, Lovelock JE, Andreae MO, Warren SG. Oceanic phytoplankton, atmospheric sulfur, cloud albedo, and climate. Nature 1987, 326:635–661.

Chase GD, Rabinowitz JL. Principles of radioisotope methodology. Minneapolis: Burgess, 1967.

Chekalyuk AM, Gorbunov MY. Laser remote sensing of phytoplankton photosynthetic activity in situ. Proc. of the XVII Congress, ISPRS, Washington, DC, August 2–14, 1992.

Chisholm SW, et al. *Prochlorococcus marinus* nov. gen. nov. sp.: an oxyphototrophic marine prokaryote containing divinyl chlorophyll *a* and *b*. Arch Microbiol 1992a, 157:297–300.

Chisholm SW. Phytoplankton size. In: Falkowski PG, ed. Primary productivity and biogeochemical cycles in the sea. New York: Plenum, 1992b:213–237.

Chitnis PR, Thornber JP. The major light-harvesting complex of photosystem. II. Aspects of its molecular and cell biology. Photosyn Res 1988, 16:41–63.

Cho SH, Thompson GA. Galactolipids of thylakoid pigment protein complexes separated electrophoretically from thylakoids of *Dunaliella salina* labeled with radioactive fatty acids. Plant Physiol 1989, 90:610–616.

Christensen JP, Murray JW, Devol AH, Codispoti LA. Denitrificaction in continental shelf sediments has major impact on the oceanic nitrogen budget. Global Biogeochem Cycles 1987, 1:97–116.

Clayton RE. Photosynthesis: physical mechanisms and chemical patterns. New York: Cambridge University, 1980.

Cleveland JS, Perry MJ. Quantum yield, relative specific absorption and fluorescence in nitrogen-limited *Chaetoceros gracilis*. Mar Biol 1987, 94:489–497.

Cleveland JS, Perry MJ, Kiefer DA, Talbot MC. Maximal quantum yield of photosynthesis in the northwestern Sargasso Sea. J Mar Res 1989, 47:869–892.

Cleveland JS, Weidemann AD. Quantifying absorption by aquatic particles: a multiple scattering correction for glass fiber filters. Limnol Oceanogr 1993, 38: 1321–1327.

Codispoti LA. Is the ocean losing nitrate? Nature 1995, 376:724.

Codispoti LA, Christensen JP. Nitrification, denitrification and nitrous oxide cycling in the eastern tropical south Pacific Ocean. Mar Chem 1985, 16:277–300.

Codispoti LA, Friederich GE, Iverson RL, Hood DW. Temporal changes in the inorganic carbon system of the southeastern Bering Sea during spring 1980. Nature 1982, 296:242–245.

Cohen P, Holmes CFB, Tsukitani Y. Okadaic acid: a new probe for the study of cellular regulation. TIBS 1990, 15:98–102.

Comolli J, Taylor W, Rehman J, Hastings JW. Inhibitors of serine/threonine phosphoprotein phosphatases alter circadian properties in *Gonyaulax polyedra*. Plant Physiol 1996, 111:285–291.

Coombs J, Greenwood AD. Compartmentation of chloroplasts. In: Barber J, ed. The intact chloroplast. Amsterdam: Elsevier, 1976:1–51.

Cooper TG, Filmer D, Wishnick M, Lane MD. The active species of "$CO_2$" utilized by ribulose diphosphate carboxylase. J Biol Chem 1969, 244:1081–1083.

Cooper TG, Wood HG. The carboxylation of phosphoenolpyruvate and pyruvate. 2. The active species of "$CO_2$" utilized by phosphoenolpyruvate carboxylase and pyruvate carboxylase. J Biol Chem 1971, 246:5488–5490.

Copin-Montegut C, Copin-Montegut G. Stoichiometry of carbon, nitrogen, and phosphorus in marine particulate matter. Deep-Sea Res 1983, 30:31–46.

Cota GF. Photoadaptation of high Arctic ice algae. Nature 1985, 315:219–222.

Cota GF, Smith WO Jr, Mitchell BG. Photosynthesis of *Phaeocystis* in the Greenland Sea. Limnol Oceanogr 1994, 39:948–953.

Cote B, Platt T. Utility of the light-saturation curve as an operational model for quantifying the effects of environmental conditions on phytoplankton photosynthesis. Mar Ecol Prog Ser 1984, 18:57–66.

Cramer WA, Crofts AR. Electron and proton transport. In: Govindjee, ed. Photosynthesis, energy convertion by plants and bacteria. New York: Academic, 1982:389–467.

Cramer WA, Furbacher PN, Szczepaniak A, Tae GS. Electron transport between photosystem-II and photosystem-I. Curr Top Bioenerg 1991, 16:179–222.

Cramer WA, Knaff DA. Energy transduction in biological membranes: a textbook of bioenergetics. Berlin: Springer-Verlag, 1990.

Cramer WA, Martinez SE, Huang D et al. Structural aspects of the cytochrome $b_6/f$ complex; structure of the lumen-side domain of cytochrome *f*. J Bioenerg Biomembr 1994, 26:31–47.

Cramer WA, Soriano GM, Ponomarev M, Huang D, Zhang H, Martinez SE, Smith JL. Some new structural aspects and old controversies concerning the cytochrome $b_6/f$ complex of oxygenic photosynthesis. Ann Rev Plant Physiol 1996, 47:477–508.

Crofts AR, Wright CA. The electrochemical domain of photosynthesis. Biochim Biophys Acta 1983, 726:149–185.

Crofts AR, Yerkes CT. A molecular mechanism for qE-quenching. FEBS 1994, 352:265–270.

Crutzen PJ. Tropospheric ozone: an overview. In: Isaksen ISA, ed. Tropospheric ozone. Dordrecht, Netherlands: Reidel, 1988:3–32.

Cuhel RL, Ortner PB, Lean DRS. Night synthesis of protein by algae. Limnol Oceanogr 1984, 29:731–744.

Cullen JJ. The deep chlorophyll maximum: comparing profiles of chlorophyll *a*. Can J Fish Aquat Sci 1982, 39:791–803.

Cullen JJ, Eppley RW. Chlorophyll maximum layers of the Southern California Bight and possible mechanisms of their formation and maintenance. Oceanol Acta 1981, 4:23–32.

Cullen JJ, Lesser MP. Inhibition of photosynthesis by ultraviolet radiation as a function of dose and dosage rate: results for a marine diatom. Mar Biol 1991, 111:183–190.

Cullen JJ, Neale PJ. Ultraviolet radiation, ozone depletion, and marine photosynthesis. Photosyn Res 1993, 39:303–320.

Cullen JJ, Neale PJ, Lesser MP. Biological weighting function for the inhibition of phytoplankton photosynthesis by ultraviolet-radiation. Science 1992, 258:646–650.

Cullen JJ, Yang X, MacIntyre HL. Nutrient limitation of marine photosynthesis. In: Falkowski PG, Woodhead A, eds. Primary productivity and biogeochemical cycles in the sea. New York: Plenum, 1992:69–88.

Dandonneau Y. Measurement of in situ profiles of primary production using an automated sampling and incubation device. ICES Mar Sci Symp 1993, 197:172–180.

Danon A, Mayfield SP. Light-regulated translation of chloroplast messenger RNAs through redox potential. Science 1994, 266:1717–1719.

Danon A, Mayfield SP. Light-regulated translational activators—identification of chloroplast gene specific messenger RNA binding proteins. Embo J 1991, 10:3993–4001.

Davenport HE. Cytochrome components of chloroplasts. Nature 1952, 170:1112–1114.

Davison IR. Environmental effects on algal photosynthesis: temperature. J Phycol 1991, 27:2–8.

Debus RJ. The manganese and calcium ions of photosynthetic oxygen evolution. Biochim Biophys Acta 1992, 1102:269–352.

Decker JP. A rapid postillumination deceleration of respiration in green leaves. Plant Physiol 1955, 30:82–84.

Degens ET, Guillard RRC, Sackett WM, Hellebust JA. Metabolic fractionation of carbon isotopes in marine phytoplankton. I. Temperature and respiration experiments. Deep-Sea Res 1968, 13:1–9.

DeMaster DJ. The marine budgets of silica and $^{32}Si$. New Haven, CT: Yale, 1979.

Demmig B, Winter K, Kruger A, Czygan F-C. Photoinhibition and zeaxanthin formation in intact leaves. A possible role of the xanthophyll cycle in the dissapation of excess light energy. Plant Physiol 1987, 84:218–224.

Demmig-Adams B. Carotenoids and photoprotection in plants: a role for the xanthophyll zeaxanthin. Biochim Biophys Acta 1990, 1020:1–24.

Dennis DT, Turpin DH, eds. Plant physiology, biochemistry and molecular biology. Essex: Longman Scientific, 1990.

Dera J, Gordon HR. Light field fluctuations in the photic zone. Limnol Oceanogr 1968, 13:697–699.

Devault D. Quantum mechanical tunnelling in biological systems. Quart Rev Biophys 1980, 13:387–564.

Devol AH. Direct measurement of nitrogen gas fluxes from continental shelf sediments. Nature 1991, 349: 319–321.

Dickson AG, Millero FW. A comparison of the equilibrium constant for the dissociation of carbonic acid in seawater media. Deep-Sea Res 1987, 34:1733–1743.

Diner BA, Petrouleas V, Wendoloski JJ. The iron-quinone electron-acceptor complex of photosystem II. Physiol Planta 1991, 81:423–436.

Dohler G, Haas FT. UV effects on chlorophylls and carotenoids of the haptophycean alga *Pavlova*. Photosynthetica 1995, 31:157–160.

Dole M, Lane GA, Rudd DP, Zaukelies DA. Isotopic composition of atmospheric oxygen and nitrogen. Geochim Cosmochim Acta 1954, 6:65–78.

Donald RGK, Schindler U, Batschauer A, Cashmore AR. The plant G-box promoter sequence activates transcription in *Sacharomyces cerevesiae* and is bound in vitro by yeast activity similar to GBF, the plant G-box binding factor. Embo J 1990, 9:1727–1735.

Douglas SE. Chloroplast origins and evolution. In: Bryant DA, ed. The molecular biology of cyanobacteria. Boston: Kluwer Academic, 1994:91–118.

Douglas SE, Murphy CA, Spencer DA, Gray MW. Cryptomonad algae are evolutionary chimaeras of two phylogenetically distinct unicellular eukaryotes. Nature 1991, 350:148–151.

Drews G. Structure and functional organization of light-harvesting complexes and photochemical reaction centers in membranes of phototrophic bacteria. Microbiol Rev 1985, 49:59–70.

Dring MJ. The biology of marine plants. London: Edward Arnold, 1982.

Droop MR. Carotenogenesis in *Haematococcus pluvialis*. Nature 1955, 175:42.

Dubinsky Z. Light utilization efficiency in natural marine phytoplankton communities. In: Falkowski PG, ed. Primary productivity in the sea. New York: Plenum, 1980:83–98.

Dubinsky Z, Berman T, Schanz F. Field experiments for *in situ* measurement of photosynthetic efficiency and quantum yield. J Plankton Res 1984, 6:339–349.

Dubinsky Z, Falkowski PG, Porter JW, Muscatine L. Absorption and utilization of radiant energy by light- and shade-adapted colonies of the hermatypic coral. Proc R Soc London 1984:203–214.

Dubinsky Z, Falkowski PG, Wyman K. Light harvesting and utilization in phytoplankton. Plant Cell Physiol 1986, 27: 1335–1349.

Duce RA, Tindale NW. Atmospheric transport of iron and its deposition in the ocean. Limnol Oceanogr 1991, 36:1715–1726.

Dugdale RC. Nutrient limitation in the sea: dynamics, identification and significance. Limnol Oceanogr 1967, 12:685–695.

Dugdale RC. Nutrient modeling. In: Goldberg ED, McCave IN, O'Brien JJ, Steele JH, eds. The sea, vol. 6. New York: Wiley, 1977:789–806.

Dugdale RC, Goering JJ. Uptake of new and regenerated forms of nitrogen in primary productivity. Limnol Oceanogr 1967, 12:196–206.

Dugdale RC, Wilkerson F. Nutrient limitation of new production in the sea. In: Falkowski PG, ed. Primary productivity and biogeochemical cycles in the sea. New York: Plenum, 1992:107–122.

Dunlap WC, Chalker BE. Identification and quantitation of near-UV absorbing compounds (S-320) in a hermatypic scleractinian. Coral Reefs 1986, 5:155–159.

Duysens LNM. Reversible changes in the absorption spectrum of *Chlorella* upon illumination. Science 1954a, 120:353–354.

Duysens LNM. Reversible photo-oxidation of a cytochrome pigment in photosynthesizing *Rhodospirillum rubrum*. Nature 1954b, 173:692–693.

Duysens LNM, Sweers HE. Mechanisms of the two photochemical reactions in algae as studied by means of fluorescence. In: Studies on microalgae and photosynthetic bacteria. Tokyo: Univ of Tokyo, 1963: 353–372.

Eaton Rye JJ, Vermaas WFJ. Oligonucleotide-directed mutagenesis of psbB, the gene encoding CP47, employing a deletion mutant strain of the cyanobacterium *Synechocystis* sp PCC-6803. Plant Mol Biol 1991, 17:1165–1177.

Edmunds LNJ, French RR. Circadian rhythm of cell division in *Euglena*: effects of a random illumination regime. Science 1969, 165:500–503.

Einstein A. Theorie der Opaleszenz von homogenen Flüssigkeiten un Flüssigkeitsgemischen in der Nähe des kritischen Zustandes. Ann Physik 1910, 33:1275–1290.

Ellis RJ. Molecular chaperones: the plant connection. Science 1990, 250:954–959.

Emerson R, Arnold W. A separation of the reactions in photosynthesis by means of intermittent light. J Gen Physiol 1932a, 15:391–420.

Emerson R, Arnold W. The photochemical reaction in photosynthesis. J Gen Physiol 1932b, 16:191–205.

Emerson R, Arnold W. The photosynthetic efficiency of phycocyanin in *Chroococcus* and the problem of carotenoid participation in photosynthesis. J Gen Physiol 1942, 25:579–595.

Emerson R, Chalmers R, Cederstrand C. Some factors affecting the long-wave limit of photosynthesis. Proc Nat Acad Sci USA 1957, 43:133–143.

Emerson R, Lewis CM. The dependance of the quantum yield of *Chlorella* photosynthesis on the wavelength dependence of light. Am J Bot 1943, 30:165–178.

Eppley RW. Estimating phytoplankton growth rates in the central oligotrophic oceans. In: Falkowski PG, ed. Primary productivity in the sea. New York: Plenum, 1980:231–242.

Eppley RW. Nitrate reductase in marine phytoplankton. In: Hellebust JA, Craigie JS, eds. Handbook of phycological methods. Physiological and biochemical methods. New York: Cambridge University, 1978: 217–223.

Eppley RW. Relationships between nutrient assimilation and growth in phytoplankton with a brief review of estimates of growth rate in the ocean. In: Platt T, ed. Physiological bases of phytoplankton ecology. Ottawa: J Can Fish Res Bd, 1981:251–263.

Eppley RW. Temperature and phytoplankton growth in the sea. Fish Bull 1972, 70:1063–1085.

Eppley RW, Coatsworth JL, Solorzano L. Studies of nitrate reductase in marine phytoplankton. Limnol Oceanogr 1969, 14:194–205.

Eppley RW, Peterson BJ. Particulate organic matter flux and planktonic new production in the deep ocean. Nature 1979, 282:677–680.

Eppley RW, Renger EH, Harrison WG. Nitrate and phytoplankton production in southern California coastal waters. Limnol Oceanogr 1979, 24:483–493.

Eppley RW, Rogers JN, McCarthy JJ. Half-saturation constants for uptake of nitrate and ammonium by marine phytoplankton. Limnol Oceanogr 1969, 14:912–920.

Eppley RW, Sloan PR. Carbon balance experiments with marine phytoplankton. J Fish Res Bd Can 1965, 22:1083–1097.

Erickson JM, Rahire M, Rochaix JD. *Chlamydomonas reinhardtii* gene for the 32,000 mol. wt. protein of photosystem II contains four large introns and is located entirely within the chloroplast inverted repeat. EMBO J 1984, 3:2753–2762.

Escoubas J-M, Lomas M, LaRoche J, Falkowski PG. Light intensity regulation of *cab* gene transcription is signaled by the redox state of the plastoquinone pool. Proc Nat Acad Sci USA 1995, 92:10237–10241.

Eskins K, Jiang CZ, Shibles R. Light-quality and irradiance effects on pigments, light-harvesting proteins and RuBisCO activity in a chlorophyll-harvesting and light-harvesting-deficient soybean mutant. Physiol Planta 1991, 83:47–53.

Evans JR, von Caemmerer S, Adams WW, eds. Ecology of photosynthesis in sun and shade. Melbourne: CSIRO, 1988.

Falk JE. Porphyrins and metalloporphyrins. New York: Elsevier, 1964.

Falk S, Leverenz W, Samuelsson G, Oquist G. Changes in photosystem II fluorescence in *Chlamydomonas reinhardtii* exposed to increasing levels of irradiance in relationship to the photosynthetic response to light. Photosynthetica 1992, 31:31–40.

Falkowski PG. Enzymology of nitrogen assimilation. In: Carpenter EJ, Capone D, eds. Nitrogen in the marine environment New York: Academic, 1983a:839–868.

Falkowski PG. Kinetics of light intensity adaptation in *Dunaliella tertiolecta*, a marine plankton chlorophyte. Photosyn Res 1984, 18:62–68.

Falkowski PG. Light-shade adaptation and assimilation numbers. J Plankton Res 1981, 3:203–216.

Falkowski PG. Light-shade adaptation and vertical mixing of marine phytoplankton: a comparative field study. J Mar Res 1983b, 41:215–237.

Falkowski PG. Light-shade adaptation in marine phytoplankton. In: Falkowski PG, ed. Primary productivity in the sea. New York: Plenum, 1980:99–117.

Falkowski PG. Molecular ecology of phytoplankton photosynthesis. In: Falkowski PG, Woodhead A, eds. Primary productivity and biogeochemical cycles in the sea. New York: Plenum, 1992:47–67.

Falkowski PG. Species variability in the fractionation of $^{13}C$ and $^{12}C$ by marine phytoplankton. J Plankton Res 1991, 13:21–28.

Falkowski PG. The role of phytoplankton photosynthesis in global biogeochemical cycles. Photosyn Res 1994, 39:235–258.

Falkowski PG, Dubinsky Z, Muscatine L, McCloskey L. Population control in symbiotic corals. BioScience 1993, 43:606–611.

Falkowski PG, Dubinsky Z, Santostefano G. Light-enhanced dark respiration in phytoplankton. Int Ver Theor Angew Limnol Verh 1985, 22:2830.

Falkowski PG, Dubinsky Z, Wyman K. Growth-irradiance relationships in phytoplankton. Limnol Oceanogr 1985, 30:311–321.

Falkowski PG, Fujita Y. Effect of light state transitions on the apparent absorption cross-section of photosystem II in *Chlorella*. In: Biggins J, ed. Progress in photosynthesis research. Dordrecht, Netherlands: Martinus Nijhoff, 1987:737–740.

Falkowski PG, Fujita Y, Ley AC, Mauzerall D. Evidence for cyclic electron flow around photosystem II in *Chlorella pyrenoidosa*. Plant Physiol 1986, 81:310–312.

Falkowski PG, Greene R, Geider R. Physiological limitations on phytoplankton productivity in the ocean. Oceanography 1992, 5:84–91.

Falkowski PG, Greene R, Kolber Z. Light utilization and photoinhibition of photosynthesis in marine phytoplankton. In: Baker N, Bowyer J, eds. Photoinhibition of photosynthesis: from molecular mechanisms to the field. Cambridge: Bios Scientific, 1994:407–432.

Falkowski PG, Hopkins TS, Walsh JJ. An analysis of factors affecting oxygen depletion in the New York Bight. J Mar Res 1980, 38:479–506.

Falkowski PG, Kiefer DA. Chlorophyll *a* fluorescence in phytoplankton: relationship to photosynthesis and biomass. J Plankton Res 1985, 7:715–731.

Falkowski PG, Kim Y-S, Kolber Z et al. Natural versus anthropogenic factors affecting low-level cloud albedo over the North Atlantic. Science 1992, 256:1311–1313.

Falkowski PG, Kolber Z. Variations in chlorophyll fluorescence yields in phytoplankton in the world oceans. Austral J Plant Physiol 1995, 22:341–355.

Falkowski PG, Kolber Z, Fujita Y. Effect of redox state on the dynamics of photosystem II during steady-state photosynthesis in eucaryotic algae. Biochim Biophys Acta 1988, 933:432–443.

Falkowski PG, LaRoche J. Acclimatation to spectral irradiance in algae (minireview). J Phycol 1991, 27:8–14.

Falkowski PG, LaRoche J. Molecular biology in studies of ocean processes. Int Rev Cytol 1991, 128:261–303.

Falkowski PG, Owens TG. Effects of light intensity on photosynthesis and dark respiration in six species of marine phytoplankton. Mar Biol 1978, 45:289–295.

Falkowski PG, Owens TG. Light-shade adaptation: two strategies in marine phytoplankton. Plant Physiol 1980, 66:592–595.

Falkowski PG, Owens TG, Ley AC, Mauzerall DC. Effects of growth irradiance levels on the ratio of reaction centers in two species of marine phytoplankton. Plant Physiol 1981, 68: 969–973.

Falkowski PG, Rivkin RB. The role of glutamine synthetase in the incorporation of ammonium in *Skeletonema costatum* (Bacillariophyceae). J Phycol 1976, 12:448–450.

Falkowski PG, Sukenik A, Herzig R. Nitrogen limitation in *Isochrysis galbana* (Haptophyceae). II. Relative abundance of chloroplast proteins. J Phycol 1989, 25:471–478.

Falkowski PG, Wilson C. Phytoplankton productivity in the North Pacific ocean since 1900 and implications for absorption of anthropogenic $CO_2$. Nature 1992, 358:741–743.

Falkowski PG, Wirick CD. A simulation model of the effects of vertical mixing on primary productivity. Mar Biol 1981, 65:69–75.

Falkowski PG, Woodhead AD, eds. Primary productivity and biogeochemical cycles in the sea. New York: Plenum, 1992.

Falkowski PG, Wyman K, Ley AC, Mauzerall D. Relationship of steady state photosynthesis to fluorescence in eucaryotic algae. Biochim Biophys Acta 1986, 849:183–192.

Falkowski PG, Ziemann D, Kolber Z, Bienfang PK. Nutrient pumping and phytoplankton response in a subtropical mesoscale eddy. Nature 1991, 352:544–551.

Fanning KA. Nutrient provinces in the sea: concentration ratios, reaction rate ratios, and ideal covariation. J Geophys Res 1992, 97C:5693–5712.

Farquhar GD, Ehleringer JR, Hubick KT. Carbon isotope discrimination and photosynthesis. Mol Biol 1989, 40:503–537.

Farquhar GD, von Caemmerer S, Berry JA. A biochemical model of photosynthetic $CO_2$ assimilation in leaves of $C_3$ species. Planta 1980, 149:78–90.

Farrell JW, Pedersen TF, Calvert SE, Nielsen B. Glacial-interglacial changes in nutrient utilization in the equatorial Pacific Ocean. Nature 1995, 377:514–517.

Fay P. Oxygen relations of nitrogen fixation in cyanobacteria. Microbiol Rev 1992, 56:340–373.

Fenchel T. Intrinsic rate of natural increase: the relationship with body size. Oecologia 1974, 14:317–326.

Fisher T, Shurtz-Swirski R, Gepstein S, Dubinsky Z. Changes in the levels of ribulose-1,5-bisphosphate carboxylase/oxygenase (Rubisco) in *Tetraedon minimum* (Chlorophyta) during light and shade adaptation. Plant Cell Physiol 1989, 30:221–228.

Fitzwater SE, Knauer GA, Martin JH. Metal contamination and its effects on primary production measurements. Limnol Oceanogr 1982, 27:544–551.

Flores E, Herrero A. Assimilatory nitrogen metabolism and its regulation. In: Bryant DA, ed. The molecular biology of cyanobacteria. Dordrecht, Netherlands: Kluwer Academic, 1994:487–517.

Flugge UI. On the translocation of proteins across the chloroplast envelope. J Bioenerg Biomem 1990, 22:769–787.

Flynn KJ, Dickson DMJ, Al-Almoudi OA. The ratio of glutamate: glutamine in microalgae: a biomarker for N-status suitable for use at natural cell densities. J Plankton Res 1989, 11:165–170.

Ford RC, Rosenberg MF, Shepherd FH et al. Photosystem-II 3-D structure and the role of the extrinsic subunits in photosynthetic oxygen evolution. Micron 1995, 26:133–140.

Fork DC, Herbert SK, Malkin S. Light energy distribution in the brown alga *Macrocystis pyrifera* (giant kelp). Plant Physiol 1991, 95:731–739.

Förster T. Intermolecular energy migration and fluorescence. Ann Physik 1948, 6:55–75.

Frank HA, Cogdell RJ. Carotenoids in photosynthesis. Photochem Photobiol 1996, 63:257–264.

Franzen LG, Rochaix JD, Vonheijne G. Chloroplast transit peptides from the green alga *Chlamydomonas reinhardtii* share features with both mitochondrial and higher plant chloroplast presequences. FEBS Lett 1990, 260:165–168.

Frenkel AW. Light induced phosphorylation by cell-free preparations of photosynthetic bacteria. J Am Chem Soc 1954, 76:5568–5569.

Freyssinet G, Sailland A. Structure and evolution of the small and large RuBisCO subunits from various photosynthetic organisms. Plant Physiol Biochem 1991, 29:517–529.

Frid D, Gal A, Oettmeier W, Hauska G, Berger G, Ohad I. The redox-controlled light-harvesting chlorophyll a/b protein kinase. J Biol Chem 1992, 267:25908–25925.

Friedman AL, Alberte RS. Biogenesis and light regulation of the major light harvesting pigment-protein of diatoms. Plant Physiol 1986, 80:43–51.

Froelich PN. Kinetic control of dissolved phosphate in natural rivers and estuaries: a primer on the phosphate buffer mechanism. Limnol Oceanogr 1988, 33:649–668.

Fujita Y, Murakami A, Aizawa K, Ohki K. Short-term and long-term adaptation of the photosynthetic apparatus: homeostatic properties of thylakoids. In: Bryant DA, ed. The molecular biology of cyanobacteria. Dordrecht, Netherlands: Kluwer Academic, 1994:677–692.

Fujita Y, Murakami A, Ohki K. Regulation of the stoichiometry of thylakoid components in the photosynthetic system of cyanophytes: model experiments showing that control of the synthesis or supply of Chl A can change the stoichiometric relationship between the two photosystems. Plant Cell Physiol 1990, 31:145–153.

Fujita Y, Murakami A, Ohki K, Hagiwara N. Regulation of photosystem composition in cyanobacterial photosynthetic system: evidence indicating that photosystem I formation is controlled in response to the electron transport state. Plant Cell Physiol 1988, 29:557–564.

Fujita Y, Ohki K, Murakami A. Chromatic regulation of photosystem composition in the cyanobacterial photosynthetic system: kinetic relationship between change of photosystem composition and cell proliferation. Plant Cell Physiol 1987, 28:227–234.

Fujita Y, Ohki K, Murakami A. Chromatic regulation of photosystem composition in the photosynthetic system of red and blue-green algae. Plant Cell Physiol 1985, 26:1541–1548.

Fujita Y, Shimura S. Photosynthesis and photosynthetic pigments of *Trichodesmium*. In: Marumo R, ed. Studies on the community of marine pelagic blue-green algae. Ocean Research Institute, Univ of Tokyo, 1975:65–71.

Gaffron H, Wohl K. Zur Theorie der Assimilation. Naturwissenschaften 1936, 24:81–92, 103–207.

Gallagher JC, Wood AM, Alberte RS. Ecotypic differentiation in the marine diatom *Skeletonema costatum*: influence of light intensity on the photosynthetic apparatus. Mar Biol 1984, 82:121–134.

Ganeshram RS, Pedersen TF, Calvert SE, Murray JW. Large changes in oceanic nutrient inventories from glacial to interglacial periods. Nature 1995, 376:755–758.

Gantt E. Phycobilisomes. Ann Rev Plant Physiol 1981, 32:327–347.

Garab G, Szito T, Faludi-Daniel A. Organization of pigments and pigment-protein complexes of thylakoids revealed by polarized light spectroscopy. Elsevier Science, 1987, 7:305–339.

Garside C. The vertical distribution of nitrate in open ocean surface water. Deep-Sea Res 1985, 32:723–732.

Geider RJ. Light and temperature dependence of the carbon to chlorophyll *a* ratio in microalgae and cyanobacteria: implications for physiology and growth of phytoplankton. New Phytol 1987, 106:1–34.

Geider RJ. Respiration: taxation without representation? In: Falkowski PG, Woodhead AD, eds. Primary productivity and biogeochemical cycles in the sea. New York: Plenum, 1992:333–360.

Geider RJ, LaRoche J. The role of iron in phytoplankton photosynthesis, and the potential for iron-limitation of primary productivity in the sea. Photosyn Res 1994, 39:275–301.

Geider RJ, Macintyre HL, Kana TM. A dynamic-model of photoadaptation in phytoplankton. Limnol Oceanog 1996, 41:1–15.

Geider RJ, Osborne BA. Algal photosynthesis: the measurement of algal gas exchange. New York: Routledge, Chapman and Hall, 1992.

Geider RJ, Osborne BA. Respiration and microalgal growth: a review of the quantitative relationship between dark respiration and growth. New Phytol 1989, 112:327–394.

Geider RJ, Osborne BA, Raven JA. Growth, photosynthesis and maintenance metabolic cost in the diatom *Phaeodactylun tricornutum* at very low light levels. J Phycol 1986, 22:39–48.

Genty B, Harbison J, Briantis J-M, Baker NR. The relationship between nonphotochemical quenching of chlorophyll fluorescence and the rate of photosystem 2 photochemistry in leaves. Photosyn. Res. 1990, 25:1772–1782.

Gibbs SP. The evolution of algal chloroplasts. In: Lewin RA, ed. Origins of plastids. New York and London: Chapman Hall, 1992.

Giersch C, Krause GH. A simple model relating photoinhibitory fluorescence quenching in chloroplasts to a population of altered photosystem II reaction centers. Photosyn Res 1991, 30:115–121.

Gillespie JH. The causes of molecular evolution. New York: Oxford University, 1991.

Giovannoni SJ, Wood N, Huss V. Molecular phylogeny of oxygenic cells and organelles based on small-subunit ribosomal RNA sequences. In: Lewin RA, ed. Origins of plastids. New York: Chapman and Hall, 1993: 159–168.

Glaser E, Norling B. Chloroplast and plant mitochondrial ATP synthases. Curr Top Bioenerg 1991, 16:223–263.

Glazer AN. Phycobilisome, a macromolecular complex optimized for light energy transfer. Biochim Biophys Acta 1984, 768:29–51.

Glover HE. Ribulose bisphosphate carboxylase/oxygenase in marine organisms. Int Rev Cytol 1989, 115:67–138.

Gnaiger E, Forstner H, ed. Polarographic oxygen sensors. Berlin: Springer-Verlag, 1983.

Golbeck JH, Bryant DA. Photosystem I. In: Lee CP, ed. Current topics in bioenergetics. San Diego, CA: Academic, 1991:83–177.

Golden SS, Brusslan J, Haselkorn R. Expression of a family of psbA genes encoding a photosystem II polypeptide in the cyanobacterium *Anacystis nidulans* R2. Embo J 1986, 5:2789–2798.

Goldman JC. On phytoplankton growth rates and particulate C : N : P ratios at low light. Limnol Oceanogr 1986, 31:1358–1363.

Goldman JC. Physiological processes, nutrient availability, and the concept of relative growth rate in marine phytoplankton ecology. In: Falkowski PG, ed. Primary

productivity in the sea. New York: Plenum, 1980:179–194.

Goldman JC, Brewer PG. Effect of nitrogen source and growth rate on phytoplankton-mediated changes in alkalinity. Limnol Oceanogr 1980, 25:352–357.

Goldman JC, McCarthy JJ, Peavey DG. Growth rate influence on the chemical composition of phytoplankton in oceanic waters. Nature 1979, 279:210–215.

Gombos Z, Murata N. Lipids and fatty acids of *Prochlorothrix hollandica*. Plant Cell Physiol 1991, 32:73–77.

Gombos Z, Wada H, Murata N. Direct evaluation of effects of fatty acid unsaturation on the thermal properties of photosynthetic activities, as studied by mutation and transformation of *Synechocystis* PCC6803. Plant Cell Physiol 1991, 32:205–211.

Goodwin TW, ed. The biochemistry of carotenoids. I. Plants. New York: Chapman and Hall, 1980.

Gordon HR, Morel A. Remote sensing of ocean color for interpretation of satellite visible imagery. A review. New York: Springer-Verlag, 1983.

Gottfried DS, Steffen MA, Boxer SG. Stark effect spectroscopy of carotenoids in photosynthetic antenna and reaction center complexes. Biochim Biophys Acta 1991, 1059:76–90.

Graham D, Whittingham CP. The path of carbon during photosynthesis in *Chlorella pyrenoidosa*. Z Pflanzenphysiol Bd 1968, 58:418–427.

Grande KD, Marra J, Langdon C et al. Rates of respiration in the light measured using an $^{18}$O isotope-labelling technique. J Exp Mar Biol Ecol 1989, 129:95–120.

Grant NG, Hommersand MH. The respiratory chain of *Chlorella protothecoides*. Plant Physiol 1974, 54:57–59.

Green BR, Durnford DG. The chlorophyll-carotenoid proteins of oxygenic photosynthesis. Ann Rev Plant Physiol Plant Mol Biol 1996, 47:685–714.

Green BR, Kühlbrandt W. Sequence conservation of light-harvesting and stress-response proteins in relation to the three-dimensional molecular structure of LHCII. Photosyn Res 1995, 44:139–148.

Green BR, Pichersky E. Hypothesis for the evolution of three-helix chl *a/b* and chl *a/c* light-harvesting antenna proteins from two-helix and four-helix ancestors. Photosyn Res 1994, 39:149–162.

Green BR, Pichersky E, Kloppstech K. Chlorophyll *a/b*-binding proteins: an extended family. Trends Biochem Sci 1991, 16:181–186.

Greenbaum E, Lee JW, Tevault CV et al. $CO_2$ fixation and photoevolution of $H_2$ and $O_2$ in a mutant of *Chlamydomonas* lacking photosystem I. Nature 1995, 376:439–441.

Greenberg BM, Gaba V, Canaani O et al. Separate photosensitizers mediate degradation of the 32 kDa photosystem II reaction center protein in the visible and UV spectral regions. Proc Nat Acad Sci USA 1989, 86:6617–6620.

Greene RM, Geider RJ, Falkowski PG. Effect of iron limitation on photosynthesis in a marine diatom. Limnol Oceanogr 1991, 36:1772–1782.

Greene RM, Geider RJ, Kolber Z, Falkowski PG. Iron-induced changes in light harvesting and photochemical energy conversion processes in eukaryotic marine algae. Plant Physiol 1992, 100:565–575.

Greene RM, Gerard VA. Effects of high-frequency light fluctuations on growth and photoacclimation of the red alga *Chondrus crispus*. Mar Biol 1990, 105: 337–344.

Greene RM, Kolber ZS, Swift DG et al. Physiological limitation of phytoplankton photosynthesis in the eastern equatorial Pacific determined from the variability in the quantum yield of fluorescence. Limnol Oceanogr 1994, 39:1061–1074.

Grossman AR, Manodori A, Snyder D. Light-harvesting proteins of diatoms: their relationship to the chlorophyll *a/b* binding proteins of higher plants and their mode of transport into plastids. Mol Gen Genet 1990, 224:91–100.

Grossman AR, Schaefer MR, Chiang GG, Collier JL. Environmental effects on the light-harvesting complex of cyanobacteria. J Bact 1993a, 175:575–582.

Grossman AR, Schaefer MR, Chiang GG, Collier JL. The phycobilisome, a light-harvesting complex responsive to environmental conditions. Microbiol Rev 1993b, 57:725–749.

Grossman, AR, Schaefer MR, Chiang GG, Collier JL. The responses of cyanobacteria to environmental conditions: light and nutrients. In: Bryant DA, ed. The molecular biology of cyanobacteria. Dordrecht: Kluwer Academic, 1994:641–675.

Gruber N, Sarmiento SL. Global patterns of marine fixation and denitrification revealed by the conservative tracer N*. Global Biogeochem Cycles 1997 (in press).

Gruerson D, Covey SN. Plant molecular biology. New York: Chapman and Hall: 1988.

Gschwend PM, MacFarland JK, Newman KA. Volatile halogenated organic carbon compound released to seawater from temperate marine macroalgae. Science 1985, 227:1033–1035.

Guerrero MG, Vega JM, Losada M. The assimilatory nitrate-reducing system and its regulation. Ann Rev Plant Physiol 1981, 32:169–204.

Guy RD, Vanlerberghe GC, Turpin DH. Significance of phosphoenolpyruvate carboxylase during ammonium assimilation. Carbon isotope discrimination in photosynthesis and respiration by the N-limited green alga *Selanastrum minutum*. Plant Physiol 1989, 89: 1150–1157.

Hader DP, Tevini M. General photobiology. Oxford: Pergamon, 1987.

Haehnel W. Electron transport between plastoquinone and chlorophyll *a* in chloroplasts. 2. Reaction kinetics and the function of plastocyanin in situ. Biochim Biophys Acta 1977, 459:418–441.

Hagar A, Stransky H. The carotenoid pattern and occurrence of the light induced xanthophyll cycle in various classes of algae. V. A few members of the Cryptophyceae, Euglenophyceae, Bacillariophyceae, Chrysophyceae and Phaeophyceae. Arch Mikrobiol 1970, 73: 7–89.

Halldal P, Taube O. Ultraviolet action spectra and photoreactivation in algae. Photophysiol 1972, 6:445–460.

Harding LWJ, Prèzelin BB, Sweeney BM. Diel periodicity of photosynthesis in marine phytoplankton. Mar Biol 1981, 61:95–105.

Harris EH. The *Chlamydomonas* sourcebook: a comprehensive guide to biology and laboratory use. New York: Academic, 1989.

Harrison WG. Nutrient regeneration and primary production in the sea. In: Falkowski PG, ed. Primary production in the sea. New York: Plenum, 1980:433–460.

Harrison WG, Harris LR, Irwin BD. The kinetics of nitrogen utilization in the oceanic mixed layer: nitrate and ammonium interactions at nanomolar concentrations. Limnol Oceanogr 1996, 41:16–32.

Hartman FC, Harpel MR. Stucture, function, regulation, and assembly of D-ribulose-1,5-bisphosphate carboxylase/oxygenase. Ann Rev Biochem 1994, 63: 197–234.

Haselkorn R. Developmentally regulated gene rearrangements in prokaryotes. Ann Rev Genet 1992, 26: 111–128.

Haselkorn R, Buikema WJ. Nitrogen fixation in cyanobacteria. In: Stacey G, Burris RH, Evans HJ, eds. Biological nitrogen fixation. New York: Chapman and Hall, 1992:166–190.

Haxo FT, Blinks LR. Photosynthetic action spectra of marine algae. J Gen Physiol 1950, 33:389–422.

Heber U. Metabolite exchange between chloroplasts and cytoplasm. Ann Rev Plant Physiol 1974, 25: 393–421.

Heber U, Kirk MR, Boardman NK. Photoreactions of cytochrome *b*-559 and cyclic electron flow in photosystem II of intact chloroplasts. Biochim Biophys Acta 1979, 546:292–306.

Heber U, Schreiber U, Siebke K, Dietz KJ. Relationship between light-driven electron transport, carbon reduction and carbon oxidation in photosynthesis. Biochem Genetic Reg Photosyn 1990, 10:17–37.

Hecky RE, Kilham P. Nutrient limitation of phytoplankton in freshwater and marine environments: a review of recent evidence on the effects of enrichment. Limnol Oceanogr 1988, 33:796–822.

Heichel GH. Prior illumination and the respiration of maize leaves in the dark. Plant Physiol 1970, 46: 359–362.

Heldt-Hansen HP, Grant NG, Olson LW. Respiration of gametangia of the aquatic phycomycete *Allomyces marogynus*. Plant Physiol 1983, 73:111–117.

Herbert D, Elsworth R, Telling RC. The continuous culture of bacteria: a theoretical and experimental study. J Gen Microbiol 1956, 14:601–622.

Herguerra JC, Berger WH. Glacial to postglacial drop in productivity in the western equatorial Pacific: Mixing rate vs. nutrient concentration. Geology 1994, 22: 629–632.

Herron HA, Mauzerall D. The development of photosynthesis in a greening mutant of *Chlorella* and an analysis of the light saturation curve. Plant Physiol 1971, 50:141–148.

Herzig R, Falkowski PG. Nitrogen limitation of *Isochrysis galbana*. I. Photosynthetic energy conversion and growth efficiencies. J Phycol 1989, 25:462–471.

Hill R, Bendall F. Function of the two cytochrome components in chloroplasts: a working hypothesis. Nature 1960, 186:136–137.

Hill WE, Dahlberg A, Garrett RA, Moore PB, Schlessinger D, Warner JR, eds. The ribosome: structure, function and evolution. Washington, DC: Am Soc Microbiol, 1990.

Hiller RG, Anderson JM, Larkum AWD. The chlorophyll–protein-complexes of algae. In: Scheer H, ed. Chlorophylls. Boca Raton, FL: CRC, 1991:529–547.

Hiller RG, Wrench PM, Gooley AP et al. The major intrinsic light-harvesting protein of *Amphidinium*: characterization and relation to other light-harvesting proteins. Photochem Photobiol 1993, 57:125–131.

Hirayama O, Inamura T. Distribution and functions of lipids in thylakoid membranes from a thermophilic cyanobacterium, *Mastigocladus laminosus*. Agric Biol Chem 1991, 55:1005–1011.

Hitchcock GL. The time course of photosynthetic adaption, the growth rate response, and variations in the pigment, carbohydrate, and protein content of *Skeletonema costatum* and *Detonula confervesa* to changes in light intensity. Kingston: Univ of Rhode Island, 1977.

Hofmann E, Wrench PM, Sharples FP, Hiller RG, Welete W, Diederichs K. Structural basis of light harvesting by carotenoids: peridinin-chlorophyll-protein from *Amphidinium carterae*. Science 1996, 272:1788–1791.

Hoge FE, Swift RN. Airborne simultaneous spectroscopic detection of laser-induced water Raman backscatter and fluorescence from chlorophyll *a* and other naturally occurring pigments. Appl Optics 1981, 20:3197–3205.

Holland HD. The chemical evolution of the atmosphere and oceans. Princeton: Princeton University, 1984.

Holligan P, Robertson J. Calcification. Global Biogeochem Cycles 1996, 2:85–96.

Holzwarth AR. Fluorescence lifetimes in photosynthetic systems. Photochem Photobiol 1986, 43:707–725.

Horton P, Ruban AV. Regulation of photosystem II. Photosyn Res 1992, 34:375–385.

Horvath G, Melis A, Hideg E et al. Role of lipids in the organization and function of photosystem II studied by homogeneous catalytic hydrogenation of thylakoid membranes in situ. Biochim Biophys Acta 1987, 891:68–74.

Houmard J. Gene transcription in filamentous cyanobacteria. Microbiology 1994, 140:433–441.

Howarth RW, Marino R, Cole JJ. Nitrogen fixation in freshwater, estuarine, and marine ecosystems. 1. Rates and importance. Limnol Oceanogr 1988a, 33:669–687.

Howarth RW, Marino R, Cole JJ. Nitrogen fixation in freshwater, estuarine, and marine ecosystems. 2. Biogeochemical controls. Limnol Oceanogr 1988b, 33:688–701.

Huber SC, Huber JL, Campbell WH, Redinbaugh MG. Apparent dependence of the light activation of nitrate reductase and sucrose-phosphate synthase activities in spinach leaves on protein synthesis. Plant Cell Physiol 1992, 33:639–646.

Hughes MN, Poole RK. Metals and micro-organisms. New York: Chapman and Hall, 1989.

Hulburt EM. Coexistence, equilibrium, and nutrient sharing among phytoplankton species of the Gulf of Maine. Am Nat 1977, 111:967–980.

Hundal T, Fosmark-Andree P, Ernster L, Andersson B. Antioxidant activity of reduced plastoquinone in chloroplast thylakoid membranes. Arch Biochem Biophys 1995, 324:117–122.

Hutchinson GE. A treatise on limnology. New York: Wiley, 1971.

Hutchinson GE. The ecological theatre and the evolutionary play. New Haven, CT: Yale, 1965.

Hutchinson GE. The paradox of the plankton. Am Nat 1961, 95:137–145.

Imbrie J, Boyle EA, Clemens SC et al. On the structure and origin of major glaciation cycles. I. Linear responses to Milankovitch forcing. Paleoceanography 1992, 7:701–738.

Ivashchenko AT, Karpenyuk TA, Ponomarenko SV. ATP synthase of bacteria, mitochondria, and chloroplasts—properties of the membrane sector F(0). Biochem USSR 1991, 56:257–266.

Jagendorf AT, Margulies M. Inhibition of spinach chloroplast photosynthetic reactions by *p*-chlorophenyl-1, 1-dimethylurea. Arch Biochem Biophys 1960, 90:184–195.

Jahnke RA, Jackson GA. The spatial distribution of sea floor oxygen consumption in the Atlantic and Pacific Oceans. In: Rowe GT, Pariente V, eds. Deep-sea food chains and the global carbon cycle. Kluwer Academic, 1992:295–307.

Jasper JP, Hayes JM, Sikes EL. Transfer of $CO_2$ from equatorial latitudes to high latitudes during the late quaternary. In: Jahne B, Monahan E, eds. Air-water gas transfer. New York: Springer-Verlag, 1995.

Jassby AD, Platt T. Mathematical formulation of the relationship between photosynthesis and light for phytoplankton. Limnol Oceanogr 1976, 21:540–547.

Jeffrey SW. Algal pigment systems. In: Falkowski PG, ed. Primary productivity in the sea. New York: Plenum, 1980:33–58.

Jeffrey SW, Hallegraeff GM. Phytoplankton pigments, species and light climate in a complex warm-core eddy of the East Australian Current. Deep-Sea Res 1987, 34:649–673.

Jerlov NG. Marine optics. Amsterdam: Elsevier, 1976.

Johanningmeier U, Howell SH. Regulation of light-harvesting chlorophyll binding protein mRNA accumulation in *Chlamydomonas reinhardtii*. J Biol Chem 1984, 259:13541–13549.

John DM. Biodiversity and conservation: an algal perspective. The Phycologist 1996, 38:3–15.

Johnston AM, Maberly SC, Raven JA. The acquisition of inorganic carbon by four red macroalgae from different habitats. Oecologia 1992, 92:317–326.

Joliot, P. Earlier researches on the mechanism of oxygen evolution: a personal account. Photosyn Res 1993, 38:214–223.

Joliot P, Bennoun P, Joliot A. New evidence supporting energy transfer photosynthetic units. Biochim Biophys Acta 1973, 305:317–328.

Jones AL, Harwood JL. Lipids and lipid-metabolism in the marine alga *Enteromorpha intestinalis*. Phytochem 1993, 34:969–972.

Jones LW, Kok B. Photoinhibition of chloroplast reactions. I. Kinetics and action spectra. Plant Physiol 1966, 41:1037–1043.

Jordan PM, ed. Biosynthesis of tetrapyrroles. Amsterdam: Elsevier, 1991.

Jovine R, Johnsen G, Prèzelin BB. Isolation of membrane-bound light-harvesting-complexes from the dinoflagellates *Heterocapsa pygmaea* and *Prorocentrum minimum*. Photosyn Res 1995, 44:127–138.

Junge W. Physical aspects of light harvesting, electron transport and electrochemical potential generation in photosynthesis of green plants. In: Trebst A, Avron M, eds. Encyclopedia of Plant Physiology, New Series. Berlin: Springer-Verlag, 1977:59–93.

Kaiser WM, Huber SC. Post-translational regulation of nitrate reductase in higher plants. Plant Physiol 1994, 106:817–821.

Kandler, O. Über die besiehurgen zwischen phosphathaushalt und photosynthese. I. Phosphat schisgelschuinugen bei *Chlorella pyrenoidosa* als Falge Licht-Dunkel-Wechsel. Z Nat 1950, 5B:423–437.

Kaplan WA. Nitrification. In: Carpenter EJ, Capone DG, eds. Nitrogen in the marine environment. New York: Academic, 1983:139–190.

Karabin GD, Farley M, Hallick RB. Chloroplast gene for Mr 32000 polypeptide of photosystem II in *Euglena gracilis* is interrupted by four introns with conserved boundary sequences. Nucl Acid Res 1984, 12: 5801–5812.

Karentz D, McEuen FS, Land MC, Dunlap WC. Survey of mycosporine-like amino acid compounds in Antarctic marine organisms: potential protection from ultraviolet exposure. Mar Biol 1991, 108:157–166.

Kasting JF. Algae and earth's ancient atmosphere. Science 1993a, 259:835.

Kasting JF. Bolide impacts and the oxidation state of carbon in the Earth's early atmosphere. Origins Life Evol Biosph 1990, 20:199–231.

Kasting JF. Earth's early atmosphere. Science 1993b, 259:920–926.

Kasting JF, Toon OB, Pollack JB. How climate evolved on the terrestrial planets. Sci Am 1988, 258:90–97.

Kautsky H, Appel W, Amman H. Chlorophyll fluoresenz und kohlensaure assimilation. Biochem Z 1960, 332:277–292.

Kautsky H, Hirsch A. Neue Theorie zur Köhlensaureassimilation. Naturwissen 1931, 19:964.

Kavanagh TA, Jefferson RA, Bevan MW. Targetting a foreign protein to chloroplasts using fusions to the transit peptide of a chlorophyll a/b protein. Mol Gen Genet 1988, 215:38–45.

Kawecka B, Eloranta P. Biology and ecology of snow algae. Acta Hydrobiol 1986, 28:387–391.

Keeley JE. Photosynthesis pathways in freshwater aquatic plants. Trends Ecol Evol 1990, 5:330–333.

Keeling RF, Piper SC, Heimann M. Global and hemispheric $CO_2$ sinks deduced from changes in atmospheric $O_2$ concentration. Nature 1996, 381:218–221.

Kehoe DM, Grossman AR. Similarity of a chromatic adaptation sensor to phytochrome and ethylene receptors. Science 1996, 273:1409–1412.

Kerby NW, Raven JA. Transport and fixation of inorganic carbon by marine algae. Adv Bot Res 1985, 11:71–123.

Kiefer DA, Chamberlain WS, Booth CR. Natural fluorescence of chlorophyll a: relationship to photosynthesis and chlorophyll concentration in the western South Pacific gyre. Limnol Oceanogr 1989, 34:868–881.

Kiefer DA, Mitchell BG. A simple, steady state description of phytoplankton growth based on absorption cross section and quantum efficiency. Limnol Oceanogr 1983, 28:770–776.

Kiene RP, Visscher PT, Keller MD, Kirst G. eds. Biological and environmental chemistry of DMSP and related sulfonium compounds. New York: Plenum, 1996.

Kilham P, Hecky RE. Comparative ecology of marine and freshwater phytoplankton. Limnol Oceanogr 1988, 33:776–795.

Kirk JTO. A theoretical analysis of the contribution of algal cells to the attenuation of light within natural waters. I. General treatment of pigmented cells. New Phytol 1975, 75:11–20.

Kirk JTO. Effects of suspensoids (turbidity) on penetration of solar radiation in aquatic ecosystems. Perspectives in southern hemisphere limnology. Davies BR, ed. 1985, 125:195–208.

Kirk JTO. Estimation of the absorption and the scattering coefficients of natural waters by use of underwater irradiance measurements. Appl Optics 1994a, 33:3276–3278.

Kirk JTO. Light and photosynthesis in aquatic ecosystems. Cambridge: Cambridge University, 1994b.

Kirk JTO. The nature and measurement of the light environment in the ocean. In: Falkowski PG, ed. Primary productivity and biogeochemical cycles in the sea. New York: Plenum, 1992:9–29.

Kirk JTO. The upwelling light stream in natural waters. Limnol Oceanogr 1989, 34:1410–1425.

Kirk JTO. Volume scattering function, average cosines, and the underwater light field. Limnol Oceanogr 1991, 36:455–467.

Kirk JTO, Tilney-Bassett RAE. The plastids. Amsterdam: Elsevier, 1978.

Kirk JTO, Tyler PA. The spectral absorption and scattering properties of dissolved and particulate components in relation to the underwater light field of some tropical Australian freshwaters. Freshwat Biol 1986, 16:573–583.

Kishino M, Takahashi M, Okami N, Ichimura S. Estimation of the spectral absorption coefficients of phytoplankton in the sea. Bull Mar Sci 1985, 37:634–642.

Klein RR, Gramble PE, Mullet JE. Light-dependent accumulation of radiolabeled plastid encoded chlorophyll a-apoproteins requires chlorophyll a. Plant Physiol 1988, 88:1246–1256.

Klimov VV, Allakhverdiev SI, Demeter S, Krasnovski AA. Pheophytin photoreduction in PSII of chloroplasts in relation to redox conditions in the environment. Dokl Akad Nauk SSSR 1979, 249:227–230.

Kloos R, Stevens E, Oettmeier W. Complete sequence of one copy of the psbA gene from the thermophilic cyanobacterium *Synechococcus elongatus*. Zeitschr Natur CA J Biosci 1993, 48:799–802.

Knoll AH. Evolution and extinction in the marine realm: some constraints imposed by phytoplankton. Phil Trans R Soc Lond B 1989, 325:279–290.

Knoll AH. Proterozoic and early Cambrian protists: evidence for accelerating evolutionary tempo. Proc Nat Acad Sci USA 1994, 91:6743–6750.

Knoll AH, Bauld J. The evolution and ecological tolerance in prokaryotes. Trans R Soc Edinburgh 1989, 80: 209–233.

Kobayashi Y, Kaiser W, Heber U. Bioenergetics of carbon assimilation in intact chloroplasts: coupling of proton to electron transport at the ratio $H^+/e^- = 3$ is incompatible with $H^+/ATP = 3$ in ATP synthesis. Plant Cell Physiol 1995, 36:1629–1637.

Koenig F. Shade adaptation in cyanobacteria. Photosyn Res 1990, 26:29–37.

Kohorn BD. Replacement of histidines of light-harvesting chlorophyll a/b-binding protein-II disrupts chlorophyll-protein complex assembly. Plant Physiol 1990, 93:339–342.

Kok B. A critical consideration of the quantum yield of *Chlorella* photosynthesis. Enzymologia 1948, 13:1–56.

Kok B. Absorption changes induced by the photochemical reaction of photosynthesis. Nature 1957, 179: 583–584.

Kok B. On the interrelation of respiration and photosynthesis in green plant cells. Biochim Biophys Acta 1949, 3:82–84.

Kok B. Partial purification and determination of oxidation-reduction potential of the photosynthetic chlorophyll complex absorbing at 700 mμ. Biochim Biophys Acta 1961, 48:527–533.

Kok B. Photosynthesis in flashing light. Biochim Biophys Acta 1956, 21:245–258.

Kok B, Beinert H. Light induced EPR signal of photocatalyst P700. II. Two light effects. Biochem Biophys Res Commun 1962, 9:349–354.

Kok B, Forbush B, McGloin M. Cooperation of charges in photosynthetic oxygen evolution. I. A linear four step mechanism. Photochem Photobiol 1970, 11:453–475.

Kolber Z, Barber RT, Coale KH et al. Iron limitation of phytoplankton photosynthesis in the Equatorial Pacific Ocean. Nature 1994, 371:145–149.

Kolber Z, Falkowski PG. Fast repetition rate (FRR) fluorometer for making in situ measurements of primary productivity. Proceedings of Ocean 92 Conference, Newport, Rhode Island, 1992.

Kolber Z, Falkowski PG. Use of active fluorescence to estimate phytoplankton photosynthesis in situ. Limnol Oceanogr 1993, 38:1646–1665.

Kolber Z, Wyman KD, Falkowski PG. Natural variability in photosynthetic energy conversion efficiency: a field study in the Gulf of Maine. Limnol Oceanogr 1990, 35:72–79.

Kolber Z, Zehr J, Falkowski PG. Effects of growth irradiance and nitrogen limitation on photosynthetic energy conversion in photosystem II. Plant Physiol 1988, 88:72–79.

Krause GH, Weis E. Chlorophyll fluorescence and photosynthesis: the basics. Ann Rev Plant Physiol Plant Mol Biol 1991, 42:313–349.

Krom MD, Kress N, Brenner S, Gordon LI. Phosphorus limitation of primary productivity in the eastern Mediterranean Sea. Limnol Oceanogr 1991, 36: 424–432.

Kromer S. Respiration during photosynthesis. Ann Rev Plant Physiol Plant Mol Biol 1995, 46:45–70.

Kübler JE, Raven JA. Consequences of light-limitation for carbon acquisition in three rhodophytes. Mar Ecol Prog Ser 1994, 110:203–208.

Kübler JE, Raven JA. Inorganic carbon acquisition by red seaweeds grown under dynamic light regimes. Hydrobiologica 1996a, 326/327:401–406.

Kübler JE, Raven JA. Non-equilibrium rates of photosynthesis and respiration under dynamic light supply. J Phycol 1996b, 32:963–969.

Kuhlbrandt W, Wang DN, Fujiyoshi Y. Atomic model of plant light-harvesting complex by electron crystallography. Nature 1994, 367:614–621.

Labahn A, Fromme P, Graber P. Uni-site ATP synthesis in thylakoids. FEBS Lett 1990, 271:116–118.

Langdon C. On the causes of interspecific differences in the growth-irradiance relationship for phytoplankton. II. A general review. J Plankton Res 1988, 10: 1291–1312.

Langdon C. The significance of respiration in production measurements based on oxygen. ICES Mar Sci Symp 1993, 197:69–78.

Larkum AWD, Barrett J. Light-harvesting processes in algae. Adv Bot Res 1983, 10:3–219.

Larkum AWD, McComb A.J, Shepherd SA, eds. Aquatic plant studies 2. Biology of seagrasses. Amsterdam: Elsevier, 1989.

LaRoche J, Bennett J, Falkowski PG. Characterization of a cDNA encoding for the 28.5 kDa LHCII apoprotein from the unicellular marine chlorophyte, *Dunaliella tertiolecta*. Gene 1990, 95:165–171.

LaRoche J, Mortain-Bertrand A, Falkowski PG. Light intensity-induced changes in *cab* mRNA and light harvesting complex II apoprotein levels in the unicellular chlorophyte *Dunaliella tertiolecta*. Plant Physiol 1991, 97:147–153.

LaRoche J, Partensky F, Falkowski PG. The major light-harvesting antenna of *Prochlorococcus marinus* is similar to CP43′, a chl binding protein induced by iron limitation in cyanobacteria. In: Mathis P, ed. Photosynthesis: from light to the biosphere. Dordrecht, Netherlands: Kluwer, 1995:171–174.

Laties GG. The cyanide-resistant, alternative path in higher plant respiration. Ann Rev Plant Physiol 1982, 33:519–535.

Lavorel J. Luminescence. In: Govindjee, ed. Bioenergetics of photosynthesis. New York: Academic 1975:223–317.

Lawlor DW. Photosynthesis: molecular, physiological, and environmental processes. London: Longman Scientific, 1993.

Laws EA. The importance of respiration losses in controlling the size distribution of marine phytoplankton. Ecology 1975, 56:419–426.

Laws EA, Bannister TT. Nutrient- and light-limited growth of *Thalassiosira fluvatilis* in continuous culture, with implication for phytoplankton growth in the ocean. Limnol Oceanogr 1980, 25:457–473.

Laws EA, DiTullio GR, Carder KL et al. Primary production in the deep blue sea. Deep-Sea Res 1990, 37:715–730.

Laws EA, DiTullio GR, Redalje DG. High phytoplankton growth and production rates in the North Pacific subtropical gyre. Limnol Oceangr 1987, 32:905–918.

Laws EA, Popp BN, Bidigare RR, Kennicutt MC, Macko SA. Dependence of phytoplankton carbon isotopic composition on growth-rate and $[CO_2](aq)$: theoretical considerations and experimental results. Geochim Cosmochim Acta 1995, 59:1131–1138.

Lazarus D. Speciation in pelagic Protista and its study in the fossil record: a review. Paleobiology 1983, 9:327–340.

Lea PJ, Miflin BJ. Alternative route for nitrogen assimilation in higher plants. Nature 1974, 251:614–616.

Lee CB, Rees D, Horton P. Non-photochemical quenching of chlorophyll fluorescence in the green alga *Dunaliella*. Photosyn Res 1990, 24:167–173.

Lee RE. Phycology. Cambridge: Cambridge University, 1989.

Lee S-H, Kemp P. Single-cell RNA content of natural marine planktonic bacteria measured by hybridization with multiple 16S rRNA-targeted fluorescent probes. Limnol Oceanogr 1994, 39:869–879.

Lee Y-K, Ding S-Y. Accumulation of astaxanthin in *Haematococcus lacustris* (Chlorophyta). J Phycol 1991, 27:575–577.

Letelier RM, Karl DM. The role of *Trichodesmium* spp in the productivity of the subtropical North Pacific Ocean. Mar Ecol Prog Ser 1996, 133:263–273.

Leverenz JW. Factors determining the nature of the light dosage response curve of leaves. In: Baker NR, Bowyer JR, ed. Photoinhibition of photosynthesis: from molecular mechanisms to the field. Oxford: Bios Scientific, 1992:239–254.

Levine RP, Ebersold WT. The genetics and cytology of *Chlamydomonas*. Ann Rev Microbiol 1960, 14: 197–216.

Levitus S. Climatological atlas of the world ocean. Washington, DC: National Oceanic Atmospheric Admin, 1982.

Lewin RA, ed. Origins of plastids. New York: Chapman and Hall, 1993.

Lewis MR. Satellite ocean color observations of global biogeochemical cycles. In: Falkowski PG, Woodhead AD, eds. Primary productivity and biogeochemical cycles in the sea. New York: Plenum, 1992:139–153.

Lewis MR, Horne EPW, Cullen JJ et al. Turbulent motions may control phytoplankton photosynthesis in the upper ocean. Nature 1984, 311:49–50.

Lewis MR, Smith JC. A small volume, short-incubation time method for measurement of photosynthesis as a function of incident irradiance. Mar Ecol Prog Ser 1983, 13:99–102.

Ley AC. The distribution of absorbed light energy for algal photosynthesis. In: Falkowski PG, ed. Primary productivity in the sea. New York: Plenum, 1980: 59–82.

Ley AC, Butler WL. Energy transfer from photosynthesis II to photosystem I in *Porphyridium cruentum*. Biochim Biophys Acta 1977, 462:290–294.

Ley AC, Mauzerall D. Absolute absorption cross sections for photosystem II and the minimum quantum requirement for photosynthesis in *Chlorella vulgaris*. Biochim Biophys Acta 1982, 680:95–106.

Ley AC, Mauzerall D. The extent of energy transfer among photosystem II reaction centers in *Chlorella*. Biochim Biophys Acta 1986, 850:234–248.

Li WKW, Goldman JC. Problems in estimating growth rates of marine phytoplankton from short-term $^{14}C$ assays. Microb Ecol 1981, 7:113–121.

Li WKW, Maestrini SY, eds. Measurement of primary production from the molecular to the global scale. Copenhagen: ICES, 1993.

Liebig J. Chemistry and its application to agriculture and physiology. London: Taylor and Walton, 1840.

Lin S, Carpenter EJ. Growth characteristics of marine phytoplankton determined by cell cycle proteins: the cell cycle of *Ethmodiscus rex* (Bacillariophyceae) in the southwestern North Atlantic Ocean and Carribean Sea. J Phycol 1995, 31:778–785.

Lindeman RL. The trophic-dynamic aspect of ecology. Ecology 1942, 23:399–418.

Lipps JH, ed. Fossil prokaryotes and protists. Oxford: Blackwell, 1993.

Littler MM, Littler DS, Blair S, Norris JN. Deepest known plant life discovered on an uncharted seamount. Science 1985, 277:57–59.

Long SP. Modification of the response of photosynthetic productivity to rising temperature by atmospheric $CO_2$ concentrations: has its importance been underestimated? Plant Cell Environ 1991, 14:729–739.

Long SP, Hallgren JE. Measurement of $CO_2$ assimilation by plants in the field and the laboratory. In: Coombs J, Hall DO, Long SP, Scurlock JMO, eds. Techniques in bioproductivity and photosynthesis. Oxford: Pergamon, 1986:62–94.

Long SP, Humphries S, Falkowski PG. Photoinhibition of photosynthesis in nature. Ann Rev Plant Physiol Plant Mol Biol 1994, 45:655–662.

Longhurst A, Sathyendranath S, Platt T, Caverhill C. An estimate of global primary production in the ocean from satellite radiometer data. J Plank Res 1995, 17:1245–1271.

Lorenz EN. The essence of chaos. Seattle: Univ of Washington, 1993.

Lorenzen CJ. A method for the continuous measurement of in vivo chlorophyll concentration. Deep-Sea Res 1966, 13:223–227.

Lorenzen CJ. Diurnal variation in photosynthetic activity of natural phytoplankton populations. Limnol Oceanogr 1963, 8:56–62.

Lorimer GH. The carboxylation and oxygenation of ribulose 1,5-bisphosphate: the primary events in photosynthesis and photorespiration. Ann Rev Plant Physiol 1981, 32:349–383.

Lovelock JE. Gaia: a new look at life on earth. Oxford: Oxford University, 1994.

Lyell C. Principles of geology [London, 1830]. Chicago: Univ of Chicago, 1990.

Maberly DJ. The plant book. Cambridge: Cambridge University, 1987.

Mabberly SC. Photosynthesis by *Fontinalis antiphyretica* I. Interaction between photon irradiance, concentration of carbon dioxide, and temperature. New Phytol 1985a, 100:127–140.

Mabberly SC. Photosynthesis by *Fontinalis antiphyretica* II. Assesment of environmental factors limiting photosynthesis and production. New Phytol 1985b, 100: 141–155.

Mabberly SC, Raven JA, Johnston AM. Discrimination between $^{12}C$ and $^{13}C$ by marine plants. Oecologia 1992, 91:481–492.

MacArthur R. On the relative abundance of species. Am Nat 1960, 94:25–36.

MacDonald FD, Buchanan BB. The reductive pentose phosphate pathway and its regulation. In: Dennis DT, Turpin DH, eds. Plant physiology, biochemistry and molecular biology. Essex: Longman Scientific, 1990: 239–252.

MacFarlane JJ, Raven JA. C, N, and P nutrition of *Lemanea mamillosa* Kutz (Batrachospermales, Rhodophyta) in the Dighty Burn, Angus, Scotland. Plant Cell Environ 1990, 13:1–13.

MacKintosh C, Beattie KA, Klumpp S et al. Cyanobacterial microcystin-LR is a potent and specific inhibitor of protein phosphatases 1 and 2A from both mammals and higher plants. FEBS Lett 1990, 264:187–192.

MacKintosh C, Coggins J, Cohen P. Plant protein phosphatases. Subcellular distribution, detection of protein phosphatase 2C and identification of protein phosphatase 2A as the major quinate dehydrogenase phosphatase. Biochem J 1991, 273:733–738.

Madsen TV. Growth and photosynthetic acclimation by *Ranunculus aquatilis* L. in response to inorganic carbon availability. New Phytol 1993, 125:707–715.

Madsen TV. Inorganic carbon uptake kinetics of the stripian macrophyte *Callitmdre caphocarpa* Serdt. Aquat Bot 1991, 40:321–332.

Malkin R. Cytochrome $bc_1$ and $b_6f$ complexes of photosynthetic membranes. Photosyn Res 1992, 33:121–136.

Malkin S, Canaani O. The use and characteristics of the photoacoustic method in the study of photosynthesis. Ann Rev Plant Phyisol Plant Mol Biol 1994, 45: 493–526.

Malkin S, Kok B. Fluorescence induction studies in isolated chloroplasts I. Number of components involved in the reaction and quantum yields. Biochim Biophys Acta 1966, 126:413–432.

Malone TC. Algal size and phytoplankton ecology. In: Morris I, ed. The physiological ecology of phytoplankton. London: Blackwell, 1980.

Malone TC. Diurnal rhythms in netplankton and nannoplankton assimilation numbers. Mar Biol 1971, 10: 285–289.

Malone TC. Phytoplankton photosynthesis and carbon-specific growth: light-saturated rates in a nutrient rich environment. Limnol Oceanogr 1982, 27:226–235.

Malone TC, Neale PJ. Parameters of light dependent photosynthesis for phytoplankton size fractions in temperate esturine and coastal environments. Mar Biol 1981, 61:289–297.

Manley SL, Goodwin K, North WJ. Laboratory production of bromoform, methyl bromide, and methyl iodide by macroalgae and distribution in nearshore Southern California waters. Limnol Oceanogr 1992, 37:1652–1659.

Mann KH. Seaweeds: their productivity and strategy for growth. Science 1973, 182:975–981.

Mann KH, Lazier JRN. Dynamics of marine ecosystems. Oxford: Blackwell, 1991.

Margulis L. Origin and evolution of the eukaryotic cell. Taxon 1974, 23:225–226.

Marra J. Phytoplankton photosynthetic response to vertical movement in a mixed layer. Mar Biol 1978, 46:203–208.

Martin JH. Glacial–interglacial $CO_2$ change: the iron hypothesis. Paleoceanography 1990, 5:1–13.

Martin JH. Iron as a limiting factor in oceanic productivity. In: Falkowski PG, Woodhead A, eds. Primary productivity and biogeochemical cycles in the sea. New York: Plenum, 1992:123–137.

Martin JH. Iron, Liebig's law and the greenhouse. Oceanography 1991, 4:52–55.

Martin JH, Gordon RM, Fitzwater SE. Iron in Antarctica. Nature 1990, 345:156–158.

Martin W, Somerville CC, Loiseaux-de Goër S. Molecular phylogenies of plastid origins and algal evolution. J Mol Evol 1992, 35:385–404.

Matorin DN, Vasil'ev IR, Vedernikov VI. Photoinhibition of primary photosynthetic reactions in natural phytoplankton populations of the Black Sea. Sov Plant Physiol 1992, 39:285–290.

Mauzerall D. Light-induced changes in *Chlorella*, and the primary photoreaction for the production of oxygen. Proc Nat Acad Sci 1972, 69:1358–1362.

Mauzerall D. Multiple excitations and the yield of chlorophyll *a* fluorescence in photosynthetic systems. Photochem Photobiol 1978, 28:991–998.

Maxwell DP, Falk S, Trick CG, Huner NPA. Growth at low temperature mimics high-light acclimation in *Chlorella vulgaris*. Plant Physiol 1994, 105:535–543.

Maxwell DP, Laudenbach DE, Huner NPA. Redox regulation of light-harvesting complex II and cab messenger RNA abundance in *Dunaliella salina*. Plant Physiol 1995, 109:787–795.

Mayfield SP, Schirmer-Rahire M, Frank G et al. Analysis of the genes of the OEE1 and OEE3 proteins of the photosystem II complex from *Chlamydomonas reinhardtii*. Plant Mol Biol 1989, 12:683–693.

Mayr E. Populations, species, and evolution. Cambridge, MA: Harvard, 1970.

Mazel D, Marliere P. Adaptive eradication of methionine and cysteine from cyanobacterial light-harvesting proteins. Nature 1989, 341:245–248.

McBride GB. Simple calculation of daily photosynthesis by means of five photosynthesis-irradiance equations. Limnol Oceanogr 1992, 37:1796–1808.

McCarthy JJ. Nitrogen. In: Morris I, ed. The physiological ecology of phytoplankton. Oxford: Blackwell, 1980: 195–233.

McDermott G, Prince SM, Freer A, Hawthornthwaite-Lawless AM et al. Crystal structure of an integral membrane light-harvesting complex from photosynthetic bacteria. Nature 1995, 374:517–521.

McDuff RE, Chisholm SW. The calculation of *in situ* growth rates of phytoplankton populations from fractions of cells undergoing mitosis: a clarification. Limnol Oceanogr 1982, 27:783–788.

McElroy MB. Marine biological controls on atmospheric $CO_2$ and climate. Nature 1983, 302:328–329.

McKay ML, Gibbs SP. Composition and function of pyrenoids: cytochemical and immunocytochemical approaches. Can J Bot 1991, 69:1040–1052.

McKay ML, Gibbs SP, Espie GS. Effect of dissolved carbon on the expression of carboxysomes: localization of Rubisco and the mode of inorganic cabon transport in cells of the cyanobacterium *Synechococcus* UTEX 625. Microbiology 1993, 159:21–29.

Medlin LK, Barker GLA, Baumann M et al. Molecular biology and systematics. In: Green JC, Leadbeater BSC, eds. The Haptophyte algae, Oxford: Clarendon, 1994:393–411.

Medlin LK, Lange M, Barker GLA, Hayes PK. Can molecular techniques change our ideas about the species concept? In: Joint I, ed. Molecular ecology of aquatic microbes. Heidelberg: Springer-Verlag, 1995:133–152.

Meeks JC. Chlorophylls. In: Stewart WDP, ed. Algal physiology and biochemistry. Berkeley: Univ of California, 1974:161–175.

Melis A, Anderson JM. Structural and functional organization of the photosystems in spinach chloroplasts, antenna size, relative electron transport capacity and chlorophyll composition. Biochim Biophys Acta 1983, 724:473.

Melis A, Thielsen APGM. The relative absorption cross-sections for photosystem I and photosystem II in chloroplasts from three types of *Nicotiana tabacum*. Biochim Biophys Acta 1980, 589:275–286.

Merrett MJ. Inorganic carbon transport in some marine microalgae species. Can J Bot 1991, 69:1032–1034.

Metz J, Nixon P, Diner B. Nucleotide sequence of the psbA3 gene from the cyanobacterium *Synechocystis* PCC-6803. Nucl Acids Res 1990, 18:6715.

Michel H, Deisenhofer J. Relevance of the photosynthetic reaction center from purple bacteria to the structure of photosystem II. Biochemistry 1988, 27:1–7.

Michel H, Deisenhofer J. X-ray diffraction studies on a crystalline bacterial photosynthetic reaction center: a progress report and conclusions on the structure of photosystem II reaction centers. In: Staehelin LA, Arntzen CJ, eds. Photosynthesis III: photosynthetic membranes and light-harvesting systems. New York: Springer-Verlag, 1986:371–381.

Michel H-P, Tellenbach M, Boschetti A. A chlorophyll b-less mutant of *Chlamydomonas reinhardtii* lacking in the light-harvesting chlorophyll *a*/*b*-protein complex but not in its apoproteins. Biophys Biochim Acta 1983, 725:417–424.

Michell BG, Kiefer DA. Chlorophyll *a* specific absorption and fluorescence excitation spectra for light-limited phytoplankton. Deep-Sea Res 1988, 35:639–663.

Miller CB, Frost BW, Wheeler PA et al. Ecological dynamics in the subarctic Pacific, a possibly iron-limited ecosystem. Limnol Oceanogr 1991, 36:1600–1615.

Mills EL. Biological oceanography: an early history, 1870–1960. Ithaca, NY: Cornell, 1989.

Milos P, Morse D, Hastings JW. Circadian control over synthesis of many *Gonyaulax* proteins is at a translation level. Naturwiss 1990, 77:87–89.

Mitchell P. Coupling of phosphorylation to electron and hydrogen transfer by a chemiosmotic type of mechanism. Nature 1961, 191:44–148.

Mitchell P. Protonmotive redox mechanism of the cytochrome b-c complex in the respiratory chain: protonmotive UQ cycle. FEBS 1975, 56:1–6.

Mitusi A, Kumazawa S, Takahashi A et al. Strategy by which nitrogen-fixing unicellular cyanobacteria grow photoautotrophically. Nature 1986, 323:720–722.

Mobley CD. Light and water: radiative transfer in natural waters. San Diego: Academic, 1994.

Molina MJ, Rowland FS. Stratospheric sink for chlorofluorocarbons. Chlorine atom-catalyzed destruction of ozone. Nature 1974, 249:810–812.

Monod J. Recherches sur la croissance des cultures bacteriennes. Paris: Hermann, 1942.

Moore RM, Tokarczyk R. Volatile biogenic halocarbons in the Northwest Atlantic. Global Biogeochem Cycles 1993, 7:195–210.

Morden CW, Golden SS. psbA genes indicate common ancestry of prochlorophytes and chloroplasts. Nature 1989, 337:382–385.

Morel A. Available, usable, and stored radiant energy in relation to marine photosynthesis. Deep-Sea Res 1978, 25:673–688.

Morel A. Light and marine photosynthesis: a spectral model with geochemical and climatological implications. Prog Oceanogr 1991a, 26:263–306.

Morel A. Optical modeling of the upper ocean in relation to its biogenous matter content (case one waters). J Geophys Res 1988, 93:10749–10768.

Morel A. Optical properties of pure water and pure seawater. In: Jerlov NG, Nielsen ES, eds. Optical aspects of oceanography. London: Academic, 1974:1–24.

Morel A. Optics of marine particles and marine optics. In: Demers S, ed. Particle analysis in oceanography. Berlin: Springer-Verlag, 1991b:141–188.

Morel A, Ahn YH. Optical efficiency factors of free-living marine bacteria: influence of bacterioplankton upon the optical properties and particulate organic carbon in oceanic waters. J Mar Res 1990, 48:145–175.

Morel A, Andre J-M. Pigment distribution and primary production in the western Mediterranean as derived and modeled from coastal zone color scanner observations. J Geophys Res 1991, 96:12685–12698.

Morel FMM, Hudson RJM, Price NM. Limitation of productivity by trace metals in the sea. Limnol Oceanogr 1991, 36:1742–1755.

Morel FMM, Reinfelder JR, Roberts SB et al. Zinc and carbon co-limitation of marine phytoplankton. Nature 1994, 369:740–742.

Mori T, Binder B, Johnson CH. Circadian gating of cell division in cyanobacteria growing with average doubling times of less than 24 hours. Proc Nat Acad Sci USA 1996, 93:10183–10188.

Morris I. Photosynthetic products, physiological state, and phytoplankton growth. In: Platt T, ed. Physiological bases of phytoplankton ecology. Ottawa: Can Bull Fish Aquat Sci, 1981:83–102.

Morris I, Syrett P. The effect of nitrogen starvation on the activity of nitrate reductase and other enzymes in *Chlorella*. J Gen Microbiol 1965, 38:21–28.

Morris I, Yentsch CS, Yentsch CM. The physiological state with respect to nitrogen of phytoplankton from low-nutrient subtropical water as measured by the effect of ammonium ion on dark carbon fixation. Limnol Oceanogr 1971, 16:859–868.

Mörschel E, Rhiel E. Phycobilisomes and thylakoids: the light-harvesting system of cyanobacteria and red algae. In: Harris JR, Horne RW, eds. Membranous structures. New York: Academic, 1987:209–254.

Morse D, Salois P, Markovic P, Hastings JW. A nuclear encoded form II RUBISCO in dinoflagellates. Science 1995, 268:1622–1626.

Mortain-Bertrand A, Bennett J, Falkowski PG. Photoregulation of LHCII in *Dunaliella tertiolecta*: Evidence that apoprotein abundance but not stability requires chlorophyll synthesis. Plant Physiol 1990, 94:304–311.

Mullet JE. Dynamic regulation of chloroplast transcription. Plant Physiol 1993, 103.

Mullet JE, Burke JJ, Arntzen CJ. Chlorophyll proteins of photosystem I. Plant Physiol 1980, 65:814–822.

Mullet JE, Klein RR. Transcription and RNA stability are important determinants of higher plant chloroplast RNA in leaves. Embo J 1987, 6:1571–1579.

Murata N. Control of excitation transfer in photosynthesis. IV. Kinetics of chlorophyll *a* fluorescence in *Porphyra yezoensis*. Biochim Biophys Acta 1970, 205:379–389.

Murphy DG. The molecular organisation of the photosynthetic membranes of higher plants. Biochim Biophys Acta 1986, 864:33–94.

Myers J. Enhancement studies in photosynthesis. Ann Rev Plant Physiol 1971, 22:289–312.

Myers J. On the algae: thoughts about physiology and measurements of efficiency. In: Falkowski PG, ed. Primary productivity in the sea. New York: Plenum, 1980:1–16.

Myers J. Photosynthetic and respiratory electron transport in a cyanobacterium. Photosyn Res 1986, 9:135–147.

Myers J. The 1932 experiments. Photosyn Res 1994, 40:303–310.

Myers J, Graham J-R. The photosynthetic unit in *Chlorella* measured by repetitive short flashes. Plant Physiol 1971, 48:282–286.

Nanba O, Satoh K. Isolation of a PS II reaction center consisting of D-1 and D-2 polypeptides and cytochrome b-559. Proc Nat Acad Sci USA 1987, 84:109–112.

Neale PJ. Algal photoinhibition and photosynthesis in the aquatic environment. In: Kyle DJ, Osmond CB, Arntzen CJ, eds. Photoinhibition. New York: Elsevier, 1987:39–65.

Neefs J-M, Van de Peer Y, De Rijk P et al. Compilation of small ribosomal subunit RNA structures. Nucleic Acids Res 1993, 21:3025–3049.

Nelson DM. Kinetics of silicic acid uptake and rates of silica dissolution in the marine diatom *Thalassiosira pseudonana*. J Phycol 1976, 12:246–252.

Nelson DM, Treguer P, Brzezinski MA et al. Production and dissolution of biogenic silica in the ocean—revised global estimates, comparison with regional data and relationship to biogenic sedimentation. Global Biogeochem Cycles 1995, 9:359–372.

Nelson JR, Wakeham SG. A phytol-substituted chlorophyll c from *Emiliana huxleyi* (Prymnesiophyceae). J Phycol 1989, 25:761–766.

Nelson N. Coupling factors from higher plants. Meth Enzym 1980, 69:301–313.

Neori A, Vernet M, Holm-Hansen O, Haxo FT. Comparison of chlorophyll far-red and red fluorescence excitation spectra with photosynthetic oxygen action spectra for photosystem II in algae. Mar Ecol Prog Ser 1988, 44:297–302.

Newman JR, Raven JA. Photosynthetic carbon assimilation by *Crassula helmsii*. Oecologia 1995, 101:494–499.

Nielsen MV. Photosynthetic characteristics of the coccolithophorid *Emiliania huxleyi* (Prymnesiophyceae) exposed to elevated concentrations of dissolved inorganic carbon. J Phycol 1995, 31:715–719.

Nixon PJ, Rogner M, Diner BA. Expression of a higher plant psbA gene in *Synechocystis* 6803 yields a functional hybrid photosystem-II reaction center complex. Plant Cell 1991, 3:383–395.

Odum EP. Fundamentals of ecology. Philadelphia: WB Saunders, 1971.

Ogren WL. Photorespiration: pathways, regulation, and modification. Ann Rev Plant Physiol 1984, 35: 415–442.

Ohad I, Koike H, Kyle DJ, Inoue Y. Mechanism of photoinhibition in vivo. J Biol Chem 1990, 265:1972–1979.

Ohad I, Kyle DJ, Arntzen CJ. Membrane protein damage and repair: removal and replacement of inactived 32-kD polypeptides in chloroplast membranes. J Cell Biol 1984, 99:481–485.

Ohad I, Kyle DJ, Hirschberg J. Light-dependent degradation of the $Q_B$-protein in isolated pea thylakoids. Embo J 1985, 4:1655–1659.

Olaizola M. Laboratory and field studies of diatoxanthin cycling and non-photochemical quenching in marine phytoplankton. PhD thesis. State Univ of New York at Stony Brook, 1993.

Olaizola M, LaRoche J, Kolber Z, Falkowski PG. Non-photochemical fluorescence quenching and the diadinoxathin cycle in a marine diatom. Photosyn Res 1994, 41:357–370.

Olaizola M, Yamamoto HY. Short-term response of the diadinoxanthin cycle and fluorescence yield to high irradiance in *Chaetoceros muelleri* (Bacillariophyceae). J Phycol 1994, 30:606–612.

Öquist G, Chow WS, Anderson JM. Photoinhibition of photosynthesis represents as mechanism for the long-term regulation of photosystem II. Planta 1992, 186:450–460.

Orellana MV, Perry MJ. An immunoprobe to measure Rubisco concentrations and maximal photosynthetic rates of individual phytoplankton cells. Limnol Oceanogr 1992, 37:478–490.

Ort DR, Oxborough K. In situ regulation of chloroplast coupling factor activity. Ann Rev Plant Physiol Plant Mol Biol 1992, 43:269–291.

Osmond CB. What is photoinhibition? Some insights from comparisons of shade and sun plants. In: Baker NR, Bowyer JR, eds. Photoinhibition of photosynthesis: from molecular mechanisms to the field. Oxford: Bios Scientific, 1994:1–24.

Osmond CB, Austin MP, Berry JA et al. Stress physiology and the distribution of plants. BioScience 1987, 37:38–48.

Osmond CB, Chow WS. Ecology of photosynthesis in the sun and shade: summary and prognostications. Austral J Plant Physiol 1988, 15:1–9.

Owens TG, Falkowski PG, Whitledge TE. Diel periodicity in cellular chlorophyll content in marine diatoms. Mar Biol 1980, 59:71–77.

Owens TG, Riper DM, Falkowski PG. Studies of δ-aminolevulinic acid dehydrase from *Skeletonema costatum*, a marine plankton diatom. Plant Physiol 1978, 62:516–521.

Owens TG, Wold ER. Light-harvesting function in the diatom *Phaeodactylum tricornutum*: I. Isolation and characterization of pigment-protein complexes. Plant Physiol 1986, 80:732–738.

Paasche E, Brubak S, Skattebøl S et al. Growth and calcification in the coccolithophorid *Emiliania huxleyi* (Haptophyceae) at low salinities. Phycologia 1996, 35:394–403.

Packard TT. The light dependence of nitrate reductase in marine phytoplankton. Limnol Oceanogr 1973, 18: 466–469.

Paillotin G, Breton J. Orientation of chlorophylls within chloroplasts as shown by optical and electrochromic properties of the photosynthetic membrane. Biophys J 1977, 18:63–73.

Pakrasi HB, Riethman HC, Sherman LA. Organization of pigment proteins in the photosystem II complex of the cyanobacterium *Anacystis nidulans* R2. Proc Nat Acad Sci USA 1985, 82:6903–6907.

Palenik B, Haselkorn R. Multiple evolutionary origins of prochlorophytes, the chlorophyll *b*-containing prokaryotes. Nature 1992, 355:265–267.

Pamatmat MM, Banse K. Oxygen consumption by the seabed. 2. In situ measurements to a depth of 180m. Limnol Oceanogr 1969, 14:250–259.

Pancic PG, Strotmann H. Structure of the nuclear encoded γ subunit of $CF_0CF_1$ of the diatom *Odontella sinensis* including its presequence. FEBS Lett 1993, 320:61–66.

Pancic PG, Strotmann H, Kowallik KV. Chloroplast ATPase genes in the diatom *Odontella sinensis* reflect cyanobacterial characters in structure and arrangement. J Mol Biol 1992, 224:529–536.

Park R, Epstein S. Metabolic fractionation of $C^{13}$ and $C^{12}$ in plants. Plant Physiol 1961, 36:133–138.

Parsons T, Takahashi M, Hargrave B. Biological oceanographic processes. New York: Pergamon, 1984.

Parsons TR, Stephens K, Strickland JDM. On the chemical composition of 11 species of marine phytoplankton. J Fish Res Bd Can 1961, 18:1001–1016.

Pasciak WJ, Gauis G. Transport limitation of nutrient uptake in phytoplankton. Limnol Oceanogr 1974, 19:881–888.

Paytan A, Kastner M, Chavez FP. Glacial to interglacial fluctuations in productivity in the equatorial Pacific as indicated by marine barite. Science 1996, 274: 1355–1357.

Perry MJ, Eppley RW. Phosphate uptake by phytoplankton in the central North Pacific Ocean. Deep-Sea Res 1981, 28A:39–49.

Perry MJ, Talbot MC, Alberte RS. Photoadaptation in marine phytoplankton: response of the photosynthetic unit. Mar Biol 1981, 62:91–101.

Phillips JN Jr, Myers J. Growth rate of *Chlorella* in flashing light. Plant Physiol 1954, 29:152–161.

Pickard GL, Emery WJ. Descriptive physical oceanography. Oxford: Pergamon, 1990.

Pirson A, Lorenzen M. Synchronized dividing algae. Ann Rev Plant Physiol 1966, 17:439–458.

Platt T. Local phytoplankton abundance and turbulence. Deep-Sea Res 1972, 19:183–187.

Platt T. Primary production of the ocean water column as a function of surface light intensity: algorithms for remote sensing. Deep-Sea Res 1986, 33:149–163.

Platt T, Bird DF, Sathyendranath S. Critical depth and marine primary production. Proc R Soc London 1991, 238:205–217.

Platt T, Gallegos CL, Harrison WG. Photoinhibition of photosynthesis in natural assemblage of marine phytoplankton. J Mar Res 1980, 38:687–701.

Platt T, Irwin B. Caloric content of phytoplankton. Limnol Oceanogr 1973, 18:306–310.

Platt T, Sathyendranath S. Oceanic primary production: estimation by remote sensing at local and regional scales. Science 1988, 241:1613–1620.

Platt T, Sathyendranath S, Ravindran P. Primary production by phytoplankton: analytic solutions for daily rates per unit area of water surface. Proc R Soc London 1990, B241:101–111.

Portis AR, Salvucci ME, Ogren WL. Activation of ribulose bisphosphate carboxylase/oxygenase at physiological $CO_2$ and ribulose bisphosphate concentrations by rubisco activase. Plant Physiol 1986, 82:967–971.

Post AF, Dubinsky Z, Falkowski PG. Kinetics of light-intensity adaptation in a marine planktonic diatom. Mar Biol 1984, 83:231–238.

Post AF, Dubinsky Z, Wyman K, Falkowski PG. Physiological responses of a marine planktonic diatom to transitions in growth irradiance. Mar Ecol Prog Ser 1985, 25:161–169.

Post AF, Ohad I, Warner KM, Bullerjahn GS. Energy distribution between photosystems 1 and 2 in the photosynthetic prokaryote *Prochlorothrix hollandica* involves a chlorophyll *a/b* antenna which associates with photosystem 1. Biochim Biophys Acta 1993, 1144:374–384.

Postgate JR, ed. Nitrogen fixation. London: Edward Arnold, 1987.

Postgate JR, ed. The chemistry and biochemistry of nitrogen fixation. New York: Plenum, 1984.

Powell TM, Steele JH, eds. Ecological time series. New York: Chapman and Hall, 1995.

Prasil O, Adir N, Ohad I. Dynamics of photosystem II: mechanism of photoinhibition and recovery processes. In: Barber JR, ed. The photosystems: stucture, function and molecular biology. New York: Elsevier, 1992:295–348.

Prasil O, Kolber Z, Berry JA, Falkowski PG. Cyclic electron flow around photosystem II in vivo. Photosyn Res 1996, 48:395–410.

Precali R, Falkowski PG. Incorporation of [$^{14}$C]-glutamate into proteins and chlorophylls in *Dunaliella tertiolecta*, a marine chlorophyte. Biologia Plant 1983, 25:187–195.

Prèzelin BB, Matlick HA. Time course of photoadaptation in the photosynthesis irradiance relationship of a dinoflagellate exhibiting photosynthetic periodicity. Mar Biol 1980, 58:85–96.

Puiseux-Dao S. Cell-cycle events in unicellular algae. In: Platt T, ed. Physiological bases of phytoplankton ecology. Ottawa: J Can Fish Res Bd, 1981:130–149.

Rabinowitch E, Govindjee. Photosynthesis. New York: Wiley, 1969.

Race HL, Hind G. A protein kinase in the core of photosystem II. Biochem 1996, 35:13006–13010.

Ragan MA, Bird CJ, Rice EL et al. A molecular phylogeny of the marine red algae (Rhodophyta) based on the nuclear small sequenced rRNA gene. Proc Nat Acad Sci USA 1994, 91:7276–7280.

Ramalho CB, Hastings JW, Colepicolo P. Circadian oscillation of nitrate reductase activity in *Golyaulax polyedra* is due to changes in cellular protein levels. Plant Physiol 1995, 107:225–231.

Raman CV. On the molecular scattering of light in water and the colour of the sea. Proc R Soc London 1922, 101A:64–79.

Ramanathan VL. Greenhouse effect due to chlorofluoro-carbons: climate implications. Science 1975, 190:50–52.

Ramazanov Z, Mason CB, Geraghty AM et al. The low $CO_2$ inductable 36-kilodalton protein is localized to the chloroplast envelope of *Chlamydomonas reinhardtii*. Plant Physiol 1993, 101:1193–1199.

Ramus J. A form–function analysis of photon capture for seaweeds. Hydrobiologica 1990, 204/205:65–71.

Ramus J. Productivity of seaweeds. In: Falkowski PG, ed. Primary productivity and biogeochemical cycles in the sea. New York: Plenum, 1992:239–255.

Rau W. Functions of carotenoids other than in photosynthesis. In: Goodwin TW, ed. Plant pigment. New York: Academic, 1988:231–255.

Raven JA. A cost-benefit analysis of photon absorption by photosynthetic unicells. New Phytol 1984b, 94:593–625.

Raven JA. Carbon: a phycocentric view. In: Evans GT, Fasham MJR, eds. Towards a model of ocean biogeochemical processes. Berlin: Springer-Verlag, 1993:123–152.

Raven JA. Division of labour between chloroplasts and cytoplasm. In: Barber J, ed. The intact chloroplast. Amsterdam: Elsevier, 1976a:403–443.

Raven JA. Energetics and transport in aquatic plants. New York: AR Liss, 1984a.

Raven JA. Implications of inorganic C utilization: ecology, evolution and geochemistry. Can J Bot 1991a, 69:908–924.

Raven JA. Inorganic carbon acquisition by marine autotrophs. Adv Bot Res 1997a (in press).

Raven JA. Photosynthetic and nonphotosynthetic roles of carbonic anhydrase and cyanobacteria. Phycologia 1995, 34:93–101.

Raven JA. Responses of aquatic photosynthetic organisms to increased solar UVB. J Photochem Photobiol Biol 1991b, 9:239–244.

Raven JA. The iron and molybdenum use efficiencies of plant growth with different energy, carbon and nitrogen sources. New Phytol 1988, 109:279–287.

Raven JA. The quantitative role of dark respiratory processes in heterotrophic and photolithotropic plant growth. Ann Bot 1976b, 40:587–602.

Raven JA. The role of autotrophs in global $CO_2$ cycling. In: Linstrom ME, Tabita FR, eds. Microbial growth on C1 compounds. Dordrecht, Netherlands: Kluwer, 1996:351–358.

Raven JA. The roles of marine biota in the evolution of terrestrial biota. Biogeochem 1997b (in press).

Raven J, Beardall J. Respiration and photorespiration. In: Platt T, ed. Physiological bases of phytoplankton ecology. Ottawa: J Can Fish Res Bd, 1981a:55–82.

Raven JA, Beardall J. The intrinsic permeability of biological membranes to H$^+$: significance for low rates of energy transformation. FEMS Mirobiol Letts 1981b, 10:1–5.

Raven JA, Beardall J. The lower limit of photon fluence rate for phototrophic growth: the significance of "slippage" reactions. Plant Cell Environ 1982, 5:117–124.

Raven JA, Farquhar GD. The influence of N metabolism and organic acid synthesis on the natural abundance of C isotopes in plants. New Phytol 1990, 116:505–529.

Raven JA, Geider RJ. Temperature and algal growth. New Phytol 1988, 110:441–461.

Raven JA, Handley LL, MacFarlane JJ et al. The role of $CO_2$ uptake and CAM in inorganic C acquisition by plants of the isoetid life form. A review, with new data on *Eriocaulon decangulare*. New Phytol 1988, 108: 125–148.

Raven JA, Johnston AM. Inorganic carbon acquisition mechanisms in marine phytoplankton and their implications for the use of other resources. Limnol Oceanogr 1991, 36:1701–1714.

Raven JA, Johnston AM. Responses of aquatic macrophytes to changes in temperature and $CO_2$ concentration. In: Yamamoto HY, Smith CM, eds. Photosynthetic responses to the environment. Rockville, MD: American Society of Plant Physiologists, 1993:102–112.

Raven JA, Johnston AM, Bin Surif M. The photosynthetic apparatus as a phyletic character. In: Green JC, Diver WL, Leadbetter BSC, eds. The chromophyte algae: problems and perspectives. Oxford: Oxford University, 1989:41–60.

Raven JA, Johnston AM, Newman JR, Scrimgeour CM. Inorganic carbon acquisition by aquatic photolithotrops of the Dighty Burn, Angus UK: uses and limitations of natural abundance measurements of carbon isotopes. New Phytol 1994, 127:271–286.

Raven JA, Johnston AM, MacFarlane JJ. Carbon metabolism. In: Sheath RG, Cole KM, eds. The biology of red algae. Cambridge: Cambridge University, 1990: 172–202.

Raven JA, Johnston AM, Turpin DH. The influence of changes in $CO_2$ concentration and temperature on marine phytoplankton $^{13}C/^{12}C$ ratios: an analysis of possible mechanisms. Paleogeogr Paleoclimatol Paleoecol 1993, 103:1–12.

Raven JA, Richardson K. Dinophyte flagella: a cost-benefit analysis. New Phytol 1984, 98:259–276.

Raven JA, Walker DI, Johnston AM et al. Implications of $^{13}C$ natural abundance measurements for photosynthetic performance by marine macrophytes in their natural environment. Mar Ecol Prog Ser 1995, 123:193–205.

Rayleigh L. On the scattering of light by small particles. Philos Mag 1871, 41:447–454.

Raynaud D, Jouzel J, Barnola JM et al. The ice record of greenhouse gases. Science 1993, 259:926–934.

Read BA, Tabita FR. High substrate specificity factor ribulase bisphosphate carboxylase/oxygenase from eukaryotic marine algal and properties recombinant cyanobacterial RUBISCO containing "algal" residue modifications. Arch Biochem Biophys 1994, 312: 210–218.

Redalje DG, Laws EA. A new method for estimating phytoplankton growth rates and carbon biomass. Mar Biol 1981, 62:73–79.

Redfield AC. On the proportions of organic derivatives in sea water and their relation to the composition of plankton. Liverpool: James Johnstone Memorial, 1934.

Redfield AC. The biological control of chemical factors in the environment. Am Sci 1958, 46:205–221.

Redfield AC, Ketchum BH, Richards FA. The influence of organisms on the chemical composition of sea-water. In: Hill MN, ed. The sea. New York: Interscience, 1963:26–77.

Redlinger T, Gantt E. Photosynthetic membranes of *Porphyridium cruentum*. An analysis of chlorophyll-protein complexes and heme-binding proteins. Plant Physiol 1983, 73:36–40.

Reid AF, Urey HC. The use of the exchange between carbon dioxide, carbonic acid, bicarbonate ion, and water for isotopic concentration. J Chem Phys 1943, 11:403–412.

Reiskind JB, Bowes G. The role of phosphoenolpyruvate carboxykinase in a marine microalga with C4-like photosynthetic characteristics. Proc Nat Acad Sci USA 1991, 88:2883–2887.

Reith M. Molecular biology of Rhodophyte and Chromophyte plastids. Ann Rev Plant Physiol Plant Mol Biol 1995, 46:549–575.

Reith M, Munholland J. A high-resolution gene made of the chloroplast genome of red algae *Porphyra purpurea*. Plant Cell 1993, 5:465–475.

Reithman HC, Sherman LA. Purification and characterization of and iron stress-induced chlorophyll-protein from the cyanobacterium *Anancystis nudulans* R2. Biochim Biophys Acta 1988, 935:141–151.

Renger G. Energy transfer and trapping in photosystem II. In: Barber JR, ed. The photosystems: structure, function and molecular biology. New York: Elsevier, 1992:45–99.

Reuter JGJ. Theoretical Fe limitations of microbial $N_2$ fixation in the oceans. Eos 1982, 63:445.

Richards L, Thurston CF. Protein turnover in *Chlorella fusca* var. vacuolata: measurements of the overall rate of intracellular protein degradation using isotope exchange with water. J Gen Microbiol 1980, 121: 49–61.

Richardson K, Beardall J, Raven JA. Adaptation of unicellular algae to irradiance: an analysis of strategies. New Phytol 1983, 93:157–171.

Riebesell U, Wolf-Gladrow DA, Smetacek V. Carbon dioxide limitation of marine phytoplankton growth rates. Nature 1993, 361:249–251.

Riper DM, Owens TG, Falkowski PG. Chlorophyll turnover in *Skeletonema costatum*, a marine plankton diatom. Plant Physiol 1979, 64:49–54.

Rivkin RB, Putt M. Diel periodicity of photosynthesis in polar phytoplankton: influence on primary production. Science 1987, 238:1285–1288.

Rivkin RB, Swift E. Diel and vertical patterns of alkaline phosphatase activity in the oceanic dinoflagellate *Pyrocystis noctiluca*. Limnol Oceanogr 1979, 24: 107–116.

Roberts DR, Kristie DN, Thompson JE et al. In vitro evidence for the involvement of activated oxygen in light-induced aggregation of thylakoid proteins. Physiol Planta 1991, 82:389–396.

Rochaix JD. *Chlamydomonas reinhardtii* as the photosynthetic yeast. Ann Rev Genet 1995, 29:209–230.

Rochaix J-D, Kuchka M, Mayfield S et al. Nuclear and chloroplast mutations affect the synthesis or stability of the chloroplast *psbC* gene product in *Chlamydomonas reinhardtii*. Embo J 1989, 8:1013–1021.

Rodriguez-Rosales MP, Herrin DL, Thompson GA. Identification of low molecular mass GTP-binding proteins in membranes of the halotolerant alga *Dunaliella salina*. Plant Physiol 1991, 98:446–451.

Ronnenberg T. The complex circadian rhythm of *Gonyaulax polyedra*. Physiol Plant 1996, 96:733–737.

Rosen R. Optimality principles in biology. London: Butterworths, 1967.

Rotatore C, Lew RR, Colman B. Active uptake of $CO_2$ during photosynthesis in the green alga *Eremosphaera viridis* is mediated by a $CO_2$-ATPase. Planta 1992, 188:539–545.

Rowe GT, Haedrich RL. The biota and biological

processes of the continental slope. Sep Spec Pub 1979, 27:49–59.

Roy H. Chaperonins—what do they really do? Plant Physiol 1992, 11:75–78.

Rundel RD. Action spectra and estimation of biologically effective UV radiation. Physiol Plant 1983, 58: 360–366.

Rutherford AW. Photosystem II, the water-splitting enzyme. TIBS 1989, 14:227–232.

Rutherford AW, Inoue Y. Oscillation of delayed luminescence from PS 2: recombination of $S_2Q_b$ and $S_3Q_b$. FEBS 1984, 165:163–170.

Ryther JH. The ratio of photosynthesis to respiration in marine plankton algae and its effect upon the measurement of productivity. Deep-Sea Res 1954, 2:134–139.

Ryther JH, Dunstan WM. Nitrogen, phosphorus, and eutrophication in the coastal marine environment. Science 1971, 171:1008–1013.

Sakamoto W, Kindle KL, Stern DB. In vivo analysis of *Chlamydomonas* chloroplast *petD* gene expression using stable transformation of β-glucuronidase translational fusions. Proc Nat Acad Sci USA 1993, 90:497–501.

Sakshaug E. Production of protein and carbohydrate in the dinoflagellate *Amphidinium carterae*. Some preliminary results. Nor J Bot 1973, 20:211–218.

Sakshaug E, Kiefer DA, Anderson K. A steady state description of growth and light absorption in the marine planktonic diatom *Skeletonema costatum*. Limnol Oceanogr 1989, 34:198.

Samson G, Bruce D. Complementary changes in absorption cross-sections of photosystems I and II due to phosphorylation and $Mg^{2+}$-depletion in spinach thylakoids. Biochim Biophys Acta 1995, 1232:21–26.

Samuelsson G, Richardson K. Photoinhibition at low quantum flux densities in a marine dinoflagellate (*Amphidinium carterae*). Mar Biol 1982, 70:21–26.

Sancetta C, Villareal T, Falkowski PG. Massive fluxes of rhizosolenoid diatoms: a common occurrence? Limnol Oceanogr 1991, 36:1452–1457.

Sandmann G, Kuhn M, Böger P. Carotenoids in photosynthesis: protection of D1 degradation in the light. Photosyn Res 1993, 35:185–190.

Sandmann G, Reck M, Kessler E, and Boger P. Distribution of plastocyanin and soluable cytochrome *c* in various classes of algae. Arch Microbiol 1983, 134:23–27.

Sarmiento JL, Bender M. Carbon biogeochemistry and climate change. Photosyn Res 1994, 39:209–234.

Sarmiento J, Orr J. Three-dimensional simulations of the impact of Southern Ocean nutrient depletion on atmospheric $CO_2$ and ocean chemistry. Limnol Oceanogr 1991, 36:1928–1950.

Sarmiento JL, Orr JC, Siegenthaler U. A perturbation simulation of $CO_2$ uptake in an ocean general circulation model. J Geophys Res 1992, 94:3621–3645.

Sarmiento JL, Siegenthaler U. New production and the global carbon cycle. In: Falkowski PG, Woodhead AD, eds. Primary productivity and biogeochemical cycles in the sea. New York: Plenum, 1992:316–317.

Sarmiento JL, Sundquist ET. Revised budget for the oceanic uptake of anthropogenic carbon dioxide. Nature 1992, 356:589–593.

Sasaki Y, Sekiguchi K, Nagano Y, Matsuno R. Detection of small GTP-binding proteins in the outer envelope membrane of pea chloroplasts. FEBS Lett 1991, 293:124–126.

Scherer S. Do photosynthetic and respiratory electron transport chains share redox proteins? Trends Biochem Sci 1990, 15:458–462.

Schmidt A, Jager K. Open questions about sulfur metabolism in plants. Ann Rev Plant Mol Biol 1992, 43: 325–349.

Schmidt-Nielson K. Energy metabolism, body size, and problems of scaling. Fed Proc 1970, 29:1524–1532.

Schnepf E, Elbrachter M. Nutritional strategies in dinoflagellates. A review with emphasis on cell biological aspects. Eur J Protistol 1992, 28:3–24.

Schoch S, Lempert W, Rudiger W. On the last steps of chlorophyll biosynthesis intermediates between chlorophyllide and phytol-containing chlorophyll. Z Pflanzenphysiol Bd 1977, 83:427–436.

Schopf JW, ed. Earth's earliest biosphere: its origin and evolution. Princeton: Princeton University, 1983.

Schopf JW. Microfossils of the early Archean Apex Chert: new evidence of the antiquity of life. Science 1993, 260:640–646.

Schrader H. Coastal upwelling and atmospheric $CO_2$ changes over the last 400,000 years: Peru. Mar Geol 1992, 107:239–248.

Schreiber U, Bilger W, Schliwa U. Continuous recording of photochemical and non-photochemical quenching with a new type of modulation fluorometer. Photosyn Res 1986, 10:51–62.

Sculthorpe CD (1967). The biology of aquatic vascular plants. London: Edward Arnold, 1967.

Seitzinger SP. Denitrification in freshwater and coastal marine ecosystems: ecological and geochemical importance. Limnol Oceanogr 1988, 33:702–724.

Seliger HH, McElroy WD. Light: physical and biological action. New York, Academic, 1965.

Sellers PJ, Bounoua L, Collatz GJ et al. Comparison of radiative and physiological-effects of doubled atmospheric $CO_2$ on climate. Science 1996, 271:1402–1406.

Setif P. Energy transfer and trapping in photosystem I. In: Barber JR, ed. The photosystems: structure, function and molecular biology. Amsterdam: Elsevier, 1992:471–499.

Setlow RB. The wavelengths in sunlight effective in producing skin cancer: a theoretical analysis. Proc Nat Acad Sci USA 1974, 71:3363–3366.

Shlyk AA. Chlorophyll metabolism in green plants. Dokl Akad Nauk SSSR 1970:1–293.

Shuter B. A model of physiological adaptation in unicellular algae. J Theor Biol 1979, 78:519–552.

Siedow JN, Umbach AL. Plant mitochondrial electron transfer and molecular biology. Plant Cell 1995, 7:821–831.

Siefermann-Harms D. Carotenoids in photosynthesis. I. Location in photosynthetic membranes and light-harvesting function. Biochim Biophys Acta 1985, 811: 325–355.

Siegenthaler U, Sarmiento JL. Atmospheric carbon dioxide and the ocean. Nature 1993, 365:119–125.

Silverman DN. The catalytic mechanism of carbonic anhydrase. Can J Bot 1991, 69:1070–1078.

Simonis W, Chube KM. Untensuchungen uber der zusammenhang von phosphathaushalt und photosynthese. Z Nat 1952, 2B:194–196.

Simpson GG. Tempo and mode in evolution. New York: Columbia University, 1944.

Singer SJ, Nicolson GL. The fluid mosaic model of the structure of cell membranes. Science 1972, 175: 720–731.

Slovacek RE, Hannan PJ. In vivo fluorescence determination of phytoplankton chlorophyll *a*. Limnol Oceanogr 1977, 22:919–925.

Smart LB, Mcintosh L. Expression of photosynthesis genes in the cyanobacterium *Synechocystis* sp PCC-803–psaA-psaB and psbA transcripts accumulate in dark-grown cells. Plant Mol Biol 1991, 17:959–971.

Smayda TJ. Phytoplankton species succession. In: Morris I, ed. The physiological ecology of phytoplankton. Berkeley: Univ of California, 1980:493–570.

Smetacek V, Passow U. Spring bloom initiation and Sverdrup's critical depth model. Limnol Oceanogr 1990, 35:228–234.

Smith DF, Horner SMJ. Tracer kinetic analysis applied to problems in marine biology. In: Platt T, ed. Physiological bases of phytoplankton ecology. Ottawa: Can Bull Fish Aquat Sci, 1981:113–129.

Smith EL. Photosynthesis in relation to light and carbon dioxide. Proc Nat Acad Sci USA 1936, 22:504–511.

Smith GJ, Zimmerman RC, Alberte RS. Molecular and physiological responses of diatoms to variable levels of irradiance and nitrogen availablity: growth of *Skeletonema costatum* in simulated upwelling conditions. Limnol Oceanogr 1992, 37:989–1007.

Smith RC, Prezelin BB, Baker KS et al. Ozone depletion, ultraviolet radiation and phytoplankton biology in Antarctic waters. Science 1992, 255:952–959.

Smith WO Jr, Nelson DM. The importance of ice-edge phytoplankton production in the Southern Ocean. BioScience 1990, 36:151–157.

Smoluchowski M. Molekular-kinetische Theorie der Opaleszenz von Gasen in kritischen Zustande, sowie verwandter Erscheinungen. Ann Physik 1908, 25: 205–207.

Somerville C, Browse J. Plant Lipids—metabolism, mutants, and membranes. Science 1991, 252:80–87.

Sommer U, ed. Plankton ecology—succession in plankton communities. Berlin: Springer-Verlag, 1989.

Song XZ, Gibbs SP. Photosystem I is not segregated from photosystem II in the green-alga *Tetraselmis subcordiformis*—an immunogold and cytochemical study. Protoplasma 1995, 89:267–280.

Spivack AJ, You C-F, Smith HJ. Forameniferal boron isotope ratios as a proxy for surface ocean pH over the last 21 Myr. Nature 1993, 363:149–131.

Staehelin A. Chloroplasts structure and supramolecular organization of photosynthetic membranes. In: Staehelin LA, Arntzen CA, eds. Photosynthesis III: photosynthetic membranes and light harvesting systems. New York: Springer-Verlag, 1986:1–84.

Steemann-Nielsen E. Marine photosynthesis with special emphasis on the ecological aspects. Amsterdam: Elsevier, 1975.

Steemann-Nielsen E. On detrimetal effects of high light intensities on the photosynthetic mechanism. Physiol Planta 1952, 5:334–344.

Steemann-Nielsen E. On the time course in adapting to low light intensities in marine phytoplankton. J Cons Int Explor Mer 1964, 29:19–24.

Steemann-Nielsen E. The use of radio-active carbon ($C^{14}$) for measuring organic production in the sea. J Cons Int Explor Mer 1952, 18:117–140.

Steemann-Nielsen E, Hansen VK. Measurements with the carbon-14 technique of the respiration rates in natural populations of phytoplankton. Deep-Sea Res 1959, 5:222–233.

Stegmann PM, Lewis MR, Davis CO, Cullen JJ. Primary production estimates from recordings of solar-stimulated fluorescence in the Equatorial Pacific at 150° West. J Geophys Res 1992, 97C:627–638.

Steinback KE, Bonitz S, Arntzen CJ, Bogorad L, eds. Molecular biology of the photosynthetic apparatus. Cold Spring Harbor, 1985.

Stitt M. Limitation of photosynthesis by carbon metabolism. I. Evidence for excess electron transport capacity in leaves carrying out photosynthesis in saturating light and $CO_2$. Plant Physiol 1986, 81:1115–1122.

Stitt M, Sonnewald U. Regulation of metabolism in transgenic plants. Ann Rev Plant Physiol Plant Mol Biol 1995, 46:341–368.

Straus NA. Iron deprivation: physiology and gene regulation. In: Bryant DA, ed. The molecular biology of cyanobacteria. Dordrecht, Netherlands: Kluwer Academic, 1994:731–750.

Strickland JDH, Parsons TR. A practical handbook of seawater analysis. Ottawa: Bull Fish Res Bd Canada, 1972.

Stumm W, Morgan JJ. Aquatic chemistry. New York: Wiley, 1981.

Subramaniam A, Carpenter EJ. An empirically derived protocol for the detection of blooms of the marine cyanobacterium *Trichodesmium* using CZCS imagery. Int J Remote Sens 1994, 15:1559–1668.

Sukenik A, Bennett J, Falkowski PG. Changes in the abundance of individual apoproteins of light-harvesting chlorophyll *a*/*b*-protein complexes of photosystem I and II with growth irradiance in the marine chlorophyte *Dunaliella tertiolecta*. Biochim Biophys Acta 1988, 932:206–215.

Sukenik A, Bennett J, Falkowski PG. Light-saturated photosynthesis—limitation by electron transport or carbon fixation? Biochim Biophys Acta 1987b, 891: 205–215.

Sukenik A, Bennett J, Mortain-Bertrand A, Falkowski PG. Adaptation of the photosynthetic apparatus to irradiance in *Dunaliella tertiolecta*. Plant Physiol 1990, 92: 891–898.

Sukenik A, Falkowski PG, Bennett J. Energy transfer in the light-harvesting complex II of *Dunaliella tertiolecta* is unusually sensitive to Triton X-100. Photosyn Res 1989, 21:37–44.

Sukenik A, Levy RS, Levy Y et al. Optimizing algal biomass production in an outdoor pond: a simulation model. J Appl Phycol 1991, 3:191–201.

Sukenik A, Livne A, Neori A et al. Purification and characterization of a light-harvesting chlorophyll-protein complex from the marine eustigmatophyte *Nannochloropsis* sp. Plant Cell Physiol 1992, 33: 1041–1048.

Sukenik A, Wyman KD, Bennett J, Falkowski PG. A novel mechanism for regulating the excitation of photosystem II in a green alga. Nature 1987a, 327:704–707.

Svensson B, Vass I, Styring S. Sequence analysis of the D1 and D2 reaction center proteins of photosystem-II. Z Nat CA J Biosci 1991, 46:765–776.

Sverdrup HU. On conditions for the vernal blooming of phytoplankton. J Cons Explor Mer 1953, 18:287–295.

Sverdrup HU, Johnson MW, Fleming RH. The oceans. Englewood Cliffs, NJ: Prentice-Hall, 1942.

Swanson RV, Ong LJ, Wilbanks SM, Glazer AN. Phycoerythrins of marine unicellular cyanobacteria. 2. Characterization of phycobiliproteins with unusually high phycourobilin content. J Biol Chem 1991, 266: 9528–9534.

Syrett PJ. Nitrogen metabolism in microalgae. In: Platt T, ed. Physiological bases of phytoplankton ecology. Ottawa: J Can Fish Res Bd, 1981:182–210.

Tae G-S, Cramer WA. Topography of the heme prosthetic group of cytochrome b-559 in the photosystem II reaction center. Biochemistry 1994, 33:10060–10068.

Takahashi JS. Circadian clock genes are ticking. Science 1992, 258:238–240.

Takahashi M, Shimura S, Yamaguchi Y, Fujita Y. Photoinhibition of phytoplankton photosynthesis as a function of exposure time. J Oceanogr Soc Japan 1971, 27:43–50.

Talling JF. Photosynthetic characteristics of some freshwater plankton dynamics in relation to underwater radiation. New Phytol 1957, 56:29–50.

Tang E. Why do dinoflagellates have lower growth rates? J Phycol 1996, 32:80–84.

Taylor FJR. An overview of the status of evolutionary cell symbiosis theories. Ann NY Acad Sci 1987, 503:1–16.

Tevini M, Pfister K. Inhibition of photosystem II by UV-B radiation. Z Naturf 1985, 40c:129–133.

Thompson PA, Calvert SE. Carbon-isotope fractionation by a marine diatom: the influence of irradiance, day length, pH, and nitrogen source. Limnol Oceanog 1994, 39:1835–1844.

Thornber JP. Biochemical characterization and structure of pigment-protein of photosynthetic organism. Encycl of Plant Physiol New Series 1986, 12:98–142.

Tilman D. Resource competition and community structure. Princeton: Princeton University, 1982.

Tilzer MM, Elbrachter M, Gieskes WW, Beese B. Light-temperature interactions in the control of photosynthesis in Antarctic phytoplankton. Polar Biol 1986, 5:105–111.

Ting CS, Owens TG. Photochemical and nonphotochemical fluorescence quenching processes in the diatom *Phaeodactylum tricornutum*. Plant Physiol 1993, 101:1323–1330.

Topliss BJ, Platt J. Passive fluorescence and photosynthesis in the ocean: implication for remote sensing. Deep-Sea Res 1986, 33:849–864.

Trebst A. Inhibitors in electron flow: tools for the functional and structural localization of carriers and energy conservation sites. Meth Enzym 1980, 69: 675–715.

Trebst A. The three-dimensional structure of the herbicide binding niche on the reaction center polypeptides of photosystem II. Z Naturforsch 1987, 42c:742–750.

Turekian KK. Global environmental change: past, present and future. Englewood Cliffs, NJ: Prentice-Hall, 1996.

Turpin DH. Effects of inorganic N availability on algal photosynthesis and carbon metabolism. J Phycol 1991, 27:14–20.

Turpin DH, Bruce D. Regulation of photosynthetic light harvesting by nitrogen assimilation in the green alga *Selenastrum minitum*. FEBS Lett 1990, 263:99.

Turpin DH, Harrison PJ. Limiting nutrient patchiness and its role in phytoplankton ecology. J Exp Mar Biol Ecol 1979, 39:151–166.

Turro NJ. Modern molecular photochemistry. Menlo Park, CA: Benjamin/Cummings, 1978.

Tyler JE, ed. Report on the second meeting of the Joint Group of Experts on Photosynthetic Radiant Energy. UNESCO Tech Pap Mar Sci, 1966.

Tyndall J. On the absorption and radiation of heat by gases and vapors and on the physical connection of radiation absorption and conduction. Philos Mag 1861, 22:167–194.

Urey HC. The thermodynamic properties of isotopic substances. J Chem Soc London 1947: 562–581.

Valentin K, Cattolico RA, and Zetsche K. Phylogenetic origin of the plastids. In: Lewin RA, ed. Origins of plastids. New York: Chapman and Hall, 1993:193–212.

Van Cappellen P, Ingall ED. Redox stalization of the atmosphere and oceans by phosphorus-limited marine productivity. Science 1996, 271:493–496.

van der Staay GWM. Functional localization and properties of the chlorophyll *b*-binding antennae in the prochlorophyte *Prochlorothrix hollandica*. PhD thesis. Univers van Amsterdam, 1992.

van der Staay GWM, Ducruet A, Aebersold R et al. The Chl *a/b* antenna from prochlorophytes is related to the iron stress-induced Chla *a* antenna (isiA) from cyanobacteria. In: Mathis P, ed. Photosynthesis: from light to the biosphere. Dordrecht, Netherlands: Kluwer, 1995:175–178.

van Niel CB. The bacterial photosyntheses and their importance for the general problem of photosynthesis. Adv Enzymol 1941, 1:263–328.

Vassiliev IR, Kolber ZS, Mauzerall D et al. Effects of iron limitation on photosystem II composition and energy trapping in *Dunaliella tertiolecta*. Plant Physiol 1995, 109:963–972.

Vassiliev IR, Prasil O, Wyman KD et al. Inhibition of PSII photochemistry by PAR and UV radiation in natural phytoplankton communities. Photosyn Res 1994, 42:51–64.

Vermaas W. Molecular-biological approaches to analyse photosystem II structure and function. Ann Rev Plant Physiol Plant Mol Biol 1993, 44:457–481.

Vermaas W, Ikeuchi M, Inoue Y. Protein composition of the photosystem II core complex in genetically engineered mutants of the cyanobacterium *Synechocystis* sp. PCC-6803. Photosyn Res 1988, 17:97–113.

Vermaas W, Vass I, Eggers B, Styring S. Mutation of a putative ligand to the non-heme iron in photosystem 2: implications for Qa reactivity, electron transfer, and herbicide binding. Biochim Biophys Acta 1994, 1184: 263–272.

Villareal TA, Lipshultz F. Internal nitrate concentrations in single cells of large phytoplankton from the Sargasso Sea. J Phycol 1995, 31:689–696.

Vincent WF, Neale PJ, Richerson PJ. Photoinhibition: alga responses to bright light during diel stratification and mixing in a tropical alpine lake. J Phycol 1984, 20: 201–211.

Vogel S. Life in moving fluids. Boston: Wieland Grant, 1981.

Volk T, Hoffert MI. Ocean carbon pumps: analysis of relative strengths and efficiencies in ocean-driven atmospheric $CO_2$ exchanges. In: Sunquist ET, Broeker WS, eds. The carbon cycle and atmospheric $CO_2$: natural variations Archean to present. Washington, DC: American Geophysical Union, 1985:99–110.

Vollenweider RA. Models for calculating integral photosynthesis and some implications regarding structural properties of the community metabolism of aquatic systems. In: Prediction and measurement of photosynthetic productivity, Pudoc: Wageningen, 1970: 455–472.

Von Wettstein, D, Gough D, Kannangara CG. Chlorophyll biosynthesis. Plant Cell 1995, 7:1039–1057.

Wallace JM, Hobbs, PV. Atmospheric science. New York: Academic, 1977.

Walsh JJ. Death in the sea: enigmatic phytoplankton losses. Prog Oceanogr 1983, 12:1–86.

Walsh JJ. On the nature of continental shelves. San Diego: Academic, 1988.

Wang SY, ed. Photochemistry and photobiology of nucleic acids. New York: Academic, 1975.

Warburg O et al. Über den Energieumsatz bei der Kohlensaureassimilation. Zeitschr physik Chem 1923, 102:236–259.

Warneck P. Chemistry of the natural atmosphere. New York: Academic, 1988.

Wassink EC, Wintermans JFGH, Tya JE. Phosphate-exchanges in *Chlorella* in relation to condition for photosynthesis. Proc Kon Ned Akad Wet 1951, 54: 41–52.

Weaver EC, Weaver HE. Paramagnetic unit in spinach subchloroplast particles: estimation of size. Science 1969, 165:906–908.

Webb KL, Burley JWA. Dark fixation of $^{14}CO_2$ by obligate and facultative salt marsh halophytes. Can J Bot 1965, 43:281–285.

Weger HG, Herzig R, Falkowski PG, Turpin DH. Respiratory losses in the light in a marine diatom: measurements by short-term mass spectometry. Limnol Oceanogr 1989, 34:1153–1161.

Weis E, Berry JT. Quantum efficiency of photosystem II in relation to energy-dependent quenching of chlorophyll fluorescence. Biochim Biophys Acta 1987, 894: 198–208.

Wetzel RG. Limnology. Philadelphia: Saunders, 1983.

Whitmarsh J, Eckert HJ, Schoneich C, Renger G. Functional size of Photosystem II determined by radiation inactivation. Photosyn Res 1993, 38:363–368.

Whitmarsh J, Samson G, Poulson M. Photoprotection in photosystem II—the role of cytochrome b559. In: Baker NR, Bowyer JR, eds. Photoinhibition of photosynthesis: from molecular mechanisms to the field. Oxford: Bios Scientific, 1994:75–93.

Whitney SM, Shaw DC, Yellowlees D. Evidence that the dinoflagellate ribulose-1,5-bisphosphate carboxylase oxygenase is related to the form II large subunit of the photosynthetic purple nonsulfur bacteria. Proc Nat Acad Sci 1995, 259:271–275.

Wignall PB, Twitchett RJ. Oceanic anoxia and the end Permian mass extinction. Science 1996, 272: 1155–1158.

Williams PJL. On the definition of plankton production terms. ICES Mar Sci Symp 1993, 197:9–19.

Williams PJL, Jenkinson NW. A transportable microprocessor-controlled Winkler titration suitable for field and shipboard use. Limnol Oceanogr 1982, 27:576–584.

Williams PJL, Robertson JI. A serious inhibition problem from a Niskin sampler during plankton productivity studies. Limnol Oceanogr 1989, 34:1300–1305.

Williams RJP. Natural selection of the elements. Proc R Soc Lond 1981, 213:361–397.

Winhauer T, Jager S, Valentin K, Zetsche K. Structural similarities between psbA genes from red and brown algae. Curr Genetics 1991, 20:177–180.

Winter K, Smith JAC, eds. Crassulaean acid metabolism: biochemistry, ecophysiology and evolution. Heidelberg: Springer-Verlag, 1996.

Woese CR. Bacterial evolution. Microbiol Rev 1987, 51:221–271.

Wolk CP. Physiology and cytological chemistry of blue-green algae. Bacteriol Rev 1973, 37:32–101.

Wong WW, Sackett WM. Fractionation of stable carbon isotopes by marine phytoplankton. Geochim Cosmochim Acta 1978, 42:1809–1816.

Wood AM, Leatham T. The species concept in phytoplankton ecology. J Phycol 1992, 28:723–729.

Wood PM. Electron transport between PQ and cytochrome C-552 in *Euglena* chloroplasts. FEBS Letts 1976, 65:111–116.

Wood PM. The roles of *c*-type cytochromes in algal photosystems: extraction from algae of a cytochrome similar to higher plant cytochrome *f*. Eur J Biochem 1977, 72:605–613.

Woodrow IE, Berry JA. Enzymatic regulation of photosynthetic $CO_2$ fixation in $C_3$ plants. Ann Rev Plant Physiol Plant Mol Biol 1988, 39:533–594.

Woodwell GM, Whittaker RH, Reiners WA et al. The biota and the world carbon budget. Science 1978, 199:141–146.

Wray GA, Levinton JS, Shapiro LH. Molecular evidence for deep Precambrian divergences among metazoan phyla. Science 1996, 274:568–573.

Wright JC. Limnology of Canyon Ferry Reservoir. II. Phytoplankton standing crop and primary production. Limnol Oceanogr 1959, 4:235–245.

Yamamoto HY, Chichester CO. Dark incorporation of $^{18}O_2$ into antheraxanthin by bean leaf. Biochem Biophys Acta 1965, 109:303–305.

Yamamoto HY, Kamite L. The effect of dithiothreitol on violaxanthin de-epoxidation and absorbance changes in the 500 nm region. Biochim Biophys Acta 1972, 267:538–543.

Yamamoto HY, Nakayama TOM et al. Studies on the light and dark interconversions of leaf xanthophylls. Arch Biochem Biophys 1963, 97:168–173.

Yentsch CS. Phytoplankton growth in the sea—a coalescence of disciplines. In: Falkowski PG, ed. Primary productivity in the sea. New York: Plenum, 1980: 17–32.

Yentsch CS, Ryther JH. Short-term variation in phytoplankton chlorophyll and their significance. Limnol Oceanogr 1967, 2:140–142.

Yoder JA, McClain CR, Feldman GC, Esaias WE. Annual cycles of phytoplankton chlorophyll concentrations in the global ocean: a satellite view. Global Biogeochem Cycles 1993, 7:181–193.

Yokota A, Iwaku T, Miura K et al. Model for the relationship between $CO_2$ concentrating mechanism, $CO_2$ fixation, and glycolate synthesis during photosynthesis in *Chlamydomonas reinhardtii*. Plant Cell Physiol 1987, 28:1363–1376.

Zehr JP, Falkowski PG. Pathway of ammonium assimilation in marine diatom determined with the radiotracer $^{13}N$. J Phycol 1988, 24:588–591.

Zehr JP, Falkowski PG, Fowler J, Capone DG. Coupling between ammonium uptake and incorporation in a marine diatom: experiments with the short-lived radioisotope $^{13}N$. Limnol Oceanogr 1988, 33:518–527.

Zehr JP, Mellon M, Braun S et al. Diversity of heterotrophic nitrogen-fixation genes in a marine cyanobacterial mat. Appl Environ Microbiol 1995, 61:2527–2532.

Zehr JP, Ohki K, Fujita Y. Arrangement of nitrogenase structural genes in an aerobic filamentous nonheterocystous cyanobacterium. J Bacteriol 1991, 173: 7055–7058.

Zipfel W, Owens TG. Calculation of the absolute photosystem I absorption cross-sections from $P_{700}$ photooxidation kinetics. Photosyn Res 1991, 29:23–32.

Zohary T, Erez J, Gophen M et al. Seasonality of stable carbon isotopes within the pelagic food web of Lake Kinneret. Limnol Oceanog 1994, 39:1030–1043.

Zuber H. Primary structure and function of the light-harvesting polypeptides from cyanobacteria, red algae, and purple photosynthetic bacteria. In: Staehelin LA, Arntzen CJ, eds. Photosynthesis III: photosynthetic membranes and light-harvesting systems. Springer-Verlag, 1986:238–251.

Zumpft WG. The denitrifying prokaryotes. In: Ballows A, Truper HG, Dworkin M, Harder W, Schleifer K-H, eds. The prokaryotes: a handbook on the biology of bacteria: ecophysiology, isolation, applications. New York: Springer-Verlag, 1992:554–582.

# Index